ETHNICITY AND FAMILY THERAPY

THE GUILFORD FAMILY THERAPY SERIES
Alan S. Gurman, Editor

ETHNICITY AND FAMILY THERAPY

Edited by

MONICA McGOLDRICK
University of Medicine and Dentistry of New Jersey and Rutgers Medical School

JOHN K. PEARCE
Cambridge Family Institute

and

JOSEPH GIORDANO
Louis Caplan Center on Group Identity and Mental Health, American Jewish Committee

Introduction by Irving M. Levine
Foreword by Harry Aponte

THE GUILFORD PRESS
New York
London

© 1982 The Guilford Press
A Division of Guilford Publications, Inc.

Printed in the United States of America

Last digit is print number: 20 19 18 17 16 15 14

LIBRARY OF CONGRESS CATALOGING IN PUBLICATION DATA
Main entry under title:

Ethnicity and family therapy.

(The Guilford family therapy series)
Includes index.
1. Minorities—United States—Mental health services. 2. Ethnology—United States. 3. Family psychotherapy—United States. I. McGoldrick, Monica. II. Pearce, John K., 1935-   . III. Giordano, Joseph. IV. Series. [DNLM: 1. Family therapy. 2. Ethnic groups—Psychology. WM 430.5.F2 E84]
RC451.5.A2E83   616.89'156   81-20198
ISBN 0-89862-040-6   AACR2

To our families,
whose traditions we hope to continue,
further enrich,
and leave to those who
will follow us.

Contributors

CAROLYN ATTNEAVE, PhD, Department of Psychology, Psychiatry, and Behavioral Sciences, University of Washington, Seattle, Washington

GUILLERMO BERNAL, PhD, Department of Psychiatry, University of California at San Francisco General Hospital, San Francisco, California

NANCY BOYD-FRANKLIN, PhD, University of Medicine and Dentistry of New Jersey, Community Mental Health Center of Rutgers Medical School, Newark, New Jersey

JANET BRICE, MS, University of Medicine and Dentistry of New Jersey and Community Mental Health Center of Rutgers Medical School, Piscataway, New Jersey

CELIA JAES FALICOV, PhD, Department of Psychiatry, University of California Medical School, and San Diego Family Institute, San Diego, California

EDWIN H. FRIEDMAN, MD, Family Center, Georgetown University Medical School, and Family Training, Saint Elizabeth's Hospital, Washington, D.C.

NYDIA GARCIA-PRETO, MSW, Family Training, Youth Services, University of Medicine and Dentistry of New Jersey, and Community Mental Health Center of Rutgers Medical School, Piscataway, New Jersey

JOSEPH GIORDANO, ACSW, Louis Caplan Center on Group Identity and Mental Health, American Jewish Committee, New York, New York

FREDDA M. HERZ, RN, PhD, Department of Nursing, Herbert H. Lehman College, Bronx, New York; Faculty, Family Institute of Westchester, Mt. Vernon, New York

PAULETTE MOORE HINES, PhD, Central Community Focus Team, University of Medical and Dentistry of New Jersey, Community Mental Health Center of Rutgers Medical School, Piscataway, New Jersey

DAVIS Y. JA, PhD, Richmond Maxi Center, San Francisco, California

BEHNAZ JALALI, MD, Family Therapy Unit, Department of Psychiatry, Yale University School of Medicine, New Haven, Connecticut

JUDITH LANDAU, MB, ChB, DPM, Formerly of the Department of Psychiatry, University of Natal, Natal, South Africa, and the Faculty of Health Sciences, University of Durban–Westville, Westville, South Africa. Present address: Philadelphia Child Guidance Clinic Training Center, and private practice, Philadelphia, Pennsylvania

RÉGIS LANGELIER, PhD, Department of Counseling, Université Laval, Quebec, Canada

JAY LAPPIN, MSW, Faculty, Philadelphia Child Guidance Clinic, Philadelphia, Pennsylvania

EVELYN LEE, MSSA, EdD cand., Department of Psychiatry, University of California Medical School, San Francisco, California

DAVID MCGILL, PsyD, Faculty, Smith College Graduate School of Social Work, Northampton, Massachusetts

MONICA MCGOLDRICK, MA, MSW, Psychiatry Department, University of Medicine and Dentistry of New Jersey, and Community Mental Health Center of Rutgers Medical School, Piscataway, New Jersey; Faculty, Family Institute of Westchester, White Plains, New York

C. F. MIDELFORT, MD, Gunderson Clinic, Lacrosse, Wisconsin; Lutheran General Hospital, Park Ridge, Illinois

H. C. MIDELFORT, PhD, Anthropology Department, Brown University, Providence, Rhode Island

EVERETT MOITOZA, EdD, Martha's Vineyard Mental Health Center, Edgartown, Massachusetts; Harvard Medical School, Boston, Massachusetts

SANDRA M. MONDYKOWSKI, MDiv, Alcohol/Psychiatry Service, Brigham and Women's Hospital, Boston, Massachusetts

JOHN K. PEARCE, MD, Faculty, Cambridge Family Institute, Cambridge, Massachusetts

ELAINE PINDERHUGHES, MSW, Human Behavior and the Social Environment, Boston College Graduate School of Social Work, Chestnut Hill, Massachusetts

CLAIRE QUINTAL, PhD, l'Institut français, Assumption College, Worcester, Massachusetts

ELLIOTT J. ROSEN, EdD, Department of Psychology, Pace University, White Plains, New York; Faculty, Family Institute of Westchester, Mt. Vernon, New York

MARIE ROTUNNO, PhD, Benton & Bowles, Inc., New York, New York

SAM SCOTT, Faculty, Philadelphia Child Guidance Clinic, Philadelphia, Pennsylvania

STEVEN P. SHON, MD, Clinical Services, California State Department of Mental Health, Sacramento, California

CARLOS E. SLUZKI, MD, Mental Research Institute, Palo Alto, California

JOHN SPIEGEL, MD, Florence Heller School for Advanced Studies in Social Welfare, Brandeis University, Waltham, Massachusetts

EVE PRIMPAS WELTS, MSW, McLean Hospital, Belmont, Massachusetts

NORBERT A. WETZEL, ThD, Family Therapy Program, Trinity Counseling Service, Princeton, New Jersey; Adjunct Faculty, Graduate School of Applied and Professional Psychology, Rutgers University, Piscataway, New Jersey

HINDA WINAWER-STEINER, MSW, Faculty, Ackerman Institute for Family Therapy, New York, New York; Adjunct Faculty, Graduate School of Social Work, Rutgers University, New Brunswick, New Jersey

Acknowledgments

We owe our greatest debt to Sophocles Orfanidis; Susy, Sarah, and Miranda Pearce; and Grace, David, and Steven Giordano, from whom we have stolen much of the time this book has required.

Many others have been instrumental and supportive in this book's development. We have had the good fortune to have a support network that would be hard to match. We are deeply grateful to our editor, Kathy Milea, whose tireless effort, creative skill, and good humor could not be measured. She labored unceasingly to help us think more logically and to write more coherently. We trust we have made full use of her wise counsel.

We are deeply indebted to Myra Wayton, who handled numerous aspects of the project, large and small. Special thanks are also due Cindy Diacik, whose good nature never failed through the typing and retyping of the manuscript and who could always be relied upon to provide for us. We also thank Ron Cody for all of his help with the ups and downs of Superwylbur, our word processing program.

Many other friends and colleagues also provided us with support through the writing and production of this book. In particular we thank Betty Carter, Joyce Richardson, Harry Aponte, Irving Levine, Rick Varieur, Tom McDonough, Marcy Ringel, Braulio Montalvo, Manuel Guttierrez, Kalliope Adamides, Helen McGoldrick, Harris Goldstein, Gianfranco Cecchin, Luigi Boscolo, Lucia Antonioli, David McGill, Merrily Stern, Eugen and Marie-France Baer, Duke Stanton, Michael and Lenore Rohrbaugh, Sandy Leiblum, Meyer Rothberg, Kitty LaPerriere, Froma Walsh, Joan Barth, Ellen Overlan, Jeaninne Stone, and Joan Craig.

We thank Gary Lamson, Director of the Community Mental Health Center of Rutgers Medical School, for providing the supportive context in which much of the work for this book was done. We appreciate the support of the Institute on Pluralism and Group Identity of the American Jewish Committee and Phil Hallen, president of the Maurice Falk Medical Fund.

We also thank Seymour Weingarten, Editor in Chief of The Guilford Press, for his efficient and unintrusive support and Alan Gurman, the Series Editor, for his friendship and good advice (always offered with amazing speed and tact). Finally, we want to thank the contributors, who took the time and patience to collaborate in this venture, struggling to articulate the values, patterns, and clinical suggestions presented here.

MONICA MCGOLDRICK
JOHN K. PEARCE
JOSEPH GIORDANO

Introduction

Having seriously changed group relationships in American society, the ethnic identity movements of the 1960s and 1970s should have also had a profound impact on the way professionals practiced in the field of mental health.

To an extent this did happen, but unevenly, haltingly, and controversially. The importance of ethnocultural factors in behavior, although more widely conceded than ever, has remained for many an add-on, to be taken less seriously than knowledge about generic interpersonal relations.

In professional circles ethnic group identity proponents often were treated respectfully but with a hidden wink that ethnic militancy made it politically necessary to mollify special group interests.

When in June 1968, I organized the National Consultation on Ethnic America at Fordham University and launched what later became known as the "new ethnicity" (or, as I prefer it, the "new pluralism") movement, the advocates for differential ethnic analysis consisted mostly of non-White minority spokesmen.

The Fordham meeting broke the simplistic non-White–White dichotomy and ushered in a remarkable decade of studies on the remaining significance of White ethnicity.

By the middle of the 1970s the theoretical and therapeutic work of John Spiegel, John Papajohn, Monica McGoldrick, and John Pearce had begun to gain greater acceptance. Simultaneously a new group therapy called "ethnotherapy" was being invented and perfected by Price Cobb, Judith Weinstein Klein, and Joseph Giordano who made important breakthroughs in the study of Blacks, Jews, and Italians.

In all of these experiments, one fact stood out. Ethnocultural factors are more powerfully played out in family relations than in any other arena.

Generously funded by the Maurice Falk Medical Fund, the multiethnic work that we had pioneered at the Institute on Pluralism and Group Identity and at our Louis Caplan Center on Group Identity and Mental Health had flowed into many streams of thought, action, and process. A new generation of researchers and therapists had begun to conduct their work with an eye on cultural differences and were beginning to write about their experiences.

So it was with a sense of excitement and anticipation that we lent our aid to the collection and editing of the fine manuscripts represented in this book. *Ethnicity and Family Therapy* represents a good beginning in breaking through the barriers toward honest dealing with the psychology of America's still vibrant subcultures. The findings and practices described here are sure to be controversial, especially when our emotions are ignited by what we read about our own group.

As a guide to practicing family therapists and to other general readers interested in cultural systems, the material presented here will prove to be endlessly fascinating and eminently useful.

IRVING M. LEVINE
Institute on Pluralism and Group Identity
American Jewish Committee

Foreword

The editors and contributing authors of *Ethnicity and Family Therapy* have brought into sharp focus an issue that is, for the most part, informally discussed in the field of psychotherapy, but one that is subliminally struggled over by therapists and patients in most therapy relationships.

An essential aspect of family therapy, whatever the school of therapy, is the negotiation, directly or indirectly, of the structures of family relationships among family members. The therapist plays an active part in furthering, facilitating, forcing, and directing these negotiations in the family. In the process, the therapist engages in negotiations between himself or herself and the family through his or her personal and professional incursions into the family's relations.

These family structures, which are being negotiated, are not simply personal arrangements among family members. They are manifestations of the values of the cultural group to which the family belongs. The therapies employed also reflect cultural values, which are inherent in their historical development. The personal interpretations and applications of the therapies by clinicians are, moreover, filtered through the personal cultural perspectives of the therapists. Cultural values, which shape the relationships between family and therapist, which influence their respective perceptions of self and others, and which affect their manner of communication, occupy space in the core of therapy.

Ethnicity and Family Therapy represents a leap ahead for the field of psychotherapy in understanding the relationships of ethnic and racial factors to the process of therapy. For the most part the authors are not anthropologists. They are experts in therapy who have made a practical study of ethnicity as a part of therapy. The chapters contain both highly academic and candidly personal interpretations of the place of ethnicity in the relationships of therapists (and their therapy) to the families they treat. Beyond the introductory orienting and theoretical chapters, the expositions are practical efforts at introducing the specific cultural structures of a wide range of ethnic groups into the conceptual and working framework of the family therapist. This in itself is both a professional stance and a political act by the editors who thereby assume the postion that ethnic difference is to be considered an active dynamic in the treatment of families, as well as a set of distinctions that are to be recognized and accepted in the societal aspect of the therapy context. The editors do not treat ethnic value structures as archaic postures that are to be erased through assimilation with the dominant social structure. Moreover, theirs is a realistic position that incorporates into the boundaries of therapy a most powerful force in the psychological and social functioning of families that has traditionally belonged to the realm of the anthropologist and the sociologist but not of the psychotherapist.

After reading this book, it will be difficult for any therapist to imagine how he or she can attempt to assess, treat, and communicate with a family without being sensitive to the cultural roots of the family and of himself or herself. One may argue, as I have, with the ethnic stereotypes depicted by some of the authors or with the nonevolving, static picture of ethnic structure presented by some of the authors. But among what experts or non-experts will one find consensus about the values and social structures of any national, ethnic, or racial group? Social values and structures are evolving and intermingling in living cultures as well as within families and individuals from these cultures. The development and change of these structures are signs of life. Debates with and among the authors is a necessary part of that evolution. But this important work thoughtfully and forcefully places the issue of ethnicity squarely in the middle of the therapist's theoretical and practical clinical considerations, where it belongs.

HARRY APONTE
UMDNJ–Rutgers Medical School

Preface

The United States is the most ethnically diverse nation in history, but this fact has not increased our ability to tolerate differences. We have regarded our society as a melting pot and have blinded ourselves to its inherent diversity. Our wish to forget cultural variations and to encourage common norms, though understandable, has been an idealistic and fallacious goal.

There are still many psychotherapists in the United States who are being trained with hardly a reference made to ethnicity. There are clinics set up to serve particular ethnic groups that have no staff who speak the group's native language. Foreign psychiatric residents are trained to do therapy on the most subtle aspects of adjustment in our society without any consideration of the major cultural gaps between themselves and their patients. In fact, most of us have gone through our entire professional educations with hardly a word mentioned about ethnicity. It is, therefore, not surprising that therapists have not appreciated the role of ethnicity in developing therapeutic models and interventions. For many reasons, some of which we have outlined in Chapter 1, the subject of ethnicity has, until recently, been almost taboo.

Problems (whether physical or mental) can be neither diagnosed nor treated without some understanding of the frame of reference of the person seeking help. We have asked the authors writing about various American groups to answer the following questions, relating them specifically to a family therapy context:

1. What do they define as a problem?
2. What do they see as a solution to their problems?
3. To whom do they usually turn for help?
4. How have they responded to immigration?
5. What are the typical family patterns of the group?
6. How do they handle life cycle transitions?
7. What may be the difficulties for a therapist of the same background or for a therapist of a different background?

The chapters highlight ethnic differences in family patterns and typical attitudes toward therapy, emphasizing positive and practical clinical suggestions. The authors have described ethnic patterns using simplified pictures of the cultures, "snapshots" frozen in time, in which the continuities with the past are emphasized. There are disadvantages in this approach, the most obvious of which is stereotyping. We are keenly aware of the perniciousness of negative stereotyping and in no way wish to contribute to that tendency in our culture, although it cannot be denied that our snapshots can be misused in that way.

There are those who argue that, therefore, ethnic generalizations do more harm than good. In our view, developing a relatively simple paradigm is the only realistic way to begin to expand our knowledge. But it is only a start. The danger of training anyone in the details of a particular ethnic group is that it will ultimately squeeze people into unreal categories and reify their culture, as we have rigidified diagnoses. We think the solution to the problem lies in maintaining openness to new experience, once we have a framework, rather than in avoiding a framework because it is not altogether accurate or complete. We hope readers will move past the stereotypes, using them as starting points from which to learn more.

We have not dealt fully with the enormous complexity of present-day ethnic families. Any single group would take many volumes to consider in depth, and most of the groups presented here are themselves combinations of a multitude of cultural groups with a widely varied heritage.

Many factors will determine the extent to which particular families will fit into the traditional paradigms presented here: migration experience, whether they lived in an ethnic neighborhood in the United States, their upward mobility, socioeconomic status, educational achievement, rate of intermarriage, the strength of their political and religious ties to their group.

Obviously no therapist can become an expert on all ethnic groups. What we consider essential is to develop an openness to cultural variability and to the relativity of our own values. We come to understand patterns only by observing differences, and thus we have presented many groups together in the same volume, rather than focusing on fewer groups in greater depth.

It is not easy to raise questions about the validity of assumptions that we have grown up with and have always experienced as part of ourselves. Writing the chapters for this book has been a far more difficult task than other clinical or academic writing (as the authors will surely testify). Our authors have had to write about their own cultures, from inside the culture. They have had to gain enough distance to describe a phenomenon when still a part of it. Many of us have gained some perspective on our own ethnicity by marrying spouses with different backgrounds (about half of the authors). Close experience of differentness increases both one's ability and one's need to understand.

Chapters 3 through 21 describe specific American ethnic groups. In addition, we have included a theoretical overview by Monica McGoldrick, and an ecological perspective by John Spiegel, who has been the guiding force on ethnicity and therapy for many years. We have also included several chapters on special issues. The case of a Vietnamese single-parent family is an excellent example of culturally sensitive intervention that transcends detailed knowledge of the group's values and customs. A chapter on the Latin Lover illustrates the importance of understanding reciprocal stereotyping in intercultural inter-action. "The Myth of the Shiksa" raises some important reservations about the ways an emphasis on ethnicity may be used to obscure family emotional process. Chapter 25 offers a model of ecosystemic assessment and demon-strates its application with Chinese families. Finally, Chapter 26 describes a model of therapy for families in cultural transition, in which the therapist works through a member of the family who is pivotal in the transition process.

This book proposes cultural profiles and specific therapeutic suggestions intended to broaden the repertoire of therapists. We urge readers to take what is presented here not as the truth, but rather as a map, which, while it covers only limited aspects of the terrain, may nevertheless be a useful guide to explorers seeking a path.

MONICA MCGOLDRICK
JOHN K. PEARCE
JOSEPH GIORDANO

Contents

I
CONCEPTUAL OVERVIEW

1

Ethnicity and Family Therapy: An Overview

MONICA McGOLDRICK

It seems so natural that an interest in families should lead to an interest in ethnicity, that it is surprising this area has been so widely ignored. Ethnicity is deeply tied to the family, through which it is transmitted. The two concepts are so intertwined that it is hard to study one without the other, and yet we have done just that.

The mental health field has paid most attention to the intrapsychic factors that shape life experiences. The study of cultural influences has been left primarily to sociologists and cultural anthropologists. And even they have tended to focus on distant cultures or other sociological trends, paying scant attention to the variety of cultural groups from all over the world that have coexisted for over 200 years in the United States. As Andrew Greeley, one of the few sociologists who has been studying ethnicity, has observed, future historians will be amazed that we have stood in the midst of such an astonishing social phenomenon and taken it so much for granted that we did not bother to study it.

> They will find it especially astonishing in light of the fact that ethnic differences, even in the second half of the 20th Century, proved far more important than differences in philosophy or economic system. Men who would not die for a premise or a dogma would more or less cheerfully die for a difference rooted in ethnic origins. (Greeley, 1969, p. 5)

Ethnicity remains a vital force in this country, a major form of group identification, and a major determinant of our family patterns and belief systems. The premise of equality, on which our country was founded, required us to give primary allegiance to our national identity, fostering the myth of the "melting pot," the notion that group distinctions between people were unimportant. Yet, we have not "melted." There is increasing evidence that ethnic values and identification are retained for many generations after immigration (Greeley, 1969, 1978, 1981) and play a significant role in family

Monica McGoldrick. Psychiatry Department, University of Medicine and Dentistry of New Jersey, and Community Mental Health Center of Rutgers Medical School, Piscataway, New Jersey; Faculty, Family Institute of Westchester, White Plains, New York.

life and personal development throughout the life cycle (Lieberman, 1974; Teper, 1977; Gelfand & Kutzik, 1979). Second-, third-, and even fourth-generation Americans, as well as new immigrants, differ from the dominant culture in values, life-styles, and behavior.

Gradually we have begun moving toward a more complex view of ourselves, which allows us to consider group differences within the whole. For family therapists this means shifting our thinking up a level to the consideration of the cultural system of families who share common history and traditions. Just as family therapy itself grew out of the myopia of the intrapsychic view and concluded that human behavior could not be understood in isolation from its family context, family behavior also makes sense only in the larger cultural context in which it is embedded. Perhaps family therapists needed, for a time, to block out other system levels in order to gain understanding of the nuclear family and then the extended family, but the time is past now when that is sufficient context. There are many specific clinical implications of shifting to this broader perspective, as we hope the chapters in this book will demonstrate.

Ethnicity: We and They

An ethnic group has been defined as "those who conceive of themselves as alike by virtue of their common ancestry, real or fictitious, and who are so regarded by others" (Shibutani & Kwan, 1965, p. 23). Ethnicity describes a sense of commonality transmitted over generations by the family and reinforced by the surrounding community. It is more than race, religion, or national and geographic origin (which is not to minimize the significance of race or the special problems of racism). It involves conscious and unconscious processes that fulfill a deep psychological need for identity and historical continuity (Giordano & Giordano, 1977). Ethnicity patterns our thinking, feeling, and behavior in both obvious and subtle ways. It plays a major role in determining what we eat, how we work, how we relax, how we celebrate holidays and rituals, and how we feel about life, death, and illness.

Our cultural values and assumptions are generally outside of our awareness. We see the world through our own "cultural filters," often persisting in established views despite even clear evidence to the contrary (Watzlawick, 1976).

The subject of ethnicity evokes deep feelings, and discussion frequently becomes polarized or judgmental. According to Greeley, using presumed common origin to define "we" and "they" seems to touch on something basic and primordial in the human psyche (Greeley, 1969). Similarly, Irving Levine (1981) has observed: "Ethnicity can be equated along with sex and death as a subject that touches off deep unconscious feelings in most people."

Indeed, there is a common tendency for human beings to fear, and therefore to reject, that which they cannot understand. The ancient Greeks called all non-Greeks "barbarians," considering them to be without culture. And the Russian word for a German is *nemetz*, which means "one who is mute," reflecting the belief that those who could not be understood could not speak at all. We tend to label that which is different as "bad" or "crazy." Thus, in more modern usage, the German may label the Italian "hysterical," while the Italian may label the German "obsessive–compulsive."

Ethnic Identity

Ethnicity is a powerful influence in determining identity. A sense of belonging and of historical continuity is a basic psychological need. We may ignore it or cut it off by changing our names, rejecting our families and social backgrounds, but we do so to the detriment of our well-being.

Even Freud, in his later works, began to look into the role of culture in identity formation. As Erikson has noted, Freud took certain principles of cultural identity for granted (Erikson, 1950). He described Freud's own deep sense of ethnic identification as consisting of many obscure emotional forces, which were all the more powerful the less they could be articulated. According to Erikson, Freud conceived of ethnic identity as suggesting a deep commonality, known only to those who share in it, and only expressible in works more mythical than conceptual.

Erikson, in his classic work on identity in 1950, began to develop a framework for understanding how the individual is linked to the ethnic group and society. He defines identity as a process located in the core of the individual, and yet also in the core of his or her communal culture. In his description the final stage of human development concerns coming to terms with our cultural identity: "For only an identity safely anchored in the 'patrimony' of a cultural identity can produce a workable psychosocial equilibrium" (p. 412).

The work of Klein (1980) with Jews, Cobbs (1972) with Blacks, and Giordano and Riotta-Sirey (in press) with Italians demonstrated the fact that if people are secure in their identity, then they can act with greater freedom, flexibility, and openness to others of different cultural backgrounds. However, if people receive negative or distorted images of their ethnic background or learn values from the larger society that conflict with those of their family, often develop a sense of inferiority and self-hate that can lead to aggressive behavior and discrimination toward other ethnic groups.

Ethnicity and the Medical Model

Until now, the medical model, with its emphasis on "diagnosing" and "curing" disease, has been the major influence on the psychotherapeutic system. This leads to a systematic inattention to "illness"—that is, to the patient's or family's perception of what is wrong—and is partly responsible for noncompliance, dissatisfaction with clinical care, and treatment failure. There is much evidence that this model is inadequate for understanding illness and the help-seeking behavior in our society. Problems (whether physical or mental) can be neither diagnosed nor treated without understanding the frame of reference of the person seeking help as well as that of the helper. Many studies (Giordano & Giordano, 1977; Tseng & McDermott, 1981; Rabkin & Struening, 1976; Harwood, 1981; Rakel, 1977) have shown that people differ in

1. their experience of pain
2. what they label as a symptom
3. how they communicate about their pain or symptoms
4. their beliefs about the cause of their illness
5. their attitudes toward helpers (doctors and therapists)
6. what treatment they desire or expect.

Kleinman, a prominent physician–researcher, has explored the culturally determined nature of the entire health care system:

> Illness behavior is a normative experience governed by cultural rules; we learn "approved" ways of being ill. . . . And doctors' explanations and activities, as those of their patients, are culture-specific. (Kleinman, Eisenberg, & Good, 1978, p. 252)

Symptoms differ so much among ethnic groups that it brings into question the usefulness of our diagnostic nomenclature (Fantl & Shiro, 1959; Opler & Singer, 1956; Singer & Opler, 1956; Tseng & McDermott, 1981). The language and customs of a culture will influence whether or not a symptom is labeled a problem. Having the diagnosis or label may even help to create the problem. For example, the absence of stuttering among certain groups of American Indians is associated with their less stringent demands for fluent speech (Eisenberg, 1977). In fact, their language has no word for stuttering.

As Tseng and McDermott (1981) have stated:

> We need to continue to examine ourselves to see on what grounds, and for what purposes, we recognize, label, and conceptualize certain emotional behavior disturbances as mental disorders and what are the sociocultural implications of our conclusions. (p. 36)

Patients' "illness" (the experience of being ill) is very different from the course of their "disease" (a physically identifiable dysfunction) and is strongly influenced by cultural beliefs (Stoeckle, Zola, & Davidson, 1964).

Almost all of us have multiple belief systems to which we turn when in need of help. We use not only the official medical or psychotherapeutic system, we turn also to religion, self-help groups, alcohol, yoga, chiropractors, and so on. We utilize remedies our mothers taught us and those suggested by our friends. Many factors influence our tendency to rely on one system or another at any given time.

Thus, patients vary markedly in their use of the health care system. Although it is estimated that more than 90% of the population experience some physical symptoms of illness at any given time, the vast majority (70–80%) of those believing themselves ill manage their problems outside the formal health care system (Zola, 1972). Of those who do seek professional attention, only about 50% are found to have any diagnosable disease (Kleinman *et al.*, 1978).

Attitudes toward health and illness are strongly influenced by ethnic factors, and studies of ethnic differences in response to physical illness (Sanua, 1960; Zborowski, 1969; Zola, 1966) have clear implications for family therapy practice. In Zborowski's classic study (1969) of physically ill patients of Jewish, Italian, Irish, and White Anglo-Saxon Protestant (WASP) descent, the Jewish and Italian patients tended to complain about their pain, while the Irish and WASPs did not. When it came to describing their pain experience, the WASPs and Jews were accurate, while the Irish and Italians were conspicuously inaccurate. The Italian patients dramatized their pain, and the Irish blocked or denied theirs. When the researchers looked at patients' expected solutions, the results again showed striking differences. The Italians worried about the effects of their pain on their immediate situation (work, finances, family), but once the pain was relieved, they easily forgot their suffering. While they wanted an immediate remedy to stop the pain, the Jewish patients found this unacceptable. They feared anything, such as a pill, that stopped the pain, because they felt it would not deal with the real source of their problem. They worried about the harmful, long-range effects of drugs on their general health. Instead, they sought a full explanation of the meaning of their pain and of its relief. The Irish patients did not expect a cure for their ailments at all. They were fatalistic and usually did not complain of or even mention their pain. Rather, they tended to view pain as the result of their own sinfulness and held themselves responsible for it. The WASP patients, on the other hand, were optimistic, future oriented, and confident in the ability of technology and science to cure disease. Operating on the "work ethic," they sought control over their pain by their own efforts.

Emotional expressiveness can lead to problems since the dominant culture tends to value emotional expressiveness less than many minority groups within it. "Americanized" medical personnel in Zborowski's study (1969) distrusted the uninhibited display of suffering exhibited by Jewish and Italian patients and saw their reactions as exaggerated. Another researcher found that doctors frequently labeled their Italian patients as having "psychiatric problems," although there was no evidence that psychosocial problems were more frequent among them (Zola, 1966). We would suppose that Jewish and Italian medical staffs would also have difficulty understanding the silence of Irish and WASP patients.

One of the first to move beyond the medical model in the psychoanalytic movement was Karen Horney, who recognized that human problems were incomprehensible apart from their cultural context:

> Thus the term neurotic, while originally medical, cannot be used now without its cultural implications. . . . One would run a great risk in calling an Indian boy psychotic because he told us that he had visions in which he believed. . . . The conception of what is normal varies not only with the culture, but also within the same culture in the course of time. (Horney, 1937, pp. 14–15)

In Horney's view, therapy was aimed at helping the patient adapt to the environment, which implied that some theory of social order, such as cultural anthropology, needed to be added to the concepts of psychoanalysis.

However, others did not follow Horney's lead in awareness of cultural relativity in psychotherapy. Even when mental health professionals have considered culture, they, like sociologists and cultural anthropologists have more often focused on international cross-cultural comparisons than on the ethnic groups in our own culture (Carpenter & Strauss, 1974; Giordano & Giordano, 1977; Kiev, 1972).

A number of important collections on ethnic differences that have appeared in the sociological literature (Glazer & Moynihan, 1975; Mindel & Habenstein, 1976; Sowell, 1981) have not, for the most part, become part of the knowledge base of family clinicians. Recent growing interest and awareness may change this pattern. New works are appearing frequently, filling in many gaps. The new *Harvard Encyclopedia of American Ethnic Groups* (Thernstrom, Orlov, & Handlin, 1980) will surely become a classic, Tseng and McDermott's *Culture, Mind and Therapy* (1981) takes a careful and much needed look at diagnostic labeling from a cultural perspective, and Harwood's (1981) collection on seven medically underserved groups is another important addition.

In recent years there has been a burgeoning literature on work with a few minority groups, notably Black (see Hines & Boyd-Franklin, Chap. 4; Pinderhughes, Chap. 5; Boyd, 1980; Block, 1981; Staples & Mirande, 1980; Allen, 1978) and Hispanic (see Falicov, Chap. 7; Garcia-Preto, Chap. 8; Bernal, Chap. 9; Levine & Padilla, 1980). Unfortunately, in the past when these groups have been studied, they have too often been presented singly or as a group representing "third world" cultures. The focus on the harmful effects of racism, poverty and political powerlessness often so dominate, that positive aspects of ethnicity—traditions, coping skills, belief systems—are ignored. While racism and poverty are enormous issues in our culture and have great impact on behavior in the health care system (Thomas & Sillen, 1972; Jacobs, Charles, Bocobs, Weinstein, & Man, 1972), focusing on them exclusively, rather than within the broader context of a pluralistic society, may obscure perspective on the relativity of all value systems.

Just as there is a paucity of material on the impact of ethnicity in individual therapy, very little has appeared in the family therapy literature on the subject. An exception is the work of Spiegel and Papajohn (1971, 1975) who have made a major advance in our conceptualizations about cultural differences by developing a framework for analyzing value orientations of a culture (see Chap. 2). They have used their schema, which is based on Kluckhohn and Strodtbeck (1961), to analyze the cultural conflicts of a number of ethnic groups (Irish, Italian, Greek, Mexican American, and Puerto Rican) as they adapt to the dominant American value structure. For example, in analyzing the time orientation (past, present, or future) of different groups, none of the ethnic groups valued the future to the extent it is valued in the dominant American value system. Clearly those who value the past or present over the future will find themselves at odds with the dominant culture and are likely to be labeled as "deviant" for this difference.

In addition to the comparative value analysis of Spiegel and Papajohn, a few family articles have appeared, on Black Americans (Boyd, 1980; Foley, 1975; McAdoo, 1977), Jewish Americans (Zuk, 1978), Slovak Americans (Stein, 1978), and Irish Americans (McGoldrick & Pearce, 1981). Also, Minuchin, Montalvo, Guerney, Rosman, and Schumer (1967) focused on the multiproblem families and developed specific techniques to deal with poor Black and Hispanic families. But the other major family models (Bowen systems, strategic, communications), while emphasizing the importance of the family context, have not made explicit reference to ethnic differences. Many family therapists view ethnicity as a superficial overlay, irrelevant in relation to more "basic" family process (Bowen, 1981; Satir, 1981).

While interest in ethnicity has grown in recent years, there has been very little systematic integration of material on ethnicity in the training of any mental health professionals (Giordano & Giordano, 1977; Pinto, 1976; Sanua, 1975). However, a few training programs are now integrating material on ethnicity into their curricula. Spiegel's group in Boston was the first to set up a program for ethnicity training. Recently a few others—Carlos Sluzki and Dora Schnitman in the Family Practice Residency at the University of California and Fred Taketomo and Joel Feiner (in press) in the Psychiatric Residency at Einstein's Bronx Psychiatric Center—have also set up seminars on ethnocultural differences.

Ethnicity and Families

Ethnicity relates family process to the broader context in which it evolves. Just as individuation requires that we come to terms with our families of origin, coming to terms with our ethnicity is necessary to gain a perspective on the relativity of our belief systems. For example, if young people experience their parents as cold, distant, and unfeeling, it may be hard for them, even with the appreciation that their grandparents were the same, to feel sympathetic to their life-styles. However, if we recognize in that "distance" the determined individualism on which the pioneers forged ahead in this country, we become connected with a fuller, more complex and accurate picture of our heritage, which may be easier to appreciate and to renegotiate.

Even the definition of "family" differs greatly from group to group. The dominant American (WASP) definition focuses on the intact nuclear family. Black families focus on a wide network of kin and community. For Italians there is no such thing as the "nuclear" family. To them family means a strong, tightly knit three- or four-generational family, which also includes godparents and old friends. The Chinese go beyond this and include in their definition of family all their ancestors and all their descendants. [Their conception of time is very different, and death does not create the same distinction it does for Westerners (Shon & Ja, Chap. 10).]

The family life cycle phases also vary for different groups. For example, Mexican Americans have a longer courtship period and see early and middle childhood as extending longer than the dominant American pattern (Falicov & Karrer, 1980). Adolescence is shorter and leads more quickly into adulthood than in the dominant American structure, while middle age extends longer going into what Americans generally think of as older age.

Cultural groups vary also in the emphasis they place on different transitions. The Irish have always placed most emphasis on the wake, viewing death as the most important life cycle transition. Italians, in contrast, emphasize the wedding, while Jews often give particular attention to the Bar Mitzvah, a transition most groups hardly mark at all. Families' ways of celebrating these events differ also. As Greeley has noted, the Irish tend to celebrate weddings (and every other occasion) by drinking, the Poles by dancing, the Italians by eating, and the Jews by eating and talking (Greeley, 1969).

Some groups celebrate Christmas most elaborately (e.g., Poles, Germans, Scandinavians, WASPs), where others emphasize Easter (Greeks and Slavs), and others the Jewish New Year, the Chinese New Year, and so forth. These customs evoke deep feelings in people that relate to the continuity of the rituals over generations and centuries.

The occupations that groups choose also reflect their values, as well as necessity. The Irish are overrepresented in politics and police work; Jews, in small businesses, medicine, and, above all, in mental health specialities; Germans, in engineering; Greeks in the restaurant business; and so on.

Every culture generates characteristic problems for itself. These problems are often consequences of cultural traits that are conspicuous strengths in other contexts. For example, WASP optimism leads to confidence and flexibility in taking initiative, an obvious strength when there are opportunities to do so. But the one-sided preference for cheerfulness also leads to the inability to cope with tragedy or to engage in mourning (McGill & Pearce, Chap. 21). Historically, WASPs have perhaps had less misfortune than most other peoples. But optimism becomes a vulnerability when they must contend with tragedy. They have few philosophical or expressive ways to deal with situations in which optimism, rationality, and belief in the efficacy of individuality are insufficient. The WASP strengths of independence and individual initiative work well in some situations, but WASPs may feel lost when dependence on the group is the only way to ensure survival.

Naturally, what behavior groups see as problematic will differ as well. WASPs may be concerned about dependency or emotionality, the Irish about "making a scene," Italians about disloyalty to the family, Greeks about any insult to their pride, or *filotimo*, Jews about their children not being "successful," or Puerto Ricans about their children not showing respect.

Groups differ also in what they see as the solution to problems. WASPs tend to see work, reason, and stoicism as the best solutions. Jewish families often consult with doctors and therapists and seek understanding and insight. The Irish, until recently, solved problems by going to the priest for confession, "offering up" their suffering in prayers, or (especially men) seeking solace through drink. Italians may prefer to rely on family support, eating, and expressing themselves. West Indians may see hard work, thrift, or consulting with their elders as the solution, and Norwegians might prefer surgery, fresh air, or exercise.

Groups also differ in attitudes toward seeking help. In general, Italians rely primarily on the family and turn to an outsider only as a last resort (Gambino, 1974; Fandetti, 1976; Rotunno & McGoldrick, Chap. 16; Zborowski, 1969). Black Americans have long mistrusted the help they can receive from traditional institutions except the church, which was the only one that was theirs (Hines & Boyd-Franklin, Chap. 4; Pinderhughes, Chap. 5; McAdoo, 1977). Puerto Ricans (Garcia-Preto, Chap. 8), Greeks (Welts, Chap. 13), and Chinese (Kleinman, 1975; Tseng & McDermott, 1981; Lee, Chap. 25) are likely to somatize when they are under stress and may seek medical rather than mental health services. Norwegians, too, often convert emotional tensions into physical symptoms, which they consider more acceptable, thus, their preference for the surgeon rather than the psychotherapist (Midelfort & Midelfort, Chap. 20). Likewise, Iranians often view medication and vitamins as a necesary part of treating symptoms, regardless of their origin (Jalali, Chap. 14). Many potential patients, perhaps even the majority, experience their troubles somatically and strongly doubt the value of psychotherapy. And many groups may tend to see their problems as the result of their own sin, action, or inadequacy (Irish, Blacks, Norwegians) or somebody else's (Greeks, Iranians, Puerto Ricans).

Cultural differences are often ascribed to class rather than ethnicity.

Class is also a major aspect of family life experience, but all differences cannot be ascribed to this factor alone. For example, Puerto Ricans, Italians, and Greeks all have similar rural, peasant backgrounds, and yet there are important ethnic differences among these groups. Puerto Ricans (see Chap. 8) tend to have flexible boundaries between the family and the surrounding community, so that child lending is a common and accepted practice. Italians (see Chap. 16) tend to have much more clear boundaries between the family and the surrounding community and extremely tight boundaries against outsiders. You can be taken in as a member of the extended family by long and close association, but the boundaries remain quite rigid between insiders and outsiders. Greeks have very definite family boundaries, are disinclined to adopt children, having deep feelings about the "blood line" (Welts, Chap. 13). Greeks are also nationalistic—a value that relates to a nostalgic vision of ancient Greece and to the country they lost under hundreds of years of Ottoman oppression. (Poles and Irish, who experienced similar foreign domination after a period of nationhood, also have intense nationalistic feelings.) By contrast, Italians, until coming to this country, defined themselves primarily by family ties, second, by their village, and, third, if at all, by the region of Italy from which they came. Puerto Ricans as a group have coalesced only within the past century or so and have developed their awareness of their group identity primarily in reaction to experiences with the United States. These differences have important implications for treatment. Each group's way of relating to a therapy situation will reflect its differing attitudes toward family, group identity, and outsiders, even though certain family characteristics such as male dominance and role complementarity are somewhat similar for all three groups.

Factors Influencing Ethnicity

Many factors will influence the ways ethnic patterns surface in a family.

Migration

Therapists need to be attuned to the stresses of migration even several generations later (Sluzki, 1979; Cassim, 1982). All families in this country have experienced the complex stresses of migration; they may be "buried" or forgotten, but they will continue, albeit at times subtly, to influence the family's outlook. Under the pressure of accommodating to the new situation, and because of the pain of what was left behind, many immigrant groups have been forced to abandon much of their ethnic heritage (Greeley, 1979; Winawer-Steiner & Wetzel, Chap. 12; Hines & Boyd-Franklin, Chap. 4) and thus have lost a part of their identity. The effects of this cutting off of the past may be all the more powerful for being hidden. Families will be more vulnerable in the present, the more they have repressed their past.

How the family adjusts to the new culture depends a great deal on whether one family member migrated alone or whether a large portion of the family, community, or nation came together.

Families who migrate alone have a greater need to adapt to the new situation, and their losses are often more hidden. Frequently, educated immigrants, who come for professional jobs, are in this situation of moving to places where there is no one with whom they can speak their native language or share customs and rituals.

When a number of families migrated together, as often happened with the Scandinavians who settled in the Midwest, they brought their network with them and were able to preserve much of their traditional heritage.

When a large part of the population or nation came together, as happened in the waves of Irish, Polish, Italian, and Jewish migration, the situation was again different, in that our nation as a whole tended to react to these large groups with prejudice and discrimination. The newest immigrants became the biggest threat to those just ahead of them, who feared losing their tenuous hold on economic security.

The reasons for migration will also play an important role, including what the family was seeking and what it was leaving behind—religious or political persecution, poverty, wish for adventure, and so forth.

A family's dreams and fears in coming to the United States become part of its heritage. Their attitudes toward what came before and what lies ahead will have profound impact on the messages given to their children, although the subject may never be mentioned directly.

The hope of returning to the country of origin may impede the family's efforts to adapt to the new situation. The film El Super depicts this touchingly in a Cuban family who kept hoping the revolution would be over so that they could return to Cuba. The state of permanent uncertainty or uprootedness is in itself profoundly stressful and will have a long-range impact on family adjustment.

Often the pain of the situation from which family members fled plays a dominant role in the family for generations, as the children of Holocaust survivors are now demonstrating.

The Languages Spoken in the Home

Family members vary in the extent to which they retain their heritage, though clearly the impact of the past diminishes as families have new experiences. The language of the country of origin will serve to preserve its culture. Often family members vary in the rate at which they learn English (Lappin & Scott, Chap. 22). It is important to learn what language(s) were spoken while the children in the family were growing up.

A 45-year-old Greek man, raised in Astoria, Queens, where his parents, who migrated in their teens, never learned to speak much English, described his mother as uninterested in his life, "ignorant and incapable of much emotional response." His marital difficulties seemed a clear reflection of his feelings about his mother, so he was asked to bring her in for one session. (The father had died some years earlier.)

It turned out that his parents had known three languages (Greek, Russian, and Bulgarian). The mother spoke English with difficulty. She had never needed to learn it, as she lived in a traditional family, where women did not go beyond the home sphere. Her husband had been her translator when necessary, since he had needed English in his business. The son had spoken Greek throughout his childhood, but had lost much of it by now, so that he and his mother could barely communicate. When given the opportunity to speak in Greek, the mother showed an astonishing understanding of the problems her son was experiencing, in spite of the fact that he practically never spoke to her, and even when he did, never discussed anything in depth.

In the session, which was conducted in part in Greek, the mother's rich traditions and complicated childhood were discussed. The family had been prominent before being forced to emigrate, a loss from which they had never recovered. They had placed all their hopes on their only son, who had done very well academically and professionally. However, he was personally isolated, unable to get in touch with the wealth of his family heritage. He was shocked to realize how much he himself had let the language barrier prevent him from making emotional contact with his mother over the years and how much that had influenced his sense of identity, in spite of having the outward trappings of success.

Race and Country of Origin

Race has also been a major factor here since those whose skin color marked them as different always suffered more discrimination than others— they could not "pass" as other immigrants might try to do. This has left immigrants who are noticeably different physically from the dominant norm with no choice about their ethnic and racial identification.

Often those who look physically similar join or are lumped together as one group, even when they are not. Certain ethnic groups who were, in fact, historical strangers, if not enemies, may be identified with each other in the United States since that is how they are perceived. A Pakistani therapist will be expected to work better with an Indian family, in spite of generations of animosity; or an Argentinian Jew, raised in a situation of antisemitic prejudice in the country of origin, may be named administrator of the Hispanic section of a clinic because of language and geographic background. Often groups who are perceived as identical feel pressure to distinguish themselves from each other. West Indians, for example, whom Americans tend to identify with American Blacks, have had a different history and usually do not perceive themselves as the same group ethnically (Brice, Chap. 6). Or, on the other hand, groups from different backgrounds may join together for common needs as Hispanic groups have tended to do.

The Family's Place of Residence

Whether or not they live in an ethnic neighborhood will influence the impact of the family's cultural heritage on their lives.

The East and West coasts, which tend to be the points of entry for most immigrants, are likely to have greater ethnic diversity and ethnic neighborhoods, and people in these areas are more often aware of ethnic differences (the East more than the West). The ethnic neighborhood provided a temporary cushion against the stresses of migration that usually surface in the next generation. Those immigrant families who moved to an area where the population was relatively stable, for example, the South, generally have had more trouble adjusting (and were pressured to assimilate very rapidly).

The therapist should be informed about the ethnic network in the community and, if it is lacking, encourage the rebuilding of connections, through family visits or letters or creating new networks. Also, when family members move from the ethnic enclave, even several generations after immigration, the stresses of adaptation are likely to be severe.

The Socioeconomic Status, Educational Achievement, and Upward Mobility of Family Members

Even though there is evidence that ethnic distinctions play a less powerful role among the most educated and upwardly mobile segments of our population, ethnicity is still often a hidden stress. Upward mobility may lead families to dissociate themselves from their ethnic roots. In addition, groups differ in the extent to which they value education or "getting ahead," and this may cause intergroup prejudice as well as intergenerational conflict.

> An Italian medical student reported great frustration with his father who had high blood pressure. When the father was finally persuaded to consult a physician, he was given medication. He decided he would take it during the week, but weekends were his own and he would take a vacation from the medication. The son had great difficulty appreciating his father's need to assert that he would not let scientific regimens take complete control of his life—his living came first.

Family members may feel compelled to make a choice between moving ahead and loyalty to their group (Lee, Chap. 25). This in itself can be a source of severe identity conflict for family members.

The Emotional Process in the Family

Emotional factors will also influence the role ethnicity plays in the family (see Friedman, Chap. 24). Some families will hold onto their ethnic identification, becoming clannish or prejudiced in response to perceived threat to their integrity. They use ethnic identification as a pull for family loyalty. For other groups, for example, Scots, Irish, or French Canadians (see Langelier, Chap. 11), such an emotional demand would not be likely to hold much weight.

Most of us have some ambivalence about our ethnic identification. It is rarely a matter of indifference. It may appear to be, but we can all imagine situations where we would be proud to be identified with our group, others where we would be embarrassed, and situations where criticism would make us feel defensive. Those most exposed to prejudice and discrimination are obviously most likely to internalize negative feelings about their ethnic identity.

Frequently traits create such toxic reactions that they can barely be mentioned for fear of sounding prejudiced. Again, the groups that have experienced the most external discrimination are under the most pressure regarding their "negative" traits.

As in any emotionally determined situation, objective discussion of ethnic characteristics becomes impossible under stress. The therapist should be sensitive to this factor. Children who have not been exposed to the same ethnic discrimination their parents have lived through may have difficulty appreciating the emotional intensity with which the parents hold to their ethnic values.

The Political and Religious Ties to the Ethnic Group

As many sociologists have observed, politics is an area strongly influenced by ethnic identification. Americans join together on the basis of various similarities: class, union affiliation, economic interests, sex, geography, or ethnicity. Since our country's beginning, politicians have been extremely sensitive to the dynamics of the ethnic vote (Winawer-Steiner & Wetzel, Chap. 12). The more a person feels ethnically identified politically, the more the sense of ethnicity will be strengthened. This factor may lie dormant at one time and be aroused at another. Similarly, religion is a force that often strengthens ethnic identification. Generations of Irish children were strengthened ethnically not only by being the most political of all American ethnic groups (Greeley, 1981; Glazer & Moynihan, 1975), but by participating in a religion that was dominated by Irish clergy. (Generations of Italian, German, and, at times, Polish children also got a fair dose of Irish ethnicity along with their catechism.) Greeks have also been unified ethnically by the Greek church, which became the center of most Greek community activities and of

"Greek school," where the next generation was indoctrinated not only about religion, but also about the ancient Greeks and pride in their ethnic heritage.

Politics and religion are commonly ignored by therapists, but they are aspects of people's lives, which may be important sources of strength in times of stress. Therapists must assess the role they may play and their interface with ethnic values.

The Family Life Cycle

All of life is motion from and toward. Families who become symptomatic have become fixed in time. In the most basic sense, therapy aims to get the family back in motion. When ethnic stresses or transitions interact with life cycle transitions, the stresses inherent in all change are compounded.

Ethnicity interacts with the family life cycle at every stage. Migration is so disruptive in itself (Hinkle, 1974), that we could say it adds an entire extra stage to the life cycle for those families who must negotiate it. The readjustment to a new culture is by no means a single event, it is a prolonged developmental process of adjustment, which will affect family members differently, depending on the life cycle phase they are in at the time of the transition.

When family members come in the young adult phase, they may have the greatest potential for adapting to the new culture in terms of career and marital choice. However, they are perhaps the most vulnerable to cutting off their heritage, leaving themselves vulnerable to disconnection at later phases of the life cycle.

> Jack Johnson was admitted to the hospital for depression and alcohol withdrawal at age 58. He had migrated alone to the United States from Norway at age 24. He lived in a rooming house for several years, sent money back to his family in Norway, but never visited, and no family members ever visited him. At age 32 he married Mary, a third-generation Irish American, and became a peripheral member of her extended family. He worked hard as a carpenter, raised five children, and rarely spoke about his background. His family rarely asked. His father had died when Jack was in his teens, and his brother wrote that his mother died after Jack had been here for about 10 years. After that he gradually gave up the minimal correspondence he had kept up with his two brothers. He brought home his earnings, and his wife managed the family.
>
> Shortly before his admission to the hospital, Jack's wife had left him. She said that after the children were gone she found the relationship with him empty and could not stand his spending his weekends drinking. Jack moved into a rooming house, did not see much of his children after the separation, and drank increasingly. His landlady finally called the police when she found him passed out on the stairs.

While it would obviously be an oversimplification to attribute all of Jack's difficulties to his immigration and being cut off from his extended family, his vulnerability to later family stress seems to have been much increased by his distance from his family in early adulthood. The distance from parents that is appropriate at that phase could not be repaired at later phases, when the need for cultural support and identification tends to increase (Gelfand & Kutzik, 1979). This left him permanently cut off, unable to maintain continuity between his heritage and his children.

Therapy involved questioning Jack in detail about his background, not only about his family but about Norway, the meaning of Norwegian customs, his attitudes about his ethnicity, and helping him reconnect with his brothers. The following year he made the first trip back to his country of origin since leaving in 1946. He took with him his youngest daughter, who was particularly excited about the reconnection, feeling she had found a part of her father she had never even known about.

Families that migrate with young children are perhaps strengthened by having each other, but they are vulnerable to the parental reversal of hierarchies. If the family migrates with small children (even more so with teenagers), there is a likelihood that the parents will acculturate more slowly than their children, creating a problematic power reversal in the family (see Lappin & Scott, Chap. 22). If the children must take on the task of interpreting the new culture for the parents, parental leadership may be so threatened that children are left without effective adult authority to support them and without the positive identification with their ethnic background to ease their struggle with life in this new culture. If the parents have support in their cultural adjustment—through their work place or extended family and friends—the children's adjustment will be facilitated and may go more easily since children generally adapt well to new situations, even when it involves learning a new language. Problems may surface, however, in adolescence, when the children move out toward their peer culture (see Bernal, Chap. 9). Coaching the younger generation to show respect for the values of the older generation is usually the first step in negotiating such conflicts.

Families migrating when their children are adolescents may have more difficulty because they will have less time together as a unit before the children move out on their own. Thus the family must struggle with multiple transitions and generational conflicts at once. In addition, the distance from the grandparental generation in the old country may be particularly distressing as grandparents become ill, dependent, or die. The parents may experience severe stress in not being able to fulfill their obligations to their parents in the country of origin. It is not uncommon for symptoms to develop in adolescents in reaction to their parents' unexpressed distress. For example:

John was admitted to an adolescent psychiatric unit in an acute psychotic state at age 17, two weeks after a visit to Greece with his parents and younger sister. He had begun acting strangely while in Greece, where the paternal grandfather had died two months previously. John's grandmother was in good health, but according to John, was severely depressed and lonely. In his psychotic talking he spoke often of taking care of her and of bridging the two worlds of Greece and the United States. John's father had begun a successful restaurant business in the United States, into which he had brought his younger brother, brother-in-law, and two cousins. John's mother had no immediate family in the United States, and missed her own parents and sisters a great deal. However, her husband had told her before they came to this country that she must never think of returning, and she obeyed.

John's dilemma, reflected, at least partially, his concern that his parents were in an impossible dilemma—cut off from their families in Greece, unable to give up the strivings they had in the United States or to reconcile themselves with what they had left behind. He felt that his paternal grandfather's death symbolized for his mother that her own parents would die without her support. He worried about her almost continuously. Therapy involved helping the family sort through their cultural conflicts. The worry and concern for the family in Greece was reframed as a sign of their loving sensitivity, while their struggle to achieve in this country was also for the family's benefit. The mother was encouraged to stay in close touch with her parents and sisters in Greece but also to develop contacts with the Greek women in her church, which she had been avoiding in her preoccupation with her own family members in Greece.

When families migrate in the launching phase, it is less often because they seek a better way of life and more often because circumstances in the country of origin make remaining there impossible. This phase causes particular difficulties for families because it is much more difficult for the middle generation to break into new work and friendship networks at this phase. Again, if aging parents are left behind, the stresses will be intensified.

The launching phase may be made more complex when children date or marry spouses from other backgrounds. This is naturally perceived as a threat by many, if not most, parents since it means a loss of the cultural heritage in the next generation. One cannot underestimate the stress it creates for parents, who themselves have had to give up their country of origin, to fear the loss of their traditions when their children intermarry.

Migration in later life is often especially difficult because families are leaving so very much behind. There is evidence that even those who migrate at a young age have a strong need to reclaim their ethnic roots at this phase, particularly because they are losing other supports around them (Gelfand & Kutzik, 1979). For those who have not mastered English, life can be extremely isolating at this phase. The need to depend on others may be particularly frustrating, as when one is forced to be in a nursing home where one cannot communicate easily.

Sometimes if the first generation is older at the time of immigration and lives in an ethnic neighborhood in the new country, its conflicts of acculturation may be postponed. The next generation, particularly in adolescence, is likely to reject the ethnic values of their parents and strive to become "Americanized" (Sluzki, 1979). Intergenerational conflicts often reflect the value struggles of families in adapting to the United States.

The third or fourth generations are usually freer to reclaim aspects of their identities that were sacrificed in the previous generations because of the need to assimilate (Rotunno & McGoldrick, Chap. 16).

Families from different ethnic groups may have very different kinds of intergenerational struggles. WASP families are likely to feel they have failed if their children do not move away from the family and become independent (McGill & Pearce, Chap. 21), while Italian families are likely to feel they have failed if their children do move away. Jewish families will expect a relatively democratic atmosphere to exist in the family, with children free to challenge parents and to discuss their feelings openly (Herz & Rosen, Chap. 17). Greek families, in contrast, do not expect or desire open communication between generations and would not appreciate the therapist getting everyone together to discuss and "resolve" their conflicts. Children are expected to respect parental authority, which is maintained by the distance parents preserve from their children (Welts, Chap. 13). Irish families will be embarrassed to share feelings and conflicts across generations and cannot be expected to do so to any great extent.

Any life cycle transition can trigger off ethnic identity conflicts since they put families more in touch with the roots of their family traditions. How the rituals of transition are celebrated can make an important difference in how well the family will adjust to the changes (Friedman, 1980). All situational crises—divorce, illness, job loss, death, retirement—can compound ethnic identity conflicts, causing people to lose a sense of who they are. The more a therapist is sensitive to the need to preserve continuities, even in the process of change, the more he or she can help the family to maintain maximum control of its context and build upon it.

Intermarriage

Obviously intermarriage complicates geometrically the picture presented by a family of a single ethnic group. Generally, the greater the difference between spouses in cultural background, the more difficulty they will have in adjusting to marriage.

For example, a WASP/Italian couple might run into conflicts because the WASP takes literally the dramatic expressiveness of the Italian, while the Italian finds the WASP's emotional distancing intolerable. The WASP may label the Italian "hysterical" or "crazy" and be labeled in return "cold" or "catatonic." Knowledge about differences in cultural belief systems can be helpful to spouses who take each other's behavior personally. In the extreme, of course, it may also be used as an excuse for not taking responsibility in a relationship: "I'm Italian. I can't help it" (i.e., the yelling, abusive language, impulsiveness). Or, "I'm a WASP. It is just the way I am" (the lack of emotional response, the rationalization and workaholism). Or, "I can't help being late, we Puerto Ricans have a different conception of time."

Cultural and religious groups have always had prohibitions against intermarriage. Until 1967 when the laws were declared unconstitutional, 19 states had laws prohibiting racial intermarriage. Until 1970 the Catholic Church prohibited intermarriage with non-Catholics unless the latter promised to raise all children as Catholic. Intermarriage is feared because it threatens the survival of the group.

The likelihood of intermarriage obviously increases with the length of time an ethnic group is in this country, as well as with educational and occupational status. For example, in a nationwide survey of Catholics, 80% said their parents were from the same ethnic background, but only 55% of this generation were married to someone from the same ethnic background (Heer, 1980).

Just as understanding of family systems (family patterns, sibling positions, life cycle stages, etc.) is important for couples, so is understanding of ethnic differences (McGoldrick, 1980). Couples may have a sudden and remarkable shift in response when they can come to see the spouse's behavior fitting into a larger ethnic context rather than as a personal attack.

Couples who choose to marry are usually seeking a rebalance of the characteristics of their own ethnic background. They are moving away from some values as well as toward others. As with all systems, the positive feelings can, under stress, become negative. The extended families may stereotype the new spouse negatively—often a self-protective maneuver—reassuring themselves of their superiority, when they feel under threat. During courtship, a person may be attracted precisely to the fiance's differentness, but when entrenched in a marital relationship the same qualities often become the rub.

Friedman, in his discussion of the "Myth of the Shiksa," describes what he calls "cultural camouflage": the universal tendency of family members everywhere to avoid responsibility for their feelings, their actions, and their destiny by attributing their cause either to factors in their own background, or to aliens (*shiksas*) from a background that is foreign (*goyische*). Friedman's point is a very important one. Families may use their ethnic customs or religious values selectively to justify an emotional position within the family or against outsiders (Friedman, Chap. 24).

But our experience is that the opposite problem is equally difficult. That is, couples often react to each other as though the other's behavior were a personal attack rather than just a difference rooted in ethnicity. Typically, we tolerate differences when we are not under stress. In fact, we find them appealing. However, when stress is added to a system, our tolerance for difference diminishes. We become frustrated if we are not understood in ways that fit with our wishes and expectations. WASPs tend to withdraw when upset, to move toward stoical isolation, in order to mobilize their powers of reason (their major resource in coping with stress). Jews, on the other hand, seek to analyze their experience together; Italians may seek solace in food, emotional and dramatic expression of their feelings, and a high degree of human contact. Obviously these groups may perceive each other's reactions as offensive or insensitive although within each group's ethnic context their reactions make excellent sense. In our experience, much of therapy involves helping family members recognize each other's behavior as a reaction from a different frame of reference (McGoldrick, 1980, 1982).

> The Carbones applied for therapy after seven years of marriage. Tony was third-generation Italian American, the youngest of three sons, from a very closeknit family. He was the first to attend college, where he did very well and where he met Ann, the middle of three daughters from a Boston Brahmin family, whose ancestors had come over on the Mayflower. Ann's father was a banker, who ruled his family tyrannically. Her mother was a quiet, soft-spoken woman, who filled her life with social activities and hostessing for her husband's business friends. She suffered chronic headaches, which she never mentioned to anyone.
>
> Tony's career plans had changed when his oldest brother was injured in a car accident and the family needed him to take over the family business. (The middle brother was considered "weak" by the family and could not be given the job.) Tony and Ann had had a romantic courtship. Tony saw Ann as the ideal American woman: blond, beautiful, wealthy, sophisticated, and quietly charming. Ann was attracted to him for his dark good looks, humor, and easy outgoing manner. She appreciated that he was not a "stuffed shirt" like her father and that he liked to have a good time and to say what he thought.
>
> However, after they moved to Tony's hometown, Ann became unhappy. She felt uncomfortable at all of the family gatherings Tony insisted she attend with him on weekends. He often went off with his brothers and father and left her with his mother and aunts. In Ann's view he became angry, impulsive, and abusive when things did not go his way. She took to having headaches like her mother and gradually became quietly addicted to painkillers and alcohol.

A major part of therapy with this couple revolved around helping each of them to understand the other's behavior in an ethnic context. Tony came to realize that Ann's withdrawal and nonresponse were not aimed directly at him but were part of a general way she had learned at home of coping with stress. Ann came to appreciate that Tony's style, far from indicating that he did not love her, reflected his deep frustration that he was not able to stay in control of her happiness as his family obligation. Both of them were relieved to learn that the other's behavior was not meant to be destructive as it appeared. And both were relieved to realize that their own behavior was not as disturbed as they were coming to feel through their mutually escalating cycles. Each spouse gradually moved to more accommodation of their differences in perception: Tony by allowing Ann the space to solve her addiction for herself, and Ann by accepting Tony's expressions of frustration as a sign of his caring. She learned to respond to him rather than withdrawing from what she perceived as rejection.

Therapy

Appreciation of cultural variability leads to a radically new conceptual model of clinical intervention. Restoring a stronger sense of identity may require resolving cultural conflicts within the family, between the family and the community, or in the wider context in which the family is embedded. A part of differentiation involves selecting from our ethnic traditions those values we wish to retain and carry on. Families may need coaching to sort out deeply held convictions from values asserted for emotional reasons. This requires raising one's consciousness beyond the level of family to a perspective on the cultural relativity of all value systems.

Defining what response is adaptive in a given situation is not an easy task. It involves appreciation of the total context in which the behavior occurs. For example, Puerto Ricans in this country may see returning to Puerto Rico as a solution to their problems. A child who misbehaves may be sent back to live with family members. This solution may not be functional from the perspective that the child will then be isolated from the immediate family. The living situation in Puerto Rico may also not be adequate to provide for the child's needs. However, it is advisable for the clinician not to counter the parents' plan but to encourage them to strengthen their connectedness with the family members in Puerto Rico with whom their child would be staying in order to make the most of their wish to rely on their own network for support.

The therapist's role in such situations, as in all therapy, will be that of a culture broker, helping family members to recognize their own ethnic values and to resolve the conflicts that evolve out of different perceptions and experiences.

Often it is very difficult to understand the meaning of behavior without knowing something of the value orientations of the group. The same behavior may have very different meaning to families of different backgrounds.

For example, clients may not talk openly in therapy for many different reasons. Black clients may be uncommunicative, not because they cannot deal with their feelings, but because the context involves a representative of a traditional "White" institution, which they never had reason to trust. The Irish client's failure to talk might have nothing whatsoever to do with resisting the institutional context, but rather with embarrassment about admitting feelings to anyone, most especially to other family members. Norwegians might be withholding out of respect and politeness not to state openly certain less than positive feelings they have about other family members. It is a courtesy having nothing to do with either the therapy context or guilt about "unacceptable" feelings.

There are many examples of such misunderstood behavior. Puerto Rican women are taught to lower their eyes and avoid eye contact. American therapists are taught to read lack of eye contact as an indication of inability to relate to others. Jewish patients routinely inquire about the therapist's credentials, which many groups would perceive as a challenge and affront but is for them a needed reassurance. Iranian and Greek patients may ask for medication and give every indication of taking it and then go home and not take it as prescribed. Irish families may not praise or show overt affection for their children, for fear of giving them a "swelled head." Therapists may misread this behavior as lack of caring. Physical punishment, commonly used by many groups (Black, Greek, Iranian, Puerto Rican), may be misread as child abuse by American therapists unfamiliar with the norms of these groups. The list of possible misunderstandings is endless. The point is that therapists must never be too quick to judge the meaning of behavior they observe.

> For example, an Italian therapist who did an excellent evaluation of an Irish family, came for supervision to discuss his "failure," because in his view he had not managed to engage them, or "put them at ease." He misunderstood their awkwardness as resulting from his failure as a therapist to establish a congenial setting. Their stiffness and embarrassment in the situation had to do with their feelings about their son's misbehavior and not with the therapist at all. This trainee had to remind himself continuously throughout his work with this family that their emotional distance did not have the same meaning for them that it did for him.

Ethnicity Training

There are many who believe that cross-fertilization from one ethnic group to another is the best antidote to the "stuckness" families experience when their cultural adaptations fail. It is often said that Irish reserve is a good balance for Italian impulsiveness, while Italian expansiveness counters Irish repression. Jewish families who become stuck in their analyzing, may be helped by the WASP ethic that pushes to resolve the matter and move on. On the other hand, the constriction of WASP methods in dealing with emotional distress may be greatly helped by the Jewish value of sorting through the painful experiences and sharing the suffering. The recent movie *Ordinary People* was an excellent demonstration of the ways in which the values of one culture (in this case the values of a Jewish therapist) may be an excellent antidote to the rigidities of another culture (in this case a WASP family trapped in its inability to deal with tragedy).

We believe the best way we can learn is by being open to new possibilities and that this is much more likely when the training takes a positive point of view. It does not help therapists to be told only what they are doing wrong, what does not work, and how inappropriate traditional therapies are for the clients they see. They need to be offered something new to try. We make it a point in these chapters and in our training to emphasize what can be done over what will not work.

This model requires clinicians to struggle consciously with their own subjectivity and to recognize the limitations of any belief system in their work. We do not mean to imply that culture is the only or even the most important contextual factor to be considered in assessing problems and behavior. Social class and religious and regional identities are also extremely important. In addition, the impact of gender on personality, development, and illness behavior, though largely ignored until recently, cannot be overestimated (Silverstein, 1981; Carter & McGoldrick, 1980; Gluck, Dannefer, & Milea, 1980; Mechanic, 1978). Only when we come to realize the context-determined roots of our values can we shift to a systemic view of ourselves as part of a helping context. Only then will we leave behind the dichotomized mythology of the doctor "diagnosing" and labeling the patient as though by some objective measures of reality. We are always a part of the systems we are trying to observe, and our participation affects our observations. This perspective is a prerequisite for understanding and intervening in the complexities of interacting systems.

In our view the most important part of ethnicity training involves the therapist coming to understand his or her own ethnic identity in a differentiated way. Similar to the emphasis that Bowenites place on the therapists' working out the relationships in their own families or origin, we think that differentiation requires going a step beyond this to a resolution of our own ethnic identity. This means, ideally, that therapists would no longer be "triggered" by ethnic characteristics they may have regarded negatively nor be caught in an ethnocentric view that their groups values are more "right" or "true" than others. No group has a corner on truth. Resolving the psychological issues of ethnic identity involves achieving a multiethnic perspective where we are open to understanding values that differ from our own and no longer need to convince others of our values or give in to theirs.

We try to teach a way of thinking more than specific information about different ethnic groups, but our experience has taught us repeatedly that theoretical discussions about the importance of ethnicity are practically useless in training clinicians. We come to appreciate the relativity of values best through specifics. Thus in our training we work a great deal through detail. How do groups differ in their responses to pain, in their attitudes about doctors, in their beliefs about suffering? Do they prefer a formal or informal style in dealing with strangers? Do they tend to feel positive about their bodies? about work? about marital intimacy? about children expressing their feelings? In other words, we try to offer rules of thumb.

Obviously the study of ethnocultural factors in therapy could hardly be based on encouraging therapists to learn the differences in values, family patterns, life cycle rituals, and attitudes toward therapy of all groups. It would be a big mistake to suggest that therapists need to become cultural anthropologists in order to be effective clinicians. So what do we expect? Even if many of us (about half) marry into another ethnic group, have close friends from other backgrounds, or live in another culture, we are still not likely to have too keen an understanding of the world view of more than a few groups. The best approach is probably for clinicians to focus on a few groups with whom they have considerable exposure as a way of training themselves to be more aware of the cultural relativity of all norms and values.

Ethnicity, like family systems, may at times be a very loaded issue for trainees. Even an objective discussion of cultural differences may trigger off disturbing feelings or memories of early ethnic experiences. The psychological scars of negative stereotyping and discrimination are often still there— the cultural memory can readily come alive with a seemingly harmless joke or ethnic reference.

In our experience there are two major resistances to ethnicity training. The first is the attitude that ethnicity is a subject we all understand, it is common sense, and there is no particular need to develop a special program to study it when there are so many other critical priorities to be covered in training. We think this issue can best be responded to through concrete, useful clinical suggestions.

The second resistance, which is more difficult to address, is an active reluctance to define ethnic differences. At times this may come from minority groups who fear that in a discussion of ethnic differences in general their own group will be lost. More often the resistance comes from deep-seated fears about labels. It is usually predictable that those who are the most upset about discussion of ethnic differences, have charged personal reasons for their reactions.

> Once in doing a presentation about the Irish I began to discuss their high tolerance for drinking, and the many functions that drinking serves in Irish culture. Suddenly a very Irish-looking woman stood up in the audience and began in a barely controlled manner to challenge me for stereotyping. I was taken quite by surprise since the Irish attitudes about drinking have been much discussed and are not particularly a matter for debate. It was not until some while later that it came out in working with this young woman that her Irish father's drinking had been the central fact of her childhood. She heard the characterization of the Irish as drinkers as a pronouncement of doom on her family, which was very painful to her.

It is extremely important in beginning ethnicity training to set up a safe context. We must make the training situation safe for stereotyping, that is, for generalizing about cultural differences. Nothing would make failure more likely than to begin training with a description of characteristics of different ethnic groups without making clear to the group the need to use generalizations, which will reflect at best only partial truths.

One of the best ways we know to do this is by describing our own reluctance to stereotype—our fears of being labeled as prejudiced or racist and the alternative possibility of not talking about differences at all.

Presentations of one group alone are rarely successful because they lead the audience to think of the exceptions to the rule. Once a number of cultures are presented together it is easier to recognize, for example, that while all Irish are not alike, they probably are, indeed, a good deal more like each other than they are like Greeks or Russians.

In training groups we often ask participants to (1) describe themselves ethnically, (2) describe who in their family experience influenced their sense of ethnic identity, (3) discuss which groups other than their own they think they understand best, (4) discuss which characteristics of their ethnic group they like most and which they like least, (5) discuss how they think their own family would react to having to go to family therapy and what kind of approach they would prefer.

Conclusion

It is hard for us to remain open to the wide range of cultural possibilities. Ambiguity and difference are threatening, and we tend to close down emotionally when confronted with too much of them. Understanding the relativity of our own ethnic biases is the best insurance against such rigidity. Yet this insight is hard to gain.

For us as therapists there are particular difficulties in stepping outside our belief systems. Not all cultures value the pursuit of insight, truth, "getting ahead," or sharing problems and feelings. By exploring our ethnic assumptions, we are led to question our primary therapeutic techniques. It is no wonder we are threatened.

The extensive geographical and class mobility in American culture, while often cutting individuals off from their ethnic heritage, increases their contact with different ethnic groups. The high rate of interethnic marriage means that many Americans will learn about ethnic differences from marriage partners.

But, at best, most Americans probably come to understand well only three or four groups in the course of a lifetime. Obviously, no therapist can become an expert on all ethnic groups. What is essential for clinicians is to develop an attitude of openness to cultural variability and to the relativity of their own values.

Some potential negative consequences of emphasizing ethnicity must also be recognized. Overly strict adherence to a particular way of doing things, under the supposition that it is an "ethnic" value, can make an ethnic group resist change and thereby impede its development. Values that were functional in another place and time often become dysfunctional when translated into modern America. Ethnocentrism, clannishness, prejudice, fear, and distrust of outsiders can prevent cooperation, reinforce exclusivity, and deepen intergroup conflicts (Giordano & Giordano, 1977; Kolm, 1973). However, the solution to these problems lies not in eradicating cultural differences but in developing their potential to become a source of cultural enrichment.

ACKNOWLEDGMENT

Special thanks to Kathy Milea, John Pearce, and Joe Giordano for the many hours of discussion and suggestions for the development of this chapter.

REFERENCES

Allen, W.R. Black Family Research in the United States: A Review, Assessment and Extension. *Journal of Comparative Family Studies, 9*, 166–188, 1978.

Block, C.B. Black Americans and the Cross-Cultural Counseling and Psychotherapy Experience. In A.B. Marsella & P.B. Pedersen (Eds.), *Cross-Cultural Counseling and Psychotherapy.* New York: Pergamon, 1981.

Bowen, M. *Georgetown Symposium,* Washington, D.C., 1981.

Boyd, N. Family Therapy with Black Families. In S. Corchin & E. Jones (Eds.), *Minority Mental Health.* New York: Holt, Rinehart & Winston, 1980.

Carpenter, W., & Strauss, J. Cross-Cultural Evaluation of Schneider's First-Rank Symptoms of Schizophrenia: A Report from the International Pilot Study of Schizophrenia. *American Journal of Psychiatry, 131,* 204–210, 1974.

Carter, E.A., & McGoldrick, M. (Eds.). *The Family Life Cycle: A Framework for Family Therapy.* New York: Gardner Press, 1980.

Cassim, H. *The Maintenance of Family Ties in Italian Immigrant Families.* Master's thesis, Hahnemann Medical College, Philadelphia, 1982.

Cobbs, P. Ethnotherapy in Groups. In L. Soloman & B. Berzon (Eds.), *New Perspectives on Encounter Groups.* San Francisco: Jossey-Bass, 1972.

Eisenberg, L. Psychiatry and Society: A Sociobiologic Synthesis. *New England Journal of Medicine, 296,* 903–910, 1977.

Erikson, E.H. *Childhood and Society.* New York: Norton, 1950.

Falicov, C., & Karrer, B. Cultural Variations in the Family Life Cycle. In E.A. Carter & M. McGoldrick (Eds.), *The Family Life Cycle: A Framework for Family Therapy.* New York: Gardner Press, 1980.

Fandetti, D. *Day Care in Working Class Ethnic Neighborhoods: Implications for Policy and Programming.* Paper presented at the Baltimore Conference on Ethnicity and Social Welfare. New York: Institute on Pluralism and Group Identity, 1976.

Fantl, B., & Shiro, J. Cultural Variables in the Behavior Patterns of Symptom Formation of 15 Irish and 15 Italian Schizophrenics. *International Journal of Social Psychiatry, 4*(4), 245–253, 1959.

Foley, V.C. Family Therapy with Black Disadvantaged Families: Some Observations on Roles, Communication, and Technique. *Journal of Marriage and Family Counseling, 1,* 57–65, 1975.

Friedman, E. Systems and Ceremonies. In E.A. Carter & M. McGoldrick (Eds.), *The Family Life Cycle: A Framework for Family Therapy.* New York: Gardner Press, 1980.

Gambino, R. *Blood of My Blood: The Dilemma of Italian-Americans.* Garden City, N.Y.: Doubleday, 1974.

Gelfand, D.E., & Kutzik, A.J. (Eds.). *Ethnicity and Aging.* New York: Springer, 1979.

Giordano, J., & Giordano, G.P. *The Ethno-Cultural Factor in Mental Health: A Literature Review and Bibliography.* New York: Institute on Pluralism and Group Identity, 1977.

Giordano, J., & Riotta-Sirey, J. *An Italian American Identity.* Unpublished paper, Institute on Pluralism and Group Identity, New York, 1981.

Glazer, N., & Moynihan, D. (Eds.). *Ethnicity: Theory and Experience.* Cambridge: Harvard University Press, 1975.

Gluck, N.R., Dannefer, E., & Milea, K. Women in Families. In E.A. Carter & M. McGoldrick (Eds.), *The Family Life Cycle: A Framework for Family Therapy.* New York: Gardner Press, 1980.

Greeley, A.M. *Why Can't They Be Like Us?* New York: Institute of Human Relations Press, 1969.

Greeley, A.M. *The American Catholic.* New York: Basic Books, 1978.

Greeley, A.M. *The Irish Americans.* New York: Harper & Row, 1981.

Harwood, A. (Eds.). *Ethnicity and Medical Care.* Cambridge: Harvard University Press, 1981.

Heer, D.M. Intermarriage. In S. Thernstrom, A. Orlov, & O. Handlin (Eds.), *Harvard Encyclopedia of American Ethnic Groups.* Cambridge: Harvard University Press, 1980.

Hinkle, L.E. The Effects of Exposure to Culture Change, Social Change and Changes in Interpersonal Relationships on Health. In B.S. Dohrenwend & B.P. Dohrenwend (Eds.), *Stressful Life Events.* New York: Wiley, 1974.

Horney, K. *The Neurotic Personality of Our Time.* New York: Norton, 1937.

Jacobs, D., Charles, E., Bocobs, T., Weinstein, H., & Man, D. Preparation for Treatment of the Disadvantaged Patient: Effects on Disposition and Outcome. *American Journal of Orthopsychiatry, 42*(4), 666–673, 1972.

Kiev, A. *Transcultural Psychiatry.* New York: Free Press, 1972.

Klein, J. *Jewish Identity and Self Esteem: Healing Wounds through Ethnotherapy.* New York: Institute on Pluralism and Group Identity, 1980.

Kleinman, A.M. Explanatory Models in Health Care Relationships. In *Health of the Family* (National Council for International Health Symposium). Washington, D.C.: National Council for International Health, 1975.

Kleinman, A.M., Eisenberg, L., & Good, B. Culture, Illness, and Care: Clinical Lessons from Anthropologic and Cross-Cultural Research. *Annals of Internal Medicine, 88,* 251–258, 1978.

Kluckhohn, F.R., & Strodtbeck, F.L. *Variations in Value Orientations.* New York: Harper & Row, 1961.

Kolm, R. *Ethnicity and Society: A Theoretical Analysis and Its Implications for the United States.* Rockville, Md.: National Institute of Mental Health, 1973.

Levine, E.S., & Padilla, A.M. *Crossing Cultures in Therapy: Pluralistic Counseling for the Hispanic.* Monterey, Calif.: Brooks/Cole, 1980.

Levine, I. Personal communication, 1981.

Lieberman, M. *Adaptational Patterns in Middle Aged and Elderly: The Role of Ethnicity.* Paper presented at the Conference of the Gerontological Society, Portland, Ore., October 1974.

McAdoo, H. Family Therapy in the Black Community. *American Journal of Orthopsychiatry, 47,* 75–79, 1977.

McGoldrick, M. The Joining of Families through Marriage: The New Couple. In E. Carter & M. McGoldrick (Eds.), *The Family Life Cycle: A Framework for Family Therapy.* New York: Gardner Press, 1980.

McGoldrick, M. Normal Families: An Ethnic Perspective. In F. Walsh (Ed.), *Normal Family Processes.* New York: Guilford Press, 1982.

McGoldrick, M., & Pearce, J.K. Family Therapy with Irish Americans. *Family Process, 20*(2), 223–241, 1981.

Mechanic, D. Sex, Illness, Illness Behavior and the Use of Health Services. *Social Science and Medicine, 12B,* 207–214, 1978.

Mindel, C., & Habenstein, R. (Eds.). *Ethnic Families in America*. New York: Elsevier, 1976.

Minuchin, S., Montalvo, B., Guerney, B., Rosman, B., & Schumer, F. *Families of the Slums*. New York: Basic Books, 1967.

Opler, M.K., & Singer, J.L. Ethnic Differences in Behavior and Psychopathology: Italian and Irish. *International Journal of Social Psychiatry, 1*, 11–17, 1956.

Papajohn, J., & Spiegel, J. *Transactions in Families*. San Francisco: Jossey-Bass, 1975.

Pinto, T. *Ethnicity and Professional Education: A Survey of Curriculum Content*. Unpublished paper, Institute of Pluralism and Group Identity, New York, 1976.

Rabkin, J., & Struening, E. *Ethnicity, Social Class and Mental Illness in New York City*. New York: Institute of Pluralism and Group Identity, 1976.

Rakel, R.E. *Principles of Family Medicine*. Philadelphia: Saunders, 1977.

Sanua, V. Sociocultural Factors in Responses to Stressful Life Situations: The Behavior of Aged Amputees as an Example. *Journal of Health and Human Behavior, 1*, 17–24, 1960.

Sanua, V. *Evaluation of Psychotherapy with Different Socioeconomic and Ethnic Groups: A Need for Rethinking in the Training of Therapists*. Paper presented at the Annual Conference of New York Society of Clinical Psychology, New York, April 1975.

Satir, V. Personal communication, March 1981.

Shibutani, T., & Kwan, K.M. *Ethnic Stratification*. New York: Macmillan, 1965.

Silverstein, O. *Fusion*. Paper presented at Conference on Mothers and Daughters. New York, February 1981.

Singer, J., & Opler, M.K. Contrasting Patterns of Fantasy and Motility in Irish and Italian Schizophrenics. *Journal of Abnormal and Social Psychiatry, 53*, 42–47, 1956.

Sluzki, C. Migration and Family Conflict. *Family Process, 18*(4), 379–390, 1979.

Sowell, T. *Ethnic America*. New York: Basic Books, 1981.

Spiegel, J. *Transactions: The Interplay between Individual, Family and Society* (J. Papajohn, Ed.). New York: Science House, 1971.

Staples, R., & Mirande, A. Racial and Cultural Variations among American Families: A Decennial Review of the Literature on Minority Families. *Journal of Marriage and the Family, 42*, 887–903, 1980.

Stein, H.F. The Slovak-American "Swaddling Ethos": Homeostat for Family Dynamics and Cultural Persistence. *Family Process, 17*, 31–46, 1978.

Stoeckle, J., Zola, I.K., & Davidson, G. The Quality and Significance of Psychological Distress in Medical Patients. *Journal of Chronic Disease, 17*, 959–970, 1964.

Taketomo, Y., & Feiner, J. An Introduction to Culture Course for Psychiatric Residents. To be published.

Teper, S. *Ethnicity, Race and Human Development*. New York: Institute on Pluralism and Group Identity, American Jewish Committee. In press.

Thernstrom, S., Orlov, A., & Handlin, O. (Eds.). *Harvard Encyclopedia of American Ethnic Groups*. Cambridge: Harvard University Press, 1980.

Thomas, A., & Sillen, S. The Illusion of Color Blindness. In A. Thomas & S. Sillen (Eds.), *Racism and Psychiatry*. New York: Brunner/Mazel, 1972.

Tseng, W.-S., & McDermott, J.F. *Culture, Mind and Therapy: An Introduction to Cultural Psychiatry*. New York: Brunner/Mazel, 1981.

Watzlawick, P. *How Real Is Real?* New York: Random House, 1976.

Zborowski, M. *People in Pain*. San Francisco: Jossey-Bass, 1969.

Zola, I.K. Culture and Symptoms: An Analysis of Patients' Presenting Complaints. *American Sociological Review, 5*, 141–155, 1966.

Zola, I.K. The Concept of Trouble and Sources of Medical Assistance. *Social Science and Medicine, 6*, 673–679, 1972.

Zuk, G.H. A Therapist's Perspective on Jewish Family Values. *Journal of Marriage and Family Counseling, 4*, 110–111, 1978.

2

An Ecological Model of Ethnic Families

JOHN SPIEGEL

This chapter will describe an ecological approach to ethnic families. We think it is important at the outset to provide you with a map of the field of family therapy within which to place this approach. Therefore, we believe it will be useful to sketch an outline of the similarities and differences among various approaches into which we may plug the ecological, or, in our terminology, the transactional field approach. Of course, a map is not an exhaustive nor an in-depth analysis but rather a quick survey of the landscape.

Commonalities

All family therapies hold in common three basic ideological assumptions. They may differ in the degree to which the assumptions are articulated or held at the center of attention, but they can be located at either the explicit or implicit level in their approach to theory, diagnosis, and treatment. They are as follows.

The Systems Approach

Family therapists pay as much attention to the family (whether nuclear or extended) as a system of interactive processes as they do the individual who happens to be the identified patient or client. It is assumed that in order to help the identified patient, the family will have to change some of the habitual—or ritual—ways in which it interacts and produces insoluble problems for the patient.

However, any variation or deviation from the basic routines of family interaction will be countered by a reaction among the members to restore the previous balance, no matter how pathological its effects for one or more family members. Such resistance is expected during the course of therapy and is usually ascribed to a homeostatic mechanism within the family system.

John Spiegel. Florence Heller School for Advanced Studies in Social Welfare, Brandeis University, Waltham, Massachusetts.

In addition, it is thought that the way the identified patient gets trapped in dysfunctional interactions is of greater concern than the particular psychopathological label that others have attached to the patient. While the clinician may focus on diagnostic terminology for particular purposes of research or epidemiology, when he or she is seeing a family, the attention goes to family process.

The Structural Approach

In general, family therapists, of whatever persuasion, are structuralists in the tradition of Levi-Strauss (1963) and Chomsky (1965), backed up by the long tradition of psychoanalysis. The observed behavior of family members is thought to be a surface phenomenon, generated by deeper and unobservable layers of structure that must be inferred.

Family theorists conceptualize these deeper structures in various ways, but all of them look for hidden patterns: distorted or disguised interactions, disqualifications, metamessages operating at a level opposite to the message conveyed, unappreciated ego masses, undiscovered coalitions, triads, rubber boundaries, pseudomutualities, schisms and skews, cultural value systems, or whatever. The task of the therapist, then, is to bring these deeper layers to the surface so that family members can change them.

The Interdisciplinary Approach

As a rule, family therapists bring their professional or disciplinary training into their understanding of family processes not as a rigid set of guidelines but as their contribution to the pooled effort involved in the treatment process. Cotherapists, for example, are usually from different disciplines since it is believed that each profession has something to give and to learn from the others.

Despite the tendencies of psychiatrists to consider themselves *primus inter pares*, theoretical and pragmatic contributions to the therapeutic process have frequently—as in the cases of Haley (1976) and Bateson (1972)—emanated from outside the helping professions. This openness to outside influences is more characteristic of family therapy than of any other treatment technology.

Divergences

The differences among the models emerge from two sets of dichotomies: (1) theoretical concepts borrowed from one field and then applied to family therapy versus a theoretical approach growing out of the direct experience with family therapy and (2) strict focus on the family itself versus inclusion of wider institutional contexts.

With respect to the first dichotomy, some family therapists have based their work on psychoanalytic or psychodynamic theory arising from work with individuals. They have simply broadened their theoretical approach to include the different family members. This approach grew out of child psychiatry, where the therapist always looked at mother–child interactions and sometimes saw one or the other parent as a part of the therapeutic process, as exemplified in the early work of Ackerman (1958). It also emerged from work with schizophrenic patients represented in the writings of Framo (1965) and Boszormenyi-Nagy (1962).

The theory of small group psychotherapy, such as the work of Bell (1961), has also been transferred and modified for application to the family as a group. Similarly, learning theory and behavior modification techniques (frequently with the addition of cognitive theoretical components), have been applied to family therapy (Mash, Hamerlynck, & Handy, 1975). Some borrowing of theory and technique is inevitable since we all stand on the shoulders of our predecessors. What is significant here is that the borrowed technique, as for the example in the behavioral approaches, is made the clinical focus.

These techniques stand in contrast to the theories and approaches that have grown out of direct experience with families, such as Bowen's Systems Therapy (1978) that grew out of work with schizophrenics and their families; the structural approach developed by Minuchin (1974) and his coworkers at the Philadelphia Child Guidance Clinic that grew out of work with Hispanic and Black families; and the problem-solving approach developed by Watzlawick, Beavin, and Jackson (1967), Haley (1976), and others in Palo Alto, California, that grew out of work, at least at first, with schizophrenics. The fundamental differences are so basic that they cannot be seen as equivalent to each other.

For example, the innovative aspects of the structural and problem-solving approaches are often so at odds with both common sense and traditional psychodynamic theory as to require a 180-degree switch in the mind set of the therapist. They both require, often from the first interview, a direct and sometimes dramatic intervention by the therapist that bypasses the surface phenomenon to get to the deeper structures activating the family interactions. This is clearly in contrast to the wait-and-see minimal interpretive techniques of the psychodynamically oriented therapists. Where the issue is "common sense," the intervention is more complex since it frequently features a paradoxical form of communication that is alien both to the logic of ordinary communications and to the interpretive procedures of the psychodynamic approach. Similarly, both the structural and problem-solving approaches tend to focus on the here and now of dysfunctional family transactions, while waiting for the past influences on current behavior (e.g., developmental childhood experiences of family members), to appear as a matter of course. However, in order to facilitate the exposure of these hidden interactions, therapists may borrow techniques, such as family sculpting or guided fantasy, from other more psychodynamic approaches.

The point we wish to make here is that we could not have predicted the emergence of these innovative approaches from a knowledge of the prior history of the field. By the same token, we cannot, at this stage, predict their relevance in the future. For example, it is not yet apparent how the technique of paradoxical communication can be useful to the human services generally.

The Institutional Context

The models discussed so far have been concerned primarily with the family as a system in its own right. The relationships between the family and wider institutional contexts stay in the background or emerge only as a context for symptomatic behavior, such as a child with a school problem or a couple involved in a court battle because of divorce proceedings. In such instances attention may be focused for a time on the characteristics of the school or the behavior of lawyers.

There are three interrelated approaches, however, that take a different, more varied, and more flexible position with respect to family systems or subsystems and that make an effort to deal with the interface between the family and the wider social system.

The first is the ecological approach proposed by Auerswald (1968, 1972, 1974). Based on a sweeping indictment of Western ideology and cognitive styles that are compared unfavorably with Eastern belief systems, his ecological program attributes the fragmentation and specialization of our service delivery institutions to the hierarchical, linear thinking about space and time in which we have all been educated. In its place, this program proposes a more complex and flexible thought structure that examines relationships. Ecological analysis has been a small but long-standing topic in the field of experimental psychology. For a review of this topic, see Berry (1980).

Where service delivery is concerned, this means transcending the firm boundaries and the associated intake policies of agencies to make the connections that individuals and families need in order to modify the dysfunctional ways in which they are maintaining (or failing to maintain) themselves in their environmental situation. For example, we all know of and complain about the inefficiencies caused by the organizational structure and work habits of social service agencies. But after a period of time, most attempts at innovative solutions of these problems get washed away by withdrawal of funding or burnout of leadership. Often according to Auerswald (1974), it is the implicit Western thought ways that cause the counterproductive fragmentation and specialization that requires attention first.

The second of these broader approaches is network therapy, as proposed by Speck and Attneave (1973) and Pattison (1977), among others. While still entailing an ecological principle, network therapy is more pragmatic and less ideological. This model assumes that any dysfunctional stalemate in the nuclear family may well be reinforced by the extended family or by friends or significant others in the neighborhood or community, or even by relatives living at a distance.

In therapy, attempts are made to assemble components from the wider systems, to reveal whatever pathological structures are being maintained by means of the network, to identify key persons involved in the reinforcing process, and to bring others into the network who may be able to provide a more benevolent, supportive function. Attention is paid to possible support systems wherever they are located and to the cultural and ethnic issues inherent in any environmental niche occupied by the family.

The third of these broader models, the transactional field approach, is associated with my own work (Spiegel, 1971; Papajohn & Spiegel, 1975). We took the word "transactions" (which is now coming into popular usage in the professional literature) from the philosopher John Dewey and the political scientist Arthur Bentley. Looking at the whole of Western civilization, Dewey and Bentley (1950) identified two principal explanatory thought ways and then proposed a third to make up for the deficiencies of the first two.

The first, "self-action," describes an entity as operating under its own internal powers or disposition. Aristotle's explanation of gravity—that a stone falls to earth because it is disposed to go back to its natural resting place—is a prototypical self-action concept. Contemporary child development studies, which are increasingly concerned with innate qualities of the human organism, are examples of this type of thinking.

The second mode of explanation, "interaction," involves thing acting upon thing acting upon thing. The origin of interactional thinking can be traced to Newton's theory of gravity, which posits a force of attraction exerted by objects upon each other over a distance of space. All stimulus-response observations and therapeutic procedures (e.g., behavior modification) grow out of interactional thinking.

Both self-actional and interactional thinking proceed in a straight line in time and space, from first to final causes. Perhaps more importantly, they suggest dependent or independent relationships rather than systems or processes; and when applied to human relations they create "blame systems" or pejorative labels. Thus, we get schizophrenogenic mothers, passive or immature fathers, delinquents, and so on, all acting or reacting in their roles as victims or victimizers in linear (or developmental) time.

To transcend these limitations, Dewey and Bentley proposed the term "transaction," which denotes system in process with system, where no entity can be located as first or final cause. In the case of the identified patient, whatever behavior is displayed is viewed within the context of the patient's ecological niche, or—in my terms—the transactional field (see Figure 2.1).

The Universe is concerned with the nonliving world in general, all the way from the cosmos to the atomic nucleus. It includes the house or dwelling

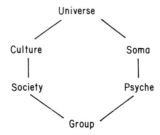

FIG. 2.1. Organization of the transactional field.

in which a family lives; the land on which that house is built; the surrounding terrain, urban or rural; the quality of the air a family breathes; and the food resources it consumes. Processes included in Universe are in transaction with processes in Soma, the anatomical structures and physiological processes within the human organism. The next focus, Psyche, takes in cognition, perception, problem-solving, conflict elaboration and reduction, emotional arousal, habit formation, and communication. Personality results from the integration of processes within Psyche, and from its transactions, on the one side, with Soma and, on the other, with the focus called Group. It is in groups such as the family, that behavior receives situational definitions and role attributions. However, groups do not exist in isolation from each other. They receive their forms and functions in accordance with their place in the larger network of social systems that we label Society. Finally, the family as a social institution, along with the other religious, educational, economic, legal, governmental, recreational, and voluntary institutions that make up Society, are anchored in a set of beliefs and values about the nature of the world and human existence known as Culture. Culture in turn contributes to the survival of a society in its ecological niche, as well as forming the basis of a people's beliefs about the nature of the Universe, thereby completing the circling of the transactional field.

Value Orientation Theory and Its Application: The United States Case

Therapeutic interventions are usually conceived as being directed at the process of conflict, anxiety, and defense systems within the individual or the family (or preferably both). The ecological approach keeps in mind that imbalance and conflict may arise from any focus in the transactional field. For example, it may begin with Society during times of economic depression, war, or rapid social change; or from Universe, as in the case of hurricanes or other natural disasters. Thus, illness, including mental illness, becomes only one aspect of destabilization, an aspect that gets overemphasized in the medical model. Making pathologies out of our imbalances and role conflicts within the family is not very helpful and may be, in fact, harmful; but making pathologies out of our value conflicts and cultural misunderstandings within ethnic or minority families can be even more harmful. Therefore, the ecological approach suggests that in families undergoing acculturation, Culture is the focus from which to begin the therapeutic process. It also recognizes that in addition to dealing with the clash of cultural norms, therapy needs to take into account the strengths within ethnic families—those cultural values that have facilitated survival in the ecological niche.

Again, the therapist working with an individual ethnic family needs to have a way to contrast his or her middle-class standards and beliefs and the values of different ethnic minorities. Table 2.1 is based on the theory of variation in cultural value orientations proposed by Kluckhohn (Kluckhohn & Strodtbeck, 1961). According to Kluckhohn, orientations are distinguished from concrete values by their levels of generality. "A value orientation is a generalized and organized conception, influencing behavior of time, of nature, of man's place in it, of man's relation to man, and of the desirable and undesirable aspects of man–environment and inter-human transactions" (Kluckhohn, 1951).

Operating within the Psyche focus of the transactional field, value orientations have three distinguishing qualities: (1) directional—they provide a program for selecting behaviors between more or less favored alternative behaviors; (2) cognitive—they provide a view of the nature of the world and of human affairs; and (3) affective—they are never taken lightly—people are ready to bleed and die for them—and they are the main reason why people and organizations become so resistant to change.

The classification of value orientations set forth in Table 2.1 is based on the following assumptions:

1. There are a limited number of common human problems for which all people in all places must find some solutions. These are:

a. Time—the temporal focus of human life

b. Activity—the preferred pattern of action in interpersonal relations

c. The Relational Orientation—the preferred way of relating in groups

d. The Man–Nature Orientation—the way people relate to the natural or the supernatural environment

e. The Basic Nature of Man—the attitudes held about the innate good or evil in human behavior.

2. Although there is variability in the solutions to these problems, this variability is neither limitless nor random but occurs within a range of three possible solutions for each of these problems.

a. Time—Past, Present, Future

TABLE 2.1. Comparison of Value Orientation Profiles

	American middle class	Italian	Irish
Time	Future > Present > Past	Present > Past > Future	Present > Past > Future
Activity	Doing > Being > Being-in-Becoming	Being > Being-in-Becoming > Doing	Being > Being-in-Becoming > Doing
Relational	Individual > Collateral > Lineal	Collateral > Lineal > Individual	Lineal > Collateral > Individual
Man–Nature	Dominant over > Subjugated > Harmony	Subjugated > Harmony > Dominant over	Subjugated > Harmony > Dominant over
Basic Nature of Man	Neutral > Evil > Good	Mixed > Evil > Good	Evil > Mixed > Good

    b. Activity—Doing, Being, Being-in-Becoming

    c. Relational—Individual, Collateral, Lineal

    d. Man–Nature—Harmony-with-Nature, Mastery-over-Nature, Subjugated-to-Nature

    e. Basic Nature of Man—Neutral/Mixed, Good, Evil.

3. All possible solutions are in varying degrees present in the total cultural structure of every society, and every society will be characterized not only by a dominant profile of first-order value choices but also by substitute second- and third-order choices. Differences among various cultures are based on the pattern of preferences for each of these solutions in a dominant-substitute profile of values.

However, in the process of sociocultural change, second-order choices may be moved into the first order and vice versa. This is often the key to understanding generational problems between parents and children or marital difficulties, either in a cross-cultural marriage or in a marriage where one spouse is adapting faster than the other.

In Table 2.1, U.S. middle-class preferences are compared with those of Southern Italian and rural Southern Irish families. Since the rank-ordered patterns for the American middle class exert the pull toward which ethnic groups move, let us begin with these mainstream values.

It is probably no great surprise that the American middle class places the Future orientation in the first-order position to the dimension of Time in human affairs. Americans plan their families, as well as their educational and occupational careers. They cut up their days and weeks into small time segments that they keep track of in little black appointment books.

This emphasis on the Future has certain implications. It places importance on novelty and transience. Anything new becomes better than anything old, whether it be a new car, a new style, or a new idea. No one wants to be old-fashioned, left behind, or outmoded in the inexorable push for change. Youth is highly regarded as the representative of the future, while the elderly have so little future left to them they tend to take a back seat and are frequently neglected.

Mainstream Americans do take time out to live in the Present, their second-order choice. A Present-time orientation occurs in recreational situations, when people are supposed to have fun and forget about the Future. Even then, they may be so aware of taking time out they start looking at their watches, thinking, "I have to go home because I have to get up early tomorrow."

The Past is in a weak third-order position. Independence Day, Thanksgiving, and other Past-time oriented holidays are used for Present-time enjoyment, not for serious reenactment of a highly valued past. Nostalgia kicks notwithstanding, we are pro progress and anti tradition.

In the Activity dimension, the Doing orientation is at the core of the U.S. life-style. The competitiveness, the striving for upward mobility in jobs and social contacts are all associated with Doing. The first question asked of a stranger is, "What do you do?" and self-esteem depends as much (if not more) on how the world views our accomplishments than on internal standards.

Whereas Doing often involves controlling our feelings to get the job done properly and thus gain recognition, the Being alternative refers to the spontaneous expression of our inner feelings in any given situation. The second-order position of Being in the U.S. pattern is the consequence of its restriction to a limited number of contexts, such as family and recreational situations.

The Being-in-Becoming orientation shares with Being a concern with what the human being is rather than what he or she can accomplish. However, it stresses the development of different aspects of the person in a rounded and integrated fashion, which distinguishes it from the nose to the grindstone quality of Doing. We recall Leonardo da Vinci who might start an engineering project, switch to painting, and then, without having finished either, turn to anatomical dissection. Developing different interests was more important to him than getting the job done within a time frame, an alien concept to most mainstream Americans.

In the Relational dimension, the first choice of the Individual orientation reflects the preference for autonomy versus responsibility to any collectivity. Children are trained from infancy to be independent and to articulate their own needs and opinions. The separation–individuation process not only begins early, but is also continuously reinforced as the children are entrusted to baby sitters, go to nursery school, sleep over at the homes of friends, go off to summer camps, and then go away to college. Adults pursue their self-interests, and if a better job beckons elsewhere a family member may just take off with a minimum of goodbye ceremony.

Every society, however, requires some responsibility to a collectivity, and the second-order choice—the Collateral orientation—in mainstream American values reflects the democratic ethos on which the nation was founded. Everyone is on the same level, and ideally power is distributed equally. At home, fathers prefer not to be strong authority figures but rather to have decisions arrived at through a family consensus. At work, the boss may assume a position of authority with an air of apologetic informality, as if to neutralize the inevitable hostility.

The Lineal or hierarchical orientation is theoretically in a weak, third-order position, but there are many ways in which it strongly intrudes itself, casting the shadow of hypocrisy upon our democratic principles. Racism is a prime example of the bias and prejudice fostered by the Lineal orientation. The bureaucratic institutions that are found in government and industry, with their tables of organization and flowcharts that channel communication from the top down (but not vice versa), are set up in lineal fashion.

Two conditions within the ecological niche require and justify the operations of the Lineal orientation: (1) under conditions of material scarcity, when a strong authority is required to control aggression and competition for the scarce resources and to prevent the war of all against all and (2) in emergency situations characterized by great danger when time pressures require the leader to count on instant and unquestioned obedience. In the history of the world these two conditions have been combined and mutually reinforcing, most of the time. Western "civilized" empires and Oceanic "primitive" tribes have fought each other for the control of scarce resources. Democracy, a relative newcomer, has made its appearance only when technology, transportation, and the sharing of raw materials has reduced the scarcity and increased the availability of material goods and possessions.

The first-order choice of the Man–Nature category, Mastery-over-Nature, is based on the assumption that there are few (if any) problems that cannot be solved with the help of technology and the expenditure of vast sums of money. We have conquered infectious diseases, gone to the moon, and split the atom. Although we still have not mastered chronic illness, especially cancer and long-term mental illness, there is hope. And while a few imbalances, like war and weather, are more elusive, they are not impossible to control. Problem solving is where it is at. If parents have problems with children, husbands with wives, wives with husbands, then let us get to work. No need to suffer.

The problem is that some problems will not go away, at least not at the wave of the human hand. In that case, we switch to the second-order choice, Subjugated-to-Nature. If the experts and specialists have been unable to help, particularly with personal problems, then an appeal is likely to be made to the Deity. Or else the trouble simply has to be endured until it goes away due to the benevolence of God or natural forces.

The Mastery-over-Nature and Subjugated-to-Nature orientations are especially dichotomous, but the latter is not quite as removed from the third-order choice, Harmony-with-Nature. This assumes that there is not necessarily a clash between humans and nature but that there are many forces and influences both in the heavens and on earth (e.g., gods, demons, angels, saints, spirits, ghosts, wee folk). Human problems are thought to arise when we have not attended properly to or kept our lives in balance with all these sources of influence. So it may be that since it has not rained, the rain god may be angry, and a rain dance may help the situation. Even though many people may secretly believe in some aspects of this orientation, Harmony-with-Nature is likely to be put down as superstition or magical by mainstream Americans.

The final category, Basic Nature of Man, has undergone a change in the course of our country's short history. The position of the Puritan settlers was that people were born evil but perfectable. But, following the lead of 19th-century Humanism, the growth of secular colleges and universities, and the popularization of psychology and the social sciences during the 20th century, the concept of original sin has been displaced by the Neutral orientation. This assumes that we are born neither good nor evil, but more like a blank slate upon which the environment, the parents, the neighborhood, and the school leave their imprint during the course of growth and development. The Neutral position generates moral pragmatism as well since punishment is no longer expected from God for sins. Although it is felt that we should avoid hurting others when possible, there are no absolute prescriptions other than those legislated into law or our own inner sense of decency.

Innate Evil, in the second-order position, is, however, a continuous possibility. Fundamentalist sects have always promoted it, and born-again Christians are attempting to resurrect it. Also, large segments of the population may experience a heightened awareness of evil in periods of national stress. For example, under the stress of post World War II recovery, many Americans became convinced that government, the motion picture industry, and the media in general, had been infiltrated by Communists.

In the third-order position is the Good-but-Corruptible orientation, a view put forth by Rousseau after contemplating the noble savages described in the reports of early South Sea voyagers. It is a view held today by only a few "flower children," most of whom have disappeared into rural settings where they can cultivate goodness far from wicked civilization.

The dominant American choices in each dimension fit together nicely. Thus, if the personal achievement implied by Doing is to be facilitated, then it is good to be able to plan for the Future, as an Individual not too constrained by family or group ties, with the optimism supplied by the Mastery-over-Nature orientation, and the pragmatic morality, with which such self-interest is justified, afforded by the Neutral view of the Basic Nature of Man.

Unfortunately, this pattern also represents something of a pressure cooker, full steam ahead with little opportunity for relaxation without guilt or lowered self-esteem. It fosters a narcissistic self-involvement and allows no room for tragedy. If an airplane crashed killing hundreds of people, somebody "goofed" or the technology is to blame, and loved ones are compensated with money. Grieving ceremonies are weak or absent, and those who have suffered a loss may need the help of a therapist to undergo the separation process. Furthermore, the dominant choices have, at least in the past, applied only to men. Women have been socialized for inferior second-order alternatives—taking care of day-to-day affairs (Present), dealing with children's and husband's feelings (Being), attending to relatives and keeping in touch with friends (Collateral). The effort of the women's movement to correct this split in sex roles has been only partially successful.

Finally, there has been some resistance to the compulsive planning for the Future and the complete ignoring of the Past. Some middle-class Americans refuse to wear watches or worry about the Future, while others connect with the Past by reading historical novels or biographies, collecting antiques, or keeping track of their family tree in the family Bible. Teenagers no longer feel they must postpone sexual experience until marriage, and, supported by moral pragmatism, there has been increased acceptance of both premarital and extramarital sex as well as homosexuality.

The Value Orientations of Italians and Irish

In the Time dimension, Italians and Irish are similar, both placing Present time in the first-order position. This is characteristic of most rural peoples for whom Time goes around in large cycles of anniversaries and holidays, seasons for sowing or reaping. The hours are marked by the position of the sun or the bell in the church steeple; and whether one looks back into the past or forward into the future, there is little evidence of, or expectation for, change. Only if there is an unusual problem will there be an appeal to the Past, usually by getting the advice of the elder generation.

The Future is last in both of these cultures, and one might wonder how such people could undertake the gigantic step of emigrating. The answer is that the rural economies of Southern Italy and Southern Ireland were depressed, and America was seen as a place of greater economic opportunities where one might live out a similar life-style with greater ease. Although many immigrants gave up farming, people from the same villages and families tended to go to the same cities in this country, forming "Little Italys" and Irish neighborhoods where, except for the shift from rural to urban settings, there was no need to undergo rapid sociocultural change.

In the Activity dimension, we again find similar profiles between the two ethnic groups. The Being orientation comes first, followed by Being-in-Becoming and then by Doing. The verbal emotionality of the Italians is well known; the Irish, on the other hand, are somewhat more restrained with strangers. Even with family members, the Irish often convey feelings more by subtle cues or by teasing than by words or direct confrontation.

Being-in-Becoming has an aesthetic quality for the Italians, an appreciation for physical qualities. For example, one Italian mother told us her children were doing very well in school. A mainstream American might surmise that they were getting good grades, but when asked why she thought this, the Italian mother said, "Because they have such beautiful eyes. All the teachers love them." For the Irish, the Being-in-Becoming orientation is more likely to find expression in appreciation for idiosyncrasies of character.

The fact that Doing occupies a last position for both Italians and Irish does not mean that there is any disposition to avoid hard work. However, when they come home, they talk very little about their work, unless they have a complaint or some scandal to share that will make food for gossip with the neighbors.

Gossip is the principal form of social control in rural communities or neighborhood enclaves where everyone knows everyone else.

In the Relational category, Italians prefer the Collateral orientation. Lateral relations are very important, and loyalty to the extended family system is demanded, as is both physical and emotional closeness. There is anguish over separation, which is to be avoided if at all possible. Italian husbands and fathers take the second-order Lineal position of authority only if there is strong disagreement within the family. Actually, because of the absence of a strong, superordinate authority, family (or neighborhood) arguments are apt to provoke collateral fission, a split that lends to protracted feuding.

The Individual orientation is not at all encouraged. If a child becomes too independent, he or she is scolded for being "willful" or for "having a big head." If the child persists he or she may be physically punished. But the next minute, acting out of the Being orientation, the parent is likely to pick up and hug and kiss the child.

Among the Irish, the first-order position is the Lineal orientation, which presents a unique problem. Husbands and fathers are supposed to be "the boss," but in rural Ireland the socialization of young men did not provide adequate reinforcement for this role. The farms were cut into such small pieces that the property could not be distributed to all the male children. Also, there was no system of primogeniture. It was up to the father to decide which of his sons would inherit the land; and he was in no hurry to make this decision as it would require him to retire to the "west room." Young men, with no source of stable income, were kept on pocket money and were unable to marry. The restless sons moved to the city or emigrated. Unable to marry, with no sexual outlets but prostitutes, the young men congregated in the pub. Thus drinking became "a good man's weakness," a forgivable and understandable indiscretion. When marriage finally occurred, the wife was likely to be the stronger person, ruling the family from behind the throne in order not to expose publicly the weakness of her husband. The men tended to overcompensate for this weakness through impulsive pugnacity. Sons were closer to their mothers than to their fathers, thus perpetuating the strain in the male role.

Since the Roman Catholic Church is the official religion for both groups, the Subjugated-to-Nature orientation holds the first-order position in the Man–Nature category. Suffering is expected as a part of our fate in this world. But where the Italians are pessimistic or resigned, the Irish tend to be stoical and tough-minded.

For Italians, the influence of the second-order Harmony-with-Nature orientation is still very strong. It has been partially assimilated into the church through the powers attributed to the local saint. There is also a fear of evil spirits, particularly of the power of the evil eye. The *Mal Ocho* is believed to be possessed by only certain people, and Italians are careful not to arouse their envy, especially where their children are concerned. Even second- and third-generation Italian Americans may continue to fear the evil eye, seeing it as the cause of family problems despite preliminary protests that they no longer subscribe to such superstitions.

Among the Irish, Harmony-with-Nature is manifested more by fanciful or mystical views of the powers in nature—elves, bog creatures, wee folk, and so on. It contributes to the Gaelic predilection for fantasy that is often so strong it interferes with the ability to distinguish fantasy from reality.

Few Italians or Irish take the Mastery-over-Nature orientation seriously. Even after exposure to American technology and problem solving, the optimism and hope associated with this view takes a long time to sink in.

In the Basic Nature of Man dimension, Italians hold a Mixed orientation in first place. They consider people to be born with the capacity to do good or evil, though some have more of one, some more of the other. No matter how the child turns out, it is not the fault of the parents but of fate. However, the Italians are aware of the potential for evil, particularly where male sexuality is concerned. Unmarried women are not allowed to date or be in the company of men without a chaperone. The Mixed orientation is also associated with a relaxed sense of morality. People will steal if given the opportunity, as guilt is not internalized and the only shame is to be caught.

For the Irish, the Evil orientation features a sharp awareness of sin and of the possibilities of yielding to temptation, which is always just around the corner. The harsher morality of the Irish Catholic Church as compared to the Italian led to this characteristic internalization of guilt. The Irish are also very reluctant to complain about pain or illness. This is associated not only with the tough-minded stoicism mentioned above but also with the notion that pain and illness may be God's punishments for sinful thinking or behavior.

Both Italians and Irish find mental illness in the family painful to acknowledge, but for different reasons. For Italians it is a blot on the family honor, a sign of bad blood lines. Or it may be a sign of witchcraft. For the Irish, it is another sign of punishment for sin. Both groups tend to somatize their emotional problems, thus seeming to lack insight.

In concluding this section, it may be helpful to point out the great cultural gap that Italians and Irish must traverse in order to accommodate to mainstream American value patterns. American first-order choice is in last place for these two groups. If accommodation is to occur without too much strain, it must be done slowly, over several generations.

Implications for Therapy

While ethnic families are attempting to understand and learn to implement the dominant value orientation patterns, those patterns themselves are undergoing change. The resulting confusion increases the stress of the acculturation process. This makes it very important for the family therapist to keep track of three acculturation issues: (1) the value patterns characteristic of the family's culture of origin; (2) where the family is in the acculturation process

—that is, what values have been or are being changed at the time of intervention; and (3) the family's understanding or misunderstanding of mainstream American values. In the case of cross-cultural marriages, there is, of course, a fourth issue: (4) what conflicts have occurred or what compromises are being made to compensate for the differences between the two native value patterns.

Middle-class therapists, no matter what their ethnic origins, have been socialized in terms of mainstream values. The therapist will be Future oriented, expecting clients to be motivated and to keep appointments punctually. He or she will also expect families to be willing to work on therapeutic tasks (Doing), over reasonable periods of time (Future), with the prospect of change before them (Mastery-over-Nature). All this is to be done while taking a pragmatic view of moral issues (Neutral), and at the very least the therapist will expect to help clients to distance themselves from any overwhelming moral burden or intense feelings of shame. And clients will be expected to separate themselves from enmeshment in the family structure and to develop increased autonomy (Individual).

If these assumptions are open to questions, then it is very important for the therapist to be aware of the differences between his or her values and those of the ethnic families and to work out a way to resolve them (Giordano & Giordano, 1977). The principal therapeutic technique employed in our ecological approach is what we are calling the "culture broker." This is a concept borrowed from Weidman (Weidman, 1973, 1975), with some modifications. The function of the culture broker also somewhat resembles Bowen's concept of the "coach" (Bowen, 1978). In this role, the therapist determines the family's value conflicts and confusions and then tries to help the family resolve them. While the therapist suggests pathways for accommodation, this is done without imposing his or her own values on the family. This requires a real effort on the part of the therapist to accept the family where it is and to respect and validate its value positions. Prior knowledge of the dominant values of the ethnic group in question is almost indispensable in such situations.

Assessment is first directed at two points: evaluating the clinical situation of the identified patient and determining his or her ethnic background and that of the spouse, as well as the characteristics of the patient's ecological niche or neighborhood. We do not take the view, subscribed to by some family therapists, that diagnosis is irrelevant. We are interested in the total transactional field and are therefore obliged to first investigate the intrapsychic processes of the identified patient and later those of other family members. Furthermore, we must maintain a liaison with other hospital departments (e.g., outpatient clinics or emergency rooms) and community mental health centers, for whom diagnosis and prognosis are important issues. However, at times we may be dealing with behavior or symptoms, such as the Puerto Rican *ataque* or the Portuguese pseudohallucination, neither of which are considered psychopathological in the eyes of the ethnic community. The following example illustrates such a case:

> A young Portuguese female whose family had been in this country for five years had made a suicide attempt. She had been depressed following the death of her mother the year before and had frequent visual and auditory hallucinations of her mother appearing and speaking to her. The patient had jumped out a first-story open window believing that she had seen and heard her mother beckoning from the street.
>
> Among the Portuguese such visual and auditory hallucinations are considered normal after the death of a loved one. The spirit of the deceased is considered to be active, hovering around, and interested in the affairs of family members. In fact, failure to encounter the spirit is often considered to be characteristic of an unfeeling or unloving child. But was jumping out a window considered reasonable in this context? As we did not know, we decided to ask the family and neighbors. There was a general agreement that jumping out a window was beyond the expected behavior, especially after a year from the time of death. This confirmed the clinical assessment we had arrived at on other grounds.

Determining the cultural and ethnic background can be simple or complex, depending upon the time since emigration, the number of generations in this country, and the number of intermarriages that has occurred. This determination should be included as routine in all family therapy, even though it may not be considered necessary with WASP families or those thoroughly acculturated into the middle class. Its routine absence is an indication of our cultural blindness—an insensitivity based in part on our false melting-pot ideology and in part on the therapist's wish to deny or ignore his or her own ethnicity.

Once we ask for ethnic or national background information, it is surprising how relevant it becomes, especially in the development of a genogram. However, it should be noted that it takes a long time to gather all the necessary information for a genogram. Many minorities are so involved in the Present and with their current difficulties, they do not want to spend much time talking about their ancestors. They want their problems fixed right now or as soon as possible. Also, people with a Present-time orientation often forget to keep appointments. Thus, it helps to make home visits as soon as possible, for many reasons. There are apt to be some family portraits, which helps with the genogram, and it is easier to see how roles are assigned in the family when observing them in their natural environment rather than in the artificial setting of an office. Furthermore, the therapist is likely to meet some family members who resist coming to the medical setting or who are suspicious of the intentions of the therapist. Such people are likely to find a reason to be absent on the first few visits but tend to get drawn in as family tensions begin to decrease.

For many of our ethnic and minority patients, their problems appear first as somatic symptoms, and such patients are often resentful about being referred for therapy, feeling let down by the doctors. Generally, we take the position that the complaints are real, and see to it that medical treatment is provided. We usually find that as we ask about the situation in which the symptoms appear or get worse, the information about family conflicts will gradually surface. After a while we will hear more about the family and less about the complaint, until we get to the point of being able to see the family. On the other hand, there are some families that can be seen sooner because of their concern about the identified patient.

Patients who are strongly oriented to Harmony-with-Nature, may believe that the symptoms or problems derive from an evil spirit, a family curse, the evil eye, or the ingestion of a magical substance (usually white powder surreptitiously placed in food or wine). In some cases these patients may simply not know where to find a native healer in this country. We will then make an attempt to locate such a person and to bring him or her into the treatment situation. Or, for example, if a Puerto Rican patient is already seeing a spiritist, he will attempt in some way to collaborate. Since native healers, root workers, spiritists, *curanderos*, and shamans are generally quite concerned with family relationships, it may be possible to work out an innovative (if unorthodox) form of family therapy. This kind of experimentation with alternative therapists has not happened too often in our work because many of them do not trust anyone connected with the medical establishment.

As is usually the case in therapy, the therapeutic contract develops out of the assessment procedure. Here we take a somewhat different tack—or so we believe—from most other family therapies. Because we are dealing with families based on Lineal or Collateral orientation, it is important to line ourselves up with the head of the family. This is normally the father, but in his absence it can be the mother or grandmother. Since the head of the family holds culturally sanctioned power, we would not be able to gain entree into the family without sincerely respecting that power and the objectives he or she has in mind for the family. Thus, we would not be able to get very far if we indicated that one of our goals was to obtain autonomy or individuation for a wife or daughter. However, we can identify with the values and goals of the head of the family, while offering a better way of implementing them, as in the case below:

A Puerto Rican family had recently moved into a mixed neighborhood, and the father was terribly worried about his 15-year-old daughter's virginity. He insisted that the mother drive the daughter to and from school and would not let her date or attend school dances or other social affairs or leave the house unaccompanied by a family member. He felt that no woman could protect herself in the unsupervised presence of an attractive or seductive boy who wanted to have sex with her. He saw American sexual permissiveness and dating patterns as a disgusting and dangerous life-style.

Meanwhile the daughter, though bright, had been doing poorly in school and was complaining of severe headaches—the reasons for the referral. In an individual interview she appeared depressed and acknowledged anger toward her father. However, she was afraid to confront him for fear of his violent anger at any sign of disobedience. The mother agreed with the daughter, thought the father was "crazy," but was also afraid to confront him openly.

The therapist considered all the possible intrapsychic dynamics in the case: incestuous attachment of the father to the daughter; his hysterical personality formation; the daughter's repressed rage and sexual attachment to the father; and the mother's envy of the daughter and her implicit use of the daughter to retaliate against the father (triangulation).

The therapist intervened through an individual interview with the father so as not to expose him to any loss of respect in front of the family—respect for the male role being of prime importance in Puerto Rican families. In the interview the therapist agreed with the father's view about the importance of maintaining control over his daughter's activities and preserving her virginity. He agreed that American dating patterns are quite permissive and that sexual intercourse under these circumstances is always a possibility, validating the father's fears. But he also pointed out that American girls usually have a great deal of unsupervised experience with boys from an early age, and that they have been trained not only how to protect themselves but also how to control their own feelings and behavior. Then the therapist explained the position of the daughter. She had been "grounded" prior to any misconduct, and it was suggested that this undeserved punishment was likely to bring out the very behavior it was designed to prevent. He then suggested to the father that it might be better to allow her some experience so that she could learn how to handle herself in these circumstances. It was further pointed out that she could come home and talk to him about it afterward.

To condense this account quite a bit, the father finally permitted the daughter to go to a church dance with her girlfriends. Nothing untoward happened, but she gave him a vivid account of the dance, and he in turn gave her some advice. Gradually the father gained confidence in her good judgment and allowed her a little more freedom. The daughter's depression lifted, and her school work improved. At this point, with the father's increased confidence in his ability to solve problems, the therapy turned to the conflict between the husband and wife.

Undoubtedly, this outcome could be explained in terms of various theories of family therapy, to which we would have no objection. For us what is important is that the family took a small step toward accommodation to mainstream American values. This small step in the process of acculturation reconciled the peer-group values working upon the daughter without undermining the Puerto Rican values important to the father's sense of self-worth and dignity.

Did we impose our own American values on this family? We would say, "No." It is true that the range of choice was increased for the family by supplying information and suggesting possibilities that were in the direction of American values. But the family adopted the direction, after giving it a trial, because it worked. There was positive reinforcement supplied by the external situation not from the therapist. Thus, a therapeutic relationship can be solidified without alienating other family members by seeming to side too much with the power holder. Such small steps can lead to a considerable reduction in tension between conflicting value systems, and, by reverberating around the transactional field, to interpersonal and intrapersonal tension.

REFERENCES

Ackerman, N. *The Psychodynamics of Family Life*. New York: Basic Books, 1958.

Auerswald, E. Interdisciplinary versus Ecological Approach. *Family Process, 7*(2), 202–215, 1968.

Auerswald, E. Families, Change, and the Ecological Perspective. In A. Ferber, M. Mendelsohn, & A. Napier (Eds.), *The Book of Family Therapy*. New York: Science House, 1972.

Auerswald, E. Thinking about/Thinking about Health and Mental Health. In S. Arieti (Ed.), *American Handbook of Psychiatry* (2nd ed.). New York: Basic Books, 1974.

Bateson, G. *Steps to an Ecology of Mind*. New York: Ballantine, 1972.

Bell, J.E. *Family Group Therapy* (Public Health Monograph No. 64). Washington, D.C.: Department of Health, Education and Welfare, 1961.

Berry, J.W. Ecological Analyses for Cross-Cultural Psychology. In N. Warren (Ed.), *Studies in Cross-Cultural Psychology*. New York: Academic Press, 1980.

Boszormenyi-Nagy, I. The Concept of Schizophrenia from the Perspective of Family Treatment. *Family Process, 1*(1), 103–113, 1962.

Bowen, M. *Family Therapy in Clinical Practice*. New York: Jason Aronson, 1978.

Chomsky, N. *Aspects of a Theory of Syntax*. Cambridge: M.I.T. Press, 1965.

Dewey, J., & Bentley, A.F. *Knowing and the Known*. Boston: Beacon, 1950.

Framo, J.L. Rationale and Techniques of Intensive Family Therapy. In I. Boszormenyi-Nagy & J.L. Framo (Eds.), *Intensive Family Therapy*. New York: Harper & Row, 1965.

Giordano, J., & Giordano, G.P. *The Ethno-Cultural Factor in Mental Health: A Literary Review and Bibliography*. New York: Committee on Pluralism and Group Identity, American Jewish Committee, 1977.

Haley, J. *Problem-Solving Therapy: New Strategies for Effective Family Therapy*. San Francisco: Jossey-Bass, 1976.

Kluckhohn, C. Values and Value Orientations. In T. Parsons & E. Shils, *Toward a General Theory of Action*. Cambridge, Mass.: Harvard University Press, 1951.

Kluckhohn, F.R., & Strodtbeck, F.L. *Variations in Value Orientations*. Evanston, Ill.: Row, Peterson, 1961.

Levi-Straus, C. *Structural Anthropology*. Boston: Beacon, 1963.

Mash, E.J., Hamerlynck, L.A., & Handy, L.C. (Eds.). *Behavior Modification and Families*. New York: Brunner/Mazel, 1975.

Minuchin, S. *Families and Family Therapy*. Cambridge: Harvard University Press, 1974.

Papajohn, J., & Spiegel, J.P. *Transactions in Families: A Modern Approach for Resolving Cultural and Generational Conflict*. San Francisco: Jossey-Bass, 1975.

Pattison, E.M. A Theoretical-Empirical Base for Social System Therapy. In E.F. Foulks et al. (Eds.), *Current Perspectives in Cultural Psychiatry*. Jamaica, N.Y.: Spectrum, 1977.

Speck, R., & Attneave, C. *Family Networks*. New York: Vintage Books, 1973.

Spiegel, J. Transactions Inquiry: Description of Systems. In J. Papajohn (Ed.), *Transactions: The Interplay between Individual, Family and Society*. New York: Science House, 1971.

Watzlawick, P., Beavin, J.H., & Jackson, D.D. *Pragmatics of Human Communication*. New York: Norton, 1967.

Weidman, H.H. *Implications of the Culture Broker Concept for the Delivery of Health Care*. Paper presented at the Annual Meeting of the Southern Anthropological Society, Wrightsville Beach, S.C., 1973.

Weidman, H.H. Concepts as Strategies for Change. In J.N. Sussex (Ed.), *Psychiatry and the Social Sciences, Psychiatric Annals* (special Miami edition), 5(8), 17–19, 1975.

II
THE PARADIGMS

3

American Indians and Alaska Native Families: Emigrants in Their Own Homeland

CAROLYN ATTNEAVE

Many professionals would find the idea of an encounter in their practice of an American Indian or Alaska Native family a remote and possible romantic notion. However, the 1980 U.S. census indicates an almost 60% increase in our American Indian population, resulting in 1.8 million Indians. The Bureau of Indian Affairs' number and the Indian Health Service's estimates that were made before the 1980 census show a number of startling demographic facts that increase the odds of such an encounter. First, the total population of American Indians and Alaska Natives in the United States reached at least 1 million during the mid-1970s. During the past two decades the population has been increasing for almost the first time since contact with Europeans in the 16th and 17th centuries was followed by devastating decimations. Second, children have always been precious to native cultures, and the spread of modern medical services to the more remote areas of the United States lowered the infant mortality rates, while adaptations to modern living have somewhat increased the likelihood of survival in adult life. It is not surprising that half this population will be under 20 years of age. In 1980 the median age of those served by the Indian Health Services was projected to be under 19 years. Whereas much of the rest of the U.S. population and economy may now be suffering from the decline of the "baby boom" of the postwar years and feeling pressures of a top-heavy age structure with the approach of more persons in retirement age than workers to support them, this is not true of many minority populations, particularly not for the American Indian or Alaska Native groups. Only 10% of these populations are 55 or over, which suggests again an emphasis on young families. These elements lead to intergenerational stress, and an emphasis on solving family problems is a major mental health priority.

Most of the available literature concerning the appropriate way to establish professional mental health relationships with this population has

Carolyn Attneave. Department of Psychology, Psychiatry, and Behavioral Sciences, University of Washington, Seattle, Washington.

been written with the reservation population in mind. Indeed, much of it was developed for and by the Indian Health Service, which began to provide psychiatric services in the late 1960s (Attneave & Beiser, 1975; Kelso & Attneave, 1981). This literature may be very tribal specific, for tribal subcultures are many and varied. Anyone working with an Indian family needs to know details of the particular tribal background of the family. It is wise, for example, to know that the Blackfeet tribe in northern Montana was a border buffer and would not take kindly to being compared with the Sioux, the Flathead, or the Shoshone, even though they may appear to the outsider to have similar life-styles, values, and problems. Perhaps this is similar to the mistake commonly made of assuming that the Basques are Spanish. Another common mistake is to generalize that all Indian populations in a region are alike, not recognizing that, even though a Navajo, a Hopi, an Apache, and someone from Laguna Pueblo may all live in the Southwest desert, each has a different language and set of traditions. Land disputes between Navajo and Hopi have been compared to problems between Israelis and Palestinians, for example, with almost as much hopelessness of ever finding acceptable and just settlement. Anyone who expects to practice in a state with an indigenous or reservation Indian population (most states west of the Mississippi, upper New York, Maine, Florida, North Carolina, rural Michigan, Minnesota, and Wisconsin) should make use of local resources such as libraries, historical societies, and Tribal offices in order to be informed.

This need for specific local information is also true of Alaska. There are Eskimo villages along the coastal areas north from Cook Inlet to the Point Barrow settlements on the Arctic Ocean. There are the Aleuts, a much less well-known people, along the Aleutian chain of islands. There are also at least two major Indian groups in Alaska. One is the Athabascan-speaking tribes, who reside in the mountains and valleys inland around the city of Fairbanks. These interior Indians are very different from the coastal tribes who are like the Indians of the northwest coast of British Columbia and Washington. The coastal tribes, who are known for their totem poles, reside along the panhandle of Alaska and its off islands and the cities of Juneau and Ketchikan.

Anchorage, as a major city and medical center, attracts Alaska Natives together with migrants from other states and Canada. The Alaska Native population of Anchorage is like that of many other cities, a mixture of young and old who are moving from a relatively isolated life into a situation of great complexity with a different set of survival needs.

The major cities of the United States all have populations of American Indians and Alaska Natives, and in some there will be second- or even a few third-generation residents. Miller and associates (Native American Research Group, 1974/1979) studied the children and families of major tribes in the San Francisco Bay area and found the Sioux and Navajo outnumbered the indigenous California Indians and other miscellaneous tribes. Chicago,

Cleveland, Dallas, Minneapolis, New York, and Boston all have recorded from 3000 to 5000 Indians living within their environs in the late 1960s. When available, the detailed analyses of the 1980 census will probably increase this number and also extend the list of cities to include such unlikely spots as Honolulu, Atlanta, New Orleans, and Miami. An appropriate estimate for many metropolitan areas is 10,000 or more. More than half the American Indian and Alaska Native population do not use reservations as a principal residence, and many thousands more live away from reservations for varying amounts of time while they seek employment, education, and other opportunities offered in more metropolitan areas.

It is most likely that it will be one of the families who have migrated in this fashion that will be encountered in a family therapist's office. Some will be referred by courts or schools or alcoholism treatment centers. Some will be among the case loads of social service agencies, and some will come, as many other clients do, because they need help and have heard about family treatment and feel it makes sense to them.

In fact, because there are good chances of this self-selection, one of the first cautions to make clear to family therapists who may find themselves facing an American Indian couple or family for the first time is to consider the odds—that probably 50% of the cases that arrive on the therapist's doorstep will be well-educated, typically middle-class people with similar problems and similar attitudes as the rest of their clientele. The underlying racial and cultural characteristics make no more or no less difference than those of a migrant family of any type that has acculturated itself to the United States for several generations. Esoteric problems of language barriers, exotic religious practices, or other strange customs will not be prominent. After all, missionaries of all denominations, from Roman Catholics to the Friends, from Fundamentalists to Episcopalians, have been at work for several hundred years. Government schools and public schools have been nibbling away in a melting pot fashion for the last century. Therefore, proceed with these couples as with anyone else—sensitively and professionally.

Above all, the therapist should not assume some affinity based on novels, movies, a vacation trip, or an interest in silver jewelry. These are among the most offensive, commonly made errors when non-Indians first encounter an American Indian person or family. Another is a confidential revelation that there is an Indian "Princess" in the family tree—tribe unknown, identity unclear, but a bit of glamour in the family myths. The intent may be to show positive bonding by the therapist, but to the Indian they reveal stereotypical thinking. Just as other clients do, the Indian client wants to be recognized as a person—a human being, not as a category. This is even more true if the family identity relating to tribal or village origin does not include the activity or content to which the non-Indian alludes. For instance a Wampanoag or Nouganset from New England or a Tlinget from Alaska is not interested personally in Custer's last stand. A Sioux may never have heard of Pope's rebellion in 1680. And for any of these, the silver and turquoise jewelry of the Southwest is as much an exotic art form as for the non-Indian.

There are, however, some guidelines for those times when the therapist may feel stuck. The ideas that follow are based on experience with a wide variety of tribal people in many parts of the United States and Canada.

While tribally specific information is a continuing need, the general principles provide a coarse screen for sifting out the major contrasts between the two cultures—that of the middle-class therapist and that of the American Indian or Alaska Native clientele. A paper by Wax and Thomas (1961) prepared to facilitate relationships between Indians and others may be a helpful supplement to the discussion that follows.

Initial Contact

The first advice is addressed directly to the non-Indian therapist: *Be yourself*. The closer to tribal traditions any Indian couple may be, the more important this advice becomes. For the professional, the initial period may be thought of as an assessment of the family and its problems. For the Indian family involved, it is a period of careful assessment of the therapist and rather little self-disclosure. In traditional ways this might consist of long periods of silence interspersed with somewhat short exchanges. What usually happens is that the short ritual of social amenities between therapist and client is stretched out over an hour or more—sometimes for more than one session. During this early period it may help the therapist to know the kinds of questions that are in the family members' minds: "Can you tolerate our silences? Our indirectness? Our uncertainty?" "What is your style? Pacing? Your interest in people?" "How much confidence do you have that problems can be solved?" This sets the stage for later work that will proceed according to the comfort of the therapist and how genuinely mutual respect can be communicated.

No guidelines for this period of initial contact can specify one set of infallible behaviors. It is rather like the Indian handshake style, which tends to be an exchange of touching and feeling rather than the firm clasp indicating sincerity that typifies most white American handshakes. To imitate it usually leads to a dead-fish offering of a limp hand, which is artificial and satisfies no one. To be aware that even in such routine gestures the therapist is being felt out and assessed may lead to self-consciousness. Yet somehow, this awareness should strip away artificiality and not only allow but even promote self-expression.

Probably all families go through this period of mutual assessment, and therapists are aware of the necessity to involve each family member in order to assure the return for a second and third session. However, hastiness, impatience, and worry over whether or not the family will return is self-defeating. If this is true about most clients, it is doubly true in working with Indian families.

If the therapist presses for information and action the family will often present a concrete problem for which concrete suggestions are expected and even wanted. If the problem is within the therapist's domain of expertise, it should be treated as expected; concretely but not as the only or most important problem in the world. This provides a context while relationships are being established. This initial problem is usually a masking problem, real but not the most serious disturbance in the family. If the problem is not in the therapist's repertoire or is beyond the limits of expertise, this too can be made clear and other possibilities of working together suggested. Substance abuse, problems with the utility company, the bill collectors, and the like, may be discussed or referred, and if these problems suggest underlying difficulty, that difficulty may be briefly offered for further exploration when the appropriate time comes.

This discussion of an initial, concrete problem allows therapist and family to find a fit for what may be differing role expectations. In most Indian settings the dominant person (the therapist) is expected to be active and the subordinate persons (the family members) show respect by quiet attentiveness. Observation of many mainstream situations reverse these expectations, for example, therapists act as attentive listeners urging family members to talk. Each therapist will have a style of asserting authority, and this observation of cultural dissonance is offered as a clue to follow if your manner is not eliciting appropriate behavior.

Cultural conditioning leads the majority of non-Indian therapists to talk more than usual as a way of eliciting opinions and thus learning about new people and situations. Equally strong cultural traditions may lead an American Indian to observe and test before talking freely to strangers. Being aware of these "natural" tendencies may also help in establishing appropriate roles and rapport.

Sometimes this initial period can be most useful for asking open-ended questions that elicit family history. Showing genuine interest without exhibiting judgmental behavior will elicit information and establish relationships that will be invaluable reference points later, but which for now are a vehicle for enabling the family to know the therapist and the therapist to know the family. This initial phase is perhaps overemphasized, but it is important to be aware that it often seems to last longer and be less active on the part of the American Indian family than for other clientele. There will be more pauses and more indirect observations by way of peripheral vision rather than direct eye contact. The therapist may have feelings of dropping some threads and picking up others. The therapist's integrity, self-confidence, and centeredness are being tested, as well as whether the therapist understands and respects the persons seeking help.

Perhaps it would be encouraging to look at an example of two very different, but successful, psychiatrists working in overlapping regions of the Southwest. Both men were well trained in traditional American medical and psychiatric skills. One spent the first year or so learning the language and culture, seeking out the traditional healers to whom he could apprentice himself, and engaging in much of the social, political, and religious life of the tribe. He became identified with the most respected leaders and healers and within that tradition effected an exchange of cultures, techniques, and skills. The second remained a Western-oriented, traditional psychiatrist. He found himself most useful to the persons caught in transition between cultures who needed to stabilize themselves around White values, White economic solutions, and White middle-class mores. While he gained understanding of the culture from repeated contact with it, he did not particularly participate in Indian social life or folkways. When the two patterns of service delivery were described, each not only recognized his own style but acknowledged that he would not change it were he to start over (Attneave & Beiser, 1975).

Both men were well respected; both were as busy as they could manage with self-referrals and tribal referrals. Both were considered competent by the Indian people. The secret of their successes was in the way each was true to his own inner convictions, allowing them to operate with respect for their patients but without pretense of desiring to be different. Those who were disturbed, or their families, soon knew what the men were like and could make use of what they had to offer. Both psychiatrists were in a region where large segments of the population could verify and pass along on the "moccasin grapevine" the characteristics of the doctors and the kind of problems with which they were useful.

In an urban setting this is not as easily done since the Indian population comes from many tribes and is often much more loosely knit. Ties that permit information to be passed along do exist in cities but less efficiently. Therefore, each encounter between an Indian family and a therapist may have to have its own period of validation. If, however, an increasing number of families appear over a year or two, the chances are good that the therapist passed the tests and that the word had been spread within the Indian community. Successive encounters with new families may be more relaxed and the initial mutual assessment period shorter. This pattern, except for its relevance to Indian and Alaska Native values, is much like the history of contacts with any cultural enclave.

Therapeutic Relationships from the Indian Perspective

There is a deep-seated cultural basis for accepting very different styles of therapeutic assistance, provided they are perceived as sincere. Underlying almost all basic Indian beliefs is a sense that each different element in the universe has its place and its function. The troubled family members at some levels will be seeking to locate themselves again in a harmonious relationship not only with one another but with the world and the universe. Not being able to discern how or where he or she had gone astray from this set of proper relationships is troubling. The authority of therapists, like that of traditional healers, comes from the fact that they know these real-life relationships, that they can assist others in finding them, and above all that they respect their own powers enough to be able to respect their clientele.

Knowing the essence of these relationships does not mean that we know the immediate answers to whatever problems are presented. What is sought is confidence in the ability to search out and to solve together, at a pace that will be comfortable and with a kind of authority that is not easily shaken by setback or failure. What is not sought is a manipulative, power-aggrandizing approach. Exploitation by non-Indians abounds in the Indian world, and any echo of it destroys the therapeutic alliance or prevents its formation in the first place.

The therapist should be straightforward about fees. Unless one works for the IHS or BIA whose services are specified by treaty, fees are understood and acceptable, although the family is often most comfortable if they are paid by a third party—governmental source, insurance, or the like. In this connection it is interesting to note that only in White society do the healers support themselves by their therapeutic work alone. In traditional settings therapists all have some other trade or means of livelihood (Bergman, 1974). An exception may be found for some healers in the retirement years, when they may have reduced needs and a sufficient reputation that the exchange of material goods and funds for these services can be a source of sufficient support. However, common majority customs are now familiar, and the therapists' fees are not apt to reduce status with their clientele.

One further custom may occasionally cause an orthodox therapist surprise and discomfort. If the therapeutic intervention is successful or if the alliance made is a good one even though it does not produce specific results desired, a gift may be offered by the family. This could be craftwork, food, or an invitation. Giving is part of traditional behavior, is deeply ingrained, and should be respected and appreciated. Above all, it should not be refused for the sake of psychoanalytical "purity."

The Source of Problems and Their Typical Forms

The source of Indian family disturbances and symptoms is not in the main different from those of other families: enmeshment and lack of generational boundaries, well-meant but misdirected efforts to forge working relationships, misunderstandings of self and others, reenactment of the results of cutoff relationships, effects associated with unfinished grief work, and the need to cope without being overwhelmed by anxiety. There are, however, some basic vulnerabilities and some particular flavors to these problems imparted by the history of Indian–White relationships and by the dissonance of basic values. The models presented in chapters on other ethnic groups not only present this dissonance but also its intensification as shifts occur over the generations. Taking some of these themes in turn may illuminate the sources of tension and trouble encountered in modern urban Indian families.

Two cautions are needed in looking at dissonance in value orientations as a background for family problems. The first is the reminder that every culture contains all the possible values. The contrasts are not between opposites but between preferences and priorities. Tension arises over rank order, not complete negation of the alternatives, in almost every instance. Values are described by English and English (1958) as themes that "define for an individual or for a social unit what ends or means to an end are desirable." Sheibe (1970) may be even closer to the usage intended here in describing values as "what is wanted, what is best, what is preferable, what ought to be done. They suggest the operation of wishes, desires, goals, passions, valences or morals." It is in this sense that the traditional values described here have been distilled from the heterogeneity of modern Indian ways of living.

No Indian or Alaska Native person today is able to live out completely a traditional life-style. All are aware of and even at times caught up in the mainstream non-Indian U.S. culture. But there are differences in rank ordering within these value categories that are sometimes overt and sometimes unconscious. Sometimes reactions to stress activate "wishes . . . passions . . . morals" in all of us. Where there is dissonance between the cultures of family and therapist, it seems most helpful to be sensitized to the broad underlying patterns in order to understand the specifics and to select our tools appropriately (Papajohn & Spiegel, 1975).

Table 3.1 summarizes the ways in which the general U.S. middle class and the American Indian and Alaska Native cultures prioritize their manner of dealing with five basic problems of relationship. Each of these will be discussed in more detail in the pages that follow.

Time

Time orientation and preference in traditional Indian and Alaska Native cultures has always been present oriented, with a reflected past and with both past and present projected as an image of the future. American Indian present time, however, is easily misunderstood by those who have not lived with it. It is cyclical rather than linear and is not limited to this minute or even this hour. It may encompass days or even months and years. It is life geared to personal and seasonal rhythms rather than ordered and organized by external mechanical clocks and calendars. The day-by-day present is organized around personal bodily needs—sleep and waking, eating and excretion, work and relaxation, social times and times of aloneness. These

TABLE 3.1. Traditional Cultural Value Preferences for U.S. Middle-Class and American Indian/Alaska Native Populations

Topic area of relationship	U.S. middle class[a]	American Indian[b]
Man to nature, environment	1.[c] Control over 2. Subject to 3. Harmony with	1.[c] Harmony with 2. Subject to 3. Control over
Time orientation	1. Future 2. Present 3. Past	1. Present 2. Past 3. Future
Relations with people	1. Individual 2. Collateral 3. Lineal	1. Collateral 2. Individual 3. Lineal
Mode of activity idealized	1. Doing 2. Being 3. Being-in-Becoming	1. Being-in-Becoming 2. Being = Doing[d]
Nature of man	1. Mixed 2. Evil 3. Good	1. Good 2. Mixed 3. Evil

[a]Data on middle-class values from ongoing work at the Florence Heller School for Advanced Studies in Social Welfare, Brandeis University, Waltham, Massachusetts. Published comparisons with other ethnic groups and discussions of implications for family stress in Papajohn and Spiegel (1975).

[b]Based on traditional values as observed and discussed in about 50 tribal groups.

[c]Order of preferred or idealized choices indicates preference of usage. If first listed behavior or attitude becomes untenable, second is utilized. If both first and second are untenable, third is adopted in a particular instance.

[d]"=" indicates either choice is possible, depending on other factors.

rhythms with their immediacy of satisfaction provide a constancy to the larger pattern rhythms of seasonal variations in weather, food sources, and times appropriate for varying activities. Religious observances follow an annual seasonal cycle, along with various social events and periods of travel for migratory groups. Mythologies relate to the seasonal variations, to the establishment of rhythmic events of food supply and social organization, as well as to the establishment of geographic features and to unique catastrophes such as drought, earthquake, fire, or flood.

Events in the life cycle, too, are established and rhythmic, and at each stage there is a focus on what is appropriate for that stage without great concern for the next or succeeding stages since the succession is felt to be inevitable. In their traditional form, the mythologies did not dwell on a past to be created again, but on wisdom from the past that could be of use today. The future was included in storing food during summer and fall for winter, in moving from summer to winter habitat, and; among a few highly organized town and village dwelling cultures, in the development of political alliances and the passing of political and socially stratified positions along the generations.

This highly satisfying solution to problems of time management came crashing into unwieldy fragments with the encroachment of the technical White society. Forced to remain in a limited geographical territory, the ecology of a life based on rhythms of nature could not survive. Wages, manufactured goods, and formal schooling (rather than apprenticeships) organized life along lines directed toward new but not always accepted goals. It is not hard to see a certain ironic patience of the early treaty Indians, as they expected the same certainties of guarantee from the White settlers that came with their own knowledge of the seasons and the relations with the natural world. It is also easy to see the disillusionment that crept in as promises were not kept, resources were destroyed, and older patterns were forbidden. Resentment and confusion, rebellion and apathy were predictable results.

The present-day Indian family will have preserved some of this natural-ness of rhythm and some distortions of it. Indian time can be both a passive-aggressive resistance to mechanistic, technical, societal ways, and it can also be a way of expressing contrasting priorities. Successful urban Indian adap-tation requires mastery of time clocks on the job. Monotonous labor, with little seasonal variation, requires passivity at one end of the scale. At the other extreme it can result in identification with the aggressor through a slavish attention to the punctuality of others. In times of stress, and in the cracks of time when enjoyment is available, the attention to natural rhythms asserts itself. The future is still unknown and unpredictable but not only because faith in the newer social paths is uncertain and their application unknown. Indeed, at times of crisis it may be helpful to recall the paralyzing effect of future shock on White middle-class youth and families in the 1960s and 1970s. Similarly, the emotionally reverberating effects of natural disasters and mass unemployment on wide swaths of ordinary U.S. populations are experiences that parallel the clash of cultures and the devastation of being a conquered people that is still experienced by many Indian families.

The immediate past, measured in one or two generations, has little to recommend its revival to the Indian population. It is grim and unlovely in the memories and myths of most families. Except for creating bonds between those who have shared similar experiences and survived (as in the boarding schools or on a reservation), the near past has little to recommend its return.

A small but highly visible group of younger militant Indians has at-tempted to revive an 18th-century version of traditional Indian life. This minority behaves as though the key to present and future were in the past—a clear difference in prioritizing of time preferences. This idealization of past time has some support from traditionalist elders since it offers a reemphasis on a set of values and a life-style that has seemed endangered. However, the narrow definition of options led these militants into nonnegotiable clashes with contemporary society. There is a heroic quality that is impractical but admired, much like the charge of the Light Brigade, a similar phenomenon in English history. The 1970s episodes at Wounded Knee can be understood in this perspective.

A family whose members include one of these activists may experience particular stress. These are very real stresses on families, some of whose members are fugitives, prisoners, or martyrs. More importantly, there is the arousal of ambivalence and a need to resolve this in a positive fashion that permits traditional values to be operationally expressed in a contemporary setting. This problem has its parallels in other minority groups such as the Blacks and Chicanos. Each individual family will require a patient and sometimes painful working through of basic issues. A non-Indian therapist needs to avoid the double binds of rhetorical argument. Consultation and reality testing will help avoid problems of overidentification and group countertransference.

In general, however, the time dimension will affect the course of therapy most directly by setting the stage for concrete immediate problems and their solution. Framing tasks in terms of natural recurring cycles of human development is effective if used cautiously. A future orientation is not a powerful motivation for this population unless firmly rooted in present satisfaction.

Relationship of Man and the Natural World

The prevailing orientation of the major society in Western civilization is toward control over nature. This attitude includes controlling other people. It is almost as if the idealized model of man as well as other aspects of the environment is that of a machine. There is a quality of omnipotence attributed to science and technology as a means of control, and for most persons (except those engaged on scientific frontiers), there is very little emphasis on understanding and working with natural phenomena. When it is unavoidable, submission to natural forces is devastating and usually considered temporary.

In traditional Indian culture the emphasis is turned completely around. Careful understanding and working in harmony with natural forces is a way of life. A few, and only a few, have control over natural forces, chiefly through unusual understanding and alliance with them. The metaphor of the hunter who understands his prey and its environment is the accepted explanation of their powers (Castaneda, 1972). Submission, acceptance of overwhelming natural events that cannot be controlled, is a part of life. Survival often depends upon stoic submission in the face of disaster as well as upon skillful anticipatory and preventive moves.

It is helpful to realize that there is considerable animism pervading the view of the forces of nature. Not only animals but plants, rocks, mountains, and bodies of water exist as personalities or as vehicles of expression for the spiritual forces of the universe.

Where a young Indian man is technically trained in the armed forces or at trade school or is employed in the demolition of natural resources by the developers of energy or minerals, his sense of power and strength is most subtly intensified by its blending with these traditional views. There are at times surging internal conflicts of ambivalence both within himself and reverberating through his family.

Machines that extend personal control over the environment may, from the Native American point of view, be more appropriately used in the urban setting, however, because in this alien environment they are part of what might be called a profane rather than a sacred frame of reference. Among some Indian and Alaska Native groups, machines, including automobiles and household appliances, seldom receive the care and reverence that are still given tools made of natural materials and that are part of rural and traditional life. This may account for abandoned snowmobiles, junk cars, and other debris of rural slums associated with Indian dwellings.

This is not always the case, however. While few Western social theorists include complex tools and machines in their definitions of nature and environment, such an inclusion sometimes occurs among Indians and Alaska Natives. For instance, in the arctic, many Eskimos make the transition from surviving in a primitive culture to being expert mechanics and airplane navigators (Kleinfeld, 1973). The principles involved are the same as those of handling dogs and hunting in the arctic. A good mechanic understands machines and works to get the most out of them; he becomes the modern "troubleshooter" as a version of the "hunter." In a similar way, the Mohawk high steel worker transfers his understanding and respect for the forces of nature to the technical skills of working with metals and gravity. He appears to defy heights when he is truly adapting himself to a new set of harmonies. Out of this he has developed both useful skills and survival ability in the White world. Not all instances of culture exchange are as successful for both worlds, however. Family therapists may find that these technical aspects of the 20th-century life need to be framed in more traditional value orientations.

There have been too few such opportunities for transfer of attitudes since the mastery over the environment extends in modern Western society to the manipulation of people as things, an exact opposite of respecting the nonhuman elements of the universe as though they were people.

Social Relationships: General Consensus and Collaterality

Perhaps the fullest understanding of the relationships between man and nature includes some understanding of the preferences in value orientations toward social relationships. Here the consensual collateral form of social organization and decision making has first preference. Whenever the needs or goals of a group conflict with individual decisions and preferences, the group takes precedence. This group reference may be the tribe, the band, the family, or any other coherent cluster of people. It is again quite under-standable that in early periods, when survival depended upon cooperative group endeavor, this form of relationship could evolve and take strong hold. In emergencies, for brief periods, an authoritarian leader might have taken charge, but this was a second choice, a temporary solution. It was not a permanent relationship for most North American tribes. Authority derived from expertise combined with problem-solving skills. Since this combination was often found in persons whose lives represented age and experience, respect for elders was thus reinforced, provided that the emergent leader might be assumed by anyone mature enough to fill it and to relinquish it as needed by the group. Some of this traditional behavior is appropriately parallel to the role of therapist to the family.

In the Southwestern Pueblo and the Northwestern Coastal tribes, a town or village of more permanent location permitted more social stratifica-tion to develop, and elements of inherited social positions were established. The choice of heirs to the power and prestige of these positions still rested on consensual support and the fulfillment of responsibility to the *pueblo* or village. In spite of talks of Indian princesses, hereditary chieftains, and the like, there was no real parallel with European royal succession or any other automatic inheritance of power.

Tribal histories never suggested the impatient solution of majority vote so revered by "democracies." If a sizable portion of the band, tribe, or village dissented, discussion continued until some compromise could be reached. Except when asked specifically to do so, no one spoke for anyone else, and each was expected to participate. Discussions could last for hours, even days, until all were heard and a group decision was reached. Tribal meetings still last for hours, and tensions can be high as one faction seeks consensus while another pushes for a majority vote.

The collateral form of social pattern must, of course, have a method of dealing with dissidents. Historically ostracism and/or the voluntary parting from the group seem to have been the most common mechanisms used when consensus could not be reached. As long as there was time to discuss endlessly and to weigh alternatives, the chances of group agreement were fairly certain. And as long as there was space for separateness for the dissidents who could calculate their chances of joining another group or of surviving in small splinter factions, group agreement as an overarching value worked quite well. When imposed limitation of reservation boundaries and bureaucratic expectations prevented this solution to unresolved differences, the system broke down and dissatisfaction festered.

But for most purposes the ideal of collaterality persists. Communal sharing of essentials such as food, clothing, transport, and materials needed for ritual is still an essential element of social continuity. Until recently there were few ways in which foodstuffs could be preserved and stored for more than the annual cycle. Often feast and famine followed one another in an expected rhythm for just these reasons. The accumulation of individual wealth was not only impractical but was strongly neutralized by the prevailing custom of sharing. The greatest respect went to those who gave the most to others, first to individuals and families, then to the band, tribe, or community. Benedict (1934), in describing the potlatching customs observed among the Kwakiutl and Haida of the Alaskan panhandle, decried the waste and power displays of an old and almost universal custom that had degenerated during the period of White contact.

However, in a positive bonding tradition, "giveaways" still persist in almost all tribes. All manner of possessions are given ritually to honor others for their help or their achievement or to acknowledge kinship ties. This practice serves as a means of recycling the good of honored dead and as means of showing respect to the living (Momaday, 1974). These ceremonial giveaways are a part of the family life cycle to make climactic events such as birth, naming, marriage, and death. Giving is also a part of day-to-day, week-to-week occasions. Accumulated wealth is less respected than generosity.

In urbanized Indian centers this pattern may take the form of potluck suppers. Giving is often associated with social gatherings called "Pow Wows." These gatherings were formerly associated with ceremonial observances but are now more like festivals where there is dancing, gambling, and feasting for several days. Where there are tribal communities, Pow Wows are usually hosted by one tribal group who expects that they (or at least some of the tribal members) will also be recipients of gifts, honor, and attention at another tribe's Pow Wow when they are the visitors and guests. In urban settings there are variations on the older rural patterns, but the festival atmosphere prevails. Non-Indians are welcome to attend but, unless invited, usually do not dance.

In addition to these formal occasions, the day-to-day life-style is also based upon sharing of material goods. Travelers and visitors are always fed, housed, even clothed or transported. A common reversal of usual mainstream custom is the presentation of gifts to the guest rather than the expectation of a bread-and-butter present or a token of flowers, wine, or candy from the guest. Among some tribes such a gift may be interpreted as an insult: It implies that the host may not have enough to share. However, non-Indians need not worry over this too much since they are extended the respect due any person. They are more apt to be caught off guard when admiring something as a polite show of interest. To be given the article is startling to the non-Indian. Knowing this pattern may help the non-Indian understand the rareness of casual comments about jewelry or accessories in the office by Indian clients.

The duty and responsibility for sharing are taught early to young children and create tension with those in school who are simultaneously being taught to be thrifty and to mark possessions as personal property. In a capitalistic mercantile society personal acquisition is important in learning to plan for an economically productive future. It is an expression of the competitive individualistic orientation that not only condones but extols success at the expense of others.

This emphasis on group collaterality and identity, including the shared possessions and rapid redistribution of excess, is again a source of ambivalence and tension for the urbanized Indian. Newly arrived families and individuals in cities have assumed, sometimes naively, that all people operate in this fashion and hence were both imposed upon by their neighbors and exploited by "streetwise city folk." Not only does this cause problems, but within White society the distribution of welfare benefits and other services only to those who qualify is incomprehensible to traditional Natives. At first hearing, welfare services are assumed to be an example of their own value system operating in White society. That there are rules, eligibility requirements, and a different sense of fairness based on rules of equity rather than obvious need seems to many Indians both paradoxical and unjust (Walster & Walster, 1975). This may be rationalized later as being similar to treaty settlement and, therefore, both capricious and unreliable.

This problem becomes even more marked when an urban Indian family establishes itself with employment or when a student receives a stipend or fellowship. The cash flow is expected by the White majority to be used with provident thriftiness and a certain self-centered protectiveness. But Indian relatives see it as something to be shared. Unemployed parents move in; siblings consume food, wear out clothing, and take up time needed for study or advancement. Students may realize that they can neither pay tuition nor study in these conditions. However, they cannot be "Indian" and at the same time be selfish about helping others whose needs are greater. This tradition hinders more promising careers than perhaps any other obstacle to adaptation into a full participation in the life of contemporary urban American society. This tradition is also an area of potential difficulty for therapy since well-meaning attempts to mobilize individual or nuclear family assertiveness may be resisted as an attack on the basic value of collateral rather than individual identity.

Being–Doing–Becoming

Traditionally there was also respect for individuality and autonomy embedded in the strong sense of collateral relationships and interdependence. At times each person might need to take charge and to be able to contribute individually. Indeed, there seems to be some inherent respect for the development of individual autonomy as long as it did not threaten the group. Probably embedded in the accumulated tribal wisdom was an appreciation that variability enriched the group itself.

Competition, individually and between groups, was a part of traditional Indian life. But this competition did not depend upon the destruction of the competitor. Competition with self, especially in mastery of appetites and skills, was part of survival. Competition in athletic activities was preparation for defense, hunting, and war, if that became necessary to the group. Competition in skills and craftsmanship was highly individualized. Rivalries were active in courtship. Group competition in games often appeared bloody and savage even though within their own rules players were scrupulously fair. This type of competition is nowadays ritualized in the Indian rodeo and in competitive dancing that easily shades into the more destructive attitude of the mainstream culture if group bonding is weakened. Trimble (1976), reviewing a number of studies, notes that need achievement is as strong in Indian communities as in White society. The ideal Indian person is one who is always in balance as a living being but who is also becoming, achieving, and growing.

Noninterference as a Way of Being

In a complex way the idealization of the innate potential in each person and the respect for autonomous, natural unfolding of personality led to a principle of Indian mores that is currently labeled "noninterference." Perhaps, in a traditional Utopia, no child would need discipline and reproof, no youth would aspire beyond the capabilities of the group to deliver, or no adult would become angry with others or self-destructive. However, minimal use of finely calibrated rewards and punishments that involved shame and ridicule, were always part of child rearing, just as ostracism controlled adult deviations.

Perhaps as a reaction to the highly manipulative non-Indian social controls, perhaps for other less obvious reasons, noninterference has been idealized by many Indians to a point of paralysis of all social assertion and control. This is sometimes extrapolated to apply to nonintervention in self-destructive behaviors as well as in those in which intervention or correction are age appropriate. It is often extended to situations in which an individual's behavior may threaten the group, for example, when a drunken driver wrecks a car.

Direct confrontation is limited to making sure the individual is aware of the consequences of behavior. Then it is left to the innate forces within the individual to operate. Choice to control or not to control the behavior is not preempted by anyone else. This attitude often bewilders social agencies and schools who feel that Indian families are "not cooperative."

As in the case of most taboos, there are sanctions for controlling other person's behaviors. They operate dramatically when life-threatening injury occurs or when mental illness exacerbates deviant behavior. Just as the White middle class has trouble defining the limits of freedom of speech, traditional Indian values post ethical problems in the clash between non-interference and the need to teach the young, punish the criminal, or protect the weak. When this paralyzing problem occurs, the family discovers the rationale for change within the context and priorities held by the Indian family.

It also may be worth noting that this Indian value, transferred into modern conceptual framework, may affect feedback of negative opinions from the family to the therapist. "Resistance" will be more covertly expressed. Humor, especially if it expresses ability to share a sense of the therapist's frustrations, may be the most effective weapon in cutting through the tangled traps that are built on this value orientation when it becomes distorted.

The individual, autonomous but still a member of a group and loyal to it and to its needs, is an ideal of traditional Indian culture. The source of the individuality is felt to be innate. Parental aspirations do not lend themselves as much to shaping and molding as to freeing the inner self of the child in order that it can become what it is destined to be.

In this sense the traditional first-order ideal value of this set, Being-in-Becoming, is a difficult concept indeed to verbalize. The present orientation is always seen in relation to the cycle of which it is a part. "Being" today is the foundation of tomorrow. A person therefore, is continually "Becoming." Self-development is never static or achieved as a goal. It cannot be hurried. However, as one *is*, one *becomes*.

The second-order values, Doing and Being, seem to have alternating valences, depending on the demands and essence of the situation at any one period of time. Doing for the sake of being busy has little place. Doing for mere self-expression is a luxury and a selfish indulgence. Doing for the sake of personal rather than group goals is tainted and suspect. Because of its complexity it is easy to see that the ideals of this sort are easily misunderstood. Observers, anthropologists, or others usually ascribe to Indians a "Being position" as the top value since they seldom mention the goals of personal growth that they would find difficult to explain without appearing competitive or selfish.

However, for the urbanized late 20th-century Indian, this value system based on Being-in-Becoming has deep roots and sometimes leads to personal conflict. To develop self in the mainstream culture requires a type of competitiveness that allows only one or a few to succeed, often at the expense of others. Even where skills of teaching, technology, or political administration can be learned from the mainstream, it is hard to return to the tribal group without some taint of this ruthless orientation.

While the dominant culture admires doing and accomplishment, it generally has no systematic way of incorporating the individual into the social unit. Success in the dominant culture depends on nebulous factors of luck, of a hope of vanquishing of obstacles both human and material, and of the possibility of recognition by the stronger, more powerful elements. Status in the White middle class tends to be discontinuous and precarious. In contrast, within an Indian society there has been continual validation by group acceptance or rejection. Individual and group success has been clear to all. This has broken down to some extent during the reservation period but is still strongly felt in kin groups. Therefore, the urban, educated person is often alienated from home and traditional recognition systems and is lost in forming new social ties.

In many families these value clashes begin with child rearing, where the pressure to be a contributing member allows children and youth to assume a share of group responsibility in the family and leads to an early development of autonomy. At the same time, the family instills the sense that each person is innately an individual whose potential is to be fostered and not forced. This leads to an apparent lack of discipline as well as what non-Indians often consider unwarranted allowing of very young children to make decisions about family disposition of livestock, goods, or services, to say nothing of whether or not to attend school and where.

Consequences of choices and behavior may, at one period in the past history, have provided immediate feedback, but in the contemporary urban world, consequences of many behaviors are remote and intangibly in the future. Intellectually, a parent may appreciate the need for one set of values to become dominant and may sense the desirability of conformity to the dominant culture. However, in many families the demands of the White society mobilize emotional antibodies that defeat the best intentions. These parents need help in ways that offer them respect while they seek appropriate child-rearing guides.

Traditional Family Organization

In each culture, patterns of value orientations are transmitted by the family, and the American Indian is no exception. However, the Indian structure contrasts with the modern "American" family in a number of significant details (Redhorse, Shattuck, & Hoffman, 1981). In modern America the basic unit is supposed to be the family of procreation, especially the nuclear family. Even though this may now be a single-parent-headed household or a blended family of stepparents and children (his, hers, and theirs), the executive functions are presumed to reside in the parent(s). Relationships with in-laws and extended family of earlier generations are much less substantial, and if enmeshment occurs, a usual move of the family therapist is to disentangle the generations.

The traditional pattern of Indian family organization was quite different, with three generations involved and multiple parental functions delegated among aunts and uncles as well as grandparents. Cousins were all considered siblings, and incest taboos applied to all. Grandparents were often more available for infant and toddler care and thus continued a relationship of mutual concern with grandchildren throughout the lifespan. The parent generation was occupied with matters of economic importance—hunting,

providing shelter, gathering or cultivating crops, preserving food, manufacturing the implements needed for both productive and ritual labors.
Parenting roles, when not given to grandparents, were shared by several
adults. Uncles and aunts often had particular disciplinary responsibilities
toward their nieces and nephews, freeing biological parents for a much
looser, more pleasure-oriented association with offspring.

Administratively, this complex family could be organized in many
ways, with an administrative focus on the oldest man or woman and with a
wide variety of roles. The results of the particular patterning constitute many
of the tribal differences, yet in each the basic outline of three (or more if
present) generational extended families was the general phenomenon of the
family.

For children the extended family meant ties from birth allowing bonding
to several parental figures. This provided a security of affection and of
standards of behavior, as well as a variety of role models. The usual family
therapist's method of separating the generations will often run counter to
this model, which is quite often firmly established in the memories of today's
urban Indian family even though it cannot be practiced in quite the same
ways (Attneave, 1977). Sometimes great efforts are made to maintain these
connections, as is vividly described in the account of the Boston-to-Nova
Scotia network of the Mic Mac Indians in *Urban Renegades* (Guillimen,
1974). Seen from the perspective of maintaining these ties, much that has
seemed incomprehensible becomes quite sensible. What is "renegade" behavior in one culture is loyalty and sustaining of group identity in another,
even though the level of subsistence remains marginal in both.

The Nature of Man: Mostly Good, Somewhat Mixed

The main orientation of the Indian toward human nature is that it is
generally good, although the existence of evil is recognized and the possibility
of its appearance in human form is acknowledged. In general, however,
human foibles and misdeeds are considered to result from lack of opportunity to develop full potential. The results are often treated as misunderstandings by individuals who do not quite fit into society.

One manifestation of evil is witchcraft, including the use of spells
against another person. A keenly sensed danger of any form of power,
including that of the therapist or healer, is that the temptation to misuse
power may be too great. Perhaps avoidance of this danger is one reason that
only a few aspire to careers of healing, leadership, and powerful community
status. It also adds wariness and caution to the behaviors of those seeking a
therapist's help.

This fear of contamination may be part of the unconscious force behind
the proverbial "bucket of crabs" phenomenon. When Indians find someone
clambering over the barriers that have penned them up or held them down,

they often seem to attack and pull down the adventuresome one—behaving like a bucket of crabs that can be safely left on the beach by a fisherman. Since they pull one another back rather than climb out using one another as a ladder, this kind of attack by kin and peers is a real threat to many who gain more education and experience in the "White man's world." There is almost inevitably a simultaneous feeling of their own unworthiness due to lack of group validation and a sense of frustration that new ideas cannot be implemented. The result is often a fear of exerting leadership. Sensitive explorations of self-defeating activity or impotence at the brink of success will be needed to discover whether they are due to real fear of contamination or to the equally paralyzing fear of the accusations of disloyalty by some members of a larger Indian community.

These leveling and inhibiting influences are part and parcel of the group collateral process, which can also be used for more healthy moves whenever it is possible to gain group support for innovative or constructive plans. However, the family therapist needs to keep in mind how deeply entrenched these group processes are and be willing to consult around the larger units, such as social networks, and even to include them in the therapeutic inter- ventions (Attneave, 1969; Speck & Attneave, 1973).

The Medicine Person as Colleague

Sooner or later in a relationship with Indian families there will arise a mention of the traditional healer—medicine person, shaman, or spiritual leader. As in the case of most of the world's religions, the leader and top authorities are more nearly alike than many of their lesser representatives. In keeping with the need for maintaining therapeutic integrity, relationships to the traditional medicine person should parallel those to a chaplain or other clergy. These are usually considered colleagues whose expertise is only partially shared. Meyer (1974) describes his work with one displaced urban- ized Indian patient who felt that her scientific training and adoption of a Christian religion had blotted her earlier beliefs from her life. However, unable to resolve her grief in any other way, she did recount an earlier loss in adolescence that had been eased by a ritual prescribed by the medicine person to whom she then related. When reassured that there was nothing alienating her new status if she were to repeat the ritual, she did so and the current ghosts were laid to rest.

Reconnection of life threads may be significant and important in success- fully adapting to current situations and problems. For this the elder and the medicine person can indeed be welcome cotherapists, if available. Often a traditional healer can act as a consultant to the family if at too great a distance for regular involvement in the therapy.

Taboo Breaking and Taboo Reversing

One of the problems of partially retained traditional attitudes and knowledge seems to be that the dramatic and the threatening, the prohibitions and the dangers, are most often retained and passed along. Elders and medicine people may often have the knowledge of how to reverse the curse, how to undo the taboo—and this may be at times almost lifesaving in nature.

For example, a woman seemed to be near death after childbirth. Her mother and an aunt who came to visit seemed helplessly convinced of this. Her symptoms did not yield to any treatment for postpartum depression, and the diagnosis, in spite of failing vital signs, did not conform to any known complications of childbirth. However, she was wasting away in the hospital, causing the staff much anguish and frustration. In a family consultation it was revealed that her husband, whom she had met in the city, was actually a cousin close enough for traditional incest taboos to be in force. In all innocence they had fallen in love and married, but the birth of the child had brought relatives together and the nature of their kinship was revealed. According to tribal tradition the penalty for incest of this nature was death, and the current parental and kin generations were all resigned to this, although at the same time they were deeply grieved by it.

A search among the elders of the tribe finally turned up a solution, equally traditional but almost lost since it had been so seldom used in contemporary times. If one of the couple could be adopted by a nonrelated family, the original family of procreation could go through a ritual mourning for its lost member, and then the marriage could be celebrated and the new child accepted. Since both families of the bride and groom were related, the result would be no real or lasting cutoffs of original relationship, only an extension of the family circle to include the new adopting family. This procedure reversed the patient's downward spiral, and the family is now thriving.

This illustration is a fairly infrequent occurrence, although one problem of boarding schools, foster homes, and urban living is the fact that youngsters do run the risk of breaking such taboos since there is no one to rehearse genealogies and inform them about the kinship ties. What is more important to be learned from the example is that within every culture there are ways of overcoming taboos. The problem for the modern Indian is often that these antidotes are not widely known, so that freedom from their restrictive weight is difficult to achieve.

Another example occasionally encountered in certain tribes is the prohibition against talking directly to a mother-in-law, a problem that can generally be neutralized by a handsome gift to indicate that open and free communication does not mean loss of respect. Many other rituals have a basis in hygiene, good health, and social order. Sometimes they can be reinstated easily with a modern twist such as the use of saunas in place of the sweat lodges that are inaccessible in city environments. This practice is showing considerable effectiveness in the rehabilitation of alcoholics in a number of Indian programs, although some health clubs would be surprised to know how they are being perceived.

Whether in terms of these practical solutions to cultural double binds or to exorcise ghosts, access to consultants familiar with specific tribal tradition is helpful. Such a person can validate and acknowledge personal achievements or provide support for proceedings with the difficult solution of the problems of living in two worlds. The therapist working with Indian families will find the elders and medicine people a resource to be used with respect (Coutoure, 1980). The agnostic therapist will find them shrewd and patient. The therapist whose convictions tie them tightly to a single faith should realize that the Indian generally lives in traditional space that allows for an ecumenical relationship, being basically able to share the same reverence with many manifestations of what is deemed essentially the same Great Spirit.

The Power of Places

Since many manifestations of spirit power in the Indian world are tied to geographic features of particular places, a return to the place of origin may include reviving old beliefs as well as seeking out family members and learning more of our origins. Family accounts that need balancing (Nagy, 1973) may include recall or reencounter with places as well as people. Indeed, those therapists who follow the Bowen model may well find this another aspect of self-differentiation that needs to be included in between-session homework. The film or videotape of someone leaving a place or being homesick for it, used by Paul and Paul (1975), suggests other emotion-laden stimuli, which might well be added to one's repertoire when dealing with Indian couples.

The Problem of Guilt

Guilt is seldom introduced into traditional Indian homes at the earlier stages of child development. Instead shaming, ridicule, and allowing a child to learn from the consequences of behavior are more modal methods of control. The process of growing up within the group is one of self-discovery, and everyone assumes that learning follows readiness. This basic pattern flowing from the value orientations already discussed may be one of the reasons that young children enter school eagerly, but in later elementary school they become troubled and disillusioned about formal learning. Teachers, youth leaders, and nearly all majority culture representatives expect to induce guilt as a means of social control and as a motivator of appropriate patterns of behavior.

It may well be that one reason guilt is not as prominent a reaction among American Indian people is the simple fact that they do not feel as though they should have control over others or their own environments. Consequently, they do not have conflicted feelings if things are not controlled. For instance, it has been noted that non-Indian adults become guilty and conflicted when they cannot control their aging parents and become defensive even while distancing these parts of their family (Strong & Spitzer, 1981). American Indian adults would attempt to convince an aging and ill parent to keep a clinic appointment, desist from a diet that would exacerbate their ailments, or do other things that are sensible in preserving their lives. However, they would feel that no matter how senile or ill, the elderly parent retains the right to make his or her own decisions, and they would feel sadness, perhaps, but not guilt if their efforts were unsuccessful.

This same attitude is extended at the other end of the age scale to a large portion of a child's life. While there are firmly set limits concerning proper and life-threatening behaviors involving others, the child is still free to choose when and whether to engage in a wide range of activities. A parent does not rush immediately to help if a child tries to climb a tree that he or she is not yet well coordinated enough to master. Neither does the parent threaten, bribe, or cajole about eating, attending school, going to bed on time, or a hundred and one other details that non-Indian parents compulsively feel must be done. Often attempts are made to persuade or distract, but if these tactics are not successful, the consequences of behavior are expected to teach their own lessons. A scraped knee or a failing grade are risks the child is presumed old enough to take. Only in this way is it presumed that children are able to learn how to control themselves and the value of conforming. Penalties may at times be severe and, as there have been cultural shifts, the delayed and accumulated effects of social penalties or the swift and deadly effects of machinery, drugs, and other products of technology do not always fit the slower paced skills, training, or social sanctions of the traditional culture.

This lack of induced guilt does not inhibit initiative in its traditional context. However, since the non-Indian has seldom appreciated children's autonomous efforts, the Indian child may simply withdraw, wait, or use passive resistance to the onslaught of scolding by teachers and other non-Indians. This pattern becomes an entrenched defense, with the result that what is seen by teachers as refreshing, if sometimes naive, behavior in young Indian children just entering school is interpreted as stubbornness or callousness in older children and as delinquency or lack of motivation in adolescents and youth.

Oedipal crisis phenomena, held by some theorists to be the stimulus to development of guilt, are traditionally diffused by multiple parental Indian family relationships. The typical problems associated with this complex are unfamiliar in traditional families. When this type of problem does appear, as housing and other trends limit families to the confines of nuclear households, it is doubly disturbing to Indian parents, who have no familiar ways of coping or resolving the crisis.

One task of the therapist working with majority culture families and with many of those with European roots may be to relieve unnecessary guilt feelings from about the age of five onward. With Indian and Alaska Native families, some efforts to demystify the differences between guilt and shame seem to be more appropriate.

Specific Family-Focused Problems

A number of contemporary problems are rooted in the contrasting family structures. In the 1950s it was not uncommon to encounter parents who had never experienced family living after early school age. The government boarding schools had removed children to a regimented institutional setting, and there were no memory patterns for dealing individually with obstreperous, active, latency-age youngsters nor for handling wisely the emerging sense of self in adolescence. Parent education and support groups and a relaxation of pressures to remove children from their "pagan and savage" homes have somewhat alleviated these problems. Nevertheless, it may take several generations for new models to be absorbed and integrated.

Ironically, many Indians are making attempts to follow a Victorian model established in government schools or the Dick-and-Jane model of the popular reading texts. These school-taught models may have been the only pictures of family life experienced by large numbers of those growing up as late as the 1940s and 1950s. In the arctic and elsewhere, the elders and parents may have spent many years in TB sanitariums while the youth were sent hundreds or thousands of miles away to government- or church-sponsored boarding schools. As the major culture struggles to evolve a tolerance of new forms of family life, perhaps the Indian traditional family will become a more viable alternative.

The Problem of Sex-Appropriate Roles

In traditional Indian society, sex roles were quite specific. The responsibility for teaching self-discipline and for establishing the proper limits and the development of skills and potential were the province of the same-sex parental figures. In general, women made the transition into the non-Indian economy with a certain amount of success more quickly than men. Their household skills and ability to nurture children made them useful in domestic service roles. Vocational nursing and other service positions followed fairly easily. Because Indian women were used to hard seasonal labor, they could do factory work, especially in food processing such as canneries, and other urban jobs. Girls persisted in school longer than boys.

Men and boys, on the other hand, often had only brute strength to market. As roustabouts and unskilled laborers, they had fewer years of employability and far more erratic employment patterns. Those jobs they did hold seldom exposed them to the intimate side of the non-Indian world, and their frustrations with the social setting of formal education left them stranded in deadend situations. Historical and contemporary unemployment rates of 70% or 80% on many reservations further impede development of male role models of success.

In traditional societies the role-specific tasks and responsibilities resulted in the contributions of each gender being equally appreciated. As this became less realistic with changes in economic patterns, the Indian family followed the mainstream pattern, especially that of lower socioeconomic strata, and experienced disintegration into female-headed households. Often in the urban environment these households also have lacked the supporting cast of extended kin. In general, Indians have not formed ties with others to the extent that the Black community has in making up a similar deficit (Stack, 1974).

Without a traditional model for raising boys and with little support from the environment to supplement this lack, single-parent Indian women feel helpless as the young boys fall into patterns of truancy and delinquency. These mothers see no way to contribute to their family's well-being. The women's liberation movement did not reach many Indian women through its appeals for increased self-respect and status since they already felt they had them. However, as the women's movement grapples with child-rearing issues and discusses and rogynous personalities, it may be a means of freeing Indian women from their inhibition in raising boys appropriately.

That this is badly needed is seen in a report by Jillek-All (1975) in which she describes the problems of young Indian men and women as they meet in urban settings. The girls and women have generally absorbed traditional tribal patterns as well as a school and media-induced desire for "freedom." They misinterpret the behavior of the boys and men including the assumption that physical familiarity will inevitably lead to marriage. The young men, on the other hand, have not been so instructed in tribal traditions. Young men, especially in urban settings, take license from their exposure to television, movies, and barroom stories to indulge and desert, exploit and cast off the Indian women, who appear so naive. Depression and self-denigration experienced by these women is reactivated as sons begin to follow the same pattern. Particularly among college women and young professionals, the sense of helplessness in dealing with boys is a family problem that may well need the sympathetic support and creative solution of the family therapist.

Otherwise there remain only the alternatives often mentioned by Indian women: interracial marriages, which create new identity strains or the self-destructive patterns of alcoholism, suicide, and apathy, which claim a heavy toll.

Alcoholism and Suicide

Perhaps this is the place to mention two negative stereotypes that haunt the American Indian: alcoholism and suicidal tendencies. Of these, suicide seems not to be as widespread as it was first thought to be. Some tribes are noted for having a rate one-tenth that of the national average, whereas others would seem to fall under the weight of a rate 10 times the national average. Shore (1975) has presented research indicating that suicide is not only a tribally specific trait but may well be a familial one within these tribes. This poses real ethical dilemmas since while identification of suicide-prone families could be helpful to those engaged in prevention, it might also accelerate the phenomenon in a self-fulfilling fashion.

There may even be some small indication that the generalization of this stereotype if having this self-fulfilling effect on at least some young people even in low-incidence tribes. Adolescents often attempt suicide or fall into a "parasuicide" category. Most of these suicidal "gestures" are efforts to remedy interpersonal strains, often directed at family members. The family therapist should be alert for indications of suicidal tendencies within the family history and not be too hasty to dismiss as unimportant an indication of being trapped with no other way out on the part of family members. The work now being done with the descendants of the Nazi holocaust may be relevant to the problems of suicidal and addictive behavior in the American Indian community.

The treatment of alcoholism is a special field in itself. If the pattern is one of occasional tension release, defiance, or binge celebrations, it can probably be handled within the usual family therapy context. In one family it was possible to negotiate a contract: The husband was to limit his drinking sprees to two holidays each year, New Year's Day and the Fourth of July. At those times he was to control himself sufficiently that he not endanger himself or others nor destroy property. His wife, at those times, would not lock him out of the house nor ridicule him in front of his children, although she was free to visit relatives or otherwise withdraw and not participate. Law enforcement officials also agreed to the compact. The sobriety and lack of recrimination during the rest of the year enabled the family to work out their other problems and, with reduced stress, the acting-out patterns of the children subsided.

However, if there is a chronicity or destructive and aggressive personality change indicating chronic alcoholism, then referral to an alcohol treatment center should be a priority. A center with Indian personnel is desirable, but in any case, until alcohol use is controlled, other interventions are of questionable effect. Support for the noninvolved family members is in order, but unless the family therapist is well trained in alcohol treatment, the use of collateral expertise is advised.

One of the nightmares arising from the prevalence of alcoholism at the present time is the physical damage of the children during pregnancy, now being labeled as the "fetal alcohol syndrome." This syndrome indicates as yet unknown limits on the child's potential, but it is clear that these children are developmentally delayed and often mentally retarded. The presence of such children in the family, with their physical stigmas and special educational needs, can be a source of embarrassment to reformed alcoholic parents.

Denial of the child's limitations is often tenaciously asserted as a protection against the parent's awareness of being the responsible agent. One of the most difficult of such cases was the child of a couple now active in Alcoholics Anonymous and well known as alcohol counselors. Their oldest child required a special educational placement due to fetal alcohol damage. The blow to the family, reinforced by puritanical preaching from the pulpit about sins of the fathers being visited on the sons, was nearly overwhelming. Skillful parental support and aid in locating appropriate special educational facilities were essential in what will probably be a long-term therapeutic relationship for this family.

Since children are considered precious and are accepted for themselves, a handicapped child is usually given all the support needed to reach his or her own level of fulfillment, but public disgrace and stigma are hard to bear. The media campaigns aimed at prevention of fetal alcohol syndrome make this particular diagnosis a difficult one for parents to accept. The aim of the campaign seems to be to frighten prospective parents into sobriety, but it offers little hope to children already born with this condition.

Strengths of Indian Families

Over the generations the Native people of this continent have been displaced into a position like that of emigrants with a major culture. However few in number, they represent significant survivors of a now alien culture. They bring durability and persistence to today's problems. This discussion has put emphasis on dissonance in values between cultures. The problems that illustrate the tensions between cultures tend to present a gloomy picture of difficulties inherent in working with American Indian families. Actually there are challenges and opportunities for real satisfaction in these contacts. One is the opportunity to work with viable, strong families. Miller's research group in the San Francisco Bay area (Native American Research Group, 1974/1979) has shown that a high percentage of families living in the cities are surviving and coping with urban life fairly well. Some are now second-generation city dwellers. One of the most interesting findings is that the families succeeding best in this migration have two characteristics: Not surprisingly, one is an openness to learning and to using the social and technical tools of the White culture. A second, more startling characteristic is the interest these families show in keeping alive the language, folkways, crafts, and values associated with their tribal identities.

Family strength is no insurance against problems. However, the therapeutic contracts by Indian families are often clear and cogent. Implicit or explicit, what is sought is a restoration of a sense of innate worth and goodness, a restoration of feelings of adequacy and of the fit of person, place, and family. A creative therapeutic alliance will enable therapist and family to untangle knots of shifting cultural skeins. The task need not be just a puzzle or a routine application of skills. At times the new insights into human strengths and variability transfer creatively to aid in the solution of problems brought to the therapist by other families. Whether or not this occurs, encounters with the strengths of Indian families and discovery of ways to work together become, more often than not, both a challenge and an adventure.

REFERENCES

Attneave, C. Therapy in Tribal Settings and Urban Network Interventions. *Family Process, 8*, 192–210, 1969.

Attneave, C. The Wasted Strengths of Indian Families. In S. Unger (Ed.), *The Destruction of Indian Families*. New York: Association on Indian Affairs, 1977.

Attneave, C., & Beiser, M. *Mental Health Service Networks and Patterns of Utilization.* Albuquerque and Rockville: Indian Health Service, 1975.

Benedict, R. *Patterns of Culture.* New York: Penguin Books, 1934.

Bergman, R. The Training of the Medicine Man as a Model for Psychiatry. In C. Tulipson & C. Attneave (Eds.), *Beyond Clinic Walls.* University, Ala.: University of Alabama Press, 1974.

Castaneda, C. *Journey to Ixtlan.* New York: Simon & Schuster, 1972.

Coutoure, J. *Next Time Try a Medicine Man.* Unpublished manuscript, 1980.

English, H.B., & English, A.C. *A Comprehensive Dictionary of Psychological and Psychoanalytical Terms: A Guide to Usage.* New York: David McKay, 1958.

Guillimen, M. *Urban Renegades.* New York: Columbia University Press, 1974.

Jillek-All, L. *Identification of Specific Psychosocial Stresses in British Columbia Indian Patients.* Presented at Second Transcultural Workshop on Native People's Mental Health, Canada, 1975.

Kelso, D., & Attneave, C. *Bibliography of North American Indian Mental Health.* Westport, Conn.: Greenwood Press, 1981.

Kleinfeld, J.S. Intellectual Strengths in Culturally Different Groups: An Eskimo Illustration. *Review of Education Research, 43*, 341–359, 1973.

Meyer, G. On Helping the Casualties of Rapid Change. *Psychiatric Annals, 4*, 44–48, 1974.

Momaday, N.S. I Am Alive . . . . In *The World of the American Indian*. Washington, D.C.: National Geographic Society, 1974.

Nagy, I.B. *Invisible Loyalties.* New York: Harper & Row, 1973.

Native American Research Group. *American Indian Socialization to Urban Life.* Final Report, NIMH Grant MH 22719, D. Miller, Principal Investigator. San Francisco: Scientific Analysis Corp., 1974. (Revised, 1979.)

Papajohn, J., & Spiegel, J. *Transactions in Families*. San Francisco: Jossey-Bass, 1975.

Paul, N.L., & Paul, B.B. *A Marital Puzzle*. New York: Norton, 1975.

Redhorse, J., Shattuck, A., & Hoffman, F. (Eds.). *The American Indian Family: Strengths and Stresses*. Isleta, N.M.: American Indian Research & Development Associates, 1981.

Scheibe, K.E. *Beliefs and Values*. New York: Holt, Rinehart & Winston, 1970.

Shore, J. American Indian Suicide: Fact and Fantasy. *Psychiatry, 8*, 86–91, 1975.

Speck, R., & Attneave, C. *Family Process*. New York: Pantheon, 1973.

Stack, C. *All Our Kin* (No. CN424). New York: Colophon, 1974.

Strong, C., & Spitzer, R. *Caring for Elderly Relatives: Its Meaning among Indians and White Families*. Unpublished report, Whatcom Counseling & Psychiatric Clinic, Bellingham, Wash., 1981.

Trimble, J. Value Differences among Indians: Concerns for the Concerned Counselor. In P. Pederson, W. Lonner, & J. Draguns (Eds.), *Counseling across Cultures*. Honolulu: University Press of Hawaii, 1976.

Walster, E., & Walster, G.W. Equity and Social Justice. In M. Lerner (Ed.), *The Justice Motive in Social Behavior*. Ann Arbor, Mich.: Society for the Psychological Study of Social Issues, 1975. (See also in this volume: Deutch, M. Equity, Equality and Need; and Schwarts, S., The Justice of Need and the Activation of Humanitarian Norms.)

Wax, R., & Thomas, R. American Indians and White People. *Phylon, XXII*(4), 1961.

4

Black Families

PAULETTE MOORE HINES
NANCY BOYD-FRANKLIN

The doctrine of color blindness in mental health has outlived its usefulness. Psychological theory, research, and practice have advanced for decades without giving significant attention to the role and implications of race. Some deny that there is any such thing as Black culture (Staiano, 1980). Attempts have been made to deny or ignore many aspects of Black heritage, and there have been many pressures for accommodation to the mainstream. However, we believe that there is a set of core values and behavior, which in its gestalt remains distinctively characteristic of and understood by a majority of Black people. The implications of this for family therapy have not been adequately explored. Consequently, as Foley (1975) has observed, if family therapy is still in its infancy, family therapy with Black families is still in the incubator stage.

This chapter has been written to sensitize clinicians to the cultural context in which Black people have lived and continue to live in the United States. It has been a challenge for us as we are particularly concerned about the injustice that is suffered when it is assumed that all Blacks fit into one mold. We wish to assert emphatically that there is no such entity as "the Black family." The diversity that exists among Black families and communities is a reality determined by a complex interplay of variables. Black families have come to the United States from many different countries over the last four centuries. By far, however, the largest group of Blacks in the United States are those of African origin whose ancestors were brought directly here as slaves. Within this group, on whom we will focus in this chapter, one finds great diversity of values, characters, and life-styles. Geographic origins, age, level of acculturation, religious background, and socioeconomic status interact to generate a host of variations that cannot be fully articulated in a single chapter.

It is also impossible to discuss cultural considerations in working with Black families without also taking into account the social, economic, and

Paulette Moore Hines. Central Community Focus Team, University of Medicine and Dentistry of New Jersey, Community Mental Health Center of Rutgers Medical School, Piscataway, New Jersey.

Nancy Boyd-Franklin. University of Medicine and Dentistry of New Jersey, Community Mental Health Center of Rutgers Medical School, Newark, New Jersey.

political realities of being "Black" in this society. Color is the predominant distinguishing fact of life of all Black Americans. While all immigrant groups have had acculturation problems, Blacks exist with the reality that the American dream was not dreamed for them. Black families continue to combat social, economic, and political hardships because of color discrimination. This reality pervades all aspects of Black family life; however, the means of coping with racism and discrimination vary from one family to the next.

An example of the diversity that can be found among Black families is evident in the authors' own family backgrounds. Hines was born and raised in North Carolina; her parents were of African and African/American Indian descent. Similar to countless other Blacks currently living in the Northeast, she migrated from the South as an adult. Boyd-Franklin was born in Harlem and raised in the Bronx by a Black family with Caribbean and Southern Black roots. Her maternal family has its roots in Jamaica, West Indies; her paternal family moved to New York and New Jersey from North and South Carolina.

Undoubtedly, our personal backgrounds and professional experiences have influenced our notions about Black culture and family patterns. The majority of our clinical work with Black families has been with low-income, inner-city families in the Northeast. A large percentage of these are families whose older members migrated north from the South. Consequently, some of the ideas we will present are applicable to a broader group, and we will also make some comparative references to middle-income Black families. However, we urge you to be cautious in making generalizations to the life-styles of Blacks in other parts of the country or from other socioeconomic groups.

Cultural Context

Blacks comprise approximately 11% of the American population. Until recent decades, the vast majority lived in the South. During the years between 1940 and 1970, over 1.5 million Blacks migrated, first, to the North and, subsequently, to the West Coast. Over 81% are now living in urban areas. This migration can be attributed largely to job opportunities. However, many failed to find the opportunities for mobility that they expected. Racism and oppression have made it extremely difficult for the majority of Black people to enter the mainstream in this country. The long-lasting effects of poverty and oppression have caused many to feel broken by the system—disillusioned and frustrated. For some, dependence on drugs and alcohol has developed into a new kind of slavery. However, as Billingsley (1968) has noted, Black families as a group have shown an "amazing ability to survive in the face of impossible conditions." For example, Blacks have made major advances in income, education, employment, home ownership, and voter participation (U.S. Department of Commerce, 1979). Although Blacks remain far behind Whites in almost every social and economic area, a growing proportion of the Black population have managed to throw off the shackles of poverty and have struggled to become upwardly mobile. However, the more remarkable aspect of African American culture has been the ability to retain a sense of peoplehood, pride in "blackness," and a psychic security that theoretically goes against all odds. The family has been and remains the basic pillar stone or source of strength for this significant accomplishment.

Families seeking clinical services more often than not do so because of their inability to solve problems in living. While it is appropriate to focus on "what needs to change," therapists frequently overfocus on deficits and ignore strengths that will assist them in helping the family to accomplish the desired changes. It is easy for non-Black clinicians, who lack a cultural frame of reference, to assume that the clinic population they observe is representative of the entire cultural group. Certainly there is little literature that focuses on the resourcefulness that has allowed Black families not only to cope with but to transcend barriers to meeting their economic and psychic needs. One of the few researchers who has focused on the adaptive strengths of Black families is Hill (1972). He attributed the survival of Black families to their strong kinship bonds; flexibility of family roles; and high value placed on religion, education, and work. These strengths will provide a framework for the remainder of our discussion of Black families and issues in family therapy. We wish to emphasize that it is important for clinicians to consider the strengths and resources that can be mobilized to assist families.

Kinship Bonds and Role Flexibility

Although influenced by the oppressive forces of slavery and today's society, the strong kinship bonds among Black families today can be traced to historical origins in Africa. It is obviously difficult when we look at a continent as large as Africa to make generalizations about history and culture; however, a number of Black scholars have argued that there were, in fact, more similarities than differences among African societies (e.g., Nobles, 1980; Mbiti, 1970).

Franklin (1969) has provided some insight into the political, social, and economic organization that was typical of West Africa. Each aspect of life was permeated by the African belief in strong kinship bonds. Political organizations tended to center around village states and local rulers. Although not all Africans were engaged in agriculture, the land was extremely important to the entire community. It was owned not by individuals but by the tribal or familial group.

A number of authors have referred to the "communalities" that the various tribes of Africa shared in the area of kinship or to an intratribal sense of collective unity (Nobles, 1980). Mbiti (1970) stresses that the "survival of the tribe" was primary and that kinship controlled tribal life and provided the sense of bonding between individuals. In effect, individuals owed their existence to the tribe (Nobles, 1980). In contrast to the European premise of "I think, therefore, I am," the African philosophy is, "We are, therefore, I am." Franklin (1969) states that the family provided the basis for the economic and political life in Africa and exerted considerable influence over its members.

Slavery was a major disruption to the close kinship and family ties. African people were torn from their homeland and their tribal life and thrust into servitude. Slaves had virtually no human rights. Men, women, and children were forced to abandon their native languages, names, occupations, mates, religions, foods, and customs (Kinney, 1971). The master's sole responsibility was to provide food and clothing. Mortality rates were high (Pinkney, 1975) and life expectancies low (Ernst & Hugg, 1976). Slave markets were developed in the New World to sell and ship slaves to less-developed areas, and families were frequently dissolved by the sale of family members.

Men and women were not allowed to legalize their marriages, either through their original tribal ceremonies or through the European rituals of their masters. Frequent changes of partner became the rule. Black men were used as breeders to increase the labor supply, and Black women were often sexually exploited by their owners. Often Black women were dragged from their husbands' beds to provide their masters with recreation—and eventually new field hands (Pinkney, 1975).

Despite extremely difficult conditions, family life remained important. Slaves sought to maintain the high value placed on the family and tribal relations of their African heritage. New family units were formed by choice as well as force to compensate for the loss of family members to the slave market. Even after free status was granted, many Blacks, hoping that lost family members might return, rejected the option of leaving the plantations. Those who were separated yearned to reunite with their relatives in the afterlife if not in this world.

It is from this heritage of shared loyalty and strong kinship bonds that Black Americans descend. Reliance on a kinship network, not necessarily drawn along "blood" lines, remains a major mode for coping with the pressures of an oppressive society. Stack (1975) reports that the Black families she studied had evolved patterns of "co-residence, kinship-based exchange networks linking multiple domestic units, elastic houshold boundaries, and lifelong bonds to three generational households." She adds that "the Black urban family . . . embedded in cooperative domestic exchange . . . proves to be an organized, tenacious, active, lifelong network" (p. 124). White (1972) has pointed to the number of "uncles, aunts, big mamas, boyfriends, older brothers and sisters, deacons, preachers, and others who operate in and out of the Black home" (p. 45).

Before we elaborate further on extended family systems and their implication for therapy, we will explore some aspects of roles and relationships within the nuclear family. These roles, as previously mentioned, have developed from a complex interplay of African heritage, accommodation to the mainstream, and attempts to cope with the stresses of oppression.

The role of the Black male as father and mate varies. But Black fathers, regardless of income, are likely to demand and to receive recognition as head of household from their wives and children. Their identity is tied to their ability to provide for their families. Yet their chances for success in fulfilling this function are often limited because of discriminatory practices (see Pinderhughes, Chap. 5). Black males have had the highest job loss rates in the labor force. When employed, the number engaged in managerial and professional jobs is relatively small. The essence of these realities is that Black males may have to expend great time and energy trying to provide the basic survival necessities for their families. This investment of Black fathers in providing for their families has been overlooked by those who stress peripheralness, or the absence of participation and interest on the part of Black fathers in daily family activities (e.g., Moynihan, 1965).

The issue of peripheralness has been vastly overstated in the literature. An absence of active involvement in daily family matters characterizes some but certainly not all Black fathers. Hill (1972) challenges this notion of peripheralness and describes the role flexibility that occurs between Black males and females in child rearing and household responsibility. Particularly when child care is an issue, husbands and wives may reverse roles. For this reason White (1972) suggests that the Black child may not learn a rigid distinction between male and female roles. We believe it is important that therapists involve fathers in family treatment. This can be accomplished in a number of ways. We may find, for example, that a father who is working two jobs cannot afford to take time off from work to participate in ongoing family therapy sessions. The same father, however, may be willing to come in the evening or to take time off to come in for a single, problem-focused session. Therapists have to be creative in their use of phone contacts and letters to keep fathers abreast of the developments in their families' treatment. This communicates respect for their position in their families. Even limited involvement in their families' therapy can decrease the potential for sabotaging and may well be sufficient for beginning structural changes that can promote the attainment of the goals that the therapist and the family are working toward. In addition, when fathers are minimally involved or not living in the home, it is not uncommon for therapists to assume without further inquiry that there are no "male models" in the home. This assumption overlooks the pervasive influence of extended family members and the likelihood that there are other male models who may be actively involved in the lives of Black children. If a therapist is aware of these individuals, he or she can introduce the option of involving these other people in helping to relieve some of the stress of a mother who may be struggling to raise her children alone.

Pinderhughes (Chap. 5) elaborates how societal forces undermine the Black male's husband/father role. The disillusionment with hard work that does not bring rewards can cause severe pressure on couple and family relationships. However, Black couples are more likely to seek therapy because of child-focused concerns than because of marital dissatisfaction. Minuchin, Montalvo, Guerney, Rosman, and Schumer (1967) have commented that discord between Black males and females tends to be dealt with indirectly, rather than through direct confrontation. Solutions to disharmony, when sought, tend to be informal. Extended family members or ministers may be consulted, and there may be long periods of separation without either partner moving to dissolve the relationship legally. Traditionally, separation has been viewed as more socially acceptable than divorce. Couples marry for life. There is also a strong tradition among Black couples of remaining together for the sake of the children. The high tolerance for suffering and the expectation that "troubles" are inevitable has been influenced undoubtedly by the strong religious orientation and upbringing of most Blacks and their history of oppression.

Black females are more likely than their mates to initiate or at least be open to therapy as a means of solving relationship problems. However, a therapist who is not sensitive to the many issues involved may get frustrated with a woman who expresses intense dissatisfaction but at the same time resists change or dissolution of the relationship. Along with the usual problems (e.g., finances, fear of loneliness) of a person contemplating separation or divorce, ambivalence may be exacerbated by issues that are not easily articulated. For example, a woman may feel empathy for her husband's frustrations with a racist society and have difficulty holding him responsible for his behavior or situation. Furthermore, most Black females are keenly aware of the extent to which they outnumber Black males. The ratio is skewed as high as 44 to 1 in some geographic and socioeconomic areas of the country. Black males have a much lower life expectancy than Black females (or Whites of either sex). Their availability is reduced also because of lower educational levels, incarceration, mental or physical disabilities, and deaths frequently associated with their greater participation in active military service and other dangerous job situations.

Black women who are often more actively religious than their mates, tend to be regarded as "all sacrificing" and the "strength of the family." Their identity is most likely to be tied to their role as mothers. Because Black women must often assume responsibilities in their families that are less frequently taken by women in Euro-American cultures, their role may be misunderstood as dominant even when it is not. Black women have historically worked outside the home and have often been the sole wage earners in times of high unemployment. One consequence of this fact is that relationships between Black couples have often been more egalitarian than those of their counterparts in the mainstream culture. Women's liberation is not a new concept to the average Black woman, regardless of social class. Scanzoni (1971) found evidence that Black females and males grow up with the expectation that each will work as an adult. Consequently, Black males do not feel as threatened by having a working mate as do many non-Black males who are just beginning to work through the conflicts of having two-career families. In families where a father and mother are both working, an older sibling may act as a substitute parent or "parental child" for younger siblings.

Extended Kinship Networks

There are a number of other important considerations specific to the role flexibility and strong kinship alliances that characterize Black families. It has become almost a cliche that family therapy involves a "systemic approach." However, with some notable exceptions (Aponte & Van Deusen, 1981; Bowen, 1976; Minuchin, 1974; Bell, 1962), that system has been seen as the "nuclear family." Given the reality that most Black families are embedded in a complex kinship network of blood and nonrelated persons, therapists must be willing to expand the "definition of family" to a more extended kinship system. Particularly as we begin to examine parenting, the extent to which extended family involvement can promote family survival becomes more apparent. Relatives expect and accept reliance on one another in times of need and often live in close proximity. Various people interchange roles, jobs, and family functions.

An aunt or grandmother may share the responsibility for child care. It is not even uncommon for a child to be informally adopted and reared by extended family members who have resources not available to the child's parents or who reside in an environment considered more "wholesome." Many clinicians automatically assume that such a practice is indicative of rejection on the part of the parent and that it is perceived as such by the child, without giving consideration to the positive aspects of this practice. Stack (1975) refers to this process as "child-keeping" and sees it as a survival measure that grew out of a recognition in the Black community of the problems and difficulties inherent in raising children with very limited economic resources. Hill (1977) also states that since formal adoption agencies have not catered to Blacks, they have had to develop their own network of informal adoption.

Elderly people also tend to be supported by the collective efforts of family members both within and outside the nuclear family. In the same manner, young adults are often aided to be self-supporting. This pattern of collective support and ties with the extended family has continued as Blacks have realized upward mobility (McAdoo, 1978). Family therapists must explore and select carefully the "significant others" who should be included in the family therapy process. Very often key members of a family's kinship network may not be willing or able to come to the clinic for regular visits. This obstacle may be overcome by scheduling a family session in the home. But home visits should not be made without prior discussion and informed consent of key family members. Many Blacks have had negative experiences with the welfare system, in which home visits were an invasive means of "checking up" on families.

One effective way to gather information about the extended family system is to use a genogram or family tree. This tool can be effective in introducing important structural questions about the roles of different family members and their relationships and conflicts (Guerin & Pendagast, 1976). There are, however, a number of cautions: First, detailed genogram information should, as a general rule, not be gathered in the first session but only after the therapist feels that he or she has joined with the family sufficiently and is trusted by them. Second, the therapist should look for an opening to obtain the desired information rather than force an agenda of data gathering. Many Black families are suspicious of what they perceive as "prying" into their lives by well-meaning therapists. For many Black families, issues such as illegitimate births, the marital status of parents, or the paternity of the children may be "family secrets" that they will hesitate to discuss with an outsider.

We find that with Black families genograms seldom completely conform to bloodlines. They are often extremely complicated if they are accurate. Because of the practice of informal adoption, there are usually indications that children and other relatives have lived at various times with different members of the extended family. To obtain accurate information, it is essential to ask who is in the family as well as who lives in the home, or valuable information may be lost. It is also important to inquire whether there are family members who live elsewhere. Often, the question, "Who can you depend on for help when needed?" will uncover key individuals in the family's support system. The existence of previous coupling relationships and marriages should also be explored.

In the exploration of role responsibilities and boundaries in the family, therapists must be extremely careful to recognize that a system may be functional even if it is very different from that which the therapist expects would work satisfactorily. Role flexibility can be a strength that can be mobilized in times of crisis, such as separation, divorce, illness, hospitalization, or death of a family member.

In some instances, however, the boundaries in a family can become so blurred that there is no clear division of responsibility or source of authority. Two examples of this are the parental child system and the three-generational system, containing a grandmother or other maternal figure. As stated previously, in many Black families, it is common for parental power to be allocated to a child, male or female, particularly if there are many children or if both parents work. "The system can function well. The other children are cared for, and the parental child can develop responsibility, competence and autonomy beyond his years" (Minuchin, 1974, p. 97). However, a family with such a structure may run into difficulty. If the delegation of authority is not explicit, the child will lack the power to carry out the responsibilities he or she attempts to assume. Or, as Minuchin (1974) states, if the parents abdicate their responsibilities, the child may be forced to become the main source of guidance, control, and decision making at a point where developmentally he or she is unprepared to handle these roles. Misbehavior in school often occurs among parental children in late adolescence. Adolescents may display their stress through delinquency, sexual impulsiveness, or inappropriate handling of younger siblings when the demands of the household conflict with their age-appropriate need to be with peers.

Minuchin (1974) describes his strategy for working with parental child families as follows: "The therapeutic goal is to realign the family in such a way that the parental child can still help the mother" (p. 98). The goal of therapy is not to eliminate the child's parental role which may be essential to the family's survival. Rather, the therapist needs to facilitate redistribution of the child's burdens or, in some instances, help the family make better use of the resources available to them.

The boundary problems presented by the three-generational system—typically involving a grandmother who plays a central role—must also be handled sensitively. An example of such a situation is the Gordon family.

The Gordon Family

In this case, a 10-year-old boy was brought for treatment because of stealing. The first session was attended by the parents and their two children. Both parents appeared bewildered and unsure of their parenting skills with the children. When it was learned that the grandmother had the primary responsibility for child care, she was asked to join the family sessions. It became apparent that the grandmother ran the household. She had her way of handling the children, and the parents had theirs.

The therapist's goal was to form a working alliance between the parents and the grandmother so that the children were no longer given conflicting messages. This was accomplished by having a number of joint meetings with the parents and the grandmother to discuss family rules, division of labor, and child-care policies. Disputes and differences of opinions were discussed. Later the children were included in sessions in order to clarify the boundaries in the family.

The therapist's role was not to evict the grandmother from the system or to alter radically this family's structure. The grandmother was an essential part of the family system. The therapist's goal was to facilitate a working alliance among the executive members of the family in a way that their roles and responsibilities were clarified and could become mutually supportive.

The following case, seen by the second author, illustrates the need for clarification of extended family roles and boundaries.

The Gallop Family

The family consisted of Ms. LaVerne Gallop; her two children, Charlie (11 years) and Mary (5 years); her mother, Mrs. Sarah Gallop; and her aunt, Ms. Pierre (see Figure 4.1). In addition, Charlie had contact with his father, Mr. Frazier, who had major input in decision making for Charlie. When Mrs. Gallop came to the clinic with Charlie, she reported that he was "out of control" at home and in school. He was frequently truant from school. He never listened to her and was involved in frequent fights at home and in the neighborhood. When the family constellation was explored, it seemed clear that Charlie's grandmother, Mrs. Gallop, had, in fact, functioned as his mother during his earlier years. In the last year, however, she had been forced to switch from a day shift to an evening shift on her job. As a result, she was not as available during the afternoons. Mrs. Gallop came reluctantly to the session. However, it became clear during the session that she did not believe her daughter was capable of parenting her son. It was also obvious that both Ms. Gallop and Charlie responded to Mrs. Gallop as the real power in the home.

At the second interview, the therapist learned that in Mrs. Gallop's absence, Mr. Frazier (Charlie's father) and Ms. Pierre (Mrs. Gallop's sister) often undermined Ms. Gallop's instructions to Charlie. Mr. Frazier lived

FIG. 4.1. The Gallop family.

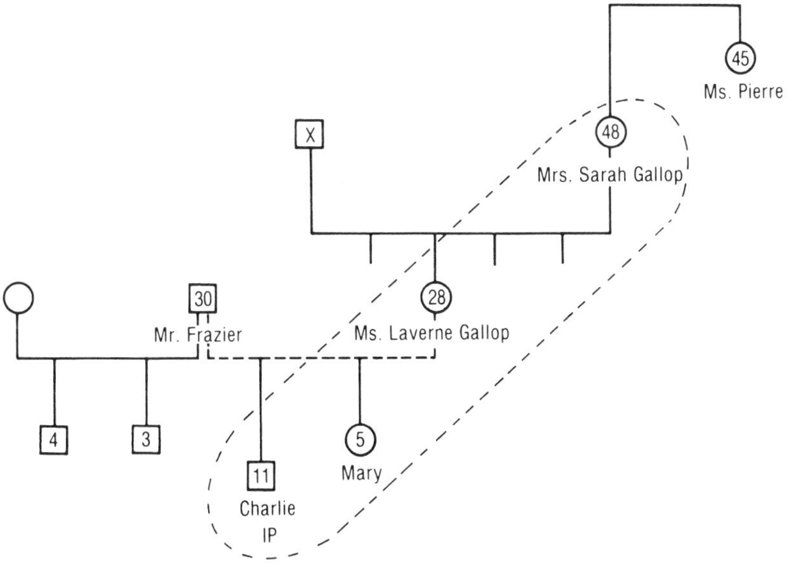

around the corner with his second family, and Ms. Pierre lived in the next building. Mr. Frazier would arrive to take Charlie for an outing even though he knew that Ms. Gallop had placed him "on punishment" and refused to let him go. Ms. Pierre was a warm nurturing person who had cared for Charlie for awhile when her sister was ill. It was to her house that Charlie would run when he became angry with his mother, and Ms. Pierre often supported his refusal to obey his mother.

With Ms. Gallop's and Mrs. Gallop's permission, a session was scheduled with Charlie's father and Ms. Pierre. In that session, the therapist was struck by the animosity between Ms. Gallop and Mr. Frazier. It was also clear that no one, including Charlie, responded to Ms. Gallop as an adult.

The adults in the family were asked to talk together to establish which problem they felt was the most serious one for Charlie. After some discussion, they were able to agree on the truancy as a major issue. Mrs. Gallop and Ms. Gallop were then asked to talk together to clarify what the rules should be for Charlie. After arguing for some time they were able, with the therapist's help, to establish a plan, which was as follows: Ms. Gallop and Mrs. Gallop would go together to the school and discuss the situation with Charlie's teacher and principal. Then Ms. Gallop would take Charlie to school for the first week in order to make sure that he arrived.

Positive and negative consequences for Charlie were discussed. He loved to go to the movies and bowling with his father. Charlie's father agreed to make these special activities contingent on a positive report from his mother. Ms. Pierre was helped to see the part she contributed to Charlie's acting out; she agreed to call Charlie's mother if he ran to her home and to return him.

Mrs. Gallop was able to say that she would like to help her daughter learn to parent effectively. The therapist encouraged Mrs. Gallop to coach her daughter. Ms. Gallop was asked to discuss the plan with Charlie and to gain his agreement to try it. The therapist established a rule that none of the other adults could intervene while this discussion was taking place. Charlie became angry at his mother at one point, and both his grandmother and his aunt attempted to intervene. The therapist blocked their intervention and helped Ms. Gallop to complete her discussion with Charlie and elicit his agreement to try the plan.

During the course of treatment various family members were seen in different subgroups in order to reinforce the new structure that had been established. For example, Ms. Gallop and Charlie's father were seen together for two sessions to help them stop triangling Charlie in their conflicts. The majority of the sessions involved Mrs. Gallop, Ms. Gallop, and Charlie. Mrs. Gallop became a cotherapist and was able to allow Ms. Gallop to deal directly with her son. After this process, Mrs. Gallop met alone with her daughter and the therapist to discuss the outcome. Finally, a number of sessions were held between Ms. Gallop and Charlie to help them discuss the problems they encountered in living together. By the end of treatment Charlie had returned to school and was doing well. His mother and grandmother had clarified the lines of authority within their family.

The three-generational issue presented here is not an uncommon problem in Black extended families. This was an underorganized family (Aponte,
1976b) in which the overcentralized power of the grandmother was no longer
available in the after-school hours. Charlie's young mother had never become
fully competent in her parental role and was at a loss about how to manage
her son. This case provides an excellent example of the importance of
working with subsystems in Black extended families. A clear parental structure needed to be introduced; later it was important that other family
members such as Charlie's father and great aunt support rather than sabotage
this structure. Subgroup meetings are particularly valuable when we are
working with underorganized families such as Charlie's (Aponte, 1976b) in
which a number of extended family members may be part of the executive
system of the family. It is important that the therapist be very problem
focused when making decisions regarding subgroup composition. This decision should be based on an analysis of who is crucial to the resolution of
the clearly defined problem.

Religion

A strong religious orientation was a major aspect of the lives of Black people
in Africa and during the era of slavery. The church was of key importance
in the escape of Blacks from the oppression of slavery. Often signals as to the
time and place of an escape were given during the religious service. Many of
the spirituals that are sung in Black churches to this day had hidden
messages and a language of resistance within them (e.g., "Wade in the
Water" and "Steal Away"). Also, many of the leaders in the Black slave
community and many post-Civil War Black politicians have been religious
leaders, such as Martin Luther King, Malcolm X, and Jesse Jackson. Outlets
for expression of feelings about their humiliation, pain, and anger were few.
Music and the ecstatic celebration of Christ's gift of salvation provided
Black slaves with a means of expressing these feelings. Spirituals such as
"Nobody Knows the Trouble I've Seen" poignantly convey these sentiments.
The highly emotional church services conducted during slavery and still
today provide a ritual of great therapeutic value.

The church also continues to serve numerous functions for members of
the Black community in modern times. In the United States Black people are
currently represented in a number of different religious groups. These include
Baptist, African Methodist, Jehovah's Witness, Church of God in Christ,
Seventh Day Adventist, Pentecostal churches, Nation of Islam, numerous
Islamic sects, Presbyterian, Lutheran, Episcopal, and Roman Catholic. The
impact of these religious groups on the lives of Black people is a complex
subject. Further reading (Nobles, 1980; Mbiti, 1970) is recommended for
therapists who wish to expand their knowledge of the various religious
philosophies and practices.

It is important that clinicians recognize the extensive role churches can play in the lives of Black people today. Therefore, let us explore a religious group that can typically be described in northeastern urban areas as a "Black church"—the Baptist religion. In the Baptist church, a Black family finds a complete support system including the minister, deacons, deaconesses, and other church members. Numerous activities such as dinners and trips sponsored by ushers, various choirs, and Sunday school provide a social life for the entire family, which extends far beyond the Sunday services and provides a network of people who are available to the family in times of trouble or loss.

> In our clinic in Newark, a family who had been seen in treatment for some time were "burned out" by a devastating fire that destroyed their home. The mother was an active member of a local Baptist church and members of her congregation mobilized quickly to help with food, shelter, and clothing. A number of families assumed responsibility for the children for several weeks until the mother could relocate.

Much more research is needed on the role of religion in the lives and mental health of Black people. Many Black men and women have had few outlets for their leadership and creative talents; the church has provided a forum for their expression. For example, the father in a family might be a porter during the week but hold a position of considerable responsibility such as a deacon or trustee in his church. A mother or grandmother who feels overwhelmed with the responsibilities of raising a family alone may find her outlet by singing in the church choir every Sunday.

Inquiries about church activities and talents that are used in the church can reinforce self-esteem and can be an effective joining strategy in working with families with active church members. Church is very important to Black families many of whose values are directly or indirectly derived from some religious doctrine.

Larsen (1976) discusses some of the issues and challenges for both religious and nonreligious therapists. He suggests that the therapist who is fortunate enough to know scriptural passages can cite biblical authority to support recommendations and can draw to some extent on the immense prestige of the Bible. Larsen (1976) writes that there is a tendency for the devout to "spiritualize" or cope by defining difficulties as God's will, "passively trusting that the problems will somehow be resolved." Religiosity is sometimes directly related to the problem the family presents and to the progress they make in family therapy as demonstrated in the following excerpt. In this case the identified patient, Karen, had been referred because of emotional outbursts at school, which involved assaultive behavior that was potentially injurious to herself and to others. Her mother, Ms. K, said during the interview that this type of behavior never occurred in her presence. Karen and her siblings, Cynthia and John, shared the fact that they had many worries. The expression of their concerns appeared to be blocked by Ms. K's religious lecturing.

THERAPIST (*to Ms. K*): Do you understand why your children worry about you?

Ms. K: No.

THERAPIST: Find out from them now.

Ms. K: Why? Do you all think I'm gonna die?

CYNTHIA: The way daddy be hitting on you.

Ms. K: Ray don't hit on me.

KAREN: When he fought you that time.

Ms. K: John, you think I'm gonna die?

JOHN: The way you two get in serious arguments sometimes (*pause*)—someone might get injured.

Ms. K: Nobody gets serious injuries. You know the Bible says everybody is gonna die but they'll come back, John.

JOHN: I know.

Ms. K: Then you all don't have anything to worry about. Jehovah tells you that you're not supposed to worry about anything like that 'cause he'll take care of his people and we'll live right back here on this earth . . . if you be good. Dying is something to get out of all this agony now.

Subsequent sessions confirmed that Karen's need to act out her anger was related to the inhibition of expression at home under her mother's strict, religious guidance. The mother's religious beliefs were also important because Karen was going through the typical preadolescent questioning of religious and other traditional values. She was clearly confused as to how to reconcile the life-style her mother advocated with the demands and stresses of the urban environment in which she lived. In order for the therapist to respond to the family's conflict, it was necessary to understand the religious premises that guided the mother's child-rearing practices. Larsen (1976) suggests that such information may be attained from the family's religious leader or from the family members themselves. What is especially noteworthy is his suggestion that we work within the confines of the family's belief system rather than attempt to modify their beliefs. The therapist's attention to their frame of reference will facilitate success in achieving credibility and in forming an alliance with the family.

A therapist's greatest resource in mobilizing a religiously oriented family may be the minister or friends from the church group.

In instances where the minister has been actively intervening in family crises, we might consider using him or her as a cotherapist. Often, family therapists who routinely contact a prior therapist of the patient, will not contact a minister who has seen the family or various family members for pastoral counseling. Yet, with religious families, it is the church network that will probably continue to support the family once the therapy ends. In fact, just as a family therapist may help a family to reconnect with its kinship network for support, one therapeutic goal for a family that has lost touch with the church network may be to help them reestablish these ties.

Work and Education

Work and education are highly valued in Black families (Hill, 1972). However, as Pinderhughes (Chap. 5) points out, the attempts of parents to instill these values in their children are potentially undermined by the realities of the racist American system. At the same time that education and hard work are presented as the route to success, parents and their children are confronted with the harsh fact that a Black person's success in the educational and work world is all too frequently dependent on factors outside of his or her personal attributes, knowledge, skills, and efforts.

Yet, the value placed on education and work is reflected in the growing proportion of Blacks who study beyond the compulsory age and the number achieving higher education and employment levels despite the opposition that has been exercised against Blacks. Education is viewed as the process most likely to insure work security and social mobility. Great sacrifices may be made so that at least one child can go to college or graduate school. It is not unusual for an older child to drop out of school to work to help a younger sibling finish. Later, the educated child may contribute to the education of other children in the family. McAdoo (1978) has labeled this process of helping those who have helped in times of need "reciprocal obligation."

Black parents generally expect their children to take advantage of opportunities that they were denied and to surpass them in achieving the "comforts of life." Youth are encouraged to pursue careers that offer the greatest security. Children who earn enough to be self-supporting and to maintain a comfortable standard of living may win as much parental approval as those who pursue a professional career. In spite of the concern about education and work opportunities, those who move too far away may be perceived as rejecting their families, particularly if they do not help family members who need assistance.

Concern about the consequences of poor school adjustment for future security is often what leads Black families to involvement in mental health systems. In addition to the typical stresses of adolescence, low-income Black youth are often faced with the need to make decisions about their work and educational goals at younger ages than their more economically advantaged counterparts. They have fewer ways of acting out their anxieties, anger, and frustration as they face an oppressive society and the expectations of parents who have limited resources to assist them in starting out as young adults. Concern for their children's futures as well as the reactivation of their own sense of powerlessness, rage, and so on, may lead parents to react to their children in ways that exacerbate the problems. It may be helpful for the therapist to help parents, in such instances, to distinguish between their own personal issues and goals and those of their children. An attempt should be made to focus on their resources that can be used to assist their children and to reinforce feelings of mastery in all concerned. The therapist may need to coach the parents regarding ways to assist their children in coping with anger and frustration that are not self-defeating. This includes acknowledging their coping capacities and helping them to share their own successful strategies with their children in a more effective way.

Emotional stresses continue to be evident for those who attain a higher social and/or educational status. Pressures to maintain close physical proximity as well as to help out needy family members may not be seen by a family as relevant to the problems with which they are dealing since they are an accepted aspect of Black family life that have promoted survival. However, therapists may need to help families resolve the conflicts involved. Even middle-income Black families are unlikely to escape the pressures of racism. For such families, there are likely to be no role models as they enter "uncharted territories." Success does not represent the same level of security as it does for their white counterparts because of institutional and economic racism (McAdoo, 1979).

Ecological Realities and the Treatment of Black Families

To work effectively with Black families, therapists must be willing to expand the context of their therapy and the definition of their own role. They must be open to exploring the impact of the social, political, socioeconomic, and broader environmental conditions on the families they treat. This is central to our concept of family therapy with all families, and it is critical in therapy with Black inner-city families.

Conceptually, the greatest clarification of this approach has been presented by Aponte (1976a, 1979) who has used the term "ecostructural" to describe this broader treatment approach. He cautions therapists always to consider a family's environment and community as relevant to the diagnostic process and planning of treatment. The ecostructural reality of poor, inner-city Black families is that external systems are likely to impinge on them. These may include welfare, the courts, schools, Medicaid, food stamps, and public housing. These systems often intrude into their lives and impact upon crucial family decisions. To treat the family without considering these systems would be a grave error. As Aponte (1979) asserts, we cannot consider the social context as an occasional concern when a family is poor. The therapist must know the social service system and be willing to make contacts with various service providers and include them in family sessions when necessary. Pinderhughes (Chap. 5) presents an excellent case example on the unnecessary stresses that can result for a family when the various service agencies involved in their lives fail to coordinate their services. Without knowledge of and access to these external systems, clinicians will seriously limit their effectiveness with inner-city Black families.

Black, inner-city families are often faced with overwhelming socio-economic problems. They may be threatened with eviction from their homes or termination of their welfare payments. These are survival issues that often take precedence over family conflicts. With such families, family therapists must define themselves as system guides and help families learn how to negotiate the complexities of the social service, bureaucratic system more effectively. It is important, as Foley (1975) points out, that the clinician not assume the family's responsibility but assist them in using available resources and contacts to help facilitate change. This approach implies not only a willingness for outreach activities but dictates a greater amount of time and energy than is usually expended with families who do not face ecological stresses. For example, if a child is referred for school problems, it may be necessary for the therapist to coordinate and arrange to meet with the child, the family, and the school officials at the school to clarify the issues and to facilitate change. This type of intervention is important also when a child is being removed from his or her home by a social welfare agency. Often, the family therapist can help the family work together with the agency to find the best possible placement for the child. Sometimes these placements can be avoided by a careful exploration with the family of the extended family members who might care for the child until the home situation is changed.

Other Considerations for Family Therapists

Given these cultural and ecological considerations, it is not surprising that Black families often hesitate to seek mental health services. The prevalence of negative attitudes toward therapy has many origins. Blacks are more likely to turn to their families, neighbors, friends, ministers, and church members in times of crisis. These persons are accorded trust that is not easily won by "outsiders." Also, there may be strong feelings against airing the family's "dirty laundry" in public. McAdoo (1979) found that the pattern of using the extended family network as the primary helping agent exists among the upwardly mobile as well as among low-income Black families. It is likely that reliance on natural support systems stimulates fewer feelings of guilt, defeat, humiliation, and powerlessness, than turning to an institution.

Many Blacks continue to view therapy as a process for "crazy people." Contacts for services are usually precipitated by crises and occur when other sources of aid have been depleted. This delay in seeking services undoubtedly influences the severity of the problem(s) being experienced and the type of treatment needed.

When a Black family does seek help from an agency, they may be confused about the relationship of the mental health center to other agencies (e.g., welfare, schools). They may be suspicious of a therapist's motives for requesting detailed, personal information or permission to contact other agencies that are servicing the family. Many have experienced the intrusion of social service workers into their private domains, sometimes to the extent of having such workers define what they "should" or "should not" be able to afford (e.g., television, phone). Even though such concerns may not be mentioned, they may indeed contribute to a family's unwillingness to co-operate once a contact for services has been made. Grier and Cobbs (1968) suggest that the issue of trust for some Blacks reflects "healthy cultural paranoia" or a refusal to identify with and trust persons differing from themselves in color, life-style, values, and so on—particularly White people. This suspiciousness is frequently a direct, learned, survival response that Black children are socialized at an early age to adopt. Because of a strong religious or spiritual orientation, Black Americans may tolerate difficulties without the inclination to explore and understand their condition. They may view emotional difficulties as the "wages of sin"; the person who manifests psychiatric symptoms may be seen as "mean" or "possessed by the devil" and may be thought to have the potential to change his or her behavior at will. Some may hold the view that emotional difficulties are a reflection of a failure to believe and practice biblical principles; to seek relief from a mental health professional rather than through prayer may signify an absence of trust in God. These attitudes may be coupled with a more pervasive belief in the inevitability of "troubles on earth." Therapy is viewed as a luxury reserved for the more advantaged who have the time and money to "lie around on couches" for years.

The concerns that many minority persons have about being misdiagnosed and treated inappropriately within mental health institutions have some basis in truth. See and Miller (1973) in their thorough review cite a number of studies that have examined Black and White differences in diagnosis, acceptance, duration, and type of treatment received. Singer (1967) studied a sample of Black and White schizophrenic patients and discovered, through his comparisons of patients of like social class, that Black patients were less likely than White patients to be given psychotherapy or other forms of treatment and were discharged sooner than Whites. Yamamoto, James, and Palley (1968) found that, while fewer than one-third of the Black patients received individual or group therapy, one-half of the White patients were given such treatment. Black patients were also more likely to be seen only briefly for medication by the therapists.

The crucial connection between these inequalities in service delivery and clinicians' perceptions of Black patients has also been established. Yamamoto et al. (1968) speculate that clinicians may frequently misinterpret the presenting picture of Black patients to mean that they will not profit from any type of "talking" therapy. Black clients can benefit from "talking" therapies if the therapy is problem-focused and culturally sensitive.

Nonetheless, Black Americans are currently utilizing mental health services in greater numbers. Our perception is that the most frequent presenting issues are poor school adjustment, acting-out behavior, depression, psychosis, drug addiction, and alcoholism. The identified patient is usually a child who has been referred by another agency such as the school, welfare department, courts, or police. This is a very important consideration since families who feel forced to come for therapy are likely to be very ambivalent about therapy.

Regardless of whether or not they come in crisis, Black families are likely to be most responsive to time-limited, problem-solving, child-focused, family therapy approaches. Active therapist participation and direction are expected. Most come to therapy with multiple problems. They may be so overwhelmed at entry that telling them therapy will be a long and difficult process is self-defeating for the therapist and the family (Foley, 1975).

Aponte (1978) emphasizes the need to help a family experience therapy as a process that can help produce immediate change(s) in their lives. He advises that from the onset, every action that the therapist takes should be goal directed. We have found his ecostructural approach to family treatment particularly effective. The therapist pursues information in a very problem-focused way. The aim is to gain enough understanding of a problem to find an appropriate solution. Insight about the causes is not necessary. Emphasis is rather on what factors are maintaining the problem and how these can be altered (Aponte & Van Deusen, 1981). The therapist focuses on what the family members say and how they react to each other, as well as how they react to the therapist's interventions. This approach minimizes the chances of being overwhelmed with data. It also maximizes the chances that the therapist will intervene on the basis of what the families present rather than on the basis of their own values, stereotypes, and so forth.

The profile of contemporary Black American families presented here has significant implications for style of therapist interactions as well as general treatment approach. Given the ambivalence that may characterize Black families, therapists may need to extend themselves to engage families and acquaint them with the therapeutic process. For example, one of the first tasks we have found helpful in the engagement process is to explore the family's feelings about seeking professional help. The family may need to be oriented to the mental health system; their myths may need to be discussed and dispelled. When outside referral is the impetus for seeking services, this task can best be accomplished at the time of referral. Hoehn-Saric, Frank, Imber, Nash, Stone, and Battle (1964) have documented the efficacy of orienting people for therapy. Among the positive results have been lower rates of premature termination and cancellation, greater satisfaction with therapy and increased goal attainment.

We must also be flexible in working with families when a request for total family participation is not met. Otherwise, even family members who are initially willing to participate in therapy may become convinced that it is not worth the stress of trying to coerce unwilling family members to join them. With the family's permission, the therapist may consider scheduling a visit on their home turf.

An unexpected request for total family involvement in the treatment of an identified client may heighten the family's feelings of guilt and responsibility. Unfortunately, blame is placed all too frequently on the family by "systems-oriented" therapists who ignore the possibility that other systems may be affecting the family's ability to resolve a difficulty. It is important for the therapist to allow for questioning and clarify the rationale for having requested family involvement. Most families will accept the explanation that they are the identified patient's (IP) greatest resource or support; they know the IP better than anyone else. They are likely to be affected by the problem and have greater potential than anyone else to help resolve it.

Another key to success in engaging the family is communicating respect. Therapists should openly acknowledge the family's strengths. They should avoid professional jargon and relate to the family in a directive but supportive manner. Assuming familiarity with adult family members before asking their permission should be avoided. The therapist who assumes the privilege of using first names prematurely may elicit unverbalized negative reactions, especially from the adult family members who may see this as showing disrespect to them in front of their children. This concern may be easily overlooked by persons who are not sensitive to the disrespect that many Blacks have experienced.

It may sometimes be desirable for the therapist to acknowlege his or her difference in ethnic background and to discuss the family's feelings on this matter early in therapy, particularly if the therapist is not Black. The therapist's own discomfort or some verbal or nonverbal indication of a family's discomfort is probably the best indicator of whether to move in this direction. If therapists have dealt with their own feelings about the racial situation in this country and are comfortable with their own feelings about working with culturally different families, they will be better able to distinguish when race is their own issue or one for a family. The risk of raising the race issue and finding it is irrelevant to a family is not likely to have a devastating effect if the therapist is secure and self-confident and can handle suspiciousness, rejection, and challenge to authority in a nondefensive manner.

Certainly, the first step for therapists is becoming familiar with the culture and accepting its rules despite the differences. This may not be easily accomplished. For example, a well-meaning therapist may unwittingly undermine much needed parental authority out of concern about the harshness of parents' handling of their children. Whether or not religion is actively practiced, the philosophy on which Black parents rear their children often had deep religious underpinnings. The biblical principle "Spare the rod, spoil the child" is commonly referred to. Physical punishment is an accepted mode of discipline and should not be assumed to be child abuse. In fact, a therapist may be more successful in assisting a family by acknowledging parents' need for a quick deterrent to misbehavior and being sensitive to concerns that their children behave appropriately in a society that will be quick to punish them for unacceptable behavior. This does not mean that the therapist has to approve or encourage the use of physical punishment. However, rather than argue for the elimination of physical punishment, the therapist can take into account the parental beliefs and values and emphasize the benefits of positive approaches.

We can easily become overwhelmed by a family who differs greatly from our own. In some instances, the issues that a family introduces may represent resistance to change. But it is important that the therapist avoid making assumptions in this direction. For example, a family's concerns about the investment of time and money in the therapeutic process may grow out of negative experiences with "helping" professionals as well as a desire to avoid an additional life demand that seems of questionable value until proven otherwise.

While ambivalence certainly affects cooperation, some families may also not recognize the importance of being present and on time for an appointment or of calling to cancel or reschedule a session. Low-income families, in particular, are likely to approach mental health services with a medical clinic frame of reference where they are used to waiting long hours for service. "Resistance" may be well grounded also in the difficulties of balancing parenting, household tasks, and one or more jobs outside the home.

Black Americans are frequently characterized by therapists as nonverbal and incapable of dealing with feelings. In some instances, Blacks who appear mute in the therapy room may talk endlessly on home turf (Jones & Seagull, 1977). Further, the lack of trust or "cultural paranoia" that was referred to previously may well limit family members' willingness to talk openly to a stranger. Third, some Black families may not communicate in the way that persons from the therapist's own ethnic group might. The therapist may need to consider working with subgroups when a family's messages to each other are so vague, complex, or incomplete that they as well as the therapist become overwhelmed. Minuchin et al. (1967) noted that for many low-income families, "affect is communicated mostly through paraverbal channels in the pitch, tempo, and intensity of the verbal messages and the accompanying kinesthetic modifiers" (p. 206). This description applies to communication patterns in many Black families. Tracking and joining a family, therefore, can become a difficult and complex process. A therapist might also consider having family members observe each other behind the one-way mirror or by using videotape playback to promote improved communication and organization. Because of the suspiciousness with which Black families approach therapy, however, it is desirable that the therapist clarify how audiotapes and videotapes will be used.

The potential for therapist burnout is heightened when working with families who live under oppressive life circumstances. One solution is to use a team of therapists who may offer feedback from behind the mirror during the family session via a bug-in-the-ear device. The therapist may also take a periodic break away from the family to discuss issues with the consulting team that the therapist, without their assistance, might overlook. Hines has been involved with several of her coworkers in the development of a program in which a multidisciplinary team of therapists meet together with a family for a planned, all-day session. Among numerous other benefits, the use of a team with differing personalities, skills, and sensitivities maximizes the likelihood that each family member will connect emotionally with at least one therapist. Team members can process together their reactions of the family session. Therapists can use each other in planning and implementing treatment strategies and follow-up with other community systems. Whatever the process, members of a team must have a good ongoing working relationship with each other.

Concluding Statement

This chapter represents a beginning. We have tried to provide a point of departure for therapists who are working with Black families. We have advocated an ecostructural approach to the treatment of Black families that takes into account their cultural and societal context and an understanding of their strengths. If this approach is to become a reality in community mental health centers and clinics that serve Black people, then our graduate schools and family therapy training programs must include a broader system orientation with an emphasis on these ethnic and ecological issues.

In the interim, clinicians working with Black families must take personal initiative in expanding their knowledge of Black culture and their contacts with community organizations and agencies. Administrators of mental health centers must promote change by supporting community outreach into schools, churches, and grassroots organizations and by advocating for the elimination of oppressive policies and practices by "helping" institutions.

Family therapy with Black families is indeed in an incubator stage of development. We must begin to establish networks of therapists and researchers working with Black families in different parts of the country if we are to provide a more complete picture of the diversity inherent in Black family life-styles. Research must include an exploration of class and other socioeconomic variables on the treatment of Black families if we are to avoid further stereotyping.

REFERENCES

Aponte, H. The Family School Interview: An Ecostructural Approach. *Family Process, 15*(3), 303–311, 1976. (a)

Aponte, H. Underorganization in the Poor Family. In P. Guerin (Ed.), *Family Therapy: Theory and Practice.* New York: Gardner Press, 1976. (b)

Aponte, H. Diagnosis in Family Therapy. In C.B. Germain (Ed.), *Social Work Practice: People and Environments.* New York: Columbia University Press, 1978.

Aponte, H. Family Therapy and the Community. In M.S. Gibbs, J. R. Lachenmeyer, & J. Sigal (Eds.), *Community Psychology: Theoretical and Empirical Approaches.* New York: Gardner Press, 1979.

Aponte, H., & Van Deusen, J. Structural Family Therapy. In A. Gurman & D. Kniskern (Eds.), *Handbook of Family Therapy.* New York: Brunner/Mazel, 1981.

Bell, N.W. Extended Family Relations of Disturbed and Well Families. *Family Process, 1*, 175–193, 1962.

Billingsley, A. *Black Families in White America.* Englewood Cliffs, N.J.: Prentice-Hall, 1968.

Bowen, M. Theory in the Practice of Psychotherapy. In P. Guerin (Ed.), *Family Therapy: Theory and Practice.* New York: Gardner Press, 1976.

Ernst, R., & Hugg, L. *Black America: Geographic Perspectives.* New York: Anchor Books, 1976.

Foley, V. Family Therapy with Black Disadvantaged Families: Some Observations on Roles, Communications, and Technique. *Journal of Marriage and Family Counseling, 1*, 29–38, 1975.

Franklin, J. *From Slavery to Freedom: A History of Negro Americans* (3rd ed.). New York: Vintage Books, 1969.

Grier, W., & Cobbs, P. *Black Rage.* New York: Bantam Books, 1968.

Guerin, P., & Pendagast, E. Evaluation of the Family System and the Genogram. In P. Guerin (Ed.), *Family Therapy: Theory and Practice.* New York: Gardner Press, 1976.

Hill, R. *The Strengths of Black Families.* New York: Emerson Hall, 1972.

Hill, R. *Informal Adoption among Black Families.* Washington, D.C.: National Urban League, Research Department, 1977.

Hoehn-Saric, R., Frank, J., Imber, S., Nash, E., Stone, A., & Battle, C. Systematic Preparation of Patients for Psychotherapy: Effects on Therapy, Behavior, and Outcome. *Journal of Psychiatric Research, 2*, 267–281, 1964.

Jones, A., & Seagull, A. Dimensions of the Relationship between the Black Client and the White Therapist. *American Psychologist, 32*(10), 851, 1977.

Kinney, E. Africanisms in Music and Dance of the Americas. In R. Goldstein (Ed.), *Black Life and Culture in the United States.* New York: Crowell, 1971.

Larsen, J. *Dysfunction in the Evangelical Family: Treatment Considerations.* Paper presented at the meeting of the American Association of Marriage and Family Counselors, Philadelphia, October 1976.

Mbiti, J.S. *African Religions and Philosophies.* Garden City, N.Y.: Anchor Books, Doubleday, 1970.

McAdoo, H. The Impact of Upward Mobility of Kin—Help Patterns and the Reciprocal Obligations in Black Families. *Journal of Marriage and the Family, 4*(4), 761–776, 1978.

McAdoo, H. *Upward Mobility and Parenting in Middle Class Black Families.* Paper presented at the Social Learning Laboratory of ETS, Princeton, N.J., May 1979.

Minuchin, S., Montalvo, B., Guerney, B., Rosman, B., & Schumer, F. *Families of the Slums.* New York: Basic Books, 1967.

Minuchin, S. *Families and Family Therapy.* Cambridge: Harvard University Press, 1974.

Moynihan, D. *The Negro Family: The Case for National Action.* Washington, D.C.: Office of Policy Planning and Research, U.S. Department of Labor, 1965.

Nobles, W. African Philosophy: Foundations for Black Psychology. In R. Jones (Ed.), *Black Psychology* (2nd ed.). New York: Harper & Row, 1980.

Pinkney, A. *Black Americans*. Englewood Cliffs, N.J.: Prentice-Hall, 1975.

Scanzoni, J. *The Black Family in Modern Society: Patterns of Stability and Security*. Chicago: University of Chicago Press, 1971.

See, J., & Miller, K. Mental Health. In D. Miller & R. Dreger (Eds.), *Comparative Studies of Blacks and Whites in the United States*. New York: Seminar Press, 1973.

Singer, B. Some Implications of Different Psychiatric Treatment of Negro and White Patients. *Social Science and Medicine, 1*, 77–83, 1967.

Stack, C. *All Our Kin: Strategies for Survival in a Black Community*. New York: Harper & Row, 1975.

Staiano, K. Ethnicity as Process: The Creation of an Afro-American Identity. *Ethnicity, 7*, 27–33, 1980.

U.S. Department of Commerce, Bureau of the Census. *The Social and Economic Status of the Black Population in the United States: An Historical View, 1790–1978* (Current Population Reports, Special Studies Series No. 80). Washington, D.C., 1979, p. 23.

White, J. Towards a Black Psychology. In R. Jones (Ed.), *Black Psychology*. New York: Harper & Row, 1972.

Yamamoto, J., James, E., & Palley, N. Cultural Problems in Psychiatric Therapy. *Archives of General Psychiatry, 19*, 45–49, 1968.

5

Afro-American Families and the Victim System

ELAINE PINDERHUGHES

An understanding of the functioning of any family requires attention to the environment with which the family interacts as well as the family's internal structure and processes. The environment is all that is external to the family. This includes not only the neighborhood, peer groups, church, school, and work place that touch family members directly, but also larger political, governmental, and economic institutions. Ideally, the environment should provide the protection, security, support, and supplies that will enhance family functioning. When these resources are "inadequate," the result may be stress and conflict within the family and failure in the individual development of its members (Germaine, 1979).

The cultural values or ethnicity of the family mediate its interaction with the external world, strongly affecting its mechanisms for coping with and adapting to environmental support of inadequacy. Thus, effective intervention with families requires knowledge of ethnic factors as they influence family functioning both internally and externally.

Afro-American Identity and the Functional Family

Afro-Americans are descendants of Africans who were brought to the United States as slaves. In this chapter we will use the term *Afro-American* rather than Black for several reasons: It refers to an identity that is cultural as well as racial. Other ethnic groups are rightly identified by culture or nationality rather than by race. "White" or "Black" is not a culture, as Irish American and Italian American are. In addition, the term more clearly differentiates descendants of American slaves from descendants of Africans in other parts of the world, such as the Caribbean and South America.

Elsewhere we have hypothesized that Afro-American ethnic identity is influenced by three cultural sources: (1) residuals from Africa, (2) identification with mainstream America, and (3) adaptations and responses to the "victim" system that is a product of racism, poverty, and oppression (Pinderhughes, 1979a).

Elaine Pinderhughes. Human Behavior and the Social Environment, Boston College Graduate School of Social Work, Chestnut Hill, Massachusetts.

The Victim System

A *victim system* is a circular feedback process that exhibits properties, such as stability, predictability, and identity, that are common to all systems. This particular system threatens self-esteem and reinforces problematic responses in communities, families, and individuals. The feedback works as follows: Barriers to opportunity and education limit the chance for achievement, employment, and attainment of skills. This limitation can, in turn, lead to poverty or stress in relationships, which interferes with adequate performance of family roles. Strains in family roles cause problems in individual growth and development and limit the opportunity of families to meet their own needs or to organize to improve their communities. Communities limited in resources (jobs, education, housing, etc.) are unable to support families properly, and the community all too often becomes itself an active disorganizing influence, a breeder of crime and other pathology, and a cause of even more powerlessness (Soloman, 1976).

This formulation of the victim system of racism and oppression is similar in some ways to Bowen's concept of the societal projection process, which, he maintains, lowers the differentiation of both scapegoated groups and the majority (Bowen, 1978).

Throughout history victimizing has exerted a pervasive effect upon Afro-American families. It is the most important of the factors enumerated by Charles Pinderhughes (1976) that have prevented Afro-Americans from having a unified culture as well as from integrating their culture with that of the American mainstream. The other factors he lists are (1) the cutoff from African culture; (2) the coercive slave culture; (3) the unpredictability of life after emancipation; (4) urbanization, which further disrupted adaptations, such as the resilient, unique Afro-American extended family; and (5) the political events of the 1960s (Black power, White backlash, etc.), which produced among Afro-Americans rapid changes in values and heightened consciousness of their identity.

Conflicting Values

The three cultural sources of Afro-American culture mentioned earlier have very different values. American values emphasize individualism, independence, autonomy, ownership of material goods, achievement, mastery, progress, youth, future orientation, efficiency, and planning. African values stress collectivity, sharing, affiliation, obedience to authority, belief in spirituality, and respect for the elderly and the past. Victim system values that are consequences of adaptation to oppression emphasize cooperation to combat powerlessness; strict obedience to authority in the context of felt oppression; strength; toughness of character; present-time orientation (since the past is painful and there is no future); suppression and channeling of feelings into music, art, and other creative activities; and belief in luck, magic, and spirituality. We want to emphasize particularly that the most severely victimized, those most totally adapted to the victim system, hold values of autonomy and isolation as a defense against the stresses that engulf them. This autonomy derives from a sense of aloneness and abandonment rather than from growth or self-actualization. Behavior based on these values includes preference for emotional expression, immediate gratification of needs, manipulation in relationships, withholding or passive aggression, oppositional or rebellious behavior, and identification with the aggressor. While these values and behaviors have an adaptive function as responses to powerlessness, they are also maladaptive for functioning in the American mainstream as persons of real power who are able to make choices and to assume responsibilities.

Values from all three value systems—African, American, and victim— are found in Afro-American families. This is why they have such diversity in values, behaviors, and family structures. For example, Billingsley (1968) identifies 12 different types of family structure and says that a large majority of families are not to be found in any single category.

Papajohn and Spiegel (1975) have described the strain that members of ethnic groups experience when they have to cope with divergent or conflicting value systems. They cite three principal solutions: (1) remaining isolated from the American mainstream and identifying exclusively with one's sub-culture, (2) identifying exclusively with American mainstream culture, and (3) integrating the two options. However, unlike other ethnic populations, Afro-Americans have not had open to them the choices of becoming exclu-sively Americanized or of integrating the two options. Never having been completely admitted to America, the remaining alternatives are either isola-tion from the American mainstream (i.e., adapting exclusively to the victim system) or identification with both cultures, without being able to integrate the two.

The current focus by Afro-Americans on blackness can be seen as an effort to cope positively with the stresses inherent in living in two cultures and also to achieve some integration. This new identity effort reinforces rather than diminishes the reality of biculturality. For Afro-Americans biculturality means enduring a lack of resolution of their value conflicts. Living in two worlds, they do not have the option of a synthesis. White ethnic groups have experienced something similar but only in the first generation. Biculturality can cause strain and take a heavy toll in emotional stress and identity confusion, but it can also create exceptional strength, flexibility, and tolerance for diversity (Knowles & Prewitt, 1968; Chestang, 1972).

Many social scientists have discussed human adaptive responses to victim systems. Among the family therapists are Aponte (1976), Minuchin (1967), Harris and Balgopal (1980), and Hines and Boyd-Franklin (Chap. 4). We will explore the effects of the victim system and biculturality upon the family at its interface with the outside world and the influence of that interface upon differentiation of family members, role functioning, role relationships, and problem solving.

The Family–Environment Interface

Afro-American families need flexible boundaries that can bend. They must closely monitor their dependency on the environment to limit their power-lessness (e.g., refuse treatment at a mental health clinic that does not understand them) and at the same time utilize supportive resources when they do exist. When the family cannot get necessary help, its internal structure may be seriously disrupted.

Families may protect themselves by maintaining rigid boundaries. While this is adaptive, rigid closed boundaries may cost them valuable support. For example, a social worker in a child guidance center in Boston found that many of the Afro-American mothers of children in treatment there did not keep appointments either because they were too depressed or because they had no one to stay with their other children. The agency staff organized a group of well-trained Afro-American college volunteers to function as sitters. In every case the mothers said they would welcome such assistance; however, only two of a group of 20 were able to use the service. When the sitters came, some mothers would not let them in; others would not leave the house.

The refusal of these mothers to let the sitters in reflects their adaptation to a hostile environment. They are distrustful of strangers and have developed rigidly closed boundaries for protection. Particularly, they do not trust strangers offering to do them a favor, gratis.

Open family boundaries can also cause problems since a family is then vulnerable to too many intrusions, some of which may be destructive. When the family space is invaded with uncoordinated, inappropriate, and even harmful, though well-intentioned interventions, it can become even more disorganized. For example, one family in treatment at a local mental health center was receiving services from the Visiting Nurse Association, a day-care center, a job-training program, and Alcoholics Anonymous. While the nurse was advising the mother to take her child to the local health clinic to test for lead poisoning as a possible cause of his overactivity, the social worker from the day-care center was advising that she learn to handle him more per-missively since excessive strictness was regarded as one of the reasons for his overactivity at school. Concurrently, a psychologist at the mental health center was focusing on the marriage as the cause of the child's behavior problems. Unable to set limits on all this "helping," the family members became more confused and in conflict with one another over what to do. Moreover, the mother's complaints about the confusion were considered to be a resistance to treatment.

Power and Conflict in Relationships

Power is an issue in any relationship. The egalitarian nature of marital relationships among Afro-Americans has been well described, as has been the undermining of male power (Billingsley, 1968; Minuchin, 1967; Staples, 1978; Harris & Balgopal, 1980). In addition, the forces of racism have hindered the development of group cohesion and have prevented the establishment of generally accepted guidelines for managing power and resolving conflict (Pinderhughes, 1976).

Thus it would seem that Afro-American families have definite vulnerability to power conflicts. Consider the diverse influences on their management of power. First, their original African cultural system, which valued collaterality and affiliation, was undermined but not totally destroyed. The residuals of African culture are still reinforcing affiliativeness rather than the individualism typical of the American mainstream. Second, adaptation to relative powerlessness, from the time of slavery to the present, has reinforced for many individuals behavior that is characterized by a dominance-submission complementarity. Behavior caused by the submissive side of this complementarity, the sense of powerlessness, includes withdrawal, isolation, passive aggression, overt aggression, dependency, accommodation, manipulation, and identification with the aggressor. When Afro-Americans have engaged in dominant behavior, they have identified with the aggressor, using the behaviors they have observed in their oppressors: aggression, domination, entitlement, projection of unfavorable attributes onto other powerless persons, and so forth (Pinderhughes, 1979b). Moreover, U.S. middle-class values emphasize mastery, possession, ownership, and power, all of which reinforce dominance in relationships.

Furthermore, the societal projection process, identified by Bowen (1978), reinforces the relatively powerless position of Afro-Americans. This process, similar to the family projection process, creates societal scapegoats of prisoners, welfare recipients, mental patients, the poor, and minorities. In this interaction, one group (the benefactors) maintains the illusion of competence at the expense of "unfortunates" by "helpfulness and benevolence." The benefactors put the unfortunates in a one down, inferior position and get angry at them for their shortcomings (Bowen, 1978). The reinforcement of dominant roles for the benefactor and submissive roles for the unfortunates can resolve overt conflict and bring order to a social system. Similarly, the assumption of dominant–submissive roles within the family can stabilize the family system.

Adaptability in Roles: Response to System Stress

Hines and Boyd-Franklin (Chap. 4) point out that one major strength of Afro-American families has been adaptability of roles. As a compensatory mechanism for the stress of the victim system, this response has until recently been regarded as deviant because it was different from the White middle-class nuclear family model of "male" and "female" role functions. Now, however, flexibility in roles is being advocated as "ideal" by feminists.

Unfortunately, when stress is very high, even this flexibility may fail to provide the necessary compensation. Under stress, the family may lose its flexibility and respond with roles marked by overfunctioning, underfunctioning, rigidity, confusion, or conflict. Any of these changes may appear when, for example, the role of provider is threatened and powerlessness is reinforced by poverty. Moreover, in many communities the victim system undermines the ability of Afro-American parents to protect their children from illegal, immoral, and violent acts. Thwarted in their preferred roles, parents may react in several ways. They may become more controlling and authoritarian than they might otherwise be to counteract the undermining of parental role and authority. Under such circumstances, family enmeshment and fusion increase and perpetuate the spiral of problem–response–problem. To prepare their children for a role in the victim system, parents may also treat them harshly. While this behavior may slip into real abuse or be carried to extremes, it may also be perceived by others as abuse when, in fact, it is not. Or parents may deny the situation, leaving the child to cope alone, which feels to the child like abandonment. Other parents may explain to the child the complexities that cause a sense of powerlessness. All of these solutions except the last can create additional problems for family members. And this last solution violates the preferred value of focusing on and experiencing the self as strong.

The role of the Afro-American mother is another example of flexibility and role compensation. This role has been both maligned and extolled. And, indeed the mother's functioning as the "strength" of the family has both adaptive and maladaptive aspects. This strength has been needed to compensate for the lack of cultural guidelines for family roles and for the undermining of the father/husband role of the male due to his lack of education, unemployment, and inability to protect his family. In extreme victimization, the male has been so undermined in his role that he has become negative, irresponsible, manipulative, exploitive, violent, remote, or absent. In these situations, if the mother cannot assume a strong role, the family is in serious trouble.

Again the family's adaptive response to victim systems stress can either resolve or reinforce problems. If the mother's role is overemphasized, for whatever reason, it can become the pathway for all interaction within the family. This requires children to relate primarily to her moods and wishes rather than to their own needs. The result is emotional fusion of the children with the mother since they no longer exist for their mother as unique, developing people, but as part of a fused group.

If being mother's child is of primary importance, then growth of self, autonomous exploration, and mastery of problems are discouraged. Development of a sense of responsibility and independence is impaired. The overprotected child and the parental child are the extreme examples of these distortions. Both of these role adaptations may be viewed as compensation for the effects of stresses from sources both outside and inside the family.

Biculturality and Identity Confusion

Biculturality, the ability to function in two worlds, is adaptive. While it requires great expenditure of energy and can lead to identity confusion, some Afro-Americans are able to become exceptionally clear about their identity and values. Such families exhibit unusual strength, are comfortable with biculturality, and exhibit remarkable flexibility, tolerance for ambiguity, comfort with difference, and creativity in their relationships with both the American mainstream and victim systems. For others adapting to these different systems can lead to value conflict and identity confusion. Identity confusion, role and power conflicts, and rigidity in relationships reinforce one another in a process in which powerlessness begets more powerlessness. Obviously the victim system has affected Afro-American families in various ways.

The adaptations developed by a given family have depended on the degree of racism, poverty, and oppression the family has experienced. Effects upon middle-class families are less because they have more resources than the poor, but even they do not escape completely. Disruptions in the family relationships and support systems that have provided a barrier against the victim system can cause great difficulty for middle-class families (Harris & Balgopal, 1980; Soloman, 1976).

Moreover, for the newly arrived middle-class family, the achievement and maintenance of middle-class status may lead to an emotional cutoff from the family of origin. McAdoo (1977) describes the problems generated when one member of a family is enabled by joint family resources to attain higher education or social achievement. The expectation of other family members for reciprocal assistance means either that he or she must go back to participating in the obligatory reciprocity stream or engage in an emotional cutoff from the family. McAdoo (1977) makes the point that either way the families may have problems.

Implications for Treatment

Therapy with Afro-American families is challenging. Therapists must understand the complexities both in the realities these families face and in the behaviors with which they respond. Without this awareness and preparation, therapists will be frustrated and confused.

A variety of treatment strategies has already been cited in Chapter 4. We offer these ideas as a supplement.

As long as racism and oppression maintain the victim system, the goal of family treatment must be to enable the family to cope constructively with those stresses and to counteract their pervasive influence. Treatment must be directed toward strengthening family structure, enhancing flexibility, and reinforcing the ability of friends, community, and the larger social system to offer effective and appropriate support. Overly closed systems, overcentral maternal roles, fused identities, and emotional cutoffs are often legitimate efforts to establish an equilibrium and to compensate for victim system stress. Altering the internal without attention to the external may only result in the system going into crisis. Minuchin (1967) affirms that where patterns of change in the family are out of phase with the realities of extrafamilial systems, therapy will fail. The therapist must strive to enhance the flexibility of boundaries at the same time that the larger social system is influenced to be more supportive. Harris and Balgopal (1980) describe the need to focus simultaneously on the problems and realities that are posed by external systems as well as on the way the family manages its relationship with them. Other objectives may include increasing differentiation among family members, promoting a clearer dual identity, and improving role functioning. Additional objectives may focus on such aspects of family functioning as communication, dominant–submissive role complementarity, and power conflicts. Since having choice undermines feelings of powerlessness, it is important to point out options whenever possible. A useful therapeutic goal may be the development of skill and comfort in making choices.

In evaluating Afro-American families the therapist must assess the degree to which:

1. external systems, such as the extended family, friends, ministers, employers, or the school, are able to support the family.

2. the family has flexible boundaries and can use appropriate external supports.

3. there is congruence in perceptions of roles among family members.

4. there is a stabilized power balance.

5. family members are differentiated.

As Boyd (1979) contends, Afro-American families use many supports which are external to the family, often incorporating nonmembers into the family. Their genograms are often "sloppy" if they are accurate. Since the network itself can become a source of stress, as in some instances of upward mobility, the network's effectiveness with the family must be assessed carefully.

Influencing the external social system to be less destructive may require the therapist to negotiate directly with other systems (see Hines & Boyd-Franklin, Chap. 4). Ecological system therapists place their major emphasis here (Auerswald, 1968). Support networks provide a cushion and supply a necessary sense of belonging (Soloman, 1976; Harris & Balgopal, 1980). Groups of all kinds may provide this support: church, school, friendship, self-help therapy, skill building, service (such as Big Sisters, Big Brothers, and elderly foster parents), political groups, or any others that teach skills in making the surrounding systems more responsive.

Therapists may need to teach families about the role the social system plays in their troubles. The therapist can point out in a positive way the adaptive value of the dysfunctional behavior yet at the same time show the problems that the behavior causes. For example, a family can be praised for their loving attempt to protect a child from the hostility of the outside world but be shown that overprotection can also be harmful to the child's development. Or an isolated and underfunctioning Afro-American father/husband may be commended for his struggle to cope with the system's undermining of his role but be helped to see that his family needs him more.

This educative approach places emphasis on recognizing the family's efforts to work on the problem. It neutralizes any negativism within the family, which, in turn, can poison the therapeutic relationship.

Families can be taught that closed boundaries, overinvestment in parenting, and other behaviors reactive to victim system stress have been adaptive for coping with powerlessness within and without the family but are maladaptive for being able to act rather than react, to make choices, or to take responsibility for family and other group interaction. The family can come to see that by engaging in those behaviors it is undermining itself. This collusion in its own victimization can be clarified and explored as a factor in dysfunctioning.

Helping the family learn the skill of resolving conflict in a way that does not oppress or exploit either party should be a high priority (Pinderhughes, 1976). Several family therapy theorists have described strategies that can be successful (Minuchin, 1967; Harris & Balgopal, 1980).

Another important priority may be the appropriate expression of feelings. For some Afro-American families it is necessary to focus on identifying, expressing, and sharing positive feelings. Feelings of anxiety, sadness, anger, and rage may be more easily expressed than genuine gratification and pleasure. Anger is a significant issue for most Afro-Americans. Experts have described the situation of Afro-Americans as requiring the ability to process large quantities of anxiety and rage continually (Grier & Cobbs, 1968; Pierce, 1970; Pinderhughes, 1973; Spurlock, 1973). Indeed, we can hypothesize that the internalizing of feelings of anxiety and rage accounts in part for the high rate of physical ailments, notably high blood pressure and heart disease, among Afro-American males.

Expressions of anger and rage may be adaptive in relieving tension, but they create many other problems in relationships. Appropriate management of anger is a crucial aspect of therapy; however, what may be most needed is education in ways to be assertive and strong rather than in expressing anger.

However, a word of caution is in order here since there are many problems involved for Afro-Americans in communicating assertively. Cheek (1976) states that "the usual black response in a state of anxiety has either been passive or aggressive—either say nothing or become loud, threatening and abusive" (p. 65). Defining assertiveness as "honest, open and direct verbal or non-verbal communication that does not have the intent of putting someone down," he emphasizes that what is assertive to Blacks often appears aggressive to Whites and vice versa (p. 18). Cheek sees assertiveness as a major social skill needed by Afro-Americans and teaches clients that "not putting anyone down" involves attention to the context of the relationship as well as to verbal and nonverbal expression. Assertiveness helps family members counteract reactions to powerlessness that get internalized in family interaction in the form of anger, put-downs, negativity, and power behavior. Focus on the management of anger should not be limited to the family's internal mechanisms. The therapist can identify external targets for appropriate expression of aggression or assertiveness. In one example Aponte helped a poor, overwhelmed mother assert herself with her child's teacher and even accompanied her to the school (Aponte, 1978). This necessary intervention with an environmental stressor of the family involved extra time and energy on the part of the therapist. The persistence of the victim system requires this kind of commitment to help the family to cope. Thus the cost in time, emotional drain, and so forth, for therapists who work with Afro-American families can make them victims too. However, unless they have the capacity to invest in this manner, intervention can be useless or even harmful.

Coping with the victim system requires skill in processing both negative and positive feelings. With some families the problem is not just that anger is inappropriately expressed but rather that it can never be expressed. When the family limits its emotional expressiveness to positive feelings only, it becomes rigid. This may be a particular problem in middle-class families.

Helping family members to define values and beliefs can enable them to increase their tolerance for difference (Bowen, 1978). The diverse sources of Afro-American identity and the need to be bicultural increase the likelihood of widely differing perceptions within the family and, thus, of value conflicts and ambivalence. As discussed earlier, these consequences can be stressful and can complicate living. Developing a tolerance for differences lessens such strains. In thinking together and putting into words their explanations of themselves and the world, family members also enhance their ability to manage these strains. And as a result they come to appreciate the complexity of Afro-American identity. For example, in one family where the children had different skin colors, a fair-skinned teenager shared his pain at being labeled "White nigger" by his Afro-American peers. Although other family members were also confused about their racial identity, the family had never discussed the problem. This exploration in therapy enabled family members to become more empathic toward this emotionally isolated youngster and, at the same time, to clarify for themselves the meaning of being Afro-American.

However, the task may be not only developing tolerance for difference, but rather achieving a common understanding among family members of the contradictions and ambiguities that characterize the roles and behaviors required for successful coping. It cannot be overemphasized that the most successful adaptation requires the ability to tolerate ambivalence, inconsistency, conflict, and polarity. For example, closeness may be characterized by vigor, toughness, negativity, and rapid alternation from distance to closeness. Accordingly, the therapist must be alert to the family's perception of contradictions in these behaviors. How much is what the therapist perceives as toughness or hostility recognized by the family as affection? How much do both toughness and affection exist together without conflict for the family? How much is the distance in relationships that the therapist sees viewed by the others as being there?

Another strategy for increasing differentiation is the exploration of functioning in the family of origin that helps the family to see itself in historical perspective. Such examination not only clarifies current functioning in the context of the past but also creates new connections and identifications that clarify confused images and integrate fragmented ones. We agree with Hines and Boyd-Franklin (Chap. 4) that this exploration is costly, painful, and can lead to frustrating practical problems. For example, in Afro-American families where parents, grandparents, or other ancestors have been white, records and legal documents have often been altered to hide their identity. Afro-Americans have also concealed such information because of feelings of shame. Indeed, recognition of the realities of life during slavery and of the vigorous oppression that followed slavery has been painful. Both Blacks and Whites have colluded in the secrecy and ignorance of Afro-American family history, in part to avoid pain. Success in uncovering the facts affords unusual opportunities for understanding the strength and endurance that has characterized Afro-American ethnicity. The opportunity to replace the gaps in knowledge with information, the feelings of shame with pride, and the identity confusion with a sense of integration and continuity through time have profound therapeutic impact (Pinderhughes, 1982).

Resistance to Change

The family's response to victim system stress may render all the above strategies ineffective. The family may be so determined to remain in charge at all costs in order to avoid compounding its powerlessness that it will not grant the therapist the power to help. Therapists may then need to try techniques that neutralize this resistance.

Therapists may do this by taking a one down position with the use of paradox. Paradoxical interventions give the power back to the family. The therapist may suggest: "Do not do anything different. Keep on doing what you are doing already, only do it more (or less, or at certain times)." Another example would be: "It is important for you two to continue fighting because if you do not, one of you might get too depressed." Telling the family to do precisely what the therapist wants them not to do (in this case to fight) may provoke the family to oppose the therapist in order to maintain a sense of power. In opposing the therapist's suggestion that they continue fighting, they must stop the fighting.

Reframing, or giving the family another way of looking at their problem, is also an important aspect of paradoxical intervention. The therapist might say, for example, "You are fighting so viciously because you love each other and are working hard at being strong, determined, and committed." The idea is to go with the resistance, not against it, and even to overload it (Galoosian, 1980).

At the same time, therapists with Afro-American families must be careful in using paradoxical interventions since they involve an element of trickery and cleverness on the part of the therapist. The use of such interventions with those whose experiences make them sensitive to manipulation can result in their feeling foolish or more victimized.

Moreover, with the use of paradox the therapist must take care that the attempt to empower the family does not leave it isolated both from the therapist and from external supports. All family members must be given support in their new roles. Without such attention, the family may feel forced to reseek its former equilibrium. This is always a risk in therapy, and most family therapists are particularly sensitive to potential detrimental effects that change can cause elsewhere in the system. It may be hard for non-Afro-American therapists to realize the extent of isolation a Black family may feel, and, therefore, the need to maintain and reinforce the supports that do exist before moving toward major shifts within the family itself.

A Case Example: The A Family
John, aged 17, was the second of four children of an affluent suburban family. One year earlier he had been arrested for breaking and entering and possession of drugs. After a psychiatric evaluation by the court psychiatrist, John and his parents began treatment.

After a year the A family was referred to a second therapist by a family friend because the treatment was not progressing. At that time the first therapist was recommending long-term residential treatment, which the family rejected. John had become more depressed and was skipping school. Conflict between the parents was increasing.

The new therapist saw the A's as an ambitious Afro-American family living in a White suburb where the family was cut off from the surrounding White community. This isolation intensified the conflict between Mr. and Mrs. A, who fought over managing the children, handling finances, and organizing the household. Mr. A had clung to rigid, traditional ideas of male dominance, obedience of children, strict discipline, and thrift. Mrs. A seemed just as dogmatic in her insistence on permissiveness and on disapproval of her husband's values. They were at war. The family's isolation also reinforced a tendency for Mrs. A to cling to her adolescent son, John, to protect him from rejection as he sought to experiment and to explore the outside world.

The more John misbehaved, the more his father became furious and threatened to throw him out, and the more his mother came to his rescue. The more protective Mrs. A became, the more Mr. A withdrew to his hobbies. The more Mr. A withdrew, the more John became frightened at the closeness with his mother, and the more he wanted to get away from the family, escalating his misbehavior.

Therapy focused on identifying this cycle and examining the family's mutual scapegoating. Both parents resisted task assignments aimed at altering the blaming and fighting over how to handle John. However, both responded to an exploration of key experiences in their families of origin and later family experiences. Initially, Mr. A could only focus on his success in school and work. Denying at first any significance to being the only Black or one of a few in high school, college, his armed services unit, and in his current position, Mr. A gradually opened up about his feelings of isolation. It had been necessary for him to be better than others to be recognized. Several times he had been skipped over for promotions because of his race, and he always had to control his feelings, no matter how deep his resentments. He had been furious at the previous therapist who had called him rigid. An effective therapeutic strategy was to relabel this rigidity as a lifelong adaptation that had enabled him to be successful in unsupportive environments.

As therapy continued, Mrs. A became noticeably more understanding. She described her Southern background and discussed her idealization of her minister father, a powerful figure in the Black community. She had similarly idealized Mr. A, who felt he could never please but had not understood why. Seeing each other in the light of his struggles and her past, they began to respond to each other with more tolerance and were able to join forces in handling John. Mr. A, having had his inflexibility recognized as a strength, was then ready to understand the way in which his toughness had been maladaptive for handling John. John resisted these changes in his parents and continued his efforts to split them. But after a stormy period of six months, he began to respond constructively. John completed high school and moved South to live with his grandmother and to begin college.

The A family was empowered to cope more effectively with external systems and to make internal changes that lessened some of its rigidity. This was accomplished by the following:

1. Therapy supported the family's refusal to send John away to residential treatment center or school. The therapist agreed with the family that this might exacerbate John's difficulties.

Sending an Afro-American child away from home is difficult. Where he or she can be sent so that the problems will be understood in the context of Black identity is a problem. A White institution that does not offer this understanding can reinforce feelings of abandonment in the patient and helplessness in the family, making them more vulnerable than ever.

2. Therapy focused on the way Mr. A's strength and endurance had been both adaptive and maladaptive. The family's history was constantly interpreted in the context of their blackness. Mr. A's behavior, which was seen by Mrs. A as unreasonable, by John as frightening, and by the former therapist as rigid, was relabeled as necessary toughness that had been adaptive. Later this strength was explored in terms of power and negative aspects. Pearce (1981) has suggested that with Afro-American spouses, exploration of mutual needs, with a focus on the ways each feels "little" and dependent on the other, is unlikely to be acceptable or helpful. What must be explored and reinforced instead is strength.

3. Therapy increased self-differentiation in family members. In this case we see illustrated the vulnerability of Afro-American families to value conflict. Explanation of early experiences in the context of their blackness reinforced tolerance for their differences and encouraged a clearer sense of the Afro-American identity.

The Role of the Therapist

Therapists with Afro-American families should be clear about their own personal qualities and their ability to conduct therapy that will empower clients. It is axiomatic that therapists should be clear about their own ethnicity and the ways in which it influences their perceptions, feelings, and behavior. This clarity safeguards against behavior that either stereotypes or fuses with clients. It is also important that therapists understand how feelings, attitudes, and behaviors are influenced by their "power gestalt," that is, their experiences with power in relation to self, family, ethnicity, race, class, sex, profession, and so on (Pinderhughes, 1979a). For no other ethnic groups have the issues of power and powerlessness been so important. Self-awareness helps the therapist not to abuse power, which is particularly important because of the powerlessness inherent in the Afro-American family's role as clients needing help. Moreover, Afro-American families look for and expect strength in the therapist—strength that is conveyed by an authoritative stance that communicates ability to interact vigorously but not oppressively, and understanding of the necessary stamina and commitment.

As therapists we are all benefactors in the societal projection process, which reinforces for helpers a sense of competence and projects upon our Afro-American clients inferiority and incompetence (Bowen, 1978). We must be aware that:

1. the sense of competence and appearance of higher self-differentiation with which we seem to be endowed may be at the expense of our clients who are victims in the societal projection process.

2. effective intervention for our clients means reinforcing in them a sense of power, competence, and higher self-differentiation.

3. we, as benefactors, must take back and own for ourselves the projections of incompetence and powerlessness.

While this appears paradoxical because in a sense our "power" is threatened, it really is not. True power will exist for both our clients and ourselves when power and competence are shared.

REFERENCES

Aponte, H. Underorganization in the Poor Family. In P. Guerin (Ed.), *Family Therapy: Theory and Practice*. New York: Gardner Press, 1976.

Aponte, H. Videotape presented at workshop of the Society for Family Therapy and Research, Boston, April 8, 1978.

Auerswald, E. Interdisciplinary vs. Ecological Approach. *Family Process, 8*, 202–215, 1968.

Billingsley, A. *Black Families in White America*. Englewood Cliffs, N.J.: Prentice-Hall, 1968.

Bowen, M. *Family Therapy in Clinical Practice*. New York: Jason Aronson, 1978.

Boyd, N. *Kinship Issues and Black Family Therapy*. Paper presented at meeting of the American Orthopsychiatric Association, Washington, D.C., April 1979.

Cheek, D. *Assertive Black . . . Puzzled White*. San Luis Obispo, Calif.: Impact, 1976.

Chestang, L. *Character Development in a Hostile Environment* (Occasional Paper No. 3). Chicago: University of Chicago School of Social Service Administration, 1972.

Galoosian, H. *Workshop on Brief Strategic Interventions with Families*, Armed Forces, Munich, Germany, 1980.

Germaine, C. *Institute on Systems Theory, Ego Psychology and Social Work Practice*. Sponsored by the Massachusetts Chapter of the National Association of Social Workers, Boston, December 8, 1979.

Grier, W., & Cobbs, P. *Black Rage*. New York: Basic Books, 1968.

Harris, O., & Balgopal, P. Intervening with the Black Family. In C. Janzen & O. Harris (Eds.), *Family Treatment in Social Work*. Itasca: Peacock, 1980.

Knowles, L.L., & Prewitt, K. *Institutional Racism*. Englewood Cliffs, N.J.: Prentice-Hall, 1968.

McAdoo, H. Family Therapy in the Black Community. *Journal of the American Orthopsychiatric Association, 47*(1), 75–79, 1977.

Minuchin. S. *Families of the Slums*. New York: Basic Books, 1967.

Papajohn, J., & Spiegel, J. *Transactions in Families*. San Francisco: Jossey-Bass, 1975.

Pearce, J. Personal communication, 1981.

Pierce, C. Offensive Mechanisms. In F. Barbour (Ed.), *The Black Seventies*. Boston: Sargent, 1970.

Pinderhughes, C. Racism and Psychotherapy. In C. Willie, B. Brown, & B. Kramer (Eds.), *Racism and Mental Health*. Pittsburgh: University of Pittsburgh Press, 1973.

Pinderhughes, C. Black Personality in American Society. In M. Smythe (Ed.), *The Black American Reference Book*. Englewood Cliffs, N.J.: Prentice-Hall, 1976.

Pinderhughes, E. Black Genealogy: Self Liberator and Therapeutic Tool. *Smith College Studies in Social Work, 52*(2), 93–106, 1982.

Pinderhughes, E. Afro-Americans and Economic Dependency. *The Urban and Social Change Review, 12*(2), 24–27, 1979. (a)

Pinderhughes, E. Teaching Empathy in Cross Cultural Social Work. *Social Work, 24*, 312–316, 1979. (b)

Soloman, B. *Black Empowerment*. New York: Columbia University Press, 1976.

Spurlock, J. Consequences of Racism for Children. In C. Willie, B. Brown, & B. Kramer (Eds.), *Racism and Mental Health*. Pittsburgh: University of Pittsburgh Press, 1973.

Staples, R.E. Black Family Life and Development. In L. Gary (Ed.), *Mental Health: A Challenge to the Black Community*. Washington, D.C.: Institute for Urban Affairs, 1978.

6

West Indian Families

JANET BRICE

A major problem that therapists have in treating Black families is a lack of sensitivity in recognizing the vast differences among Black cultural sub-groups. In the professional literature, there are few if any cultural distinctions between a Black person born in the West Indies and one born and raised in the United States.

Therapists are often unaware of the fact that British West Indian family structure, roles, child rearing, and ethnic identity are different from that of American Blacks. This cultural "blind spot" sometimes creates distrust, problems in communication, and resistance to therapy.

This chapter will discuss cultural factors that may play a role in the treatment of British West Indian families.[1] It will look at family structure, attitudes toward emotional disturbances, and differences between West Indian and American Blacks.

To understand the British West Indian family, we must first appreciate its cultural context—the historical heritage, migration, and demographics of its people.

Historical Heritage

The West Indies are a group of islands in the Caribbean Sea, stretching from the northern coast of Venezuela, to the southern end of Florida, to the eastern end of the Yucatan Peninsula. While some of the islands have gained their independence, many are still colonies of France, Great Britain, the Netherlands, and the United States.

The West Indian people are a particularly heterogeneous group in terms of race, religion, and culture. Blacks, the descendants of the West Africans who were enslaved and brought to the islands in the 16th century, make up from 50% to 85% of the population, depending on the island (Lane, 1981). Whites, the descendants of the British, French, Spanish, and Dutch explorers

1. The West Indian people are a heterogeneous group that is strongly influenced by American, British, Dutch, French, and Spanish cultures, as well as by its African roots. To reflect the rich diversity of this region is beyond the scope of this chapter.

Janet Brice. University of Medicine and Dentistry of New Jersey and Community Mental Health Center of Rutgers Medical School, Piscataway, New Jersey.

that settled the West Indies, make up only 5%,[2] and those four languages are spoken in the West Indies. The islands are predominantly Protestant; some islands are Catholic. There are also some Moslems, Jews, and other religions, as well as influential folk or tribal religions (e.g., in Haiti). The rest of the population is mixed, and they are referred to as "Mulattos." Minority groups in the islands include the East Indians and Chinese.

The lives of the Black people on the islands were strongly affected by slavery, which had an impact on stable relationships, as it did on American Blacks. Family members who came from Africa together were separated on the auction block and sold to different plantations, whose owners dictated who would mate with whom. There was no guarantee that the parent–child unit would stay together (Clarke, 1957).

Emancipation of West Indian Blacks took place earlier than did that of their American counterparts and contributed to the shaping of the Black family. Freed Blacks strived for economic independence so that the men could be the true heads of their families and answer to no authority. Land ownership became associated with an independent income, stable relationships, and marriage. In Clarke's (1957) study of Jamaica, she explains that what differentiated the situation in the British West Indies from that in the southern United States was the fact that British West Indian slaves could become upwardly mobile. The Black landowners became the Black upper class. The illegitimate Black children of White plantation owners, the Mulattos, formed the middle class.

Although the scars of slavery are still embedded in the memories of many Blacks, early emancipation, ownership of land and business, and numerical dominance have provided them with a strong sense of ethnic identity and identification with their particular island culture. British West Indians migrating to the United States bring this strong sense of ethnic–cultural identity with them.

Migration

The migration of West Indians to the United States dates back to the early 19th century. In the 1850s there were only a few hundred West Indians immigrating to the United States each year. By the end of the century, the number had only risen to approximately 1000 per year (Ueda, 1980). Blacks who came to the United States at that time were predominantly middle-class Mulattos from the British-owned islands; 55% were skilled, 31% were un-

2. Guadeloupe and Martinique belong to France; Bermuda, the Caracas, Cayman, Leeward, Windward, Turk, and part of the Virgin Islands are colonies of Great Britain; Puerto Rico and the remaining Virgin Islands are under U.S. government rule; and the Netherland Antilles are Dutch. The remaining islands, including the Commonwealth of the Bahamas, Barbados, Cuba, the Dominican Republic, Haiti, Jamaica, Trinidad, and Tobago, are independent (Ploski & Marr, 1976).

skilled, 14% were school children or elderly; 9% were professionals, 7% were white-collar workers, and 41% were unemployed dependents (Ueda, 1980).

Where people settled was dictated by the mode of travel they used. Immigrants traveled by steamship and were likely to settle in the coastal cities where there were large ports. During the first three decades of the 20th century most West Indians were living in New York, Massachusetts, and Florida.

The second big wave of immigration occurred in the 38-year span between 1940 and 1978. These immigrants were slightly older than their predecessors, well educated, and skilled.

Usually one family member migrated to the United States and became established. Because it was relatively easier for women than men to secure employment, many more women came over by themselves, and the ratio of men to women dropped significantly from early groups of immigrants. If other relatives were in the United States, the individual lived with them. Other family members were sent for later. Several West Indian families often shared an apartment or house, with each family owning a bedroom. However, when a family moved out, the remaining families did not necessarily move into the other rooms. In an effort to make some money, they would rent the empty bedroom.

One advantage to migrating in this fashion was that the family was not scattered throughout the city. People were available to give each other emotional and financial support. The disadvantages were the crowded conditions and the new immigrants' longing for their spouses, parents, or children who had been left behind.

Family members were not the only friendly faces that the newly arriving immigrants met. Because so many of the islands resembled small towns, the probability was very high that if an individual ran into a fellow islander, he or she might have known the other's family back home. Even in instances where the two immigrants did not know one another, they were able to reminisce about certain places and celebrations particular to their island. Thus, a support system evolved to help ease the stress of acculturation.

Demographics

But even with these support systems, British West Indians, like other ethnic groups, have faced and still face the problems of adjusting to a new culture. The weather in the United States changes and can be cold and brutal compared to the warm tropical temperatures of the islands. The weather dictates what people do and when they do it, which may be somewhat disconcerting for a people accustomed to tropical temperatures all year round. Modes of dress and daily diet are unfamiliar. Although jobs are available, there are many times when a skilled British West Indian immigrant must take work that does not utilize his or her training, for example, the mop and pail of domestic work is often referred to as "West Indian pen and ink."

One of the most difficult things British West Indians have had to cope with was physical and psychological isolation. Many of the cities in the United States are equal in size to some of the West Indian islands. Visiting extended family members was relatively easy on each island because the country is so small. In the United States, however, traveling to see relatives or going to work becomes a lengthy and complicated endeavor. At home, people knew their neighbors and were familiar with local shopkeepers, clergy, and teachers. By comparison, the urban atmosphere seems cold and distant. People who are used to living in their own homes and being outdoors now live in cramped apartments far removed from the countryside.

Aside from their physical separation from their families, British West Indians' experience of racial discrimination adds to their difficulties. While racism has been part of the history of the Caribbean, and continues today in various forms on the islands, it is perceived and experienced differently by British West Indians than by American Blacks, which may create psychological problems for some West Indians.

British West Indians and American Blacks

American Blacks tend to define people as either Black or White. West Indians, in contrast, make three distinctions: Black (or Negro), colored, and White. These color distinctions represent points on a continuum from African to European. The lighter you are, the closer you are to the European end of the continuum and the higher your status in Caribbean society (Garvey, 1973). Dominquez (1975) describes the situation in this way:

> To lump the arriving immigrants together with Afro-Americans (as is often done phenomenologically by the layman) is to relegate some immigrants who are phenotypically Caucasian to the lowest ranks of American society. Furthermore, a large number of these immigrants are of physically mixed ancestry (e.g., Caucasian and Negroid) but do not perceive themselves as black (as do light skinned Afro-Americans) because their society of origin acknowledge the existence of physically intermediate populations as phenomenologically distinguishable. Differing historical circumstances having to do with the existence of a lower European-African ratio in the Caribbean than in the U.S. lead to the social and public acknowledgement in these countries of intermediate racial categories.

A light-skinned British West Indian who comes to the United States is in a dilemma. In the islands, he or she had a certain amount of status, at least more than a Black person. In the United States, however, Whites reject the

British West Indian as "another Black," while Blacks may reject or look down on the West Indian because of his or her refusal to identify with other Blacks.

British West Indians, who are sensitive to potential exploitation from a powerful nation (Dominquez, 1975), share ambivalent feelings about the United States with American Blacks. But unlike American Blacks who were brought to this country in slave ships, and have a long history of negative experience here, British West Indians have come here voluntarily, looking for educational and occupational advancement. Like American Blacks, they are cut off from their African roots, but unlike American Blacks, they retain an ethnic identity associated with their island or region and view themselves as immigrants (Best, 1975).

The two groups differ considerably in their attitudes toward the possibility of social mobility. They both have a strong desire to advance, but they disagree on the extent to which they can control their own destinies in a country with a White majority. American Blacks believe that no matter how hard Black people work, their color will prevent them from being justly rewarded. For some, the frustration has resulted in "learned helplessness," so that they view efforts to break the cycle of poverty as futile.

British West Indians, as a result of having lived in a predominantly Black society, have had different experiences. Even if they are not well educated, they come to hope, and sometimes expect, that their chldren and grandchildren will achieve more. There is evidence for this in the fact that West Indians "have been disproportionately overrepresented among Black professionals" (Sowell, 1981). And the U.S. value of hard work, which was learned primarily from the British, has meaning for the British West Indian (see Chap. 21 on British Americans).

It is precisely those British West Indians who are most impressed with the superiority of European culture who "make it" in the Caribbean or in the United States (Glantz, 1978). As a consequence—so runs the argument— the Black immigrant in the United States is not only more apt to be forceful and enterprising than either the native American or the stay-at-home, but is also more likely to believe that hard work and self-abnegation can lead eventually to reasonable prominence as a professional, local leader, small property owner, small business man, or landlord (Bryce-LaPorte, 1972).

British West Indians' attitude about money has also been consistent with their British origins and has helped them to make their way in the United States. Because of their future orientation, they have been very thrifty and would sacrifice in the present in order to have something in the future.

British West Indians have always kept in mind their ethnic identity in their attempts to make a place for themselves in the United States. British West Indians frequently spoke in terms of a region, of being British, of coming from a particular island, or of being from the West Indies. They asserted these identities to distinguish themselves from other Blacks in America.

Family Relationships

Marriage, which occurs with more frequency among the West Indian upper classes, carries a great deal of status in the British West Indies. For example, someone's spouse and children are commonly referred to as his or her "Christian family." A man saves every penny he can because he is not considered eligible for marriage until he can provide his intended wife with a house and economic security. Some of his money goes to his family, and the rest is put aside for purchasing a house. Since this saving process takes a number of years, the average age for a British West Indian at the time of marriage is almost 10 years older than the average age of a person marrying in the United States (Schlesinger, 1968).

In marriage, the man's primary responsibilities are economic. As the head of the household, he is expected to support his wife and their children. A husband failing to provide for his family is seen as not fulfilling his role, and this is grounds for divorce. The woman who contemplates marriage anticipates a better life for herself. She is not expected to work outside of the home or to do housework (Clarke, 1957); her primary task is child rearing.

Although marriage is a very valued union, it is not the only type of family pattern among West Indians. There are many other types of union, and we will discuss the two most prevalent ones—purposive and nonpurposive.

Purposive unions involve an arrangement in which a man and woman choose to live together to test their compatibility. During their time together, which sometimes lasts several years, they may have children. The sex roles follow those of a patriarchal marriage. This union is known as "faithful concubinage" in Jamaica (Schlesinger, 1968), "*ménage*" in Martinique (Horowitz & Horowitz, 1963), and "living" in Trinidad (Voyandoff & Rodman, 1978).

In nonpurposive unions the woman is referred to as housekeeper or domestic arranger. She cooks, cleans, and launders. The man does not look upon the woman as his equal and, therefore, does not contemplate marriage.

Fidelity is important in marriage, and adultery is grounds for dissolving a marriage. But the West Indian woman often enters marriage totally ignorant about sex and is far more concerned about being a good mother than a good sexual partner to her husband (Henry & Wilson, 1975). Her duties revolve around child rearing, and a married woman without children is viewed as deviant. The job of child rearing includes socialization and discipline. Spankings are the primary form of punishment and are often accompanied by a scolding or "tongue lashing."

Children are supposed to show a great deal of respect for their elders. It is considered impolite for them to talk back to or disagree with an older person since adults are certain that their life experiences guarantee that they know what is best for children.

There are considerable differences in the socialization of female and male children. Girls are taught obedience and are discouraged from being assertive. Domestic training is emphasized in the belief that confining a young girl to the house and garden will keep her out of trouble (Schlesinger, 1968; Henry & Wilson, 1975). Girls are expected to be pretty but never sexually alluring and sex education is usually denied them. Girls date boys whom their parents know extremely well. If there are not enough opportunities for a girl to meet appropriate young men, she is not permitted to go out.

Male children are socialized to be responsible. Achievement is emphasized, and education is valued as a means to an end, not as a goal in and of itself. Boys are encouraged to seek respectable and stable professions and to choose fields of study that offer opportunities for advancement and upward mobility.

There is a strong bond between mothers and sons, and a son is doted on regardless of his sibling position. If her husband is absent, there is a tendency for the mother to lean on her male children. A son's closeness with his mother continues even after he marries, and sons are expected to take care of their mothers.

Although the mother has chief responsibility for raising the children, British West Indian children have warm and loving relationships with their fathers. Unfortunately, this close relationship between fathers and children is frequently disrupted by lengthy separations. The family's economic situation determines the likelihood of this—the poorer the family, the more likely the father will have to search for work away from the community.

Sometimes it is the children who are separated from their families. "Child lending" is a fairly common occurrence in the islands. This is a practice whereby school-aged children are sent to live with extended family members. In some families, this is done because the mother may be forced to work or has died at a young age. In other families, a child may be sent to live with a relative to have easier access to education. Sometimes the arrangement may be made for the benefit of the relative. For example, a child may be sent to be a companion to a childless woman or a woman whose children are all grown (Sanford, 1974).

Therapy with British West Indian Families

British West Indians are a very proud and strong people who believe in handling their own problems. Pain is endured without much evidence of suffering. Religion is very important as a guide to solving problems and for communal support, and God is believed to supply strength. When the endurance level has been reached, a family member will confer with other members, usually elders. If a person outside of the family is consulted, it will probably be the local pastor. He is not necessarily sought out in order to provide answers but to provide further emotional support and to buttress the family's faith.

Folk beliefs also exert a strong influence on West Indians. Some families in crisis will consult a practitioner of *obeah* (witchcraft).

> How obeah works, and indeed it may, is of course as complex a question to consider as is the understanding of any form of psychotherapy. It is not simply a matter of suggestion or the credibility of unsophisticated people. Nor can it be adequately explained on the basis of an abreaction and a "release of repressed hostility." While suggestions are made and hostility is evoked, they function as therapeutic processes because they are put into language of such socially signifi-cant content. Symbols of religion, violence and death particularly subserve the most intense emotional relationships for Virgin Islanders and structure the events of the environment into organized wholes. When the obeahman says that a neighbor is envious or covetous and that hostility exists, he is generally not far from the truth. When such a relationship is put into the metaphors and the rest of the symbolic apparatus of obeah, then it gains an overwhelmingly vivid quality of meaning and reality. (Weinstein, 1962, pp. 153–154)

The West Indian family finds it difficult to admit that there is a problem it cannot handle. If a family does go to a mental health professional, it often does so for a child's problem, which may come from a school, or a medical complaint, which may come from a physician who was unable to find a physiological basis for the client's symptoms.

Once the family is referred, the therapist should have little trouble getting its members to come in because British West Indians seriously consider the advice of professionals (i.e., teachers and doctors). However, the therapist must choose a time for an appointment that will not require the father or mother to miss work. West Indians take the adage "time is money" very seriously.

West Indians are not likely to challenge the authority of the therapist. They may respond best to an older male therapist because this is syntonic with the cultural respect most feel for men and elders. If the therapist does not fit this image, he or she may include extended family elders, such as a grandmother, in the treatment. This would help to demonstrate that the therapist recognizes the value of older people, as well as to provide the therapist with information from another generation.

> Let us consider the case of the C family. Mr. and Mrs. C have five children. The first four were born and raised in Jamaica, and the fifth, a girl, eight years younger than her nearest sibling, was born and raised in the United States. Mr. and Mrs. C entered therapy because they were having trouble with their youngest girl. She did not listen to them, was rude, and came and went as she pleased.

The therapist discovered that Mr. and Mrs. C were disciplinarians who were, however, inconsistent with the youngest child. Mrs. C, in particular, seemed ambivalent about carrying through on threats to punish her. Mrs. C's mother was invited to a subsequent session. Her views on discipline and her observations of Mrs. C in the role of mother were taken into account. The grandmother stated that her generation believed in "directing" the children, that is, that parents provide strong direction by virtue of experience. She did not countenance the permissiveness that went on in the United States. Eventually, the therapist found out that Mrs. C's ambivalence about discipline had to do with her conflict about assimilating in the American mainstream. It helped Mrs. C to have her mother come in and state her viewpoint and acknowledge the excellent job Mrs. C had done with the other children.

Family members tend to be quite stoical and have a covert agreement among themselves not to reveal feelings. The therapist's efforts to amplify feelings could be threatening, and the middle-class British West Indian family is most likely to respond to a therapeutic approach that is educational.

Bowen systems therapy is in many ways very compatible with West Indian cultural perspectives on receiving help. The therapist is portrayed as a teacher, and therapy is viewed as research and self-change. British West Indians value education and upward mobility, and this approach recognizes their desires to use their own resources to improve themselves. It also respects what has happened in the past and what the older generation has to say about it. Among British islanders, wisdom is said to come from experience.

If we consider the extensive role played by extended family members in the rearing of children, it would be crucial to examine the history of symptoms across generations. The multigenerational perspective could serve to lower anxiety by taking the focus away from the "identified patient" and by putting some distance between the symptom and the nuclear family. In working with West Indian families, the therapist cannot get away from discussing events that have occurred in at least three generations.

Bowen systems therapy does not emphasize emotionality, which is a very appropriate tack to take among West Indians. Considering the tremendous amount of rational thought that is given to decisions about marriage, work, and finances, it is likely that questions aimed at feelings will reach a dead end.

The therapist who is helping someone to differentiate from his or her family will meet with difficulty. Socialization in the British West Indies emphasizes the obligations children have to their families. This is particularly important if the family has made sacrifices that enabled the child to get ahead. In trying to achieve individualization, the best place to intervene may not be with the parent, but with the grandparents of the patient. The therapist might want to find out who is the oldest living relative in the United

States and who is the oldest living relative in the islands. If both of those individuals are living, it is important to find out which one is called upon for advice. Detriangulating the people most closely involved with the key figures would start the ripple effect of change throughout the rest of the system.

Bowen systems therapy is not suitable for all West Indian families. It is not structured, is intellectual, and requires a great deal of time for the family to do the research. Thus, it is not appropriate for a low socioeconomic West Indian family that is facing a crisis. Such families would benefit from a goal-directed, explicitly structured, and time-limited therapeutic experience.

For some patients who are "stuck," strategic interventions may have an appeal because the therapist's interpretations align him or her with the family. Prescribing the symptom takes away the need for that individual to resist.

> Take, for example, the K family. They came to the Community Mental Health Center because one of their sons was giving them a great deal of trouble. He had been living with his mother's sister. The trouble started when he had been reintegrated into his nuclear family. After taking a detailed history, the therapist hypothesized that the boy's behavior was his way of testing his parent's loyalty. In essence, he wanted to know if they really loved him, and his criterion was whether or not they would send him away again. The therapist empathized with the parents, agreeing that there was really nothing they could do. They had tried a variety of disciplinary measures, all of which had failed. They were commended for their patience. The therapist then suggested that perhaps the boy did not want to be a part of this family. Perhaps he wanted to return to his aunt's house. The therapist told the boy that his behavior indicated that. If he continued to behave in the same manner, his plan would be successful. Since the boy really wanted to be included in his nuclear family his behavior had to change in order to achieve that goal.

Summary

It is important for therapists who treat West Indians to be sensitive to the fact that they came from a unique heritage that is varied in its subcultures. Their history of enslavement, colonization by Europeans, migratory labor, and migration to the United States has had profound effects on their family system and their behavior.

The strength of the West Indian family lies in the fact that it is so closely knit, something that can work to a therapist's advantage. Throughout history, West Indian families have had an important resource in extended family members. Such enmeshment was, and still is, adaptive because it has provided individuals with both emotional and practical support in times of stress. The therapist working with these families will find his or her work rewarding because they are truly motivated to help one another.

REFERENCES

Best, T. West Indians and Afro-Americans: A Parnership. *The Crisis, 82,* 389, 1975.

Bryce-LaPorte, R.S. Black Immigrants: The Experience of Invisibility and Inequality. *Journal of Black Studies, 3,* 29–56, 1972.

Clarke, E. *My Mother Who Fathered Me.* London: Allen & Unwin, 1957.

Dominquez, V. *From Neighbor to Strangers.* New Haven: Yale University, Antilles Research Program, 1975.

Garvey, M. The Race Question in Jamaica. In D. Lowenthal & L. Comitas (Eds.), *The Consequences of Class and Color.* New York: Anchor Books, 1973.

Glantz, O. Native Sons and Immigrants: Some Beliefs and Values of American-Born and West Indian Blacks at Brooklyn College. *Ethnicity, 5,* 189–202, 1978.

Henry. F., & Wilson, P. Status of Women in Caribbean Societies: An Overview of their Social, Economic and Sexual Roles. *Social and Economic Studies, 24,* 165–198, 1975.

Horowitz, M., & Horowitz, S. A Note on Marriage in Martinique. *Marriage and Family Living, 25,* 1963.

Lane, H.U. (Ed.). *The World Almanac and Book of Facts.* New York: Newspaper Enterprise, 1981.

Ploski, H., & Marr, W. *The Negro Almanac: A Reference Work on the Afro-American.* New York: Bellwether, 1976.

Sanford, M. A Socialization in Ambiguity: Child Lending in a British West Indian Society. *Ethnology, 13*(4), 393–400, 1974.

Schlesinger, B. Family Patterns in the English-Speaking Caribbean. *Journal of Marriage and the Family, 30,* 149–154, 1968.

Sowell, T. *Ethnic America.* New York: Basic Books, 1981.

Ueda, R. West Indians. In S. Thernstrom, A. Orlov, & O. Handlin (Eds.), *Harvard Encyclopedia of American Ethnic Groups.* Cambridge: Harvard University Press, 1980.

Voyandoff, P., & Rodman, H. Marital Careers in Trinidad. *Journal of Marriage and the Family, 40,* 157, 1978.

Weinstein, E. *Cultural Aspects of Delusions.* New York: Free Press, 1962.

7

Mexican Families

CELIA JAES FALICOV

This chapter makes specific clinical suggestions to guide therapists who work with Mexican American families. The suggestions are meant to be a general framework with which to approach families in a clinical situation. Effective family therapy requires that the therapist raise relevant contextual questions, avoid errors of assessment due to ethnocentric or stereotypic views, and set up appropriate treatment goals and culturally consonant interventions. These can be accomplished only with knowledge about the cultural characteristics of the Mexican family's life cycle and structure, and information about the family's adaptation to their new culture.

Generalizations about some aspects of Mexican history and migration, family interactional patterns, and the effects of cultural transition on the Mexican family system will be presented first, as a background for the clinical suggestions and examples that will follow. The model presented is based on observations made during extensive clinical work with a Mexican American population in the midwestern and western United States, reviews of the literature, and discussions with colleagues and trainees.

Mexican History and Migration

Most Mexicans are *mestizos*, that is, of mixed Spanish and Indian descent. They trace their native heritage back to Indian groups that built great civilizations in Mexico long before the Spanish explorers arrived in the 1500s. During the 17th, 18th, and 19th centuries, Spain extended its rule over the region that is now Mexico, California, and the southwestern United States. The Spaniards and the Indians learned much from each other, but, in general, the Spaniards took Mexico's riches and kept the Indians poor. Roman Catholic priests from Spain taught Catholicism to the Indians who often combined it with their own religions. Many Spanish men took Indian women as mates. Because of such unions, some Indian domestic arts and child-rearing practices were preserved.

Celia Jaes Falicov. Department of Psychiatry, University of California Medical School, and San Diego Family Institute, San Diego, California.

During the 1600s and 1700s the Spaniards and Mexicans established missions and communities that later became important cities in the United States, such as Santa Fe, Los Angeles, and San Antonio. In 1821, Mexico won its freedom from Spain, but 300 years of Spanish rule left a strong imprint.

Today, the Spanish and Indian heritages are so fused that it is difficult to separate them, as the following examples illustrate. Nearly all Mexican people belong to the Roman Catholic Church, but Indian villages still combine ancient religious practices with Catholic ones. Sorcery, witchcraft, and ancient herbal lore exist along with Western medical practices and beliefs. The linkage of family honor to the daughter's virtue can be traced to Spanish tradition. The privileged position of the oldest son in the family is traced by anthropological studies to Mayan tradition. These and other Indian and Spanish traditions influence the Mexican family today.

It is tempting to reduce many of the attributes observed in Mexican people, such as courtesy, formality, submission, dissimulation, or hermeticism to generalizations about an "oppressed servant" mentality, a counterpart to the "psychology of the master" developed during the centuries of foreign domination, as some authors have attempted to do (Paz, 1961). To avoid the pitfall of linear causation, however, the Mexican traits in this chapter should be considered only as observations. Knowledge of the historical circumstances in which these traits emerged provides part of the context, but not a simple cause–effect explanation for these cultural traits. The influence of the diverse components of an historical event are reciprocal; cultures are molded by their circumstances, which in turn are molded by the culture.

The geographical proximity between Mexico and the United States has resulted in continuous interaction between the two countries. A popular Mexican sentiment about this interaction is summarized by the refrain "Pobre México! Tan lejos de Dios y tan cerca de los Estados Unidos!"— Poor Mexico! So far from God and so near the United States! During the 1820s, Mexico allowed many Americans to settle in their territory, which is now Texas. In 1835, the Americans led a revolt against the Mexicans and established the Republic of Texas. The conflict over Texas became the chief cause of the Mexican War (1846–1848), in which the United States gained most of the land that is now Arizona, California, Colorado, Nevada, New Mexico, Utah, and Wyoming. Over 75,000 Mexicans who lived in those areas became U.S. citizens. To this day, many people within this ancestral group consider the southwest United States to be, if not politically, at least culturally, Mexican.

After the discovery of gold in California in 1848, settlers from the eastern United States poured into the West. Racial, religious, language, and other cultural differences became sources of conflict between the Mexican people and the Anglo-American newcomers. The two groups lived apart. Each had its own schools, stores, and places of entertainment in its respective *barrio*, or neighborhood. Gradually and mostly through discrimination and injustice, Mexicans lost their private property and most of their rights and became workers in a land that now belonged to English-speaking Americans.

Although Mexico has a variety of landscapes and climates, most of its land is dry, mountainous, and unsuitable for agriculture. Industrial and technological developments have been slow. More than one-third of the people work extremely hard and live in total poverty, while the population grows about 3½% a year, mostly because of the high birth rate. Therefore, work opportunities in the United States have always been a powerful magnet.

The Mexican American population began to grow rapidly in the early 1900s when thousands of Mexicans fled the violence of the Mexican Revolution of 1910. Many were recruited by American railroads, mining companies, and farm owners. But because of the severe unemployment of the Great Depression of 1910, thousands of Mexican immigrants were deported or were pressured by the U.S. government to return to Mexico. During World War II a new wave of Mexicans immigrated to the United States. Many were *braceros*, farm workers who had been issued temporary work permits.

At present, many Mexicans continue to enter the United States daily in search of better economic opportunities. Most frequently, immigrants come from the northern bordering states and central rural areas of Mexico. Recently, lack of employment opportunities in Mexico has prompted immigration from large urban centers like Mexico City and Guadalajara. Since the 1960s, however, the majority of Mexican immigrants are no longer granted U.S. legal alien status. Fear of detection and a sense of anomie and social alienation permeates the lives of these nondocumented immigrants. Predictably, they shun medical and psychological treatment.

It is estimated that well over 6.5 million Mexican Americans live in the United States, making them the second largest minority group in this country. Most of them live in cities. Like most other minority groups, Mexican Americans suffer discrimination in housing, education, and jobs. They work hard at low-paying and low-prestige jobs, are often exploited by employers, have very high unemployment and school dropout rates. The school dropout rate is probably caused by a combination of language difficulties, racial prejudice, and cultural dissonance. In spite of their high unemployment, many Mexican Americans do not receive welfare aid. In part, their non-document status precludes this possibility, but also many are too proud to accept a type of financial support that they regard as a negative sign of acculturation.

Although there are Mexicans who have lived in the southwestern states for several generations, census figures for 1970 estimate that the majority of Mexicans living in the United States were either born in Mexico or born to parents who are Mexican born (Hernandez, Estrada, & Alvirez, 1973). The census also indicates that a large majority of Mexican Americans specify Spanish as their native tongue or the language spoken in their homes as children. The predominant religion is Roman Catholic. In border areas like southern California, Jehovah's Witnesses, Pentecostal, and other evangelical faiths have some followers among Mexican Americans.

Cultural Family Patterns

The literature on the traditional Mexican family structure and values is extensive (Alvirez & Bean, 1976; Grebler, Moore, & Guzman, 1973; Madsen, 1964; Peñalosa, 1968) and, although not geared to clinical problems, can provide a framework for understanding public norms or cultural ideals. The scope of this chapter does not allow a thorough review of this literature, but cultural ideals relevant to family treatment will be summarized in this section.

Two points need to be remembered before genealizing about cultural family patterns. First, broad cultural generalizations do not do justice to regional, generational, socioeconomic, and idiosyncratic variations in lifestyle found in Mexican American families. Thus, descriptions and analyses of values and norms that may be valid at the macrosocial level need refinement and qualification at the microsocial level. Second, cultural norms tend to refer to the *public* reality of how relationships or behaviors "ought" to be. These internalized behavioral prescriptions sometimes do not coincide with *private* realities, that is, how things "really" are for each family. Both public (cultural) and private (idiosyncratic) norms govern family relationships and combine to make every family unique; both public and private aspects need to be considered and evaluated in the therapeutic situation.

Knowledge of the cultural ideals that influence the family's development and organization and awareness about the changes introduced by the processes of migration and acculturation can provide crucial guidelines for assessing and intervening in family therapy. The cultural characteristics of the Mexican American family life cycle and its therapeutic implications have been described elsewhere (Falicov & Karrer, 1980). The emphasis of this section will be on the cultural norms that govern family organization.

The generalizations that follow pertain primarily to the cultural background of poor and working-class families from northern and central Mexico who have migrated to the United States during the past three or four decades. The descriptions that follow apply only to Mexican families that come from rural or semirural areas and poor or working-class socioeconomic levels. Marked differences between Mexican lower and upper or middle socioeconomic levels exist in the circumstances and values that influence family life, and these should not be minimized.

Mexican Family Organization

In Mexican society, the nuclear family is embedded in an extended family network. The boundaries of the nuclear family are flexible with respect to the inclusion of relatives such as grandparents, uncles, aunts, or cousins (Madsen, 1964). Children who are orphaned or whose parents are divorced may be included in the household of relatives, along with adults who have remained single, become widowed, or divorced. Vertical or lateral kinship ties up to third and fourth cousins are often close. The children's godparents, or *compadres*, are often considered to be part of the extended family. Close friends of the parents are often called "uncle" or "aunt" by the children.

Interdependence, both intergenerational and lateral, characterizes this supportive network. Many family functions, such as caretaking and disciplining of children, financial responsibility, companionship, emotional support, and problem solving are shared. This tendency to extend kinship ties and to rely on relationships beyond the nuclear family has been called "familism" (Alvirez & Bean, 1976; Mindel, 1980). To facilitate the functioning of the kinship network, affiliation and cooperation are stressed, while confrontation and competition are discouraged. A corollary of these tendencies is "personalism," that is, a focus on relationships rather than on tasks (Levine & Padilla, 1980).

Both a high degree of cohesion and of hierarchical organization are normal for Mexican families. Patterns of interaction are characterized by generational interdependence and loyalty to the family of origin; high levels of affective resonance, interpersonal involvement, and controls; a tendency for individuals to live in families—of origin, of procreation, or extended—at every developmental stage; and the fact that all life cycle events and rituals are family celebrations and affirmations of their unity. It is important to emphasize that in spite of this high degree of emotional proximity and interdependency, hierarchies are clearly defined. Rules are organized around age and sex, as they are the most important determinants of authority, with older males being attributed the greatest centrality.

The family protects the individual, and it demands loyalty. The values of family proximity, cohesiveness, and respect for parental authority are present throughout an individual's lifetime. Autonomy and individual achievement are not particularly emphasized. Honesty and the preservation of one's *dignidad* (dignity) is another fundamental value. Individuals pride themselves as being *pobre pero honesto* (poor but honest) and as being able to describe their family network in the same manner. This constellation of values influences when and how the stages of the life cycle are lived and defines many aspects of interpersonal transactions, including the boundaries and operations of the nuclear family subsystems.

Nuclear families usually live in households nearby but separate from the extended family and thus preserve their boundaries and identity. Families are usually large, consisting of the parents and four, five, or more children. Birth rates among Mexicans are substantially higher than among Anglo-American families, at all socioeconomic levels (Bean, 1973). The large size is a major structural influence on many aspects of family life.

MARITAL SUBSYSTEM

Traditional views about family life and Roman Catholicism exert important influences upon attitudes toward marriage and divorce. Although it is changing rapidly with the influence of urbanization, the traditional division of labor that is functional for an agrarian society, whereby the husband assumes the instrumental role of provider and protector of the family and the wife the expressive role of homemaker and caretaker, is still the predominant public norm.

This complementarity of roles is supported by male and female cultural ideals rooted in Spanish antecedents and expressed in hierarchies of male dominance and female submission. The ideal of *machismo* or *muy hombre* (manliness or virility) dictates that men be aggressive, sexually experienced, courageous, and protective of their women (who include mother, sisters, and wives) and their children. The female counterpart of this ideal is a humble, submissive, and virtuous woman, devoted to her home and children. Although in most Mexican marriages there is outward compliance with the cultural ideal of male dominance and female submission, this is often a social fiction. In the reality of their private lives, Mexican American families may include husbands who are domineering and patriarchal (Peñalosa, 1968), who are submissive and dependent on their wives for major decisions, or who follow a more egalitarian power structure (Hawkes & Taylor, 1975). Couples find their own balance of power and control, which may even change over time or in different contexts.

In some cases, the culturally prescribed organization of male dominance and female submission can lead to extreme complementarity or to attempts to balance the relationship with another culturally acceptable but less openly discussed norm, that of *hembrismo* or *marianismo* (Stevens, 1973), that is, the undercover power and family centrality of the self-sacrificing mother.

Since the launching of young adults occurs primarily through marriage, during the early stages of family formation, boundary problems and loyalty conflicts with the families of origin are common. In addition, and mostly for economic reasons, many Mexican marriages have been affected by the practice of patrilocal residence, whereby young brides go to live with their husbands' families. In these situations, the working out of the mother-in-law and daughter-in-law relationship is crucial to the success of the marriage. According to the traditional ideal, the daughter-in-law was supposed to have the same obligations as a daughter and to perform many domestic chores under the supervision of her mother-in-law. Even if they only temporarily live with the husband's family, most young women no longer tolerate this role and thereby create marital conflict.

Ideally, there should be a certain formality in the relationship between spouses. No deep intimacy or intense conflict is expected. Respect, consideration, and curtailment of anger or hostility are highly valued. The waning of satisfaction in marriage is a matter of popular folklore and it may be hinted at among same-sex friends, but direct confrontation of marital difficulties is uncommon. Romantic ties are secondary to the preservation of the marriage. Rather, it is the existence of children that validates and cements the marriage. It is thought that *el amor de madre* (motherly love) is a much greater force than wifely love. Father too, is obligated and genuinely wants to do his best for the children. Since the relationship between parents and children is considered to be *more* important than the marital relationship, the couple enjoys little freedom from parental functions during the child-rearing stages. The boundary between the marital and children's subsystems is generally preserved, but the rules against direct expression of hostility or resentment between spouses may result in alliances with the children or with relatives living in the same household.

The large number of children, their relatively late departure from the family, and their intense connectedness with the parents during adulthood prolong the parenthood cycle and allow the marital couple to maintain a focus on parental and grandparental functions. Thus, Mexican parents may never experience an empty nest.

The majority of Mexican families remain two-parent families throughout their lifetimes. The number of divorces is considerably smaller than for Anglo populations (Alvirez & Bean, 1976). However, common-law marriages and desertions are not infrequent among the urban poor.

PARENT-CHILD SUBSYSTEM

Following the cultural prescriptions for the behavior of men and women, the parental functions are complementary. The Mexican father disciplines and controls while the mother provides nurturance and support. Both engender the *respeto* (respect) of children. While the word *respeto* is the same as the English respect, studies indicate that the internalized meaning of the word varies. For Anglo-Americans, it reflects a fairly "detached, self-assured egalitarianism." For Mexicans, it implies a relationship involving a "highly emotionalized dependence and dutifulness, within a fairly authoritarian framework" (Diaz-Guerrero, 1975). In general, the status of parents is high and that of children low. Thus, complementary transactions between parents and children are stressed while symmetrical transactions are discouraged or tolerated only in jest.

Hierarchies are clearly defined, and most parents would not expect or want to be friends with their children. But most would agree that parents and children should care about and enjoy each other. During late childhood and throughout adolescence children are expected to help with housework, child care, cooking, and errands. These are family duties for which no monetary reward is received or expected. In general, children and adolescents are not encouraged to work outside of the home. Boys and girls are scolded or punished for disobedience, poor manners, rudeness, or doing things without permission. Girls are often punished for coming home late. Shaming or belittling the child, deception, promises, and threats are common child-rearing methods.

In spite of the emphasis on good behavior, parents give a great deal of nurturance and protection to young children and adopt a relaxed attitude toward the achievement of developmental milestones or the attainment of skills related to self-reliance. Mexican parents are less pressured than Anglo-American parents to achieve developmental goals or to correct minor deviances from the norm. In fact, there is a basic acceptance of the child's individuality. Parents will describe their children as shy, slow, or talkative without making any value judgments as long as the child is fairly obedient and respectful.

The role of the mother is idealized and equated with self-denial and abnegation. When her patience is exhausted a mother may become nervous or upset but not angry or resentful of the children. Father protects mother and demands that children obey and help her, but he is not usually involved with the caretaking of household and children. He is usually playful and affectionate toward young children, but his primary role with older children is to discipline them and to expect obedience. The polarization of protective nurturance and authoritarian control between mother and father occasionally develops into a rigid pattern. Although mother is supposed to support father's disciplinary measures in his presence, she may covertly disagree with him. In his absence, she may allow behaviors of which he does not approve but at the same time instill fear of the father as a means of control. Children may ask her for things they do not dare ask of their father directly. Father may be softened up through mother's mediation rather than the children's persuasion. This pattern perpetuates a lack of direct contact between father and children and reinforces the mother's centrality. At each step, the punctuation of this interactional pattern is supported by cultural norms.[1]

Extended family members such as grandparents, uncles, aunts, and godparents perform many parental functions. They provide nurturance and support for young children, and their presence in the community exerts a controlling influence on adolescents. They also provide a type of individual attention to children that is usually difficult for parents to provide in large families.

1. Sociologists regard this type of alliance between mother and children as functional when parental role segregation is high (such as in the patriarchal households of technologically simple societies) and will not label this pattern as "pathological stable coalition" in need of change.

SIBLING SUBSYSTEM

Because of the large number of siblings, there are complex allocations of roles, division of labor, and individual compatibilities that stimulate the formation of several subgroups within the sibling group. The ties among siblings are very strong in the Mexican family tradition. Fraternal solidarity is an ideal that parents instill in children from an early age. During childhood, siblings—along with cousins—are constant companions. Parents encourage children to have their own siblings and cousins as their playmates, and children seem to be happy to do so. It is common for Mexican children to know few peers or have few friends other than their siblings. Competition and fighting among siblings is discouraged, while cooperation, sharing, and even sacrifice for a sibling are stressed. Parents accord authority to the older siblings and, as in most large families, usually delegate some supervisory and caretaking functions to them. Although some siblings attempt to establish a more egalitarian relationship during adulthood, age hierarchies continue to be compelling. During adolescence, there is segregation by sex within the sibling group that prevents cross-sex companionship but allows for complementary functions such as the girls doing household chores for the boys, who in turn, chaperone and protect the girls.

During adulthood, emotional support, advice, or practical help among siblings is usual. Because of the closeness and life-long association, life cycle events in the family of one sibling may have repercussions upon the family of another sibling. Or a younger, unmarried or widowed sibling, niece, or nephew may come to live with an older sibling or aunt in a mutually favorable relationship. But this "permanent visitor" may also form a coalition with one family member against another.

Quarrels and resentments among adult siblings are common. They may be caused by favoritism of the parents for one sibling over another, by disagreements about inheritance, by unpaid debts, or by the persistence of a controlling attitude on the part of an older sibling that is no longer acceptable to a younger one. Rifts among siblings, however, are seldom permanent. Life cycle rituals or crises, such as an illness or loss of a job, usually reunite siblings.

Relationships between cousins are often close, particularly between *primo hermanos* (first cousins), and resemble sibling relationships.

GODPARENTS AND COPARENTS

The custom of *compadrazgo* deserves special attention as an extension of the family. By this custom two sets of relationships are established: one is between *padrinos y ahijados* (godparents and their godchildren); the other is between the parents and the godparents who become *compadres* (coparents). Most Mexicans and Mexican Americans have *compadres* living in the same town and use their help in a variety of ways (Keefe, Padilla, & Carlos, 1978a).

The original function of godparents was to provide security for the godchild. Godparents are equivalent to an additional set of parents who act as guardians or sponsors of the godchild and care for him or her in emergencies. Godparents may be chosen from among members of the extended family or from outside of it. Families vary as to whether they ask the same or different sets of godparents to serve for all of their children. Families also vary on the reasons behind the choice of a particular set of godparents. Poor families may seek a wealthier family; rural families may choose a city family; others may have political favors in mind; and still others will base their choice on friendship or emotional reasons.

The two most important types of godparents are those of baptism and marriage since these two events are probably the most important life cycle rituals for Mexicans. The godparents of baptism assume responsibilities throughout the child's lifetime. The godparents of marriage contribute to the expenses of the wedding and, at least in theory, can function as mediators between the couple in case of quarrels or separations.

It is interesting that Mexicans have extended the *compadre* system beyond the original Roman Catholic religious occasions, such as baptism, communion, or confirmation and have *compadre* systems for secular activities. For example, in small towns there may be godmothers at social dances who act as chaperones for young girls.

Godparents and godchildren and *compadres* have a formal relationship with each other. *Compadres* often exchange many favors, including lending money. They believe that because they have avoided intimacies, such as discussing personal matters or drinking together, business can be conducted correctly.

The relationship between uncles and nephews, although less formal and more intimate, has some of the qualities of security and help that characterize the relationship between godparents and godchildren.

Effects of Cultural Transition on the Mexican Family System

With the exception of the Mexican American population of the southwestern United States, the majority of the Mexican families who live in the United States are immigrants. Their sociocultural context and their social identity have drastically changed. They are in a state of cultural transition that ranges from cultural alienation and marginality to cultural integration, often mediated by a stage of cultural duality. In their family scenario, values of the past coexist with the values of the present, imparted through the school, church, neighborhood, or place or type of employment. The process of migration and acculturation adds constant change and a complexity that needs to be kept in mind when discussing cultural patterns.

Migration produces a transitional crisis in the family with predictable stages (Sluzki, 1979). Not only must individual family members adapt to the cultural transplantation, but the family unit itself must often be reconstructed. New patterns of interaction emerge as a result of changes in family composition, that is, separations and reunions of family members during the migratory process that require structural and functional reorganizations. Other family reorganizations stem from changes in the rules that define roles, boundaries, and hierarchies within the family as a result of acculturation processes. Although these patterns are necessary and largely adaptive to the circumstances of the Mexican immigrant, over time they may become dysfunctional and bring families to the mental health clinic. Only a few of these family reorganizations will be mentioned here. For a more extensive discussion, see Falicov (in preparation). Some of these family changes are related to the fact that immigration usually involves separation from extended family and friends. These losses prompt a regrouping to accomplish nurturance and instrumental functions and may increase the cohesiveness of the nuclear family to compensate for the initial sociocultural isolation. While initially crucial for survival, this cohesiveness may lead to a dysfunctional enmeshment.

Other organizational problems may result from migrations that involve prolonged separations among nuclear family members as when father migrates first and mother reorganizes with the children into a one-parent family supported by the extended family in the native country. When some families reunite a second reorganization takes place, analogous to the incorporation of a stepfather into the family unit, but other families may never fully recover from the separation. Further imbalances may occur during the process of acculturation. For example, family members may experience acculturation at different speeds and with varying styles as a result of a division of roles that is functional to the survival of the family. A wife may stay at home and become increasingly isolated and loyal to the original culture, while her husband is learning the new language and values. Or the children may become sociocultural and language intermediaries between the parents and Anglo-American society, weakening the authority of the parents and aggravating generational conflicts.

Cultural values evolve as part of a process of change linked to stages of acculturation. Differences in many areas of life can be described for the Mexican newly arrived in the United States, the Mexican American who has resided in this country for a decade or more, and the Chicano who was born in this country (Karrer & Falicov, 1982). The cultural norms that govern family life gradually change and begin to resemble American norms, or the old norms clash with the new ones and cause internal dissonance or conflict with external norms, or eventually an integration of old and new norms may take place.

In spite of inevitable acculturation, there is evidence that Mexican American families who have resided in the United States for several generations preserve many identifiable threads of the original culture. Even families who are upwardly mobile become acculturated but not assimilated and many retain their language and ethnic identity (Gordon, 1964; Teske & Nelson, 1976). This is probably due at least in part to Mexico's proximity. Trips to and from the native land help renew the ties, maintain a group of reference, activate a support system, and reaffirm ethnic identity. Often the family plans for a permanent reunion of the family of origin and even of the extended network in the adoptive country (Carlos & Sellers, 1972).

A recent comparative study indicates that Mexicans move toward and within the kin network while Anglo-Americans move away from the kin network (Mindel, 1980). This persistence of the extended family is adaptive to situations of poverty, environmental stress, and the sociocultural isolation of the ethnic neighborhood. As in the native village, the presence of extended family members in the community exerts many supervisory pressures upon children and adolescents. Thus, the extended family often acts as a partial buffer against the stresses of acculturation. When these community influences are missing they must be supplied by the parents through restrictions on children's activities, selection of friends, and increased discipline, which in turn tend to increase intergenerational conflicts.

The reestablishment of the three-generational arrangement results in a complex and rich situation with the presence of members who know the old culture, others who are most aware of the stresses of adaptation to the new one, and still others, the younger ones, who represent the new culture.

Therapeutic Process

The aspects of the therapeutic process discussed in this section are some general comments about the therapist's and the family's cultural values; appropriate therapeutic approaches; the formation of a therapeutic alliance and the initial interviews with Mexican Americans; and arriving at a problem definition and corresponding therapist's role and interventions.

Therapist–Family Interaction

Family therapy involves transactions between two sets of cultural values, the values of the therapist and the values of the family. The training of therapists has usually been permeated by the U.S. middle-class values of individualism, egalitarianism, self-determination, self-fulfillment, future orientation, achievement, and optimism. These values beget expectations about the behavior of clients, set standards for what constitutes mental health, and are implicit in theories of problem formation, the mechanisms of change, and even cure. Thus, the therapist expects the family to keep appointments and be on time, to take responsibility for their own actions, to solve problems, to plan for the future, and to express verbally all of their concerns. In contrast, traditional Latin American ideals stress family interdependence and loyalty, age and sex hierarchies, collectivism and continuity, affiliation and cooperation. A Mexican American family may want the therapist to be casual about keeping appointments, to take the initiative for change, and to give advice or educate them as to the solution to their problems.

Cultural values are most significant during the early phase of therapy, when family and therapist are attempting to develop common grounds. Above all, the cultural norms of a family need to be understood and respected. However, there are situations where the goal of therapy may be "to counter the culture bind," that is, oppose a cultural norm (Whitaker, 1976). "Living the culture" and its ideals can inhibit the development of personal identities and lead to a dysfunctional exaggeration of the customary cultural patterns. Families may indeed benefit from exposure to different cultural values; for example, a Mexican father locked in rigid authoritarianism might benefit from a therapist who can model egalitarianism, and by the same token, a task-oriented WASP might benefit from exposure to a therapist from a person-oriented culture.

The families on which the following clinical observations are based generally come to therapy at the suggestion or mandate of the school, the court, or some other agency—most often for a problem with one of their children. The therapist needs to find out who and how compelling the referral source is and whether the family agrees with the recommendation. The presenting problems are varied, but there are usually specific symptoms in the children, such as school phobias; learning problems; enuresis and encopresis; truancy or other forms of disobedience and minor delinquency; nervous tics; night terrors; hair pulling; excessive masturbation. Upon exploration, other problems may emerge. Among the most common are financial difficulties, unemployment and/or alcoholism in the father, health complaints in the mother, and marital or parent–child conflict.

It is likely that the family has already turned to other sources for help, which varies with the type of problem experienced. For marital or parent–child conflicts, relatives and clergymen are frequently consulted. For problems with children, a wide range of helpers, including relatives, friends, *compadres*, priests, or family physicians are consulted. For emotional problems, such as anxiety and depression, which the individual does not connect directly to a family situation, a physician is most often consulted (Keefe, Padilla, & Carlos, 1978b). In cases of severe illness or recent death in the family, religious people may turn to propitiatory religious practices for solace and hope for recovery. Among the most common are promise making, offerings to the church (such as medals, amulets, or candles), prayer offerings, and votive promises that usually include deprivation of some physical comfort (Nall & Speilberg, 1978). The use of folk medicine occasionally surfaces when treating families of Mexican descent who maintain two systems of beliefs and practices regarding illness and health. The most prevalent is modern Western medicine, but some families still practice *curanderismo* (rural folk medicine) either before, after, or simultaneously with modern remedies (Rubel, 1960; Torrey, 1972; Kiev, 1968). In recent years, the role of the *curandero* appears to have become increasingly circumscribed to the treatment of specific symptoms associated with folk illnesses, such as *susto*, *mal de ojo*, or *empacho*. [For an excellent comprehensive description of folk illnesses, see Gonzalez (1976).]

Mexican Americans tend to attribute their emotional problems to two main causes: family conflicts and financial difficulties, in that order (Moll, Rueda, Reza, Herrera, & Vasquez, 1976). Because of the belief that many emotional problems are the product of social interactions between nuclear or extended family members or between one family member and someone from the larger community and because of the great importance attributed to the family in general, family therapy is easily accepted as an approach to individual symptoms. It is interesting that even folk illnesses are often attributed to interpersonal problems, such as envy.

Although a family may appear to be tentative and guarded, the members usually do want treatment, and from early on the therapist is respected as an authority on human relations. A word should be said here about the common misconception that Mexican fathers are difficult to engage in family therapy. It is possible that negative stereotypes about Mexican *machismo*, which emphasize the male's reluctance to ask for help, result in the therapist being hesitant to engage the father, and the stereotypes, therefore, act as a self-fulfilling prophecy. To counter this negative preconception we can argue that positive cultural meanings of *machismo* include loyalty, fairness, responsibility, and family centrality. These qualities can become a bridge, rather than a barrier, in engaging Mexican American fathers in family therapy (Ramirez, 1979). Very few fathers refuse an invitation extended by a therapist who appreciates the positive side of *machismo* and emphasizes both the father's centrality as the head of the household and the therapist's willingness to help his family. Another common misconception is that Mexican fathers have difficulties in accepting a woman in the authority role of therapist. Women professionalism is more widespread in Latin America than in the United States, and, in general, Mexican people who have had very limited access to educational opportunities value the knowledge and manners of an educated person regardless of sex.[2]

Therapeutic Approaches

Inevitably, the therapist's theoretical orientation, a type of subculture in itself, plays a role in the conceptualization of the problem, the goals delineated, and the methodology used to achieve them. Mexican American families of lower socioeconomic levels appear to respond best to a brief and

2. An interesting bit of relevant peasant mythology indicates that young women from small villages who go to work in the city, upon their return are regarded by the local people as a kind of *bruja* (witch) because of their assertiveness, manners, and aspirations. The term *bruja* is an ambivalent one but commands considerable admiration and even fear (Lewis, 1951).

problem-oriented approach that redefines the problem in interactional terms centered on the relationship between parents and children. The cultural emphasis on hierarchies within the family lends itself to a structural family therapy approach (Aponte & Van Deusen, 1981; Haley, 1976; Minuchin, 1974) that emphasizes generational boundaries in contrast to approaches sponsoring equal rights for all family members.

Within a problem-oriented framework, an emotive and dramatic tone is more appealing than an efficient, highly structured, and contractual approach such as behavior modification. When feelings are subtly elicited by the therapist, Mexican Americans respond much more openly than when they are asked to describe and explain their feelings and reactions. An experiential communication approach with emphasis on "telling it like it is" or "baring one's soul" or interpretations about nonverbal behavior will be threatening insofar as it challenges inhibitions about personal disclosure and supports symmetrical interactions. On the other hand, indirect approaches to change such as the use of positive reframing or paradoxical interventions utilized by the Brief Therapy Center of the Mental Research Institute (Weakland, Fisch, Watzlawick, & Bodin, 1974) can be very effective with Mexican families who are resistant to change.

Culture-specific modifications of widely used structural and strategic approaches such as Haley's (1976) first interview format are necessary to facilitate the formation of a therapeutic system, the definition of the problem, and the appropriate goals and interventions. Some guidelines are offered in the following sections to help arrive at such culture-specific adaptations.

Forming a Therapeutic Alliance

SOCIAL PHASE

There are significant variations from one culture to another in the styles of communication among strangers (Hall, 1959, 1976). With Mexicans, initial encounters tend to be formal, polite, and reserved. However, once a relationship is established, hugging or touching and impromptu visiting are common, and over time friendships tend to assume the quality of kinship. Americans, in contrast, are generally casual and friendly—often using first names from the time of introduction. Yet, when social intimacy does develop (usually after a considerable amount of time), individuals customarily continue to maintain a certain distance.

Taking these differences into account, the therapist should address the Mexican American family in a polite and formal manner, using last names to introduce himself or herself and when speaking to the adults. An informal and egalitarian approach, second nature to Americans, may be confusing or actually considered improper by Mexican American clients; direct questioning, informal use of language, and expectations of full disclosure may increase suspicions and sharpen defenses. However, keeping appropriate distance in forming a therapeutic alliance does not negate the value of warmth, playfulness with children, humorous remarks, or praising a clever statement.

A social phase that transmits the therapist's interest in the persons involved rather than focusing on procedures (such as referral sheets and precise dates) is essential, given the cultural emphasis on *personalismo*. When the family and the therapist have had more prolonged contact, it is not unusual for the family to invite the therapist to its home either to observe something for therapeutic purposes or to participate in a social occasion, like graduation from school. Gifts and homemade items are sometimes offered to the therapist during treatment or at termination.

Whenever possible, it is advisable for the therapist to use the mother tongue since lack of proficiency in English is common among Mexican Americans. With acculturated or American-born clients there may be some question as to which language is in fact dominant. Those clients who speak English with difficulty have the added demands of decoding and encoding (Pitta, Marcos, & Alpert, 1978). This can produce anxiety, blocking of expressiveness, or even a failure to integrate affect with experience. Unless the therapist's goal is to decrease the emotional reactivity, it is preferable to use Spanish, if only because it is the more emotionally charged language.

Whether the family speaks Spanish or English, the Mexican linguistic style tends to vary from public to private situations. In public, it is prone to allusions, indirect statements, and guardedness; while in private conversations—reserved only for intimate relationships—it may be bolder and more direct (Paz, 1961). These patterns of disclosure have implications for therapy. A tone of acceptance that avoids direct confrontation or demands for greater disclosure is desirable throughout treatment. The use of humor, allusions, and diminutives soften the directness and are often more effective forms of delivery because they mirror cultural transactional styles. Disclosure can be facilitated when the therapist becomes a philosopher of life through story telling, anecdotes, and humor. Use of analogies, proverbs, popular songs, or a mysterious, unexpected communication that transmits an existential sense of the absurd, the impossibility to win, or the reversals that life plays is consonant with Mexican cultural themes. These types of communication introduce flexibility into the family system while building the therapeutic alliance, and it is possible to use them in conjunction with structural interventions aimed at producing change in the family organization.

Since cultural norms emphasize the importance of the parent–child dyad over the marital dyad, during the initial stages a focus on parent–child interactions is more readily accepted than a focus on marital issues or on issues concerning the parents' families of origin. A Mexican woman, for example, feels more challenged to perform as a mother than as a wife, companion, or sexual partner. Furthermore, a therapeutic focus on individual needs over familial needs will meet with resistance. For example, it is unwise to try to convince a Mexican mother that she needs time for herself when attempting to decrease her involvement with her children. This goes against the cultural ideal of maternal self-sacrifice. Instead, it is preferable, for example, to motivate her to teach the children responsibility by planning to do one or two fewer things for them without letting them know which ones. This can be explained to the mother as allowing the children to develop necessary survival skills.

Although women who are interviewed alone or with their children often blame their husbands for creating marital and family problems, only highly acculturated or middle-class couples contemplating separation or divorce are likely to request marital treatment. Mexicans see satisfaction in marriage as the result of good fortune and wise choices, not as something to be attained by working on the relationship. Rather, they tend to search for compensation in other areas of their lives, particularly in their relationship with their children. Another obstacle to open discussion of marital difficulties is the value Mexicans place on curtailing public displays of anger or hostility between spouses. These injunctions against direct expression of aggression prompt the widespread use of *indirectas*. These take various forms, such as criticism by allusion ("*one* that I know never finishes her work," "*some* people never change"), self-deprecation, use of the diminutive in a cutting way, and belittlement (Lewis, 1951). While these patterns may seem dysfunctional to a therapist from another culture, according to Diaz-Guerrero (1975), the degree of "truth" between a husband and a wife should not be measured by how well it corresponds to the therapist's values of openness and directness but by whether it helps the couple get along.

If it appears necessary to address issues of marital harmony, this should definitely be postponed until a strong therapeutic alliance has been established. In the initial stages therapeutic leverage can be obtained by appealing to the parents' interest in the well-being and happiness of each child, the siblings' relationship, or the family as a whole.

The search for strengths and the genuine use of praise that gives the family a sense of its own dignity and the appreciation of the therapist have a strong impact. Explanations about the reasons for dysfunction or direct confrontation tend to increase the Mexican American family's sense of insecurity and may be perceived as disapproval by the therapist rather than as stimulus for change.

GATHERING INFORMATION

Some exploration of the family's immigration pattern is useful in establishing a frame of reference. It is good to begin with questions about how long the family has been in the United States, who immigrated first and who has been left behind, and what stresses were experienced by the various members of the family. (For the American-born family of Mexican descent, it is preferable to explore these origins only when they appear to be relevant.) The family's alliances and splits may be manifested in the losses or gains expressed. When the course of migration is discussed, the therapist should not get bogged down in details or become too interested in apparent contradictions about dates or events. The family's evasiveness may be an attempt to conceal their illegal status or their economic hardships back home. At this stage, it is important that the therapist be empathetic with the plight of the immigrant family, while stressing positive aspects of immigration such as the fact that immigrants seek a better life for themselves and their families. If the therapist has had similar experiences in his or her family, sharing them may facilitate the therapeutic encounter. However, the therapist needs to be cautious about commenting on cultural similarities with a client family that may either not exist or that the family may not want to acknowledge at a given point. General statements that suggest human kinship, such as "I like holding babies" or "I am a mother of young children, too" have a wide, effective range (Minuchin, 1974).

The proximity of the extended family and their involvement with the nuclear family should also be explored to decide whether their presence in the sessions is desirable. A considerable number of families have a maternal or paternal relative living with them. Often a Mexican American family will spontaneously bring a relative to the session who has either driven them to the clinic or who is visiting with the family.

In moving to a discussion of the presenting problem, addressing questions to the father first, then to the mother, then to other adults, and finally to the older and younger children, respects traditional age/sex hierarchies and conveys *respeto*. A neutral opening that allows the family to choose its own spokesperson is also appropriate. However, if an adolescent son or daughter begins the session, it is usually symptomatic of a weakened executive system and contrary to the public sociocultural norms. Redirecting the opening to the parent helps reestablish culturally consonant generational boundaries and build trust in the therapist.

Asking the family their ideas about why the presenting problem exists may elucidate cultural beliefs about illnesses and their origin in the family. Questions about what approaches have already been tried and how these have worked can also provide information about views on the "inheritance" or social origins of the problem or other theories that point to alliances and splits within the family.

During the initial stages, it is not advisable for the therapist to challenge the family's verbal statements that their life-style follows culturally prescribed norms, even if their actual behavior suggests otherwise. For example, a wife may say that her husband is the "boss," although the therapist and the rest of the family are all aware that she is dominating the therapy session and the family. These observations need to be placed in their cultural context and internally noted—but not verbalized. They are equivalent to what Ferreira (1963) has labeled "family myths," but since they are supported by the culture, they can also be labeled "cultural myths." As such, they represent a sort of "official party line" that should not be questioned initially. Instead, the family's capacity for change can be probed through the use of culturally consonant approaches. If the wife appears to support her husband publicly although she seems to disagree with him covertly, the therapist might ask her to go beyond her role of quiet supporter and to be even more supportive by providing him with new ways or ideas about child rearing rather than to encourage her to express her disagreement openly. If it appears that the husband should assume a more ascendant role and be regarded as more influential by his family, the family interactions can be reframed in the context of what "ought to be" according to the culture. The therapist could interpret the wife's frequent glancing at her husband as she talks as asking for his approval or guidance. This can transform the family's experience of him from a passive man to a silent, powerful patriarch.

In these approaches, the public reality of cultural values is used to form a coalition with external forces such as religion, society, or culture to exert leverage for change (or for stability) in the private, idiosyncratic relationships within the family. Jackson (1965) described a similar use of values as interpersonal tactics or homeostatic devices used by family members on each other.

Awareness of the developmental norms, child-rearing practices, and the family organization dictated by the culture is helpful, but if the therapist does not know a cultural norm or wishes to hear the family present what a particular norm means to them, he or she can ask questions such as: "How old do you think your daughter should be before she wears lipstick? . . . goes out on dates?" This approach has the advantage of acknowledging the parents' authority and can bring out difficult topics such as sex, pregnancy, or family secrets. The therapist should *not*, however, make an issue of his or her ignorance since this would tend to decrease the therapist's authority and create greater cultural distance from the family.

The current sociocultural context is another major influence to be considered when evaluating the family's adaptation. It is necessary, for example, to assess the safety of the neighborhood—the crime rate; gang-related activities—before assuming excessive restrictiveness on the part of the parents. All of this information becomes relevant to the appropriate definition of a problem.

CLOSURE

Families usually provide sufficient information in the first session to allow the therapist to formulate a working hypothesis that can be summarily described to a family. However, to close the first interview with an explicit "contract" may be too task oriented for Mexicans, who tend to be person oriented. A general agreement about what the treatment approach will be and an estimate of the number of sessions can be made; but treatment objectives should be phrased simply and focused on either the specific symptom or on improving parent–child relationships.

It is possible to send the family home with a task that is not too elaborate, one that is phrased as something the family might try should the opportunity arise. This approach is more consonant with Latin American culture, which values serendipity, chance, and spontaneity in interpersonal relationships. Unlike Anglo-Americans, Latin Americans would not be comfortable with the idea of scheduling certain times to be intimate, express affection, or resolve problems. Thus, failure to perform a task of that nature assigned in therapy should not be mistaken for a lack of motivation.

Finally, because of the cultural emphasis on cooperation either out of respect for authority or because of affiliation with peers, Mexicans feel that it is impolite to disagree, and this, too, may interfere with the formation of a therapeutic alliance. In fact, there is a popular proverb that says, "Mexicans have a hundred ways of saying no without ever saying it." A Mexican family may seemingly accept—by not overtly rejecting—the terms of the treatment suggested by the therapist, even though they are covertly resistant to what is being presented. Encouraging the family to express their reactions (both positive and negative) to the proposals may pay off and begin to establish a tone of mutuality.

Problem Definition and Selection of Therapist's Role

Understanding the family's cultural norms and present social context is perhaps the single most important factor in defining the family's problem and selecting the appropriate role for the therapist in the treatment process. In our experience, we found that four types of behavior and problem patterns, and corresponding treatment goals and interventions, need to be distinguished: cultural patterns, situational stress patterns, dysfunctional patterns of cultural transition, and transcultural dysfunctional patterns. This typology of problems has been developed from the study of Mexican American families, but it could probably be applied to other ethnic families in cultural transition.

CULTURAL PATTERNS

Cultural patterns include culturally determined belief systems, developmental norms, and family roles and rules. For example, a 5-year-old child sitting on his mother's lap or a 3-year-old child drinking out of her bottle, although not in line with Anglo norms, are not patterns in need of change. These child-rearing practices are consonant with Mexican ideals that stress nurturance as opposed to autonomy. To cite another example, the cultural variations in perferred physical distance observable between strangers are also noticeable among family members. An office that has a couch that comfortably seats three Mexican American family members, accommodates only two Anglo-American family members. To judge the Mexican American family as overinvolved, or overprotective, would be to conceptualize as deviant or pathological patterns that are the cultural norm and that should be respected as such. These patterns do not require intervention on the part of the therapist, who becomes a "cultural observer."

In fact, generally, the therapist will not see a Mexican American family unless one of the following dysfunctional patterns is also present.

SITUATIONAL STRESS PATTERNS

Situational stress patterns occur at the interface between the family and society. They include problems of social isolation; of lack of knowledge about social or community resources; or of dissonance between the normative expectations of the home and of the school,[3] peer group, or other institution. Often it is difficult to distinguish the multiple situational problems created by poverty from those caused by migration.

If these problems impair the family's ability to cope with internal demands, then the therapist needs to become a "social intermediary" or "matchmaker" between the family and the community. Specific strategies geared toward the alleviation of environmental stress and help with the adaptational process have been described by Minuchin (1974). Erickson (1975) has also discussed the use of social networks in clinical practice. The therapist who is proficient at network analysis can mobilize the family to use existing networks or can facilitate the building of new reciprocal relationships in the community. Networks based on mutual aid can give economic, emotional, and educational assistance, which are invaluable resources for families struggling with the problems of cultural adaptation. One immediate resource for communal activities is the parish or parochial school. Priests, if sensitive to problems of poverty, can offer significant spiritual support, especially when dealing with physical illness, old age, and death. Other resources can be provided by extended family, friends, and neighbors. Godparents, for instance, can have supportive and auxiliary functions as advocates for the child, temporary relief for the parents, or intermediaries between the school and the family. Given their relative emotional distance from the family's problem, they may be more effective in those roles than grandparents are.

Some examples of therapeutic action with families and concomitant action in the living or working environment are illustrated by the research team directed by Elkaïm (1980) in an impoverished district of Brussels. Elkaïm stresses the concept of "defamilization," that is, the refusal to reduce the causes of a symptom solely to the family context and to ignore the economic, social, cultural, and political dimensions.

As a social intermediary it is often necessary for the therapist to assume an active role as a link between the family and appropriate institutional, neighborhood, or network resources. Simple and instrumental explanations

3. For further definition and specific discussion of the difficulties in developing effective approaches to deal with the problems of sociocultural dislocation between the home and the school, see Montalvo (1974).

and solutions should be considered, first, before searching for complex and purely psychological aspects. The following example illustrates many of the points relevant to a situational stress pattern and its management:

> An elderly lady, Mrs. R, was referred to a mental health center by a priest. She had been seeing him because she was depressed and irritable and had been losing weight. Mrs. R was in an isolated situation within the ethnic neighborhood. She had migrated from Mexico eight years before to live with her two sons and an older single daughter. Two years ago the sons had moved to a nearby city in search of better jobs, and Mrs. R had remained with her daughter who spoke no English and did not work. Among other questions, the therapist asked, "Are you losing weight because you have lost your appetite?" Mrs. R quipped, "No, I've lost my teeth, not my appetite! That's what irks me!" Indeed, Mrs. R had almost no teeth left in her mouth. Apparently, her conversations with the priest (an American who had learned to speak Spanish during a South American mission) had centered on the emotional losses she had suffered recently as the cause of her "anxious depression" without considering the practical issues. As an undocumented immigrant, Mrs. R had no medical insurance, did not know any dentists, and had no financial resources. It was necessary for the therapist to help find dental care for Mrs. R. Finally, a university dental clinic agreed to have her seen by supervised practicum students. This required a long trip to another part of the city to an institution that had no Spanish-speaking personnel. Mrs. R also needed reassurance that her undocumented legal status would not result in any consequences for her or her sons.
>
> The next step was to enlist the cooperation of a bilingual neighbor, Rose, to accompany Mrs. R to her appointments at the dental clinic. Rose was willing to do it. To reciprocate (and with only a hint on the therapist's part), Mrs. R began to do some baby-sitting for Rose's young baby.

DYSFUNCTIONAL PATTERNS OF CULTURAL TRANSITION

Dysfunctional patterns of cultural transition are interactional patterns reflecting organizational changes that initially helped to accomplish the immigrant's objectives but eventually became rigid and hampered some aspect of the family's functioning. Normal developmental stresses can be intensified, or developmental transitions—such as becoming independent and leaving home—can become more problematic when the family must be organized to adapt to a new environment. For example, given parents' long-standing dependency on their older children to be intermediaries with the larger culture, parents who might otherwise work out a gradual separation find it impossible to do so. Younger siblings, too, may cling to an older brother or sister who appears to be much less old-fashioned and more understanding than the parents.

Some studies indicate that the stresses of acculturation and parent–child cultural dissonance may play a major role in the occurrence of delinquency

(Doob, 1970; Bogardus, 1943–1944) and drug abuse (Vaillant, 1966; Alexander & Dibb, 1975) in young people. Although comparable data do not exist for Mexican Americans, there is also evidence (Szapocznik, Scopetta, & Tillman, 1978) of an epidemic of abuse—and frequent overdose with sedatives and tranquilizers among middle-aged Cuban women who were challenged in their maternal role and were in intense conflict with their Americanized adolescent children.

To deal with these types of problems, the therapist can assume the role of cultural mediator or of family intermediary. Acting as a "cultural mediator," the therapist can challenge the present dysfunctional pattern by labeling it a deviation from the family's cultural heritage. For example, the idea can be conveyed to the parents that the children have too much power for their own good by using statements like: "In Mexico, children know how to behave, but they get here and forget. You need to go back to the old traditions."

The culture's life cycle rituals can also be used to deal with developmental impasses linked to cultural transition. The therapist can encourage the family to perform "initiation rites" or *fiestas* at times such as engagements, weddings, baptisms, and graduations (from kindergarten on through graduate school). Occasionally, a therapist might suggest that it is the absence of such a ritual that is causing confusion about whether a certain stage has been reached, and the family could be encouraged to invent a ritual. For example, while Mexican girls have a *quinceañera* (cotillion) at age 15 to announce their entrance into womanhood, there is no equivalent ritual for boys. A family having difficulty letting go of an adolescent son could be urged to invent a ritual to symbolize the son's entrance into manhood. Sometimes, the appearance of other developmental requirements can facilitate the resolution of developmental transitions. Often a mother's depression about her daughter's marriage may be resolved when the daughter bears a child or when her own mother begins to require more of her attention. With those families who practice Catholicism, prayer and religious rituals (e.g., the mass and the sacraments of baptism, eucharist, and penance) can also be used for therapeutic purposes.

As a family intermediary the therapist's function is to clarify expectations, to "translate" family members' "cultural" behavior to one another, to justify conflict, to encourage compromise and negotiation, and to correct or ameliorate structural imbalances that have resulted from the cultural transition. The following case illustrates interactional patterns prompted by cultural transition (as well as some cultural and situational patterns) and the various components of the role of the therapist as family intermediary.

> Javier, a 16-year-old boy, was referred by his school for persistent truancy. Nine years ago, his family, consisting of mother, father, and four younger siblings, had moved from Tijuana, Mexico, to San Diego, California, to

better their economic situation. Javier was bilingual and served as the family interpreter in their dealings with outside institutions, but he preferred to speak English and was clearly more acculturated than his parents.

The father began the session by complaining bitterly about Javier's unruly behavior, lack of cooperation with his mother, and lack of respect toward his parents. The mother appeared to agree with her husband's views about Javier, although she protested that she did not need much help around the house. (This interaction between the parents could be recognized as culturally patterned.)

Whenever the father escalated pressures for compliance, Javier would become more rebellious and would threaten to leave home to find a job. Because of Javier's higher degree of acculturation, he had considerably more power in the outside world than did his parents. And, influenced by the greater degree of autonomy he observed in his American peers, it was difficult for Javier to assume a dependent and submissive attitude toward his parents. The father, defeated in his attempts to control his son, would turn to the mother and blame her for not raising the son properly, for being too "soft," and for not demanding enough of him. This situation would easily escalate into a parental conflict of mutual accusations. An inquiry about the father's occupation and present employment revealed that he had hoped to set up his own small business as a car mechanic after moving from Mexico. He had not succeeded and was supporting the family precariously with his occasional small jobs. Although he was very proud of his competence and honesty as an automobile mechanic (he proudly displayed a very old letter of recommendation from a client in Tijuana, which he always carried with him) he refused to go to work in a company under an Anglo foreman. In his view, "they [Americans] don't respect us Mexicans, and when you turn around they exploit you." It was clear to the therapist that the father's position in the family was further debilitated by his unemployment. The dilemma was how to approach a discussion of this subject without undermining him further.

The therapist decided to express her admiration for the father's integrity. He had remained honest in a business where there is so much dishonesty and had maintained his pride in his Mexican identity in spite of the financial difficulties it had occasioned him. The therapist then asked him if his family appreciated him. Father was obviously moved and said he did not know. The son intervened saying that his father was very stubborn and should let him find a job to help the family. Mother remarked that she also wanted to look for a job, but her husband would not allow it. This interaction gave the therapist the opportunity to reframe the son's opposition as showing care and concern for the family. Perhaps he had tried to grow up too fast and had tried to be practical in a rather American way, but the values of loyalty and solidarity—in contrast to Anglo values of individualism or "selfishness"—were obviously successfully inculcated by the parents.

The conflict between the parents and Javier was labeled as an understandable "misunderstanding" that often occurs between immigrant parents and their children because of apparent value differences. The therapist cited her own family as one in which those types of misunderstandings occurred.

Clarification of the different viewpoints in a positive light was a necessary step to creating bridges, emphasizing similarities, and narrowing the cultural gap between father and son. It was also necessary to decrease the son's power while encouraging his right to autonomy in certain areas and supporting the parent's authority in others. Therefore, Javier was asked what kind of job he would be able to get, thereby uncovering the fact that his job opportunities were almost nil. It seemed advisable, then, that he use his last year of school to prepare himself for the job market. The father was asked to reassure his son and his wife that he would take care of the financial situation. The father was willing to try his best to ensure the welfare of the family without abandoning his dignity. To create a more delineated boundary between the parental subsystem and Javier, the school counselor's cooperation was enlisted in dealing with Javier's plans for the future. The therapist continued to work with the parents with a focus on removing roadblocks to the employment of the father.

Another effective method of cultural mediation in families is for a therapist to interview separately—first, the parents and second, the siblings—and then to bring the whole family together for a feedback session with the therapist. Because of the sibling subgroup's large size and greater degree of acculturation, it is extremely influential. In a separate interview the siblings can negotiate issues they might not bring up with their parents present. Or their cooperation may be enlisted to extricate an overprotected or a parental child from the parental subsystem. Parents will tend to respect the feelings that siblings have for each other as a sign of sibling solidarity.

A therapist who speaks both Spanish and English has other options for cultural strategies. For example, a blurred generational boundary can be more clearly delineated by talking to the parents in Spanish and to the children in English. Or, when the generational boundary is excessively rigid, greater permeability can be achieved by asking the children to make an effort to communicate with their parents in Spanish. If both the family and the therapist are bilingual, mixing both languages during the session highlights the contrast between the old and the new and becomes a metaphor for the necessity for integrating both sets of values, as well as the language.

TRANSCULTURAL DYSFUNCTIONAL PATTERNS

Dysfunctional family patterns may be aggravated by cultural adaptation, but they belong to categories of universal or, at least, transcultural human problems. A limited range of repetitive interactional behaviors, developmental impasses, hierarchical imbalances with rigid coalitions, or other boundary problems are characteristics of dysfunctional family systems probably found everywhere. Often, Mexican American families, like other families, come to therapy with problems of this nature, although the content may be organized around culture-specific issues.

When family therapists are confronted with dysfunctional behavior that clearly transcends cultural patterns, the more traditional techniques of family therapy must be used, tempered by accommodating therapeutic goals to fit cultural definitions of universal values and using knowledge of each family's culture to select the timing and content of the therapeutic strategy.

The process of individuation, for example, is universal, but its characteristics, which include quantity and quality of differentiation, behavioral markers, timing, and implementation, vary from culture to culture. Thus, a therapist perceiving a need for greater individuation in a 9-year-old Mexican American boy, may encourage him—in the Anglo pattern—to seek friendships outside the home by joining a neighborhood club or to take more responsibility by getting a newspaper route. On the other hand, his parents may feel that giving him a few household chores or allowing him to run an occasional errand—duties that do not warrant payment or an allowance— are sufficient acknowledgment of more maturity.

Unfortunately, much of what has been said and written about the "typical" Mexican family assumes inherent pathology (Montiel, 1973). Such ethnic stereotyping may lead the therapist to form precipitous conclusions and to omit necessary therapeutic action. For example, an emphasis on the behavioral pattern of enmeshment as merely a cultural stylistic preference may lead to overlooking instances of dysfunctional enmeshment. In the following case, the focus on the child at the expense of the marital relationship, the self-sacrifice of the mother, and the extreme closeness between the mother and the child all had a culturally consonant quality, but the degree and rigidity of these behaviors and the consequences for family members were clearly dysfunctional.

Frank G, Jr., 9 years old, was referred by Children's Hospital for night terrors and multiple fears. The following history of the family was obtained.

Mrs. G was born and raised in Mexico. She remained at home through her 20s and was very attached to her parents, particularly her mother, in an intensely ambivalent relationship. Her mother did not want her to study nursing (which she eventually did after much struggle) for fear that she might get sexually involved with somebody while away in school. After finishing nursing school, she returned home and sometime in her 30s, she met Mr. G, who was an older single man. She felt, however, that she could not marry and leave home until her mother died. Following her mother's death, she married Mr. G and went to live with him in the United States.

Mr. G came from a very poor Mexican American family, and early in his life he became a street boy, successfully fending for himself, but being suspicious and distant from others.

Their initial marital adjustment went smoothly until Frank, Jr. was born. At that time, in their own words, the "apple of the discord" was planted. Mother and son became a very close dyad. They began to sleep in the same bed, displacing father to the living room sofa. Disagreements around handling the boy mounted, with mother always protecting him while father was becoming the peripheral "ugly monster" who, according to mother, was brutal and uncaring. During the interview, father did not appear at all brutal or primitive; on the contrary, he seemed to make more sense and to be more cogent about what type of family environment Frank, Jr. needed than did his wife.

This family's first attempts to get help with Frank, Jr.'s extreme fears and dependency on mother started around the time he entered kindergarten. After seeking treatment at several agencies, mother and son were hospitalized and placed under heavy sedation during a mutual psychotic episode when Frank, Jr. was 6 years old. At that time, the psychiatrists felt this was a hopeless case and advised sending the boy to Mexico to live with relatives; the family complied. Mother said separation from the boy was like death to her.

After some time Mrs. G began to recover, and the relationship with her husband improved. Mr. G returned to the matrimonial bed and the discord subsided, until the relatives in Mexico reported that Frank, Jr. was having nightmares. Mother went to fetch the boy and brought him home, where he again displaced father from the marital bed to the sofa, presumably because of the boy's night terrors. Subsequently, Frank, Jr. developed terrors about going anywhere alone, including to the bathroom. Mother and boy constituted an undifferentiated unit. Emotionally, father was locked out of this rigid triangle.

Because he appeared to be the only hope for change, the therapist supported and engaged Mr. G in many ways during the sessions. When he began to respond, Mrs. G could not tolerate her husband having a voice in the family and refused to have him in the sessions. Seeing her for a half-hour alone prior to the conjoint sessions proved fruitless. She always repeated: "Poor me and poor little boy."

A paradoxical task requiring much greater involvement of mother and child was attempted next. The mother was to monitor each and every activity of the boy, including going to school with him. This required asking permission from the principal and the teacher for her to sit next to the boy in the classroom and in the lunchroom. Contrary to expectations, rather than becoming dismayed and exhausted by this daily project, she readily agreed to do it. Father got upset by her willingness to do such a crazy thing and tried to interfere with setting up this task.

The principal and the teacher were contacted to develop a collaborative therapeutic plan. They agreed to sabotage the mother benevolently by always agreeing that she could be everywhere with the son but simultaneously frustrating her with innocent confusion of schedules, making her wait long periods in the office to fill out elaborate forms, making her ask permission from different teachers for special activities, and so on. The principal and the teacher told the mother they would schedule private conversations with Frank, Jr. to help him overcome the "embarrassment" he must feel since he still needed his mother so much.

Gradually, Frank, Jr. began to react by complaining that the boys were making fun of him and telling his mother he was not such a baby. During one of the sessions a conversation about growing up took place and Frank, Jr., who had become quite articulate, said that he wanted to live in his own apartment—with no mother, father, or wife, but with two pets, a cat and a dog, which he would train to live together from a very early age, because "if you get them old, they fight all the time." Father readily saw the connection between the pets and his parents and said, "The boy is right, perhaps the trouble between my wife and me is that we are like a cat and a dog who got married when we were too old to learn to live with each other and have children." Somehow this insightful remark seemed to summarize the universality of the key issues involves in this case.

Summary

Social, cultural, and medical anthropology; cross-cultural psychology; and sociology are disciplines that contain valuable knowledge about culture, family, and mental health. However, it would be an exceedingly difficult, compartmentalized, and lengthy undertaking to extract from these disciplines knowledge of cultural variations relevant to the therapeutic context. The task of building a theoretical model of family therapy that takes into account cultural variation can be facilitated by sharing the empirical knowledge gathered by practitioners.

This chapter offers a conceptual framework for family assessment and intervention that takes into account the sociocultural background and normative expectations of the Mexican American family. The problems presented by families who have migrated within the last three generations are classified as situational, cultural transition, and transcultural dysfunctional patterns. Each of these patterns requires specific therapeutic roles and interventions. The need to develop culturally attuned approaches and interventions at various phases of the treatment process (forming a therapeutic alliance, defining problems and goals, and choosing strategies) is emphasized and illustrated through clinical examples.

ACKNOWLEDGMENT

I am indebted to Betty M. Karrer for her valuable contribution during an earlier phase of this work and to Jill Metcoff for her thoughtful suggestions.

REFERENCES

Alexander, B.K., & Dibb, G.S. Opiate Addicts and Their Parents. *Family Process, 14,* 499–514, 1975.

Alvirez, D., & Bean, F.D. The Mexican American Family. In C. Mindel & R. Habenstein (Eds.), *Ethnic Families in America.* New York: Elsevier, 1976.

Aponte, H.J., & Van Deusen, J. Structural Family Therapy. In A.S. Gurman & D.P. Kniskern (Eds.), *Handbook of Family Therapy.* New York: Brunner/Mazel, 1981.

Bean, F.D. Components of Income and Expected Family Size among Mexican Americans. *Social Science Quarterly, 54,* 103–116, 1973.

Bogardus, E.S. Gangs of Mexican American Youth. *Sociology and Social Research, 28,* 55–66, 1943–1944.

Carlos, M.L., & Sellers, L. Family, Kinship Structure and Modernization in Latin America. *Latin America Research Review, 7*(2), 95–124, 1972.

Diaz-Guerrero, R. *Psychology of the Mexican: Culture and Personality.* Austin: University of Texas Press, 1975.

Doob, C.B. Family Background and Peer Group Development in a Puerto Rican District. *The Sociological Quarterly, 11,* 523–532, 1970.

Elkaïm, M. Family System and Social System: Some Examples of Interventions in an Impoverished District of Brussels. In M. Andolfi & I. Zwerling (Eds.), *Dimensions of Family Therapy.* New York: Guilford, 1980.

Erickson, G.D. The Concept of Personal Network in Clinical Practice. *Family Process, 14*(4), 487–498, 1975.

Falicov, C., & Karrer, B. Cultural Variations in the Family Life Cycle: The Mexican American Family. In E. Carter & M. McGoldrick (Eds.), *The Family Life Cycle and Family Therapy.* New York: Gardner Press, 1980.

Falicov, C.J. Families in Cultural Transition: An Ecosystemic Model. In D. Schnitman & C. Sluzki (Eds.), *Cross-Cultural and Transcultural Issues in Family Health Care.* In preparation.

Ferreira, A. Family Myth and Homeostasis. *Archives of General Psychiatry, 9,* 457–463, 1963.

Gonzalez, E. The Role of Chicano Folk Beliefs and Practices in Mental Health. In C.A. Hernandez, M.J. Haug, & N.N. Wagner (Eds.), *Chicanos: Social and Psychological Perspectives.* St. Louis, Mo.: C.V. Mosby, 1976.

Gordon, M. *Assimilation in American Life: The Role of Race, Religion and National Origins.* New York: Oxford University Press, 1964.

Grebler, L., Moore, J., & Guzman, R. The Family: Variations in Time and Space. In L.T. Duran & H.R. Bernard (Eds.), *Introduction to Chicano Studies, A Reader.* New York: Macmillan, 1973.

Haley, J. *Problem-Solving Therapy.* San Francisco: Jossey-Bass, 1976.

Hall, E.T. *The Silent Language.* Garden City, N.Y.: Doubleday, 1959.

Hall, E.T. *Beyond Culture.* Garden City, N.Y.: Encore Press, Doubleday, 1976.

Hawkes, G., & Taylor, M. Power Structure in Mexican and Mexican American Farm Labor Families. *Journal of Marriage and The Family, 31,* 807–811, 1975.

Hernandez, J., Estrada, L., & Alvirez, D. Census Data and the Problem of Conceptually Defining the Mexican American Population. *Social Science Quarterly, 56*(4), 671–687, 1973.

Jackson, D. The Study of the Family. *Family Process, 4,* 1–20, 1965.

Karrer, B., & Falicov, C.J. *The Acculturation of the Mexican Family: Therapeutic Implications.* Manuscript submitted for publication, 1982.

Keefe, S.E., Padilla, A.M., & Carlos, M.L. *Emotional Support Systems in Two Cultures: A Comparison of Mexican Americans and Anglo Americans.* Los Angeles: University of Califiornia, Spanish Speaking Mental Health Center, 1978. (a)

Keefe, S.E., Padilla, A.M., & Carlos, M.L. The Mexican American Family as an Emotional Support System. In J.M. Casas & S.E. Keefe (Eds.), *Family and Mental Health in the Mexican-American Community* (Monograph No. 7). Los Angeles: University of California, Spanish Speaking Mental Health Center, 1978. (b)

Kiev, A. *Curanderismo: Mexican-American Folk Psychiatry.* New York: Free Press, 1968.

Komarovsky, M. *Blue Collar Marriage.* New York: Vintage Books, 1962.

Levine, E.S., & Padilla, A.M. *Crossing Cultures in Therapy.* Belmont, Calif.: Wadsworth, 1980.

Lewis, O. *Life in a Mexican Village: Tepoztlan Restudied.* Urbana, Ill.: University of Illinois Press, 1951.

Madsen, W. *The Mexican-American of South Texas.* New York: Holt, Rinehart & Winston, 1964.

Mindel, C.H. Extended Families among Urban Mexican Americans, Anglos and Blacks. *Hispanic Journal of Behavioral Sciences, 2*(1), 21–34, 1980.

Minuchin, S. *Families and Family Therapy.* Cambridge: Harvard University Press, 1974.

Moll, L.C., Rueda, R.S., Reza, R., Herrera, J., & Vasquez, L.P. Mental Health Services in East Los Angeles: An Urban Community Case Study. In M.R. Miranda (Ed.), *Psychotherapy with the Spanish Speaking: Issues in Research and Service Delivery* (Monograph No. 3). Los Angeles: University of California, Spanish Speaking Mental Health Research Center, 1976.

Montalvo, B. Home–School Conflict and the Puerto Rican Child. *Social Casework, 55*(2), 100–110, 1974.

Montiel, M. The Chicano Family: A Review of Research. *Social Work, 18*(2), 22–23, 1973.

Nall, F.C., & Speilberg, J. Social and Cultural Factors in the Responses of Mexican Americans to Medical Treatment. In R.A. Martinez (Ed.), *Hispanic Culture and Health Care: Fact, Fiction and Folklore.* St. Louis, Mo.: C.V. Mosby, 1978.

Paz, O. *The Labyrinth of Solitude: Life and Thought in Mexico.* New York: Evergreen Books, 1961.

Peñalosa, F. Mexican Family Roles. *Journal of Marriage and the Family, 30*(4), 680–689, 1968.

Pitta, P., Marcos, L.R., & Alpert, M. Language Switching as a Treatment Strategy with Bilingual Patients. *The American Jounal of Psychoanalysis, 38,* 255–258, 1978.

Ramirez, R. Machismo: A Bridge Rather than a Barrier to Family Counseling. In P.P. Martin (Ed.), *La Frontera Perspective: Providing Mental Health Services to Mexican Americans.* Tucson, Ariz.: La Frontera Center, 1979.

Rubel, A.J. Concepts of Disease in Mexican-American Culture. *American Anthropology, 62,* 795–814, 1960.

Sluzki, C.E. Migration and Family Conflict. *Family Process, 18,* 379–390, 1979.

Stevens, E. Marianismo: The Other Face of Machismo. In A. Pescatello (Ed.), *Female and Male in Latin America.* Pittsburgh: University of Pittsburgh Press, 1973.

Szapocznik, J., Scopetta, M.A., & Tillman, W. What Changes, What Stays the Same and What Affects Acculturative Change? In J. Szapocznik & M.C. Jerrers (Eds.), *Cuban Americans: Acculturation, Adjustment and the Family.* Washington, D.C.: COSSMHO, The National Coalition of Hispanic Mental Health and Human Services Organizations, 1978.

Teske, R.H., & Nelson, B.H. An Analysis of Differential Assimilation Rates among Middle Class Mexican Americans. *The Sociological Quarterly, 17,* 218–235, 1976.

Torrey, E. *The Mind Game: Witchdoctors and Psychiatry.* New York: Emerson Hall, 1972.

Vaillant, G.E. Parent–Child Cultural Disparity and Drug Addiction. *Journal of Nervous and Mental Disease, 142,* 534–539, 1966.

Weakland, J., Fisch, R., Watzlawick, P., & Bodin, A.M. Brief Therapy: Focused Problem Resolution. *Family Process, 13*(2), 141–168, 1974.

Whitaker, A. The Hindrance of Theory in Clinical Work. In P. Guerin, Jr. (Ed.), *Family Therapy, Theory and Practice.* New York: Gardner Press, 1976.

8

Puerto Rican Families

NYDIA GARCIA-PRETO

In times of stress Puerto Ricans turn to their families for help. Their cultural expectation is that when a family member is experiencing a crisis or has a problem, others in the family are obligated to help, especially those who are in stable positions. Because Puerto Ricans rely on the family and their extended network of personal relationships, they will make use of social services only as a last resort (Badillo-Ghali, 1977).

The intent of this chapter is to provide family therapists with a beginning framework for working with Puerto Rican families. It provides some information about history, cultural values, family patterns, and the effects of migration and culture shock on the family. Clinical examples have been used to illustrate certain typical family patterns and therapeutic interventions that are culturally appropriate.

While this chapter makes reference at certain points to middle-class families and discusses Puerto Rican culture in general, the sections on migration and therapeutic intervention focus primarily on the problems of the low-income Puerto Rican family. These are the families who are usually referred to social welfare agencies and mental health centers.

Puerto Rican culture has been influenced by several different races and ethnic groups, and a present-day Puerto Rican family may consist of a mother who is White, a father who is Black, and children who are various shades of color. Their cultural ancestry may be a mixture of African, Taino, Corsican, and Spanish, though their ethnic identification will be Puerto Rican.

Not only are there differences among families, but members of a single family may also differ. These differences depend upon whether the formative years were spent in the United States or Puerto Rico, the balance achieved between the old culture and the demands and stresses of the new environment, and the rewards provided by the American milieu (Mizio, 1974).

Despite subcultural and interfamily differences, certain characteristics are common to Puerto Ricans. Families, especially in the continental United States will exhibit these characteristics in varying degrees depending on their

Nydia Garcia-Preto. Family Training, Youth Services, University of Medicine and Dentistry of New Jersey, and Community Mental Health Center of Rutgers Medical School, Piscataway, New Jersey.

level of acculturation. It is also important to note that because Puerto Ricans did not solidify as an ethnic group until the 1800s, the definition of their family patterns is probably less fixed than that of many other groups.

Historical Background

Before the Spanish settled Puerto Rico in 1500, the native population of the island was Taino Indian. What we know about these Indians is based primarily on retrospective archaeological studies conducted by Franz Boas (1940) and the writings of Fray Ramon Pane (1505). It is believed that most of the Taino died of hunger, overwork, or suicide shortly after the Spanish invasion (Fernandez-Mendez, 1970). Of those who survived, the men generally worked for the Spaniards and the women became their consorts.

Even though the Taino way of life soon faded, a few remnants of their culture are still visible. For instance, the value that Puerto Ricans place on preserving a peaceable demeanor is reminiscent of Taino tranquility; emphasis on kinship and dependence on the group are also Taino characteristics of Puerto Rican culture. Some of the physical characteristics of Puerto Ricans—skin color, hair texture, and bone structure—have also been identified as Indian. The names of certain fruits and vegetables (e.g., *yuca, guineo*) are believed to be Indian, as are the names of a number of towns (e.g., Yubucoa and Humacao).

In contrast, the Spanish influence is widely evident today. The Spaniards brought their language, literature, and food preferences to Puerto Rico, as well as the Roman Catholic religion and its rituals for birth, marriage, and death. Other Spanish legacies include the family's patriarchal structure and the double standard regarding sexual behavior. In addition, the pride, dignity, and flamboyance of Spaniards are important ingredients in Puerto Rican culture. Many aspects of Spanish culture, such as the Catholic worship of saints and belief in an afterlife and the strong sense of family obligation, blended well with the Indian culture. This may account for some of the difficulty in sorting out Puerto Rican traits that are distinctly Taino.

The Spaniards brought African slaves to the island to work in the production of sugar cane (Wagenheim & Wagenheim, 1973). The Africans in turn contributed their language, food, musical instruments, religion, and medicine men to the cultural mix of the island. They also carried with them the fatalism of an enslaved race. Although there were fewer slaves in Puerto Rico than on other islands, such as Haiti, Jamaica, or Cuba, Puerto Ricans suffered the same horrors as slaves elsewhere. For example, slave owners gave little regard to maintaining the stability and permanence of the slave family and often took slave women for their consorts. Although the slaves were freed in 1873, most remained poor and dependent on their previous owners.

In 1898, the United States invaded and colonized Puerto Rico. In 1900, a U.S. governor was appointed to head a civil government made up of island residents. The United States retained the power to veto any laws they might pass and the resident commissioner, who represented Puerto Rico in the U.S. House of Representatives, had no vote. The United States also mandated the use of English as the language of instruction in the public schools. Considering that few people on the island—not even the teachers—spoke English, this was perhaps the cruelest aberration imposed on the people of Puerto Rico.

In 1917, the island's participation in its own government was increased. A bill of rights was established and U.S. citizenship was granted. At the same time, military service became obligatory for all eligible males. Puerto Rico elected its first governor in 1948, and in 1952 it became a commonwealth. With this latter change, Spanish was reinstituted as the language of instruction in public schools, with English becoming the second language.

Real political power over Puerto Rico, however, still rests in the U.S. House Committee on Insular Affairs and the Senate Committee on Territorial and Insular Affairs. Puerto Ricans continue to have little power over the fate of their island since they have no vote in U.S. elections. The political party in power favors statehood for Puerto Rico. However, there is a large group that prefers the present structure, and a smaller but active group that favors independence.

The migration of Puerto Ricans to the United States began in the early 1900s. The granting of U.S. citizenship to Puerto Ricans in 1917 facilitated the process. They came primarily to the northern cities of the United States in search of jobs, education, political refuge, and adventure. Another motivation for migration has been the desire to solve family problems. For instance, a relative abroad may need help with child rearing, marital problems, or a sick relative. Other familial reasons are avoidance of difficult situations, such as the aftermath of a marital separation or legal difficulties.

After World War II the rate of migration increased, peaking in 1952 when it surpassed 52,000 (Rodriguez, Sanchez-Korrol, & Alers, 1980).

Although Puerto Rican communities in the Northeast have continued to expand, by 1969, there were more people returning to Puerto Rico than arriving in the United States (Rodriguez et al., 1980). Since no special documents are necessary for travel, migration from the island to the mainland continues to be marked by a back and forth movement that has strongly influenced Puerto Rican family life. "This phenomenon reinforces many links to the island, although it also reflects repeated ruptures and renewal of ties, dismantling and reconstruction of familial and communal networks in old and new settings" (Rodriguez et al., 1980, p. 2).

The Puerto Rican Economy

In addition to the historical blending of various ethnic and racial groups, economic factors have formed different subcultures in Puerto Rico. Originally, Puerto Rico was an agrarian society. The emphasis was on land and property ownership. This resulted in a two-class society—the rich and the poor.

After the U.S. invasion, industrialization rapidly affected all segments of the population. The towns and urban centers grew in size, and the populations became differentiated into classes or sociocultural groups.

The differences among wealthy landowners, ecclesiastical and lay officials, craftspersons, merchants, and subsistence farmers became more marked. One of the most important developments was the growth of a middle class. This new group was composed of people having varied occupations and income. They represented a new trend, a new set of values that ascribed major importance to the symbols of personal achievement and wealth.

Industrialization also appeared in rural areas. A value system based on cash began to replace one that had been based on personal relationships and services. Sugar, tobacco, and coffee became the most important products. Different geographic regions specialized in the production of each. As a result of the special ways in which these crops were cultivated and the distinctive environments of the regions, different subcultures developed.

The small farmers of tobacco and subsistence crops, known as *jibaros*, are a rural people of mixed ethnic origins. They have been characterized as laconic but shrewd and honest. They strive for upward mobility and value individual effort (Manners & Steward, 1953). Sugar cane workers have been found to have a stronger identification with the community than other groups (Wolf, 1952). Coffee growers have been known to have more patriarchal families with less flexibility in sex roles and family structure. Differences in occupational history will influence Puerto Rican attitudes, even after migration, and are based largely on the different demands on the daily lives of these groups.

Sugar cane workers own no land and live on wages earned during four or five months of the year. The rest of the year they must depend upon each other and unemployment benefits, therefore, they tend to avoid competition and to maximize mutual aid among neighbors. They are also informal about marriage, separations, and child-rearing practices.

In contrast, the coffee growers live a more isolated existence in the mountains. Having little contact with their neighbors, they must depend upon the extended family system for economic and social support. The roles of men, women, and children are clearly defined, with the husband being the authority who controls his wife and children.

The third group, the middle class, exhibit less group identity and emphasize competition and upward mobility. The U.S. pattern of feminine independence (Papajohn & Spiegel, 1975) has also influenced middle-class Puerto Rican women. Women in this group usually work, and many have professions. This may account for the apparent decline of male dominance and the increase of female autonomy. Middle-class children tend to remain dependent for longer periods than children from other classes. Unlike the children of the sugar cane workers and coffee growers, the middle-class children are not expected to do things for themselves. They are expected to finish high school, to attend college, and to qualify for occupations that will maintain their middle-class status.

The Puerto Rican upper class, in comparison to the other groups, is relatively small. It is distinguished by its wealth, prominence, and extreme Americanization (Manners & Steward, 1953).

Families will also present different styles of communication depending on their origins. For example, poor rural families, especially, tend to be soft-spoken, polite, and deliberate. They are less verbal and have a slower pace than urban middle-class families. In terms of seeking help, families who originate from sugar cane regions will probably use community resources more readily than descendants of coffee growers because of their dependence on the community for help.

As a result of these sociocultural differences, therapists working with Puerto Rican families are likely to observe marked contrasts in family structure, values, and patterns of socialization. Recognizing these variations will help therapists to make more accurate assessments and to provide appropriate interventions. For instance, when working with a rural family we may obtain better results with an approach that is experiential rather than verbal.

Cultural Values

It is difficult to treat Puerto Rican culture as an undifferentiated entity. Genralizations tend to obscure important differences. For instance, we may say Puerto Ricans emphasize spiritual and human rather than commercial values. However, while this may be true for those in the lower classes, persons in the middle and upper classes value possessions as highly symbolic of personal worth.

On the other hand, in order to present a paradigm of the culture, generalizations are necessary. The following section focuses on values that have been characterized as Puerto Rican and that seem to permeate all classes and groups.

Belief in Spirituality

Puerto Ricans celebrate life. They emphasize spiritual values and are willing to sacrifice material satisfaction for spiritual goals. For them being is more important than doing or having (Papajohn & Spiegel, 1975). They live for the present; the future and past are not given much attention. Puerto Ricans, though not resigned, are accepting of fate.

The majority of Puerto Ricans are nominally Roman Catholics, al-though the Protestant denominations and Pentecostal sects have been growing on the island since the turn of the century (Fitzpatrick, 1976). Their Roman Catholic ways of worship, however, are different from U.S. catholicism, which is so strongly flavored by the Irish. Most Puerto Ricans have some distrust of organized religion, the Church, and the priest, and believe they can make contact with God and the supernatural without the clergy. They tend to personalize their relationship with God by creating a favorable ambience through special relationships with the saints, who become their personal emissaries to God. Promises and offerings are made, prayers said, and candles lit, all in attempts to show gratitude and faith. They will call on the Church primarily for weddings, christenings, and funerals.

A significant proportion of the Puerto Rican population believe in spiritism. Spiritism is the belief that the visible world is surrounded by an invisible world inhabited by good and evil spirits who influence human behavior (Delgado, 1978). According to this belief, spirits can either protect or harm, as well as prevent or cause illness. Every person is seen as having spirits of protection. This protection can be increased by good deeds or decreased by evil deeds. Spiritist beliefs also include the use of incense, candles, and powders, which are alleged to have magical properties to cure illnesses and ward off the "evil eye."

Dignity of the Individual

Puerto Ricans define self-worth in terms of those inner qualities that give them self-respect and earn them the respect of others. For example, if a man is able to protect and provide for his family and is honorable and respectful in his behavior, he experiences a sense of justifiable dignity and expects the respect of others.

This form of individualism is often referred to as "personalism." It stems from the social situation in most Latin American countries where the rich and the poor are fixed in their socioeconomic status, with little chance for mobility. Focusing on inner qualities allows a person to experience self-worth regardless of worldly success or failure. This is in clear contrast, of course, to American individualism, which values achievement above all else.

Respect for Authority

Respect is vital in the Puerto Rican culture. Respect acknowledges another's social worthiness and makes everything possible or impossible; it is the social grease in the flywheel of interpersonal relationships. Not to show the proper respect to the Puerto Rican male assaults the very core of his manliness and the integrity of his family and puts in question his self-esteem as a human being (Puerto Rican Congress of New Jersey, 1976).

Respect plays a major role in preserving the network of close, personal relationships. Children learn how to relate to others according to their age, sex, and social class. Respect for authority is first learned in the home and then expands to the outside society, especially when dealing with superiors. The rules of respect are complex. For instance, Puerto Ricans think that a child who calls an adult by his or her first name without using "Doña," "Don," "Sr.," or "Sra." is disrespectful. To make direct eye contact with strangers, especially women and children, is also unacceptable.

Control of Aggression

Puerto Ricans fear losing impulse control and expressing violence. Aggression in Puerto Rico is controlled by pressure from the group, which may be the extended family, the community, or both. Further, the repression of aggression is culturally reinforced by the system of *compadrazgo*, the mutual aid expectations among family members, and the social rules of respect. The need for Puerto Ricans to preserve an appearance of outward dignity and calm may require suppression and repression of assertiveness and aggressiveness at the expense of inner psychological needs (Rothenberg, 1964). For women, common outlets for aggression are gossip (often about sexual behavior) and psychosomatic complaints (such as headaches, stomach or body aches, and fatigue). Drinking, verbal threats, and angry political discussions against the government and large corporations are some of the ways in which men commonly release aggressive feelings.

Family Structure

Puerto Ricans value the family's unity, welfare, and honor. Family ties and relationships are intense, and visits are frequent even if family members are not living in the same household (Mizio, 1974). Separations are cause for extreme grief, and reunions are cause for extreme joy. The emphasis is on the group rather than on the individual. There is a deep sense of family commitment, obligation, and responsibility. The family guarantees protection and caretaking for life as long as the person stays in the system. Leaving the system implies taking a grave risk (Papajohn & Spiegel, 1975). The focus is on the extended family system rather than the nuclear.

The Nuclear Family

Traditionally, Puerto Rican families have been patriarchal. The husband, as head of the family, is free to make decisions without consulting his wife. The husband's major responsibility is to protect and provide for his family. He is expected to be a dignified, hardworking, *macho*. *Machismo* (maleness, virility), to the Puerto Rican man, is a desirable combination of virtue, courage, romanticism, and fearlessness (Abad, Ramos, & Boyce, 1974).

It is the woman's responsibility to care for the home and to keep the family together. The husband is not expected to perform household tasks or to help with the child rearing. This arrangement results in wives assuming power behind the scenes, while overtly supporting their husband's authority. This can work as long as she does not challenge him openly.

The cultural rule of respect plays an important role in maintaining the marital relationship. Respect in marriage was eloquently defined by a male client who said to his wife: "Respect between husband and wife means that as a wife you must be loving, considerate, and never have negative thoughts about me."

Maldonado-Sierra and Trent (1960) observe that a woman may rebel against the expected role of submission to men by expressing "thinly repressed hostility toward her husband through passive–aggressive manipulation of the males in her family." For example, a woman who discovers that her husband is having an affair, may refuse to have sexual intercourse with him, complaining of body aches and nervousness.

In fact, as in American culture, sexuality is a major issue in Puerto Rican families. *Machismo*, according to Sluzki (Chap. 23), dictates that a man must signal that he is always ready for sex. In most situations, seductive behavior is expected from him when interacting with women who are not members of his family system. The paradox is that virginity is very important in traditional Puerto Rican culture and that a man is also responsible for protecting the honor of the women in his family.

Women are taught to repress or sublimate their sexual drives and usually regard sex as an obligation. From infancy they are trained to be extremely modest, which often leads to shame about their bodies. The double standard about sex usually continues after marriage. Only men are free to engage in extramarital affairs. Puerto Rican couples often do not communicate about this issue. "Intimate relations" are not openly discussed, especially in front of children or strangers. This reluctance may be due to the distance that is encouraged between boys and girls during childhood.

Even when entering consensual unions women are expected to be virgins and to remain faithful. Although consensual unions are rapidly declining, they are still common among poor Puerto Ricans who have no property rights related to marriage and are not well instructed in any religious faith (Fitzpatrick, 1976). These unions are not regularized by civil or religious ceremonies but have been culturally and officially accepted. The moral quality of the union is judged in terms of the respect one person holds for the other. People will openly admit that they are living consensually except to strangers who might not understand. This practice is changing for economic reasons. For example, Social Security benefits and pensions depend upon having a marriage certificate.

Traditionally, the pattern has been to marry young and to have many offspring. Children are seen as the poor man's wealth, the caretakers of the old, and a symbol of fertility. Parents—in particular the mother—feel obligated to sacrifice for them. During infancy they are loved and enjoyed by all of the adults in the family. Expectations from them are limited prior to age 2, when formal training begins. This training is primarily the responsibility of the mother and the maternal grandmother (Nieves-Falcón, 1972).

Children are expected to show gratitude by assuming responsibility for younger siblings and older parents. If children are not obedient, passive, and respectful, they are punished. Unlike WASP or Jewish families, Puerto Ricans do not see their children as individuals with minds of their own. Parents often talk harshly to their children, demanding to know why they did something and then proceeding to answer the question themselves or to complain about the child's refusal to answer before he or she has the chance to speak. Spankings are acceptable as discipline. Parents may hesitate to reward good behavior for fear that children will lose their feelings of respect. These restrictions may cause strain in the family and lead the child to act out feelings outside the home.

The mother has the major responsibility for disciplining the children, but the father is expected to be the real enforcer. However, at times the mother plays the role of mediator between the father and children, forming an alliance with the children that tends to isolate the father from the family.

The Extended Family

The family is usually an extended system that encompasses not only those related by blood and marriage, but also *compadres* (godparents) and *hijos de crianza* (adopted children whose adoption is not necessarily legal). *Compadrazgo* is the institution of *compadres* and *comadres* (coparents). It is a system of ritual kinship with binding mutual obligations for economic assistance, encouragement, and even personal correction (Mizio, 1974). Sponsors of children at baptism become *padrinos* (godparents) to their *ahijados* (godchildren) and *compadres* (coparents) to the parents. The functions of godparents are to provide security for the children and to offer help in times of crisis. The choice indicates not only admiration and respect for the person, but a wish to include them in the family (Abad *et al.*, 1974).

Transferring children from one nuclear family to another within the extended system in times of crisis is a common practice in Puerto Rico. Giving children to a mother, sister, *compadre*, or neighbor for temporary care in times of crisis is not seen as neglect by the child, the natural parents, or the community. The others assume responsibility as if the children were their own. This is not to say that some children may not be adversely affected psychologically or experience rejection and loss or that the parents do not experience pain and loss. However, unless the practice is regarded as a problem by the family, it is better for a therapist not to criticize or attempt to alter such arrangements.

Marriage in Puerto Rican culture is still considered much more a union of two families than it is in the United States (Fitzpatrick, 1976). The extended family is a source of strength for the couple, and its absence may cause stress and tension in the marriage. For example, women usually depend on other women in the extended family for help with child rearing and domestic tasks since the husband is not expected to share these responsibilities. Without the help of the extended family, she may experience those tasks as unbearable and begin to demand the husband's help. He may resent it and become argumentative and distant, often turning to drink, gambling, and affairs. The extended family also provides a measure of control for aggression and violence. Without relatives to intervene in the arguments and to advise the spouses to respect each other, couples may have serious difficulties.

Life Cycle Issues

Birth, marriage, and death are the most important events in the Puerto Rican life cycle. The first two are very happy occasions celebrated by the family and community.

The family meets together when there is a death to comfort each other and to pray for the dead. Religious rituals such as masses, rosaries, and *novenas* (prayers to the saints) are said to help the dead and the living. Crying, screaming, and *ataques* (hysterical convulsive reactions) are common ways of mourning at a funeral. Despite these visible expressions of grief, there is an underlying acceptance of death in the Puerto Rican culture. Puerto Ricans envision the dead in an invisible world inhabited by spirits who have some influence over the living. A person's potential for power and peacefulness may be perceived as being greater in the afterlife.

Patterns of Handling Stress

Puerto Ricans tend to attribute stressful situations to external factors and to express stress through somatic complaints. When in distress they turn to their families who ordinarily recommend visiting a physician. If the problem is perceived as nonphysical, then it is usually categorized as spiritual. Examples of spiritual problems are guilt, shame, sin, disrespect for elders or for family values (Padilla, Ruiz, & Alvarez, 1975). In these cases the family will probably suggest a visit to the clergy.

There is also a significant probability that Puerto Ricans in distress will be treated by a spiritist rather than by a mental health professional (Garrison, 1977a). Such persons are believed to have special faculties that enable them to have some control over spirits. However, most Puerto Ricans who go to spiritists consult physicians as well (Delgado, 1978). They often consult spiritists when the illness is psychosomatic and doctors tell them there is nothing physically wrong with them (Delgado, 1978). They go to a spiritist because spiritism, unlike most treatment modalities based on psychoanalytic theory, takes into account the family situation and cultural milieu when evaluating and treating behavior (Sager, Brayboy, & Waxenberg, 1972). Spiritism helps to alleviate anxiety and focuses on change by helping individuals gain control over their lives and by positive reframing of dysfunctional behavior (Delgado, 1978).

Rogler and Hollingshead (1961) describe the work of a spiritist with clients who would be described as schizophrenic by mental health professionals. The healing of illness usually takes place in group ceremonies known as reunions or seances but may also be done individually. During these sessions the medium tries to contact the spirit world to determine which spirits are influencing the person's condition. An attempt will be made to convince the spirits to help rather than to harm. The help of those spirits that already protect the person will also be enlisted. The medium will interpret and treat by prescribing ointments, herbs, massages, and prayers to help the individual gain spiritual strength.

Symptoms that a mental health professional will classify as personality disorders and psychoses, the spiritist will interpret as spiritual. For example, the spiritist may tell people with hallucinations that they are developing faculties that enable them to communicate with the spirits. The behavior will be defined as meaningful rather than sick. The group, which is usually composed of neighbors and family, will serve as a primary group where problems are discussed, interpreted, and understood within a culturally accepted belief system.

Research in this area may lead to innovative interventions. Due to the significant role that spiritists appear to play in the mental health care delivery systems in Puerto Rican communities, attempts have been made by a number of therapists to use them as resources (Abad et al., 1974; Garrison, 1977b). Ruiz and Langrod (1976) and Garrison (1977b) have used the spiritist as a consultant in cases where patients are deeply involved in the belief. This method has caused controversy among therapists and in the Puerto Rican community. However, it is an example of an intervention that takes into consideration cultural beliefs.

Puerto Ricans may also handle stress by having *ataques de nervios* (nervous attacks). *Ataques* have been clinically labeled as the "Puerto Rican Syndrome" and resemble conversion reactions expressed in hyperkinetic episodes (Fernandez-Marina, 1961). Abad and Boyce (1979) describe patients in a state of *ataque* as falling to the floor with thrashing of limbs, grinding of teeth, and clenching of fists. The patient displays an altered state of consciousness of a dissociative nature not unlike the unconsciousness seen in true epileptic seizures. This behavior may also be a culturally learned and sanctioned symptom precipitated by repressed anger or sexual tension (Garrison, 1977b). Anger, which is usually precipitated by discord in social relationships, is discharged, and secondary gains, such as being able to exercise control over one's family or to receive protective care and attention from others, may result. Whatever guilt may be associated with the aggressive behavior is alleviated by claiming amnesia.

Migration and Its Effect on Family Structure

Poverty and racism are two major factors adversely affecting the Puerto Rican migrant's quality of life in the continental United States (Mizio, 1979). U.S. census figures cited for March 1977 showed that while 9.4% of all Americans were below the poverty level, 38.8% of mainland Puerto Ricans (more than 1.7 million) were earning below that level. The median income for all U.S. families was $14,958 per year; Puerto Rican families averaged only $7669. More than 64% of all Americans graduated from high school, but only 30.6% of Puerto Rican adults did so (U.S. Bureau of Census, 1977). The census also found that the dropout rate is higher for Puerto Rican youngsters born on the island than for those born in the United States.

Island-born youngsters are more likely to have difficulty communicating in English, to be unemployed, and to be poor. The cycle of poverty often begins on the island. Poor families from rural areas and urban slums are limited by lack of education, training, and ability to speak English. For example, the Puerto Rican who migrates from a slum in San Juan will probably settle in a slum in the Bronx. If unemployment was a problem for the family in Puerto Rico, it will also be very limited in New York City. Fewer difficulties are experienced by middle-class families who come from urban centers in Puerto Rico and have marketable skills.

Racism, a reality of this society, not only affects the Puerto Rican's economic situation, but also presents serious problems for the family. Tomas (1967) describes how color affected his self-image and his relationships with other members of his family. Rabkin and Struening (1976) found that non-White Puerto Ricans were more frequently admitted to mental health hospitals than White Puerto Ricans. When a family arrives in the continental United States, it is often perceived as interracial and its members as White, Black, and non-White. The family's exposure to the racial prejudice in this country may lead to resentment, rejection, and splits in the family.

Puerto Ricans on the mainland quickly find that some of their cultural attitudes are not reinforced by U.S. society. Culturally Puerto Ricans learn to be dependent on the group and the community and are rewarded for submissive and respectful behavior. Conflict and anxiety are experienced when they confront a society that frowns on passivity and expects independent individualistic behavior. The rules of respect that bind relationships in Puerto Rico are not understood here. For instance, the concept of *machismo* in this society has negative connotations causing conflicts for the traditional Puerto Rican man. When traditional cultural values are not reinforced by society, they cease to be functional. This culture shock tends to produce significant changes in Puerto Rican family structure.

Conflict in the marital relationship may erupt when the traditional sex roles are reversed. Sometimes the woman is able to obtain employment and the man may have to stay home to take care of the children. This shift in roles does not become problematic as long as the woman continues to accept the traditional view of family life. Puerto Rican women have always been influential in the home as well as in the island's political and academic life (Fitzpatrick, 1976). This may be in part because a large percentage of women have always worked to supplement the family's income. In 1920 women constituted 25% of the work force in Puerto Rico (Fernandez & Quintero, 1974).

However, the wife who becomes the breadwinner will tend to feel more independent and self-confident. As a result the husband is likely to feel emasculated, especially if she openly challenges his authority. If the husband is unable to regain his dominant position through employment, he may experience panic and confusion. The wife in turn may develop contempt for her spouse when he no longer fulfills his macho role (Mizio, 1974). Some women may also experience emotional pain and feelings of helplessness in such a situation. Marital discord and separation are common outcomes.

Another important point about Puerto Rican family structure is the increasing number of female-headed households, especially on the mainland (U.S. Bureau of Census, 1977). This indicates an increase in divorce and separations among Puerto Ricans. This may be because on the mainland it is easier for women to obtain help from social agencies, thereby lessening their economic dependence on men.

The language issue places strain on parent–child relationships. Children have an easier time learning English and are often asked to interpret for their parents. The dependence on their children to express their wishes, concerns, and conflicts places Puerto Rican parents in an inferior and powerless position. Asking the child to speak for his or her parents is also contrary to the cultural expectation that children should be quiet in front of strangers.

There were also fewer differences between the expectations of the family and of the larger society in the island. Children and adults shared more activities together since the family was the main vehicle for recreation. Puerto Rican children in the United States are likely to rebel against their parents' rigidity and to reject their customs, which they view as inferior to the American way of life.

Children who are caught in the conflict of cultures and loyalties may develop a negative self-image, which can inhibit their chances for growth and accomplishment. The parents, thwarted at every turn, may give up.

A sense of distance may begin to separate children from their parents, who often feel they have lost control. Parents usually react by imposing stricter rules, using corporal punishment, and, if necessary, appealing to the traditionally accepted values of respect and obedience, which are seen as a solution. Parents of adolescents, especially daughters, may become extremely strict and overprotective due to the lack of support from outside systems and the realistic fears of crime, drug addiction, and different sexual mores (Badillo-Ghali, 1977).

In Puerto Rico parents were able to rely on other adults in the extended family and the community for help with discipline, which they cannot do in the United States. The lack of extended family and friends may also precipitate feelings of loss and isolation. Individuals may feel obligated to fulfill roles and functions that were previously performed by others in the extended system. Consequently, they may experience extreme anxiety. In Puerto Rico the nuclear family was never expected to take care of all of their needs. Understandably, they may feel overwhelmed and resentful.

Although Puerto Ricans on the mainland experience the effects of migration and culture shock more intensely, families on the island are also affected. Growing exposure to American culture through education, the media, and the back and forth movement, have significantly influenced family structure. In general, the family has been changing from an extended system with traditional Hispanic values to a nuclear family with modern American values.

For example, traditional patterns of sexual behavior are changing as both island and mainland families are becoming more tolerant of sexual freedom. Family obligations and responsibilities, which guaranteed security and the individual's worth, are often modified. Especially in the upper and middle classes, obligations to extended family members may be acknowledged but dropped if they become too burdensome.

Therapeutic Techniques and Issues

Engaging the Puerto Rican family in a warm and personal relationship during the first interview is critical. Haley (1971) discusses the importance of the initial interview and emphasizes that the therapist should take advantage of the crisis and intervene as rapidly as possible to bring about change. Although the therapist should be active and work toward change, he or she should not get down to business immediately (Mizio, 1979). Establishing a personal relationship, rather than one that is distant and professional, is crucial to the outcome of therapy.

The language factor may be a major issue and a barrier in therapy. When the family is unable to speak English, conducting the interview in Spanish is necessary in order to engage them. Older Puerto Ricans are often hesitant and afraid to learn English. It is humiliating when they try to speak English but are not understood and are asked to repeat themselves. Using children as interpreters is problematic because it shifts the family structure by placing children in a superior position. Asking the child to speak for his or her parents violates the cultural expectation that children should be quiet in front of strangers. Parents may be hesitant to discuss intimate issues or conflicts in front of children. A child may feel pressured to be accurate and clear and frustrated when unable to meet those expectations due to lack of verbal skill in both languages. The child may also feel ashamed of his or her parents and view them as inferior. Mizio (1974) observes that children who experience their parents' pain may feel tremendously responsible for the family's burden and may be crushed in the process.

Even when Puerto Rican families speak English, lack of fluency may lead to distorting information or vagueness (Gonzalez, 1978; Marcos, Alpert, Urcuyo, & Kesselman, 1973). Also, when the therapist is able to speak Spanish but is not familiar with the culture, he or she may overestimate or underestimate the degree of dysfunction in a family. Knowledge of the culture allows for greater understanding of the nuances of communication that the family uses, such as colloquialisms and nonverbal expressions. When there are no Spanish-speaking therapists, the use of interpreters, preferably Hispanic adults, is advisable. However, it has been found that reliance upon translators, even Hispanics, introduces distortions that result in limitations and frustrations for both therapist and client (Abad & Boyce, 1979).

The therapist can help the family relax by asking the members to take off their coats, by providing comfortable chairs in a warm and personal setting, and, when possible, by offering coffee. An informal conversation, such as asking whether they had any difficulties finding the office, may ease the situation. If the family was referred by another agency, using the name of the referring person, stating that the person seemed concerned about them, and expressing a wish to assist them in whatever way possible will be a respectful and personal way of opening a discussion about the presenting problem.

Asking the family when the problems began, what types of solutions they have tried, and what are their expectations for change will help the therapist explore family history and assess the role that cultural differences, socioeconomic factors, and generational conflicts play in the situation. Knowing where they live and who is helpful in the extended family and in the neighborhood will help the therapist determine what support systems are available for the family.

Puerto Ricans are likely to respond to a therapist who is active, personal, and respectful of the family's structure and boundaries. They may speak more easily to a woman about emotional problems since women handle those concerns in the family. They may take directives more readily from a male therapist because of the authority men have in the culture.

During this process the husband should be addressed first, the wife second, and then the children, according to age, following the traditional family structure and boundaries for authority. In cases where the woman does all the talking, attempts should be made to help the man comment on her statements. If he agrees with her it would be important to reinforce their unity and reframe his quiet behavior as a sign of silent strength. If they disagree, it would be important to modify the disagreement. This may be accomplished by pointing out that their ability to view the problems from different perspectives increases the alternatives for solutions.

Puerto Ricans may not easily accept an agency's expectation that they keep scheduled appointments due to the informality of the culture and the environmental circumstances that make this difficult. In some cases home visits may be the only way of initiating or maintaining a relationship (Mizio, 1979). Pittman, Langsley, Flomenhaft, DeYoung, Machotka, and Kaplan (1971) found that therapy in the client's home gave the client an increased opportunity to reveal his or her health and maintain freedom of movement when anxious. With Puerto Ricans, home visits can be used effectively by therapists to personalize their relationship with the family and to increase the level of trust. The therapist's influence in the system will automatically increase if the family is able to relate to him or her as they would to a *comadre* or *compadre*.

The use of a genogram (Guerin, 1976) can be helpful in determining who is in the family. However, this information will be given only when there is trust, such as in the case of the Cruz family.

> Both Mr. and Mrs. Cruz had been previously married and each had children from their first unions. The three oldest children, Noemie, 17, Miguel, 15, and Pedro, 14, were Mr. Cruz's children. Margot, 11, was Mrs. Cruz's child, and Jose, 5, was Mr. and Mrs. Cruz's child. All the children lived at home with them. Mr. Cruz's children saw their mother sporadically. Mrs. Cruz's daughter had very little contact with her father. This information was obtained only after the family had begun to trust the therapist.

Blended families, such as the Cruz family, are common among Puerto Ricans on the mainland (Fitzpatrick, 1976). Carter and McGoldrick (1980) have found that with remarried families whose presenting problems are child focused, it is beneficial to help the stepmother back off and the father to take charge of his children. With Puerto Rican families, however, suggesting this shift may be dangerous and confusing if not presented carefully. The therapist is likely to alienate the stepmother if she feels that her position in the family is undermined. Traditionally, it is the woman who is responsible for child rearing, and she is the person who disciplines on a day-to-day basis. It is a cultural expectation that children should respect all adults, and a common practice for adults to raise children who are not their own. Consequently, it is not unnatural for a stepparent to expect respect from children and for children to view this expectation as natural.

For example, in the Cruz family the children had lived with their mother for three years after the divorce. She had remarried and the stepfather had been abusive. The mother was unable to protect them, and the father had gained custody. Pedro had always been close to both his mother and his father. He was very hurt by his mother's apparent lack of interest, and his father's absence from home, due to work, was adding to Pedro's feelings of loneliness and rejection. Since Pedro was unable to speak to anyone at home or outside about his feelings of hurt, anger, and conflictual loyalties to parents, he was expressing his conflict at school and with his stepmother.

Therapy, in this case, focused primarily on helping the father take charge of the discipline, especially with Pedro and Miguel. It was emphasized that this shift was needed because both Pedro and Miguel were at an age when they needed their father to teach them how to be men. Mrs. Cruz was encouraged to support her husband by telling him whenever the children were being disrespectful. They were able to accept this suggestion since it is a Puerto Rican expectation for fathers to teach their sons how to be men and for mothers to teach their daughters how to be women.

Another therapeutic goal was to help the children reconnect with their natural mother, and to help Mr. and Mrs. Cruz negotiate with her regarding visits with the children.

The value of rebuilding mutual trust among broken and dysfunctional relationships has been emphasized by Boszormenyi-Nagy and Spark (1973). Bernal (Chap. 7) has found that helping Hispanic families who have migrated to the United States reconnect family ties is vital to their growth. This is especially true with Puerto Ricans because of the back and forth migration that often leads to repeated cutoffs and breaks in the family system.

Most Puerto Ricans who seek help usually arrive in a state of crisis and expect the same treatment that they receive in a hospital's emergency room. They are generally referred to mental health centers by schools, hospitals, social service agencies, or the court. A few may come voluntarily to ask for medication or other concrete services. The presenting problems are usually somatic complaints and nervousness, but they may also be about the situation at home. These families are often isolated without support systems, and connecting them with community networks such as churches, social clubs, relatives, and spiritists (when the client is involved in that belief) may lessen their isolation and provide natural support.

When clients believe in spiritism, it is important not to put down their beliefs but to help them express their explanations and expectations for the present difficulties. If the client believes that herbal baths and prayers to guardian spirits will provide strength, the practices should not be discouraged. At the same time the client should be encouraged to make choices and to take responsibility for the consequences. The goal would be not to change the belief but to help clients gain self-trust and control over their lives.

Since many of the family problems presented are basically social, learning to deal with environmental stresses needs to be part of the therapy. The therapist's willingness to meet the family's request for concrete services and to act as their advocate is an important vehicle for establishing a trusting relationship (Mizio, 1979). For instance, in the case of the Martinez family, helping the mother deal with the school alleviated the stress at home.

> Mrs. Martinez, a 34-year-old separated Puerto Rican female, was referred by the school to a mental health center for therapy. She had left Puerto Rico with her two sons, Mario, 8, and Hector, 2, after separating from her husband. Mario, who enrolled in a bilingual class, refused to do schoolwork and disturbed the other children in the classroom. At the time of the referral Mrs. Martinez had been living in the United States for only five months.

A meeting between Mrs. Martinez and the teacher was facilitated by the therapist. The goal was to agree on the classroom behavior they expected from Mario. They were helped to formulate a strategy that improved the child's behavior. This process increased Mrs. Martinez's sense of personal power.

The therapist also gave Mrs. Martinez tangible advice about setting consistent and clear limits for her son at home. She had been most worried about Mario's physical expression of anger. She saw this behavior as similar to her husband's violent outbursts. Frustrated by her inability to control Mario, Mrs. Martinez often spanked him. This, in turn, caused her to feel guilty about her own loss of control. The therapist gave Mrs. Martinez advice, which met the expectation that most Puerto Ricans have when they go to a professional for help. The therapist, who wanted to ensure the mother's cooperation with the task, engaged her in the formulation of a plan that seemed feasible.

A large percentage of the Puerto Ricans who seek help are women. They often complain about their husbands' drinking, abusive behavior, and general absence from the home. They may have attempted to change the situation at home by threatening to leave their husbands. Their lack of resources, however, makes carrying out this threat difficult. Since they are unable to change the situation at home, they experience themselves as failures. Their relatives and the other women in the community often advise them to be strong and accepting. This advice reflects the cultural belief that it is the woman's role to hold the family together. There is a tendency among Puerto Ricans to admire a woman who "carries her cross."

Wives are usually ambivalent about accusing their husbands. On the one hand, they feel disloyal and, on the other hand, they feel betrayed. They try to clarify that their husbands are basically good human beings. They believe that their husbands' behavior is caused by the alcohol, the lack of job opportunities, the friends, and, in general, the way of life in this country.

Mrs. Conde illustrates the bind in which some of these women find themselves.

> During the past five years Mrs. Conde has come to therapy on different occasions when the situation at home has reached a crisis. In therapy she claims to feel embarrassed about coming with the same problem and not taking steps to change it. She wants to do things by herself but feels helpless. She wants the therapist to help her think clearly. She states that she wants to go away from her husband and her family of origin to a place where she can live in peace with her children. She holds back for fear that she will not be able to handle the children, especially her son, alone. She would prefer to say home and help her husband. She does not want to talk about him behind his back, but he refuses to seek help.

Women like Mrs. Conde often drop out of therapy when the crisis is over and return when another crisis arises.

As a rule, it is highly unusual for Puerto Ricans to initiate therapy for marital problems. Those who do are more likely to be acculturated into the American society. Most of the families who seek help present problems that are child focused. However, marital conflicts are commonly observed in these families. In most cases the couple will resist therapeutic attempts to explore these conflicts directly. A typical response may be that the husband will refuse to come in again. In general, Puerto Rican men refrain from asking for help. Abad *et al.* (1974) attributed this avoidance to their sensitivity to any situation that threatens their *machismo* image.

Often wives will ask therapists to convince their husbands to come to therapy. The therapist should assess the situation carefully before interpreting the request as manipulative. Puerto Ricans who ask an outsider to intervene in this fashion usually feel powerless and embarrassed. They view authority figures as influential and this type of request as legitimate. Pushing the woman to do the convincing herself may alienate her and result in her withdrawal from therapy. In some cases a call from the therapist will prove more effective because of the cultural rules of respect for authority. Every effort should be made to include the husband in therapy by appealing to his sense of responsibility and to his traditional role as head of the family. The following case illustrates this situation.

> Mr. and Mrs. Arce were referred to therapy by a local Puerto Rican community agency. They were having difficulties managing their children, especially a 12-year-old son. Therapy focused on helping the parents set clear limits and provide a reward system for the children. The parents appeared distant and angry and had difficulty working together. The therapist commented that they seemed to be having difficulties and that she sensed tension between them. They denied any difficulty and quickly agreed on an issue.
>
> The next therapy session was attended by Mrs. Arce alone. She stated that her husband had refused to come. He did not believe in therapy and was angry with her for seeking help. It was her fault, he felt, that the children were disobedient and disrespectful. She went on to complain about his lack of interest in her, his absence from the home, and his outbursts of anger. She wanted the therapist to call her husband and ask him to come to therapy.
>
> The therapist called Mr. Arce and told him that his absence had shown how much his wife needed his help to discipline the children. The husband's traditional role in the family was supported, and his boundaries regarding intimate matters were respected. An attempt to personalize the relationship was made through a home visit. The therapist supported the wife by involving the husband in the family as a father. Uniting them as parents strengthened generational boundaries and had a positive effect on the children's behavior. In the privacy of their home they were able to perceive the therapist as a friend and as part of their support system. The trust level was heightened enabling them eventually to share more about their relationship.

Regardless of the therapist's ability to engage Puerto Rican couples in therapy, he or she will find that it is extremely difficult and embarrassing for them to talk about sexual problems and physical abuse. Talking about issues concerning lack of respect, jealousy, and problems with in-laws will be easier. If the man refuses to come in, the woman may be coached to mobilize the extended family for support. In cases where the extended family is not available or supportive, the therapist may help to break the cycle by mobilizing external systems such as welfare, child-care facilities, and women's self-help groups to support the woman.

The engagement of children in therapy should vary depending upon their ages. Since young children may be shy and frightened in front of strangers, playfulness and physical contact with them may be more appropriate than conversation. If adolescents are unable to speak in front of their parents, it may be necessary to see them alone. Due to respect and fear they might not be able to speak about sex, drugs, problems at school, or cultural conflicts at home and in the community. The goals consequently would be to help adolescents express their concerns, to help them share with their parents those issues that are relevant to the family problems, and to find ways in which parents and child can compromise.

Sometimes discussing the family's migratory process will clarify conflicts caused by contrasts between cultural values. Redefining roles in terms of privileges and responsibilities may be helpful.

The therapist can be helpful by encouraging the parents to discuss their genuine concern for the child and their fears that the behavior may lead to serious problems. By asking the parents to tell the child about their love, concerns, and fears, the therapist can help them relate to their children in a more positive manner.

General Approaches

The structural approach to family therapy has been used effectively to engage Puerto Rican families in a personal and trusting relationship (Minuchin, Montalvo, & Guerney, 1967). This emphasis that the approach places on engaging the family in such a relationship is a reason for its success with Puerto Ricans. Some other reasons for its success, according to Canino and Canino (1980), are that it uses the family and extended family as integral components of the therapy; it considers stressful external life events like migration, poor housing, and unemployment as part of the family's context and, therefore, as contributors to the development and maintenance of symptomatic behavior; it is present, concrete, and goal oriented, factors that have been found successful with low-income groups.

A method such as the one used by Selvini-Palazzoli, Boscolo, Cecchin, and Prata (1978), in which the therapist gives the family a brief evaluation of the problem and a prescription at the end of the first session, may be helpful in engaging the family in therapy. Puerto Ricans are likely to respond positively to the group's respectful objective and personal style. Giving a positive connotation to the family's behavior will also aid the engagement. The group's clear assumption of authority in the session will suit Puerto Ricans who expect the therapist to be the expert and leader.

Conclusion

Puerto Ricans underutilize mental health services. An explanation may be that the therapist and the family have different expectations from therapy, which are largely determined by their sociocultural context. Lack of knowledge about the family's frame of reference may limit the therapist's ability to engage the family in a trusting and personal relationship.

There is a pressing need to take new directions that are culturally appropriate when providing services to Puerto Ricans. For instance, since Puerto Ricans under stress are likely to go to medical clinics rather than mental health centers, those settings may have to shift their boundaries to provide therapeutic interventions that respond to the crisis presented. Agencies that treat Puerto Ricans may need to operate on a walk-in basis and with considerable flexibility. Due to the complexity and multitude of problems presented by these families, more than one therapist may need to intervene. A team of therapists who are familiar with the language and culture may increase the efficiency of treatment.

Garcia-Preto, Katonak, Leiderman, and Lopez-Greenspun (to be published) have been using a team approach to work with Hispanic families in crisis. The team functions as a temporary bridge to extended systems of support, helping the family through crisis. They can thus provide the human resources and flexibility needed to make various interventions on the spot with multiproblem families. For example, they are able to work as cotherapists, meet separately with different subsystems in the family, and contact other agencies to help the family deal with environmental stresses. Personalizing the therapeutic relationship, connoting cultural values positively, and facilitating the family's connectedness to others in the community have proven to be effective techniques. The "no show" and the dropout rates have lessened for families seen in this way. Further research in this area may lead to innovative interventions.

There is evidence that family therapy conducted in the client's home has proven successful with multiproblem Puerto Rican families (Hardy-Fanta & MacMahon-Herrera, 1981). This area deserves further exploration. In general, wider use of family therapy as a treatment modality for Puerto Ricans is recommended since they usually seek help as family units and frequently for family problems.

REFERENCES

Abad, V., & Boyce, E. Issues in Psychiatric Evaluations of Puerto Ricans: A Socio-Cultural Perspective. *Journal of Operational Psychiatry*, *10*(1), 28–30, 1979.

Abad, V., Ramos, J., & Boyce, E. A Model for Delivery of Mental Health Services to Spanish Speaking Minorities. *American Journal of Orthopsychiatry*, *44*(4), 584–595, 1974.

Aponte, H. The Family–School Interview: An Eco-Structural Approach. *Family Process*, *13*(3), 303–312, 1976.

Badillo-Ghali, S. Culture Sensitivity and the Puerto Rican Client. *Social Casework*, *55*(1), 100–110, 1974.

Boas, F. *Puerto Rican Archeology*. New York: Academy of Sciences, 1940.

Boszormenyi-Nagy, I., & Spark, G. *Invisible Loyalties: Reciprocity in Intergenerational Family Therapy*. New York: Harper & Row, 1973.

Canino, I., & Canino, G. The Impact of Stress on the Puerto Rican Migrant: Some Treatment Considerations. *American Journal of Orthopsychiatry*, *50*(3), 232–238, 1980.

Carter, E.A., & McGoldrick, M. Forming a Remarried Family. In E.A. Carter & M. McGoldrick (Eds.), *The Family Life Cycle*. New York: Gardner Press, 1980.

Delgado, M. Folk Medicine in Puerto Rican Culture. *International Social Work*, *21*(2), 46–54, 1978.

Fernandez, C.C., & Quintero, R.M. Bases de la Sociedad Sexista en Puerto Rico. *Revista/ Review InterAmericana*, *4*(2), 1974.

Fernandez-Mendez, E. *La Identidad y Cultura*. San Juan: Instituto de Cultura Puertorrequeña, 1970.

Fernandez-Marina, R. The Puerto Rican Syndrome: Its Dynamics and Cultural Determinants. *Psychiatry*, *24*, 79–82, 1961.

Fitzpatrick, J.P. The Puerto Rican Family. In R.W. Habenstein & C.H. Mindel (Eds.), *Ethnic Families in America: Patterns and Variations*. New York: Elsevier, 1976.

Garcia-Preto, N., Katonak M., Leiderman, S., & Lopez-Greenspun A. *Family Therapy with Hispanics; A Team Approach*. To be published.

Garrison, V. Doctor, Espiritista, or Psychiatrist? Health Seeking Behavior in a Puerto Rican Neighborhood of New York City. *Medical Anthropology*, *1*(2), 65–188, 1977. (a)

Garrison, V. The Puerto Rican Syndrome: In Psychiatry and Espiritismo. In V. Crapanzano & V. Garrison (Eds.), *Case Studies in Spirit Possession*. New York: Wiley, 1977. (b)

Gonzalez, J. Language Factors Affecting Treatment of Schizophrenics. *Psychiatric Annals*, *8*, 68–70, 1978.

Guerin, P.J. Evaluation of Family System and Genogram. In P.J. Guerin (Ed.), *Family Therapy*. New York: Gardner Press, 1976.

Haley, J. Approaches to Family Therapy. In J. Haley (Ed.), *Changing Families—A Family Therapy Reader*. New York: Grune & Stratton, 1971.

Hardy-Fanta, C., & MacMahon-Herrera, E. Adapting Family Therapy to the Hispanic Family. *Social Casework and the Journal of Contemporary Social Work, 62*(3), 138–148, 1981.

Maldonado-Sierra, E., & Trent, R.D. Neuroses and Traditional Beliefs in Puerto Rico. *International Journal of Social Psychiatry*, *6*, 237, 1960.

Manners, R.A., & Steward, J.H. The Cultural Study of Contemporary Societies: Puerto Rico. *American Journal of Sociology*, *59*(2), 123–130, 1953.

Marcos, L., Alpert, M., Urcuyo, L., & Kesselman, M. The Language Barrier in Evaluating Spanish Speaking Patients. *Archives of General Psychiatry*, *8*, 655–659, 1973.

Minuchin, S., Montalvo, B., Guerney, B.R. *Families of the Slums: An Exploration of Their Treatment*. New York: Basic Books, 1967.

Mizio, E. Impact of External Systems on the Puerto Rican Family. *Social Casework*, *55*(1), 76–83, 1974.

Mizio, E. *Puerto Rican Task Report—Project on Ethnicity*. New York: Family Service Association, 1979.

Nieves-Falcón, L. *Diagnóstico de Puerto Rico*. Rio Piedras: Edil, 1972 (paperback).

Padilla, A.M., Ruiz, R.A., & Alvarez, R. Community Mental Health Services for the Spanish-Speaking/Surnamed Population. *American Psychologist, 30*, 892–905, 1975.

Pane, F.R. Account of the Antiquities—Or Customs of the Indians. In K. Wagenheim & O.J. Wagenheim (Eds.), *The Puerto Ricans*. New York: Anchor Books, 1973 (paperback).

Papajohn, J., & Spiegel, J. *Transactions in Families*. San Francisco: Jossey-Bass, 1975.

Pittman, F.S., Langsley, D.G., Flomenhaft, K., DeYoung, C.D., Machotka, P., & Kaplan, D.M. Therapy Techniques of the Family Therapy Unit. In J. Haley (Ed.), *Changing Families—A Family Therapy Reader*. New York: Grune & Stratton, 1971.

Puerto Rican Congress of New Jersey. *Folk Medicine in a Homogeneous Puerto Rican Community*. Trenton, N.J.: Author, 1976.

Rabkin, J., & Struening, E.L. *Ethnicity, Social Class and Mental Illness* (Paper Series No. 17). New York: Institute of Pluralism and Group Identity, 1976.

Rodriguez, C.E., Sanchez-Korrol, V., & Alers, J.O. *The Puerto Rican Struggle: Essays on Survival*. New York: Puerto Rican Migration Research Consortium, 1980 (paperback).

Rogler, L., & Hollingshead, A.B. The Puerto Rican Spiritualist as a Psychiatrist. *American Journal of Sociology, 67*(1), 12–22, 1961.

Rothenberg, A. Puerto Rico and Aggression. *American Journal of Psychiatry, 20*(10), 962–970, 1964.

Ruiz, P., & Langrod, J. The Role of Folk Healers in Community Mental Health Services. *Community Mental Health Journal, 12*, 292–398, 1976.

Sager, C., Brayboy, T.L., & Waxenberg, B.R. Black Patient–White Therapist. *American Journal of Orthopsychiatry, 8*(3), 128, 1972.

Selvini-Palazzoli, M., Boscolo, L., Cecchin, G., & Prata, G. *Paradox and Counterparadox: A New Model in the Therapy of the Family in Schizophrenic Transaction*. New York: Jason Aronson, 1978.

Tomas, P. *Down These Mean Streets*. New York: Knopf, 1967 (paperback).

U.S. Bureau of Census. *Persons of Spanish Origin in the United States* (Current Population Reports Series, No. 317:20). Washington, D.C.: U.S. Government Printing Office, 1977.

U.S. Commission on Civil Rights. *Puerto Ricans in the Continental United States—An Uncertain Future*. Washington, D.C.: Author, 1976 (paperback).

Wagenheim, K., & Wagenheim, O.J. (Eds.). *The Puerto Ricans*. New York: Anchor Books, 1973 (paperback).

Wolf, K.L. Growing Up and Its Price in Three Puerto Rican Subcultures. *Psychiatry, 15*, 401–433, 1952.

9

Cuban Families

GUILLERMO BERNAL

Since 1959, nearly 850,000 Cubans have migrated to the United States. This migration has had unique characteristics that distinguish it from other Hispanic or Latino groups. To conduct effective family therapy with Cubans, a critical understanding of socioeconomic, political, cultural, and historical issues is necessary.

Cuba is the largest island in the Caribbean. It is 780 miles long from east to west, it ranges from about 25 to 125 miles in width, and it has a total area of 44,218 square miles (about the size of Pennsylvania). Some historians have suggested that Cuba's historical significance is out of proportion to its size (Foner, 1962). Perhaps this is, in part, because of the strategic geographical position Cuba has occupied throughout history. Cuba, which is centrally located in the Caribbean between the Florida and the Yucatan peninsulas, has occupied a significant strategic position by its proximity to all points north, south, east, and west. To the Spaniards, Cuba was the key to the Americas. Traffic that was bound for Mexico, Peru, and other points in South America generally stopped in Havana, making it an important mercantile and commercial port. At different historical periods, control of the entry into and exit from the Caribbean and the Americas was possible through Cuba.

The economic, political, and military importance that Cuba had for Spain did not go unnoticed by the United States, an emerging powerful nation 90 miles from its shores. While Spain attempted to maintain its grip of her last colonies, Cuba's War of Independence attracted attention and subsequent intervention by the United States.

In 1898, during the Spanish–American War, the United States invaded Cuba, Puerto Rico, the Philippines, and Guam. While Puerto Rico, the Philippines, and Guam became colonies of the United States, Cuba was able to obtain its independence. However, independence was achieved at the cost of a military base (Guantanamo Bay Base) and the Platt Amendment, which gave the United States the right to intervene in the internal affairs of Cuba. After numerous political upheavals and continued foreign intervention, the Platt Amendment was dropped in 1933.

Guillermo Bernal. Department of Psychiatry, University of California at San Francisco General Hospital, San Francisco, California.

Nevertheless, Cuba remained tied to U.S. economic and political interests until the revolution in 1959. To present an analysis of the historical developments that preceded the revolution is beyond the scope of this chapter; there are a number of volumes available on this topic (e.g., Castro, 1972, 1975; Thomas, 1971, 1977).

It is worthwhile, however, to review briefly some of the reasons that a revolution took place in Cuba. First, prerevolutionary Cuba was essentially a one-crop economy dominated by the U.S. economy. The political strategy of the United States was to support any government irrespective of its human rights policy and its constitutionality so long as such governments protected the interests of the United States. Prior to the revolution, the unemployment rate in Cuba was generally 25%. Perhaps most importantly, the ownership of land was concentrated in so few hands that less than "eight percent of Cuban farms accounted for seventy-one percent of the total viable land" (Foner, 1962, p. 8).

The triumph of the Cuban revolution in 1959 led to the first experiment with socialism in the Americas. In a manner similar to how Spain tried tenaciously to maintain its grip on Cuba, it appears that the United States has attempted to reassert its control of this Caribbean island. When the United States was faced with the reality of losing economic control of Cuba, the new government was denounced, blockaded, and eventually invaded. Fears were fueled about the Soviet threat only 90 miles away. This volatile political situation affected the way in which Cubans were initially received: The United States was to welcome with open arms all those fleeing from communism.

While the United States has had a great deal of impact on Cuba, Cuba also has had impact on the United States. The radical programs instituted by the revolutionary government affected the country at social, political, and economic levels. Such measures produced dissatisfaction with certain sectors of the Cuban population. Those sectors left Cuba in an unparalleled migration, primarily to the United States. The suddenness of the Cuban migration, its size within relatively brief periods, and its predominant middle- and upper-class composition, particularly during the early migration waves, seemed to both magnify its impact and set up a special situation in relation to other Latinos in the United States. While the first waves of immigrants left for political reasons, subsequent waves left for family and/or economic considerations.

The Cuban Migration in Context

The impact of Cubans has been greatest in the major metropolitan areas, such as Miami, New York and New Jersey, Chicago, and, to a lesser degree, Los Angeles. Along with other Latinos, such as Mexicans and Puerto Ricans, Cubans comprise a large and rapidly increasing ethnic group in the

United States. Cubans, while representing only 6% to 7% of the Latinos in the United States, have been considered a success story.[1]

The relative success of Cubans in the United States is linked to the unique aspects of the Cuban migration and the nature of its historical context (Casal, Prohias, Carrasco, & Prieto, 1979). For example, in sharp contrast to the characteristics of Mexicans and Puerto Ricans (see Chaps. 7 and 8), the Cuban migration of the 1960s was (1) overrepresented by Whites and therefore were less likely to experience racial barriers; (2) disproportionately composed of the upper and middle classes of society; these sectors had educational resources, business know-how, financial backing, and a set of values shared by the dominant U.S. culture; and (3) aided by major federal programs, such as the Cuban Refugee Program, to facilitate educational, training, work opportunities, and so on (Casal et al., 1979).

The migration of Cubans to the United States dates back to the 19th century. The focus here will be on the phases of migration since 1959. Most Cubans in the United States today have arrived since that time or have parents who migrated since the revolution in 1959.

Three phases of migration may be identified (Amaro & Portes, 1972; Perez-Stable, 1981). The first phase was from 1959 to 1965 and had two waves. The first wave was from 1959 up to the time of the Bay of Pigs invasion of April 1961. This wave of immigrants was composed of persons connected to the Batista dictatorship and of persons and families from the upper and upper-middle classes. The strategy of this group was to settle temporarily and to wait until a return was possible under a more favorable political and economic climate. The second wave during this phase was composed of persons leaving from the time of the failure of the Bay of Pigs invasion up to 1965. Amaro and Portes (1972) refer to these individuals as the "real refugees" since these left with no idea of possible return. This group

1. Hernandez (1974) provides an appendix on the periodical literature on Cuban exiles. Of particular relevance to the claims of the Cuban "success story" are "Flight from Cuba: Castro's Loss Is U.S. Gain," in U.S. News and World Report, May 1971, pp. 74–77, and "Cuba's New Refugees Get Jobs Fast: Opportunities in the U.S.," in Business Week, March 1966, pp. 69. In an attempt to dispel myths about the Cuban migration, Perez (1976) conducted an interesting study of 1970 U.S. census data. He compared Cuban-born to foreign-born populations in the United States that had migrated from 1960 to 1970. Perez found, contrary to previous reports, that Cubans had a high rate of unemployment, had lower numbers in professional and administrative categories, had a lower family income, and had more people at the poverty level than the foreign-born immigrants.

Perhaps one of the most complete documentations of the Cuban migration and Cubans as a minority group was a needs assessment study conducted by Hernandez (1974) and Prohias and Casal (1973). Elsewhere, Casal and Hernandez (1975) provide an extensive review of the literature on Cubans in the United States. These studies showed that Cubans, when compared to other Latinos or Hispanics, appeared as "relatively" successful. Clearly, there are problems with such comparisons due to the qualitatively different aspects of Mexican and Puerto Rican migrations as well as the sociohistorical context that has been markedly different from that of the Cubans (see, e.g., Bernal & Flores-Ortiz, 1980).

was primarily from middle class and professional sectors of Cuban society who could not adapt to the revolutionary changes and feared the consolidation of the revolution.

The second phase began in 1965 and ended in 1973. The Camarioca port was opened to Cuban émigrés who wished to pick up their relatives by boat. Approximately 5000 people left prior to the negotiations that resulted in the "Freedom Flights" or airlift from Havana to Miami. Cubans leaving at this time were more likely to be middle and lower-middle class and were composed of small businessmen, skilled laborers, and so forth. They were migrants who resembled the traditional immigrants who came to the United States in search of better economic opportunities.

Although the first two phases of the Cuban migration had important class differences, there were similarities that are useful to point out. These early waves of Cuban immigration were not representative of the Cuban population as a whole (Fagan, Brody, & O'Leary, 1968). These first two phases of immigrants were predominantly White and somewhat older and there were more females than males (Casal et al., 1979).

The third phase was punctuated with the events leading to the Peruvian Embassy incident in April 1980. This most recent wave of nearly 125,000 people has been the largest group of Cubans to arrive in the United States in any one previous year. To date, there exist no reliable data on the characteristics of this group. Unzueta (1981), reporting on data obtained from the first 61,000 Cuban "entrants" of this phase processed in Miami, indicated that the group is relatively young (between the ages of 15 and 35), predominantly male, and may be as high as 40% "non-White." The educational level was estimated to range between sixth and ninth grades. The population of this phase of immigrants can be divided into two broad groups: a marginal population and a sociopolitical dissident population (Spencer, Szapocznik, Santisteban, & Rodriguez, 1981). A sizable percentage of this third phase were poorly educated "lumpenized" (or antisocial) elements that managed to live on the fringes of Cuban society and looked to the United States as the land of easy living (Perez-Stable, 1981). A smaller sector of this population was comprised of former political prisoners and other discontented groups that were awaiting entry permits from the United States. Still, another sector of this population was comprised of individuals who had family in the United States and wished to be reunited.

The problems that this third phase of immigrants face are many. One complexity is that for better or worse, this new group is a product, albeit marginal, of a socialist society. First, their values are likely to clash with the values held in U.S. society. Second, many in this third phase lack connections to natural support systems outside of Cuba (Unzueta, 1981). Third, this group will face the racial, educational, and class barriers, as well as the difficulties of adaptation and assimilation.

Clearly, with Cuban families, an appreciation of the historical and political issues, as well as an understanding of the phases of migration constitute important considerations in the evaluation and engagement in family therapy. Of equal importance is the cultural legacy of Cubans, to which we turn our attention below.

Cuban Cultural Heritage

Cuban culture may be considered to be a blending of Spanish and African cultural patterns (Bustamante & Santa Cruz, 1975; Ortiz, 1973). The method and speed of Spanish colonization determined the historical course of various American nations. In Cuba, unlike Mexico, the indigenous population was virtually decimated. This accounts for the relatively weaker influence that indigenous culture has had on the predominant values and cultural patterns.

There are a number of characteristics that are generally found among Latino groups (see Chaps. 7 and 8). In the areas of language, religion, philosophy of life, family structure, and sex roles, there are probably more similarities than differences among Cubans, Mexicans, Puerto Ricans, and other Central and South Americans. The differences that do exist between Cubans and other Latinos result primarily from class, greater degree of European and African influence, and the unique historical connection to powerful nations (i.e., Spain, the United States, and the Soviet Union) that shapes the world view and reinforces a sense of specialness of Cuba. The following material attempts to sketch some important aspects of the Cuban cultural heritage.

Language

The Spanish language[2] is probably one of the most important aspects of Cuban family life. However, the severity of the cutoff from the culture of origin coupled with the political sanctions against reconnecting with Cuba has pushed many families toward "decubanized" overassimilation. The price of "relative" success may be the loss of language and, by inference, a loss of ethnic identity. An important part of therapy might be to facilitate the recapture of the language and the return to the cultural roots, that is, to facilitate a "recubanization."

Religion

Catholicism remains the major religious preference of many Cubans. Although the number of Cuban Catholics appears to decrease over time in the United States (Rogg & Cooney, 1980), the Church remains a strong base of

2. Parenthetically, it should be noted that while the Spaniard attempted to eradicate all vestiges of Indian culture, the indigenous legacy is apparent in everyday language. Words such as *Cuba*, *guajiro* (peasant farmer), *guayaba* (guava), and *caiman* (crocodile) (Ortiz, 1974; Valdez Bernal, 1978) are considered indoamericanisms. Additionally, the Spanish spoken by Cubans is influenced by the language and culture of the Yoruba and other African peoples.

influence and support for families. The religious community may be used as an important resource in therapy as it is often the place where many Cubans, particularly older Cubans, turn to for support from outside the family in times of crises.

Folk-healing traditions that combine the heritage of Spanish Catholic medical and religious practices with African and other belief systems are common with certain sectors of the population. For example, Santeria (Gonzales-Wippler, 1975) is a religion that combines the beliefs of the Yorubans (Africans from South Nigeria) with those of Catholics. In Cuba, this religion is known as *lucumi* and in Brazil as *macumba*. Also, *espiritismo* (Morales-Dorta, 1976) has been described as a faith-healing system that predominates in Puerto Rico but may be found in parts of Cuba (e.g., the Oriente region). The spiritist practice is centered on a medium as a counselor or healer who helps clients by such practices as exorcizing spirits causing illness. *Santeros* and *espiritistas* are generally found in Cuban and other Latino communities throughout the United States. With some families, mobilizing the support systems available through *santeros* and *espiritistas* can serve as important resources that, when combined with family therapy, have powerful healing effects.

Value Structure

Recently, a number of investigations aimed at studying Cuban values have been conducted with Cubans in Miami (Szapocznik, Scopetta, Arnalde, & Kurtines, 1978; Szapocznik, Kurtines, & Hanna, 1979). In their study with Cuban adolescents, using the Kluckhohn and Strodtbeck (1961) model of value orientations, Szapocznik, Scopetta, Arnalde, and Kurtines (1978) found that Cubans tended to value "lineality," "subjugation to nature," "present time," and "doing" orientations. In a replication of these studies with an adult outpatient Cuban population, Szapocznik *et al.* (1979) found that Cubans differed from Anglos in temporal, relational, and person–nature orientations.

These studies support the cultural characteristics of *personalismo* in interpersonal relationships; that is, an orientation toward people and persons over concepts and ideas. An orientation toward the "lineality" or hierarchy of the family was also supported. Additionally, a value on action, doing, and the present were shown to be important aspects of the Cuban value structure. Szapocznik, Scopetta, Arnalde, and Kurtines (1978) argue for the development of treatment modalities that are in synchrony with the value systems of Cubans in the United States. They suggest the use of a modified form of structural family therapy (Minuchin, 1974). While this approach is useful with Cubans, a contextual approach (Boszormenyi-Nagy & Krasner, 1980) is more inclusive since cutoff and legacy issues may be integrated with structural dimensions of therapy.

Cuban values need to be considered in light of the experience of migration. Of particular importance are the values and principles transmitted to the children and how these values may have been influenced by the migration. For example, some families promote the values of acquiring knowledge and learning and emphasize "here and now" experiences *porque eso no te lo puede quitar nadie* (because no one can take that away from you). With other families, the focus on the present is lived out through an overemphasis on consumer and material values. With the latter families, the emphasis on consumerism may serve as a means of asserting that they are better off in the United States. Other families may have a dual emphasis on educational experiences and consumerism.

At the root of these behavioral patterns and values there is often a shared "existential" reality. For many Cuban families who suffered major losses in Cuba, who faced difficult struggles in the United States, who encountered contradictions between Anglo and Cuban values, the sense that their reality can be radically transformed when least expected is heightened. Thus, values and issues related to "existence" may predominate over "essence." How these issues are manifested with Cuban families will vary widely as a result of the phase of migration, the adaptation to life in the new context, and the linkage maintained to the family in Cuba.

The Family

The Cuban family structure is founded on "familism," the cultural attitudes and values toward the family. The family is the most important social unit in the life of Cubans. The Cuban family is characterized by a bond of loyalty and unity, which includes nuclear and extended family members, as well as the network of friends, neighbors, and community.

Adherence to the traditional family hierarchy of the man as provider depends largely upon social and economic factors. If the husband is unable to find work, he not only loses face, self-esteem, and possibly the *respeto* (respect) of his wife and children, but he is likely to develop marital and intergenerational difficulties. Similarly, when the wife must work outside the home, her new role as economic provider can affect the power balance of the family.

The nature of Cuban marriages and sex roles largely depend upon social class, level of acculturation, stage of migration, religion, and social status in the United States. Nevertheless, elements from the legacy of the Spaniards who brought the notions of *machismo*, female purity, and female marital fidelity may be found in contemporary Cuban relationships. *Machismo*, or maleness, is a largely misunderstood term originally intended to describe the male role as patriarch or autocratic ruler of women and children within the culture. The attribution of dominance and authority to the male, compounded by the emphasis on female virginity prior to marriage and fidelity to her husband thereafter, often result in asymmetrical and oppressive marital arrangements.

The pressures for female purity tend to be reinforced by religious ideology. Women, in the traditional sense, are encouraged to emulate the Virgin Mary. Within the contemporary cultural context, women are, at times, dichotomized into those who are pure like the virgin (*madonas*) and those who are not (prostitutes). As a result, child-rearing patterns emphasize the protection of girls to insure their innocence until marriage. To this day, the traditional practice of *chaperonas* during courtship is maintained by certain families. In the clinical context, the presentation of a rebellious young woman may signal value conflicts between the older and younger generations that probably should be the focus of therapy. Issues of sex roles, *machismo*, and virginity are difficult to deal with for most families. Because of the cutoff from the culture of origin for Cubans, such patterns of conduct that are maladaptive in the new context may be tenaciously held onto in order to support the notion of a Cuban identity.

Acculturation (Szapocznik & Herrera, 1978), adaptation, and adjustment (Rogg & Cooney, 1980) are significant factors affecting the Cuban family in the United States. For example, Cuban women tend to acculturate at a slower rate than do men (Szapocznik, Scopetta, & Tillman, 1978). This situation, compounded by the pressures of the immigrant status and history, often leads to role conflicts when economic conditions push Cuban women to work outside the home. The conflict between the culturally prescribed role ideal and the actual roles of both mother and worker can produce emotional difficulties, marital disharmony, and intergenerational conflicts.

For example, Cubans who migrated during the early phases were primarily from upper- and middle-class backgrounds; therefore, in the clinical context, it is important to consider what postmigration changes may have occurred at the socioeconomic level of the families. If the shifts were downward, how have the parents adapted to this lower status? If the wife was working outside the home for the first time, how did the husband adapt to this change? How did the couple handle changes in traditional marital roles when the wife was not only working for the first time but perhaps was earning more income than her husband? How were the children affected by such changes? Was the housework distributed among the group or was the mother's full-time housework compounded with her full-time employment? Clearly, an upward shift in socioeconomic status may also produce changes in role positions and family structure.

Several independent researchers have indicated that younger Cubans and second-generation Cubans are acculturating at a faster rate than are older and first-generation Cubans. These faster rates of acculturation for younger Cubans (Gil, 1968; Rogg, 1974; Szapocznik, Scopetta, & Tillman, 1978) have produced added stresses and conflicts for Cuban families. Parents are threatened since their authority is questioned and challenged. Children often reject cultural values they view as outmoded (Rogg & Cooney, 1980) and may thrust themselves into a rebellious rejection of Cuban cultural attitudes and behaviors.

The effects of acculturation on Cuban men's and women's views of their roles and their families is a complex one. In working with Cuban families, it is important to recognize that acculturation variables along with socio-economic factors may obfuscate cultural issues and conflicts.

Characteristics

It may be worthwhile to mention, at the risk of stereotyping, some traits that have been considered characteristically Cuban. For example, Bustamante and Santa Cruz (1975) point out that Cuban *choteo*, or humor, and an "exaggerated self-criticism" at one time served a defensive function in the social reality of Cubans. Rubenstein (1976) referenced Manach's (1955) study of *choteo*, and Ortiz (1974) refers to *choteo* as a typical Cuban phenomenon and a type of humor that has been defined as ridiculing or making fun of people, situations, and/or things. *Choteo* often involves exaggerating things totally out of proportion. As Rubenstein (1976) notes, *choteo* may signify taking "matters lightheartedly . . . to modify [situations] through jokes or satirical expressions or gestures" (p. 70).

Almost a precondition for *choteo* is the *tuteo*, the informal form of addressing others. Rather than using the polite or formal *usted* (you), Cubans have a tendency to use *tu* in many interpersonal situations as a means of diminishing distance and establishing familiarity and *personalismo*.

Another characteristic is a sense of "specialness" that many Cubans have about themselves and their culture. Perhaps this specialness stems from the cultural fusion that occurred among European, African, and, to a lesser extent, indigenous cultures. This unique fusion has achieved varied forms of expression through music, art, and literature. For example, the *son* is a basic Afro-Cuban genre produced through the union of Yoruba rhythms and Spanish lyrics. The son, as well as the rumba, mambo, charanga, guaguanco, and cha cha cha, are at the root of what today is known as *salsa* music in the United States.

The sense of specialness may also stem from the geopolitical importance Cuba has had in relation to powerful nations throughout its history. Previously, it was noted that Cuba held a strategic position in relation to Spain and her other colonies. Later, Cuba became a favorite neocolony for the United States with strong economic and military links. Today, as the first socialist state in the Americas, Cubans continue to hold a special position that has been without parallel in the western hemisphere.

Clearly, the sense of specialness many Cubans hold about themselves may have facilitated their adaptation to new environments and may be connected to their "relative success." While notions of specialness are often the driving force behind important accomplishments, extreme manifestations of specialness are at the root of chauvinism, classism, and racism.

In certain non-Cuban cultural contexts, *choteo* and *tuteo* may converge to appear as inappropriate, intrusive, and histrionic. A sense of specialness may be viewed as arrogance and/or grandiosity. When these false impressions are taken together with the sometimes rapid rate and high volume of speech of some Cubans, it is not surprising to find misdiagnoses of manias or hysterical reactions in clinical settings.

Clinical Considerations[3]

To involve Cubans in therapy requires skills in family therapy and sensitivity to cultural issues. Knowledge of the Spanish language is often necessary. For a therapist who does not speak the client's language, much can be missed or frankly misunderstood. Through the language, the therapist can gain a grasp of the cultural issues and may be able to reach older family members for help in resolving intergenerational problems.

Bernal and Flores-Ortiz (1982) have outlined a set of general guidelines for the engagement and evaluation of Latinos in therapy. The focus here will be on the interface between sociohistorical issues and cultural processes that appear to be particularly relevant to the family evaluation and treatment of Cubans in the United States.

The *contextual* framework developed by Boszormenyi-Nagy (e.g., Boszormenyi-Nagy & Spark, 1973; Boszormenyi-Nagy & Krasner, 1980) is most helpful in approaching the task of evaluating and treating Latinos in general and Cubans in particular. The contextual model is an inclusive framework that incorporates psychological, interactional, structural, and ethical–relational dimensions of family processes. Because of the severity of the dysjunction[4] and cutoff from culture and family of origin, legacy and loyalty issues are particularly critical with Cuban families. Nevertheless, a thorough assessment entails not only loyalty and legacy dimensions but also the stages of family development (Carter & McGoldrick, 1980), a study of the relationship the symptom may have to the family structure, and a differentiation of life stress events from a chronic condition.

In the evaluation of Cuban families, the following factors are especially important to ascertain: (1) the migration phase associated with the family; (2) the degree of connectedness to the culture of origin; and (3) a differentia-

---

3. The considerations presented here are by no means exhaustive and should be viewed as only a beginning of understanding the manifestation of cultural processes that may facilitate the engagement and treatment of Cuban families.

4. Throughout this chapter, the terms "rejunction" and "dysjunction" are used to signify, respectively, moves toward and away from building trust in family relationships (Boszormenyi-Nagy & Ulrich, 1981).

tion between the stresses of migration from differences in cultural values and family developmental conflicts.

In working with Cuban families, it is important to inquire how long the family has lived in the United States. This will provide information about the migration phase and will serve as an initial means of assessing differential levels of acculturation in the family (Padilla, 1980; Szapocznik & Kurtines, 1980). Generally, families acculturate at different rates, which may in itself cause added stress (Szapocznik, Scopetta, & Tillman, 1978). Thus, length of time in the United States is a critical question during the evaluation.

Other important questions regarding the migration are: Why did the family move? Who initiated the move? Was there family support for the move or was it a reaction to family difficulties at home? Were there family members in the United States already? Was someone in the family delegated to serve as a bridge and bring the family little by little? (Bernal & Flores-Ortiz, 1982). Further, it may be useful to ask about the political, social, and family pressures that preceded the move.

Which members of the family remained in Cuba is an important matter. Many Cuban families have been split over political issues, and others have been completely uprooted and transplanted elsewhere. Nevertheless, most Cubans have family ties to relatives or friends in Cuba. An analysis of these areas can provide important information about invisible obligations (Boszormenyi-Nagy & Krasner, 1980) that may be affecting the family. Also, as Sluzki (1979) has noted, "the anecdotes that consolidate roles of heroes and villains, victims and oppressors, remain frequently as family myths and appear repeatedly as themes of family feuds or unmentioned skeletons in the closet" (p. 383).

At times, the crises of migration and the family developmental cycle (Bernal & Flores-Ortiz, 1982) may be so blurred with cultural processes that a differentiation between these is difficult. Nevertheless, it is useful to distinguish among migration, transcultural processes, and conflicts in relation to family development. Often the family system becomes dysfunctional because the migration and subsequent adaptation processes interfered with the stages of family development. For example, migration-related tasks such as finding work, providing for food, clothing, shelter, learning a new language, and protecting the family from a new environment often preempt the completion of family developmental tasks (Bernal & Flores-Ortiz, 1982). Thus, when such a disruption occurs, the end result may be a disruption of the whole family developmental sequence, which may lead to symptomatic behavior.

Of particular importance in evaluating Cuban families are the conflicting value orientations related to dependence versus independence. Cuban values of "interdependence" in an "independent" value-oriented context can lead not only to adaptational and intergenerational difficulties on the part of clients but to misattributions on the part of therapists. Therapists need to be sensitive to these issues and clear about the use of labels such as "fusion," "undifferentiated ego mass," and "enmeshment" since healthy interdepend- ence for Cubans may appear as pathological dependence to the non-Latino (Bernal & Flores-Ortiz, 1982).

The value conflicts or binds that different children of Cuban families have experienced vary widely. During the early phases of migration, many Cuban families dissuaded their children from identifying with North Ameri- can culture and discouraged contact with Cuba in an effort to promote "anticommunist" values. Thus, the youth in many families were faced with the dilemma of having to negate both "North Americanism" and "Cubanism." These children had few or no models to affirm, save those of the pre-1959 Cuba.

Azicri (1981) refers to the early stage of the development of Cuban communities in the United States as one of "decubanization" followed by a stage of "recubanization." For our purposes, Azicri's framework may be modified to include a "pseudocubanization" stage characterized by the "frozen culture" group that identified and promoted the values of pre-1959 Cuba. Decubanization as a process is apparent with the "cultureless" group of Cubans that rejected identification with Anglo and Cuban values. Another younger sector became decubanized by assimilating Anglo values and reject- ing Cuban values; this has often resulted in intergenerational family prob- lems. It is the decubanized "generation gap" Cubans of the early phases of migration who often bring their families into treatment.

Examples are offered below to illustrate some common problems Cuban families have in the United States. Case material has been selected from the three phases of migration discussed above to highlight demographic differ- ences and the significance of the sociohistorical and political contexts.

Consider the following case of an upper-middle-class professional Cuban family who migrated in the early 1960s.

The Martin Family

The Martins are a White Cuban family of seven who migrated from Havana to Miami in the early 1960s, were relocated by the Cuban Refugee Center in Philadelphia, and returned to Miami 10 years later. The parents had been professionals in Cuba and indicated that they initially came to the United States with the idea that it would be a "temporary" stay until the political situation in Cuba settled down. They had never intended to migrate per- manently, but circumstances left them no choice.

The presenting problem that led the family to seek help was the behavior of the youngest child—a 16-year-old daughter who was perform- ing poorly in school and was abusing marijuana and amphetamines. While this symptomatic behavior occurred 14 years after the family migrated, it soon became clear that the adolescent paid a heavy price as a result of structural changes that occurred with the family due to the migration. Everyone in the family paid a high price in terms of loss of their culture and natural supports, but the youngest child, who developed into a rebellious adolescent, paid the heaviest price.

Soon after the family's relocation to Philadelphia, both parents worked long hours and the oldest son, aged 13, was placed in a parental role with respect to the other children. This restructuring was necessary so that the chores at home could be done while the parents worked. When the oldest son graduated from high school and left for college, the second oldest son took charge of running the household and disciplining the other children. By the time the parents had the time to "parent" the daughter, she was used to being on her own. The parents were now in their late 50s, and their adolescent daughter was struggling for a greater degree of "independence," was refusing to speak Spanish, and was generally rejecting the Cuban culture.

During the initial four to five evaluative sessions, it became apparent that the stage-specific tasks of the adolescent leaving home and the parents moving toward integrating the loss and accepting their old age could not be accomplished for a variety of reasons. Principally, the adolescent was deprived of parenting, because both parents needed to work. Her older brothers, acting as surrogate parents, did not have the skills to encourage her moves toward independence and encouraged instead a restrictive dependence that had a suffocating impact on her.

The difficulties erupted when the daughter blossomed into full adolescence and the time for her to leave home approached, as had been modeled for her by her older siblings. The difficulties during this period were further compounded because the daughter had not made a contribution to the family as the older brothers had when they were teenagers (i.e., playing a disciplinary role, taking care of the other children). At an invisible level, however, her contribution was the near-delinquent behavior that kept the parents focused on her and not on the realities of growing old.

An area of complexity with the Martin family was that within a Cuban cultural context, a teenage daughter is not expected to be fighting for independence through misbehavior or drug abuse. Expectations for children, particularly girls, are that they leave home at the time when they are getting married. In this case, migration issues and cultural norms converged to exacerbate the difficult stage of separating parents and adolescents.

The Martin family illustrates some aspects of the Cuban experience that are unique to this group.[5] Clearly, the loss of culture, family, and country is significant for any family that migrates. However, the Martins, like most Cubans who came to the United States, could not return to nor visit Cuba, and returning to Cuba remained an issue for them for nearly 18 years. They hoped that things would change politically.

The family became dysfunctional when parental values and expectations (Gonzalez Reigosa, 1976) of the Cuba of 1960 were placed on the daughter;

---

5. For an excellent illustration of the struggles of Cuban families in the northeastern United States, see *El Super*, a film by Andres Jimenez released in 1978.

this is a pattern found with many Cuban families. In this case it is interesting to note that the daughter's rebellious behavior occurred at a time when her parents began to accept her as a grownup and coincided with her moving out of her parents' house to live with one of her older brothers. As she began to make connections with her Cuban cultural roots, her sense of ethnic identity became stronger, which eventually led her to connect with her family in Cuba. The daughter began to shift from a decubanized position of assimilation to the U.S. culture or from the generation-gap Cuban (Gonzalez Reigosa, 1976) to a position of gradual recubanization (Azicri, 1981) and genuine biculturality. Interestingly, the parents' wish to return to or reconnect with Cuba was actualized by their daughter, who served as an important bridge between families that had been disconnected for nearly two decades.

A common strategy of some Cuban families who attempt to restabilize after the disruption of migration is to act as though the migration did not occur and to make efforts to continue living as if they were still in Cuba. The same behavior patterns are expected from family members, the same values are clung to, the same activities and rituals are maintained. In short, a pseudocubanization is at work here. It is as if the culture of origin were frozen in time (Gonzalez Reigosa, 1976) and recreated continuously in the new environment. Although initially adaptive as a coping strategy, such rigidification of the parent culture can eventually lead to dysfunctional patterns.

The following case of a working-class White Cuban family, who left in 1970, illustrates some of the above issues and may be representative of the second phase of migration. However, in this case disturbed family relationships, while affected by the cutoff seemed to have preceded the migration.

The Diaz Family

The Diaz family migrated from Oriente, Cuba, in 1970. Since that time they have lived in the San Francisco Bay area. The family consisted of four sisters and one brother. (The parents had died in Cuba.) They were from a working-class family and were in their late 50s or 60s. None had ever married or had children; they all lived together in the same apartment.

The presenting problem was the bizarre behavior of the second oldest sister who was eventually hospitalized in a psychiatric unit when she became disruptive at home. The identified patient was labeled as delusional (i.e., she complained that sparks from the electric current were bothering her and would spit on her and that the water from the faucet was contaminated with saliva). She had not been a problem before except shortly after the migration from Cuba. The family reported that in 1950, this sister had been briefly hospitalized in Cuba for a "mental problem."

The Diaz family was unusually resistant to meeting as a group. The siblings said that their sister needed help, that she was sick, and that she had become intolerable. However, they agreed to meet for several sessions to help in an evaluation. The primary avenue for the engagement of the family was through focusing on their life in Cuba and the difficulties they had had here. The youngest brother recounted a story of the many hours of volunteer work he had had to do so that the family could obtain a permit to leave the country. When they finally left, two other sisters chose to stay in Cuba. They had no other family in the United States except each other and thus had to help each other even more. They maintained little or no contact with the relatives in Cuba, who had sided with the revolutionary government. Recently, the family had received a letter from an older sister in Cuba who was ill. Though at this time visits to Cuba were possible, the family vowed never to return unless things had changed politically. It was a month or two after receiving the letter that the sister developed "psychotic" symptoms.

One of the key elements in understanding the Diaz family was an appreciation for the delicate family and political conflicts that affected them. Engagement was facilitated by affirming their conflict and acknowledging both the importance in and difficulty of connecting with family in Cuba. As the family began to reveal more about their struggles, its need to remain close to each other could be appreciated. Subsequently, the family members were able to develop a plan to connect with the ill sister in Cuba; this seemed to reduce family tension and the symptomatic behavior. The degree of disconnectedness maintained by the family with other family members in Cuba revealed loyalty conflicts that underlay the behavior of the symptomatic sister.

In the above cases, the Martin family shows how the experience of migration appeared to have disrupted the family's development. The therapist's intervention was based on facilitating the family's move through a particular developmental phase. Their disturbed relationships, which appeared to have preceded their migration, were intensified by this process. In such instances, the therapist needs to engage the family in a therapeutic process to deal with patterns and processes of a more long-standing nature.

In both cases, attention to specific cultural differences facilitated the engagement process in therapy. For example, the Diaz family was engaged by allowing them to discuss important political matters, relatives, and life in Cuba. Many families maintain a certain image of Cuba fixed on the time that they left. These images often develop into myths and have an organizing function, particularly when families go through major crises such as migration. With Cubans, these myths have been shared by large sectors of the Cuban community in the United States.

The cutoff experience from culture and country of origin was perhaps most acute for Cubans migrating during the third phase of immigration. Most of these individuals left under highly stressful conditions and with the knowledge that the likelihood of returning and reconnecting with Cuba was minimal. Consider the following case of a young Black Cuban who arrived through the Mariel boat lift.

The Gonzalez Family

Juan and Frank were first cousins who arrived during the 1980 influx of immigrants from Cuba. The presenting problem was Frank, a Black man in his late 20s, youngest of five siblings, and prior construction worker. Frank was brought to a psychiatric emergency room by his cousin after exhibiting "strange behavior," which included threats with knives, incoherent speech, "loud language," and spontaneous outbursts of anger. The precipitating events that lead to psychiatric hospitalization were multiple and included (1) a conflictual relationship between Juan and Frank; (2) separation from the natural support systems (e.g., family and work); and (3) a stressful, if not traumatic, migration. Both Juan and Frank were involved in the boat lift experience and awaited resettlement for many months at a midwestern camp for Cuban entrants.

Nine months after their arrival, Frank established communication with his family in Cuba. He started receiving angry and blaming letters from his mother. The letters stated he was a bad son and was unbalanced. After receiving these letters, he started to act strange, would become irritated for no apparent reason, and would stare into the sky.

After a four-week hospitalization, Frank continued in outpatient treatment, which included psychotropic medications. Both he and his cousin attended these sessions on a regular basis. It soon became apparent that a major issue was Juan's wish to leave Cuba and go to Miami, which Frank had opposed but went along with anyway for the adventure.

Eventually, a second hospitalization was necessary as Frank developed seriously depressive symptoms, including suicidal and homicidal ideas. Juan had previously reassured Frank that he would not leave him while he was ill, but as soon as he got better, they were to go their own ways. This knowledge maintained Frank's dysfunctional behavior. At this time, Frank was familiar with the ward, the staff, and the expectations in the hospital. These issues were addressed during the second hospitalization, which was somewhat more productive. Nevertheless, at times he became unexpectedly angry and agitated.

During the second hospitalization, family and individual sessions were continued and the focus was on immediate reality considerations, such as, setting up separate living arrangements for Juan and Frank while still maintaining a connection, establishing links to the Cuban resettlement service in San Francisco as well as to other service agencies (e.g., bilingual education and English classes), and making connections with relatives in Miami. The emphasis was on mobilizing support and resources, which was done in a structured format where specific contingencies were set up to maximize Frank's participation in activities, groups, and posthospitalization treatment plans. The themes in therapy, appropriately enough, centered around loss of country and family, in particular, mother, separation, anger, and frustration.

The Gonzalez family needed crisis intervention aimed at mobilizing resources to ease the traumatic migration and adaptation to the new environment. The symptomatic behavior and dysfunction of one family member seemed to be connected not only to the experience of migration, but also to the relationship difficulties between Frank and Juan, which appeared to be long standing in nature.

In the Gonzalez case, issues of migration were central. While the Martin family and, to a lesser extent, the Diaz family could employ defenses such as that their stay would only be temporary or that they would wait out the political situation, the Gonzalez family knew otherwise. They had lived most of their lives under socialism. Furthermore, their sense of cultural and family cutoff was probably greater than that of Cubans from the other phases of immigration. On the one hand, the Gonzalez family had witnessed the mass demonstrations in Cuba repudiating and rejecting those who were leaving. On the other hand, they did not feel exactly welcomed in the United States. In fact, there is evidence suggesting that this group was rejected by sectors of the Anglo, Afro-American, and Latino communities. Also, adding insult to injury, sectors of the Cuban communities in the United States have been at best distant to this group for fear of having their image tarnished (Perez-Stable, 1981) by these new migrants. Thus, the cutoff is intensified since they have been repudiated back home and many have experienced rejection in their new environment.

The Gonzalez family appeared to have been functioning on the fringes of Cuban society, while the Martin and Diaz families, although differing in social class, appeared to have been well integrated in their society of origin. Compared to Cubans from the first two migration phases, people and families such as Frank and Juan Gonzalez are likely to encounter racial, educational, and class barriers hampering the adaptation process. Cultural factors may further impede their adaptations. While Cubans from the prior phases of migration tend to be "present" oriented, this new group is "very present" oriented (see, e.g., Szapocznik, 1981), if not focused on the immediate gratification of needs and impulses. Characteristically, this group tends to establish intense emotional relationships and to value "collateral" or group and community support systems (Szapocznik, 1981), as compared with the lineality and hierarchial family structures valued by Cubans who migrated during the 1960s.

Summary and Implications

The degree of connectedness that Cuban families maintain to their birthplace, culture, and roots is an important element in the assessment of the Cuban families in the United States. This dimension is apparent in the case examples presented above. As previously noted, loyalty and legacy issues are particularly visible with Cuban families. A therapeutic framework such as the contextual approach (Boszormenyi-Nagy, 1979) has useful applications for the work with Cuban families. Boszormenyi-Nagy and Krasner (1980) emphasize that the roots and legacies of our family can never be substituted. These bonds outlast physical and geographical separations and significantly influence the extent to which various family members can freely make commitments to relationships beyond the family of origin (Boszormenyi-Nagy & Krasner, 1980).

The clinician must continually assess the degree of connectedness and the possibilities of rejunctiveness (Boszormenyi-Nagy & Krasner, 1980) to the family of origin, extended family, and culture of origin, as well as to the new culture. Such data have implications for the family's adaptation and adjustment and can facilitate the identification of cultural and relational resources, understanding of intergenerational and loyalty conflicts, and developing of a broader view of the family's context.

It is important to identify where in a spectrum of Cuban cultural identity an individual and/or his or her family are situated. At one end of the spectrum, the frozen culture Cubans may be identified. These were first-generation Cubans who wanted no or little involvement with North American culture. Their adaptation strategy was to resist acculturation at all costs and to hold on to the image and values of pre-1959 Cuba.

Many younger family members were pushed to still another side of the spectrum in response to the static culture and ideology proposed by the first group. Decubanization arose as a response to pseudocubanization. Here two additional groupings may be identified. One has been described as a culture-less younger sector of the first generation. Since many came as youngsters, this group rejected the values of the frozen culture as well as the values of the new culture. While marginal to some extent, Gonzalez Reigosa (1976) describes this group as seeking self-definition through individual pursuits.

A more assimilated and decubanized second generation of Cubans comprise the third group. Their coping strategy was to assimilate and become North Americans. This younger generation's values, at times, may be at the opposite pole of their parents' values. Conflicts with this generation gap sector of Cubans center around value differences that appear to be a result of different degrees of acculturation.

The bicultural Cuban is the fourth group that falls on the recubanization (Azicri, 1981) side of the spectrum and may include individuals from the cultureless and generation gap groups. These are Cubans who have resolved the dilemma of culture conflicts through involvement in *both* Cuban and Anglo cultures, thus developing a new and creative coping strategy. Recent research (Szapocznik & Kurtines, 1980) suggests that Cubans with connectedness to both Cuban and Anglo cultures are more adaptive and functional.

Between 1978 and 1979, nearly 100,000 Cubans in the United States have visited Cuba. For many it was their first visit in nearly 20 years. As a result of *el diálogo* (Castro, 1978),[6] Cubans who longed to be reunited with

---

6. An analysis of the issues concerning "el diálogo" (the dialogue) between Cubans in the United States and Cubans in Cuba is available (Azicri, 1979; Casal, 1978). A contrasting view is available in the September 1979 issue of *Reunión* (*Boletín del Instituto de Estudios Cubanos*) by M.C. Herrera.

their families and others who were searching for a reaffirmation of their cultural identity and heritage were able to do so. A recent publication, *Contra Viento y Marea* (Grupo Areito, 1978), provides autobiographical descriptions of the conflicts and struggles of young Cubans who in spite of political, social, economic, and family pressures eventually reconnected with their cultural roots.

With Cuban families, perhaps more than other Latinos in the United States, the changing political and sociohistorical contexts are a critical consideration. Political events continue to affect the lives of Cuban families in the United States. An understanding of such forces, an appreciation of the changing character of the various waves of Cuban immigrants, and familiarity with the cultural heritage are all essential components in effective work with Cuban families in the United States.

ACKNOWLEDGMENT

The following individuals have made important contributions to this chapter, and I am gratefully indebted to them: Ana Isabel Alvarez, Manolo Gutierrez, Monica McGoldrick, and Eliseo Perez-Stable.

REFERENCES

Amaro, N., & Portes, A. Situación de los Grupos Cubanos en Estados Unidos. *Aportes*, No. 23, 6–24, 1972.

Azicri, M. Un Análisis Pragmático del Diálogo entre Cuba del Interior y del Exterior. *Areito*, *V*, 4–7, 1979.

Azicri, M. El Desarrollo Político de la Comunidad Cubana en E.E.U.U.: Un Análisis del Presente y Projeción Futura. Paper presented at the Seminar on the Situation of the Black, Chicano, Cuban, Native American, and Puerto Rican Communities in the United States, Havana, November 1981.

Bernal, G., & Flores-Ortiz, Y. *Latino Families in Therapy: Socio-Historical and Cultural Differences*. Unpublished manuscript, University of California, San Francisco, 1980.

Bernal, G., & Flores-Ortiz, Y. Latino Families in Therapy: Engagement and Evaluation. *Journal of Marital and Family Therapy*, *8*(3), 357–365, 1982.

Boszormenyi-Nagy, I. Contextual Therapy. In I. Zwerling (Ed.), *The American Family*. Philadelphia: Smith, Klein, & French Laboratories, 1979.

Boszormenyi-Nagy, I., & Krasner, B.R. Trust Based Therapy: A Contextual Approach. *American Journal of Psychiatry*, *137*(7), 767–775, 1980.

Boszormenyi-Nagy, I., & Spark, G. *Invisible Loyalties*. New York: Harper & Row, 1973.

Boszormenyi-Nagy, I., & Ulrich, D.N. Contextual Family Therapy. In A.S. Gurman & D.P. Kniskern (Eds.), *Handbook of Family Therapy*. New York: Brunner/Mazel, 1981.

Bustamante, J.A., & Santa Cruz, A. *Psiquiatria Transcultural*. Havana: Editorial Científico-Técnica, 1975.

Carter, E.A., & McGoldrick, M. (Eds.). *The Family Life Cycle: A Framework for Family Therapy*. New York: Gardner Press, 1980.

Casal, L. Fidel Castro: Invitación al Diálogo. *Areito*, *V*, 5–9, 1978.

Casal, L., & Hernandez, A.R. Cubans in the U.S.: A Survey of the Literature. *Cuban Studies/ Estudios Cubanos*, *5*(2), 25–51, 1975.

Casal, L., Prohias, R., Carrasco, J., & Prieto, Y. The Cuban Migration of the Sixties in its Historical Context. In L. Casal, R. Prohias, & S. Carrasco (Eds.), *Black Cubans in the*

United States. Unpublished manuscript, Project Sponsored by the Ford Foundation, Office of Latin America and the Caribbean, 1979.

Castro, F. *Revolutionary Struggle.* Cambridge: M.I.T. Press, 1972.

Castro, F. *Discursos* (Vol. I). Havana: Editorial de Ciencias Sociales, 1975.

Castro, F. *Entrevista de Fidel con un Grupo de Periodistas Cubanos que Escriben para la Comunidad Cubana.* Havana: Editorial de Ciencias Sociales, 1978.

Fagan, R.R., Brody, R.A., & O'Leary, T.J. *Cubans in Exile: Disaffection and the Revolution.* Palo Alto, Calif.: Stanford University Press, 1968.

Foner, P.S. *A History of Cuba and Its Relation to the United States* (Vol. I). New York: International Publishers, 1962.

Gil, R.M. *The Assimilation and Problems of Adjustment to the American Culture of One Hundred Cuban Refugee Adolescents.* Unpublished master's thesis, Fordham University, New York, 1968.

Gonzalez Reigosa, R. Las Culturas del Exilio. *Reunión: Boletín del Instituto de Estudios Cubanos,* 89–90, September 1976.

Gonzalez-Wippler, M. *Santeria: African Magic in Latin America.* New York: Anchor Books, 1975.

Grupo Areito. *Contra Viento y Marea.* Havana: Casa de las Américas, 1978.

Hernandez, A.R. *The Cuban Minority in the U.S.: Final Report on Need Identification and Program Evaluation.* Washington, D.C.: Cuban National Planning Council, 1974.

Herrera, M.C. El Diálogo: Apuntes y Reflexiones. *Reunión: Boletín del Instituto de Estudios Cubanos,* 125–126, September 1979.

Kluckhohn, F.R., & Strodtbeck, F.L. *Variations in Value Orientations.* Evanston, Ill.: Row, Peterson, 1961.

Manach, J. *Indagación del Choteo.* Havana: Editorial Libro Cubano, 1955.

Minuchin, S. *Families and Family Therapy.* Cambridge: Harvard University Press, 1974.

Morales-Dorta, S. *Puerto Rican Espiritismo: Religion and Psychotherapy.* New York: Vantage, 1976.

Ortiz, F. *Contrapunteo Cubano del Tabaco y el Azucar.* Barcelona: Editorial Ariel, 1973.

Ortiz, F. *Neuvo Catauro de Cubanismos.* Havana: Editorial de Ciencias Sociales, 1974.

Padilla, A.M. (Ed.). *Acculturation: Theory Models and Some New Findings.* Washington, D.C.: Westview, 1980.

Perez, L. *Cuban Exiles in the United States: Myths, Realities, and the Role of the Researcher.* Paper presented at the 71st Annual Meeting of the American Sociological Association, September 1976.

Perez-Stable, E.J. *Cuban Immigration: A Socio-Historical Analysis.* Presentation at the Bicultural Association of Spanish Speaking Therapists and Advocates (BASSTA), San Francisco, February 1981.

Prohias, R.J., & Casal, L. *The Cuban Minority in the U.S.: Preliminary Report on Need Identification and Program Evaluation.* Boca Raton: Florida Atlantic University, 1973.

Rogg, E.M. *The Assimilation of Cuban Exiles: The Role of Community and Class.* New York: Aberdeen, 1974.

Rogg, E.M., & Cooney, R.S. *Adaptation and Adjustment of Cubans: West New York, New Jersey.* New York: Hispanic Research Center, 1980.

Rubenstein, D. Beyond the Cultural Barriers: Observations of Emotional Disorders among Cuban Immigrants. *International Journal of Mental Health,* 5(2), 69–79, 1976.

Sluzki, C.E. Migration and Family Conflict. *Family Process, 18*(4), 379–390, 1979.

Spencer, F.W., Szapocznik, J., Santisteban, D., & Rodriguez, A. *Cuban Crisis 1980: Mental Health Care Issues.* Paper presented at the Southeastern Psychological Association, Atlanta, March 1981.

Szapocznik, J. *Transcultural Processes in Mental Health: Concepts Relevant to Cuban Refugees.* Paper presented at Human Service Training Center Symposium on Transcultural Processes in Mental Health and Human Services Delivery to Cuban and Haitian Refugees, Miami, March 1981.

Szapocznik, J., & Herrera, M.C. (Eds.). *Cuban Americans: Acculturation, Adjustment, and the Family*. Washington, D.C.: COSSMHO, 1978.

Szapocznik, J., & Kurtines, W. Acculturation, Biculturalism, and Adjustment among Cuban Americans. In A.M. Padilla (Ed.), *Acculturation: Theory Models and Some New Findings*. Washington, D.C.: Westview, 1980.

Szapocznik, J., Kurtines, W., & Hanna, N. Comparison of Cuban and Anglo-American Cultural Values in a Clinical Population. *Journal of Consulting and Clinical Psychology*, *47*(3), 623–624, 1979.

Szapocznik, J., Scopetta, M.A., Arnalde, M., & Kurtines, W. Cuban Value Structure: Treatment Implications. *Journal of Consulting and Clinical Psychology*, *46*(5), 961–970, 1978.

Szapocznik, J., Scopetta, M.A., & Tillman, W. What Changes, What Remains the Same, and What Affects Acculturation Change in Cuban Immigrant Families. In J. Szapocznik & M.C. Herrera (Eds.), *Cuban Americans: Acculturation, Adjustment, and the Family*. Washington, D.C.: COSSMHO, 1978.

Thomas, H. *Cuba: The Pursuit of Freedom*. New York: Harper & Row, 1971.

Thomas, H. *The Cuban Revolution*. New York: Harper & Row, 1977.

Unzueta, S.M. *The Mariel Exodus: A Year in Retrospect*. Unpublished manuscript, Metropolitan Dade County, Office of the County Manager, Dade County Court House, Miami, 1981.

Valdez Bernal, S. *Indoamericanismos no Aruacos en el Español de Cuba*. Havana: Editorial de Ciencias Sociales, 1978.

10

Asian Families

STEVEN P. SHON

DAVIS Y. JA

In exploring the uniqueness and cultural distinctiveness of the Asian American family, it is crucial to examine, first, exactly what culture is, and, second, how Far Eastern cultures have been viewed historically by Americans.

In the development of human civilization, an enormous diversity of cultures has evolved and has left their impact on succeeding civilizations. Within each culture, similar patterns of physiological need for survival, shelter, food, and procreation have dictated behavioral responses that in large part were influenced by the environmental context and prior contributing cultures. These behavioral responses, or customs, were derived from an early age when behavior was shaped by the available means of survival and by the environmental context. Each culture through survival learns a particular pattern of adaptation controlling its environment. Benedict (1959) writes:

> The life history of the individual is first and foremost an accommodation to the patterns and standards traditionally handed down in his community. From the moment of his birth the custom into which he is born shapes his experiences and behavior. By the time he can talk, he is the little creator of his culture, and by the time he is grown and able to take part in its activities, its habits are his habits, its beliefs his beliefs, its responsibilities his responsibilities. (pp. 2-3)

Culture then is survival but shaped by an environmental, historical, and social process taking on specific structures such as language, leadership, kinship, and religion. Culture is also a process or a strategy of behaviors involving communications, beliefs, and values.

As cultures emerge, it is inevitable that uniquely different groups meet and are absorbed into one another. This process of incorporation may at

Steven P. Shon. Clinical Services, California State Department of Mental Health, Sacramento, California.

Davis Y. Ja. Richmond Maxi Center, San Francisco, California.

times be conflictual. The perception of one culture by another may be distorted because of its lack of familiarity or its potential threat.

The peoples of East Asia, including the Chinese, Japanese, and Koreans, have evolved a unique cultural form and process that has unfortunately been maligned, stereotyped, and considered "enigmatic" by Westerners for hundreds of years. The term "mysterious East," as coined by Western civilization, has only served to disguise the reality of several complex civilizations that have their own unique customs, traditions, and deeply rooted familial systems based on political and religious foundations that are thousands of years old. Miller (1969) indicates that America has two images of China, the "favorable image [of] ancient greatness and hoary wisdom" and the unfavorable image of a "stagnating, perverse, semi-civilized breeding ground for swarming inhuman hordes." This favorable/unfavorable image partially stems from the competition for resources.

Park (1950) believes that when interethnic groups first make contact, they compete, accommodate, and finally assimilate. Yet there may be some disagreement about this "pluralistic" notion of cultural assimilation for Asians in America. In a capitalist society where competing classes struggle, the physical appearance of Asians has been a difference that has led, and continues to lead, to racial and cultural oppression. Physical appearance and language are, of course, the most prominent differences between Asians and Westerners.

East Asia has the distinction of evolving the longest continuing recorded civilization in the world. Its formidable history provides a background, very different from that of the West, in which East Asian cultures must be understood. Further differences between East and West occur in philosophical approaches to life that are dictated in the East by traditional systems such as Confucianism and Buddhism. These systems do not stress independence and autonomy of the individual but rather that the individual is superceded by the family. Further, the family adheres to the Confucianistic tradition of specific hierarchical roles established for all members. Rules of behavior and conduct are formalized in members' roles to a greater extent than in most other cultures. An individual's response and adherence to this code of conduct becomes not a reflection of the individual but of the family and kinship network to which he or she belongs. This extended family network, the "clan," is responsible for maintaining the status of the family name or lineage. Relationships among husband, wife, and in-laws are strictly prescribed as are relationships between children and parents. Male offspring are valued more than females, and the expectations of each sex are quite different. Historically this was necessary in order to continue under an oppressive dynastic rule and to maintain a large labor force capable of heavy manual and agricultural labor.

In addition to the general distinctions of East Asian cultures from Western cultures, distinctions among the various East Asian groups are also crucial. For Western observers, the differences among Chinese, Japanese, and Koreans may seem minimal, but nothing could be further from the truth. The most obvious difference is language, but the historical, social, and economic developments of the separate nations have also been very different. While it is extremely important to keep in mind the differences among East Asian groups, as well as between East Asian and Western groups, in this chapter we will concentrate on the common features of family structure and function that exist among East Asian groups. Certainly, throughout the centuries there have been numerous contacts among the cultures of the Far East. Buddhism and Confucianism in their varying contemporary forms are, for example, derived from common experiences in early periods of religious and political exchange. This has led to many similarities in family structure.

Key factors to be considered when applying the concepts presented here to any particular Asian family are its social class, geographical origin, birthplace, and generation in the United States. Although the concepts to be discussed will be applicable to most Asian American families, they will be far more applicable to recent immigrants with strong traditional ties. They will be least applicable to later-generation Asian Americans, such as Sansei (third-generation) Japanese Americans.

For East Asian immigrant families cultural transition during immigration was, and continues to be, an extreme hardship. China by the late 1800s had suffered years of continuing famine, war, and economic devastation by Western European powers. These difficult times forced many Chinese from Kwantung Province near the port city of Canton to leave their country, initially as sojourners, to come to America. They came during the California gold rush of 1848 to find a piece of "gold mountain." For Japanese Americans, immigration began in the 1890s when recruiters from Hawaii and the West Coast urged them to seek work as agricultural and mining workers, thus filling the void created by the racist congressional Exclusion Acts of 1882 that halted the influx of Chinese laborers. Beginning in 1903, Koreans were recruited to work on the Hawaiian plantations and for West Coast agriculture. Many Koreans also immigrated as political refugees after the occupation and annexation of Korea by the Japanese following the Russo-Japanese War.

Asian American families felt the greatest pressures during their early struggle for survival and economic security. This "transition" was accomplished at times with success, but more frequently with conflict and alienation. The Asian American family's language, customs, beliefs, and structure began to shift and change. This change in turn had major emotional and psychological consequences for which they are to this day continuing to pay.

This chapter will examine the Asian family structure, basic principles influencing family process and dynamics, issues arising out of cultural transition, forms of family dysfunction, and the implications for therapy.

East Asian Family Structure

The structure of families from East Asian cultures is dominated by Confucianistic principles, with their strong emphasis on specific roles and the proper relationships among people in those roles. Before learning about these relationship patterns, it is important to understand that the concept of time surrounding the existence of East Asian families is different from that of American families. Within American families the emphasis is on the single nuclear family, which has a time-limited life span. The general view is that two individuals who are independent adults meet, court, marry, and have children. They rear their children to become responsible, self-sufficient individuals who will ultimately leave home and repeat the process.

However, within the traditional East Asian framework the family is not time limited. The concept of the family extends both backward and forward. The individual is seen as the product of all the generations of his or her family from the beginning of time. This concept is reinforced by rituals and customs such as ancestor worship and family record books, which trace family members back over many centuries. Because of this continuity, the individual's behavior has a different importance and consequence. Personal actions reflect not only on the individual and the nuclear and extended families, but also on all of the preceding generations of the family since the beginning of time. And individual actions will impact upon all future generations as well. Therefore, there is a burden of responsibility that transcends the individual's personal concerns.

Marriage

In examining the more traditional East Asian family we will begin with the process of the marriage. The choice of mate is often heavily influenced by the families on both sides. While the tradition of arranged marriages is disappearing, there is still frequently a much stronger influence by the family on mate selection than there is for other cultures in the United States. Traditionally, a person does not marry without the blessing of his or her family.

Within the traditional East Asian framework, marriage does not mark the creation of a new family but rather the continuation of the man's family line. The woman is considered to have left her family of origin and to have become absorbed into the family of the man. Under this patriarchal system the status of the wife is quite low; her position is lower than that of her husband, lower than that of her husband's parents, and lower than that of her husband's older siblings.

Within the traditional Confucian framework a woman has three pathways to follow, all of which involve subservience to a man. In her youth she must follow and obey her father. In her adulthood she must follow her husband. In her later years she must follow her oldest son. We will see later that while traditional families may follow this form on the surface, the real dynamics create a different situation.

Roles of Mother and Father

Within the nuclear family subsystem roles and expectations are fairly clearly defined. The father is the leader of the family. He makes the decisions, and his authority is unquestioned. While his authority is great so, too, is his responsibility. Within the eyes of the community, the successes or failures of the family as a whole and of its individual members begin with the influence of the father. It is expected that he will provide for the economic welfare of his family. The responsibility of providing food, clothing, and shelter rest squarely on his shoulders. He enforces the family rules and is the primary disciplinarian. Because of this, he is frequently seen as somewhat stern, distant, and less approachable than the mother.

The traditional role of the mother is of the nurturant caretaker of both her husband and children. Until recently, women were not free to engage in the same kinds of work and activities as men, and the care of the family was seen as their central roles. The mother's energy and creativity were to be channeled primarily into raising her children. The mother is clearly the emotionally devoted, nurturant parental figure who feeds the children, cares for them when they are sick, listens to their difficulties, and frequently intercedes with the father on their behalf. The strongest emotional attachments, therefore, tend to be with the mother.

This dynamic is quite important in the later life of the mother, after the father has died and the oldest son has inherited the reins of the family. Because of the great emotional attachment the oldest son feels toward his devoted mother, the wishes of the mother are frequently respectfully attended to by the son. Thus, although the oldest son is the ruler of the family, it is frequently the mother who rules this son and, therefore, the rest of the family. This, then, becomes the reward of the woman in the later years of her life. The influence of the wife and mother is more covert, through her ability to influence primary male figures, as contrasted to the overt authority influence of males.

Roles of Sons and Daughters

Within traditional East Asian cultures, sons are clearly more highly valued than are daughters. Most of these societies have only recently industrialized; it is understandable that sons were considered more helpful in agrarian-oriented societies. During very difficult times newborn female infants were left to die. The family name and lineage is passed through the male side, while married females are absorbed into the husband's family. Females are raised for the families of others; sons are raised to marry, bring women into the family, and have children who will broaden and extend the family line.

The most important child is, of course, the oldest son. Like his father, he frequently receives better treatment and commands more respect, but he must also shoulder more responsibility. He is expected to be a role model for his siblings as well as to have authority over them. Younger siblings are expected to follow the guidance of the oldest son, not only as children but throughout their adult lives. When the father dies the oldest son takes over the leadership of the family, a task for which he has usually been groomed throughout his life. The pressures and expectations upon this role may cause conflict within this son, and it frequently becomes a pivotal point of conflict within the family as a whole. If the oldest son abdicates this role either through his actions (generally by displaying lack of responsibility) or by outright refusal, the next son generally fulfills it. However, with the recent loosening of traditional attitudes toward women throughout East Asia, the vacated role of an oldest son may more frequently be filled by a daughter. The most important issue is that the role is filled. However, the daughter, in spite of greater freedom of choice in mate and career, is still seen primarily as the caretaker of the household.

Issues of Obligation and Shame

Obligation

Highly developed feelings of obligation govern much of the traditional life of people from East Asian cultures. Shame and loss of face are frequently used to reinforce adherence to prescribed sets of obligations. This section will examine some of these concepts.

As stated earlier, American society has tended toward the ideals of the self-sufficient, self-reliant individual who is the master of his or her fate and chooses his or her own destiny. High value is placed on the ability to stand on your own two feet, or pull yourself up by your own bootstraps, or do your own thing. In contrast, Asian philosophies tend toward an acknowledgment that individuals become what they are because of the efforts of many things and many people. They are the products of their relationship to nature and other people. Thus, heavy emphasis is placed on the nature of the relationship among people, generally with the aim of maintaining harmony through proper conduct and attitudes.

In such a context, the concept of obligation is crucial. The tendency toward reciprocity in America is heavily toward contractual obligation, agreed upon freely among individuals and groups. Within Asian cultures, contractual obligations exist and are important, but the unspoken obligatory reciprocity that arises out of human relationships has a greater impact on the personal life of the individual. Obligation is incurred in two ways. The first is through the relationships of ascribed roles or status, such as those of parent to child, teacher to pupil, and employer to employee. There is a great emphasis on the hierarchical or vertical nature of the relationship. The second is through actions that incur obligation because of their kindness or helpfulness. At times obligations to different individuals may conflict and be a source of great anxiety.

The greatest obligation of East Asians is to their parents, who have brought them into the world and have cared for them when they were helpless. The debt that is owed can never be truly repaid; and no matter what parents may do the child is still obligated to give respect and obedience. This is illustrated by the following Confucian analect. Confucius said,

> In serving his parents, a son may gently remonstrate with them. When he sees that they are not inclined to listen to him, he should resume an attitude of reverence and not abandon his effort to serve them. He may feel worried, but does not complain. (Chan, 1963, p. 28)

Shame

Shame and shaming are the mechanisms that traditionally help reinforce societal expectations and proper behavior. The East Asian concept of *tiu lien* (loss of face) embodies the social concept of shame. Hu (1975) describes the concept of *tiu lien* as follows:

> "*Loss of lien*" is felt acutely, for it entails not only the condemnation of society, but the loss of its confidence in the integrity of *ego*'s character. Much of the activity of Chinese life operates on the basis of trust. As the confidence of society is essential to the functioning of the ego, the "*loss of lien*" has come to constitute a real dread affecting the nervous system of ego more strongly than physical fear. (p. 452)

There is a vivid illustration of the use of shaming and loss of face by a Chinese American family in Jade Snow Wong's autobiographical account of Chinese girlhood in *Fifth Chinese Daughter*:

> [When] Jade Snow picked up and kept a bright piece of cloth that fell from the pack of a visiting peddler, her wrongdoing was publicly displayed. She was told to sit outside the Wong household all day, holding the piece of cloth until the peddler returned, and when people asked her politely why she was passing her time in so peculiar a fashion, she was to confess her crime time and time again in public expiation of her guilt. (Chun-Hoon, 1971, p. 53)

The concepts of shame and loss of face involve not only the exposure of your actions for all to see, but also the withdrawal of the family's, community's, or society's confidence and support. In societal structures where interdependence is so important, the actual or threatened withdrawal of support may shake the individual's basic trust that there will be others to rely upon and raise his or her existential anxiety of being truly alone to face life. Thus, the fear of losing face can be a powerful motivating force for conforming to family and societal expectations.

The Japanese concept of *amae* (Doi, 1973) should be briefly discussed here. *Amae* is a word that has no exact equivalent in Western European languages, although it is felt by Doi to be universally found among human beings. It embodies the concept of passive love, which also includes the idea that we may take advantage of others' love and goodwill. According to Doi, it "would seem to arise first as an emotion felt by the baby at the breast towards its mother . . . and corresponds to that tender emotion that, arising in earliest infancy, was labeled by Freud, 'the child's primary object choice'" (p. 20). While Doi describes in detail the aspects of *amae* in terms of its corollaries in psychoanalytic theory, its impact on Japanese society, and its expression in psychotherapy, we shall focus on just one aspect of Doi's discussion of *amae*, that is, the relationship of *amae* to obligation and shame.

The Japanese term *giri* roughly means social obligation. However, obligation is not just seen as being a burden or debt but also as involving an opportunity to display affection and heartfelt gratitude. A relationship involving *giri* provides an opportunity for *amae* to be expressed and gratified. Therefore, love, both active and passive, is expressed through the fulfillment of obligations, or *giri*.

When shame is incurred, it includes the withdrawal of support and often the suspension of obligatory relationships. Thus, Doi (1973) states that "the man who feels shame must suffer from the feeling of finding himself, his *amae* unsatisfied, exposed to the eyes of those about him when all he wants is to be wrapped warm in his surroundings" (p. 55).

The web of obligation and fear of shame are frequently crucial parts of the life of East Asians and Asian Americans who seek or are referred for treatment. These feelings can affect their behavior and perceptions of the world and their presentation of material in therapy. It can envelop the relationship with the therapist in ways that the therapist does not understand unless he or she is familiar with the cultural themes discussed above.

The Communication Process

Western society values the ability to express ideas and feelings openly. We are encouraged to speak our piece, tell it like it is, or let it all hang out. We are often told that openness and honesty are the best policies. Verbal openness and expressiveness is certainly one of the desirable attributes of the so-called "good therapy candidate."

Within most Asian cultures there is a different attitude toward open and free communication of thoughts and feelings. What may be communicated between individuals and in what manner is determined largely by very specific characteristics of the individuals, which, in turn, define the relationships. Some of these characteristics are age, sex, education, occupation, social status, family background, marital status, and parenthood (whether or not one has children). These specific characteristics will influence behavior such as who will bow lowest, initiate the conversation, change subjects, speak more softly or loudly, look away first when eyes meet, and be most accommodating or tolerant. Even the structure of the language changes in regard to syntax, word endings, and terminology depending upon the attributes of the individuals and the nature of the relationship. Situations where knowledge about personal attributes is unknown generally cause anxiety, for the individual may be unsure about how to behave and in what style to communicate. Ambiguous situations tend to be a source of anxiety and are avoided. Frequently the therapeutic relationship carries many aspects of this ambiguity.

The anxiety aroused in ambiguous situations frequently involves the fear that a social error in behavior or speech will be made and the person will invoke a loss of face. In such situations withdrawal, silence, and watchfulness for correct cues is usually the proper behavior.

Because harmonious interpersonal relationships are so highly valued, direct confrontation is avoided whenever possible. Therefore, much of the communication style of Asian groups aims at being indirect and talking around the point. Directness, which may lead to disagreement, confrontation, and loss of face for both people is often avoided. There is a reliance on the sensitivity of the other person to pick up the point of conversation.

For example, consider this story of two Malaysian families. A daughter from a higher-class family fell in love with the son of a lower-class family. The son approached his parents and told them that he wanted to marry the girl from a higher-class family. His mother said she would approach the girl's family to see if it were acceptable to them. She made an appointment with the girl's mother and went to the home on the proper day. She was greeted by the mother and was shown into the sitting room. Refreshments were brought in consisting of tea and bananas. The two mothers talked about the weather and other things, but they never mentioned their children. After a period of time the boy's mother thanked her hostess politely and left. Upon returning home she told her son that the marriage was unacceptable and, therefore, not possible. The boy's mother knew this because in Malaysia tea and bananas are not generally served together. The girl's mother had given the message that her daughter and the other mother's son did not belong together. By doing it in this way she avoided direct discussion, which may have led to hurt feelings and a loss of face, not only for the boy's mother whose son was rejected, but also for the girl's mother who would have caused the other mother embarrassment and shame.

The Family in Transition

Issues of Adjustment

Generally, in the immigration process the Asian family undergoes two interrelated levels of adaptive cultural transition. The first is a physical or material transition in which economic security, education, and language are major barriers that the family must overcome. The second is the cognitive, structural, and affective transition in which the family psychologically attempts to incorporate various features of their new environment so that it becomes familiar, controllable, and supportive and allows for increased confidence and security. Coping with the emotional concomitants of the transition is seldom overtly acknowledged, but it is often problems in this area that bring the family into dysfunction. Although the following discussion focuses on each adaptive level separately, they are linked and are discussed within the framework of a third factor, the environmental context in which the immigration process occurs. Miller's (1969) statement on the exclusion of Chinese in 1882 is still applicable to this day: "The melting pot is mythical, and . . . Americans always had in mind a cauldron in which the immigrant was cleansed of his foreign ways" (p. 192).

A major aspect of the family in transition is its need for economic security about the basic necessities of life—shelter, food, and clothing. One of the means by which this may be accomplished is for all adult members of the family to begin employment immediately upon arrival in the United States. With their earnings, the Asian immigrants hope to purchase a home and/or a small business such as a restaurant, laundry, grocery, or fruit stand. In the meantime, renting a small apartment must suffice despite the worst possible conditions of deterioration, overcrowding, lack of heat, and insect and rodent infestation.

Employment for parents is primarily limtied to working-class jobs with six-day work weeks, 10 to 12 hour days, often below minimum wage, and with few or no benefits. Furthermore, without some basic English language skills, most working adults are trapped in employment that provides little access to vocational mobility or advancement. Often employment is restricted to restaurant work or garment sweatshops. But given the length of the work week, time to learn the language is almost impossible for parents of growing children. This bind of inadequate employment and poor housing is justified by parents in hope of future benefits.

For purposes of long-term security, the most prevalent investment is to send the children to school in hopes that professional careers, such as that of an engineer or doctor, would provide the means for successful achievement, not only for that child, but for the parents who made this educational and professional achievement possible.

However, the sacrifice of the short-term needs of adequate shelter and clothing often means the sacrifice of socialization and important basic child-rearing functions for long-term material security. Furthermore, the short-term sacrifices often occur over periods of time as long as 10 years or more, as families become mired in a continuing cycle of self-sacrifice for little or no gain. The loss of familiar environmental and social support networks makes the family's functioning more difficult.

Beyond the actual physical adjustments and necessary adaptation, the cognitive component of the family's functioning must undergo severe trauma. Each family member experiences a process of cultural separation that includes the loss of supportive coping mechanisms such as friends, peers, and familiar recreational/vocational opportunities. Upon arrival in the United States, without the language and the familiarity of the culture, Asian families are confronted with a bewildering life-style and culture. Their reactions are complex but generally fall within a framework of response patterns.

The initial phases of cognitive reactions may include (1) cultural shock or surprise at the disparity between what was expected and what actually exists, (2) disappointment at what exists, (3) grief at the separation and loss of what was left behind, (4) anger and resentment, (5) depression because of the current family situation, (6) some form of acceptance of their situation, and (7) mobilization of family resources and energy. This framework attempts to look at a generalized schema of responses that each family member undergoes. Obviously there are many variations, and the order may differ from one family to another.

In general, the response of a family is to mobilize its resources using its *traditional* problem-solving methods. This response may mean emphasizing even more the expectations and demands that each member's role in the family carries. All are expected to respond with great efficacy and energy. The hierarchical structure that may have held up under stress in East Asia will again be expected to provide the foundation on which the family can depend in order to adjust and survive in the new environment. Yet, obviously, the family is not in the environmental context that created the extended family network. The very supports on which the family depended may be missing. The extended network, which assisted the family in East Asia, may be absent in the United States. It is the breakdown of the family structure that leads to dysfunction.

Creation of Dysfunction

Because of the adherence to traditional methods of problem solving, such as reliance on hierarchical authority, male domination, and separation between material and emotional giving, the family in cultural transition frequently cannot adapt to the necessary changes. This inability to adapt may aggravate any of the phases of cognitive response described earlier. Furthermore, a family member's failure to handle a particular cognitive phase may lead to dysfunction within the total family system.

One crucial function of the family structure is to provide a framework of mutual interdependence such that each family member may rely upon another for mutual support. But the shift in culture often removes this possibility. For example, changes for the family may result from the loss of the extended family network. Relatives and close friends are often no longer available to provide support to the nuclear family. This network traditionally "kept it within the family" yet allowed problems and difficulties to be resolved outside of the core nuclear family.

Without close friends, relatives, or extended family, interpersonal relations are limited to the nuclear family. Given the rigidity of family roles, the problems experienced within the family may have little or no outlet for expression or resolution. Tensions and stress may evolve from any one or more of the phases of cognitive functioning, although generally there seems to be greater frequency of dysfunction in later phases such as those of grief, anger, and depression.

An important factor in the family's ability to withstand the pressures of cultural transition is each member's strength in incorporating a system or strategy of defense that has withstood prior threats. Adult members of the family who have previously developed good adaptive responses to their native environment may find that those mechanisms no longer work well in their new environment. Youth who are just beginning to incorporate a framework of adaptive functioning and are testing their abilities for the first time may experience the cultural trauma as far too great an obstacle for their embryonic egos to withstand. It is often these youth who "act out" and become the identified patient leading to family dysfunction.

For youth, learning the English language and academic excellence are crucial. Parents have high expectations in these areas. However, these expectations are often impractical and beyond the ability of their children. For instance, English acquisition may not occur during the first two years of the immigrant youth's schooling. Yet the parents may expect their child to succeed without understanding the time necessary for language acquisition. The youth may recognize his or her own inability to fulfill the parents' expectations, but the parents may not. The youth, therefore, may become isolated, blaming himself or herself or external authority figures for the problems. The inability to function in school is a failure to fulfill the primary requirement of a youth's role in the traditional family. In acting out, the youth may withdraw from the family, distancing himself or herself from other family members. Disruptions in communications may occur, changing from a nonverbal, passive mode to a more overt and direct challenge of authority. The parents, especially the father, whose authoritative role is in question, often respond by intensifying the traditional hierarchical stance, demanding more compliance and greater respect from the youth. This only exacerbates the problem, leading to an absolute breakdown in communication and disruption of the family process.

Another factor influencing the problem of transition is found in the Western orientation of individualism, independence, and assertiveness, particularly in attitudes toward authority, sexuality, and freedom of individual choice. For youth, acceptance of the Western orientation is often preferable because of the need for acceptance by the larger society and because of previous and continuing degradation of Asian culture based upon racism. These factors only serve to alienate the individual further from his or her own culture.

For the parents, dysfunction often occurs when roles change or shift. Failure to fulfill a particular traditional role, or the shift into a different role, may present problems that the parents have difficulty resolving. For the mother, a passive, accepting, and nurturing role is expected. She is expected to continue child rearing and providing for the emotional needs of her family. Unfortunately, because of the economic needs of the family, the immigrant wife may assume the role of a significant breadwinner, thereby encroaching upon her husband's primary role. Unless the husband can accept this change and integrate his wife's new role, conflicts will occur. Frequently, the wife accepts this new responsibility, but she also demands more respect and consideration for this double duty. She feels that this increased recognition is necessary because of her new responsibilities. In addition, this may weaken the supportive link between herself and the children, leading one or more of the children to experience increased vulnerability.

For the husband, the demand on him to share his primary role may lead to conflict and dysfunction within the family. If he cannot accept shared responsibility, he may feel that his wife is undermining his authority. Furthermore, he may feel inadequate when pressing his demand for obedience and respect from his children and wife because he feels he cannot fulfill the traditional requirements of the husband's and father's role. A further threat is the father's view of himself in the context of the Asian American community. If he fails in his role as father and provider he has brought shame and dishonor, not only to himself, but to the family lineage as a whole. Dysfunction may occur through a distancing or withdrawal from any involvement in the family. Conversely, he may demand even greater respect from his family as a means of reassuring himself and of hiding his feelings of inadequacy. His feelings of frustration and anger may be displaced onto his children or his wife who has usurped his role.

Treatment

Entering Treatment

The process of entering treatment is not an easy one for Asian Americans. Mental health resources are used only as a last resort. Most centers in San Francisco, which treat large numbers of Asian Americans, report a higher proportion of diagnoses of severe disturbance, for example, psychosis, among their Asian American clients than among their White clients. This is not necessarily a reflection of greater severity of mental illness among Asian Americans, but rather that Asian Americans generally seek treatment only when all else has failed. There are three major reasons for this pattern of utilization: (1) a lack of familiarity with Western mental health concepts, (2) a problem-solving approach that is internally oriented, and (3) social stigmatization.

Lack of familiarity with Western mental health concepts is changing very slowly. Western concepts are still fairly new in East Asia and among Asian Americans. Most mental health terminology is not even directly translatable because there are no equivalent concepts for the terms in East Asian cultures. The average person believes that someone is either normal or "crazy," a rather strict dichotomy. In this context a person only seeks help from outsiders if he or she is "crazy." There is often little understanding of the concept of a continuum of behavior during which early intervention may deter or prevent things from becoming worse.

Problem solving within East Asian cultures is supposed to occur primarily within the family context. There is a strong dictum that issues are kept within the family and solved there. This is illustrated by one of the Confucian analects.

> The Duke of She told Confucius, "In my country there is an upright man named Kung. When his father stole a sheep, he bore witness against him." Confucius said, "The upright men in my community are different than this. The father conceals the misconduct of the son and the son conceals the misconduct of the father. Uprightness is to be found in this." (Chan, 1963, p. 41)

Thus, bringing a problem to an outsider such as a therapist may be very shameful. It is a statement that the father, or mother, or both have failed the family. The strictest confidentiality does not lessen the knowledge that they have in some way not fulfilled the expectation of the family line.

This leads to the third reason for poor use of mental health services, social stigmatization. Within Asian cultures the status of the family in the eyes of the community is very important. This concern is frequently difficult for Americans to understand because in the United States there is much less of a class orientation status than in East Asia, where seeking mental health treatment reflects very seriously upon the family. The three most common reasons seen as the cause of the "craziness" may be traced to the family. First, it may be seen as a hereditary trait that runs in the family line. Second, it may be seen as a punishment for past behavior of the family (similar to karma). Finally, it may be seen as a reflection of poor guidance and discipline by the family leader. People may believe that any one or all of the above reasons together are the cause of "craziness" in a particular family. In any case, the family is less likely to be accepted and less likely to find good marriages, which are important in maintaining the family line.

For these reasons the family is not likely to seek help from a mental health agency until they have exhausted not only their own internal resources but also the resources within their cultural community, for example, herbalists, acupuncturists, and ministers. They frequently enter therapy feeling ashamed and defeated, often with a family member whose behavior is psychotic, violent, or suicidal, and can no longer be controlled. If a child is the identified patient, frequently the family has been forced against its will by the school to seek treatment. The therapist must be sensitive to all of these issues if he or she is going to engage the family successfully in treatment.

Therapeutic Alliance

Sue and McKinney's (1975) study of 17 community mental health centers in Seattle revealed not only that Asian Americans grossly underutilized mental health services, but also that of those that did seek services, 52% dropped out after the first session. Of the 48% who returned, the average number of therapy sessions was only 2.35. These statistics, which are not different from other urban areas, seem to imply the absence of the development of an initial relationship and alliance between therapist and client.

In discussing the successful development of a therapeutic alliance with Asian families, it is important to examine the process from the perspective of the client's role expectations of the therapist. The family, especially the parents, perceive the therapist as the knowledgeable expert who will guide the family behavior in the proper course of action. He or she is seen as an authority figure and is respected as such. However, the therapist may quickly lose this respect if he or she does not fulfill most of the expectations of the family, and the family may then withdraw from treatment.

The family expects that the authority figure will be more directive than passive. A frequent mistake of therapists in the initial visit is that they tend to wait for the process of the session to flow from the family in the hope of observing the family interaction with as little interference as possible. This passive initial approach is quite often seen by the family as a lack of knowledge or skill. Once such a judgment is made, the family is not likely to return. Therefore, the therapist must take a more directive stance initially. Being directive does not mean that the therapist should tell the clients how to live their lives; rather, it involves directing the process of the session. Thus, the therapist may direct the family as to who speaks first, how much time each person will speak, and what should be the focus of the dialogue. Taking command of the process is generally the expected and respected course of action for the therapist.

In working with families with East Asian cultural heritages, the importance of understanding traditional roles cannot be overemphasized. Although assimilation and acculturation may have greatly modified Asian Americans, the majority of them are immigrants or children of immigrants and as such still carry some of the traditional family values. Showing the proper respect for the roles of the family members is essential in developing and continuing a successful alliance.

The father often feels ashamed and defeated for having to turn to outsiders for help. He may be too proud to state this openly and if he feels that he is being slighted or criticized, the chances are that he will feel offended and not return. Reinforcing his role within the family initially is, therefore, extremely important. This may be done in simple ways such as addressing initial inquiries, explanations, and requests first to the father. The following case illustrates some of these points.

F, a 24-year-old son of immigrant parents, had been admitted to an in-patient unit with a diagnosis of schizophrenia, paranoid type. He had been on the unit about two weeks before he was transferred to me (SS).

The previous therapist related that F had probably been psychotic for two to three years before his parents brought him in. He had been started on medication and was being seen in individual therapy and in family sessions. The previous therapist said that the family sessions had fallen apart and that there had been trouble with the father. Father had not always given F his medication correctly when he had gone home on passes and also had not always brought him back to the unit at the proper time. In the family sessions, father did not have much to say. The therapist wondered how much he really cared about F because of his reticence to speak and the fact that he kept F at home for two to three years before any treatment was sought. In trying to work around father the therapist had attempted to work more with mother and older brother who were quite verbal and expressive. Shortly after this, the family stopped coming to sessions.

In order to reconnect, I called the family and was able to arrange a family session in their home. Upon arrival, I was offered tea and cookies as refreshment. First, I politely refused, then, after mild urging, I allowed myself to be talked into it, which was the proper etiquette. In the next 20 to 30 minutes F was not even mentioned. Instead we went through the ritualistic small talk that was important in allowing time to find out about me and vice versa, without being too direct. I found that this was a very close, traditional family. The two oldest sons were married and lived within six blocks of the parents. They, their families, and the younger sister were all at the family session. I discovered that father cared very much for F. I realized that he did not speak or understand English very well but felt too ashamed to admit it. He already felt ashamed for having to bring his son in for help, which meant he had failed in some measure as a father. It was clear that he had gotten the instructions of the previous therapist confused because of his poor English. When the therapist tried to work around him by giving instructions to the mother, it was a severe insult and caused great loss of face, so he pulled the family out of sessions. Throughout the session I addressed all of my explanations, comments, and instructions first to father even though I knew he did not understand everything and that others would have to translate later. However, this preserved his primary status. Later we talked about delegating some responsibilities around F's medication and transportation to others, which finally occurred after father gave permission and okayed each assignment. At the end of the evening, the family expressed much gratitude that I had taken time to come to their home when they knew I did not have to. Father assured me that everything would be done to see that things went smoothly, and from that time forward the family sessions and treatment plan proceeded without any difficulties.

The role of the mother must also be understood and respected within the context of her role expectations within the family. Issues involving the children reflect upon her self-esteem as a mother. We must remember that in the traditional family, the children are primarily her responsibility, as well as her resource for the future. Frequently, issues around perceived dependence of children and overprotection of the mother are raised by American therapists who are unfamiliar with traditional family dynamics of Asian families. Therapists do not always understand that within the family mutual interdependence is stressed and expected. This is not to say that individuation does not occur or is not promoted, but it is constantly tinged with the subconscious knowledge of the relationships and obligations between the individual and other family members.

Because of the American emphasis on self-reliance and independence, therapists often interpret relationships between the children and mother as symbiotic and overdependent. Such a relationship should not be assumed unless the therapist has a good understanding of the dynamics of the normal range of traditional East Asian families. When the therapist does make such an erroneous interpretation, part of the solution that is frequently prescribed is further physical separation and the development of greater outside interests for the children. A common result of this is that the family leaves therapy. It *must* be kept in mind that the children are the resource for the mother in her older age. Her reward for enduring many things in her early life comes through her children's devotion when she is older. A therapist who attempts to weaken the bonds between mother and children, however well intended, will face great resistance and will frequently lose the family.

The role of the eldest son frequently stimulates intense conflict. Since he is the oldest, he is expected to be the most respectful to the parents and at the same time to be a role model and provide direction to the other siblings. In many ways he is expected to be the most traditional, yet he cannot help being influenced by American values that are contradictory to many of those of his parents. Other siblings may more easily evade the traditional expectations placed upon the oldest, although they too have their respective roles according to sex and birth order as described earlier. It is important that the therapist be familiar with the various role expectations of each sibling so that embarrassment, resentment, and loss of face can be avoided. For example, a therapist might make a serious error in directly encouraging an older son to follow the dictates of a younger sister.

The Communication Process in Treatment

For therapists who are not used to the communication style of Asian families, the communication process in therapy may seem to be difficult and frustrating. In this section three topics will be discussed: the revelation of information, the expression of feelings, and the process of disagreement in therapy.

THE REVELATION OF INFORMATION

Before revealing family conflicts and secrets to a therapist, the family will try to develop a trusting and comfortable relationship or alliance. As described earlier, part of this involves finding out some information about the therapist. If the therapist is uncomfortable with this and gives information very reluctantly, it is likely the family will, in turn, feel uncomfortable about revealing information. This does not mean the therapist must tell his or her life story, but he or she must give enough information so that the family has some perspective about their therapist.

As issues about and problems within the family arise, the therapist will frequently find that they are minimized and discussed indirectly. Again, this tend to be a cultural communication style, and the therapist is expected to read between the lines in order to grasp the major issues. If the therapist is not patient or sensitive to this style and feels that the family is not straightforward, difficulties in therapy may arise. The family may perceive the therapist as too blunt, pushy, and insensitive. They may become extremely uncomfortable with the therapist's attempts to be more direct and open and to speed up the process. If the therapist is patient and successfully grasps the downplayed issues and indirect messages, the family will gradually respond as time goes by. However, this may be a long process and the typical Asian family may never feel as comfortable with that process as the average middle-class American family would.

THE EXPRESSION OF FEELINGS

As discussed earlier, Asians have a very different attitude toward open communication of feelings from that of Americans. The therapist must be aware of this, as well as of the fact that open communication becomes even more difficult in front of an outsider. Certain feelings, such as love, are frequently not expressed in the open way that they are in the United States. In East Asia, love and affection are ordinarily expressed openly only to infants and so much so, that by Western standards it would seem that the infant is being pampered and indulged. From the expression of love during these early years there develops a strong sense of basic trust, in the Eriksonian sense. After these early years, the child rapidly becomes incorporated into his or her role in the family structure and learns to live by the more rigid guidelines and expectations of the family and the community. Affection is no longer expressed as openly. In our experience it is unlikely that children whose parents were born in East Asia have observed their parents embrace, kiss each other, or say, "I love you." Instead, love is traditionally expressed through certain actions. Thus, if a father works hard to provide food, shelter, and clothing for his family and demonstrates understanding through good guidance and direction, he is expressing his love for his family.

Difficulties in expression of feelings may arise in Asian American families with children born in the United States. They are often confused when they observe, both in the families of friends and in the media, that American parents are expressive and affectionate. They often wonder if this difference means that their parents love them less. The therapist must be careful not to judge the parents as unloving or uncaring but rather to see the problem as a difference in cultural styles of expression. The therapist may then bring better understanding to both parents and children and help resolve an important area of misunderstanding.

THE PROCESS OF DISAGREEMENT

The process of disagreement between family members and therapist needs some discussion. We must remember that the therapist is looked upon as a knowledgeable expert. Thus, a measure of status and respect is automatically conferred upon the therapist. If the therapist is helpful in resolving some issues within the family, the esteem for the therapist will rise further. However, this may be a double-edged sword, for the family members may feel less able to disagree with the therapist or express any negative feelings toward him or her. To express feelings of anger or criticism toward someone of high status (a professional) and who has been helpful (obligation is incurred) would generally be considered disrespectful.

The therapist must, therefore, be perceptive with regard to nonverbal cues in the family, such as changes in voice inflection or facial expression. These may provide indirect cues such that someone is in disagreement or has some feelings of anger but is trying not to express them overtly. If the issues stimulating such feelings are not perceived and dealt with, the family may drop out of treatment without the therapist ever knowing why.

The therapist may find that lower status individuals within the family will not easily express negative feelings, such as anger, toward those in higher roles, for example, child to parent. In most circumstances, to do so would be considered disrespectful. Because of this, the individual may either suppress such feelings or, if in touch with them, be reluctant to express them openly. Often they are internalized and may appear as self-recrimination and self-criticism. There must be a great deal of education and delicate restructuring before the family members feel comfortable enough to express such feelings openly. The therapist should not push the family too hard for there are many families that never feel comfortable deviating from this cultural style of expression. In such instances the therapist must be aware of the subtle behaviors and cues that indicate such feelings and find methods of resolution. We have frequently found the structural family therapy model (Minuchin, 1974) quite helpful because of its emphasis on actively restructuring the interactions in the family to create change rather than relying on direct and open expression of feelings as a necessary part of the process of therapy.

Therapist Race

For the non-Asian therapist, the particular value and belief system of a different race and culture may be a barrier to understanding and working through of the particular needs and problems of the family. A key element in the therapeutic process is the ability of therapists to explore their own feelings, attitudes, and stereotypes about Asian Americans. Often the only experiences with Asian culture may be through stereotyped media portrayals or service workers in restaurants or laundries. Some may have experienced formal contact with one or two Asian friends in school or at the office. But these limited experiences may provide little or no understanding of the cultural transition difficulties of the Asian family. This is especially true given the non-Asian therapist's lack of experience and knowledge of the Asian family cultural orientation. Because of the complexities of Asian family systems, an Asian therapist is generally preferable. However, there are insensitive Asian therapists who have never seriously pursued an understanding of their own culture, language, or class. A sensitive non-Asian therapist is preferable to an insensitive Asian. But generally a degree of cultural similarity helps in the understanding of the Asian family's cultural transition in a frequently hostile environment. A therapist who has the language skills, is familiar with the class background of the family, and has had personal working experience with immigrant families can make the difference between success and failure in therapy with Asian American families.

Summary

We have offered an overview of the common cultural themes that are found within Asian American families and that affect the process of therapy with these families. We believe that knowledge of the concepts and principles discussed can be helpful in the treatment of dysfunctional Asian American families. Again, we wish to remind you that there are only Chinese families, Japanese families, Korean families, Vietnamese families, and so on. Therefore, the themes discussed in this chapter will have their own variation depending upon the ethnic origin of the family. The scope of this chapter does not allow for an in-depth discussion of each ethnic variation. Thus, the therapist treating a family of a particular Asian ethnic group is encouraged to obtain further information about that group through additional reading and by consultation with therapists of that particular ethnic group.

REFERENCES

Benedict, R. *Patterns of Culture*. Boston: Houghton Mifflin, 1959.

Chan, W.T. *A Source Book in Chinese Philosophy*. Princeton, N.J.: Princeton University Press, 1963.

Chun-Hoon, L. Jade Snow Wong and the Fate of Chinese-American Identity. *Amerasia Journal*, *1*(1), 52–63, 1971.

Doi, T. *The Anatomy of Dependence*. New York: Harper & Row, 1973.

Hu, H.C. The Chinese Concepts of Face. In D.G. Haring (Ed.), *Personal Character and Cultural Milieu*. Syracuse, N.Y.: Syracuse University, 1975.

Miller, S. C. *The Unwelcome Immigrant*. Berkeley: University of California Press, 1969.

Minuchin, S. *Families and Family Therapy*. Cambridge: Harvard University Press, 1974.

Park, R.E. *Race and Culture*. New York: Free Press, 1950.

Sue, S., & McKinney, H. Asian Americans in the Community Mental Health Care System. *American Journal of Orthopsychiatry*, *45*(1), 111–118, 1975.

11

French Canadian Families

RÉGIS LANGELIER

Franco-Americans[1] have settled throughout the United States, but their largest concentration is in New England. One out of every seven persons in New England is of French Canadian descent, constituting the largest non-English-speaking ethnic group in that area. Yet, while some cities and towns boast voter lists with a majority of French surnames, Franco-Americans go almost unnoticed. They have traditionally been quiet and unassuming as a group and have led very private lives, characterized by persistence in preserving their language and culture.

Up to this time, nothing has been published on psychotherapy with Franco-Americans. The task is made more difficult by the lack of research in counseling members of this ethnic group and by the variations within the group itself: urban and rural; educated and noneducated; first, second, third, or fourth generation in the United States. An anthropologist warns us:

> My own research and experience indicate that there is considerable variation in the "Franco-American" experience. Variation in linguistic experience, in geographical origin, in degree of assimilation, in age groups, and educational levels is enormous. In fact, it is often extremely difficult to arrive at a definition of "Franco-American"; it is, in reality, a political term. For example, many fully bilingual residents who come from 100% French homes and are of French mother-tongue, would never identify themselves as Franco-American because of the political connotations. (Sorg, 1980)

In spite of these differences, we believe that it is still possible to arrive at certain common characteristics of a family profile to enable therapists to deal more effectively with Franco-American clients. We will describe how Franco-Americans have been shaped by a pervasive Catholicism, by their dedication to duty and their conservatism, and, up to recent times, by their linguistic isolation and pride in the French language. Two sections of this chapter, "Family Patterns" and "Family Therapy," make use of material collected in a survey of 35 persons, educators and psychotherapists, currently working professionally with Franco-Americans.

1. In this chapter the term "Franco-American" refers to the descendants of French Canadian immigrants. Those who came directly from France to the United States and their descendants are not included. For information on the immigration from France, see Higonnet (1980).

Régis Langelier. Department of Counseling, Université Laval, Quebec, Canada.

Historical and Cultural Introduction
CLAIRE QUINTAL[2]

Franco-Americans, sometimes called French Canadians, are descendants of farmers who left Quebec in massive numbers between 1860 and the 1920s. The flow slowed considerably when growing industrialization and urbanization in Canada created jobs, thus reducing the necessity to immigrate to the United States.[3]

The French Canadians who came to the United States did not have far to go to reach New England. Unlike other ethnic groups in the United States (except the Chicanos) Franco-Americans did not have to cross an ocean. Having sold all of their belongings *à l'encan* (at a public auction), they simply took a train. They came into New England[4] with their own traditions, language, and religion, all of which were totally alien to native New Englanders.

Though the Franco-Americans were immigrants in New England, they had been North Americans for generations. French Canadians descend from 17th-century settlers of the New World. Their ancestors explored the continent, fought and won wars, often with Indians as allies. But they also fought and lost. Indeed, they lost the last battle and, abandoned by France, became subjects of the British monarch in the 18th century.

Although defeated by the English, most French Canadians were not subjected to overt persecution. The Acadians, French colonists of what are today Nova Scotia and New Brunswick, however, suffered severely. They were brutally deported, starting in 1755. Many ended up in Louisiana, where they are known as Cajuns. Some Acadians escaped deportation by hiding out in the woods.

French Canadians "hid out" from the English in a psychological sense. They lived apart and turned in upon themselves. In isolated rural settings, dominated culturally, as well as religiously, by the Catholic Church, they led simple lives. Education was minimal. Early marriage and the begetting and raising of children were given the highest priority by the Church hierarchy, which saw large families as the only hope for the future of the race. Few French had come originally. There were only 60,000 French Canadians and

---

2. "Historical and Cultural Introduction" by Claire Quintal, l'Institut français, Assumption College, Worcester, Massachusetts.

3. Pierre Anctil (1979) estimates that approximately 5 million United States citizens are descendants of French Canadian immigrants, 2,225,000 of whom live in New England. It has been variously estimated that of the 2,225,000 descendants of francophone Canadians living in New England, some 200,000 are of Acadian stock—the French peoples of what are today Nova Scotia, New Brunswick, and Prince Edward Island.

4. Many also settled in upstate New York, and large numbers of emigrants went to the Midwest where most of them engaged in farming.

fewer than 15,000 Acadians in the French colonies at the time of the conquest, when the population of the 13 American colonies was 1,610,000. Further French immigration was totally cut off by the English victory.

Life on a three-generation family farm was rewarding in some ways. Farms, even marginal ones, can usually manage to feed one more mouth, so there was room for children. Simple goals could be set and achieved. Life, though difficult, was not without gaiety; and there was emotional security in this stable, well-ordered existence.

But the increasing population, when combined with the shortage of good land and the stresses of farming so far north, where the growing season is very short, produced a flood of emigrants, lured by prosperity in the United States.

When French Canadians left Canada for New England, they usually came to cities where relatives or friends had preceded them. They had a place to go and a family to receive them; often, they even had a job waiting.

Family and religion are central to the lives of Franco-Americans, just as they had been for their French Canadian rural forebears. The family handed down its essentially conservative, traditional values through the generations, aided by the powerful impact of the Catholic Church's code of behavior. It is a rigid code, particularly about sexual matters. Until quite recent times, the Church's teaching on moral matters was dominated by priests and nuns trained in the seminaries and novitiates of Quebec, where the doctrine of original sin was emphasized and human nature viewed with profound pessimism. In *Visions of Gerard*, Jack Kerouac, himself a Franco-American, summed up the view of self that resulted from this teaching:

> But you bumbling fool you're a mass of sin, a veritable barrel of it, you swish and swash in it like molasses—You ooze mistakes thru your frail crevasses. . . .
> (1963, p. 41)

Life was seen as full of temptations, offering opportunities to sin rather than to strike out constructively and to choose wisely. Franco-Americans had defeatism in their blood. They set limited goals. They settled for less and had to be content since the best reward of all—paradise—could be attained if they had been faithful—in the fullest sense of the word—to Mother Church and to Mother tongue—language being perceived as the guardian of their faith.

As a result of being constantly subordinated to strong authority at home, within the Church, and at work (where Franco-Americans rarely occupied positions of authority), anger and resentment were and are often intense. Franco-Americans felt helpless in the face of powerful outside forces. They could count only on themselves as individuals, or, as was more often the case, as individuals surrounded by a caring family.

As the speakers of one of the privileged languages of the world—French—Franco-Americans could have regarded their language as a badge of honor. Such an ability could have enhanced their status within any community. But educated Americans admired only Parisian French. The French spoken in New England with a rural accent was disdained. It lacked the polish, sophistication, elegance, and style which are associated with the French from France. Thus, the French language, to which Franco-Americans were profoundly loyal, also became a badge of inferiority.

Franco-Americans distrusted outsiders. No one, they felt, not even members of other ethnic groups who, like Franco-Americans, have been the butt of prejudice, could truly understand their special position. They saw themselves, because of their religion and their language, as better than they were judged to be, but they were well aware that they were looked down upon. Survival as a separate entity, against all odds, became a mystique.

In spite of this mystique of *survivance* (survival) as an ethnic group, Franco-Americans did not support their own. They were unwilling, for example, to act in unison in political matters. Suspicion of the "other" ran too high. The "other" could be someone of another religion or of another nationality, or simply be a member of another Franco-American parish, even a Franco-American neighbor. These attitudes had been learned through a succession of generations enclosed within isolated communities.

Franco-Americans felt forever attacked and conquered by outside forces. In the 1920s they were dealt a particularly demoralizing blow in the one area where they were most confident, religion. In the *Sentinelle* affair, Franco-Americans struggled against their Irish-controlled Roman Catholic hierarchy, demanding some degree of autonomy in their own parishes; the Pope excommunicated their leaders.

Franco-Americans have been pitted against the Irish ever since they arrived in New England. They tend to see the Irish as arrogant and brash, although they respect Irish success in church and secular politics. Franco-Americans can, like the Irish, be articulate, witty, and colorful, but within the secure framework of home or parish, and usually in French.

Franco-Americans have been "put down" since birth: first, by parents fearful of raising an arrogant child whose chances of fitting into a life of adversity, and eventually getting into heaven, would be diminished, and, second, by religious teachers and priests for whom pride is thought to be the ultimate sin. They share the pervasive sense that since they have been born into a group whose chances of material and personal successes are problematic, they will be happier with their lot if they do not strive to rise above their lowly station in life. This upbringing discourages taking chances for the sake of future success. Those who do not dare to achieve the very best of which they are capable, feel lasting bitterness. Toward those who have taught them excessive humility and caution, they harbor ambivalent feelings—both respect and resentment.

Collectively, Franco-Americans spent much of their meager resources building a network of parish elementary schools, staffed by religious orders. As early as 1904, they even had a college that they could call their own, Assumption College in Worcester. But only parents of means could afford anything other than the local parish schools. Those who could not afford to go to private Catholic colleges, rarely went beyond high school. However, some young men of promise were subsidized by their parish priests to attend the classical colleges of Quebec.

Thus, the religious upbringing of Franco-Americans, coupled with a lack of education and worldly ambition, led them, at an early age, into the same mills where their parents had toiled before them. They were content to work for little return, having accepted, seemingly without question, that fallen man had to work by the sweat of his brow, but convinced that heaven would be reward enough for their lives of uncomplaining, dutiful labor.

Family Patterns

Franco-American family patterns have changed since World War II. It is vital to distinguish between prewar and postwar generations. Also, college-educated Franco-Americans living in a large city or the suburbs are less likely than their high-school-educated counterparts, living in the little Canadas of New England textile towns, to fall into the traditional family patterns attributed here to Franco-Americans. However, among those who have not gone beyond high school and who have remained in the little Canadas or in rural areas (some 20% of the population), it is fairly safe to assert that sex-specific roles are well defined, with almost no sharing of tasks between husband and wife. Marriages are not companionate but oriented toward traditional roles and expectations. The husband's responsibilities are to exercise authority, to punish misbehavior, and to provide protection and economic support. The wife's responsibilities are to oversee the family's welfare, to manage the daily household activities, to plan leisure time activities, and to rear and educate the children. Authority is almost always the man's prerogative, and although in recent times the father has been losing ground as the sole authority figure in the Franco-American family, he still exercises most of the overt power (Chassé, 1975; Woolfson, 1975).

The father is not only the authority figure and economic provider for the family; ideally he is also a moral leader who, in difficult times, provides the family with affection, attention, and support and is responsible for creating a climate of security. According to Garigue (1968), "men regard it as normal for their wives to depend on them and to trust in them" (p. 159). Such confidence stimulates a man's affection for his wife and his desire to protect her from, for example, any critical comments from other family members. A husband's affection should be expressed, above all, when his wife is weary or ill. Then he must show his love and make life easier for his wife and their family.

The Franco-American mother is the heart of her family, and a kind of "sainthood" is ascribed to her (Benoit, 1935; Chassé, 1975). She is a powerful emotional force and a moral support for the entire family (French, 1976). She acts as a mediator in family relationships and prevents direct confrontation. As one therapist in our survey succinctly put it, she is the agent of "regression to the mean," either in the relationship between a harsh father and his children or as a rule reinforcer herself when her husband is too lenient. She is expected to assist and to please her husband without challenging his authority. She exercises influence by covert persuasion, especially persuasion that will increase her husband's acceptance of her children's unorthodox behavior. This strategy has probably had greater impact on final decision making than has been generally acknowledged in sociological assessments of Franco-American families.

Early marriage and the prompt assumption of parental responsibilities characterize the transition into young adulthood for less-educated Franco-Americans. The arrival of children is the most important step in the early marital life cycle. For the young women, childbirth—especially the arrival of the first born—is the *rite de passage* into adulthood. While children of either sex are welcome, male children are particularly desired and are as a rule more indulged (French, 1976).

After marriage the woman is likely to forsake her peer group orientation for that of her new marital role, but the man "continues his peer group membership all through his adult life, with such interests often superseding those of his immediate family" (French, 1976, p. 336).

Children are raised to be honest, loyal, and hard working. Woolfson (1973), in a study of the value orientations of French Canadian and Franco-American school children, writes: "They tend to value responsibility, self-control and obedience" (p. 12). Franco-American families emphasize conformity, respect for authority and institutions, family loyalty, religious principles, and self-control.

Upward mobility and acculturation are resulting in liberalization in third-generation families as they move to mixed neighborhoods and make friends with mainstream Americans. But child management by means of punishment rather than positive reinforcement is still generally the rule.

Parent–child relationship patterns among French Canadians have been studied by Garigue (1968), who finds that while children are oriented toward both parents, they reveal a preference for the mother. They see the father more as a manager, the mother more as a friend. Children feel confidence in and strive to ally themselves with their mothers. They treat their fathers with respect tempered by emotional distance and lack of spontaneity. It appears that Franco-American patterns are similar.

From the point of view of structural family therapy, it could be said that fathers and mothers have enmeshed boundaries with power apparently shared in relationship to the children. This is particularly true in matters where problems cannot be solved by the exercise of paternal authority or maternal sentiment. Children have little or no power, and the boundaries between them and their father are rigid. Father has undisputed power to scold or otherwise punish those with lesser power.

Looking at the Franco-American family from this perspective, we can describe the politics of four specific subsystems: mother–son, father–daughter, mother–daughter, and father–son. The first two cross-sex pairs are characterized by stronger ties than are the latter same-sex pairs. In dysfunctional families where the marital coalition is relatively weak or absent, these cross-sex parent–child alliances are intense and the possibility of emotional fusion is high. In addition to these parent–child subsystems, we must consider sibling relationships. These are generally characterized by friendship and mutual aid.

It is usually of therapeutic value to encourage awareness of individuality in parent–child relationships by sorting out the different roles within the family, such as the difference between what is expected of the eldest and the youngest, and by looking at actual differences between them, such as interests and special aptitudes. This process is also useful in improving the relationships among brothers and sisters.

Franco-Americans are taught very early that anger is not an acceptable emotion. Aggression within the family is either not allowed or, if it is vented, it is done only in controlled ways such as participation in athletics. The controls are too rigid, and when anger eventually does erupt, it is often expressed in destructive ways such as verbal or even physical abuse. Rage is vented at children by screaming and spanking, but such conduct is regarded as weakness. Among adults, rage is more often expressed indirectly by prolonged silences or sometimes by pounding objects, slamming doors, and self-punishment. For women, expression of rage is a problem. There is no acceptable outlet. Coldness, withdrawal, and a martyred stance may be the indirect consequence of women's rage.

Franco-Americans are not demonstrative, but they do indicate the desire to be less inhibited in showing affection. Feelings of intimacy and attachment tend to be expressed nonverbally. For example, love can be expressed by togetherness—family reunions and gatherings. As one of our respondents said while describing the demonstration of affection among peers or among those of different generations: "We don't even have to speak to each other, just being there, just a glance and we know we love each other." A more direct or verbal approach to feelings is avoided, with delicate subjects treated in a joking, off-hand manner that belies their depth and sensitivity. According to another respondent, familial affection is often played down because of general sexual anxieties that have long been common in Franco-American families. Guilt feelings about sex seem to derive from religious teachings influenced by Jansenism.[5]

The rigidity of the moral code tended to interfere with warm and affectionate expressions of feeling among family members. Such blocking and consequent painful shyness in some individuals may lead us to overlook their genuine sensitivity, tenderness, nurturing warmth, and longing for love.

Family rituals play an important role in traditional Franco-American culture. They center around church attendance, parish activities, and family gatherings. Among the most significant are Sunday mass, church weddings, *de rigueur* baptisms, large wakes, and Christmas midnight mass followed by *le Réveillon*, an all-night festivity. Also customary are Sundays with extended family and leisure time and holidays spent with family instead of friends.

Tensions are generated when the younger, more acculturated generation does not pay much attention to these rituals. A family member who does not obey the unwritten rules brings on criticism, derision, and scorn. Regular visits to the older, high-status members of the family hierarchy can, however, placate the family critics.

Rural Franco-American families are keeping the old family traditions very much alive. These families find most of their pleasures in family and extended family activities and are devoted to the Church. Urban lower-class families, as we have said, are also relatively resistant to acculturation.

Although grandparents or elderly parents, when senile and in need of nursing care, are now often sent to homes for the aged, old age brings considerable status, more so than in the dominant American culture, to both men and women. However, as French (1976) says, "If both grandparents survive, it is the female who has the higher status. Most social and religious events, as well as Sunday after Mass visits, require a stay with *mémère* (a corruption of *grand-mère*, or grandmother). Grandmothers are revered and respected as repositories of knowledge about the entire family kinship network" (p. 343). After the death of grandparents, kinship ties throughout the family often weaken.

In the past, to counterbalance the dispersal of the children in large families, where some stayed in Canada and others migrated to the United States, many families made systematic efforts to maintain kinship ties (extending even to third cousins), to foster loyalty among immediate household

5. Jansenism is a 17th-century doctrinal system that denied free will and maintained that human nature is corrupt. Originally Jansenism was a Roman Catholic mystical movement, primarily within some French religious orders. Jansenists, religious professionals, strove to surrender the self and to achieve ecstatic mystical union with God. In addition they held human nature to be evil and damnation certain without God's grace, which could not be earned. Their theological pessimism was expressed in a general harshness and moral rigor. These ideas, although condemned by Rome as heretical, were extended to the secular life in France and in Ireland with unfortunate consequences.

members, and to encourage frequent visiting and mutual assistance among relatives (Barkan, 1980). Today, except for the rural and lower-income families, for whom the family remains the major focus of social activities, the network of extended family relationships is scattered and usually limited to weddings and funerals.

There is disagreement among mental health professionals concerning the role of religion and more specifically the influence of the parish priest on the Franco-American family. Some respondents report the priest to be no more than a figurehead. Others report that the parish priest is still consulted. The truth appears to lie somewhere in the middle. Certainly, religious teachings still affect most Franco-Americans, regardless of their religious involvement, and breaks with the faith leave scars. It is likely that even if the Church's influence has waned, its historical impact is deeply embedded in today's Franco-Americans, for example, in feelings of guilt and inferiority, and in values that seem almost old fashioned—order, compliance, and hard work.

Because Catholicism, especially French Canadian Catholicism, has traditionally opposed intermarriage and divorce, Franco-Americans have married among their own. However, in the 1940s a trend began, so that now 50% or more of Franco-Americans marry outside of their own ethnic group, though usually within the Church (Dugas, 1976). This is the result of more frequent contact with other ethnic groups in military service during World War II and of attendance at public schools. Those who intermarry tend to wed members of the other Catholic minority groups, such as Italian, Irish, and Polish.

Divorce is increasing among Franco-Americans though it has not yet reached the national rate. These emerging changes in marital patterns cause confusion and conflict among Franco-Americans who, as every other group, must rethink their traditional expectations.

The old revere the past and are deeply attached to their French language, culture, and religion. The middle aged are less committed to their traditional culture, and the young ignore their ethnic history. Those who do know it object to cultural discrimination, but they usually object only within the privacy of their own families or within official Franco-American organizations. Little is done about the complaints. Many respondents reported that the younger generation is generally ignorant not only of Franco-American history and tradition but also of past and present discrimination. Young Franco-Americans today, except for some who live in rural areas, are becoming assimilated into American society. Many young Franco-Americans do not want to be associated with their ethnic group at all. For example, in 1974, 2000 Franco-American students at a major university in New England were invited by Professor Donald G. Dugas to become part of a Franco-American support group or simply to drop by to speak with him. Ten persons responded.

These signs of assimilation contrast with opinions that Franco-Americans are "more ethnocentric than Americans" (Gardner & Lambert, 1972) and "the most unassimilable of all [ethnic] groups in New England" (Gunther, 1947). They suggest, rather, the possible impending death of Franco-Americans as an important ethnic group (Dugas, 1976).

Certain recent trends, such as bilingual education, as well as the founding of new societies devoted to the study and preservation of Franco-American culture, point to possible reemergence of Franco-American ethnicity.

Family Therapy

Franco-Americans have a history of self-help and of accepting advice from kinship networks or the local priest rather than from outsiders, who are viewed with suspicion and mistrust. Frequently clannish, Franco-Americans are reluctant to acknowledge the need to turn to mental health workers and resent any implication that they should do so. Personal problems, especially family issues, are considered too intimate and private for a stranger (therapist). Thus they operate according to a familiar blue collar ethic: work the situation out as best you can—then try to be tolerant.

First- and second-generation Franco-Americans perceive therapy as a shameful experience, a violation of their "pride" in being able to manage their own affairs. As Woolfson (1975) observes, "Recourse to outside aid, be it the Church or the social agency, is an indication that the family cannot handle its own affairs—it is a defeat only accepted as a last resort" (p. 13). Needless to say, there are few geriatric or middle-aged self-referrals for social services, and the mere thought of such a step brings to the surface hidden fears of violating the sacredness of family secrets. In addition, the experience of poverty and poor education fosters an outlook in which spending money for tangibles that gratify is preferred to spending money for intangibles, such as therapy, which show no immediate, visible, or material gain.

A major depressive episode may have to occur before a Franco-American family or individual seeks help, and since therapy is a last resort, the therapist can expect to find neither hope, nor motivation, nor a sophistication about self or others. Franco-Americans can be engaged in therapy but are usually very slow about revealing themselves to the therapist and exhibit obvious fear of being found out. Therefore, they proceed in a very tentative manner with family attitudes favoring the withholding of information. Therapeutic interventions can take a long time and at times may be impossible.

The majority of Franco-Americans do not seek insight or value clarification; instead, they are somewhat cynical and unable to articulate how they might change. The therapist can also encounter resistance based solely on his or her credentials. One respondent articulated this problem with perceived difference in status: "The social status that comes with the years of formal education and the PhD title can also act as additional inhibiting factors, making the distance between counselor and patient abysmal in the Franco-American's view."

Therapy will be influenced by experience with confession, as exemplified by the following scene. Shrouded with secrecy, in the dark confessional sits the priest, an instrument of God, who is sworn never to reveal to any person the sins confessed to him. The supplicant whispers his sins into the priest's compassionate ear, feeling abjectly guilty, but on completion arises from the kneeling position with a sense of deliverance!

> "Very well, that's all? Well then, say your rosary and fifteen Hail Mary's."
> "Yes, my father."
> The gracious slide door slides. Gerard is facing the good happy wood, he
>   runs out and hurries lightfoot to the altar, fit to sing—
> It's all over! It was nothing! He's pure again!
> —Kerouac, *Visions of Gerard* (1963, p. 49)

Over time, such confessional experiences make people reluctant to speak out face to face, in daylight, in an open space, to a person not bound by the same religious rules as is the priest.

The Franco-American projects the fantasy of the powerful parish priest onto the therapist who may use it as a chance to give advice and solve problems but who must also attempt to help the client work through this mistaken attribution. Such clerical transference is predictable and often continues throughout the therapy.

The therapist preferred by Franco-Americans would be male, the same age or older, married, Catholic, and also Franco-American. But, if the clients feel too negatively about being Franco-American, they either may not want to admit their ethnicity or to associate with other Franco-Americans (Paradis, 1980).

Since French is the primary language for first- and often second-generation Franco-Americans, these individuals must limit their choice of therapist to the parish priest or a lay counselor who speaks their language. As with other groups not raised as English speaking, subtle misunderstandings between the therapist and the consulting family may easily produce cross-cultural and intrafamily confusion. As Woolfson (1975) points out,

> The therapist must be sensitive to the fact that many Franco-Vermonters speak English as a second language with what appears ease and comprehension. But one cannot assume that there is near native control. If an ongoing process of translation is taking place, then there are many chances for misunderstanding. (p. 15)

Franco-Americans are most commonly referred for family therapy because of a child with school problems or an acting out teenager, perhaps involved in drug abuse. The family is guarded or cautious about going into sensitive family issues and requests help only for the offspring. The child's disruption is seen as a blow to parental control. The father is usually extremely hesitant about approaching a clinic, but once he is there he wants to cooperate and can be very important in the therapeutic process. This is in line with Gurman and Kniskern's (1978) general finding that "the father plays a major role in the efficacy of family therapy initiated because of a child or adolescent identified patient." However, this is a difficult experience, for the father sees himself as the key authority figure, family rule maker, and breadwinner. Particularly in low-income families, parents have a hard time accepting a child's interpretation of what is happening. Parents, and especially the father, are afraid of either losing control or losing a position of authority within the family.

Alcohol abuse, a common problem for men, is typically associated with strong denial of the problem by both sexes. Wives accept heavy drinking in their men as long as they continue to be providers for the family. When an alcoholic husband slips into long periods of heavy drinking, the wife, after intense frustration and with sympathetic support from members of the family, may separate from him. It is at this point, when they are shocked and intensely stressed, that rehabilitation is sought by the husband and family.

Family therapy referrals may be made because of major depressions, particularly associated with deaths, divorces, or other major losses, or of anxiety disorders associated with separation or phobias.

The most common defense mechanisms used by Franco-Americans are denial, displacement, sublimation, and rationalization. What we can directly observe is the blaming of others for personal inadequacies and failures, the tendency to scapegoat outsiders, the assumption of a martyred stance, and the explaining away of tyrannical or oppressive behavior by citing the authority of the Church's restrictive edicts. There seems to be a tendency to believe that problems are a passing phase. Franco-Americans tend to deny that significant family problems have long-range effects. Considering their tendency to look toward the Church for structure, it is common to see an inability to distinguish between personal values and religious dogma.

Taboo areas for discussion in family or therapeutic encounters are incest, homosexuality, leaving the Catholic Church, talk of the dead in ways that are derogatory. Needless to say, the process of family therapy is hindered by unspoken rules and unconscious rigidities and denials. For example, in one family therapy case where the issue was primarily focusing on grief over the father's death, the family could not bear to talk about him, it was taboo. He had been idealized, and the distortions that they were collusively protecting prevented them from dealing with themselves.

Taking into account the Franco-American family's pessimistic outlook and lack of enthusiasm for outsiders, the ability of the therapist to establish rapport becomes paramount. Empathy, warmth, and genuineness, sometimes referred to as the client-centered therapeutic triad (Raskin & Van Der Veen,

1970), are the keys to motivating a family's return for the second interview. This triad addresses the best of the hidden qualities within the families that seek help. Appropriate self-disclosure by the therapist may also help build a relationship with the family (Jourard, 1968; Ivey & Simek-Downing, 1980). In addition, the provision of definite structure in early sessions decreases anxiety. Intensive brief therapy usually can be regarded as solidly launched in the fourth or fifth session—when the therapist is certain that the Franco-American's qualities of persistence, endurance, and iron tenacity have been invested into the therapeutic relationship.

A sensible strategy, one that makes use of what would otherwise be obstacles, is to frame therapeutic tasks as ways to "fulfill our duty," be it as spouse, parent, church member, or therapy participant. Duty is the supreme value. Therefore, if the therapist defines problem-solving sessions and home-work tasks as "duties," then they shall be done! Unambiguous assignments, such as family meetings at home for discussion of problems, will be carried out. Therefore, direct advice, positive reinforcement, and therapeutic consistency work well, with a cognitive approach to depression being effective. The following case illustrates the above points.

Mr. and Mrs. Noir, a college-educated Franco-American couple in their 30s, had been married for 11 years. Mrs. Noir made the initial contact and described the problem as Mr. Noir's moods. During the first session Mrs. Noir described her husband's condition, with only occasional acknowledgment by him. Mr. Noir's "moods" appeared to be moderate to severe depression. At times he thought of suicide.

The evaluation included an individual session with Mr. Noir in which he seemed more willing to discuss the family problems. He expressed general pessimism about life and the inevitable badness of relationships. He described his father as passive and withdrawn and his mother as domineering and overly concerned with appearances. He could not recall ever seeing his parents argue.

Mrs. Noir said that she was happy, yet presented a world view that was strikingly negative. She said her mother was a sad person but very much in control of the family. Her alcoholic father worked long hours and was distant from the family. She could remember very few, if any, expressions of conflict between her parents.

Initially the therapy required the establishment of a warm and supportive atmosphere. Confrontation and/or attempts at insightful exploration seemed inappropriate considering their lack of experience and understanding of conflict resolution. Mr. Noir's initial reticence in therapy appeared in this case to be due to fear of the conflict resolution process rather than to fear of outsiders.

Each felt that they had very little impact on each other or on the wider world. A didactic approach was used: The therapist focused on the cognitive aspects of their demoralization. He taught them to recognize repetitious self-reproaches that only led them into blind alleys. He taught them to "stop [those] thoughts" and to intentionally shift their attentions to recognizing and planning more constructive behaviors (Beck, 1976). For example, Mr. Noir took on the responsibility to take his wife out "on the town" to a place that he picked out, at least once a week. The therapist emphasized the responsibility and duty of each family member to practice these constructive behaviors in order to maintain a truly warm and supportive family. Gradually, they were able to change their cognitive behaviors, and their morale was improved.

Paradoxical methods also work well. The therapist can say, "You're doing the very best you can, therefore I suggest you continue doing it." The family is likely to "resist" by coming up with a new way to perpetuate the status quo.

In crisis situations, and most families are first seen in an advanced stage of crisis, Franco-Americans will probably respond best to planned change and behavior modification approaches with the teaching of concrete conflict–resolution problem-solving skills and role playing.

Since communication patterns, and problems, in Franco-American families are fairly obvious, the therapist can work to enhance communication of positive and constructive messages in the early sessions. This enhances awareness of positive emotional bonding within the system.

A Franco-American daughter was leaving home to live with a Jewish boyfriend and to go to college. Everyone in her family disapproved—she was breaking all the rules—and she felt cut off. A meeting of the daughter and her four brothers was arranged (she was not willing to invite her parents). The focus of the meeting was not her defection, not confrontation, but a general discussion of how in the past, during difficult times, they had still found ways to help each other.

They wanted to think of themselves as a warm and supportive family, and this was the basis for the conduct of the session. In order to have focused on her defection and to have a reasonable chance of being constructive, it would have required that the family have skills in conflict resolution that they did not have.

Particularly strong ties exist between the dyads, mother–son and father–daughter. Bowen's (1978) interview technique of instructing family members to listen to one another and distinguish between thoughts and feelings is helpful in encouraging more constructive contact between father and son and mother and daughter.

In addition, since many Franco-Americans tend to rely on nonassertive, passive–aggressive behaviors as outlets for their hostility, anger management must be stressed. They must learn to recognize when they are angry and practice self-assertion. Emotional reeducation is a must to sustain long-term change.

The Franco-American's ego is blocked by an overly dominant superego, and some basic transactional analysis explanations often integrate well into their world view. Understandably the use of unstructured experiential exercises for ventilation is not helpful; they feel threatened and confused. Modeling, both verbal and nonverbal, of appropriate ways to express emotion is helpful. Some therapists report that humor and hyperbole are helpful in facilitating the awareness of personality problems such as nonassertiveness, repression of hostility, and paranoia. Humor can be useful as well in dealing with intimacy issues and taboo areas such as anger toward parental figures or disobedience of Church dogma. Considering Franco-Americans' tendency to take themselves and life too seriously, to lose perspective, and to be pessimistic, it may be very helpful to illustrate a situation to the point of absurdity. This "may often help [them] gain perspective on their overly intense involvement in a rigid position and reduce what was threatening and serious to triviality" (Carter & Orfanidis-McGoldrick, 1976).

One particular caution about working with the Franco-American family is their tremendous need to protect the mother from any negative comments by other family members. This is, of course, homeostasis maintained by the mother herself. She may shrewdly assume a martyred role that intensifies guilt in family members. The therapist must avoid becoming an agent in this maneuver by embarrassing or criticizing her. On the contrary, in order to transform the family system, the therapist may intervene to unbalance the system by forming a coalition with the mother against other members. However, as Haley (1976) points out, those who were criticized soon should be praised to recreate balance.

In working with the whole or extended family, it seems to be more productive to focus "on matters that harmonize with the value of having a warm and supportive family, e.g., finding how family members are attempting to help each other and making plans for future support. Approaches that rely for their success on the stimulation of open conflict, like network therapy, may be disastrous" (Pearce, 1980, p. 109). Franco-Americans avoid conflict at all costs and use obvious (and effective) delaying techniques. One caution, however, is that the levels of power in the family organization must be recognized and accepted by the therapist. When the hierarchy is confused or when some members are vying for power in the family (a previously absent father trying to reestablish himself or a parentified child establishing dominance over siblings), we might use family genogram techniques to map the levels and pockets of influence. Grandparents, especially grandmothers (the key parental advisor) are often a bridge among family members. It seems likely that the more the therapist works with the parents to put them back in charge, the better the results they will get within the entire network.

Summary

In summary, therapy with Franco-American families has a predictable profile: It begins with crisis and moves slowly as they resist change with covert defensive maneuvers. The therapist, by appealing to the Franco-Americans' sense of duty and their shared desires to have a warm and supportive family, will in time be able to engage them in cooperative problem solving, emotional reeducation, and the relearning of coping strategies.

The measure of success with Franco-American families will be behavioral change rather than insight or psychic restructuring.

ACKNOWLEDGMENT

This chapter would not have been possible without the help of the respondents to my survey, mentioned earlier, as well as the help of those therapists who spent long hours in conversation with me, sharing their experiences. In particular I would like to thank: André Léo Chabot, Paul P. Chassé, Maxine Daigle-Robichaud, Donald G. Dugas, Al Dussault, Ernest B. Guillet, Raymond G. Lacasse, Pamela Langelier, Lorraine Asselin Moynihan, Jean-Marc Nicole, John K. Pearce, Armand L. Quintal, Claire Quintal, and Richard Varieur.

REFERENCES

Barkan, E.R. French-Canadians. In S. Thernstrom (Ed.), *Harvard Encyclopedia of American Ethnic Groups*. Cambridge: Harvard University Press, 1980.

Beck, A. *Cognitive Therapy*. New York: International Universities Press, 1976.

Benoit, J. *L'Ame Franco-Américaine*. Montreal: Editions Albert Lévesque, 1935.

Bowen, M. *Family Therapy in Clinical Practice*. New York: Jason Aronson, 1978.

Carter, E., & Orfanidis-McGoldrick, M. Family Therapy with One Person and the Family Therapist's Own Family. In P.J. Guerin (Ed.), *Family Therapy*. New York: Gardner Press, 1976.

Chassé, P. *The Family*. Unpublished paper, Franco-American Ethnic Heritage Studies Program, Assumption College, Worcester, Mass., 1975.

Dugas, D.G. Franco-American Language Maintenance Efforts in New England: Realities and Issues. In *Identité Culturelle et Francophonie dans les Amériques*. Quebec: Les Presses de l'Université Laval, 1976.

French. L. The Franco-American Working Class Family. In C.H. Mindel & R.W. Habenstein (Eds.), *Ethnic Families in America*. New York: Elsevier, 1976.

Gardner, R.C., & Lambert, W. *Attitudes and Motivation*. Rowley, Mass.: Newbury House, 1972.

Garigue, P. The French Canadian Families. In B.R. Blisher (Ed.), *Canadian Society: Sociological Perspectives* (3rd ed.). Toronto: Macmillan of Canada, 1968.

Gunther, J. *Inside U.S.A.* New York: Harper, 1947.

Gurman, A.S., & Kniskern, D.P. Research on Marital and Family Therapy: Progress, Perspective and Prospect. In S.L. Garfield & A.E. Bergin (Eds.), *Handbook of Psychotherapy and Behavior Change: An Empirical Analysis*. New York: Wiley, 1978.

Haley, J. *Problem Solving Therapy*. San Francisco: Jossey-Bass, 1976.

Higonnet, P.L.R. French. In S. Thernstrom (Ed.), *Harvard Encyclopedia of American Ethnic Groups*. Cambridge: Harvard University Press, 1980.

Ivey, A.E., & Simek-Downing, L. *Counseling and Psychotherapy*. Englewood Cliffs, N.J.: Prentice-Hall, 1980.

Jourard, S.M. *Disclosing Man to Himself*. Princeton, N.J.: Van Nostrand, 1968.

Kerouac, J. *Visions of Gerard*. New York: McGraw-Hill, 1963. (1st ed., 1958.)

Paradis, F. Counseling the Culturally Different. *Le F.A.R.O.G. Forum, University of Maine*, 8(1), 1980.

Pearce, J.K. Ethnicity and Family Therapy: An Introduction. In J.K. Pearce & L.J. Friedman (Eds.), *Family Therapy: Combining Psychodynamics and Family Systems Approaches*. New York: Grune & Stratton, 1980.

Raskin, N.J., & Van Der Veen, F. Client-Centered Family Therapy. In J.T. Hart & T.M. Tomlinson (Eds.), *New Directions in Client-Centered Therapy.* Boston: Houghton Mifflin, 1970.

Sorg, M.H. Personal communication, 1980.

Woolfson, P. *Value Orientations of French-Canadian and Franco-American School Children in Border Communities in Quebec and Vermont.* Unpublished paper, Department of Anthropology, University of Vermont, 1973.

Woolfson, P. Traditional French-Canadian Family Life Patterns and Their Implications for Social Services in Vermont. In *A Franco-American Overview* (Vol. 2). Cambridge: National Assessment and Dissemination Center for Bilingual/ Bicultural Education, 1975.

SUPPLEMENTARY REFERENCES

Abramson, H.J. *Ethnic Diversity in Catholic America.* New York: Wiley, 1973.

Anctil, P. La Franco-Américanie ou le Québec d'en Bas. *Cahiers de Géographie du Québec, 23*(58), 39–52, 1979.

Anctil, P. *A Franco-American Bibliography, New England.* Bedford, N.H.: National Materials Development Center, 1979.

Doane, A.W., Jr. *Occupational and Educational Patterns for New Hampshire's Franco-Americans.* Manchester, N.H.: New Hampshire Civil Liberties Union, Franco-American Research Project, 1979.

Guérin, L. The French Canadian Family: Its Strengths and Weaknesses. In M. Rioux & Y. Martin (Eds.), *French Canadian Society.* Toronto: McClelland & Stewart, 1964.

Gifford, B., & Lee, L. *Jack's Book: An Oral Biography of Jack Kerouac.* New York: St. Martin's Press, 1978. (Also in paperback, New York: Penguin Books, 1978.)

Giguère, M. *Number and Percent of Persons with French Mother Tongue: States, Counties (Parishes), Places of 10,000 or More, SMSA's of 250,000 or More, and Urban and Rural Residence, New England and Louisiana, 1970.* University of Southern Maine, Portland, Franco-American Files, no date.

Giguère, M. (Ed.). *A Franco-American Overview* (Vols. 3 & 4): *New England* (Vols. 1 & 2). Cambridge: National Assessment and Dissemination Center for Bilingual/ Bicultural Education, 1981.

Kerouac, J. *The Town and the City.* New York: Harcourt, Brace, Jovanovich, 1950.

Kressel, K., & Slipp, S. Perceptions of Marriage Related to Engagement Conjoint Therapy. *Journal of Marriage and Family Counseling, 1,* 367–377, 1975.

Lauvrière, E. *La Tragédie d'un Peuple: Histoire du Peuple acadien, de ses Origines à nos Jours* (2 vols.). Paris: Editions Bossard, 1922.

O'Connor, P.A. Coalition Formation in Conjoint Marriage Counseling (Doctoral Dissertation, University of Southern California, 1974). *Dissertation Abstracts International, 35,* 4717–4718, 1975.

Perreault, R. One Piece in the Great American Mosaic: The Franco-Americans of New England. *Le Canado-Américain, 2,* 9–51, 1976.

Plante, D. *The Family.* New York: Farrar, Straus, & Giroux, 1978.

Plante, D. *The Country.* New York: Atheneum, 1981.

Rosen, B.C. Race, Ethnicity and the Achievement Syndrome. *American Sociological Review, 24*(1), 47–60, 1959.

Rumilly, R. *Histoire des Franco-Américains.* Woonsocket, R.I.: L'Union Saint-Jean-Baptiste d'Amérique, 1958.

Scully, R. To Be French in North America. *Canadian Forum, 55*(655), 6–12, 1975.

Slipp, S., Ellis, S., & Kressel, K. Factors Associated with Engagement in Family Therapy. *Family Process, 13,* 413–427, 1974.

Sorrell, R.S. *The Sentinelle Affair (1924–1929) and Militant Survivance: The Franco-American*

Experience in Woonsocket, Rhode Island (PhD Dissertation, State University of New York at Buffalo, 1975). Ann Arbor, Mich.: University Microfilms, 1975.

Tremblay, M.A. The Needs and Aspirations of the French-Canadian Family. In G.L. Gold & M.A. Tremblay (Eds.), *Communities and Cultures in French Canada.* Toronto: Holt, Rinehart & Winston of Canada, 1973.

Vicero, R.D. *Immigration of French Canadians to New England, 1840–1900: A Geographical Analysis* (PhD Dissertation, University of Wisconsin, 1968). Ann Arbor, Mich.: University Microfilms, 1977.

12

German Families

HINDA WINAWER-STEINER
NORBERT A. WETZEL

Research about specific aspects of German American family life is relatively sparse. This contribution presents an impressionistic view of German Americans and the relationship of their history and culture to the therapeutic context.

We have sought to highlight those elements of the German American experience that can be helpful to the ethnically sensitive therapist in the development of his or her particular approach to the treatment of German American families.

It is hoped that the following will serve as groundwork for further study of this rich, diverse, and complex ethnic group.

> At the opening of a workshop devoted to family therapy and ethnicity, participants introduced themselves by identifying their ethnic backgrounds. One man presented himself as a German American and added that he had never before shared that in a professional or social context. He then related how, during his childhood, aspects of the German culture began to disappear, particularly in church where English songs and hymns replaced the German texts he had known so well as a small child. He had learned to suppress his "Germanness."

This reluctance to claim a German heritage is not unusual. It is also not surprising if we consider that in today's popular media, in which the plight of other ethnic groups is portrayed sympathetically, there is little with which German Americans can identify positively. Indeed, "Holocaust" recalls only negative, painful associations to the homeland. On television, in general, Germans are either characterized as evil, incompetent, or mad; or they are simply not represented at all (Shenton & Brown, 1976).

Hinda Winawer-Steiner. Faculty, Ackerman Institute for Family Therapy, New York, New York; Adjunct Faculty, Graduate School of Social Work, Rutgers University, New Brunswick, New Jersey.

Norbert A. Wetzel. Family Therapy Program, Trinity Counseling Service, Princeton, New Jersey; Adjunct Faculty, Graduate School of Applied and Professional Psychology, Rutgers University, Piscataway, New Jersey.

It seems as though Germans either are forgotten or are not forgiven. It is ironic that, despite the positive relationship between the United States and West Germany, German Americans are barely visible as an ethnic group. In national elections, for example, they have not been addressed as an important voting bloc in almost 30 years (Rippley, 1976). Today, we rarely, if ever, hear of the "German vote" in national elections.

The present, relatively low profile of German Americans as an ethnic group provides a sharp contrast to the past. Americans from Germany are one of the oldest and largest immigrant groups in the history of the United States. Their contributions to American life have been as basic as frankfurters and beer and as consequential as agricultural innovations and nuclear power.

In this chapter we will first bring the characteristics of the German American culture into sharper focus. We will then address the relationship of these characteristics and of the current image of German Americans to the practice of family therapy.

Origins and Demography

The Immigrants: Their Settlement and Contributions

While there were German settlers as early as 1607 in Jamestown (Furer, 1973), the "official" beginning of German immigration to the New World is marked by the arrival of the *Concord*, the German *Mayflower*, in 1683. The settlers from the *Concord* founded, under the leadership of Franz Daniel Pastorius, Deutschstadt (Germantown), Pennsylvania, the first German settlement in the American colonies.

Although small German settlements were established in North Carolina (1710), Virginia (1714), South Carolina (1729), Georgia (1735), Maine (1736), and Ohio (1801), throughout the 18th century, Pennsylvania continued to lead as a home for Germans. In 1790, 33% of Pennsylvania's population was German. (Germans constituted 12% of the population in Maryland, 9% in New Jersey, and 8% in New York.)

Among the many accomplishments of colonial Germans were improved farming methods, the rapid establishment of schools, a flourishing press, and the first bible in America. Their technological contributions included the first papermill and glassmaking factory, as well as the famous Conestoga wagon, now a symbol of American pioneer history.

Germans played a major role in the establishment of the colonies as a nation. At the Continental Congress in 1776, Pennsylvania cast the decisive 13th vote in favor of independence from Great Britain. In the Revolutionary War, Germans provided not only fighting soldiers, but influential generals (Muhlenberg, von Steuben). Molly Pitcher, the familiar figure to American elementary school children, was also German.

In the next century, immigration spread westward along the Erie Canal to the Great Lakes and the prairies. Cincinnati became a leading German

American city. Between 1850 and 1900, Germans were never fewer than one-fourth of all foreign-born Americans. In 1882, there were a quarter of a million Americans of German descent in the United States.

Notable among the many contributions of 19th-century Germans were their leadership in farming, business, industry, and education and their prominence in science, medicine, and music. Enthusiastic participation in sports and public family recreation were typical German practices that have since become American traditions.

During the Civil War, Germans were active politically and militarily. In the South they are credited with having supported antislavery publications and with keeping Missouri in the Union. Northern German-speaking regiments were quite common. Though Germans had been opposed to slavery since colonial times (some on religious grounds, others because they were family rather than plantation farmers), they tended not to be politically active. However, during the Civil War, the enthusiastic support of the antislavery effort and of the Union was effectively organized and inspired by Carl Schurz, one member of the prominent group of intellectual refugees known as the "Forty-Eighters." Schurz, an outstanding German American, became a Union general; he was also the U.S. senator from Missouri and later the secretary of the interior.

In the 20th century, German immigration declined. The greatest numbers of Americans of German background were living in the large cities of the Midwest (Cincinnati, Louisville, St. Louis, Chicago, Milwaukee, Cleveland, and Toledo). By 1930 German immigrants were living in rural areas only in Minnesota, Iowa, and several western states. Germans constituted a major proportion of Wisconsin. New York, however, from the turn of the century until 1970, led other states as a home for German Americans.

Individual German Americans (e.g., Pershing and Eisenhower) have continued to achieve recognition, but not as representatives of an ethnic group. An exception were those who sought refuge from Nazi Germany. This group, predominantly though not exclusively Jewish, included so many outstanding contributors to the arts and sciences (e.g., Mann, Tillich, Fromm, Erikson) that their immigration has been characterized as "one of the largest transfers of intellectual talent from one nation to another in human history" (Sowell, 1981, p. 67).

Perspectives on a Hidden Culture (Hall, 1976)

In the United States in 1972, there were 25.5 million Americans of German descent; they were 12% of the population, second only to the British (14%). Despite their numerical strength, German Americans in the 1970s were the least visible of American ethnic groups (Conzen, 1980).

Today, with the exception of certain regions that are traditional centers of German culture, signs of German American life are barely visible. Though there are numerous historical societies, many of the "little Germanies" of earlier times are gone. What remains are only a few sausage shops and cafes and an occasional Octoberfest celebration. The East, which historically has had a high population of Germans, only has traces of a distinctively German American culture. Exceptions are enclaves in small areas and special groups of Germanic heritage, such as the Amish and Mennonites of Pennsylvania.

Full exploration of the basis for the decline in ethnic profile is beyond the scope of our discussion. However, aside from the long history of immigration, consideration of the following interrelated phenomena may be helpful in our understanding of the experience of German Americans as an ethnic group in the United States: (1) a high degree of diversity among German immigrants; (2) assimilation; and (3) the two world wars in the 20th century.

DIVERSITY

Germans in America are a heterogeneous group. Germans referred to in this chapter are those "born in Imperial Germany, and in the various states that coalesced to form it in 1871 and the governments that succeeded it after 1918." Swiss Germans, Austrians, and Alsatians also have shared in what is generally considered the German culture (Conzen, 1980, pp. 405–406). The dimensions and diverse characteristics of German culture in Europe were defined by region rather than by political boundaries. For example, Swiss Germans and their neighbors in Baden, Germany, are more similar in language and mannerisms than are those from Baden and their Prussian compatriots.

A study of the cultural, national, and familial history of German-speaking people must consider that the differences among the various German "tribes" always remained strong, and they never quite melted into a uniform national culture. Many of the German tribes that lived on German territory and eventually formed the German language, spoke and still speak quite different dialects. The various regional groups have their own typical rituals and customs, idiosyncrasies of family life, and prevalent values.

The immigrants, as well, varied with respect to regional origin, occupation, and religion. In 1683 the earliest immigrants to Pennsylvania were primarily Pietists and Mennonites from the Rhine regions in western Germany. They were mainly tradesmen, professional farmers, weavers, tailors, shoemakers, and carpenters.

In the early 18th century, Palatinates (from southwestern Germany) were the main immigrant group. This group was so predominant that the term "Palatines" was often used to refer to Germans in general. Among them were the Swiss Mennonites, Baptist Dunkers, and Moravian Brethren who came to the New World seeking religious tolerance. Besides members of the Lutheran and the Reformed Churches, other religious groups represented were Anabaptists, Quakers, Schwenkfelders, and Amish. They were largely landless farmers and workers who emigrated for economic reasons. Their land had become overpopulated or had been devastated by Louis XIV's armies. Many bought passage by commitment to indentured servitude, often up to seven years per adult passenger and up to age 21 for young children.

Early 19th-century immigrants from Germany came to the United States, primarily to improve their economic lot from a land devastated by poor harvests in 1816 and 1817 or by Napoleonic wars. Later, the most prominent were liberal political refugees of the unsuccessful revolution of 1848—the "Forty-Eighters."

In contrast to the earlier immigrants who were farmers, in the 20th century, many were educated professionals. After World War II, the relatively smaller numbers of immigrants represented a cross section of the German population.

We can, therefore, talk about a cultural unity of the German people only in a limited sense. Until the middle of the 19th century, the identity of the families of German immigrants in the United States was determined more by the culture (and religion) of the area from which they originated than by their common German heritage. This might explain the plurality of present-day German American family cultures.

Religious Differences. The basic religious division in the pluralistic German nation originated in the Reformation of the early 16th century. For several centuries different German regions were, for political reasons, either Catholic or Protestant.

The religious affiliation of the German immigrants is important because Catholicism and Protestantism have different values and traditions that specifically affect the lives and cultures of families. Catholic Germans tend to be more tradition oriented and guided by the authority of the Church. Protestants put more emphasis on individual responsibility and conscience. [The correspondence between the rise of capitalism and the Protestant "work ethic" in Germany is the theme of Max Weber's (1905) famous essay.]

In the New World, religion was central to the family life of the early settlers. It formed a bond among them as a group and between them and the fatherland. While colonial Germans were primarily Protestants, in the 19th century, Roman Catholics increased to one-third of the German American population. Again, religion and culture were intertwined. The church supported the culture; the desire to maintain the culture fostered church membership, which created some competition between Protestants and Catholics. The latter had to use the German language in order "to retain members who might otherwise leave their hierarchically organized church for the familiarity of German-speaking Protestant or secular groups" (Conzen, 1980, p. 418). But the far more fierce religious rivalry of this period was between the Germans and the more powerful Irish for domination of the American Catholic Church.

The relationship among religion, culture, and language gradually became less important as Germans became Americanized. By 1916 only 11% of the German Catholic parishes used the mother tongue exclusively. Protestant churches, particularly the Lutherans, continued to use the German language in services and other church activities. However, most Protestant denominations were unable to retain a strong, purely ethnic character.

Although most Germans were Catholics or Protestants, there were minority groups that, for religious reasons, had a different ethnic experience, although they are linguistically and culturally German (Smith, 1950). The Mennonites, for example, one of the Anabaptist groups that emigrated from various parts of Europe, do not belong to the major Protestant denominations.

German Jews in the New World identified with both their Jewish and their German heritages (Goren, 1980). In Europe, German-speaking Jews had made notable contributions in science, philosophy, and the arts (e.g., Freud, Marx, Kafka, Mendelssohn, Heine). Similarly, in the United States, German Jews were prominent in many fields. However, their experience as Jews and as Germans in the United States warrants separate, more extensive consideration in view of the complex cultural heritage, the history of the Jews in Germany and, above all, the Holocaust.

ASSIMILATION

Assimilation is a very complex phenomenon: "The very size of the German immigration, its religious, socioeconomic, and cultural heterogeneity, its skills, time of arrival and settlement patterns all combined to ensure a gradual process of acculturation and assimilation" (Conzen, 1980, p. 206).

The process of assimilation was, at times, externally imposed as part of the rivalry for domination among ethnic groups. For example, soon after the establishment of the new nation, a competition between the Germans and the English began. Benjamin Franklin predicted a clash between Anglo-Americans and Germans. Where German culture remained intact for a long time, Anglo-Americans feared that Germans might become dominant. Franklin believed that either the English would absorb the Germans or be absorbed by them; a stable cultural pluralism could not exist. Several generations later in the *New York Tribune*, Horace Greeley advocated the forced assimilation of all German groups. Sentiments of this sort prompted state legislatures to institute educational programs designed to anglicize German children (Billigmeier, 1974).

Often, German organizations gradually accommodated to the non-German environment simply to survive. One indication was the admission of non-Germans into German American societies and the transition to the use of English in the transactions of these societies. However, the most powerful and sudden impact on German American culture—on its flourishing press and its highly developed network of clubs and organizations—was the entry of the United States into World War I.

The two world wars had a profound impact on the fate of the German culture in the United States. During World War I there was nationwide suppression of German language and culture. German Americans were in a loyalty conflict: "loyalty to the Kaiser or the Flag." There was a general "climate of harassment, including a ban on German-composed music, the renaming of persons, foods, and towns, vandalism, tarring and feathering, arrests for unpatriotic utterances, and even a lynching in Collinsville, Illinois in April 1918. Public burnings of German books were frequent" (Conzen, 1980, pp. 422–423).

This suppression of cultural identity appears in dicussions with clients of German heritage: An older working-class couple who had immigrated in the early part of this century described how the German American club they attended was under constant FBI surveillance during World War I.

> This period was followed in hardly more than a decade by the Nazi era. . . . The German American Bund was never a major force in [New York], but it did exist. The revulsion against Nazism extended indiscriminately to things German. Thereafter, German Americans, as shocked by the Nazis as any, were disinclined to make over much of their national origins. (Glazer & Moynihan, 1970, p. 312)

Another client, an academician, was repeatedly embarrassed during his childhood to acknowledge his German heritage because of the strong anti-German feelings during World War II.

The discomfort about German ethnicity is found among psychotherapists as well. In a supervisory group, when considering a German American family in treatment, a discussion of the relevance of the family's ethnic background revealed that two members of the group, who had previously identified themselves as Polish were, in fact, half German. When asked, one explained that she simply considered herself Polish. The other, after some reflection, said that in a group that was half Jewish, she had been reluctant to acknowledge her German heritage.

World War II left German Americans with almost nothing positive with which they could identify. Germans had committed barbarian, atrocious crimes, and Germany was the outcast among the nations of the world.

One's Germanness, therefore, out of necessity, had to be toned down and, at the very least, experienced carefully and secretly. Ethnic origin for German Americans may be associated with a profound loss of ethnic identity and pride.

Characteristics of the German National Heritage

It is difficult to determine specific aspects of the "national character" that the immigrants brought with them from Germany. Apart from epistemological issues (Bateson, 1976), the diversity of the immigrants' background precludes simple answers (Parsons, 1970).

Most German American families are aware of some facets of their cultural heritage. Older family members are often knowledgeable about history, have a sense of past events, and can recall names and facts that are part of their German background.

Their sense of history and appreciation of tradition is part of the German legacy. German Americans have the capacity to look at themselves, to study their own backgrounds, and to scrutinize their past.

Proximity, Space, and Structure

Some aspects of the German cultural and familial heritage were connected with external factors. Geographically situated in the middle of western Europe, Germany was confined within borders that allowed for little natural expansion. People had to learn to live together peacefully within a small area. Explosive forces from within (internal frictions, rivalries, overpopulation, lack of natural resources) or enemies from outside (against which there was little natural protection) could endanger survival.

Indeed, the quest for *Lebensraum* (space for living) is a theme of German national and familial history. The available space had to be used intensively. German society was, therefore, highly structured. Living in proximity, people developed a need for clear and, at times, rigid boundaries; complex social hierarchies helped to define each other's territory.

To this day, in Germany, the boundary that designates the interface between family unit and surrounding society is rather well defined. The transition between inside and outside the family is regulated, and there are certain formalities that need to be respected when entering a German house.

The houses of middle-class families are usually surrounded by a fence or bushes that delineate the property between houses. In Germany, "yards tend to be well fenced; but fenced or not, they are sacred" (Hall, 1966, p. 135).

Similarly, the friendship patterns of middle-class families are clearly regulated (Salamon, 1977). There is a clear distinction between acquaintances, neighbors, and colleagues with whom one socializes and personal friends with whom much more open and intimate relationships exist. Usually, the distinctive use of *Sie* and *Du* symbolizes this difference.

Boundaries help protect the family's private space. This privacy is highly valued. German politicians, for example, do not involve their families in public life. The family's life is protected against intrusions from the outside that might endanger the members' well-being. Conflicts and emotional upheavals that the family experiences as embarrassing can be contained within the family sphere "where they belong."

Inside the family, the space is also clearly structured. In the cool, central European climate, houses are solidly constructed. The doors in contemporary German homes are usually closed. At the table, during meals, everyone has his or her assigned place. Similarly, early German American homes were noted for their construction, effective heating systems, and suitability for productive indoor life (Billigmeier, 1974).

Emotional Restraint, Sentimentality, and Gemütlichkeit

Another characteristic trait of the German heritage is the polarity of emotional restraint and sentimentality.

Affection, anger, and emotion in general do not get expressed easily. People seem to contain what they might experience as too explosive through boundaries, structure, and emotional control.

The Germanic style of handling emotions is very different from that of the Mediterranean nations. In the German tradition people are not encouraged to show emotions openly or to display affection, grief, or anger in public. Passions get repressed or sublimated in work or art (literature, music, etc.). The work of Thomas Mann, one of the most "German" writers (Hatfield, 1951; Jens, 1976), is an example of immensely rich human experience contained in a highly artful form. Perhaps the most powerful example of this phenomenon is the music of the German masters.

An acceptable form of the overt expression of emotion within the Germanic culture is the tradition of *Gemütlichkeit*, which, still found in homes of first- and second-generation German Americans, provides an interesting contrast to emotional restraint. There is no word in the English language that accurately renders the meaning of *Gemüt* (disposition, temper, heart) or *Gemütlichkeit* (geniality, comfort, warmth). German Americans introduced it to the New World as their way of making themselves feel "at home": the experience of familiarity, emotional closeness, and fun. "One of the most important changes wrought by German immigrants was their promotion of numerous forms of innocent public family entertainment . . . the German 'jovial, yet orderly activities,' their 'hearty and harmless diversions' made an impression on other Americans" (Sowell, 1981, p. 60).

Particularly in communities that have maintained their ethnic character, *Gemütlichkeit*, in the form of Sunday strolls, family visits, a pleasurable glass of wine or beer, and so on, is part of the German capacity to share feelings of warmth and conviviality; it is central to family life. On home visits, paticularly with the older generation, people are usually invited to a drink of tea or wine. The wife may set the table with her "good linen" and *Porzellan* (china) on which she serves coffee and home made *Kuchen* (cake). People observe these customs to make visitors feel comfortable and welcome with almost ritualistic accuracy and care.

German American Values

FAMILY LIFE

Among all of the diverse German immigrant groups, family life was highly valued. The family was considered the place of mutual support, of strength in times of crisis. Loyalty was owed first to the family.

Often, particularly in rural areas, work and family life were integrated just as in the German "household family" of the 16th to 18th centuries (Weber-Kellermann, 1977; Billigmeier, 1974).

Even today, under different circumstances, the relationships among the members of the German American extended family systems are strong and well organized through visits, calls, or letters. German American families live apart from their extended families, and the blurring of boundaries between nuclear and extended families that we see in other cultures is rare in German American family systems. There is emotional attachment and there are strong feelings for extended family members. Children are expected to love their parents and to take care of them in their old age. In many ways the legacy of family life and its importance as described in 17th-century German "housebooks" (a series of "normative" descriptions of family life) proved to be very persistent in the lives of German Americans (Weber-Kellermann, 1977).

WORK

The work ethic, manifested in a respect for thoroughness, solid craftsmanship, and attention to detail, was transplanted from the fatherland to the New World. Other Americans admired the German settlers' skills, diligence, and industriousness. This is significant especially in the area of farming (in 1870 Germans constituted 33% of all foreign-born farmers). "No group of immigrants was more important than the Germans in introducing new methods of agricultural production" (Billigmeier, 1974).

Germans were also noted for their technical abilities. "Skilled technicians, engineers and scientists were drawn into American industrial enterprises, large and small, in every major field of manufacturing, in every region of the country. Their contribution to the industrial development of the United States is extraordinary" (Billigmeier, 1974, p. 99).

Contemporary German Americans take their work seriously and are conscientious about meeting their responsibilities. Success in work is a source of pride and self-esteem that is important for German Americans. The exploration of the occupational or professional responsibilities of German American clients should, therefore, be an integral part of the beginning phase of therapy.

EDUCATION

The emphasis on education is part of the heritage of all of the German groups that immigrated into the New World.

German Americans have been contributing to American education since the earliest periods of American history. In 1714 the first German American pedagogue, Christopher Dock, introduced the now familiar fixture of every American classroom, the blackboard. In 1750, he published the *Schulordnung*, which was recognized as the first pedagogy work in the United States.

Franz Danielle Pastorius, *Bürgermeister* (Mayor) of colonial German-town, established a school that provided daytime classes, as well as night school for those who worked during the day or who were too old for regular, day classes.

The intellectually oriented "Forty-Eighters" (political refugees of the failed revolution of 1848) were critical of educational standards in the United States and worked toward school reform. They spread knowledge about European pedagogical theories of which few Americans seemed aware. Some attempted to improve the quality of public education, while others established German private schools. In this period German secular and religious schools appeared all over the United States. Institutions, like the German American Teachers' Seminary in Milwaukee, were founded to maintain high standards of education (Conzen, 1980).

Another significant German contribution to American education was the Kindergarten, the first of which was started in Wisconsin by Margaretha Schurz, wife of famous Carl Schurz.

German American parents undergo considerable hardships and are willing to sacrifice in order to give their children a "good" education. Children in turn are expected to work hard and do well in school. College education is highly valued. Children who fail in school or who have little interest in studying are a source of serious concern, and at times this may prompt the parents to seek professional help. Academic achievements of the children are a greater source of pride for their parents than is financial success.

A SENSE OF JUSTICE

While there is less emphasis in German American families on expression of emotions, they seem to be sensitive to issues pertaining to justice between family members and between the generations. People notice whether there is a fair balance between entitlements and obligations in the household and in the extended family. It is a high praise if a parent or relative is called "just" or if it is said that he or she contributed in an extraordinary way to the well-being of the family. This carries greater weight than if a person is character-ized as warm or loving. The tradition of the "household family" is reflected here: For the survival of the family, the tangible, economic contribution and cooperation of family members was more crucial than was their affective relationship (Weber-Kellermann, 1977). German Americans, similar to their forebears in Europe, seem to rely less on what might appear to them as the transient nature of feelings and more on the fair and honest give and take of established family relationships. In therapy it is important, therefore, to guide German American families toward reconciliation and rebalancing of interpersonal justice (Boszormenyi-Nagy & Ulrich, 1981).

Family Patterns

Certain roles and relationships can be found among most German American subgroups. Family patterns differ, however, according to time of immigration, region of origin, economic class, religious affiliation, and extent to which German culture has been supported in the area of settlement.

Men and Women

German American family structure and role complementarity reflects the legacy from the fatherland. The husband/father is the head of the household and the leader of the family. The wife takes his name, adopts his family and friends, and gains his social status.

The early Pennsylvania German Americans (now called "Pennsylvania Dutch") assumed that a male-dominated social order was proper and that women had special responsibilities only in certain areas, which were called *kinner, kich, un karrich* (children, kitchen, and church), a phrase not unknown in modern Germany. The husband ran the farm, operated the mill, and concerned himself generally with economic enterprise (Parsons, 1976).

As his forebear and European counterpart, the German American father has a gay, even sentimental, side but also a stern side. Underneath the usually self-controlled, reserved, at times unduly strict and stubborn attitude are hidden intense emotions and sentiments. These are often experienced as overwhelming and potentially destructive.

> At Christmas and Easter his childlike joy in making others happy came to its full unfolding. For weeks he aroused the imaginations of his numerous grandchildren with secret hints and poetic letters. The spirit which made the child's world dear to him also showed in his great partiality to nature, particularly in a love for flowers. . . . In contrast to this sunny, gay side of his nature, a certain sternness, often bordering on harshness, characterized his nature in spite of all his goodness and benevolence. Stern with himself, and of a pronounced honesty, he was rather too easily inclined to judge others only from his standpoint. (Frank, 1971, p. 59)

The father's "stubbornness" led to a conflict with his son which was never reconciled.

Rational, and somewhat distant, the husband/father is often emotionally less available to the children than is their mother. He is supposed to be a hard worker and provide the material needs for his family. It is his right to make the major decisions or to ratify the common decisions of the couple. He takes care of the family car, does repairs around the house, and handles the family's finances. He might meet some of his friends to drink and to socialize; on the other hand, his wife would be unlikely to do this.

German American women were regarded as hardworking, dutiful, and subservient and were respected for these qualities. Among the early Pennsylvania Germans, a wife's contribution was highly valued by her husband. She was cook, seamstress, nurse, laundress, baker, teacher, clothmaker, and supervisor of household production. Her role was indispensable in this early rural economy, and she "was the living example of frugality and duty in action" (Parsons, 1976). Unlike their British contemporaries, German American women helped at harvesting and in strenuous farm work.

The home-oriented role of women was highly adaptive for families with "family businesses" in both rural and urban settings (Weber-Kellermann, 1977). The image of the hardworking mother persists in this description from early 20th-century Wisconsin:

> In the store she was always dad's "right hand man." In the home she did a fantastic amount of work. . . . Yet I cannot recall that she ever appeared weary from work. . . . She was strong physically, with great vitality and energy. Activity was a necessary requirement. Brought up on a farm she worked side by side with her brothers, Gustav and Henry, and with her father. (Kletzien, 1975, pp. 9–10)

In more contemporary families, the wife's main task is the housework. A clean house and the neat appearance of husband and children are her responsibilities and a source of pride. Above all, it is her "chore" to raise the children with whom she is more involved than is her husband. In many ways, wives and mothers are the emotional power center of the family, although for outside appearances the leadership of fathers and husbands is not challenged. German American women appear emotionally more open and available than do their husbands.

Marital Complementarity

The marital relationship and the division of "labor" between the parents tend to solidify the complementarity of a rational, dominant leader and an emotional, submissive nurturer. Yet, the father is not lacking in emotions and might even be quite sentimental. The mother can also effectively lead the family. It is the cultural context, among other influences, that determines who plays what role (Bateson, 1976; Willi, 1978). It is the familial context that maintains the polarity within which each of the partners develops attitudes and behavior patterns that correspond to their roles.

One of the tasks in therapy with German American families is, therefore, to help them to gain greater flexibility of role patterns and to increase the spectrum of acceptable responses toward each other. For example:

> In a family in which the father was characterized as distant and authoritarian, the daughter complained to him that he had no feelings. The father was unable to respond. The therapist suggested that the father's reticence was not a sign that the father had no feelings, but that he was overwhelmed by a wealth of feelings. With this support for his "hidden" sentimental side, the father became more expressive and the father–daughter dialogue continued on a more emotional level. The daughter began to experience her father quite differently.

Most German American families talk about an "authoritarian, stern, tyrantlike father" and a "warm, loving, subservient mother" somewhere in their family background. Descriptions of a harsh, feared, and unapproachable father are common among German American families in therapy and in the German culture (Kafka, 1954; Glaser, 1976; Willi, 1978).

To what extent German American families have a significantly higher number of "authoritarian" fathers/husbands than do other ethnic groups is unclear. From a systemic perspective, we must consider not only the typical polar and complementary relationship of both marital partners, but also the entire family structure. The "patriarchal" family, in turn, would have to be viewed in relation to economic conditions and societal issues in general. It is known, for example, that traditional Swiss and German family structures are very similar, although the societal context is not (König, 1974).

Specific research does not support the idea that German fathers before World War II were more "authoritarian" than their American counterparts (Koomen, 1974). It might be that studies of the characteristics of an "authoritarian personality" (Adorno, Frenkel-Brunswik, Levinson, & Nevitt, 1950; Mitscherlich, 1973; Mitscherlich & Mitscherlich, 1975; Erikson, 1950, 1962; Schatzman, 1976) and those of Hitler's family background (Stierlin, 1977; Langer, 1972) have been generalized in an attempt to explain the most puzzling part of Germany's recent history (Dicks, 1950; Pribilla, 1946–1947a, 1946–1947b).

Parents and Children

German infants and young children are raised with more structure, greater limits on spatial exploration, and more precise schedules than are American children. This attitude reflects the historical German concern for spatial and structural issues. "German parents tend to be more controlling than American parents" (Koomen, 1974, p. 634; Devereux *et al.*, 1962).

> As perceived by American and German adolescents, American parents are less strict with their children and give them more autonomy. German parents tend

to use more "punitive" and American parents more "rewarding" and "neutral" child rearing methods, in attempting to influence their children. (Rabbie, 1965, p. 307)

Due to this legacy and their roots in a highly structured homeland, German Americans grow up in families that tend not to encourage open expression of affection or anger, joy or disappointment. The overall family climate and emotional atmosphere is much more favorable to tasks and doing than to nurturance and emotions. Disagreements between parents and children are settled through the decisions of the parents without a lengthy period of verbalized anger, accusations, and mutual compromising. Children are rewarded less for airing feelings than for politeness in verbal expression, appropriate table manners, or fulfillment of their household chores.

Life Cycle Issues

German American families seem to have difficulties in making the transition from a family with small children who need to obey their parents to a family with teenagers who are being asked for age-appropriate cooperation and who need a different kind of guidance. Fathers, in particular, usually find it very taxing to be challenged in their authority by their adolescent offspring. Parents are quite successful in teaching their children practical and intellectual skills, but they seem less oriented toward teaching them social and relational qualities that vary according to the age and sex of their children.

Parents and children in German American families talk less openly about the struggles of increasing autonomy for the children and the pain of the separation process than do families of other ethnic groups. If things do not go well, the children may leave home and cut themselves off from their parents as adults, without forming an extended family network. The process of individuation and continuing relatedness (Stierlin, Rücker-Embden, Wetzel, & Wirsching, 1980) in German American families tends to have an either–or quality to it. Parents or children might give up their contact with each other altogether rather than negotiate their differences.

Therapists, therefore, frequently have to reopen the intrafamilial dialogue. They have to be empathic and supportive to both "sides" of the adolescent struggle: Fathers can learn to live with continuing challenges and to share their own inner world, while mothers can learn how not to interfere with the developing confrontation. Adolescent sons and daughters need the therapist as a model for combining challenge with respect in their struggle for individuation within the ongoing familial relationship. Because of the strong push for education, it is less likely that the children in German American families are unable to leave at all; rather, the transition into adulthood can be abrupt and without open sharing of the concomitant feelings.

Reflections on German Americans in Therapy

Entering Therapy

German American families find it difficult to begin therapy. The tradition of the rural and urban household family, where work and home life were integrated, emphasizes self-sufficiency and the resolution of problems within the family. Coming to therapy violates a tacit rule of German American families: "do it yourself."

German Americans, therefore, come for treatment when they feel they have no alternative: the marriage is on the verge of collapse and divorce is impending, or there is a debilitating symptom that seriously interferes with the family's functioning. Seeking outside help is connected with a sense of failure; hard work, responsible behavior, and conscientiousness have not been good enough.

One second-generation mother remarked, "I would take my child to therapy only after I had done everything in my power and left no stone unturned in trying to solve the problem in the family."

The therapist who bypasses this phenomenon in the initial moments of therapy, risks shutting himself or herself out of the family. It may be helpful to take some time to track the decision-making process involved in coming to therapy. The therapist may then have the opportunity to enter the family by commenting on their decision to begin therapy in a way that is syntonic with the values of self-sufficiency and hard work, that is, by pointing to the work the family has already done in its effort to resolve the problem.

The Initial Interview

As with the entrance to the well-constructed German home with its fenced front yard, a stranger does not enter the family abruptly. During the initial interview, there is often an air of emotional restraint around the German American family, as illustrated in this vignette.

> When Mrs. Gruenewald finished explaining her view of her daughter's acting-out behavior, the rest of the family fell silent. The four children sat motionless, alternately staring at the floor, each other, or their father. Mr. Gruenewald shifted from one uncomfortable posture to another and sighed intermittently. Questions from the therapist were answered monosyllabi-cally by the children. Mother became anxious. "Talk," she said. "That is what we came here for." The harder she tried, the more deadly the silence.
>
> The therapist eventually congratulated the couple for having raised very loyal children, who were not easily convinced that a stranger should be let into their family. Their caution was viewed as protective of the family unit. Here Mr. Gruenewald opened up: "Yes, the one time we had to deal with a therapist, it was an ordeal."

The therapist who is accustomed to the more histrionic style of Italian families or the high verbal productivity of Jewish families need not be discouraged. The Germanic style of forming relationships is more structured and includes a sequence of steps over time. The joining process is generally slow and proceeds through certain stages, but once they are established, relationships are intense and lasting.

Inside or Outside

The therapist's position outside the German American family is analogous to standing in the hallway of a contemporary German home. There are many doors, all of which are closed. It appears as if he or she is not invited in. Yet the closed doors simply mean that entry is not automatic, that the doors need to be opened from within. The stranger to the family must knock and wait to gain entry. Only the *Hausherr* (master of the house) has the authority to open the doors for the guest, even if he or she is welcomed by both spouses. It is important in the joining process to respect the family's value of father's authority.

Reaction to Therapy

Once the therapist is invited into the family, German Americans are responsible about therapy and take it seriously, just as any other task that needs to be done. Appointments are generally kept, and it is rare that they are missed without good reason. In this respect, they are similar to Anglo-American families. They are conscientious about fees and about the therapist's requirements regarding who should attend the sessions. Therapy is considered a task that requires serious attention. Of course, this does not mean that German American families respond to the therapist's interventions better than do others. Compliance with the therapist's suggestions and submissiveness to his or her authority may very well be typical German American ways to let the therapist fail (Bateson, 1976). It is quite possible that the family follows through with the therapist's suggestions, but in such an exaggerated or formal way, that the task becomes ridiculous or meaningless or may undermine the therapist.

Therapeutic Styles

Therapists who overaccommodate and become too casual in trying to make the family feel at home, risk not being taken seriously. They may be regarded as amateurs who are oblivious to the delicate process of entering a family. German Americans, in other words, expect a professional context in therapy.

In a culture where people are very sensitive to clear, although at times subtle, hierarchies of power and authority, the therapeutic stance to which the German American family is likely to be most responsive would be one not only of empathy but of authority as well. The therapist is viewed as the expert and has authority to which the family can relate.

While therapists might appropriately suggest using first names (including the therapist) with families of different ethnic heritage, this might be considered "unprofessional" by German Americans, particularly more recent immigrants and the older generation.

Therapeutic styles that emphasize physical contact beyond a handshake between therapist and family are usually not advisable, at least not during the beginning phrase of therapy. Considering the German American sense for spatial boundaries, the handshake can be useful as a way of differentiating between the therapeutic context and the outside, to punctuate beginning and ending of a session, and to express mutual respect between therapist and family.

The Family in Treatment

The complementarity of marital and parental roles in German American families (fathers provide for the family and mothers are involved with household and children) and the dutiful adherence to the work ethic can be observed in therapy. Fathers rarely complain about their role. As one man of German descent put it, "The first third of my life I worked for my mother, the second third for my wife and my children, now I want to enjoy myself." That meant he did not want to work two jobs anymore as he had done all his life.

This sense of duty and responsibility for the family can grow so strong and all encompassing that it drives people into untenable situations.

> Mr. F, a successful lawyer, regularly overworked to the degree that when he reached the point of sheer exhaustion, he needed the excuse of severe depression in order to grant himself some rest. Although his wife stated that she was willing and able to work, both could not, in fact, tolerate her contributing to the family income. That would have contradicted their understanding of what was expected of him.

In such a rigidly complementary system, it is generally counterproductive to question the ethnic values. Rather, the therapist needs to devise an intervention that supports the values of work and duty and the complementarity of roles to an even greater extent.

In therapy we can use characteristics of German American fathers as an asset. Because of the seriousness and work orientation of German American fathers, they are amenable, for example, to an assignment of a task in which the father is to take charge of one of the children. While the role may be unfamiliar, the notion of working diligently on a given task is not. His own understanding of his function in his family facilitates his readiness to follow the therapist's directives.

Similarly, mothers in German American families do not generally express dissatisfaction with their roles. It is not unusual to meet a wife who has adhered to her subservient role for years and has contained enormous rage, which eventually brings the family to therapy. Defiance of the authority of the father may be acted out through subtle undermining, generally through the children. On the surface, however, it would always appear as though the father were in control, and the effort to maintain this appearance is highly collusive and well entrenched in the family's modus operandi. It is difficult, therefore, to overcome this polarization of roles.

> Karen and Peter Hoffman came to therapy because three weeks earlier, after eight years of marriage, Karen announced that she was leaving. Peter was bewildered. He had no idea that there had been any problem in the marriage and could not understand her present motives. Stuck in their complementary roles and confined by their emotional restraint, both spouses had been unable to communicate effectively. Karen revealed that she had felt dominated by and subservient to Peter throughout the years of their marriage. Through many tears, she explained that she had never thought of telling Peter how she felt. She did not understand her feelings herself and could not imagine how he would.

Within the context of these fixed roles, the expressiveness of the mother can make it difficult for the father to be more emotionally involved with the children. Here it is helpful to reduce mother's activity and to increase father's contact with the children. Because of his respect for the authority of the therapist and his orientation toward work, the father is likely to carry out this task, at least so it seems. Mother, however, feeling isolated from her husband might find this suggested change difficult to accept. Even with the therapist's support, mother may covertly undermine father's involvement with the child.

The therapist needs to consider mother's feeling of loss of emotional contact. It is essential to realize that she has lost part of her contribution to the work of the family, which she may value highly. It may be helpful, therefore, to acknowledge her reduced involvement as difficult work and treat it as such with special recognition and/or specific tasks.

In treating families of German American heritage, we are sometimes struck by the lack of expression of feelings despite the severity of their problems. It is difficult to decide whether this is an indication of the family's need for privacy and emotional restraint or if it is part of the dysfunction of the family system.

> The Strumpf family presented with a 16-year-old daughter, whose parents had gone through enormous hassles to have their daughter treated for

scoliosis and to have her wear a brace. Recently the daughter refused to wear the brace and got caught smoking marijuana. Despite the stress on everybody, the family's conversation centered around logistical, medical, and legal issues. None of the accompanying emotions were shared. Explorations into the family of origin of both parents revealed their German heritage, of self-sufficient, hardworking, performance-oriented ancestors, who left little space for emotional issues.

The therapist's most important asset is his or her awareness that the greater the emotional restraint within the family system, the more explosive the underlying feelings (as symbolized by the daughter's acting out). Here the turning point was the therapist's praise of the parents for having put aside their disappointment in their daughter in order to work harder at taking care of her.

The Ethnic Heritage as Therapeutic Issue

The therapist who is interested in multigenerational issues will discover, in work with German American families, that it takes a while for the family members to be comfortable enough to discuss the family's memory about the disappearance of the German culture.

The need to be cautious about their German background has caused, in some families, an atmosphere of suspicion toward the surrounding society. As a result, in most families, attitudes toward their German heritage are very ambivalent. This ambivalence is far from being resolved and might also be directed toward the therapist who belongs to a different ethnic group.

Exploration of a German American family's background might stir up therapists' forgotten memories and hidden prejudices. They might have to learn to accept their own suppressed German American heritage. On the other hand, therapists with different ethnic backgrounds will have to deal with their group's misconceptions and stereotypes about German Americans.

Clients are usually quite able to sense the negative, judgmental attitude behind their therapist's friendly facade. Ethnic stereotypes will invariably be communicated to the family. It is better to recognize one's own limitations as a therapist and to discuss openly whether or not treatment with a therapist of different ethnic background might be fruitful. Jewish therapists, in particular, need to be careful not to overestimate their tolerance in view of the pain of Jewish–German history.

German Americans as an ethnic group have, by and large, experienced the loss of their own culture. The ethnically sensitive therapist might, therefore, be particularly attentive to signs of other losses and might explore how the family has dealt with them. Intergenerational work with German Americans from a family therapy perspective, coaching family voyages, and guiding through operational mourning have proven to be most effective in coping with loss in the family context (Bowen, 1978; Paul & Paul, 1975).

Summary

Family therapy with German Americans remains largely an unexplored field of study. Therapists who do work with German American families need to be aware of the characteristics of German American family systems. Not the least of these characteristics is the loss of their distinctive culture in present-day America.

The authors hope that these reflections stimulate the observations of their colleagues in the field and lead to applications in clinical practice. German Americans, their "typical" family structure, and the very ambiguity of their ethnic context provide a challenge for the development of the ethnic perspective in family therapy.

REFERENCES

Adorno, T.W., Frenkel-Brunswik, E., Levinson, D., & Nevitt, S.R. *The Authoritarian Personality.* New York: Harper, 1950.

Bateson, G. Morale and National Character. In *Steps to an Ecology of Mind.* New York: Ballantine, 1976 (paperback).

Billigmeier, R.H. Americans from Germany: A Study in Cultural Diversity. Belmont, Calif.: Wadsworth, 1974 (paperback).

Boszormenyi-Nagy, I., & Ulrich, D. Contextual Family Therapy. In A. Gurman & D. Kniskern (Eds.), *Handbook of Family Therapy.* New York: Brunner/Mazel, 1981.

Bowen, M. *Family Therapy in Clinical Practice.* New York: Jason Aronson, 1978.

Conzen, K.N. Germans. In S. Thernstrom, A. Orlov, & O. Handlin (Eds.), *Harvard Encyclopedia of American Ethnic Groups.* Cambridge: Harvard University Press, 1980.

Dahrendorf, R. *Society and Democracy in Germany.* New York: Anchor Books, 1967.

Devereux, E.C., Bronfenbrenner, U., & Suci, G.J. Patterns of Parent Behavior in the United States of America and the Federal Republic of Germany: A Cross-National Comparison. *International Social Science Journal, 14,* 488–506, 1962.

Dicks, H.V. Personality Traits and National Socialist Ideology. *Human Relations, 3*(2), 111–154, 1950.

Erikson, E.H. *Childhood and Society.* New York: Norton, 1950.

Erikson, E.H. *Young Man Luther: A Study in Psychoanalysis and History.* New York: Norton, 1962.

Frank, L.F. German-American Pioneers in Wisconsin and Michigan. In H.H. Anderson (Ed.), *The Frank–Kerler Letters, 1849–1864.* Milwaukee: Milwaukee County Historical Society, 1971.

Furer, H.B. (Ed.). *The Germans in America 1607–1970.* Dobbs Ferry, N.Y.: Oceana, 1973.

Glaser, H. *Sigmund Freud's Zwanzigstes Jahrhundert.* Munich: C. Hanser, 1976.

Glazer, N., & Moynihan, D.P. *Beyond the Melting Pot.* Cambridge: M.I.T. Press, 1970 (paperback).

Goren, A.A. Jews. In S. Thernstrom, A. Orlov, & O. Handlin (Eds.), *Harvard Encyclopedia of American Ethnic Groups.* Cambridge: Harvard University Press, 1980.

Hall, E.T. Proxemics in a Cross-Cultural Context: Germans, English, and French. In *The Hidden Dimension.* Garden City, N.Y.: Doubleday, 1966.

Hall, E.T. *Beyond Culture.* Garden City, N.Y.: Anchor Books, 1976.

Hatfield, H. *Thomas Mann.* Norfolk, Conn.: New Directions Books, 1951 (paperback).

Jens, W. Der Letzte Bürger: Thomas Mann. In *Republikanische Reden.* Munich: Kindler, 1976.

Kafka, F. *Dearest Father.* New York: Schocken Books, 1954.

Kletzien, H.H. *New Holstein*. New Holstein, Wisc.: New Holstein Reporter Press, 1975 (paperback).

König, R. *Die Familie der Gegenwart, Ein Interkultureller Vergleich*. Munich: C.H. Beck, 1974.

Koomen, W. A Note on the Authoritarian German Family. *Journal of Marriage and the Family, 35*, 634–636, 1974.

Langer, W. *The Mind of Adolf Hitler: The Secret War-Time Report*. New York: Basic Books, 1972 (paperback).

Mitscherlich, A. *Society without the Father: A Contribution to Social Psychology*. New York: Jason Aronson, 1973.

Mitscherlich, A., & Mitscherlich, M. *The Inability to Mourn. Principles of Collective Behavior*. New York: Grove Press, 1975.

Parsons, T. The Link between Character and Society (with W. White). In *Social Structure and Personality*. New York: Free Press, 1970 (paperback).

Parsons, W.T. *The Pennsylvania Dutch*. Boston: Twayne, 1976.

Paul, N., & Paul, B. *A Marital Puzzle*. New York: Norton, 1975.

Ploetz, K.J. *Auszug aus der Geschichte*. Würzburg, Germany: A.G. Ploetz, 1968.

Pribilla, M. Das Schweigen des Deutschen Volkes. *Stimmen der Zeit, 139*, 15–33, 1946–1947. (a)

Pribilla, M. Wie war es moglich? *Stimmen der Zeit, 139*, 81–101, 1946–1947. (b)

Rabbie, J.M. A Cross-Cultural Comparison of Parent–Child Relationships in the United States and West Germany. *The British Journal of Social and Clinical Psychology, 4*(4), 298–310, 1965.

Rippley, L.J. *The German Americans*. Boston: Twayne, 1976.

Salamon, S. Family Bonds and Friendship Bonds, Japan and West Germany. *Journal of Marriage and the Family, 38*, 807–820, 1977.

Schatzman, M. *Soul Murder: Persecution in the Family*. Harmondsworth, England: Penguin Books, 1976 (paperback).

Shenton, J.P., & Brown, G. (Eds.). *Ethnic Groups in American Life*. New York: Arno, 1976.

Smith, C.H. *The Story of the Mennonites*. Newton, Kans.: Mennonite Publication Office, 1950.

Sowell, T. *Ethnic America*. New York: Basic Books, 1981.

Stierlin, H. *Adolf Hitler: A Family Perspective*. New York: Psychohistory Press, 1977.

Stierlin, H., Rücker-Embden, I., Wetzel, N., & Wirsching, M. *The First Interview with the Family*. New York: Brunner/Mazel, 1980.

Weber, M. *Die Protestantische Ethik und der Geist das Kapitalismus* [The Protestant Ethic and the Spirit of Capitalism] (T. Parsons, Trans.). New York: Scribners, 1958. (Originally published, 1905.)

Weber-Kellermann, I. *Die Deutsche Familie. Versuch einer Sozial-geschichte*. Frankfurt: Suhrkamp, 1977 (paperback).

Willi, J. *Therapie der Zweierbeziehung*. Rowohlt: Reinbek b. Hamburg, 1978. (Translation: *Couples in Collusion*. New York: Jason Aronson, 1982.)

13

Greek Families

EVE PRIMPAS WELTS

It is unusual for Greek people to seek psychotherapy of any kind. Greek family members, particularly fathers, are confident that they alone know the causes of their problems and how best to solve them. If they feel powerless, they are likely either to overdo attempts to control their families or to sink into fatalistic resignation. If misfortune comes their way, they assume that the causes of the problems come not from themselves, but from somewhere outside the family—the malice of neighbors, the envy of competitors, or perhaps the "evil eye." They rarely expect anything good to come from outsiders (Blume & Blume, 1970).

If Greeks do go to a clinic or private practitioner, it is likely that they were sent by an authority—a court or school. In situations where they go voluntarily, though they might appear to be cooperative in seeking help, just under the surface is the opposite tendency, the desire to rebel against the therapist's authority. Since Greeks are intensely family oriented, the entire family may appear, whether all are requested to come or not. This could mislead the therapist into thinking that they are interested in family therapy. In fact, they would find most ways of doing family therapy, particularly expressive and exploratory approaches, objectionable.

Any family therapy with Greek Americans must take into account the basic characteristics of their Greek culture. This chapter will focus on four key elements of the Greek culture. First, Mediterranean Greeks are a mercurial and paradoxical people. Holden (1972) describes them as constantly oscillating between opposites:

> Spirit and flesh, ideal and reality, triumph and despair—you name them and the Greeks suffer or enjoy them as the constant poles of their being, swinging repeatedly from one to the other and back again, often contriving to embrace both poles simultaneously, but above all never reconciled, never contented, never still. (p. 27)

What is constant is "the leaping spark of tension that is the only certain characteristic of Greekness" (Holden, 1972, p. 33).

Second, Greeks take tremendous pride in individual achievement and think of themselves, basically, as individuals. The potentially chaotic com-

Eve Primpas Welts. McLean Hospital, Belmont, Massachusetts.

bination produced by extreme individualism and volatility is moderated by two other influences: their *philotimo*, literally "love of honor," and rigidity of family roles.

The third cultural element, honor, is important in all Mediterranean cultures, but it is, perhaps, even more important to Greek men, as will be shown later.

The fourth element is a rigid family role definition: Fathers are the masters of their households. They expect to be obeyed by all family members. They expect to lead, protect, criticize, and know best. Wives' and children's roles are secondary. Generational boundaries are rigidly maintained. This pattern of relationships, in which power and authority are held by the eldest in conformity with traditional rules, is called "lineal" in the Kluckhohn (1951) value orientations scheme (see Chap. 2).

In order to understand Greeks, these four elements and their interactions must be integrated. We must understand a family led by an unquestioned leader, the father, in which role definitions may require more than wife, sons, or daughters can manage and, also, in which individual achievement in the outside world is considered essential to the pride of father and family. Assimilation in the United States naturally moderates these demands, but assimilation and the loss of old values is actively avoided. Greeks have always been a people who have traveled to find better opportunities,[1] but have remained very much Greeks, intensely nationalistic, and culturally apart. Half the Greeks in the world live outside of Greece, and the Greek nation still claims them as her own. They have only to set foot on Greek soil to resume citizenship. So the relationship of Greek Americans to Greece is a bit special, like the Greeks themselves.

History

History is important to Greeks. They look back with pride at the glories enjoyed, the oppressions endured, and their final freedom won against heavy odds.

There is controversy about cultural similarities between the ancient Greeks of the classical era (500 B.C.) and modern Greeks of today. In the intervening 2400 years, the Greeks repeatedly had been invaded and ruled by outsiders, but there seems to have been a good deal of cultural continuity (Holden, 1972). Modern Greeks think fondly of their ancestors of the classical period. They admire the heroic individualism of the greats: Aristotle, Plato, Aeschylus, Sophocles, and, of course, the Homeric heroes—wily

1. Emigration from Greece still continues as enterprising Greeks search out opportunities abroad. Australia has been particularly attractive and Melbourne has a large Greek-speaking community (Stagoll, 1979).

Odysseus and reckless Achilles. They do not identify with a collective cultural accomplishment but with the achievements of individuals, the foremost of a still vital race of individuals.

At the close of the classical period, the third century B.C., when Alexander the Great conquered all of the Middle East, the center of Greek prosperity and vitality shifted across the Aegean Sea to Asia Minor,[2] and mainland Greece (the territory that makes up most of modern Greece) began a long, demoralizing descent into poverty and obscurity (Renault, 1975).

The brief empire of Alexander was followed by the long rule of the Roman Empire, in which, at first, Greece was a backwater. But in the fifth century A.D. the Emperor Constantine built a second capital, Constantinople, on the 900-year-old site of a Greek city-state, Byzantium. It was intended to be only an administrative center for the eastern half of the Roman Empire, but pressure from northern barbarians extinguished Rome, and the East was all that was left. Gradually the people of the eastern Empire began to speak Greek and to adopt Greek culture.

In the West, the Roman Catholic Church had inherited a practical, political role from the Roman Empire, but the Eastern Orthodox Church, always subordinated to the power of an emperor, turned to the more mystical, otherworldly side of the Christian faith. The Byzantine Empire, united with nation, race, and tribe by that shared faith, was considered to be of secondary importance. Inevitably, Greek culture blended with aspects of the surrounding oriental cultures.

The Byzantine Empire lasted 1000 years. It was finally extinguished by the next power on the rise, the Turks who took Constantinople in 1453.

The Turks were an exclusively military people. They conquered in the name of Islam and quickly moved to fresh conquest. They tolerated Christians and Jews as People of the Book like themselves, who erred only in their failure to accept the Prophet. They used Greeks to rule the Ottoman Empire through the previously existing religious and civil bureaucracies. The Turks were content and avoided interfering when taxes were promptly paid and children were provided to serve in their armies. When taxes were not paid or they were otherwise crossed, which happened more frequently as the Ottoman Empire decayed into disorder, the cruelty of the Turks was terrible (Braddock, 1972).

The Ottoman Empire lasted 400 years. The peasants in mainland Greece rebelled (1821–1827) in a war of mutual extermination in which English and French naval forces determined the final outcome by sinking the Ottoman

2. The center of Greek life remained in Asia Minor until 1922, when the Greeks were disastrously defeated in an attempt by the Turkish to reestablish a new version of the Byzantine Empire. One and one-quarter million Greeks were expelled from Anatolia in an "exchange of populations" (400,000 Turks). Most of these Greeks returned and consequently repeopled mainland Greece.

fleet. The heroes of this bloody war are celebrated by Greek rural people, more than the forgotten heroes of classical Greece. In 1827 Greece began its existence as a state in the modern sense.

Immigration

In 1976 the U.S. Immigration and Naturalization Service listed the total number of Greeks who had immigrated to the United States since 1820 at about 640,000. Greek Americans now number between 1.3 and 3 million (Saloutos, 1980).

From 1900 to 1920 the first great wave of Greeks left for the United States. These Greeks came primarily from Asia Minor, where they were under pressure by the Turks to leave, and from Peloponnesus, the southern peninsula of mainland Greece, which was the poorest, least developed part of the Greek world. These Greeks, almost entirely men, came to the United States reluctantly, driven by their poverty and intending to stay only long enough to make money with which to return, buy good land, and live out a respectable and comfortable life in Greece (Kourvetaris, 1976; Bernardo, 1981; Saloutos, 1980).

Since 1961 a second wave has brought almost 200,000 more Greeks to the United States. Many of these new arrivals came from the cities, are much better educated than the earlier immigrants, and are more Europeanized than the rural Greeks. This chapter will focus, primarily, on the earlier immigrants (1900–1920). Like many other ethnic groups, these Greek Americans have preserved cultural patterns that were contemporary at the time of the emigration. Again, like other ethnic groups, it is impossible to predict which elements of the old culture will persist in any particular family.

In the United States, the Greeks settled in northern cities such as New York and Chicago. In areas where the Greek population was sufficiently large, they formed "Greektowns" where they could speak Greek and attend the Greek Orthodox Church. They sent their money home, traveled back and forth when they could afford to, and eventually brought over wives to settle permanently.

In the western United States, the Greeks worked on the railroads and in the mines. Because there were fewer Greeks and no Greektowns for the women, the men often married non-Greeks. As a result, their families are not ethnically Greek in religion or customs, although they have Greek names.

Greek men detested working for others. To have an employer, particularly a non-Greek, was a violation to their pride and an affront to their self-esteem. They took pride in controlling their own business—striking the best bargain possible and beating the competition. Even very long hours of work in their own businesses were preferable to being employed by others (Moskos, 1980). If employed by others, they often held down several jobs in order to accumulate some capital and to hasten the day when they could be on their own.

Greeks have done very well economically. Their only business liability is their difficulty in cooperating with others, even other Greeks, in trade associations or large organizations. They enjoy competing but not cooperating. In terms of the Kluckhohn relationship value orientations, they prefer, in decreasing order, lineal, individual, collateral relationships. They like to run their businesses with a strong, controlling, authoritarian hand: a preference for lineal relationships. In doing so they feel confirmed in their worth as individuals: a secondary preference for individualism. Yet they are not used to putting aside their individual interests for the sake of a larger group: the collateral relationships being least preferred.

The Family

Details of the family roles are important because the inability to perform them adequately is a frequent cause of distress. The roles themselves are taken for granted; that is, they are not ordinarily discussed. The therapist must know in advance what is expected.

Sex roles are highly stereotyped with little overlap between men and women. Men must work and provide. They rarely assist with household or child-rearing tasks. They seek the status of *nikokiri*, or master of their house, and value the companionship and compatibility of their wives (Salamone, 1980). Women, in return, cater to the men's desires, want to build up men's self-esteem, and wish to be considered good wives. As long as there is mutual agreement about these goals, marriages remain stable (Sanders, 1962).

Men

Greek men are authoritarian fathers and husbands. They are loving but, particularly to outsiders, appear to be emotionally distant. They are parsimonious with praise and generous with criticism. A Greek proverb, "A man should love his wife with his heart, but never his lips," illustrates Greek men's feelings.

Greek fathers often tease their small children in a way that may seem sadistic to non-Greeks. For example:

> A Greek-born cab driver, speaking with fondness of his beloved 4-year-old daughter, described taking down his suitcase before leaving for work and telling the child he was going off to Greece without her. At first she would not believe it and accused him of teasing. Only after he had convinced her that he was telling the truth, had heard her pleading and seen her tears, did he tell her that he was, after all, only teasing.

Teasing is intended to toughen the children and make them cautious. Within the family, children learn that teasing is part of being loved.

Greek men revere their mothers, which often irritates wives who are second in priority. It is traditional for men to consider women, other than their mothers, to be emotional, controlling, quarrelsome, talkative, and silly. Boys are taught by their parents that they are superior to their sisters, who, in turn, have been taught to accept their inferiority. While these patterns are changing, vestiges of the male sense of superiority and dominance over women remain.

Men are sensitive to public opinion and often cannot tolerate their wives working outside of the home or family business. They fear that their neighbors will think that they are unmanly or failures and unable to support the family. Greeks can be very sensitive to insult and are always on the lookout for wounds to their pride. If their *philotimo* is hurt they may never forgive and forget.

Greek Americans still believe that a woman's place is in the home, although many women work in their husbands' restaurants, stores, and other businesses. Husbands see themselves not as exploiters but as the protectors of their wives, sisters, and daughters. Protecting women was a traditional part of Greek men's *philotimo*. The virginity of his daughters was an extension of a father's honor. Under conditions of terrible poverty his daughters' virtue might, indeed, be all that a proud man really had. Failure to protect them could become a lasting dishonor, a shame that would come freshly alive with each remembering.

An obvious reason for the traditional protection of virginity was the reality that a dishonored daughter would have difficulty marrying well. She would remain a permanent and conspicuous stain on the family honor (Peristiany, 1965).

Family honor is extremely important to Greeks. Breaking the rules can have terrible implications that dishonor the entire family, and, therefore understandably, would be anticipated with intense anxiety. For example, men worship their mothers and expect to care for them in old age (Zotos, 1969). If they fail in that responsibility it means not only that they are dishonored by their own failure to discharge an obligation but that their mothers are retrospectively dishonored as mothers since they could never have been good if they raised bad sons. Similarly, failure of a son to pay the respect owed his father shames both the father and the son (Peristiany, 1965). The depth of feelings for these matters cannot be overemphasized.

In rural Greek culture the idealization of fathers was made possible by projection of hostilities onto the Turkish oppressors, corrupt politicians, and priests who cooperated with the Turks. Each family learned that they could rely on their in-group, defined as those concerned people or family members (not necessarily all), friends, and friends of friends. From the in-group, one is due unlimited respect, concern, and loyalty, collaterally. Families neither expected favors nor gave them in the struggle for survival, in contrast, for example, to Jews who consider giving to the poor a religious obligation and a blessing for the one who gives.

In the prosperous United States the situation is entirely different: The individuality and hard work of fathers and their upwardly mobile children are usually rewarded with success. Families so favored with success are less likely to continue to see the outside world as hostile. Also, the value of hierarchy in family relationships conflicts with the U.S. preference (at least on the surface) for equality and democracy. It is inevitable that, as children who do their parents' bidding and strive for success become better integrated into American society, they will be increasingly influenced by American nonlineal family values. They will learn to "play ball" with others (Papajohn & Spiegel, 1975).

Women

Greek American women are expected to comply with tradition. Marriage is considered essential. A woman who does not marry before 30 loses status in the community and is criticized for her spinsterhood. Women are, as we have said, well protected. [Margaret Mead (1953) observed that Greek women seldom knew the word for genitals.]

For most women, motherhood is regarded as fulfillment. They aspire to be good mothers whose children are well behaved, stay out of trouble, and succeed in adult life. Childbirth is totally female oriented. The idea that fathers might be present at birth to share the experience is alien. Greek women want their mothers and sisters, not their husbands, present for support when giving birth.

Women's chief security in a male-dominated society is their indispensability as bearers of children, sexual companions, and, often, laborers helping to earn the livelihood for the family. Women, who are now being educated in professions, are facing special problems and conflicts since they are still expected to fulfill the traditional obligations of wives and mothers.

When marriages were arranged, young women learned to avoid falling in love. Mates were chosen for practical reasons and love for some other man would only have complicated matters. Many Greek American women are still taught that they should marry for status (i.e., financial security) not love. Many young women achieve the illusion of free choice and avoid open confrontation with their families by seeing to it that they only fall in love with men who will please their parents.

Women who have passive husbands usually maintain them as figureheads, while they establish their own rules. There is a folk saying that acknowledges the influence of women: "The husband is the head, but the wife is the neck which decides which way the head will turn." Few women would embarrass their husbands (and, therefore, the family) by overtly demonstrating greater strength.

When angry, Greek women seldom raise their voices at their husbands. They justify their obedient silence with an ominous proverb: "Beware of silent rivers" (Zotos, 1969). When they do rebel, they may be joined by their children in passively resisting paternal authority.

Children

Greek family life is extremely close and child centered. Children are included in most social activities and are rarely left with baby-sitters or other non-family members. Grandparents are often caretakers while parents work. Greek children receive abundant love and attention up to the age of 10 or 12. Then their fathers stop playing with them and suddenly expect achievement and compliant behavior; the children may feel abandoned by this change. Extreme emphasis is placed on the future achievement of children (Katakis, 1976).

Girls between the ages of 6 and 10 are required to assist their mothers with household chores; they later assume heavier agricultural burdens or work in the family business. In Greece, girls were considered an economic liability. They required a *prika* (dowry) to marry, had to be carefully guarded, and were only temporarily contributing members of the household since their marriage would make them a productive part of their husband's family.

Male children are still preferred today, even in urban areas and in the United States (Sanders, 1962). Having a son is a wife's main source of prestige and validation (Slater, 1971). In rural Greek culture breast-feeding is continued longer for boys than girls (Vassiliou & Vassiliou, 1970). As in other Mediterranean cultures, a woman's cultivation of and identification with her son is both a pathway to power and compensation for her helplessness in a male-dominated society.

Many parents favor one child (usually a son), though not necessarily the eldest, brightest, or most successful. These parental preferences cause jealousy and resentment among siblings, even though most parents appear loving to all of their children. Jealousy and competitiveness between extended family members is intense as it is with Mexicans and Italians (Papajohn & Spiegel, 1975). In times of crisis or tragedy, the rivals will pull together, but otherwise cooperation is unusual.

Greeks take blood lines seriously. It is unusual for an extended family to accept an adopted child as a real family member. If they do adopt, Greek Americans prefer to adopt Greek-born children.

There is little opportunity for Greek children to sort out their feelings by talking. Children soon learn when it is permissible to rush into a family group and get attention and when they should stay away because the adults are intent upon something else. If they are not obtrusive, they can hang around the fringes and observe (Sanders, 1962).

Children do not often hear parental feelings articulated. Instead parents give advice and direction. Children are not allowed to talk back. The disrespectful child who challenges paternal authority risks being rejected or disowned.

Parents consider some emotions, such as uncertainty, anxiety, and fear, to be weaknesses that must be hidden from the children. A doubting child who asks, "Why?" usually finds that father replies, "Because I said so." and mother replies, "Because your father said so." The father is the final authority. This serves the Greek American child well in the American school system: Greek children obey, take instruction easily, and please teachers by being constantly respectful (Papajohn & Spiegel, 1975).

Greek mothers are totally responsible for the way their children turn out. Furthermore, their responsibility never ceases, regardless of the ages of their offspring. Fathers rarely admit responsibility for their children's unacceptable behaviors, only pride in their accomplishments. Mothers often protect a child who is naughty by hiding the facts from the father for fear that he may punish too severely. This collusion with the child reinforces father's powerful image as a threat. However, if a child over 14 years old gets out of hand, the mother may likely seek out the father, who is still feared and respected since she has lost her disciplinary effectiveness because of her earlier permissiveness.

Children are urged to study hard, though parents may not understand or help in their school work. Therefore, educated children, particularly in the first generation in the United States, are thrust into the situation of parenting themselves while also relating as though they are still dependent. Dutifully, they ignore the contradiction. Although a generation ago most Greek American parents were not well educated, they invested heavily in education as a pathway for their children to attain a better life, higher status, and a professional identity. They urged them to obtain an education, which is all the more valuable because it is something that cannot be taken away from them—perhaps a response to the experience of Turkish oppression and repeated wars. In contrast to all other areas of life, children may be forced into near total autonomy regarding major decisions such as selecting a college, planning an academic program, or choosing a profession.

But, to the parents, their offspring will always remain "children," no matter what status or professional achievements they attain. They will be expected to honor advice given freely by the older generation. This attitude contrasts with cultures where children are better educated than their parents and parents acknowledge their achievement by accepting their grown children as peers.

Education of children naturally increases the rate of acculturation. A language barrier between generations may form, and children learn ideas that they cannot share with their parents. Communication between Greek-born parents and their American-born children may then become limited to "kitchen Greek."

Since Greek parents discourage dialogue with children, adolescents rarely turn to their parents to discuss thoughts, feelings, or changing life values. Contact remains loving and loyal but somewhat superficial and ritualized around meals, holidays, and family gatherings. Family loyalties are intense, and adult children do not hesitate to ask their parents for financial help or child care. Parents readily offer assistance, despite the material or physical sacrifice it may entail. They assume the same assistance will be offered them when they need it. Greek Americans do not separate from their parents yet are perceived as mature and adult by their community.

It is not at all unusual for Greek American parents to move many miles to live near one of their children. This is in contrast to Jewish parents who may move to retirement communities far away from their children and expect the children to travel to visit them. Greek parents view their children's homes as extensions of their own territory. If one parent is widowed, the children are expected to take in the surviving parent.

In the absence of a father (or after his death), the eldest son assumes full authority. The line of succession for authority follows the birth order downward in the male line. Daughters are expected to care for aging parents. When there are no daughters, the responsibility falls to the youngest son. As long as family members are alive it is imperative that aged parents not be put into nursing homes or be cared for by *kseni* (strangers). The family must care for its own, as illustrated by this case.

> An adolescent in a psychiatric hospital, after having been physically abusive and potentially homicidal toward his family, was to be sent to a half-way house. The family withdrew him from the hospital against medical advice and gave him his own clearly separate space within the house rather than have him leave their home. He was their responsibility, not to be passed on to strangers.

Yet there is no taboo on extruding family members who have brought shame to the family or who have been grossly disobedient to the father.

Marriages

Greek couples, when in conflict, are often locked in rigid positions of blaming their spouses for disappointments in the belief that since one is right the other must be wrong. It is noteworthy that when a couple becomes a family, by the birth of a child, the rules change.

> One woman, believing her husband was intellectually and culturally inferior, inconsiderate, and insensitive to her needs, was ready to make a commitment to the marriage if she became pregnant because he would be

a "good father" and the negatives would be balanced. Having a child made the earlier, personal complaints irrelevant since she would attain validation of her womanhood and success as a wife.

Becoming a mother is a required step in gaining status within the Greek American community, and the quality of intimacy in marital relationships is considered secondary in importance to the quality of families as child-rearing enterprises. Ironically, a precarious balance in marital relationships can be maintained by scapegoating a child (Katakis, 1976). When a child is not scapegoated, excessive and even destructive child-centeredness may be an alternative cohesive force.

Dr. Robert Ravich, who has studied dyadic interaction patterns extensively using the Ravich Interpersonal Game Test,[3] observes that

> Greek men want to dominate the situation and go to great lengths to do so. They want to discover the essence of the situation and are often capable of doing so. Once discovered, they seek to take advantage of their knowledge even if it leads to trickery, subterfuge, and destruction of the situation. Their wives know this and follow the male lead, joining in what he is doing. This "following" has the effect of totally disrupting the situation and both find themselves without structure. Then the couple is at a loss for what to do, because the rules and meta-rules have been completely undermined. They try to restructure, but the task is difficult. Trust is not easy because they do not know whether the spouse will go back to following the rules or defect and again undermine the situation. Considerable tension is involved in all of this, which is tolerated, or not, according to the personalities of the two people. (1981)

These findings concur with the summary of Story Sequence Analysis by Katakis, who writes: "In general, the observed husband–wife relationship could be characterized as distant, forced, and minimal. Open conflict was avoided. Disagreements were covered up" (Katakis, 1976, p. 5).

Vassiliou (1969), in a study of Athenian Greeks, has described similar difficulties:

> Women are perceived to be ingratiating and contemptuous in their relationship to men (whether fathers, husbands, brothers, grooms). They are seen as giving affect, but at the same time as cheating the male while fearing him. . . . Although women (whether daughters, wives, sisters or brides) are not supposed to compete, to rival, or even grow impatient with males. Men may annoy, quarrel with, scold, or reprimand women. They help, admire, enjoy, feel sympathetic toward the women in a "mother" or "daughter" role, but do not show

---

3. The Ravich Interpersonal Game Test (RIG/T) is a dyadic interactional test that is nominally structured as competitive by the award of imaginary pennies for a task that is quickly completed. But the task can be secretly disrupted at almost any time by the other person. The test generally requires good verbal communication to coordinate the efforts of each partner established in the test. Couples demonstrate their interactional patterns. For further explanation of RIG/T, see Ravich (1969).

love, or express understanding when she is in a "woman" role. On the contrary, they are expected to express hostility. . . . The wife is not supposed to make as many demands of the husband as he on her, or she should have no demands at all. She should give love and care and should not expect reciprocity. She should obey and assume responsibility and blame if something goes wrong. It is expected that interpersonal conflict will be resolved without discussion or explanation through the wife's submission to the husband. The husband is not expected to submit to the wife. (p. 124)

Under these difficult circumstances the white lie is a customary manipulation. It is used to avoid embarrassment and shame and to minimize intense feelings such as hurt pride, rejection, or anger.

Unhappiness in marriage is felt by all three generations who usually live in close proximity and share space. Women are expected not to discuss domestic tensions outside the family. Doing so is considered to be defiance of the husband and would risk bringing shame or criticism on the family (Rodman, 1967).

Church approval is required for divorce, and Greeks in their homeland enjoy one of the lowest divorce rates in Europe (*Hellenic Chronicle*, 1980). The divorce situation is similar for Greek Americans, although the divorce rate is rising rapidly for both groups. Until recently, divorce was looked upon as a tragedy for a woman. The Greek word *zontochira* (divorcee) is translated as "living widow." Divorcees often have difficulty remarrying because they are seen as "used" women. When traveling in Greece, many Greek American divorcees pass themselves off as widows to prevent sexual harassment to which they would otherwise be subjected. Widows, considered "blameless" for their status, are treated more respectfully. They are likely not to consider remarriage out of loyalty to and respect for their deceased husband.

Mixed Marriages

When a Greek man marries a non-Greek woman, the wife is less likely to remain as securely tied to her family as is he to his, unless she is from a similarly family-oriented culture such as Italian. If his family speaks Greek and she does not, she is likely to feel excluded by their continued use of Greek. She may want to make her own nest with her husband and children, especially if she values individuation. This will conflict with the lineal orientation of Greek families, and a struggle for control will begin with his family becoming very critical of her.

When a Greek woman marries a non-Greek man, he will find that he has chosen a good, loyal housewife and mother to his children. She will be a satisfactory sexual partner since she has been brought up to believe that wives must be sexually accommodating to their husbands. But, if the man expects to separate his wife from her family to start a new, autonomous family unit, he is in for a surprise. He will soon discover that she is unwilling to give up her family and tradition. Nor will she be anxious to absorb him into her family if he is unfamiliar with Greek language and customs. Instead, he will be excluded from conversations and many of the interactions with her family. Having achieved her (required) social standing as a married woman, she may well refuse to alter her life-style and to accommodate to his cultural expectations.

If her husband's life is professionally demanding or full in other areas, the marriage is more likely to work. When job requirements force a geographical separation from her family, she may resist the move, but a good wife must follow her husband. Overall, the rate of divorce in mixed marriages is much higher than in marriages between Greeks.

Therapy

Family therapy with Greek Americans can only lead to improved behavior if lineal relationship values and the need for privacy are respected. The therapist must be active in a relationship with the family in which the traditional values of achievement, productivity, cleverness, seriousness, and exemplary honor are supported. Throughout the therapy, the parents, particularly the father, must retain a sense of being in control.

Therapy techniques must be modified to be compatible with these baselines. For example, behavior modification is acceptable when the father approves of and controls the entire treatment. Video- or audiotape feedback can be used if the father controls the making of and playback of the tapes and through their use feels in control of the therapy (Paul, 1981). Assertiveness training is acceptable when it is used to help in dealing with people who are outside of the family, thereby advancing the interests of the family. Positive reframing works well when it indicates appreciation of traditional values. In general, a here-and-now problem-solving stance is most likely to be effective. The therapist says, in effect, "What else can you do that works for you?" This approach counters the feeling of Greek Americans that they have no options.

Brian Stagoll has developed effective ways of working with first-generation Greek Australians: Using his "benign authority" as a physician, he reframes presenting problems as physical wherever possible. For example, to overcome the stigma of labeling a problem with a psychiatric diagnosis, he may call it exhaustion. He then joins the family by encouraging the supportive efforts of the family and members of the in-group such as the Orthodox priest or the husband's best man. Then he shifts the focus to transitional conflicts such as the transition of married partners from focus on relationships with their parents to their needs as a couple. He helps to maintain the family's sense of being in control by acknowledging his lack of familiarity with Greek traditions and soliciting their guidance. He reinforces the family's expertise on its own operations. Stagoll adapts structural techniques (that were developed in work with more collateral cultures, like Puerto Rican and Black) and paradoxical directions as when he tells a depressed Greek grand-mother who is overinvolved with her daughter to have absolute bed rest with only her grandchildren caring for her—bringing her tea every three hours. (She lasted half a day in bed before she got up, feeling much better.)

Unfortunately, the list of therapies and techniques that are unlikely to work with Greek Americans is long. Psychodynamically oriented therapy, family or individual, requires tolerating an awareness that the causes of problems often lie within oneself. Psychodrama, Gestalt, and group therapies add the additional burden of public exposure and shame. Structural family therapy, as it is usually done, calls for a greater degree of joining together and flexibility in family roles than is ordinarily acceptable in Greek families. Strategic techniques that are intended to escalate stress in order to produce second-order change will usually get the therapist fired as an incompetent, who makes things worse. Medications are often requested and appreciated, but frequently they are not actually taken. Child guidance approaches are upsetting because they imply that the parents do not know what is best for their children. Art and dance therapy are seen as frivolous. The quest for person-to-person relationships in Bowen systems therapy violates the rules against rigid boundaries between generations. Individuation from the family is seen as an offense against the lineal relationship rules, the greatest betrayal of all.

When the therapist does behave in an unacceptable way, the family may say nothing to the therapist directly, out of respect, and just drop out.

The Therapist

The sex, age, and discipline of the therapist are important. Male therapists are more likely than female therapists to be seen as challenging the father's authority. Male therapists should always be deferential to and respectful of fathers. They should also be formal and authoritative. This is what the family expects of a man. Female therapists, particularly those who have been raised to defer to males, will be less threatening. Traditionally, middle-aged women are expected to be conciliatory and supportive. However, the very existence of a female therapist doing a "man's job" does threaten tradition. Younger therapists must be very careful to show constant respect and deference.

Insanity is seen as incurable, serious, and permanently stigmatizing to the entire family (Safilios-Rothschild, 1968; Koutrelakos, Gideon, & Struen-ing, 1978). Because psychiatry is associated with insanity, psychologists or social workers may be more acceptable, particularly to more assimilated Greek Americans who have some idea of the possibility of getting psycho-logical assistance.

Greek Orthodox priests can provide helpful support, but they are not sought as therapists. Sometimes, because of memories of corruption of the Church in Ottoman Empire times, they are not trusted. In addition, since priests' families are a part of the Greek community, Greeks dread the possibility that their secrets might be exposed. A Greek proverb states: "If you never tell your secret to your friend, you will never fear him when he becomes your enemy" (Bucuvalas, Lavrakas, & Stamatos, 1980).

If, as Stagoll recommends, it is possible to reframe symptoms as a physical illness, then it is possible to work with the local Greek Orthodox priest and the network associated with his church to provide support and assistance. Church activities are important to Greek Americans and are a potential resource.

The Family's Behavior

As was said earlier, entire Greek American families are likely to appear at the office or clinic, whether asked to or not. They will want the therapist to cure the offending individual immediately. They will appear to be cooperative and compliant in the initial session, but therapists must remember that the family may soon show the other side of their feelings about authority.Their rebelliousness will surface after they have left the session and will soon take the form of failure to appear for appointments, cancellations, changes of schedule, and unwillingness to end the session on time (Samouilidis, 1978). At any point they may drop the treatment.

Therapeutic approaches that require a commitment to a course of treatment involving a series of sessions will be rejected. Sometimes the therapist may have to negotiate each new session on the basis of the content and conclusions of the current session. Handling of payment is consistent with this tenuous commitment. They will want to pay at each session to discharge their obligation and facilitate quitting. Dependency on outsiders is unacceptable.

More traditional Greek Americans will view emotional and mental problems as "nerves," physical problems that reflect the inability to deal with stress. Common complaints are headaches, dizziness, ringing in the ears, weakness, shortness of breath, fainting, tachycardia, or peculiar physical sensations (Samouilidis, 1978). It is unwise to offer a psychological interpretation for a physical symptom because it will imply that the person is out of control, that is, crazy, which will put the therapist one-up on the patient.

Physical problems require physical cures; therefore medications are usually requested.[4] The family may inquire in great detail about the medica-

4. Some older people still use *vendouzes*. In this treatment a coin, wrapped in a fine, oil-soaked cloth, is placed on the part of the body that is in pain, usually the back or chest. The cloth is ignited and then covered by a small wine glass. As the oxygen is burned, a vacuum is created, drawing out the "evil spirits" or "bad blood" (Georges, 1964).

tion and exactly how it should be taken, but this does not mean that they will actually take it. That decision will be made later, and the therapist may never know for sure.

Depression or melancholia is also traditionally considered a physical condition. It is considered sadness that follows loss or trauma, or it is attributed to the "evil eye."

A therapist doing an evaluation may be seen as an intruding "outsider" who is trying to learn family secrets rather than a helper. This is particularly likely if the parents are from rural Greece. Second- and third-generation Greek Americans or more recently arrived, better-educated Greeks are more likely to be cooperative. However, even they may be hesitant to give personal information until they feel that they know and trust the therapist.

Feelings of anxiety are not comfortably expressed in Greek families where rationalization and denial are the customary defenses. Mistrust or paranoia come naturally and do not imply the degree of psychological disturbance that they might in the wider culture. Samouilidis (1978), a Greek psychoanalyst, writes: "The mistrust is a mixture of externalized lack of inner confidence and a rebellious attitude toward authority" (p. 227).

Although Greeks may not show their warm feelings in such a formal situation as therapy, they are comfortable with a very wide spectrum of emotions—happiness, pride, love, loss, depression, and sadness.

Most parents want the therapist to support their version of "good advice" for their children. They are often looking for an ally not an objective evaluation of the family's dysfunction. Children are encouraged to "tell" the therapist about some misdeed or unacceptable behavior. Parents expect the therapist to scold the children in support of parental values. A therapist is often seen as a moral advisor and is asked to reform the character of an errant family member. This attempt of the parents to triangle the therapist is difficult, though not impossible, to avoid. Redefining "intent," rather than passing judgment on behavior is a wise move for the therapist. For example:

> A 17-year-old girl, in therapy for violating her parents' curfew, was ashamed to tell her friends she had to leave a party so early. The therapist focused on the conflict the girl experienced between wanting to obey her parents and not wanting to put herself and them in an embarrassing position by leaving early. In her conflict she had not thought of the option of phoning to let her parents know that they need not worry about her safety. The girl demonstrated regret for the pain she had caused her parents, and with the support of the therapist, the family came to understand the difficulty their rules created for her pride and integrity.

When a therapist encourages the children to speak up, it is often perceived by parents as encouragement for them to be disrespectful. A therapist who asks parents to reveal their more serious feelings to children is violating family rules. The Greek American father wants his children to see him as infallible and full of strength.

Many Greeks believe that physical punishment is an appropriate discipline for their children (and wives). To criticize a father for striking his child without acknowledging this act as a painful duty, done in the service of good parenting, is insensitive. For protective service workers to forbid physical punishment is a gross presumption and insult. The therapist is more likely to keep a father involved in therapy by pointing out that his child, in an American environment, will find it hard to perceive him as a good parent if he continues physical punishments.

Grandparents must be accepted as intimately involved with, and even a controlling part of, the family, although language barriers may prevent them from actively participating in office interviews. If the grandparents live in the home, the children can often act as interpreters.

The therapist may never get a complete picture of the family if all family members are present. Family therapists, who refuse to see individuals alone, will have difficulties because most Greek families assume the therapist will not speak honestly before a child or "sick" relative. When family members are seen individually or in subgroups, they are likely to share sessions (and distortions) with other family members, while withholding personal thoughts and feelings from both the therapist and family. A responsible family representative may contact the therapist privately after the session to learn the therapist's "real" opinion (Samouilidis, 1978). It is helpful to ask the father for permission to separate the family into subgroups of parents or children.

The Therapist's Behavior

Therapists must be very careful about trying to "join" the family. The Greek family is a closed system, and it is rare for a non-Greek to be allowed into the family.

Since problems were traditionally dealt with by a member of the in-group—a wise person in the family or a close friend—therapists will be seen, at best, as friendly outsiders who are there to render a service.

As previously mentioned, a male therapist, although deferring to fathers, is expected to be formal and authoritative. Like the father, he will have influence. A female therapist can reach the family by being nurturing and by functioning as mediator. This is acceptable because women as mothers are the main source of expressed love and affection and are expected to look after the needs of all household members. They give emotional support and mediate between father, children, and extended family members. Cotherapists of each sex could combine traits of both.

While Greeks argue freely among each other to prove themselves right, they are bound by traditional attitudes toward authority not to argue with therapists. The therapist should be concerned when the same questions or requests for advice are asked repeatedly. It probably indicates that the family does not accept the therapist's interpretations, explanations, or directives and is continuing to look for something else, perhaps the magic of medications or something akin to religious exorcism.

Neutrality on the part of the therapist is read as agreement. This makes the Bowen approach of active detriangulation and neutrality within the session difficult. A nondirective therapist is likely to be regarded as doing nothing—abandoning the family and making it solve its own problems.

Greeks want advice but have difficulty taking it from someone outside the family. A major task of the therapist is helping them either to see that they knew how the problem should be solved all along or, if the advice must be seen as coming from outside, how taking the advice is in their best interest.

The therapist, who has been asked for specific instructions and who may have made attempts to verify that there was clear understanding about the instructions, may be confused by their inaction. When the family does not follow through, they may say that they forgot, that they did not understand, or that there was no movement or change—a way of saying that the therapy is failing. Rational debates on the pros and cons of any behaviors are far more successful than interpretations of resistance.

Couples

Any approach that allows families to maintain control of themselves is best. Dr. Norman Paul reports video playback as useful with Greek Americans, especially in the severe marital problems he has treated. He asks the couple to be in an active viewing position and to be in charge. They are, in a sense, their own therapists. The intensity of self-righteousness, which he observes but the couple does not, is conspicuous in the Greeks and Greek Americans whom he has treated (Paul, 1981). Overall, Greeks are filled with "shoulds" and are reluctant to explore genuine feeling and their "real" selves.

For couples locked in rigid blaming, therapeutic interventions should be geared toward helping to examine communications and exploring alternative behaviors. At least at first, these efforts are either not understood or brushed aside in an intense effort to persuade the therapist that each, alone, is in the "right." The therapist should be patient and should be not put off by these obstacles.

The white lie, previously mentioned in connection with the avoidance of marital conflict, also appears in therapy. It is used to avoid embarrassment and shame and to minimize intense feelings such as hurt pride, rejection, or anger. By not always giving details, Greek Americans may mislead the therapist, even when closely questioned. Similarly, sincere efforts are made by Greek Americans to avoid hurting the feelings of the therapist (Samouilidis, 1978). The therapist should accept these evasions. Greek Americans do not believe that the truth will make you free, and the therapist should not attempt to impose the love of truth upon them.

Termination usually occurs quickly. Once the crisis that brought them to therapy has passed, they are ready to go. Having decided to stop, they do not understand a request by the therapist to come in and "talk about it." An invitation by the therapist to stay to learn to "better understand themselves" is likely to be countered with, "we already know ourselves."

Summary

The therapist should show deference to and respect for the father who will need to feel in control of the therapy. Then, avoiding confrontation and sticking to a cognitive approach, with the focus kept on what works best for the family, the therapist should encourage discussions of possible alternatives that are syntonic with Greek American ethnic traditions. The therapist must be cautious about innovations and must respect the need to conform to family rules.

REFERENCES

Bernardo, S. *The Ethnic Almanac.* New York: Doubleday, 1981.

Blume, R., & Blume, E. *The Dangerous Hour: The Lore and Culture of Crisis and Mystery in Rural Greece.* New York: Scribner's, 1970.

Braddock, J. *The Greek Phoenix.* New York: Coward, McCann & Geoghegan, 1972.

Bucuvalas, E., Lavrakas, C., & Stamatos, P. *Treasured Greek Proverbs.* New York: Divry, 1980.

Georges, R. *Greek-American Folk Beliefs and Narratives.* Unpublished doctoral thesis, Indiana University, 1964.

Hellenic Chronicle. Boston, August 8, 1980.

Holden, D. *Greece without Columns: The Making of the Modern Greeks.* New York: Lippincott, 1972.

Katakis, C. An Exploratory Multi-Level Attempt to Investigate Inrapersonal and Interpersonal Patterns of 20 Athenian Families. *Mental Health Society, 3,* 1–9, 1976.

Kluckhohn, C. Values and Value Orientations. In T. Parsons (Ed.), *Toward a General Theory of Action.* Cambridge: Harvard University Press, 1951.

Kourvetaris, G. The Greek American Family. In C. Mindel & R.W. Habenstein (Eds.), *Ethnic Families in America.* New York: Elsevier, 1976.

Koutrelakos, J., Gideon, S., & Struening, E. Opinions about Mental Illness: A Comparison of American and Greek Professionals and Laymen. *Psychological Reports, 43,* 915–923, 1978.

Mead, M. (Ed.). *Cultural Patterns and Technical Change.* Paris: UNESCO, 1953.

Moskos, C. *Greek Americans: Struggle and Success.* Englewood Cliffs, N.J.: Prentice-Hall, 1980.

Papajohn, J., & Spiegel, J. *Transactions in Families.* San Francisco: Jossey-Bass, 1975.

Paul, N. Personal communication, 1981.

Peristiany, J.G. *Honour and Shame.* London: Trinity Press, 1965.

Ravich, R. The Use of an Interpersonal Game-Test in Conjoint Marital Psychotherapy. *American Journal of Psychotherapy, 23,* 217–229, 1969.

Ravich, R. Personal communication, 1981.

Renault, M. *The Nature of Alexander.* New York: Pantheon, 1975.

Rodman, H. Marital Power in France, Greece, Yugoslavia and the United States: A Cross-National Discussion. *Journal of Marriage and the Family, 29*(2), 320–325, 1967.

Safilios-Rothschild, C. Deviance and Mental Illness in the Greek Family. *Family Process, 7,* 100–117, 1968.

Salamone, S. *The "Nikokiris" and the "Nikokira": Sex Roles in a Changing Socio-Economic System.* Paper presented at symposium, Modern Greek Studies Association, Philadelphia, 1980.

Saloutos, T. Greeks. In S. Thernstrom (Ed.), *Harvard Encyclopedia of American Ethnic Groups.* Cambridge: Harvard University Press, 1980.

Samouilidis, L. Vicissitudes in Working with Greek Patients. *The American Journal of Psychoanalysis, 38,* 223–233, 1978.

Sanders, I. *Rainbow in the Rock: The People of Rural Greece.* Cambridge: Harvard University Press, 1962.

Slater, P. *The Glory of Hera: Greek Mythology and the Greek Family.* Boston: Beacon Press, 1971.

Stagoll, B. Towards a Multicultural Society: Family Therapy with Greek Families. *The Australian Journal of Family Therapy, 1*(2), 61–68, 1979.

Vassiliou, G. Aspects of Parent–Adolescent Transactions in the Greek Family. In G. Kaplan & S. Lebovici (Eds.), *Adolescents: Psychosocial Perspectives.* New York: Basic Books, 1969.

Vassiliou, G., & Vassiliou, V. On Aspects of Child Rearing in Greece. In E.J. Anthony & C. Koupernik (Eds.), *The Child in His Family.* New York: Wiley-Interscience, 1970.

Zotos, S. *The Greeks: The Dilemma between Past and Present.* New York: Funk & Wagnalls, 1969.

14

Iranian Families

BEHNAZ JALALI

Iranian immigrants comprise a small, but steadily growing, ethnic group in the United States. Iranians living in the United States are now under stress, and their families may well come to the attention of the mental health professionals. Therefore, it may help therapists to know about Iranian cultural characteristics, family structure, and modes of symptom presentation, in order to enhance their therapeutic skills and understanding.

Most Iranian families in the United States are first-generation immigrants and, therefore, have many of the same characteristics as families in their homeland. They mainly come from several specific socioeconomic groups, and since social class is a central factor in Iranian society, it is particularly important to understand this class structure as it is related to migration to the United States.

Social class structure in Iran is more clearly defined with a greater number of distinct identifiable elements than is true in the United States (for more details, see Bill, 1972). Therapists should be sensitive to the importance of these distinctions to an Iranian family and should not assume similarities with other Iranians that the family itself may not experience. For example, the therapist should not assume that financial situations alone clarify the class distinctions of the family and should take pains to inquire about the family's background, belief in traditional values, and exposure to Western values. The vast majority of Iranians who have migrated to the United States are from the elite, modernized, educated and business classes, which have been exposed to Western education and values. For this reason we will mainly focus on the characteristics of these groups, but we should realize that they reflect, in fact, a relatively small portion of the actual Iranian population, which is primarily rural and agrarian. Moreover, we need to understand the basic Iranian cultural characteristics that are deeply rooted in each individual, irrespective of social class. The groups we will discuss have emerged during the last 40 years, when modern education became a vehicle for power and influence (Baldwin, 1963). Members of this new class often express new philosophies and ideas. They relate to other classes

Behnaz Jalali. Family Therapy Unit, Department of Psychiatry, Yale University School of Medicine, New Haven, Connecticut.

through their operational function and performance rather than through wealth, family ties, or property (Bill, 1973).

There have been three waves of Iranian immigrants to the United States. The first wave occurred between 1950 and 1970 and was composed mostly of people from large Iranian cities. They had an understanding of Western culture and mostly were highly educated and/or affluent. They belonged primarily to the elite and the professional middle-class groups. Between 1967 and 1969, out of the total 2143 new Iranian immigrants, more than half were engineers, doctors, and dentists. Teachers and scientists accounted for another 20%.

The second wave of immigration was from 1970 to 1978. This group was both affluent and city oriented and came from various social classes who, during these years of economic boom and rapid growth, had become wealthy. Like those of the first wave, most second-wave immigrants were professionals and were in a favorable position for gaining employment. Therefore, as immigrants, they were often able to remain in the social class they had enjoyed in Iran.

Statistics for the period 1970 to 1975 show that of 14,500 Iranian immigrants about 4065 (30%) held advanced degrees, with about one-third of this group being physicians (Askari, Cummings, & Izbudak, 1977). Some were from less-Westernized families and were more rooted in the traditional culture. Therefore, they had less prior contact with Western influences and were not as prepared as the first wave to manage the cultural change.

While economics was a factor in immigration, other social factors such as professional opportunities, the structure and condition of the employment system, and opportunities for children were also important (National Science Foundation, 1973). Others came for political reasons such as opposition to the existing regime.

Second-wave immigrants are scattered all over the United States, with the highest concentration in the Northern, Eastern, and West Coast urban centers.

The immigration of educated Iranians to Western countries is part of the process of the so-called "brain drain" that has been depriving many developing nations of its educated citizens. One out of four Iranian college students are abroad, and the majority of these (41%) are in the United States (Adams, 1958). Usually, these students had not intended to immigrate permanently when they left Iran. A variety of personal, occupational, and family reasons—including marriage to Americans—change their minds. Foreign-educated Iranians who do return often experience problems in adjustment to their homeland culture. This factor alone may keep them abroad or encourage them to return.

The third wave of immigrants arrived in the United States from 1978 to 1980, during the period immediately before and after the Iranian revolution. They emigrated for a variety of reasons including personal and economic security. This is a more heterogeneous group than earlier Iranian immigrant groups in terms of education and age. Perhaps the major element they have in common with the earlier immigrants is that most are affluent. Some have had exposure to Western culture, others have not. Unlike the first two waves, many were forced to leave Iran. Like those from any culture who are forced to flee for political or economic reasons, members of this group experienced extreme cultural shock. This was marked by great feelings of alienation, frustration, and depression as they attempted to adjust to a foreign culture. Some had to break ties with their families, at least temporarily, and destroy the integrity of the family unit. Their future remains uncertain; they have lost their social positions and power; and many cannot even practice their professions. They often have such strong ties to their homeland that they are reluctant to settle and acculturate. This group is under a great deal of stress and possibly constitutes the population that will have the highest incidence of symptomatology and problems in adjustment.

National and Cultural Characteristics

It is important for any therapist who has contact with Iranian patients to understand their cultural characteristics. These characteristics are interwoven into their everyday life and interactions with family members, friends, fellow workers, and people in authority, including the therapist.

Given the regional and ethnic diversity among Iranians, it is unlikely that we could construct a single profile with universal applicability (Banuazizi, 1977). In addition, there are contradictions within the culture itself. Iranians have taken on a number of cultural characteristics to ensure their self-preservation and to cope with political instability and turmoil of many centuries. They are individualistic and fatalistic and are nostalgically tied to the past (Haas, 1946).

Iranians are proud people who believe deeply in their own uniqueness. This sense of uniqueness has its roots in Iran's history. They have had to survive several foreign invasions and repeated internal turmoil. Time after time, Iran has managed to absorb cultural influences without losing its own identity and continuity. For example, with the invasion of the Arabs, the Islam religion was assimilated into the culture. In fact, most of the religion's rules became the governing laws of Iran. However, while they accepted Islam, they opted for a new branch of it, called Shiism. This differentiates them from most of the Moslem world who are Sunnis. Currently, 98% of Iran's population are Moslem, and 93% of these adhere to Shiism. Shiism is a highly emotional, and mystical, form of Islam that focuses on a series of martyrs: the 12 divinely designated descendants of the prophet, or the Imams.

Important characteristics of Moslem religion that were merged with the culture include submission and obedience to God; certain prescribed rituals;

and strict concepts of good versus bad, clean versus unclean, and *Haram* (forbidden) versus *Halal* (permitted) acts. For example, adultery and the consumption of alcohol and pork are forbidden acts. Bodily excretions and certain animals are considered unclean, and contact with them necessitates following a specific ritual to cleanse oneself.

The spoken language of Iran is *Farsi* (Persian), which has Indo-European roots. Even though the Arabic alphabet has been integrated into the Persian language, it is distinctly different from the Arabic language spoken by Lebanese, Jordanians, Iraqis, and so forth. (The spoken language of the ethnic populations near Iran's borders merge with those of the neighboring countries. For example, the Arab ethnic population who live near the Iran–Iraq border speak Arabic, and the Kurds who live in the northwest speak Kurdish.)

Basic cultural characteristics of Iranians are individuality, respect for authority, traditionalism, integrity, and enjoyment of life (Gable, 1959; Arasteh, 1964). Iranians have a strong sense of individuality, which has ensured their self-preservation. Individuality is especially evident in the diversity of their opinions and behavior (Arasteh, 1964). In general, they do not conform readily.

Iranians' sense of individuality has always been so powerful, that authoritarian controls have had to be exerted to ensure their allegiance and support. People in power are authoritarian in order to guarantee the submission and respect of their subjects. However, Iranians simultaneously accept the authority and resist indirectly. Or they may passively accept authoritarian treatment from their superiors and act in the same manner toward their inferiors. Other ways in which Iranians express their individuality has been the creativity in their art, poetry, literature, and philosophy.

Iranians have a sense of cultural, historical, and individual pride, which may account for their boastfulness, impatience with learning, and difficulty in admitting mistakes (Zonis, 1976).

One basic philosophy of the culture is the belief that this world and its material belongings are not worthwhile. This theme is evident in the Sufi philosophy common in Iran that started to grow in the beginning of the ninth century. Its doctrine has some links with Islam, but it also regards other philosophies and religions such as Zoroastrianism, Buddhism, Christianity, and Neoplatonism as shadows of the central truth that it seeks. Sufism essentially seeks to give the individual a spiritual union with God devoid of the rituals and intermediaries of religious hierarchy. Through a process of self-renunciation, spiritual realization, and concentration, the individual may reach a stage of unity with God (Arasteh, 1964). Iranian epicurean poets, such as Khayyam, also express the theme that since life is short, we should enjoy the present. This bitter hedonism is expressed through poetry and literature and has become part of the Iranian philosophy of life.

Iranians live for the present, and their greatest concern is to extract the most from it. Plans are not necessary since the future is either uncertain or preordained (Gable, 1959). Iranians may work five to six days a week only to spend all of their earnings on the seventh day having fun. They have learned to live with uncertainty, distrust, and cynicism (Zonis, 1976), all of which reflects a long history of adaptation of political circumstances. There is a sense of mistrust in interpersonal relationships. Individuals must always be on guard to protect themselves. They fear that others will take advantage of their trust. Trusting relationships exist mainly with family members and life-long friends.

There is a deep-rooted cultural belief in fate, or *Taghdir*, and Iranians are expected to accept the outcome with grace. Iranians' respect for strength and submission to the authority of superior forces is part of this concept of fate (Vreeland, 1957). This attitude has decreased visibly among the educated group over the past 20 years. They are more likely to believe that it is up to the individual to change his or her own life.

Iranians are very hospitable, and guests are treated with unusual courtesy and generosity. This hospitality is present at all social levels. There is a tendency toward toleration of verbal exaggeration (Gastil, 1958). Since Iranians try to avoid publicly criticizing or embarrassing one another, truthfulness is avoided if it brings harm to another (Arasteh, 1964). They express disagreement through use of socially acceptable humor and wit.

Friendships are very important. They often begin in school and are close, intimate, and of long duration. Friends remain loyal and are likely to meet regularly, make mutual demands, have high expectations of each other, and exchange favors. There is also a large circle of less intimate friends and acquaintances on whom a person relies and who are an important part of Iranians' social and professional life.

Iranians rely on a social code that prescribes correct behavioral patterns toward those in each position in the hierarchy. People in lower ranks respond to others in higher ranks with deference, politeness, and respect even though they may feel resentment and hostility toward them.

Iranians are emotionally expressive people regardless of sex. Both men and women show their tears, anger, and affection easily. Kissing and hugging as a way of greeting are common both between men and between women but are less socially acceptable between a man and a woman.

The Western preoccupation with time is not present since Iranians' philosophical view of life is oriented to the present. Since pride and identification with their occupation is more important than the materialistic rewards of a profession, Iranians will not perform a job that they consider beneath them. For example, Iranians do not perform well on assembly lines.

There is a predictable pattern to conflict resolution. When conflict develops in families and among friends, fighting ensues and overt communication stops. This may last days, weeks, or months. Eventually, mediators may be used to reconcile the two. These mediators are extremely important because they facilitate compromise, while allowing each party to save face by not "giving in."

Family Structure and Relationships

There is little research on the Iranian family apart from information generally available on Iranian life, consisting of accounts of travelers, anthropologists, outside observers, and some scanty research data based on studying a small segment of the population or a specific social class. In this chapter we have put together formulations based on personal, cultural, and treatment experiences with Iranian families.

The family is the most significant element of Iranian culture and society. The individual's total life is dominated by the family and family relationships in a way similar to other nonindustrial countries (Gable, 1959). People rely on family connections for influence, power, position, and security. The importance of the family as a social unit for Iranians dates back to Zoroastrian times (pre-Islam period), when rearing children and duties of children toward their parents were considered sacred.

The extended family has traditionally been the basic social unit. This goes along with the predominantly agrarian nature of the society. (About 75% of the population is engaged in agriculture.) In villages and tribes the maintenance of this pattern is crucial for survival in hard times and is, therefore, generally preserved. However, in urban areas, geographical dispersion of the extended family and differences in status and material holdings diminish the significance of the extended family as a functional unit. Still, the family has preserved its significance as an important psychological and bonding entity. The hierarchical organization of the society is apparent in the ascending order from the family, to the village, to the tribe, and, finally, to the country (Wilber, 1963).

The Traditional Family Structure

The traditional Iranian family unit is patriarchal: The father is the undisputed head of the family. Sons and their wives may live in the father's household or compound. An extended family consisting of a couple, their unmarried children, plus their married sons with their wives and children, is common among many segments of the population. Old Iranian houses were built to accommodate this life-style. A wall surrounded the home to ensure privacy, and each nuclear family had its own sleeping quarters. Many extended families continue to maintain close ties, and frequent marriages between cousins serve to strengthen these ties.

The father holds his authority over his wife, children, and grandchildren. No one dares to question his decisions openly. Authority in the extended family is almost always invested in the oldest man—a father who is head of his household. This man may discipline his younger brothers and sisters, as well as his nieces and nephews. It is the patriarch's responsibility to unify the group and to resolve internal conflicts. Religious laws define a wife's relationship to her husband as one of submission. A husband expects his wife to take care of the home and children, and her actions at home and in public must help his and the family's status. The father expects respect and obedience from others in the family, and in turn he supports them materially and socially. He is expected to be a strict disciplinarian, but he is also a provider of affection and love. The father is the only legal guardian of his children, and he allows more freedom to his sons than to his daughters. A father's authority gives him an incredible amount of influence and power. At times he may make decisions for his children, even when they are adults. When the father dies, the sons in the family move into separate households, with the eldest inheriting the authority and accepting the responsibility of looking after his mother and any unmarried brothers and sisters.

The mother has a different sort of authority and power, which is more subtle and indirect. It depends in part on the kind of relationship that she has built through the years with her husband, sons, brothers, and the other women in the family. In public, women address men in a different and more reserved fashion than in private; for example, they may add words to their names like *agha* or *Khan*, which is an indication of respect and formality.

The mother never openly disagrees with the father, but she may have other relatives—such as her children or her mother-in-law—intervene on her behalf. Through them, she expresses her opinions or requests. Iranian women are particularly close to their children and devote a great deal of time to them. When a conflict arises between the father and children, the mother tries to intervene and mediate. She attempts to soften the father's attitude at the same time that she encourages her children to respect his authority (Nyrop, 1978).

Mothers are also very affectionate toward their children, especially their sons. They attempt to persuade their sons rather than give them orders, but they try to dominate their daughters. Sons show a great deal of love and devotion toward their mothers and when married, they encourage their wives to be friendly with them. If, as in many instances, the relationship between the mother-in-law and daughter-in-law becomes conflictual, the son/husband serves as mediator.

Relationships between brothers and sisters are complex. There is an attachment between brothers and sisters that stems both from bonding and responsibility. A brother assumes the role of supporting his sister, but if his sister behaves inappropriately, a brother's disapproval is as powerful as a husband's. Should a sister lose her husband, her brother automatically becomes her main male protector.

Possibly, the most difficult relationship is between fathers and sons. The father continuously dominates his son but also encourages him to take on more responsibility. Identification with the father is strongly encouraged and supported because it is assumed that he will someday take on his father's role. He will become not only the head of his own nuclear family but possibly the patriarch of the extended family as well. This pattern stimulates conflict since both submission and competition are expected at the same time.

Marriage

Women marry at an earlier age than do men and are generally 10 to 15 years younger than their spouses. In traditional families women marry at about age 16 to 18, but among urban modern families it is later, typically at age 22 to 25. This is especially true among the most Westernized families, in which men try to develop economic independence before marriage. There are financial demands made on the man by the woman's family prior to marriage, which depend upon the family's wealth and social status. When marriage occurs, the two families become united. Ideally this strengthens both families, who join their wealth and increase their power and influence. Women must obtain the agreement of their fathers in order to marry whereas men do not have this legal prerequisite, although it may be a moral one. Depending upon the social class and tradition of the family, premarital sex for women may be looked upon with disdain and contempt. If the man has had premarital sex with several other women, however, it is tolerated. On the other hand, if a woman has premarital relations, she may be considered a loose woman and will consequently become stigmatized.

In traditional rural and urban families, the parents choose the ideal young woman for their son and arrange meetings and do the negotiations with her family. If these arrangements go well, a time is set for the wedding. At the marriage ceremony a sum of money, of *Mehr*, is guaranteed to the wife in case her husband dies or divorces her. Very few meetings occur between the man and the woman until they officially marry. When they do meet, it is usually in the presence of the family. Arranged marriages and betrothals at birth are declining somewhat. But they are still common, as are marriages between cousins.

A woman gains status when she gets married, and this status increases when she has a child, especially if it is a boy (Arasteh, 1964). Sons are regarded as economic assets, and Iranians desire large families with as many male children as possible. Generally, the woman goes to live among her husband's relatives; however, she maintains close ties with her family. Conflicts among in-laws are a common source of stress. Prior to the family protection laws of

1967, men were allowed to have as many as four wives, whereas women could have only one husband. Polygamous marriages invariably led to rivalries and jealousies among the wives as each competed for the husband's attention and favor. However, the first and oldest wife maintained a senior position.

A Moslem man may marry a non-Moslem woman, but a Moslem woman cannot marry a non-Moslem man unless he converts to Islam. Also, men can divorce their wives; but the reverse is not true unless there is an exceptional situation. The father is the legal custodian of the children and he retains this custody after a divorce. A woman once divorced carries a special stigma, and she loses face in the society and with her family. She has less chance of remarrying than does a divorced man. She has very little chance of marrying a man who has not married before.

Depending upon the amount of wealth, the traditional family usually has a number of servants who stay with the family for years. The servants' children or relatives may be retained to replace or supplement the help when the established servants are old and can no longer work. Servants are usually treated well by the family and are provided with food and clothing for themselves as well as for their children and relatives. Wealthier families may also have nannies who take a very active role in rearing their children. The relationship between the nanny and the child may become a very special one and is sometimes even closer than the relationship between the child and the mother (Arasteh, 1964).

The mother receives guidance and advice in rearing children from her mother, her mother-in-law, and her other relatives. Because of a relatively high infant mortality rate, the mother is fearful of losing her children. This fear often takes the form of an old belief in the evil eye that still survives to some degree in the middle and upper classes. The evil eye has both supernatural and personalized aspects. It is believed that people out of envy, jealousy, and hostility may wish misfortunes upon others. The evil eye explains the occurrence of misfortunes and focuses fear on outsiders and on their envy. As a result people refrain from making comments on the health, beauty, or even intelligence of a young child for fear that they may make them vulnerable to the evil eye (Arasteh, 1964).

Child Rearing

Children are the focus of attention and affection from both the nuclear and extended families and may be spoiled by aunts, uncles, and grandparents. This is especially true of young boys. As children grow older, they are expected to be polite and respectful toward adults. The Iranian child is typically well mannered and can sit quietly for hours in the presence of adults.

Boys tend to bully their sisters and sometimes tyrannize their mothers, but their naughtiness and aggressiveness is affectionately praised at the same time that they are scolded. Both parents are more permissive toward their sons than toward their daughters. A girl is expected to be submissive and to give in to her brother. The male child learns to respect his father's authority and dominance, yet he learns self-assertion and a degree of independence in his relationship to the rest of the family. Boys grow up believing themselves distinctly superior to girls, but by adolescence, they are also strongly protective of them.

Discipline is maintained mainly by the father and consists of scolding or slapping. There is no specific pattern to the punishment; depending upon the mood of the moment, a child may be punished for a trivial misbehavior, while at other times a child may be ignored, laughed off, or overlooked, for a more serious act. For example, a child may be slapped if he or she misbehaves in public or in front of the family's guest, yet the same misbehavior might only merit a scolding in private.

It must be understood that since the authority of the parents, especially the father, is visible and respected, simply his expression of disapproval and scolding is quite effective. Often the consequences of bad behavior do not even need to be spelled out. Western methods of disciplining, such as withholding favorite foods or sending children to their rooms, are rarely used. Also important is that adult married children are still considered by their parents to be children.

Child training involves many prohibitions that are expressed repeatedly by the parents. For example, children are told to be obedient, to behave like adults, and to be quiet. However, most of the social learning occurs through experiences with either the peer group or the extended family unit.

Life Cycle and Tradition

Parents gain more respect and power as they get older. In their older age, parents may retain their own residence and be looked after by the children or they may live with one of them. There are no nursing homes.

When death occurs, the mourning ceremonies are an important function for the family and the neighborhood where the person has lived. Mourning is expressed quite openly especially by women, to the point that they often faint out of extreme grief. The neighborhood and the community are very much involved in supporting the bereaved emotionally, soothing them, bringing food, visiting often, and talking with them about the deceased person.

No formal funeral homes exist, and the dead body may remain in the home for one to two days—in a secluded area of the house in the presence of a clergyman reciting prayers. Then the body is taken to the cemetery. The mourning lasts for three days; a memorial for the dead is held by the family on the seventh day, the 40th day, and the first-year anniversary. On these occasions the extended family, friends, and community visit the grieved, and the dead are remembered. It is generally believed that a person is judged after death and, depending upon the sum total of his or her acts during his or her life, is sent to hell or heaven (Nyrop, 1978).

Wealth passes from husband to wife and children, but the shares are unequal—sons receive a full share, daughters a half-share, and the wife a smaller share. However, the wife can own property in her own name, whether from an urban or rural background.

The traditional family has a structure that is relatively immune to conflict and tension. While to an outside observer this structure may appear as a source of conflict, the values and roles are internalized and accepted as norms, and conflicts are at a minimum. Women generally accept their husbands' dominance, at least on the surface, and complain little about it outwardly. Family loyalties and the sense of obligation go a long way. Foreigners are repeatedly astonished that Iranian women accept the situation when their husbands bring their mothers, sisters, and other relatives to share their home.

Modern Family

Upper- and middle-class families in urban areas of Iran are caught between the pull of traditional religion and culture and a change toward more Western patterns in family relationships. The development of mass media and modern schools has changed the attitudes of urban children toward traditional values. These influences have also altered family relationships and the function of the family in the society at large. However, these modern developments have not penetrated all levels of society, and the traditional forces remain strong. In the villages, the family still retains its function of educating children and transmitting cultural roles and values. Also among urban families who have not been exposed to Western education, literature, or movies, life remains essentially the same. (Interestingly, a trend toward traditionalism grew through the middle 1970s in the midst of Westernization.)

The major effects of industrialization and urbanization on the modern family have been the weakening of parental authority and the increased freedom of choice of marriage partners. As offspring loosen the ties with the traditional norms and values, they often experience conflict between their desires for independence and their strong sense of duty toward their fathers.

Among the upper and middle classes, married men tend to set up households separate from their families of origin, perhaps even in a different neighborhood. But ties remain and visits are frequent. The attitude toward women remains conservative, and premarital sex is not common. The spouse is usually chosen from the same social group, though now often without the interference of parents. Sometimes parents are only notified of the decision to marry, but their approval is sought and *Mehr* is still guaranteed. Clearly the traditional customs coexist with modern values.

Western education and travel abroad have profoundly changed the role of women and have resulted in demands for change in family relationships. More women have sought higher education, and currently 37% of all university students in Iran are women. During the 1960s many women sought employment outside of the home. The majority, however, do not contribute much to the finances of the family. Women in modern families marry at a later age than their traditional counterparts; and with no servants, child caretakers, and housekeepers, they have fewer children. It must be realized, however, that even though a portion of women have become educated and emancipated, traditional culture has a strong grip and sex roles are enormously difficult to change. The modern Iranian woman appears to have adjusted well to the dual role and, therefore, male–female conflicts are minimized.

The Western influence and break with tradition have caused families to become more oriented toward the nuclear family and have led to a partial breakdown of the extended family. Consequently, family members have become conflicted about their obligations and sense of responsibility toward elders.

The modern urban family encounters many stresses that threaten its stability. Cultural standards of social behavior are abandoned in favor of Western norms of more freedom of expression. There is a striving and competition to achieve more status and wealth. The father may resent the fact that his children do not respect his authority in the same way that he responded toward his own parents. He may also have ambivalent feelings toward his professional wife.

When there is family tension because of emotional distance or physical separation from the extended family, either the extended family may become hesitant to provide support and advice or the nuclear family may be reluctant to assume a dependent position and seek advice from them.

Immigration

Modes of Adaptation

Different modes of adaptation of migrant ethnic families have been described elsewhere (Jalali & Boyce, 1980). Wintrop and Gaviria (1975) have described other modes in a study of immigrant Peruvian physicians in the United States. The mode of adaptation to the new culture among Iranian families vacillates between acculturation and holding onto the old culture. Iranians, at times, preserve aspects of their culture no matter how Westernized they have become in appearance, mode of thinking, behavior, and language. It is not yet clear how these patterns will develop over several generations in the United States. The number of second-generation Iranian adults is still small, and it is therefore hard to comment on this. The most common modes of adaptation are the following:

1. Denigrating the old culture. Some families sever the old ties, avoid Iranians, and denounce the old traditions and beliefs. This amounts to an effort to deny their cultural origin by adopting the external features of a stereotyped American. Habits and perceived values (often materialistic) may often be copied.

2. Denying the new culture. The new becomes so frightening that the old cannot be abandoned. Families turn inward, associating only with Iranians and attempting to reproduce a microculture similar to the one in the home country. They eat the same foods, follow the same traditions, and criticize the Western culture's values and belief systems. However, the children in these families, due to contact with the outside world through schools and friends, become acculturated and conflicts frequently develop in the next generation.

3. Biculturation. This is perhaps the best mode of adaptation. The family attempts to bring the two cultures together and tolerates the conflict and anxiety of crossing the cultural boundaries. Important attachments to the old culture are maintained along with a productive assimilation of the new culture. The old ways are not toally abandoned; rather, the family attempts to blend the best of two worlds and incorporates the old with the new. Therefore, they can integrate without disrupting their basic sense of identity.

Often some family members adhere to one mode of adaptation while the other members are using another mode. In these instances, the family becomes especially prone to internal conflicts across generations.

Modes of Adaptation to the United States

In the United States family relationships remain very important, although these relationships have undergone some transformation. Ties to the family are less close, mainly because the extended family is not geographically available. The father retains some of his authority; the mother, even though she has more social freedom, maintains many traditional patterns.

Decision making lies with the nuclear family. The extended family is informed afterward, though at times they may be consulted for their special expertise. The sense of obligation to the family exists but is ambivalent.

The First Wave

The first wave of Iranian immigrants, due to their prior exposure to the West through education, media, and travel abroad, adjusted easily to the new culture. They also had marketable skills and were affluent, which allowed them to survive the insecurities of a new environment.

Many Iranians married Americans, which also facilitated acculturation. However, as might be predicted because of cultural differences, the American spouse often became a source of conflict especially when not accepted by the Iranian spouse's extended family. Conflicts would erupt, especially when the extended family arrived for long visits. Problems in communication with the extended family arose because of differences in values, life-styles, customs, and habits. No one felt at ease. The extended family felt resentful and resented; the Western spouse found it hard to grasp the intricate system of the Iranian extended family.

Immigrant Iranians who married Iranian spouses did better, particularly if well educated. Less-educated and more traditional Iranian spouses were less employable and did not speak English as well. They usually retreated from the new experiences, while the other spouse was employed and fully exposed to the new environment. Their American-born children usually grew up with very little command of their native language, even if both parents were first-generation Iranian Americans. (This is even more likely if one parent was American.) Children strongly influence the reciprocal behavior of their parents through exposure to the new culture in school and peer relationships. This, in turn, has a secondary effect on child rearing. They become a vehicle to acculturate their parents into the details of the new culture. The most prevalent modes of adaptation in this group are biculturation or denigration of the old culture.

First-Wave Immigration Case

A 42-year-old first-generation Iranian physician from a middle-class family was referred with his 38-year-old American spouse for treatment because of their chronic marital conflicts. He had immigrated to the United States about 12 years ago. They had two children, one son, age 8, and one daughter, age 5.

The couple's relationship had been fraught with difficulty for some years because the husband was chronically ambivalent about making a commitment to stay in the United States. He would occasionally entertain serious thoughts of returning to Iran and leaving his job and home here. The husband's extended family still resided in Iran, and four or five of them at a time periodically visited the couple for two to four months. These visits were always a source of stress for the couple. The wife never felt accepted by her husband's relatives and resented the intrusion into their life.

The couple disagreed about child rearing, male–female roles, socializing, and other cultural issues. Each tried to claim superiority to the other by ridiculing aspects of the other's culture. Their son was repeatedly triangulated as each tried to bring him up their own way. The husband insisted on frequent entertaining and would spend several evenings a week with his male Iranian friends. The wife wanted more time together as a family and a couple. Even though the husband was quite open and Western in his thinking, he would repeatedly accuse his wife of being aggressive and would demand more traditional and submissive behavior from her. She demanded that he share in domestic tasks and decisions. Actually, he had adjusted and changed in response to some of these demands. However, when his extended family visited he would revert to old ways, refusing to share any domestic tasks and attempting to dominate his wife.

The therapist attempted to focus the couple on the problems in their marriage, highlighting their differences and similarities and encouraging them to accept the differences in the other person. The husband was encouraged to teach his wife Farsi so that she could communicate better with him and his extended family. She was encouraged to resolve conflicts with her in-laws on a one-to-one basis instead of pressuring and triangulating her husband. Surprisingly, his sister responded quite positively to her sister-in-law's request for privacy and control of the household affairs. The wife was encouraged to ask her in-laws about recipes for ethnic food and supplies of ethnic herbs and spices, to which the extended family's response was overwhelmingly positive. She was encouraged to talk to her mother-in-law about her husband's childhood.

The husband was instructed to support his wife when she needed it but generally to let her work out her own relationship with his family. The extended family then began to accept her more and actually began to brag about her new talents. No attempts were made to cut down on the number and length of the extended family's visits, but arrangements were made for the relatives to visit other members of the extended family during their stay. As the two families were getting along better, the husband's high priority for the integrity of his nuclear family became evident.

The Second Wave

The second wave of Iranian immigrants share similarities in adaptation to the first wave. Many tradition-bound families were in this second group.

Initially these families were enthusiastic and excited about their immigration. Later, however, they started to miss their extended families, neighborhoods, and communities and felt isolated and alienated in the new culture. This second wave is especially prone to the development of conflicts between generations. Their children are exposed to school peers and acculturate easily. Later, they attempt to dissociate themselves from the old culture. They may ridicule their parents, reject ethnic food, and set themselves apart from their parents. Fathers, in particular, are threatened by these changes in their offspring and may blame the new culture and criticize its values.

These families are also prone to develop marital conflicts. Women welcome more social freedom and assert themselves, which further threatens their spouses.

Second-Wave Immigration Case

A 56-year-old Iranian businessman, a rug merchant and recent immigrant of three years' duration, his 48-year-old wife, and their 20-year-old son were referred for treatment. The identified patient was the son who had been failing in school. The son refused to study or seek a job and spent his time at home engaged in ritualistic obsessive–compulsive behavior, using drugs, driving recklessly (which led to several accidents), and engaging in other irresponsible behavior. He was the youngest child in the family and had been babied by both the immediate and extended families. The father refused to come for treatment on a regular basis and insisted that his son was spoiled and that life in the United States was too permissive.

The father came from a very traditional family and followed in his father's business. He expected his son to become a businessman like himself and to take over the management of his business some day. The father believed that his son needed a strict approach to straighten him out. He himself experienced problems adjusting to the new culture and in turn blamed the son's problems on the new culture. At home he was a strict and domineering man, who expected his wife to be submissive.

The mother presented as a pleasant, passive, and compliant Iranian women who appeared more adjusted to life in the United States than did her husband, but she missed the closeness of the extended family. She behaved in a passive–aggressive manner toward her husband and exerted her power in a subtle way. She was devoted to her children, especially her son, and called him her "baby." She clearly babied him. She was certain that he would grow out of his behavior and cited examples from her extended family where this had happened.

The son was a verbal young man who ridiculed his parents' traditional ways, especially his father's. He had no intention of going into his father's business, but he had no other plans either. He was quite Americanized in his appearance, language, and manners. He believed in having a good time but was caught between his parents' expectations and his own search for identity. The family therapist joined with the father, acknowledged his hierarchical position in the system, and labeled him as an experienced and strong man of the world whose wife needed his support, guidance, and strength.

The mother was encouraged to leave some of their son's discipline to the father since their son needed a "man's guidance" at his age. She was also encouraged to make more contacts with her extended family members both here and in Iran to occupy her time. The father and the son were instructed to teach each other about the old and the new cultures. All of these maneuvers were used without undermining the cultural role of the parents. No attempts were made to encourage the father to become less authoritarian or the mother to become less close to her son. All of the therapeutic techniques used were within the mode of cultural roles.

The Third Wave

The third wave of Iranian immigrant families, as described earlier, comprise a very special group prone to high psychosocial stresses and development of psychological symptoms.

The integrity and the unity of the family system has been disrupted by political, ideological, and physical separation. Some have been forced to flee their homeland but hope to return to it someday. This subgroup's entry to the new culture has occurred under traumatic conditions and at times has been marked by disappointments, failures, and hopelessness.

If this group of Iranian immigrants cannot use their skills or professions, they will have financial worries. They also worry about their extended families back home and have difficulty merging with their subgroup in the United States. All of these factors contribute to a determination to resist becoming acculturated, which makes them feel alienated from their surroundings.

Children's ability to cope with their new environment depends considerably on their parents' ability to cope with their conflicting loyalties, anxiety, and worry. They may feel unaccepted and shy, may avoid peer relationships, or may develop school problems. They may also delay learning the new language, which makes any change even more difficult.

Most of these families suffer cultural, physical, and emotional isolation, and the strain of their predicament naturally afflicts their psyche. Common symptoms among this group include anxiety, insomnia, and depression.

Third-Wave Immigration Case

A 45-year-old Iranian mother of five children presented with multiple depressive and somatic symptoms, including chest pains. She had arrived in the United States only weeks after the Iranian revolution to put all of her children in school here. Her husband, a businessman, had stayed behind to take care of financial matters and to support the family while they resided in the United States. The hope was that he would join them someday. She felt socially isolated and missed the closeness and support of extended family and neighborhood. She was constantly worried about her husband's safety. On the one hand, she yearned to return to Iran, and, on the other hand, she could not face the separation from her children, aged 12 to 19.

The mother demanded that the therapist provide her with vitamins, tranquilizers, and a quick recovery. She requested diet instructions and claimed to be weak. She called the therapist at all hours of the day and night, only to repeat her complaints and to ask for advice and support.

The children were clearly under stress and missed their father. They found it hard to concentrate on their studies or to adjust to the new environment, school, and housing. They tried to soothe their mother but to no avail, and at times the whole family would cry together.

The therapist initially resisted the requests for vitamins and tranquilizers, only to be besieged by the mother and her family with evidence that she was indeed deteriorating day by day. He finally gave her minor tranquilizers and vitamins, only to be told later that she had a whole cabinet full of vitamins and tranquilizers that she had brought from Iran. She had magical expectations of the medication provided by the physician/therapist. She insisted that the therapist make a home visit, which he finally did.

The patient and her children were living in a cramped apartment very isolated from the community. They all longed for their large, beautiful home and their friends and relatives in Iran. Their only solace was an occasional long distance telephone call to the father in Iran.

The mother was encouraged to make contact with the few relatives that she had in the United States, to purchase a car so that she could mobilize herself, to attend an evening English class, and to encourage her children to socialize and develop new friendships instead of hovering over her. The therapist attempted to emphasize the mother's strength and courage in coping with the new situation. At the end of her brief therapeutic contact, she had improved considerably. However, she continued to take large numbers of vitamins and attributed her recovery to them.

Treatment Issues

The American therapist's lack of familiarity with Iranians' cultural expression of psychological stress and mistrustful view of outside helpers often leads to misunderstandings. This may result in problems in the therapist–patient relationship. The following segments highlight some of these issues.

Cultural Modes of Presentation of Symptoms

Problems are frequently expressed in somatization and projection. Somatic symptoms indicating psychological distress are discussed below.

1. Heart distress may be explained as symptoms such as aching, pounding, fluttering, rapid heart beating, pains, or discomfort. Even though these symptoms might indicate heart distress, they almost always indicate a complex set of physical sensations associated with anxiety, and they can be traced to interpersonal problems, sorrow, or worry (Good, 1977). Other forms of heart-related symptoms that reflect depressed moods are comments such as "My heart is closed in" and requests for the therapist or doctor to "open it up," which in essence means a request for sympathy and listening. The brain is the center of the mind, but the heart is the center of emotions. The heart as the subject of emotional experience expresses affect (Good, 1977).

2. Weak nerves, tired nerves, shaking hands, lack of sensations, and numbness may indicate neurological problems, but these symptoms are most often equivalents of depression and anxiety.

3. General body pain, exhaustion, lack of strength are additional somatic symptoms.

4. Complaints of upper gastrointestinal pains, weak stomach, weak liver, problems in digestion, or a vitamin deficiency are also somatic symptoms.

Clearly, physical symptoms are more acceptable than psychological symptoms and have less stigma attached to them. Persons with these symptoms can make demands of the family for special privileges, caretaking, or other changes in family behavior. It is thus difficult to convince these patients that they may have psychological problems, and, therefore, it is important not to confront them directly about the meaning of the symptoms but to go along with the presenting complaint and make subtle interventions.

Problems are also projected onto outside events, people, or forces, such as grief, failure in school, or heartbreak. Usually the precipitating stress is seen by the family as the sole cause, and they may not talk about the larger cultural factors unless questioned in detail about their situation.

When Iranians face problems, they usually turn to friends or relatives for advice and support. Women turn to women; men turn to men; younger people turn to parents or older relatives; and friends gossip about problems to other relatives or friends. Only as a last resort do they turn to an outside "helper" or "doctor." By this time a whole network of people are aware of the problem even though the confidants are all sworn to secrecy.

Cultural Patterns of the Therapist/ Doctor-Patient Relationship

We must understand the roots of the doctor–patient relationship in the home country in order to develop a perspective on its complex nature here. Iranians are ambivalent, even mistrustful, of the "helper's" expertise, although in specific instances people may develop a trusting and special relationship with one physician and assign him or her special healing powers. Iranians are also doctor shoppers; they commonly go from one specialist to another, requesting medications and demanding quick results. This particularly holds true if the illness is serious or difficult to diagnose. If cure is not imminent, the patient will visit another doctor in hope that he or she will express a different opinion about the presenting problem, which, of course, can only increase the mistrust of the patient toward the previous physician.

Families usually take an active part in decisions about the course to follow such as which specialist to consult. Therefore, family support is essential in ensuring continuity of care (Good, 1976). If satisfaction is not achieved and the patient is not diagnosed or treated adequately from the family's viewpoint, the family will then consider sending their ill family member to Europe or the United States for treatment. However, the family and the patient may also disagree with the foreign physician's diagnosis. Iranian doctors tend to view most of their patients as exaggerating their symptoms and holding beliefs that are not scientifically based. For this reason they often prescribe vitamins, minor tranquilizers, and intramuscular medications to at least partially satisfy the patient.

Iranians who become patients in the United States usually trust American physicians more, but they still insist on getting prescriptions for vitamins and on no laboratory tests. Special diets that recommend the avoidance of certain foods, herbs, or spices have been a basic therapeutic element in traditional Iranian medicine. Therefore, patients often expect their physicians to order certain diets for specific illnesses. Actually, these are the same remedies with which they are familiar but were not satisfied previously. If the physician does not prescribe medications, the patient becomes convinced that the correct diagnosis has not been made. Patients screen the information they give to the physician and are usually embarrassed to provide personal information, such as about sexual problems.

Noncompliance with physicians' orders is common and is not evidence of a personal rejection of a particular physician. Also nonmedical health care professionals may be treated with particular mistrust. It must be understood that nonphysician professionals are not involved in direct patient care in Iran, and even the nurse's role is based on a pure medical model.

Family Therapy with Iranian Families

The referral of an Iranian patient for therapy is almost always made by an internist and is accepted by the patient with great reluctance. The Iranian patient responds positively to a call for a family interview since it deemphasizes the identified patient.

Therapists should be prepared for the Iranian patient's modes of problem presentation, as well as for the demands for quick results and medication. An understanding of the family background, degree of traditionalism, length of stay in the United States, and special circumstances surrounding their immigration is essential. The patriarchal organization of the family is to be acknowledged by addressing fathers first and as the head of the family. The therapist should not attempt to change cultural power hierarchies or role patterns since this will alienate the family.

Every attempt should be made to involve the extended family in therapy if they are available. Most often, such invitations are accepted readily. However, family therapists should be aware that extended family members will act as experts and authorities on family matters in the sessions. Depending upon the therapist's skill, he or she may ally with these family members and when possible, use them as cotherapists.

Compared to Westerners, Iranians are neither conforming nor obedient patients. Even though they may appear to follow the therapist's suggestions and orders, we can be sure that they will modify the suggestions to suit their own evaluation of the situation.

Men Iranian patients have difficulty following a woman therapist's directions and recommendations. They will also avoid discussing painful feelings, personal concerns, weaknesses, vulnerabilities, and sexual matters with a woman therapist. Women patients will use the same avoidances with a man therapist. Therefore, addressing personal issues within a marriage therapy context should be done with utmost tact and scrutiny. A man and woman cotherapy team approach is desirable if at all possible.

Cultural family patterns such as closeness of mother to her children, especially to boys, and her permissive attitude toward them should not be confronted directly. Instead, the therapist should try to strengthen the child's other relationships, such as peer and father–child relationship, in order to weaken mother–child bonds. Similarly, the mother may be encouraged to team up with the father to present a united front when disciplining the child.

The most effective family therapy technique with Iranian families is either the structural or the strategic problem-oriented approach possibly because the power-hierarchical orientation matches the culture. The Iranian family usually responds positively to directives and may actually request them.

Finally, therapists will help by encouraging their Iranian patients to ventilate their feelings, by listening to them with empathy and compassion, by developing an appreciation of their cultural isolation, and by treating real symptoms as they emerge.

REFERENCES

Adams, W. *The Brain Drain*. New York: Macmillan, 1968.

Arasteh, A.R. *Man and Society in Iran*. Leider, The Netherlands: E.J. Brill, 1964.

Askari, H., Cummings, J.T., & Izbudak, M. Iran's Migration of Skilled Labor to the United States. *Iranian Studies, 10*, 3–35, 1977.

Baldwin, G.B. The Foreign-Educated Iranian: A Profile. *The Middle East Journal, 17*, 264–270, 1963.

Banuazizi, A. Iranian "National Character": A Critique of Some Western Perspectives. In L. Carl Brown & N. Itzkowitz (Eds.), *Psychological Dimensions of Near Eastern Studies*. Princeton, N.J.: Darwin Press, 1977.

Bill, J.A. *The Politics of Iran, Groups, Classes and Modernization*. Columbus, Ohio: Charles E. Merrill, 1972.

Bill, J.A. The Plasticity of Informal Politics: The Case of Iran. *The Middle East Journal, 27*, 131–151, 1973.

Gable, R.W. Culture and Administration in Iran. *The Middle East Journal, 13*, 407–421, 1959.

Gastil, R.D. Middle Class Impediments to Iranian Modernization. *Public Opinion Quarterly, 22*(3), 325–329, 1958.

Good, B.J. Medical Change and the Doctor–Patient Relationship in an Iranian Provincial Town. In K. Farmanfarmaian (Ed.), *The Social Sciences and Problems of Development*. Princeton, N.J.: Princeton University Press, 1976.

Good, B.J. The Heart of What's the Matter, the Semantics of Illness in Iran. *Culture, Medicine and Psychiatry, 1*, 25–58, 1977.

Haas, W.S. *Iran*. New York: Columbia University Press, 1946.

Jalali, B., & Boyce, E. Multicultural Families in Treatment. *The International Journal of Family Psychiatry, 1*(4), 475–484, 1980.

National Science Foundation. *Immigrant Scientists and Engineers in the United States*, 1973.

Nyrop, R.F. *Iran, A Country Study*. Washington, D.C.: The American University Press, 1978.

Vreeland, M.M. *Iran*. New Haven, Conn.: Human Relations, Area Files, 1957.

Wilber, D.N. *Contemporary Iran*. New York: Praeger, 1963.

Wintrop, R., & Gaviria, M. Foreign Medical Graduates who Return Home after U.S. Residency Training: The Peruvian Case. *Journal of Medical Education, 50*, 167–175, 1975.

Zonis, M. *The Political Elite of Iran*. Princeton, N.J.: Princeton University Press, 1976.

15

Irish Families

MONICA McGOLDRICK

> But I, being poor, have only my dreams;
> I have spread my dreams under your feet;
> Tread softly because you tread on my dreams.
> —W.B. Yeats

What follows is a greatly simplified outline or paradigm within which to consider Irish American families. The characterizations may or may not be accurate in any individual instance, and we hope it will be read in the spirit of providing a few provisional hypotheses to help therapists understand their Irish families. Describing ethnic patterns necessitates using cultural stereotypes or simplified pictures of the culture. There are obvious disadvantages to this, and these generalizations are meant to serve only as a framework within which to expand clinical sensitivity and effectiveness. The paradigm in this chapter is used not as "fact," but rather as a map which, although covering only limited aspects of the terrain, may nevertheless provide a guideline to an explorer seeking a path. This focus has meant emphasizing certain characteristics which may become problematic and ignoring certain others, such as the Irish people's great hospitality and charm, which are not problematic. By no means is it meant to add to any tendency toward negative labeling or stereotyping of the Irish.

In a previous paper we have discussed family patterns and values of Americans of Irish Catholic background and have offered some general therapeutic suggestions (McGoldrick & Pearce, 1981). This chapter expands that discussion, focusing on the therapeutic implications of particular Irish American patterns.

The Irish are a paradoxical people. There is a saying: "The Great Gaels of Ireland are the men that God made mad, for all their wars are merry, and all their songs are sad." There is a striking charm, joviality, and clannishness when the Irish band together for a cause (especially a moral or political cause), and yet they seem to suffer from a sense of isolation, sadness, and tragedy. As Patrick Moynihan observed after President Kennedy's assassination: "I don't think that there is any point being Irish if you don't know that the world is going to break your heart some day" (Duff, 1971). The Irish will

Monica McGoldrick. Psychiatry Department, University of Medicine and Dentistry of New Jersey, and Community Mental Health Center of Rutgers Medical School, Piscataway, New Jersey; Faculty, Family Institute of Westchester, White Plains, New York.

fight against all odds, and yet they have a strong sense of human powerlessness in relation to nature (Spiegel, 1971a, 1971b). The culture places great
value on conformity and respectability, and yet the Irish tend toward eccentricity. Their history is full of rebels and fighters, and yet they tend to be
compliant and accepting of authoritarian structures. They place great stock
in loyalty to their own, and yet they often cut off relationships totally. They
have a great sense of responsibility for what goes wrong, and yet they
characteristically deny or project blame outward.

The paradigm outlined here draws on historical Irish traits, some of
which are more obvious in the culture of modern-day rural Irish (Scheper-
Hughes, 1979) than in Irish Americans. Recent clinical experience with
Irish Americans indicates that—perhaps as a result of Vatican II—much
of the guilt and rigidity that plagued the Irish for so many years is rapidly
diminishing. The folkways, values, and family patterns of American Irish
Catholics[1] will be discussed as they pertain to the Irish in therapy. The
description is based on clinical experience over the past six years, ethnicity
seminars, review of the literature, and discussion with colleagues.

Acculturation affects ethnic groups in various ways; there have naturally
been many changes in the Irish in America as a result of intermarriage,
upward mobility, and geographical relocation. However, this chapter will
focus on the cultural continuity: the ways in which Irish Americans retain
the cultural characteristics of their Irish heritage.

The Paradigm

The Irish in Context

Extreme poverty was the rule in Ireland; there were few natural resources
and those there were were controlled by the British. Rapid population
increase, continual subdivision of the land, and exorbitantly high rents
contributed to the overdependence of the Irish on potatoes. For many
years the potato was almost the only food of the Irish, leaving them extremely

1. According to the Census Report of 1971, nearly 7% of Americans (13.3 million people)
claimed Ireland as their ancestral home (U.S. Bureau of the Census, 1971). It seems, however,
that the actual numbers are much larger since the Census did not provide a way to list multiple
ethnic origins. The Census did not break ethnic groups down by religion, but it appears that the
Protestant Irish constitute a fair percentage of this group (Blessing, 1980). However, today the
Protestant Irish do not tend to think of themselves as Irish. The Catholic Irish peasants were a
group far apart in culture and values from the Protestants and Scots Irish, who had begun
immigrating in fair numbers to this country before the revolution. The Protestant Irish have the
lowest rate of endogamous marriage of any ethnic group, and their sense of ethnic identity
seems to have largely disappeared (Fallows, 1979). Thus, we will confine this chapter to Irish of
Catholic background who do, in fact, form a distinct ethnic unit, although, of course, many Anglo
Irish influenced Irish culture (Shaw, Swift, Wilde), and many even played a major role in the
revival of a sense of Irish culture through the arts (Yeats, Synge, Lady Gregory, Douglas Hyde)
and politics (Wolf Tone, Emmet, Constance Markievicz, and Charles Stewart Parnell).

vulnerable to the frequent failures of the potato crop. Even though during the years of the famine more than enough other foods were produced to feed the population, these foods were exported by the British, and the Irish, without their main staple—the potato—came into desperate conditions of starvation (Woodham-Smith, 1963). This was the major precipitant of the massive Irish immigration more than four generations ago that led more than a million Irish peasants to immigrate to the United States in less than two decades (Woodham-Smith, 1963; Sowell, 1981).

Although immigration subsequently declined, by 1930 almost 5 million Irish had arrived in this country, and even today some continue to come (Bernardo, 1981). In fact, no country has given up a greater proportion of its population to the United States than has Ireland (Munch, 1980).

Many in the original immigrant generation that came in the 1840s and 1850s wanted to forget the hundreds of years of English oppression they had endured and the desperate poverty they were fleeing. Although many continued to demonstrate concern for the fate of Ireland, the majority of the next generation thought of themselves primarily as Americans and gradually intermarried with other ethnic groups, but mostly of Roman Catholic religion. Their Irishness was a sentimental part of their lives, and often they knew little of their heritage.

Even when they lack self-awareness, the Irish seem to retain more of their cultural characteristics than most other ethnic groups (Greeley, 1977, 1981; Greeley & McCready, 1975). Perhaps this is because (1) their assimilation did not require them to give up their language, (2) parochial schools run primarily by Irish nuns and priests transmitted Irish cultural values to generations of Irish American children, and (3) Irish values, strongly influenced for many centuries by British domination, permitted the Irish to assimilate without giving up their own deeply rooted culture.

Although they had been farmers in Ireland, their fondness for company led the Irish to cluster together in the Irish neighborhoods of Boston, New York, Chicago, and other major U.S. cities. They became, as did later immigrant groups, the builders of the America of their time. The men worked on the railroads, the Brooklyn Bridge, and the Erie Canal. They also took up other occupations for which their heritage prepared them: saloon keeping, the priesthood, policework, politics, civil service, and, as they moved up, the law (Potter, 1960). Irish women became domestic servants, factory workers, boarding house keepers, and, later, nurses and teachers.

The Church

Just as in Ireland, the primary cultural force and national unifier of the Irish in America was the Catholic Church. Early missionaries such as St. Patrick had established a strong Church in Ireland, which became a cultivated religious tradition and the main source of high culture for continental

Europe from the eighth to tenth centuries. Later, amidst the struggles with the British, religious loyalty became closely tied with the Irish desire to recover their land and heritage. Although the Irish had been a homogeneous cultural group for 2000 years, there had never been an Irish nation; Irish national unity developed on loyalty to the Church and hatred of the English.

Jansenism, a French mystical movement that had been expelled from France, dominated the Irish Church. The Jansenists emphasized personal holiness and condemned the evil nature and untrustworthy instincts of human beings. The Irish Roman Catholic Church, banned by the English, isolated from external influences, and possessed by a grim theology, became rigid, authoritarian, and moralistic. The Church's control was increased by holding the key to salvation in a land where this life offered so little. The Church also offered the only institutional protection in the face of political oppression. Priests came to exercise extraordinary authority, more so than in France, Italy, or Spain.

Through parochial schools, the Catholic Church in America continued to have a pervasive impact on the social and cultural training of Irish children. More than other ethnic groups, the Irish struggled with their sense of sin and guilt. Irish schizophrenics, for example, are commonly obsessed with guilt for sins they may not even have committed. In contrast, Italian schizophrenics often act out their fantasies and impulses without subsequent remorse (Opler & Singer, 1957; Singer & Opler, 1956). Italians, though also Catholic, tend to place responsibility for their problems outside of themselves; their experience of guilt is limited primarily to violations of family loyalty.

Basic to the Irish character is the belief that people are bad and will suffer deservedly for their sins. The myth of badness, related to the concept of original sin, is the unquestioned conviction that no matter how hard we try to be good, we will fail because it is human nature to be evil and prone to sin.

The rigidity of the Church led to a moralistic vision among the Irish and a tendency to righteousness. Their love of dreams and mystery reinforced the power of the rules of the Church. For generations the parish, rather than the neighborhood, defined the family's context. The Church demanded absolute obedience to its rules and no right thinking Irish Catholic dared to question its decisions nor those of its representatives, the local priests.

For these reasons the changes created by Vatican II are profound. Now, for the first time, people have the option of deciding issues for themselves. This has been very stressful for many Irish Catholics who were raised with the security that there was a clear, definite source of authority in their lives. Once anything about the Church could change, their whole foundation was shaken (Wills, 1971). It is important to learn where the Irish stand in relation to the Church since they are unlikely to be neutral about its meaning in their lives (Wills, 1971). The struggles of Catholics to make sense of religion and to fit its rules and strictures into their lives cannot be minimized. A priest–counselor, particularly one with moderate views, can be an ideal resource for Catholics struggling with Church values.

Sex

In this historical context, sex has, not surprisingly, been called "the lack of the Irish" (Messinger, 1971). The Irish viewed sex as extremely dangerous. As a consequence of sexual repression, they also avoided tenderness, affection, and intimacy. Members of Irish families are often isolated from each other; when things go badly, the family atmosphere may become sullen, dour, and puritanically rigid. Messinger, a contemporary anthropologist who studied the cultural patterns of a remote Irish island community, described them as one of the most sexually naive groups in the world: "[They are] a cold, frustrated, sexless, repressed people, with little emotional flexibility and practically no capacity to give themselves in intimate relationships. Emotions are kept under control by internal guilt feelings and external ridicule" (Messinger, 1970, p. 276). This group of islanders is far from the norm, but there is perhaps an element of truth even in this extreme example.

Even the traditional dance, the Irish jig, reflects and, indeed, caricatures repression of bodily experience: the skilled dancer agilely moves only his or her feet while keeping the rest of the body as motionless as possible. This contrasts boldly, for example, with Greek dancing, where the physical suppleness and contact between dancers reflect very different attitudes toward the body.

Talking and Dreaming

The greatest natural resource of the Irish was their verbal talent. For 2000 years the poet has been the most valued member of Irish society, wit its greatest art form, and satire its most penetrating mode of attack (Colum, 1967). Poets were the only citizens allowed to move freely around Ireland, and, like the Church, they contributed to the cultural unity of the country (Chadwick, 1970). (Even today writers are the only members of Irish society exempt from paying taxes.) The splendor of the ancient epics, in striking contrast to the relative simplicity of life indicated by archaeological remains (Chadwick, 1972), indicates that the Irish have always used creative imagination to elaborate where the gifts of this world were lacking.

Side by side with the belief in sin, and partly counterbalancing it, is the Irish belief in dreams. One Irish novelist has described the Irishman as "struggling, through century after century . . . seeking a synthesis between dream and reality . . . with a shrewd knowledge of the world and a strange reluctance to cope with it" (O'Faolain, 1949, p. 17). For hundreds of years the Irish lived an impoverished life on a misty island, which had very few natural resources and was dominated by a foreign oppressor. Probably their ability to weave dreams was crucial to their survival. Historically, they have valued fantasy and dreaming more, perhaps, than any other Western European culture. Even third-generation Irish Americans have been shown to turn to compensatory fantasy more than others when frustrated (Stein, 1971).

The Irish tend not to believe that their dreams will come true. They may, however, value them more than objective truth. Life is organized around one's dreams. For example, when accused of being an inveterate liar, a character in a recent Irish novel explains: "It's a poet's way of reaching for truth" (Flanagan, 1979, p. 166). Their dreams and the sense of innate sinfulness seem to reinforce each other (McGoldrick & Pearce, 1981; Pearce, 1980). Together they give the Irish character a many leveled complexity, as intriguing as it is puzzling.

As a character in a play by George Bernard Shaw said:

> Oh, the dreaming! the dreaming! the torturing, heartscalding, never satisfying dreaming. . . . An Irishman's imagination never lets him alone, never convinces him, never satisfies him; but it makes him that he can't face reality nor deal with it nor handle it nor conquer it; he can only sneer at them that do . . . and imagination's such a torture that you can't bear it without whiskey. . . . You nag and squabble at home because your wife isn't an angel, and she despises you because you're not a hero. (Shaw, 1975, p. 909)

Yet, while the Irish know the hopelessness of their dreams, they do not speak of it openly. We might call this "denial," but it is more like the experiencing of separate alternating realities. As part of acceptance of the dreaming mode the Irish show a much greater tolerance for nonrealistic thinking and language than do, for example, the Jews, who value correct thought (Wylan & Mintz, 1976; Zborowski & Herzog, 1952). The Irish are not fond of the truth because they often fear it will reveal how bad they are. So the therapist who assumes that the love of truth will carry therapeutic work along is likely to be disappointed.

The paradox of the general articulateness of the Irish and their inability to express inner feelings can be puzzling for a therapist who may have difficulty figuring out what is going on in an Irish family (Spiegel, 1971a, 1971b). Family members may be so out of touch with their feelings that their inexpressiveness in therapy is not a sign of resistance, as it would be for other cultural groups, but rather a reflection of their blocking off inner emotions, even from themselves. Thus, although the Irish have a marvelous ability to tell stories, when it comes to their emotions, they may have no words.

The Irish often fear being pinned down and may use their language and manner to avoid it. The affinity of the Irish for verbal innuendo, ambiguity, and metaphor have led the English to coin the phrase "talking Irish" to describe the Irish style of both communicating and not communicating at the same time. Some have suggested that, in the extreme, this style of communication is responsible for the high rate of schizophrenia found among the Irish (Murphy, 1975). It is likely that their tradition of verbal obscurity was at least in part due to their history of oppression by the British. (Black Americans are another oppressed people who developed verbal mechanisms to disguise meaning.)

Scheper-Hughes (1979), who studied families in modern rural Ireland, describes group conversation as characterized by "double-talk, obfuscation, interruption, and nonsequiturs." Family therapists may be familiar with this ambiguous and mystifying communication of many Irish American families.

Hostility and Aggression

Like the modern Irish, the ancient Celts had a reputation for being "bombastic, belligerent, and sentimental, a terror to their enemies and a joy to their friends" (Corry, 1977, p. 22). Pugnacity rather than romance was usually the theme of their tales, and occasionally the entire struggle was determined by whose skill in verbal attack and ridicule was greater (Evans, 1957). Though the Irish have a well-deserved reputation for bravery and resourcefulness—even against great odds—in fighting their enemies, the terms "the fighting Irish" and the "wild Irish temper" do not refer to the direct expression of anger within the family. Fighting was and is encouraged only against outsiders and for a just and moral cause, particularly religion or politics. Except under the guise of wit, ridicule, sarcasm, or other indirect humorous expression, hostility in the family is generally dealt with by a silent building up of resentments, culminating in cutting off the relationship, often without a word—a form of social excommunication for interpersonal wrongdoing.

Humor

The Irish sense of humor is one of their greatest strengths and offers them one of their few avenues for expression of disallowed feelings. The importance of their ability to exaggerate and to use humor is indicated by the many expressions the Irish have for this: malarky, blather, blarney, hooey, the gift of gab. Humor allows for sharing of misfortune and the overcoming of difficulties, while its indirectness softens the sting of an attack.

Irish joking often has a mystifying and double-binding character; the listener is not able to gauge the intent and may be the butt of a joke even if he or she jokes back. The Irish form of banter says one thing and means another. It is often used to avoid responsibility for or closeness with others. Teasing and ridicule are especially common in Irish family relationships. Unfortunately, their facile ability to joke can at times leave family members frozen in emotional isolation and unable to get close to anyone.

Politics

Irish history may also clarify the apparent contradiction between Irish compliance with Church authority and their tendency to go beyond the law in their political behavior. By the 18th century all remnants of the Irish nobility had fled, and Ireland was completely controlled by the English. These largely absentee landlords took from the impoverished peasants whatever they could and abolished their liberties. In politics, as in religion, the Irish came to operate on the basis of personal loyalty and pursued their political causes with passionate conviction. Not surprisingly, the Irish have been the most political of all American ethnic groups (Greeley, 1977; Greeley & McCready, 1975; Shannon, 1963; Sowell, 1981). Greeley (1977) has attributed this more to family patterns than to an interest in government: "The Irish young person is so busy calculating the implicit unspoken conflicts over power in his family that he has a predisposition to be interested in the experience of power wherever it occurs" (p. 207).

Respectability

The imposition of the penal laws by the British to control and subjugate the Irish shaped the Irish character. Aside from a deep sense of resentment, they developed a longing for respectability that they carried with them to their new country. John Corry in *The Golden Clan* (1977) has commented:

> One can never underestimate the way the American Irish shunned anything improper. . . . Propriety has been the curse of the Irish since they came to America, building respectability layer on layer. . . . [They] often fight so hard to be accepted that they can never be themselves at all. (pp. 148, 154)

To this day, Irish families will exhibit a strong desire to be liked and accepted and are very concerned with appearances (Greeley, 1971). They will make every effort to avoid drawing attention to themselves through deviant behavior.

Emotional Problems

While the Irish are unlikely to seek help for neurotic problems (Roberts & Myers, 1954), they have had a strikingly high rate of hospitalization for psychosis (Rabkin & Struening, 1976; Murphy, 1975; Malzberg, 1964; Sanua, 1970; Torrey, 1980). According to the World Health Organization statistics, the Irish in Ireland have had the highest rate of mental illness in the world (Walsh, 1968). Until recently, Irish Americans had the highest psychiatric admission rate of ethnic groups in this country, especially for schizophrenia, organic psychosis, and alcoholism (Malzberg, 1964; Pollock, 1913; Roberts

& Myers, 1954; Torrey, 1980). However, they rarely complain of hysterical, psychosomatic, or hypochondriacal symptoms (Kelleher & Copeland, 1974; Kelleher, 1972) or marital problems, and if they do seek therapy, they are more likely to have anxieties, phobias, or obsessive–compulsive problems.

Drink and Food

While the overall rate of mental illness among Irish Americans has fallen during the past 25 years, the Irish—both in Ireland and in the United States—continue to have a very high incidence of alcoholism (Rabkin & Struening, 1976; Clare, 1974; DHEW, 1971; Hyde & Chisholm, 1944; Murphy, 1975; Stivers, 1976; Walsh & Walsh, 1973). Alcoholism is tolerated as "a good man's weakness." Ireland's damp climate, which has forced people to be confined indoors, might be enough to make anyone seek to repress physical sensations with alcohol. In any event, alcohol has been their universal disqualifier and solution: It dulls the pain, keeps out the cold, cures the fever, eases the grief, enlivens the celebration, allows them all manner of expression, and even cures a hangover—"a hair of the dog that bit you" (Stivers, 1976). Because the Irish are not responsible for what is done under its influence, alcohol made anything, but particularly aggression, permissible. It was "the Creatur made him do it." As one group of researchers put it: "It is remarkable that the Irish can find an outlet for so many forms of psychic conflict in this single form of escape" (Roberts & Myers, 1954, p. 762).

Not only is alcohol taken on every conceivable occasion, but it is, to a significant extent, the social substitute for food (Bales, 1962). The Irish have shown much more interest in alcohol than in their cuisine, undoubtedly a result of generations of near starvation. The Irish have shown a surprising lack of interest in what they eat, frequently not bothering to prepare their food well even when they have ample resources. In fact, fasting has been regarded with almost superstitious awe by the Irish for centuries (Scherman, 1981). The Irish certainly made a virtue of necessity, but there are many indications, even from early Irish history, of their lack of concern about worldly comforts (Scherman, 1981). While food provides Jews and Italians with a major source of emotional solace and sharing, the Irish may at times be embarrassed to enjoy good food. The pub rather than the family table was the center of Irish life, with profound implications for the family system.

Considerable alcohol use is tolerated, especially by men, without being seen as a difficulty. Alcohol abuse has thus become a serious problem for the Irish and the cause of much family disruption.

Irish women are much less likely to be drinkers than are Irish men, but they do drink more than women from other ethnic groups, usually quietly, "sipping sherry." When their drinking does get out of hand, it is extremely embarrassing for the family, the more so since women are supposed to be the strong ones in the family.

The male alcoholic cycle in an Irish family may correspond to the religious cycle of sin, guilt, and repentence, allowing brief periods of emotional contact without threatening the rigid distances usually maintained within the family. The partner and counterfoil of the "no good drunk" of an Irish family is the "sainted mother." The alcoholic cycle often goes as follows.

1. When not drinking the husband is depressed, the wife repressed, and they are distant.

2. The husband begins to drink, moving away from the wife, who pursues him, communicating her disapproval or apprehension.

3. When drunk, the husband may move toward the wife angrily or amorously. The wife may then engage with her husband, but in time the intensity will be too much and she withdraws.

4. Later, out of guilt for his anger or amour he will withdraw or beg forgiveness. She then may come close again, forgiving or condemning him, but in time she is more likely simply to withdraw in martyred silence.

5. Finally he gives up and settles back into depression while she continues her martyrdom and repression of her resentment.

The alcoholic himself may appear explosive, outgoing, and charming, expressing many of the feelings otherwise repressed in the family. His behavior may be quite unlike the Irish as otherwise portrayed in this paradigm. The wife of an alcoholic is more likely to seek support for her martyrdom than a change in her role or situation since a favorable change is beyond her expectations. Thus the family will probably not seek help for an alcohol-related problem or any other problem until it has become so serious that someone outside the family, such as the police, a doctor, or a school authority, suggests it.

Suffering

The Irish sense of personal guilt often leads them to assume that their suffering is deserved. The Irish say of others: "He'll get his." The unspoken corollary of that judgment is: "I'll get mine." The guilty will be punished. If you are suffering, it is because you are guilty and should suffer. In Jewish culture, by contrast, suffering is a shared experience that is felt to protect the family magically and increase its power (Zborowski & Herzog, 1952). The Irish find virtue and sanctity in silent suffering or in "offering up" their pain to God "in imitation of Christ." In life one makes efforts to improve, but the inner conviction is that the efforts will fail and the Irish tend to get uncomfortable if things go too well for too long. It is often said by Irish Americans that the tragedies of the Kennedys followed from their having had too much success (Galbraith, 1982).

The Irish have a much higher tolerance for physical pain than most other cultural groups (Sternbach & Tursky, 1965; Tursky & Sternbach, 1967; Zborowski, 1969; Zola, 1966). Studies of different cultural responses to physical pain show that the Irish tend toward confusion and inaccuracy in describing their pain and that they are silent and uncomplaining about their suffering even to close family members (Zborowski, 1969; Zola, 1966). They often do not seek medical help even when they obviously need it (Zborowski, 1969). They do not seek suffering, but they do expect it and are less likely than other ethnic groups to seek relief (Zborowski, 1969; Zola, 1966).

Thus, when the Irish do admit something is wrong, it would be well for the therapist to take them seriously; they are unlikely to be exaggerating. Given the limited expectations of the Irish for happiness in this life, change is likely to come very slowly. They are so resigned to their fate that no matter how bad things are already, they believe they could always be worse.

Heinrich Böll has aptly described this remarkable attitude in his *Irish Journal* (1967):

> When something happens to you in Germany, when you miss a train, break a leg, go bankrupt, we say: it couldn't have been any worse; whatever happens is always the worst. With the Irish it is almost the opposite; if you break a leg, miss a train, go bankrupt, they say: it could be worse. Instead of a leg you might have broken your neck, instead of a train you might have missed Heaven, and instead of going bankrupt you might have lost your peace of mind, and going bankrupt is no reason at all for that. . . . And if you should die, well, you are rid of all your troubles, for to every penitent sinner the way is open to Heaven, the goal of our laborious earthly pilgrimage. . . . With us, it seems to me, when something happens, our sense of humor and imagination desert us; in Ireland that is just when they come into play. (p. 104)

Death and the Family Life Cycle

It is not surprising that for the Irish death has been by far the most celebrated experience of the life cycle, reflecting the sense that life is to be endured and death is a release from suffering. The Irish love to get together for any social occasion, but the most prominent social gathering has always been the wake. There the extended family would gather, tell jokes, drink, and reminisce about the deceased. Although the emphasis on the wake as a social gathering is similar to Black American customs, the Irish joking at wakes is very different from the openly expressive mourning of Blacks. The Irish emphasis on death is comparable to the Italian focus on marriage and the Jewish focus on the Bris and Bar Mitzvah, each of which reflects the very different values held by those cultures.

Family Patterns

While acculturation for many cultural groups has placed great strain on their traditional family ties and structure, it is possible that life in America actually strengthened the Irish family by increasing the achievement options for men and offering them greater flexibility for relationships in the family. This description will focus more on the traditional patterns that may become problematic at times for Irish American families.

Although the Irish never had a cult of romantic love, they did have a surprising number of female heroines and rulers such as the wild, self-willed Queen Maeve (Chadwick, 1970). Irish women have traditionally dominated family life. As one author has stated: "The Irish wife was often the brains, the manager, the savings bank, the realist for the notional and unrealistic husband. . . . The Irish woman had a hardy spirit, an undaunted courage, and, in asserting herself, an uninhibited brass" (Potter, 1960, p. 90). Irish women have also enjoyed a greater degree of independence relative to women in other cultures. For example, unlike other ethnic groups, the rate of immigration of Irish women was higher than that of Irish men (Biddle, 1976; Kennedy, 1978; Walsh, 1973). Irish families often paid as much attention to the education of their daughters as to their sons (Blessing, 1980), and there is an overrepresentation of Irish women in professional and white-collar jobs (Blessing, 1980).

Typically the Irish woman found her social life primarily through the Church, which, by its veneration of the Virgin Mary, also reflected the Irish view of women as independent and dominant (Kennedy, 1978). Indeed, Irish women have always been considered morally superior to men. Women tended to think of men as needing to be carefully handled or manipulated. Women bore their responsibilities and burdens stoically, "offering them up." As was said of one rich Irish American matriarch, "She coped with her life mostly by ignoring her problems and saying her prayers" (Corry, 1977, p. 186). Family researcher Theodore Lidz (1968) describes the pattern thus:

> The Irish American child may grow up influenced by the mother's tendency to treat her husband like a grown-up child, pretending to believe the fabricated tales he tells her and admiring his ability to tell them; and while she seems to defer to her husband's authority, she holds the family reins tightly in her own hands, at the same time ceding to the Church a superordinate authority which must not be questioned. (p. 52)

Traditionally fathers in Irish families have been shadowy or absent figures, and husbands dealt with wives primarily by avoidance. Studies of psychiatric patients have indicated that Irish men tend to view women as the main source of anxiety and power, while Italians usually focus on the husband (Opler & Singer, 1957; Singer & Opler, 1956). A masterful description of a man's reaction to women is given in *The Iceman Cometh* (O'Neill,

1957) by Hickey, who is tormented by his guilt about his wife's moral superiority and belief in her "pipe dreams."

> It kept piling up. . . . I got so I thought of it all the time. I hated myself more and more, thinking of all the wrong I'd done to the sweetest woman in the world who loved me so much. I got so I'd curse myself for a lousy bastard every time I saw myself in the mirror. . . . Christ, I loved her, but I began to hate that pipe dream. . . . Sometimes I couldn't forgive her for forgiving me. I even caught myself hating her for making me hate myself so much. There's a limit to the guilt you can feel and the forgiveness and the pity you can take. You have to begin blaming someone else too. I got so sometimes when she'd kiss me it was like she did it on purpose to humiliate me, as if she'd spit in my face. But all the time I saw how crazy and rotten of me that was, and it made me hate myself all the more. You'd never believe I could hate so much, a good-natured happy go lucky slob like me. (p. 239)

Because of the difficulty dealing with feelings, the Irish have trouble in close relationships, especially marriage. The Irish place less emphasis on marriage than do other cultures, and romance in marriage is not a central concept. Partners tend to resign themselves to an emotionally distant relationship. Physical or emotional separation has been the primary way of dealing with problems. Traditionally, help, if needed, was sought from the priest (who was perhaps not always the best authority on marital problems).

> One patient described that when he went to the priest for counsel about his wife's lack of interest in sex, he was told that he was thinking more of this world than he was of the next, and that if they were having that much trouble they should live as brother and sister. The man sought no further counsel for many years. The marital relationship worsened, with unfortunate consequences for the children, who bore the brunt of the parents' frustration.

Irish distancing may be baffling or frustrating to someone from a culture that takes for granted more intense interactions, and it naturally presents difficulties for contemporary Irish who marry Italians, Jews, or Hispanics. Whereas the Irish may see distancing as merely the best temporary solution to interpersonal problems, others may see it as abandonment.

The method of family inheritance probably increased the lack of closeness in man–woman relationships. The Irish did not practice primogeniture, and fathers usually decided only late in life which of the sons would inherit the land (Arensberg, 1937; Arensberg & Kimball, 1968). Only the son who inherited had the means to marry. In part as a result, the Irish in Ireland have had the lowest rate and oldest age of marriage in the world (Humphreys, 1965; Kennedy, 1978).

Celibacy was considered by the Church to be the highest state one could attain, and an enormous number of Irish men and women remained celibate. Marriage was considered "permission to sin." Until recently the Church taught—and most Irish believed—that one should only have sex for the purpose of procreation. Divorce and affairs have always been less common among the Irish (Greeley, 1971), although pregnancy prior to marriage has not been unheard of. Instances of premarital pregnancy are perhaps related to the tendency to dissociate unacceptable behavior or feelings. According to Church teachings, one must fight continually the "temptation to sin," which can never be anticipated directly. It was considered a far greater sin to use contraceptives than to become pregnant as a result of a moment of passion. Just as they repress the experience of their physical bodies, the Irish will try to deny the "evil" part of themselves. Momentary lapses of the moral strictures are seen as predictable because human nature is viewed as basically evil (Spiegel, 1971b) and forgiven as inherent moral weakness.

Children

The Irish tend to view people moralistically: as good or bad, strong or weak, villain or victim. Through the process of labeling and mythmaking, the family often designates a good child and a bad one, and they may ignore aspects of a child's behavior that do not fit his or her designated role. In one Irish American family, for example, the mother always spoke about her three children as "my Denny, poor Betty, and that Kathleen." The good child, usually a "pet son," is characterized as high achieving, religious, conforming, and respectable. The bad one, or the black sheep, is seen as weak, incompetent, shy, and perhaps with a weakness for alcohol. Although mischievous, rebellious, rule-breaking behavior is typical of the bad child, the characterization is often used to refer to a loafer, a dreamer, or a "ne'r do well."

Discipline in Irish families is maintained by ridicule, belittling, and shaming (Barrebee & von Mering, 1953; Spiegel, 1971a, 1971b). In families where alcohol is abused, discipline is often inconsistent and harsh. The extreme prohibition against sexual expression may actually increase the likelihood of periodic outbursts of aggressive or sexual acting out, especially under the influence of alcohol; it is possible that incest or child abuse is made more likely by the cultural prohibitions against all emotional expression since this leaves families struggling to control feelings that are just below the surface.

Children in Irish American families are generally raised to be polite, respectable, obedient, and well behaved. Typical familial injunctions would be: "What will the neighbors think?" "Don't make a scene"; "That's a sin"; or "You'll go to hell." Children rarely are praised by their parents, and they are not usually fussed over or made the center of attention for fear of spoiling them or giving them a "swelled head" (Barrabee & von Mering, 1953). When asked by the therapist if she praised her children, one Irish American mother characteristically replied, "Why yes, all the time. Why Kevin here, he's not so bad" (Pearce, 1980). This strict and restrained attitude toward children may be very hard for a therapist from a more permissive or expressive culture to understand, just as it may be difficult for the Irish to understand the strong focus on and permissiveness toward children encouraged by many groups in the United States.

Probably because of the lack of closeness between the parents, the strongest axis in the Irish family is the mother—son tie (Barrabee & von Mering, 1953). The mother's highest hopes are for her brightest son, who until recently was steered to the priesthood to ensure his salvation.[2] In Ireland, entering the priesthood not only "saved his soul" but it was the only way a son could get an education without emigrating. Obviously it also meant that his mother would not lose him to another woman.

Frequently, the mother's idealization of her son is not realistic but rather an instance of Irish dreaming. This puts the son in a bind. Her underlying conviction is that men are weak and will let you down, yet she idealizes her son in a way he cannot openly reject. But he knows he is not what she dreams he is because indirectly she lets him know it. Greeley (1977) speculates that Irish sons have a compulsion to please their mothers that is built upon the mother's controlling them by starving them for affection. Irish sons are in a particularly difficult position because, unlike Jewish sons, they are not allowed to be angry and resentful if their mothers induce guilt or play the martyr.

Beyond the mother–son tie, family members tend to stick to their own sex and generation in forming relationships. There is evidence that father–daughter relationships are often tense (Greeley, 1975), probably due to the father's fear of repressed sexual impulses.

Extended Family

Extended family relationships among the Irish are often neither warm nor affectionate, despite an air of joviality and clannishness, and may be governed by a sense of duty or obligation. Though privately they may long desperately for some greater degree of human contact, the Irish may not have nor want much contact with the extended family. Even in situations of extreme need, the Irish often do not solicit help from family members (Stein, 1971). They are also considerably less likely than Italians and Jews to visit with relatives (Greeley, 1971). While siblings may meet for holidays out of a sense of loyalty, there is often a sense of emotional isolation and they may not actually enjoy each other.

---

2. By contrast, Italians have traditionally been less positive about their sons entering religious life since it meant they would leave the family rather than perpetuate it by marrying and having children, which was the first priority. As Gambino (1975) has noted, Italian Americans, even relatively religious ones, regarded a clerical career for their relatives as wasteful.

In Irish families tensions and anger may build up over long periods of time without resolution and finally lead to an emotional cutoff of the relationship. This is a strikingly common pattern and is in marked contrast to the enmeshment of Italian, Jewish, or Greek families. In such groups, when conflicts lead to cutting off of the relationship, the hurts will be dealt with openly, at great length, and many efforts will be made to polarize family members around the issues. Among the Irish such conflicts are often never mentioned at all. The Irish may feel such a deep sense of pain about their responsibility, that they want to deny it. There is such a pronounced tendency among Irish family members to deny or defuse personal responsibility and distort the actual flow of events, that it is often difficult for an observer to discern what has actually occurred (Spiegel, 1971a, 1971b).

Typically, one extended family member (usually a woman) is of central importance for the family. It is usually essential to get permission of this matriarch, most often a grandmother or senior maiden aunt, if therapeutic progress is to be made.

The Irish have a tremendous respect for personal boundaries, are enormously sensitive to each other's right to privacy, and will make strong efforts not to impose or intrude on one another. The Irish in older age have a much more independent, active view of themselves than the elderly of other ethnic backgrounds (Cohler & Lieberman, 1979).

Irish Americans in Therapy

When the Irish go for therapy, they will probably not look their best: outgoing, poetic, and colorful. Therapy is often viewed like confession, where you tell your sins and seek forgiveness. They may not understand their feelings and will certainly be embarrassed to admit them. Irish clients often take a one-down position, seeing authority as vested in the therapist. Although the Irish feel deep guilt and responsibility for their problems, they are likely to externalize them and will often blame others for them (de la Fontaine, 1940). As one member of an Irish family put it: "Pride means not admitting you're wrong, even if you know you are." This creates a dilemma for the therapist. The family will feel even more embarrassed if the therapist discovers their "sins."

The Irish are known for their hospitality and politeness, which seem to derive from a genuine selflessness in relationships. This probably stems directly from the attitudes with which children are raised—namely, with an emphasis on never letting them get a "swelled head." A therapist from a different culture may find it hard to comprehend how the Irish can be so lacking in a sense of self-importance. It is almost as though the Irish suffer from a national inferiority complex (Galbraith, 1982). This may also lead to problems when clients fail to let the therapist know that they are extremely inconvenienced by a therapeutic arrangement or that the therapy is not meeting their needs. While clients from other backgrounds may be quick to demand that plans be made to suit their convenience or that the therapist solve their problems, the Irish can have enormous difficulty with such self-assertions.

In spite of their paradoxical characteristics, the Irish can be very gratifying to work with because of extreme loyalty and their willingness to follow through on therapeutic suggestions. They are also apt to accept the therapist readily; they may not question credentials (Sanua, 1960; Spiegel, 1971a, 1971b; Zborowski, 1969; Zola, 1966), even when it may be in their best interests to do so. Unfortunately, their responsiveness can become a hazard when it produces compliance without real motivation for change. The therapist must help them develop a genuine investment in the process of change and not rely on their politeness, sense of responsibility, and obligation to duty.

Establishing a working alliance is a crucial aspect of dealing with Irish families. Therapists may have a tendency to be complacent when faced with Irish compliance and not appreciate the extent to which they may go along with things without really involving themselves in a personal way and without revealing crucial emotional issues to the therapist. They may have little belief in their own ability to change situations (Zborowski, 1969). They may seek help if told to do so and may carefully follow through on instructions, without ever really investing themselves in the process of change or believing in its efficacy.

> Madge O'Brien, after an extended course of family therapy, had changed her behavior considerably, responded willingly to all suggestions, never missed a session, and never challenged what the therapist said. On the day of the last session, after reviewing the fairly successful course of therapy, which had involved her setting much more clear limits on her son's behavior and her husband taking a more active role in the family, said, "Well, all in all, it was just God's will. My Joey was just different, and now God has answered my prayers and straightened him out."

She failed to recognize her own role in the problem or to appreciate the importance of behaving differently. However, as often happens with the Irish, small changes may be registered as large gains in the family in spite of the many aspects of family relating that remain unaltered.

Mrs. O'Brien reflected a typical Irish attitude about therapy. She was as loyal and responsive as she could be, but there were many levels on which therapy had not touched her. She had her religious dreams, hopes, and prayers and had made no attempt to integrate them in therapy, although she had learned a new "therapeutic reality." The therapist became an authority, like the priest, whose instructions were to be followed.

The Irish will probably respond more readily to a fairly structured problem-focused (especially child-focused) approach. Brief, goal-oriented therapy with a specific plan and a right and wrong way clearly spelled out (like behavior modification) would be likely to have appeal. On the other hand, vague, introspective, open-ended emotive therapy would be very threatening.

Using sessions to plan strategies or tasks to be done in private, at home, would be preferable to dramatic or emotional scenes or restructuring of the family in the session. Bowen systems therapy (Bowen, 1978), though open-ended in goals, may have considerable appeal because of its emphasis on loyalty and personal responsibility and its respect for individual and private boundaries. Family members often take to this approach and make striking moves on their own with minimal therapeutic input.

The Irish are apt to be very threatened by therapy directed at uncovering hostile or erotic feelings and might respond better to the use of positive reframing of the strategic brief therapy models (Haley, 1973; Selvini-Palazzoli, Boscolo, Cecchin, & Prata, 1976, 1980; Papp, 1980; Weakland, Watzlawick, & Fisch, 1974). These methods would encourage them to change without exposing their inner feelings, which might only increase their anxiety and their conviction that they are bad and deserve to suffer. In other words, by using the somewhat mysterious, paradoxical, and humorous techniques of which the Irish are themselves such masters, we may help them to be more directly assertive and expressive.

Some opening of communication to increase emotional connectedness can be extremely useful. The Irish family's sense of isolation can be so great that a therapist may not realize how much it means to them just to talk to each other about thoughts and feelings. On the other hand, the use of touching exercises or nonverbal techniques may be highly threatening. Bowen Systems Therapy again may be helpful because of the emphasis on open personal relationships with all family members without requiring exposure in front of the therapist. In addition, family members often relate on many levels at the same time, and the subtlety and ambiguity may be confusing to an outsider. A Jewish therapist's interest in clarifying many levels of meaning or a WASP therapist's pursuit of truth within the family may miss the mark completely.

The Irish family would probably prefer the therapist to keep a friendly distance. A sense of humor is a great asset in working with the Irish (as it is with all cultures), but only within the framework of a rather serious and businesslike attitude. Any personality style too loud or out of the ordinary is likely to make the family extremely uncomfortable. Swearing, for example, is likely to be viewed as crude or sacrilegious. It would also present a major obstacle for the therapist to espouse values different from the Church's norms, such as encouraging abortion, which is still total anathema in the Church, or even birth control, which is officially unacceptable.

Given Irish attitudes toward marriage, sex, and intimacy, the therapist must not move too quickly from the presenting problem to intimate relationships. In fact, some Irish families may stop therapy before ever dealing with marital issues, even though such issues are central to the discomfort and isolation of family members.

Although the father and other family members may fail to see the need for his presence, it is important for the therapist to involve him in therapy. While the mother may be the one who usually handles family affairs, the father's inactive or inconsistent role may be central to the imbalance of the family.

Although Irish men will often find a woman therapist intimidating, the strong role of women in Irish families makes them generally more comfortable with a woman therapist than are families from countries such as Greece or Italy.

The therapist may encounter conscious withholding, especially when interviewing the whole family together, because of the Irish prohibitions against sharing personal information with those of the opposite sex or of a different generation. Also, in large groups, family members may hide behind jokes or superficial story telling to handle their anxiety. Candor usually increases when the therapist interviews fewer people together. The individual session is in this sense the easiest, although in this context the fear of intimacy may increase clients' anxiety.

The therapy of Irish alcoholism is much too complex to cover in this chapter. Readers are referred to Ablon (1980), Berenson (1976), Carter (1977), Davis, Berenson, Steinglass, and Davis (1974), and Johnson (1973) for a more complete discussion of the topic. Therapists should be cautioned to take an alcohol history, even if the family does not present this as an issue, and to appreciate the degree to which the family may tolerate heavy drinking without labeling it a problem. The Johnson (1973) Intervention Approach to alcoholic families carefully structures family members' expression of feelings in relating to the alcoholic. The emphasis is on preparing family members to discuss the consequences of drinking in a planned confrontation. Angry outbursts are prohibited. This method seems well suited to helping Irish families come to terms with alcoholism in a task-oriented, controlled, and structured way (McBride, 1981). Even after the drinking has stopped, one must be careful to move very slowly in helping an alcoholic family to open up emotionally (Berenson, 1976). The expressive difficulties for which the alcohol serves as a facilitator can be extreme, and they cannot be overcome quickly. Helping alcoholic families integrate into their lives the adaptive aspects of drinking behavior without the alcohol is especially important for the Irish, who tend to have such rigid splits in their feelings between what is allowed and what is considered intolerable (Berenson, 1976; Davis et al., 1974).

Irish strengths, particularly humor, their sense of responsibility, and their loyalty are the best avenues of entry into the family. In working with the Irish, the therapist must often read between the lines, whether of blustering or of muted compliance, to ferret out what is really troubling them. If these underlying needs and wishes are exposed too early in therapy, the client may not feel relieved or understood but may instead feel exposed and embarrassed. Therapy requires a delicate balance of sensitivity without exposing awareness of what is going on too soon. It is also important for the therapist to be patient and willing to leave much unsaid or unchanged since the family may have limited goals relative to the culture's general expectations for family functioning. A therapist's push for more work may be seen as an accusation that they are still bad and have not done well. The therapist must let them change in minimal ways and withdraw, if that is their need. They will then be free to come back when problems develop again.

When the Irish do engage emotionally in therapy, they are often seeking forgiveness or absolution. Therapists must wend their way around this trap since granting absolution keeps the client in a one-down position. The many levels of self-recrimination, attempts at self-justification, tales told to show how it was someone else's fault, and so on, are ploys in this strategy. The Irish are raised to be selfless. They have extreme difficulty articulating their personal needs.

Given the Irish embarrassment about their feelings, on the one hand, and their wish to be responsive to suggestions, on the other, tasks that can be carried out at home may promote communication more successfully than directly confronting family members in therapy. Tasks focused on presenting symptoms that structure family interactions at home, address maladaptive family communication problems without unmasking them directly in sessions. There are many advantages to doing this. It fits with the Irish expectation of doing penance for their sins; it provides structure within which to organize their behavior; it spells out a right and wrong way; and it spares them public exposure in therapy. This clarity is important to those who fear doing wrong. It also provides a sense of success early in therapy, which may be especially important for the Irish who are preoccupied with feeling they are bad and have done wrong.

With family members who are obsessed with guilt, anxiety, and fear of losing control, ritualizing the badness puts structure and limits on it. Not only can guilt be limited by structuring time to feel it, but anger can also be ritualized so that the emotion can be expressed to a limited extent, without the person fearing it will get too far out of bounds. For example, couples can be instructed to carry out fights as suggested by Erickson (Haley, 1973) at given times and in a place where they will not be disturbed.

An important intervention in working with the Irish is dealing with cutoffs in the extended family. The Irish are much more likely to be cut off than enmeshed, in spite of the hidden intensity of many Irish families. Efforts to help them reconnect may do a lot to lessen feelings of emotional isolation. However, this work requires respect for personal boundaries, for the family's need to preserve a degree of distance, and for leaving certain things unspoken.

Child-Focused Families

Perhaps the most common referral of an Irish family is for a child's behavioral problem that has led the school or court to suggest they seek help. Families rarely seek therapy of their own accord but are likely to follow through on a referral from an outside authority. It is important for the therapist to be aware of the embarrassment that a behavioral problem will create for the family. Whereas a Jewish family may get most upset about underachievement or eating problems in their children and an Italian family about disloyalty to the family, the Irish wish to be respectable is of primary importance and a rebellious child is a source of great humiliation, as the following case illustrates.

> The Morans came for therapy when their 17-year-old daughter, Megan, admitted to her mother that she was the major source of drugs for her high school because she thought she was about to be arrested. Her mother told this to the woman she kept house for, who suggested she seek counseling for her daughter. Both mother and daughter preferred not to involve the father or younger brother because "they wouldn't understand." However, they complied with the therapist's request that everyone attend.
>
> In the initial family interview the parents were utterly embarrassed about their daughter's behavior. They had both suspected her drug involvement but preferred not to confront her until she brought things to a head herself. Both parents, who had been born in Ireland, presented as very well-meaning people, who struggled all their lives to make a living. They smiled awkwardly throughout the interview, trying to cover up their sense of shame and embarrassment about the situation. When the father was asked about his concern for his daughter's selling $1000 worth of drugs a week, he replied: "Well, you know, I don't like to be nosey with people. . . . If I think somebody is doing something, if a girl is pulling up her stocking, I make noise so I don't embarrass her or something like that."
>
> When the mother was asked if she had discussed the situation with anyone in her family, she replied: "Oh no. . . . It's too embarrassing. . . . It's not really something you want to brag about, is it?" The parents' embarrassment made it very difficult for them to handle the problem. The mother was so concerned about what the neighbors thought, that she had stopped relating to several of them, for fear they would ask questions. When the daughter got upset, the mother, instead of responding, would go around the house closing the windows while the father went down to the basement to avoid any conflict. Mrs. Moran had been trying in vain to control her daughter by reference to religion. To such attempts, Megan responded with jokes about her mother being "Holy Mary" and how the

local priest had run off with a parishioner and yet her mother was trying to get her to go to confession.

As therapy moved along, a major task became to involve the father more directly in the family and to help the mother to back off from the daughter. Both the mother and daughter agreed things would work out better if the father handled the discipline. He admitted reluctantly that he had to back off from his daughter because "She'd bring out the animal in you. Megan is a Cassius Clay behind it all. She can't be beaten or embarrassed." He feared he would become violent if he let himself engage in struggles with her and could not imagine being able to use a moderate response.

Therapy consisted of eight very difficult, awkward sessions, focused to a small degree on clarifying family patterns and much more on developing behavioral prescriptions to be carried out at home. The daughter's behavior changed, and the father shifted somewhat in relating to her, although he found this very difficult and embarrassing. No one in the family enjoyed the sessions, although they admitted at the end that things had improved, and Megan, who had been on the verge of being a high school dropout, graduated. On follow-up a year later, Megan was working for the police department, a common Irish solution for dealing with aggression, and was going to accompany her father on a trip to Ireland to visit relatives.

The conflict of parent and child values in the Moran family is more striking than it would be in a fourth-generation Irish American family and reflects many of the specific generational difficulties of immigrant families. However, a number of patterns are typical, including the awkwardness, embarrassment, and difficulty in dealing with feelings; the roles of the parents in the family; the fear of losing control; the mother's attempt to call on Church authority as a source of control; the family's discomfort in therapy; and the family's continuation of therapeutic movement on their own.

Therapy with Couples

It is dangerous for therapists to move into the area of marital problems unless asked to do so, and it is not too often that they are asked. Couples who do present with marital problems most often have difficulty establishing or maintaining an intimate relationship because of inhibitions in dealing with tenderness, sex, or hostilities.

What is often surprising in dealing with Irish couples is the extent to which they avoid dealing with the important emotional issues within the relationship. One woman, who applied for help after her husband developed cancer, said that she had decided five years previously that she was going to leave him as soon as her children were grown. She had never mentioned this to him or even told him of her dissatisfactions.

The inability of many Irish Americans to express their warm feelings, if their whole lives have been spent with almost no display of affection, may be extremely difficult to overcome. Frequently, the inhibition of one partner is intensified, however, by the demands of the other, who feels he or she is being cheated. This can set up in the other partner a complex web of guilt and resentment that makes a show of spontaneous warmth by the other even more difficult. Helping the spouse to reduce the intensity of the demand and reframing the other's distance as inhibition rather than intentional with-holding can be useful. In general, the use of positive connotation, which gives a caring interpretation to behavior, is likely to be of much more use than traditional psychiatric interpretations for clients who are so likely to blame themselves for whatever is going wrong and to feel incapable of changing things. Structuring the distance and intimacy will increase the couple's sense of control over their feelings.

> Kevin and Mary Dugan, an attractive but constricted couple in their mid-30s, sought marital therapy after seven years of marriage. Mary had just confessed to Kevin that she had had two affairs in reaction to his lack of affection and sexual response. Both relationships had ended because she had talked of nothing but Kevin. Kevin, who was particularly constricted emotionally, sat through the first hour showing no emotional expression whatsoever, in spite of Mary's tears, upset, and escalating tension, which seemed to have no release. Kevin came from a very religious family in which his father never expressed any emotion and his dominant mother devoted her life to her Church activities. In dealing with his wife, he seemed to feel defeated before he began. He felt he was doomed to offer an inadequate response. Occasionally he would try to tell her that he felt inarticulate and out of touch with his feelings. She would argue him down, saying he was wrong and could be articulate if he tried because he was very intelligent and successful. He would then either withdraw or respond that she was so overwhelming that he just could not take it. She was hypersensi-tive to this criticism and would protest that if he would just be specific, she would try to change. After a few minutes both would withdraw in hurt silence, feeling somehow guilty and martyred at the same time, without understanding what kept going wrong when they meant so well in the relationship. Kevin would try to express his fear of failure; Mary would feel blamed and in turn accuse him of being irrational; he would withdraw, feeling blamed, from which she would infer that she was creating his feeling; and the pattern would recycle.

Therapy involved several aspects:

1. Prescribing the symptom. It was recommended that Kevin and Mary Dugan go slowly and not try to express too much or change their pattern too quickly since change could be upsetting.

2. Ritualizing the badness. The couple was instructed to let themselves feel bad, guilty, and hopeless at given times in order to fully understand their experience. This is reminiscent of "examining one's conscience," a require-ment before confession. The rationale here was that it was important for them to experience this so that they would not be disappointed when they regressed in the future after they had made improvements.

3. Structuring their attempts to change their ways of communicating. Structuring was done to give them a sense of control over their feelings. Very short periods were assigned for dealing with emotions. They were instructed to express their annoyance for five minutes at a time (which might be considered a form of paradoxical penance).

Later on they were instructed to help each other do relaxation and breathing exercises. This was more acceptable than recommending direct focus on their sexual relationship, which, for a long while in therapy, seemed only to embarrass them and heighten their anxiety.

4. Coaching each on working out relationships with extended family. Work on relationships with extended family was structured to allow them the space to do this work privately, while the discussion of it in joint sessions helped open up the emotional context within which they were working. This work was most important in helping them lower the reactivity in their relationship with each other.

Therapy with Extended Family

Problems in dealing with extended family include cutoffs, secrets, indirectness, and eccentricity. The atmosphere is often characterized by dourness, on one hand, and humor, which obscures serious emotional issues, on the other. The concern to keep up appearances is hard for the Irish to overcome. The power of the unspoken rules may be difficult for an outsider to appreciate. The family may act pleasant, humorous, and hospitable and yet take any emotional exposure to outsiders as a severe breach of family rules, not to be forgotten. Thus, it is often much better to coach family members to work on their relationships at home, rather than to have family sessions where they are brought in together. The extent to which family members can be emotionally and physically cut off from the family may be extreme. Older unmarried relatives may be totally out of contact with other family members or may form isolated units of siblings or parent and child, who maintain almost no communication with other parts of the family. The most important point about this isolation is the care with which changes must be approached. It takes time and patience, which may be extremely frustrating for a therapist from a more emotionally open culture. It is also crucial to appreciate that a review of the underlying emotional issues in the family may not be experienced as relieving.

This attitude appears related to the Irish preference for dreams over truth. As Potter (1960) has put it, "The Irish preferred the poetry of unreality to the prose of fact" (p. 96). Ambiguity is somehow easier for them to handle. They are very uncomfortable with spelling out realities, if they are even aware of them.

Mary Dogerty, aged 50, the oldest of three living siblings, sought therapy for problems related to feeling "driven" and fears of imminent failure, in spite of having a highly successful career. In describing her family background she said she had always felt upstaged by her younger sister and that she was the one who always got into trouble in school. She felt this increased her mother's preference for her sister and led Mary to strive even harder to get attention. During our work on Mary's extended family, a session was held with her mother, Rose, aged 80, who came in with her unmarried sister, Kitty, aged 70, with whom she lived. Although Mary had great dread of her mother's and aunt's reactions to the session, they "put on a good front," joking and telling stories about their own backgrounds and Mary's childhood. They particularly joked about Mary's misbehaviors, making light of them, although Mary had earlier described to the therapist feeling totally incapable of winning attention or approval in her family. It was almost impossible to get at any loaded issues in the session. When Mary would raise a subject on which she felt sensitive, her mother or aunt would wink or joke and say, "That's our Mary, always worrying or making trouble." As the session ended and they were putting on their coats to leave, the mother took out her wallet and said, "I don't think I showed you a picture of my third daughter, Elizabeth, who, unfortunately died at age five. She looked just like Mary—just the picture of Mary!"

It was impossible to deal with the implications of the mother's remark at that moment, but it opened up for Mary a whole new understanding of her relationship with her mother. They had never in their lives discussed the similarity between Mary and Elizabeth, and, in fact, Mary said in the next session that her mother had not mentioned Elizabeth at all in many years. Later exploration of Mary and her mother's relationship and its complication by Elizabeth's death when Mary was 2 helped Mary develop a very different perception of her mother and an appreciation of the pain she had suffered at the loss of her child, which she had never been able to share with anyone.

Such meetings may at times be the only way for the therapist to gain a sense of what is happening in the family. The benefits of the session may take a long time to evaluate. A family session that had seemed largely wasted proved in the long run to have been a major turning point in the relationship of Mary and her mother and, consequently, the rest of the family. This example is rather typical of the way secrets are kept in an Irish family. The silence around them becomes mystifying. Feelings go underground, leading to cutoffs, emotional isolation, and often eccentricity. This repression can create a rigid, dour, tension-filled atmosphere, full of unspoken resentments perhaps covered by joking, and can be very difficult for family members to tolerate. Coaching a family member to return to this kind of family requires great sensitivity to the anxiety involved.

One young woman, whose father had been a successful journalist and the rebel of his family, had great difficulty establishing a relationship with her sole surviving aunt, who was the principal upholder of "Irish Catholic values" for the family. This aunt had been the spinster sister who had remained at home to care for her aging parents until their deaths. She had built up a lifetime of unspoken resentments about her role, in spite of the secondary gains of being a martyr, similar to the heroine of *Final Payments* by Mary Gordon (1979). The aunt never missed sending cards for birthdays or Christmas, but when the niece attempted to make more personal contact, she resisted it strongly, agreeing to meet only rarely and for short visits and limiting discussion strictly to the topics she chose. Initially the niece was quite put off by this behavior, describing her aunt as "a prune with doilies on the chairs." She was annoyed that her "openhearted" approaches were rebuffed for no apparent reason. It took several years of letters and gradually more personal phone calls before she was able to learn enough about the family background to realize that the resentment she was experiencing had been carried down in the family for several generations. This aunt had become the repository of unforgotten slights, "offering up" her family burdens in her prayers for the family's return to the Church. Church rules had been used in the service of bolstering her self-righteous indignation, which covered her sense of betrayal and hurt that her efforts on behalf of the family had never been reciprocated or appreciated.

In families such as this the work obviously proceeds slowly. However, the long-run benefit to family members of such pursuit is often powerful in overcoming their painful sense of isolation and vulnerability.

Conclusion

Because of Irish indirectness and difficulty in dealing with feelings at the moment, it is easy to be misled about the success of an intervention. Surprisingly often, a move that the Irish cannot make at the time they are in therapy will be carried out at some later point because they feel a deep sense of responsibility and are extraordinarily conscientious about what they feel they should do. This is particularly true about moves toward resolving issues with extended family, which may be strongly resisted at first but carried out diligently later on.

The Irish can be satisfying to work with, provided the therapist can accept the family's limited goals for changing internal attitudes and can be content with helping the family solve specific problems or increase its connectedness in a limited way. Their lack of verbal appreciation may not reflect their true response to therapy (since it is often difficult for the Irish to express their gratitude openly). What is impressive is how much a small gain for one or two family members can be registered as a large gain in the total functioning of the family. This may be particularly so with Bowen coaching. Follow-up where only minimal shifts were apparent in therapy often reveals that the family has continued to move slowly but continuously. As one young man said in describing family therapy which, because of the family's lack of verbal response had not seemed successful: "Family therapy changed us deeply. It was the first time I ever heard my family say what they thought about each other."

ACKNOWLEDGMENTS

Thanks are due many friends, colleagues, clients, and relatives whose experiences contributed to this chapter. Special thanks to Helen Cahalane McGoldrick and to Kathy Milea for their editorial help and suggestions and to my coenthusiast on ethnicity, John Pearce, for the many hours of discussion of the Irish and for his insights and suggestions on the manuscript. Thanks also to Charles Thomas Galbraith for his careful scrutiny of the manuscript and for his many suggestions.

REFERENCES

Ablon, J. The Significance of Cultural Patterning for the "Alcoholic Family." *Family Process, 19*(2), 127–144, 1980.

Arensberg, C. *The Irish Countryman.* Garden City, N.Y.: Natural History Press, 1937.

Arensberg, C., & Kimball, S. *Family and Community in Ireland* (2nd ed.). Cambridge: Harvard University Press, 1968.

Bales, R.F. Attitudes toward Drinking in the Irish Culture. In D. Pittman & C. Snyder (Eds.), *Society, Culture and Drinking Patterns.* New York: Wiley, 1962.

Barrabee, P., & von Mering, O. Ethnic Variations in Mental Stress in Families with Psychotic Children. *Social Problems, 1,* 48–53, 1953.

Berenson, D. Alcohol and the Family System. In P. Guerin (Ed.), *Family Therapy: Theory and Practice.* New York: Gardner Press, 1976.

Bernardo, S. *The Ethnic Almanac.* New York: Doubleday, Dolphin Books, 1981.

Biddle, E.H. The American Catholic Irish Family. In C. Mindel & R. Halberstein (Eds.), *Ethnic Families in America.* New York: Elsevier, 1976.

Blessing, P.J. Irish. In S. Thernstrom (Ed.), *The Harvard Encyclopedia of American Ethnic Groups.* Cambridge: Harvard University Press, 1980.

Böll, H. *Irish Journal.* New York: McGraw-Hill, 1967.

Bowen, M. *Family Therapy in Clinical Practice.* New York: Jason Aronson, 1978.

Carter, E. Generation after Generation: The Longterm Treatment of an Irish Family with Widespread Alcoholism over Multiple Generations. In P. Papp (Ed.), *Family Therapy: Full Length Case Studies.* New York: Gardner Press, 1977.

Chadwick, N. *The Celts.* London: Penguin Books, 1970.

Chadwick, N. *The Everyday Life of the Ancient Celts.* New York: G.P. Putnam, 1972.

Clare, A. Mental Illness in the Irish Emigrant. *Journal of the Irish Medical Association, 67*(1), 225–231, 1974.

Cohler, B.J., & Lieberman, M.A. Personality Change across the Second Half of Life: Findings from a Study of Irish, Italian, and Polish-American Women. In D.E. Gelfand & A.J. Kutzik (Eds.), *Ethnicity and Aging.* New York: Springer, 1979.

Colum, P. (Ed.). *A Treasury of Irish Folklore* (2nd rev. ed.). New York: Crown, 1967.

Corry, J. *The Golden Clan.* Boston: Houghton Mifflin, 1977.

Davis, D.I., Berenson, D., Steinglass, P., & Davis, S. The Adaptive Consequences of Drinking. *Psychiatry, 37,* 209–215, 1974.

de la Fontaine, E. Cultural and Psychological Implications in Casework Treatment with Irish Clients. In *Cultural Problems in Social Casework.* New York: Family Welfare Association of America, 1940.

Department of Health, Education and Welfare. *First Special Report to U.S. Congress on Alcohol and Health*. Washington, D.C.: Health Services and Mental Health Authority, 1971.

Duff, J.B. *The Irish in the United States*. Belmont, Calif.: Wadsworth, 1971.

Evans, E.E. *Irish Folkways*. London: Routledge & Kegan Paul, 1957.

Fallows, M.A. *Irish Americans: Identity and Assimilation*. Englewood Cliffs, N.J.: Prentice-Hall, 1979.

Flanagan, T. *The Year of the French*. New York: Holt, Rinehart & Winston, 1979.

Galbraith. C.T. Personal communication, 1982.

Gambino, R. *Blood of My Blood: The Dilemma of Italian Americans*. Garden City, N.Y.: Anchor Books, 1975.

Gordon, M. *Final Payments*. New York: Ballantine, 1978.

Greeley, A.M. *Why Can't They Be Like Us?* New York: Dutton, 1971.

Greeley, A.M. *That Most Distressful Nation*. Chicago: Quadrangle, 1972.

Greeley, A.M. *The American Catholic*. New York: Basic Books, 1977.

Greeley, A.M. Creativity in the Irish Family: The Cost of Immigration. *International Journal of Family Therapy*, *1*(4), 1979.

Greeley, A.M. *The Irish Americans*. New York: Harper & Row, 1981.

Greeley, A.M., & McCready, W. The Transmission of Cultural Heritages: The Case of Irish and Italians. In N. Glazer & D. Moynihan (Eds.), *Ethnicity: Theory and Experience*. Cambridge: Harvard University Press, 1975.

Haley, J. *Uncommon Therapy: The Psychiatric Techniques of Milton H. Erickson, M.D.* New York: Norton, 1973.

Humphreys, A. The Family in Ireland. In M.F. Numkoff (Eds.), *Comparative Family Systems*. Boston: Houghton Mifflin, 1965.

Hyde, R.N., & Chisholm, R. Studies in Medical Sociology: III. The Relation of Mental Disorders to Race and Nationality. *New England Journal of Medicine*, *231*, 612–618, 1944.

Johnson, V.E. *I'll Quit Tomorrow*. New York: Harper & Row, 1973.

Kelleher, M.J. Cross-National (Anglo-Irish) Differences in Obsessional Symptoms and Traits of Personality. *Psychological Medicine*, *2*, 33–41, 1972.

Kelleher, M.J., & Copeland, J.R.M. Assessment of Neurotic Symptoms in Irish Female Patients. *British Journal of Psychiatry*, *124*, 554–555, 1974.

Kennedy, R.E. *The Irish: Marriage, Immigration and Fertility*. Berkeley: University of California Press, 1978.

Lidz, T. *The Person*. New York: Basic Books, 1968.

Malzberg, B. *Social and Biological Aspects of Mental Disease*. Utica, N.Y.: St. Hospitals Press, 1940.

Malzberg, B. Mental Disease among Native Whites in New York State 1949–51, Classified According to Parentage. *Mental Hygiene*, *48*, 478–499, 1964.

McBride, H. Personal communication, 1981.

McGoldrick, M., & Pearce, J.K. Family Therapy with Irish Americans. *Family Process*, *20*(2), 223–244, 1981.

Messinger, J.C. Sex and Repression in an Irish Folk Community. In J. Marshall & L. Suggs (Eds.), *Human Sexual Behavior*. New York: Basic Books, 1970.

Messinger, J.C. Sexuality: The Lack of the Irish. *Psychology Today*, 41–44, February 1971.

Midelfort, C.F. *Conference on Working with Norwegian Families*. Piscataway, N.J.: Rutgers Medical School, July 1, 1980.

Munch, P.A. French-Canadians. In S. Thernstrom (Ed.), *The Harvard Encyclopedia of American Ethnic Groups*. Cambirdge: Harvard University Press, 1980.

Murphy, H.B.M. Alcoholism and Schizophrenia in the Irish: A Review. *Transcultural Psychiatric Research*, *12*, 116–139, 1975.

O'Faolain, S. *The Irish: A Character Study.* Old Greenwich, Conn.: Devin-Adair, 1949.

O'Neill, E. *The Iceman Cometh.* New York: Vintage, 1957.

Opler, M.K., & Singer, J.L. Ethnic Differences in Behavior and Psychopathology: Italian and Irish. *International Journal of Social Psychiatry, 1*(1), 11–17, 1957.

Papp, P. The Greek Chorus and Other Techniques of Family Therapy. *Family Process, 19*(1), 45–58, 1980.

Pearce, J.K. Ethnicity and Family Therapy: An Introduction. In J.K. Pearce & L. Friedman (Eds.), *Family Therapy: Combining Psychodynamic and Family Systems Approaches.* New York: Grune & Stratton, 1980.

Pollock, H.M. A Statistical Study of the Foreign Insane in New York State Hospitals. *State Hospitals Bulletin,* 10–27, 1913.

Potter, G. *To the Golden Door.* Boston. Little, Brown, 1960.

Rabkin, J.G., & Struening, E.L. *Ethnicity, Social Class, and Mental Illness* (Working Paper Series). New York: Institute on Pluralism and Group Identity, 1976.

Roberts, B., & Myers, J.K. Religion, National Origin, Immigration and Mental Illness. *American Journal of Psychiatry, 110,* 759–764, 1954.

Sanua, V.D. Sociocultural Factors in Responses to Stressful Life Situations: The Behavior of Aged Amputees as an Example. *Journal of Health and Human Behavior, 1,* 17–24, 1960.

Sanua, V.D. Immigration, Migration, and Mental Illness. In E.B. Brody (Ed.), *Behavior in New Environments.* Beverly Hills: Sage, 1970.

Scheper-Hughes, N.D. *Saints, Scholars, and Schizophrenics.* Berkeley: University of California Press, 1979.

Scherman, K. *The Flowering of Ireland: Saints, Scholars and Kings.* Boston: Little, Brown, 1981.

Selvini-Palazzoli, M., Boscolo, L., Cecchin, G., & Prata, G. *Paradox and Counterparadox.* New York: Jason Aronson, 1976.

Selvini-Palazzoli, M., Boscolo, L., Cecchin, G., & Prata, G. Hypothesizing—Circularity—Neutrality: Three Guidelines for the Conductor of the Session. *Family Process, 19*(1), 3–12, 1980.

Shannon, W.V. *The American Irish.* New York: Macmillan, 1963.

Shaw, B. *Complete Plays* (Vol. II). New York: Dodd, Mead, 1968.

Singer, J., & Opler, M.K. Contrasting Patterns of Fantasy and Motility in Irish and Italian Schiozphrenics. *Journal of Abnormal and Social Psychology, 53,* 42–47, 1956.

Sowell, T. *Ethnic America.* New York: Basic Books, 1981.

Spiegel, J. Cultural Strain, Family Role Patterns, and Intrapsychic Conflict. In J.G. Howells (Ed.), *Theory and Practice of Family Psychiatry.* New York: Brunner/Mazel, 1971. (a)

Spiegel, J. *Transactions: The Interplay between Individual, Family and Society* (J. Papajohn, Ed.). New York: Science House, 1971. (b)

Stein, R.F. *Disturbed Youth and Ethnic Family Patterns.* Albany: State University of New York Press, 1971.

Sternbach, R.A., & Tursky, B. Ethnic Differences among Housewives in Psychophysical and Skin Potential Responses to Electric Shock. *Psychophysiology, 1*(3), 241–246, 1965.

Stivers, R. *The Hair of the Dog: Irish Drinking and American Stereotype.* University Park, Penn.: Penn State University Press, 1976.

Torrey, E.F. *Schizophrenia and Civilization.* New York: Jason Aronson, 1980.

Tursky, B., & Sternbach, R.A. Further Physiological Correlates of Ethnic Differences in Response to Shock. *Psychophysiology, 4*(1), 67–74, 1967.

U.S. Bureau of the Census. *Characteristics of the Population by Ethnic Origin: November 1969* (Current Population Report, Series P-20, No. 221). Washington, D.C.: U.S. Government Printing Office, 1971.

Walsh, D. Some Influences on the Intercountry Variation in Irish Psychiatric Hospitalization Rates. *British Journal of Psychiatry, 113,* 15–20, 1968.

Walsh, D., & Walsh, B. Validity of Indices of Alcoholism: A Comment from Irish Experience. *British Journal of Preventive and Social Medicine, 27*, 18–26, 1973.

Weakland, J., Watzlawick, P., & Fisch, R. Brief Therapy: Focused Problem Resolution. *Family Process, 13*(2), 141–168, 1974.

Wills, G. *Bare Ruined Choirs.* Garden City, N.Y.: Doubleday, 1971.

Woodham-Smith, C. *The Great Hunger.* New York: Harper & Row, 1963.

Wylan, L., & Mintz, N. Ethnic Differences in Family Attitudes toward Psychotic Manifestations with Implications for Treatment Programmes. *International Journal of Social Psychiatry, 22*(2), 86–95, 1976.

Zborowski, M. *People in. Pain.* San Francisco: Jossey-Bass, 1969.

Zborowski, M., & Herzog, E. *Life Is with People.* New York: Schocken Books, 1952.

Zola, I.K. Culture and Symptoms: An Analysis of Patients' Presenting Complaints. *American Sociological Review, 5*, 141–155, 1966.

16

Italian Families

MARIE ROTUNNO
MONICA McGOLDRICK

For Italians, the family has been the thread that has provided not only continuity in all situations, but also the training to cope with a difficult world. *La Via Vecchia* (the old way), revered by Italians, symbolizes a value system organized primarily around protecting the family.

This chapter will focus on the character and family patterns of Southern Italians and the implications of these patterns for American families of Italian heritage. The historical, psychological, and sociological background offered here will, we hope, give therapists a framework and a context for understanding their Italian American clients.

What is generally referred to as "Italian" by most Americans is not representative of all Italian culture. It applies primarily to those Italians who trace their ancestry to the southern section of Italy, commonly known as the Mezzogiòrno, who constituted the vast majority of Italian immigrants to the United States. By virtue of geography and economy, Southern Italians have developed different customs, life-styles, nuances in language, and food preferences from their Northern Italian neighbors.

Because of industrialization, Northern Italians have had the benefit of a thriving economy and a relatively prosperous existence. In contrast, Southern Italians, who have relied on farming for their livelihood, have tended to be poorer, less educated, and somewhat more fatalistic in their outlook on life. As one researcher has described it:

> The Northerner is a modern capitalist who seeks wealth as a means of acquiring the material objects he wants; the Southerner seeks wealth as a means of commanding obedience and respect from others. While the North has accepted the modern ethic that power follows wealth, the South clings to the medieval tradition that wealth comes from power. (Ianni & Reuss-Ianni, 1972, p. 16)

Poverty and the hope of a better life led to a large-scale Italian immigration to the United States in the late 19th and early 20th centuries. To date more than 5 million Italians have settled in the United States. The vast

Marie Rotunno. Benton & Bowles, Inc., New York, New York.

Monica McGoldrick. Psychiatry Department, University of Medicine and Dentistry of New Jersey, and Community Mental Health Center of Rutgers Medical School, Piscataway, New Jersey; Faculty, Family Institute of Westchester, White Plains, New York.

majority of them—almost 4 million—came from Southern Italy between 1880 and 1920 (Nelli, 1980). Since the 1960s, the rate of Italian immigration has again risen, making Italy at present the prime source of European immigration (U.S. Immigration and Naturalization Service, 1977). For an outstanding study of recent Italian immigrant families and the implications of their experiences for therapy, see Helene Cassim's study, "The Maintenance of Family Ties in Italian Immigrant Families: A Case Study" (1982). Italians constitute 11.2% of all immigrants to this country, ranking second only to Germans (U.S. Department of Commerce, 1977).

Historical Background: Its Impact on Core Values

While all cultures value the family, for Italians it is their primary orientation (Tomasi, Tomasi, & Engles, 1970; Gambino, 1973, 1974; Barzini, 1965). It is seen as one's greatest resource and protection against all troubles. This attitude can be directly linked to the constant influx of foreigners, changing governments, and overwhelming natural disasters: floods, volcanoes, earthquakes, and famines that have characterized Italian history.

Italy occupies a strategic location on the Mediterranean Sea, and for centuries it has served as a crossroads from western to eastern Europe. Because it was considered desirable to be in possession of "the boot," as Italy was called, it was continually beset by invaders throughout the Middle Ages and on into the Renaissance. The State and wealthy landowners provided no protection against outside forces, and transition of power from one group to another was the rule. Since alliances changed frequently, it was dangerous to be too trusting of anyone with whom they did not have personal connections. Outsiders were viewed with great skepticism and one's sense of personal responsibility extended only to the network of relatives and close friends.

During this period, pilgrimages to and from Rome, the center of the Catholic Church, were also commonplace. This meant an additional flow of foreigners who were a constant and often hostile presence. The Church itself, with its great wealth and properties, was perceived as the ally of the State and wealthy landowners. It was not viewed as a source of comfort or protection by the peasant class.

Italians, who were exploited by the ruling classes, learned to define themselves by their associations with their families and their immediate neighbors. Mutual rights and obligations were powerful and binding on all members of the family (Ianni & Reuss-Ianni, 1972; Femminella & Guadagno, 1978), and allegiance to the family surpassed all other loyalties. Outsiders, even if they had a high level of contact with the family, "were considered important only if they could serve the welfare of the family" (Cassim, 1982). The worst misfortune was to be without a family. Separation from one's family was tantamount to spiritual death. The family consisted, first, of all *cognates* (blood relatives) and all *affines* (relatives by marriage).

Beyond the family came the *comparaggio* (godparents). After their families, Italians belonged not to Italy, but to their *paisani* (village neighbors). Peasants banded together against invading armies, resulting in a territorial camaraderie among neighboring villages.

These historical factors had profound consequences for the Italian character. Against a backdrop of impinging hostile forces, Italians came to rely primarily on their families and on internal resources. Value was placed on the personality traits that would provide a cushion against external instability. Adaptability and stoicism became ethnic trademarks. Rather than attempting to alter the course of events, they took pride in their ability to cope with difficult situations. Resilience became more than an attitude; it became a way of life.

As if to mitigate this fatalistic view, Italians learned to take maximum advantage of the present. They took great pleasure in gatherings and festivals. They developed the ability to experience intense enjoyment, whether in eating, celebrating, fighting, loving, or drinking. Food, in particular, developed a central place both in family celebrations and in daily life. Eating together was at the center of Italian life. Even today eating is a major sensuous experience for Italians, and food is considered a primary source of emotional and physical solace. At Christmas, for example, Italian families may eat for hours, going from one special course to the next. While famous for their wines as well, drinking has historically been viewed only as an accompaniment to the eating ritual. Italians have had a very low rate of alcoholism because drinking was done in context—at the family table.

Italians also found it beneficial to cultivate social skills. Guile, charm, and graciousness could be acquired with a minimum of nourishment from the environment, and a certain degree of power and prestige could be gained by cleverness, a pleasant manner, and a warm smile. Those Italians who successfully manipulated the social milieu were able to shape the events and people in their world in a small way—rewards that, historically, were not vulnerable to being removed by the government, the Church, or the wealthy landowners.

The Immigrants

Between 1900 and 1910, more than 2 million Italians, mostly peasants from Southern Italy, immigrated to the United States. The clash of cultures was enormous. Italian cultural attitudes were in direct contrast to American core values, which emphasize individualism, independence, and personal achievement over group affiliation. By 1910 almost half the Italians who had come to America in the previous 10 years had already returned to Italy.

Of those who stayed, most showed a definite preference for urban living (Bleda, 1978; Ragucci, 1981; Vecoli, 1978). They settled primarily in "little Italies" in cities throughout the mid-Atlantic States and New England. This pattern was largely influenced by the importance they placed on family and neighborhood connections and relationships in which children felt obligated to remain close to aging parents (Campisi, 1948; Fandetti & Gelfand, 1976; Vecoli, 1978; Ragucci, 1981).

Like the Poles, another group whose territory was always threatened (see Chap. 18), Italians took pride in home ownership, not wanting to rent, which would leave them dependent on outsiders. They wanted their homes for comfort, not as showpieces. Home was a symbol of the family, not a status symbol, and the family table was at its center. Even now third-generation Italians with extravagant homes often spend most of their time around the kitchen table, while the other rooms remain unused except when outsiders are entertained.

Finding it difficult to maintain many of their former ties, Italians also learned through necessity to join forces with other Italian immigrants. Out of this grew their first nationalistic awareness of sharing a common heritage with other Italians (Nelli, 1980).

Once they were settled, Italians tended not to move or travel. Many spent their whole lives in the same neighborhood, often without even visiting other parts of the city or town. Even second- and third-generation Italian women may have fears of being out of the safe context of their home environment. One Italian American client, in talking about the difficulty he had getting his wife to move 20 miles away from her original neighborhood, said that for her it was like moving "south of the border." It took four years for him to get her to agree to go, even though it meant a substantial improvement in their living situation. The wife responded, "Yes, and it has taken me 20 more years to get used to the new place." And this was in spite of the fact that she took her mother with her when the family moved.

Achievement, Work, and Education

The disdain for spatial mobility was paralleled in the negative view Italians held toward upward social mobility. The first-generation Italian immigrant interpreted the "American dream" as the opportunity to obtain steady work and provide food and shelter for the family. The value of work was defined not in the abstract but as the visible result of their skill and effort. As Papajohn and Spiegel (1975) have described it:

> The values of individual achievement, planning for the future, and striving to improve his status in the American social system were irrelevant. The law that forced him to send his children to school when they could be working to contribute to the family finances was viewed as an intrusion to be resisted as long as possible. Even children were expected to contribute financially to the family. The child who found himself drawn into the middle-class value system of his teachers and developed strong achievement drives found little support for

these aspirations in the home. Career ambitions were shunned if they seemed to risk alienation from the family and loss of the broad base of societal support provided by the extended family unit. (p. 105)

Italians have viewed education and vocational training as secondary to the security, affection, and the sense of relatedness the family had to offer, and they have not tended to do well academically (Ragucci, 1981; Vecoli, 1978). Identity was derived from the affiliation with the family, not from one's occupation or personal success. This attitude is in contrast to other ethnic groups, such as the Jews, who often made enormous sacrifices so that children could receive the education their parents did not have. Going to college was not expected and, in fact, was often actively discouraged because it was viewed as a threat to family solidarity. One Italian father (second generation) who was expressing regret that he had not fostered his daughter's education said about her: "What did she need an education for? I never had an education. We thought she was smart enough to knock 'em over without an education. And besides that, she had the family, so what did she need calculus for?" This father's attitude is not unique. There is even an old Sicilian proverb that says: "Do not make your children better than yourself" (Ianni & Reuss-Ianni, 1972). To understand this, it is crucial to consider the threat that learning placed on the family system. Education meant that a young person would come under the influence of outside authorities and perhaps leave home to study.

Even work was viewed within the context of its value to the family. Working as a domestic in someone else's home was frowned upon as a usurpation of family loyalty. Work was related to in a person-oriented way (Gans, 1962). Italians scrupulously avoided even appearing to exploit friends. Mutual trust was not to be jeopardized no matter what. "While middle-class Americans view the lack of interest in careers and professional advancement of Italian-Americans as a deficiency in the characters, Italian-Americans view the achievement-oriented activity of Americans as disgracefully selfish" (Papajohn & Spiegel, 1975, p. 109).

Italians, not wanting to work for outsiders, often started family businesses. The businesses naturally added to family solidarity. Italian family businesses are different from those of other groups. For example, Jews may have cutoffs or deep resentments from one generation to the next as a result of competitiveness among family members in business. Italians are more likely to have problems of enmeshment in the family business since everyone is supposed to participate. Even dysfunctional family members are often supported within the system. While this may happen for periods of time in Jewish family businesses, if people are not all contributing to the endeavor, the family is more likely to break up eventually. In Italian families, the problem more often comes if a family member does not want to enter the business. He (since women enter the business usually only as spouses) will usually be torn by a sense of loyalty and obligation and will feel the need to remain in the business no matter what. For example, a son who is educated may be brought back to the family business if something happens to his father or brothers and he is the only one viewed as capable of handling it. For an outsider (e.g., the spouse of the educated son) this commitment to family at the expense of all personal goals may be very difficult to understand and may be interpreted as lack of love for her.

Of course, these characteristics have been mitigated as Italian families of the second and third generations have become assimilated. An excellent example of the shift in attitudes is offered in Ianni and Reuss-Ianni's *A Family Business* (1972). This study of a mafia family illustrates the dependency of the first generation on family and personal ties and shows how more recent generations have moved into the professional world as lawyers and accountants.

Religion

In addition to having been at odds with the core American (primarily WASP) values, Italians have also encountered the hostility of the Irish, who dominated the Catholic Church in the United States and ran the parochial schools where Italians frequently sent their children. As Nelli (1980) states, Italians in America found the Church a "cold, remote, puritanical institution, controlled and often staffed, even in Italian neighborhoods, by the Irish. Even devout Italians resented the Irish domination of the local church and early demanded their own priests" (p. 553).

Far from the asceticism of the Irish Catholic Church, Italians prized church rituals more for their pageantry, spectacle, and value in fostering family celebrations and rites of passage than for their religious significance. As one Italian American, raised in a neighborhood with an Italian church, expressed it: He never had a sense of God as anything but a benign friend of the family until going into an Irish Catholic Church where he was frightened by the priest's sermon about the day of reckoning (Lomonaco, 1980). Most Italians have continued to view the Church as a source of drama and ritual not as a source of authority. However, because the Church has stood for tradition, family, and community, Italians still tend to support it.

Family Patterns and Roles

Italians have two words for walls, one for the internal walls of a building and one for the walls bordering on the outside. This distinction, not made in English, may well reflect the importance Italians place on boundaries. Within the family context itself, all emotions are viewed as understandable. Italians do not have the problems with disallowed feelings that some cultural groups do. Although there are clear values for right and wrong behavior, they are based primarily on how they affect the family. Disgrace to the family is considered the most grievous crime Italians could commit. Taking advantage of strangers may even be admired as cleverness, while taking advantage of a family member would be censured severely as betrayal. At all times, and at all costs, family honor is to be preserved. In time of family crisis, the Italians' first recourse has been, of course, the family. The major difficulty in an Italian system develops when family and individual values conflict.

There is virtually no such thing as a separate nuclear family unit in Italian culture. The network of significant others is usually large, including aunts, uncles, cousins, *gumbares* (old friends and neighbors), as well as godparents, who assume a role of great importance in child rearing. Unlike WASPs, who raise children to be independent and self-sufficient above all else (and who think themselves failures if their children do not leave home on schedule), Italians raise their children to be mutually supportive and to contribute to the family. Separation from the family is not desired, expected, nor easily accepted.

It is not unusual for parents and grandparents to maintain daily contact as seen, for example, when a father of two adolescents went to his mother's home (next door) for dinner rather than eat with his nuclear family. Generally, each family member has a well-delineated role that dictates both the pattern and frequency of contact with various other family members.

The following discussion refers to traditional Italian patterns that are changing rapidly. Therapists must naturally judge for themselves the extent to which these patterns still apply to any particular Italian family.

Father

The father has traditionally been the undisputed head of household, often authoritarian and rigid in his rule setting and guidelines for behavior. A kind of benevolent despot, he usually takes his responsibility to provide for his family very seriously. In addition, all male social activities occurred regularly and were considered important. Even work was not to interfere with this. Therefore, fathers traditionally were often out of the home for either business or pleasure and might not have much interaction with other family members. But as the ultimate authority on "living," they were available for consultation on major decisions. They tended to be viewed as the family sage who could provide the right solution to any problem and commanded the ultimate respect from wife and children.

In keeping with the cultural emphasis on food, Italian men pay a great deal of attention to whether their wives can cook as well as their mothers, which leads women to take great pride in their culinary skills. One Italian patient stated that his marriage almost broke up during the first two years until he got his mother to teach his non-Italian wife how to cook. The same man described his later hospitalization in the back ward of a state hospital as disastrous, not because of the generally wretched conditions but because he "nearly starved to death, the food was so horrible."

Any situation that erodes the Italian father's authority is likely to have a pronounced negative impact on him. The changing role of women in our culture may naturally place great strain on an Italian man who was raised in a traditional context. Giordano and Riotta-Sirey (1981) found that Italian women were very likely to fear violence from men, even if they had never experienced this. One study showed a very low rate of heart disease among Italian men, as long as the community remained closely knit with cohesive social groups and no challenge to the traditional role of the man as head of household (Ragucci, 1981; Stout, Morrow, Brandt, & Wolf, 1964; Bruhn, Philips, & Wolf, 1972; Wolf, Grace, Bruhn, & Stout, 1973). Cassim's (1982) recent study of Italian immigrant families indicated that the fathers were under the greatest psychological stress of all family members.

The adolescence of his children may be particularly difficult for the Italian father since it is the nature of adolescents to question parental and societal values. This is likely to be perceived as disrespect and defiance—an utterly intolerable insult to the father's self-image as head of the family. When his children mature and lose their dependence on him, another difficult period is likely to ensue. As Italian American children attempt to separate from their families of origin, feelings of severe depression, abandonment, and worthlessness are frequently noted in their fathers. This may be expressed in angry outbursts and conflicts over control of the young adults' decisions. Clinicians need to keep this in mind when they are dealing with the sometimes profound reaction an Italian father may have to the apparent advancement (marriage, job relocation, etc.) of his children. The independent strivings of his daughter will be perceived as especially threatening.

Mother

If the Italian father is the head of the family, the Italian mother is its heart. She is the family's emotional sustenance. While yielding authority to the father, she traditionally assumes total control of the emotional realm of the family. Her life centers around domestic activities, and she is expected to receive her primary pleasure from nurturing and servicing her family. Her personal needs take second place to those of her husband, and in exchange she is offered protection and security from all outside pressures or threats. It is common even among second- and third-generation Italian Americans for the wife not to drive a car and for the husband to drive her whenever she needs to go out. This pattern is not usually perceived as a problem by either partner, though to an outsider it may appear to reinforce an extreme degree of dependence.

The status of women in Italian families is paradoxical. Men are the central authority figures (Opler & Singer, 1957; Fantl & Schiro, 1959; Stein, 1971), and women are considered the servers of men. The mother, however, plays a very powerful role, especially in her son's affections (as his wife will hardly fail to notice). Among second-generation Italians, more women worked, but a far lower percentage went to college than did women from other ethnic backgrounds (Vecoli, 1978). It would appear that they could work to help the family, but education for personal development was a different matter. Obviously, by the third generation these patterns change considerably.

Intimacy in marriage is not a high priority (Arenson, 1979). The mutual support and complementarity of roles between husband and wife relate to their obligations to the entire family of at least three generations, not to marital sharing of emotions. Given this heritage, young couples of Italian background may not have models within their extended families for resolving marital issues through negotiation and role flexibility as is encouraged in most marital therapy.

Children

There is a marked role differentiation between sons and daughters in Italian families. Though both are permitted to leave home when they marry, sons are given much greater latitude prior to marriage. A bit of acting out is expected, even subtly encouraged, as a measure of manliness. Proficiency in the sexual domain is especially important, not only to fulfill the masculine image, but also to exemplify a sense of mastery in interpersonal relations—a core Italian value. Although cultivating social skills is considered important for girls as well, they are more restricted than their brothers and boy cousins. They are given more guidance and supervision and, in particular, are taught to eschew personal achievement in favor of respect and service to their parents. Frequently, young Italian women say their adult status was never really accepted by their parents, even after success in career and marriage, until they produced children themselves.

Traditionally, Italian men were trained to control themselves emotionally—to be cautious and understated in their emotional reactions, especially with outsiders. This has nothing to do with embarrassment or inhibition about expressing feelings, as it may with Irish or WASP men. Rather it reflects the historical need to protect themselves against dangerous exposure to outsiders. Women, on the other hand, were allowed to express their emotions freely, but were kept out of "men's business."

One study, done some years ago, which may still have applicability, indicated that Italian mothers were commonly oversolicitous of their sons (Barrabee & von Mering, 1953). Fathers were shown to relate to children in a more rigid way, with little overt display of affection. Mothers tended to act as the buffer between father and sons, and neither parent showed much interest in their children's personal problems.

The lack of concern about children's personal problems in no way reflects a lack of caring about their children but rather the priority of concern for the family as a unit. Children socialized to American values, however, may experience this as a rejection of their individual needs.

Generally speaking, Italian children have shown less conflict about accepting their ethnic background than have other groups but have shown more conflict about their upwardly mobile aspirations, which their families perceive as threatening. This contrasts with other ethnic groups, such as Jews and WASPs, who are more likely to feel anxious that they will not live up to their parents' upwardly mobile ambitions (Barrabee & von Mering, 1953).

> The Marconi family, consisting of an immigrant construction worker, his first-generation wife, and their two children, Willie, 13, and Lisa, 12, illustrate some of the patterns described above. They were in many respects "typically" Italian. The father was the silent but powerful head of household; the mother was a housewife who had a very close and openly affectionate relationship with both children, but particularly with Willie—the identified patient. Willie was performing very poorly in school but was extremely successful socially and was often chided for his "expertise in manly pursuits." He was overprotective of his sister, screening her boyfriends and attempting to regulate much of her behavior. Lisa, even at 12, favored domestic activities, modeling herself after her mother and claiming that she wanted to be a good wife and mother when she grew up.

As might have been expected, the family sought treatment only when Willie's acting out became excessive. His academic difficulties alone did not justify treatment. They merited attention only when coupled with failure in the more important social realm. This demonstrates not only the low priority of educational issues, but also the ways in which various roles develop in the context of the Italian family.

Extended Family

Extended family plays a central role in all aspects of Italian family life including decision making, and it is essential in working with Italian American families to learn the whereabouts and level of contact with relatives. Usually many members of the extended family live in the same neighborhood, if not on the same block or in the same building.

A daughter, rather than a son, is generally expected to assume major responsibility for sick or aging parents. Respect for and responsibility toward older family members is a strong norm in the group, and families have great resistance to admitting older relatives to nursing homes (Fandetti & Gelfand, 1976; Ragucci, 1981). At times these responsibilities may put great strain on the system, but a therapist would do well not to interfere with such arrangements. It is often more helpful to seek ways to support family members since their anxiety may only be heightened if they neglect what they believe is their duty.

The Effects of Acculturation

Becoming integrated into American life has not been without its price for Italians. Integration has been accompanied by a confusion of identity that has left second- and third-generation Italian Americans feeling not quite American and certainly not Italian in the sense of the traditions described above (Tomasi *et al.*, 1970). For example, second-generation Italian Americans often find that sticking close to home is not heavily rewarded in America, and they begin to question the tremendous allegiance to family. In fact, they may be in continuous conflict with family members who feel neglected or abandoned. They may simultaneously experience an internal bewilderment—or even despair—as a result of the opposite message they are receiving from society. The second generation may have the greatest problem developing a positive sense of identity since they are most vulnerable to the internalization of negative images that the larger culture has about them. In order to accomplish the complex task of assimilation, this group has often denied a good portion of their Italian heritage (Greeley & McCready, 1975). The result has sometimes been a discomfort with signs and symbols of ethnicity, such as names, styles of dress, and language. In the attempt to belong, the old culture was merely put aside, though not without a great deal of conflict and loss. By the third generation, family ties have generally loosened, reflecting values preferred by the larger culture. In-group solidarity having diminished, Italian Americans may in some cases feel a void or sense of cultural and personal anomie. The film *Saturday Night Fever* is an extremely sensitive portrayal of the void Italian Americans may experience in distancing from their roots.

A shift in family roles has gone hand in hand with the breakdown of family ties. In the transition from the first to the second generation, Italian fathers may lose their high status and their power in decision making. However, what is actually the product of shifting cultural values is often experienced as a loss of self-esteem on the part of the Italian man. As he begins to share power with his wife, the Italian husband is likely to feel that the discrepancy between present attitudes and those prevailing in his father's time results from his personal failure to command the proper respect. Thus, he may exhibit an increase in defensiveness and insecurity regarding his "maleness." Often this is manifested clinically as depression.

> Joe, a middle-aged, second-generation Italian, had attained modest economic success as a salesman. He reported a global disinterest in living. He felt that his wife was not humble enough and that his children answered him back to an excessive degree. In reality, his wife and children were merely independent thinkers who questioned (rather than passively accepted) Joe's dictates. Consequently, he felt challenged, compromised, and insulted. Unfortunately, he was caught in the delicate balance between living as his father had lived—with absolute obedience from his family—

and living with contemporary values. This clash between old ways and his present experience seemed to him to be a reflection of his personal ineptitude.

This father's posture is an understandable product of Italian American assimilation. An initial step toward resolution of this problem would be the involvement of other family members in therapy and a reframing of their behavior as something other than an insult to the father. The father could be complimented for creating a family in which each member took individual initiatives that reflected positively on the family.

Similarly, second-generation Italian American women have moved away from the center of domestic life and are more likely to be employed outside the home than were their mothers. They may have completed some high school and perhaps college or vocational school as well. Unlike her grandmother, a third-generation Italian woman may be solidly advancing outside the domestic sphere and is no longer defined primarily by her role as wife and mother.

Second- and third-generation mothers are also more likely to foster their children's advancement than were their forebears. If this entails departure from the home for educational or vocational purposes, they tend to be more supportive than were immigrant or first-generation parents. Indeed, there is a changing view toward education, with children being more often encouraged to stay in school and to seek employment outside the confines of the neighborhood.

In American culture, the conflicts between the value of family and of education, in particular, have made the period of adolescence extremely stressful for Italian families. Frequently, the second-generation Italian American adolescent has broken away from the family and replaced it with the gang, developing a strong peer culture. This reflects the ongoing need for a tight, close system and fits with the common Italian trait of being gregarious and having a wide social circle (Rabkin & Struening, 1976). It has also been common for Italians who do go to college to live at home and commute, allowing the younger generation a transitional phase between the American ideal of going away to college and the need to preserve family ties.

By the third generation, most Italian Americans have, at least to some degree, accommodated to the prevailing norms and have adopted the customs, life-style, and language of the larger culture. They often have looser connections with nuclear and extended family members. Many have married non-Italians, moved to different neighborhoods, and developed relationships with other nationalities. Ironically, it is these third-generation Italian Americans who sometimes embrace the very same aspects of culture their parents saw as manifestations of being "just off the boat." Much of the tension about cultural identity has subsided, and they are generally able to internalize American core values without rejecting their Italian ethnicity.

Implications for Family Therapy

Italians have had lower rates of psychiatric hospitalization in this country than most other immigrant groups (Sanua, 1970). This was also true for Italian immigrants to England (Cochrane, 1977), although one Canadian study showed a low rate only for Italian men (Murphy, 1978).

The relatively low utilization of mental health facilities and other social support facilities by Italians reflects their tendency to turn to the family for support (Rabkin & Struening, 1976). The primacy Italians give to the family leads them to relate to all problems within this context. Indeed they have been much less likely than other immigrant groups to form mutual aid societies or other community-based groups because of the primacy of the informal family support system (Vecoli, 1978).

For this reason, family intervention would seem the treatment of choice. However, since everyone outside the family is mistrusted until proven otherwise, gaining acceptance as an outsider is the first hurdle in dealing with Italians. Anyone who tries to break the close bonds of the Italian family collides with their cultural norms and is likely to be treated with suspicion. The therapist must not take this initial mistrust personally.

Italians have similar attitudes toward medical professionals. Entrusting their well-being to a physician requires a trust that often takes years to accrue, and Italians refrain from seeking outside help until the situation has reached a point of dire emergency (Twaddle, 1969). Roberts and Myers (1954) found Italians reluctant to enter a hospital, even for a severe physical illness, out of a deep-seated fear of doctors and the belief that a "hospital is a place where one goes to die" (p. 109).

Therapy with Italian families involves not so much helping them deal with any particular emotional issue (such as death, sex, or hostility), as facilitating the renegotiation of system boundaries that tend to rigidify— holding insiders (family members) in and keeping outsiders (everyone else) out. Given the previously mentioned distrust of nonfamily members and the strong tendency to use family resources to solve difficulties, the problem is likely to have reached a serious level by the time an Italian family seeks help. However, it is important to distinguish between a severe presenting problem and a dramatic presentation of a problem that may be exaggerated in hopes of getting an immediate response (Zola, 1963, 1966; Zborowski, 1969).

Italians have a penchant for histrionics. They are often much more interested in engaging and entertaining their listener than in conveying thoughts accurately. Characteristically colorful in their talk, they also express more emotional tension and hostility when under stress than many other groups—notably the Irish, to whom they are often compared (Tsushima, 1968; Singer & Opler, 1956; Opler & Singer, 1957; Fantl & Schiro, 1959; Greeley & McCready, 1975; Stein, 1971; Sternbach & Tursky, 1965; Zola,

1966; Zborowski, 1969). This may take the form of loud-pitched voices, elaborate gesturing, or arguments among family members. In early visits with an Italian family, as in any good evaluation, it is important to be alert to the differences between style and content. As has been noted by Papajohn and Spiegel (1975): "Bragging, dramatic impersonation either by impromptu acting or by telling long circumstantial tales, and histrionic exaggeration are part of everyday behavior. In Italy and in Italian-American communities, life would seem colorless without these touches of the *commedia dell'arte*" (p. 109).

The expressive intensity of the Italian family may be overpowering to a therapist from a more restrained culture in which, for example, powerful verbal expressions would be interpreted literally. For Italians, words are not meant literally. They give expression to the moment; their purpose is not logical or measured. This difference is extremely important in intermarriage, where the non-Italian spouse may be emotionally overwhelmed or devastated by the partner's words, especially those expressed in anger. The Italian partner is often totally unaware of the impact he or she is making. The intensity and expressiveness of the Italian spouse in other areas, such as enjoyment, charm, and emotional warmth are usually sources of appeal to a spouse from a more restrained background.

In therapy Italians tend to give rather detailed narratives of how their problems began, albeit in a rather diffuse way. They are likely to spend a great deal of time discussing the emotional impact and the social context of the problem, as well as any physical sensations (Zola, 1966). They have been shown to have a lower pain threshold than other groups, reflecting their sensitivity to their immediate physical experience (Sternbach & Tursky, 1965; Tursky & Sternbach, 1967). Where WASPs emphasize inability to function and Jews fear of the implications of their illness for longevity, Italians emphasize their pain experience and wish for its relief (Twaddle, 1969). A large study of symptomatology among soldiers of different ethnic backgrounds showed Italians to be much more symptomatic than several other ethnic groups (Croog, 1961).

Italians tend to somatize and have much concern and awareness about the connections between their emotional and physical well-being. Bodily attention is focused especially on malfunctions of the gastrointestinal tract and the liver (Ragucci, 1981). In fact, for some reason, first-generation Italian Americans of all ages ascribe their physical complaints more often to the liver than to any other part of their body (Ragucci, 1981).

The differences in definition of "appropriate" emotional expression may lead to problems in diagnosis. Italians have been found to have a high rate of affective disorders (Roberts & Myers, 1954). A Boston study of Italian Americans in a medical clinic showed that when no organic base for their illness could be found, they were more often labeled as having "psychiatric problems" than were other groups. This occurred despite the fact that there was no evidence that psychosocial problems were more frequent among them (Zola, 1973).

Another comparative study done in a health care setting (Zborowski, 1969) indicated that when having difficulty, Italian patients were much more preoccupied than were other groups with getting immediate relief. Where Jews, for example, worried about the long-range effects of drugs given to relieve pain, Italians had little such concern. They wanted medication and worried more about the effects of their pain on their present situation— work, finances, family. Once the pain was relieved, they easily forgot their sufferings and manifested a happy disposition.

Since the family experiences considerable distress when a member cannot carry out valued roles and tasks, the social and family relationship consequences of any problem will be among the primary concerns of Italian Americans (Zola, 1964; Ragucci, 1981). Much of their initial recounting may also be attempts to justify their behavior and to gain reassurance from the therapist that they are not to blame. It is extremely important to convey this reassurance.

Aside from the strong emotional tone that will probably characterize the first meeting, the therapist should anticipate certain frequent presenting complaints. For example, an Italian family is unlikely to seek treatment for a marital issue. There will be a great investment in perpetuating the view that the husband–wife relationship—the mainstay of family life—is basically solid, however much conflict there may be on the surface. Italians can more readily accept psychiatric help if the problem defined involves their child. Even in these circumstances, Italian parents are likely to contact mental health services only after consulting with family and neighbors and upon referral from a third party.

The intense, negative cultural valence experienced by the family seeking therapy will compound the content of the presenting problem. Because parents are more receptive to assistance for their children, joining the family around a child-focused problem is one method of breaking through family resistance. Such intervention would be tolerated best in the form of "advice" rather than "exploration" since parents expect to be given some direct help in no uncertain haste. If the family is in "crisis," it is essential that the therapist avoid lengthy discussion or evaluation and give them some response to their problem. Though quick solutions to complex problems are impossible, even a seemingly benign or insignificant suggestion might be sufficient to hold a family until more subtle and enduring interventions can be determined. An important caution, however, is not to offer advice that undercuts the family's authority. Emphasizing the family's wisdom and use of its own resources is best in offering any suggestions.

While Italian families may appear to talk openly and engagingly, even in the initial contact, sharing real family secrets is an entirely different matter.

Italian families are full of "secrets," as the therapist will soon learn by asking a question that is out of bounds. The existence of secrets may be puzzling to the therapist since the family seems to talk openly about all kinds of issues, including sex, bodily functions, and hostility. The content of the secret is often not important. Secrets tend to be aimed more at preserving the boundaries of the system—clarifying who is inside and who is not. Therapists must deal delicately with secrets, being aware of the sense of betrayal families will feel if the boundaries are crossed. The content of secrets is often not important to therapy, and the therapist is advised to proceed on the assumption that the secret is a boundary-keeping maneuver until clinical evidence indicates otherwise. Pushing the family to tell their secrets will usually only heighten mistrust and resistance. In general, therapists must adjust the depth and range of topics addressed to the degree of their closeness with family members and not press with questions that might jeopardize their position with the family.

The newest method of Selvini Palazzoli (Selvini Palazzoli & Prata, 1982) for working with very rigid families revolves totally around getting the parents into a collusion with them to "keep a secret to the grave," excluding everyone else in the entire family from information about the therapeutic suggestions. The power of secrets as boundary markers in Italian families makes this ritual an extraordinarily good strategy with them. In general Selvini-Palazzoli considers a family member's offer to reveal a secret as one of the major "snares" in family therapy (Selvini Palazzoli & Prata, in press).

Italians typically manifest overt denial of difficult problems. It is characteristic that "hot" issues are not openly discussed. This again can be misleading since we might expect such an expressive people to relate pertinent issues easily. On the contrary, with Italians it is of particular value to attend to what is not being said. Though underlying issues are prominent in therapy with all individuals, regardless of ethnic background, they are of special relevance to Italians. They do more sidestepping than most in the initial stage of therapy, which is an outgrowth of their unwillingness to expose private subjects to outsiders.

This presentation and the related "dancing" around issues fit into the Italian cultural context. While Italians may talk readily about most life experiences, even incest, violence, death, or antisocial behavior, family members are ashamed about having to go outside of the family for help. The implication is that if they had greater control over themselves, their impulses, their family, and so forth, these problems would never have developed to the point of needing an outsider. Indeed, it is somewhat ironic that control in this sphere is emphasized, while lack of control over outside events (e.g., disasters) is accepted. It is almost as if to compensate for perceived lack of control over the external environment Italians emphasized the ability to maintain control over their own families. In any case a sense of humiliation, particularly for fathers, in being unable to control their families may at times make Italians difficult to engage. They may fear that therapy is some form of punishment that is merely to be endured on directive from some outside authority (or referring agency). This belief could clearly interfere with the therapeutic process and should be dealt with in early sessions, perhaps by connoting the family positively for its strength in seeking help when needed.

The therapist must somehow move from the position of "mistrusted outsider" to the point of being granted authority to deal with the Italian family. Frequently Italians put a therapist through many tests of loyalty and skill in establishing authority. The resistance to treatment revealed in the continuous testing and retesting of the therapist's loyalty and authority may be very trying for a non-Italian therapist. One example of this was a family who continuously initiated discussion of the therapist's motivation.

> There were five teenagers in this family who were particularly provocative. In the beginning, they made fun of the cotherapists, saying all they were interested in was their high fee. After some time, the therapists moved away but continued to commute to the area monthly to see the family. At this point the teenagers began saying that the therapists were fools to work for so little money since the commute was so long. The therapists (both WASPs), who felt that their behavior with the family was consistent, were put off by this. Only when the comments were considered in the light of Italian values did they come to see this suspiciousness and testing as reflecting the Italian mistrust of the motivations of outsiders and the need to reassure themselves that the therapists were worthy of being trusted with personal business.

Another example of distrust is the case of a family who requested that the therapist provide erroneous information to the school to prove unflinching loyalty, despite the illegalities involved. This latter case also illustrates the Italian bias in favor of personal loyalty over objective rules for right and wrong, especially in dealing with bureaucracies. Unlike WASPs, who generally respect institutions and institutional rules for propriety, Italians (like Greeks, Turks, and Iranians) have had little reason to develop trust in such systems. They tend to assume that the smart person will take advantage of government bureaucracies and social agencies.

As therapy proceeds with Italian Americans, there are various patterns that we may expect to confront. For example, significant crisis periods are likely to accompany the separation of family members. Although this is almost a truism in any family where strong bonding exists, it is especially so with Italians and may take unusual forms. Events that are surrounded with much celebration and fanfare in other families might propel an Italian family into considerable conflict, for example, a job promotion that necessitates moving away from the family, acceptance into a prestigious university that is far from home, and, of course, getting married. While these experiences may be sources of advancement or personal growth for the individual, they are likely to be experienced negatively if they weaken the "collective" sense of family.

Not surprisingly, such strong emotional ties result in frequent symbiotic-like relationships between parents and children, and Italian families may not achieve the level of differentiation that predominates in the larger culture. Therapists are often perplexed or even overwhelmed by this enmeshment, as when the father, mother, and grandparents insist on making the decisions for a hospitalized young adult schizophrenic.

Although such enmeshment often creates problems, it would be an error to label it pathogenic in and of itself. In fact, if emotional fusion is not overtly present, the therapist should probe for it. Its apparent absence could indicate the aforementioned "buried" issue. Considerable work, and indeed the primary task in therapy with Italians, often revolves around helping family members to disengage from the system to some degree in order to attain an equilibrium that will be comfortable for all. However, the common therapeutic goal of disengaging young schizophrenics from their families of origin and arranging alternate living arrangements when they leave a psychiatric hospital may be so unacceptable as to be inappropriate for many Italian families. Therapists may need to work patiently for a minimal establishment of boundaries within such systems, such as arranging for the schizophrenic to live on a separate floor in the house or to have some other territorial and emotional boundaries established within the home.

Therapeutic goals often reflect core American ideals—individualism, mastery over problems, and economic advancement. These are not particularly compatible with Italian core values. Italians may not take as an inalienable right their ability to master the problems they confront. Centuries of experience have failed to give them a sense of control over their environment or their fate. The most they may expect is to get a portion of their needs met through their own personal attributes, and it is understandable why they often choose an indirect method (cunning, guile, or cleverness) to achieve a measure of personal efficacy and power. Again, this tendency is not necessarily indicative of sociopathic inclination but is instead a reflection of an historically successful method of obtaining rewards. Rather than trying to eliminate these behaviors, treatment might be geared toward utilizing them in a socially appropriate manner.

Another difference in values is that Italians may not value going on vacation as the best reward for their labors. While vacationing is a powerful American value, it means going away from home and for Italians may thus be of little interest. The younger generation may have trouble handling their parent's disapproval of their wishes to go on trips. Encouraging them to be respectful of their parents' values while maintaining their right to disagree will usually help deflect the younger generation's guilt and ease the parents' sense of anger and rejection. If the younger generation can learn to manage their differentiation without defiance and can maintain a loving posture toward the family while separating from it, a lot of pain will be avoided on both sides.

Once the therapist wins the family's trust, most of the therapy will revolve around helping family members differentiate without cutoffs occurring. The next real problem for the therapist becomes how to terminate therapy and leave the family when the time comes. The therapeutic issue becomes how to extricate oneself from the system. Families may attempt to absorb therapists into the system and to make them auxiliary family members.

> A touching example of this was a family seen for three sessions because the 25-year-old daughter had become agoraphobic and would not leave the house. Three other siblings also in their 20s were still living at home. In the first session the family expressed much distrust of the therapist and had great reluctance in exposing their "family business." The therapist labeled the family as the daughter's greatest resource, connoted positively the family's caring, and reframed the phobia of the daughter, who in the past had experienced so many painful separations, as a wish to spend more time in close connection to her family. At the second session the therapist suggested that discussing the daughter's giving up her phobias would be premature at the moment because she needed more time to absorb the warmth of the loving family circle to prepare for eventually going out on her own. By the third and last session the daughter had gotten a job through her brother's help, had begun dating, and was no longer phobic. She expressed much thanks to the therapist and gave her a purse as a gift. The family invited the therapist to a barbecue. When the therapist said she could not come as she was leaving the area, the mother said, "Well come when you get back to town. You're always welcome." As the family left, each woman in turn hugged the therapist and the father shook her hand heartily, thanking her for all she had done for them.

Somehow, the therapist must find ways to avoid becoming sucked into the system as a member while being sufficiently engaging to maintain respect and connection. The special techniques developed by the Milan Group seem particularly well suited to the enmeshment of Italian families. They maintain an acceptable connection with the family as well as adequate distance by using the stance of doctor–consultant who asks questions and then gives an evaluation and a prescription. The group places much emphasis on keeping out of the family process, using a team, a one-way window, and videotaping as tools for this. Their focus is on gathering information about the evolutionary connections among family members that are rigidifying the family process, impeding flexibility, and prohibiting further family development. They aim for an intervention that is dramatic enough to create new motion in the family and yet leaves the therapists out of the actual changes. They take great pains to keep their focus and interventions on the family as a whole, a factor of special importance with Italian families. By carefully addressing themselves to the family's myths and values, as well as to their systemic interdependencies, the Milan Group tries to push the family toward a new pattern.

Bowen systems therapy (1978) also focuses on understanding and shifting the family process while staying out of the system, but it avoids dramatic interventions. This avoidance could prevent the engagement necessary for Italian families to make use of Bowen's approach. However, the Bowen model appears to be the treatment of choice with Italians who have already distanced from their families since its primary focus is differentiation through personalized connectedness. An important problem for Italian Americans who move away from their families is the sense of loneliness and isolation they may feel, despite success by "mainstream" criteria—money, education, social status. Often, young Italian Americans seek therapy for support in cutting off from their families in attempts at pseudoindependence. Therapists may mistakenly foster this by emphasizing the individual experience over the need to maintain interpersonal connectedness. The family context is so deeply rooted for Italians that other structures will usually be shallow and inadequate by comparison.

Therapists would do best to encourage Italian Americans to negotiate their individuality within the family, even though this is a painful process and not easily accomplished. Because of the deep meaning of family to Italians, the price they pay for emotional disconnection is high. They are usually relieved and grateful to find ways to become reconnected to their families without becoming engulfed. Coaching such family members usually involves encouraging them to space out family contacts while advocating a high degree of emotional expressiveness while they are with their families. Clients need to be prepared at each step of differentiation to deal with their family's intense reactions, which include feelings of betrayal, abandonment, and rejection.

While therapists are often trained to seek truth for truth's sake, Italians more often want to prove themselves right and to preserve their family's honor. They commonly request confirmation and commitment from others in the form of: "Am I right or wrong?" These direct demands for support cannot be greeted by silence or intellectualized distancing but require at least a response that respects and responds to the intensity of their wish for connection. It is crucial for the therapist to validate the family as a whole, as well as to promote the sense of identity of its individual members. The therapist must not pursue goals counter to the family's views of itself and its needs. Even more than with other groups, it is necessary to give the family credit for change.

Therapists trained to value independence and individuality must realize that Italians may interpret these values as selfish and believe instead that family members are bound to work out each other's relationships and problems. For example, if an Italian American family accepts the middle-class concept of the independent nuclear family handling its own affairs, the grandparents may feel betrayed.

> In one such family, the grandparents visited their granddaughter at a residential school every week and continuously told the school authorities how to handle her. The granddaughter was in conflict with her parents, who felt undercut by the grandparents whenever they tried to establish regulations for their daughter. During a therapy session with the whole family, the parents confronted the grandparents with their wish to raise their daughter by themselves. The grandparents became anxious and threatened. "Why?" said the grandmother. "What did I do that's so bad? A grandmother that overloved a child and worried about her a lot. What's wrong with that?"

For these grandparents, the level of their involvement was absolutely consistent with their values. For the parents their actions were "intrusive" and "inappropriate." Obviously such enmeshment may be dysfunctional in our culture, but offhand labeling of it as pathological will only increase family anxiety. Even as family members are encouraged and helped to differentiate, the positive aspects of family caring must be stressed.

Summary

Though several striking departures from American customs have been out-lined, it may be most constructive to consider these ethnic proclivities as potential strengths, rather than impediments, to therapy. To name one, the ability to capitalize on interpersonal qualities has tremendous social poten-tial. Though sometimes confused with "manipulation," there are numerous instances in which skill in social exchange can be of value.

Another example would be Italian resourcefulness, which has over time become a finely honed skill in the face of adversity. Italians have learned to utilize environmental support effectively and to extract whatever good is possible from a seemingly hopeless situation.

While the enmeshment characteristic of Italian families certainly creates difficulties and conflicts for them in U.S. culture, Italian families provide much that people from less supportive cultural environments lack. In fact, research indicates that their emotional problems increase markedly when they lose these family supports (Rabkin & Struening, 1976). Researchers who studied Italians in Boston found the incidence of schizophrenia and manic–depressive disorders inversely related to the population density of Italian Americans in the area (Mintz & Schwartz, 1976). Interestingly, they did not find that social class was positively correlated with mental disorder for this group, as it is with so many other ethnic groups.

Similarly, Fitzpatrick (1969), a sociologist who studied rates of delin-quency in several communities, found that the rate of delinquency in the Italian community was only one-seventh as great as in a neighboring area. He attributed the lower rate of delinquency among Italians to their highly developed intermediate structures. The local politicians, lawyers, and police, as well as stores and banks controlled by local merchants, provided "linking mechanisms" with the larger structures of the city, while at the same time maintaining the group's ethnic identity.

The strength of the Italian family can also be a source of solidity and reinforcement in times of stress, providing both stability and structure. In fact, Italian families are among the most stable in the United States today. They exhibit a low rate of divorce, a low rate of single-parent households, and a relatively low rate of hospitalization. Instead of placing their sick, elderly, or mentally disabled family members in the care of outsiders, the family prefers to care for their own. Extended family are extremely important in this regard because they enrich the environmental support systems and increase the available resources. Network therapy would be particularly appropriate in working with Italian families since it acknowledges the family's primary resource and promotes maintenance of gains after therapy has ended.

A therapist who places any value before that of the family either will be rejected or will set family members against each other and against core aspects of their identity. The therapist who remains too distant will be perceived as cold and unfeeling and will be shut out. On the other hand, the therapist who responds too emotionally is likely to be drawn into the system and become immobilized in the emotion and drama of it. Thus, some intermediate stance may be most constructive. Where family members are attempting to cut off from the family, the therapist needs to help them remain emotionally connected. Where their enmeshment is leading to family dysfunction, the therapist needs to cultivate the family's tolerance for individuation.

Therapists may be frustrated by the Italian family's demand for immediate solutions. If a therapist operates on the assumption that change occurs through long evaluation and discussion of problems, Italian families will be exceedingly difficult to help. If, however, the therapist focuses on mobilizing the family's own natural supports and does not try to replace this value with one that regards therapy as the primary source of help, there is a much better chance of constructive intervention.

Although "talking things over with a therapist" may not be particularly valued by Italian Americans as a means of solving problems, the notion that the family is the basic healing context—a fundamental assumption of family therapists—probably meets nowhere with better understanding than among Italian families. Their concern for each other is a tremendous asset that needs to be addressed and channeled for effective therapeutic change.

ACKNOWLEDGMENTS

Our thanks to Joe Giordano, Olga Rabke, Gianfranco Cecchin, Luigi Boscolo, and Helene Cassim for their support and helpful suggestions which have been integrated into this chapter, although the authors bear full responsibility for the opinions expressed.

REFERENCES

Arenson, S.J. Rankings of Intimacy of Social Behaviors by Italians and Americans. *Psychological Reports, 44*, 1149–1150, 1979.

Barrabee, P., & von Mering, O. Ethnic Variation in Mental Stress in Families with Psychotic Children. *Social Problems*, No. 1, 48–53, 1953.

Barzini, L. *The Italians.* New York: Bantam Books, 1965.

Bleda, S.E. Intergenerational Differences in Patterns and Bases of Ethnic Residential Dissimilarity. *Ethnicity, 5*, 91–107, 1978.

Bowen, M. *The Use of Family Therapy in Clinical Practice.* New York: Jason Aronson, 1978.

Bruhn, J.G., Philips, B.V., & Wolf, S. Social Readjustment and Illness Patterns: Comparison between First, Second, and Third Generation Italian-Americans Living in the Same Community. *Journal of Psychosomatic Research, 16*, 387–394, 1972.

Campisi, P. Ethnic Family Patterns: The Italian Family in the United States. *American Journal of Sociology, 53*, 1948.

Cassim, H. *The Maintenance of Family Ties in Italian Immigrant Families: A Case Study.* Master's thesis, Hahnemann Medical College, Philadelphia, 1982.

Cochrane, R. Mental Illness in Immigrants to England and Wales: An Analysis of Mental Hospital Admissions—1971. *Social Psychiatry, 12*, 25–35, 1977.

Croog, S.H. Ethnic Origins and Responses to Health Questionnaires. *Human Organization, 20*, 61–69, 1961.

Fandetti, C.V., & Gelfand, D.E. Care of the Aged: Attitudes of White Ethnic Families. *Gerontologist, 16*, 544–549, 1976.

Fantl, B., & Schiro, J. Cultural Variables in the Behavior Patterns and Symptom Formation of 15 Irish and 15 Italian Female Schizophrenics. *International Journal of Social Psychiatry, 4*(4), 245–253, 1959.

Femminella, F.X., & Guadagno, J.S. The Italian American Family. In C.H. Mindel & R.W. Habenstein (Eds.), *Ethnic Families in America: Patterns and Variations.* New York: Elsevier, 1978.

Fitzpatrick, J. *The Role of White Ethnic Communities in the Urban Adjustment of Newcomers.* Paper presented at the Chicago Consultation on Ethnicity, 1969.

Gambino, R. La Famiglia: Four Generations of Italian-Americans. In J.A. Ryan (Eds.), *White Ethnics: Life in Working-Class America.* Englewood Cliffs, N.J.: Prentice-Hall, 1973.

Gambino, R. *Blood of My Blood: The Dilemma of Italian-Americans.* New York: Doubleday, 1974 (paperback).

Gans, H. *The Urban Villagers.* New York: Free Press, 1962.

Giordano, J., & Riotta-Sirey, J. *An Italian American Identity.* Unpublished paper, Institute on Pluralism and Group Identity, New York, 1981.

Greeley, A.M., & McCready, W. The Transmission of Cultural Heritages: The Case of Irish and Italians. In N. Glazer & D. Moynihan (Eds.), *Ethnicity: Theory and Experience.* Cambridge: Harvard University Press, 1975.

Ianni, P.A., & Reuss-Ianni, E. *A Family Business: Kinship and Social Control in Organized Crime.* New York: Russell Sage, 1972.

Lomonaco, S. *Presentation on Italian American Families.* Introduction to Culture Course, Albert Einstein College of Medicine, Bronx Psychiatric Center Residency Program, July 1980.

Mintz, N., & Schwartz, D. Urban Ecology and Psychosis: Community Factors in the Incidence of Schizophrenia and Manic Depression among Italians in Greater Boston. *International Journal of Social Psychiatry, 10*(2), 101–118, 1976.

Murphy, H.B.M. European Cultural Offshoots in the New World: Differences in Their Mental Hospitalization Patterns: Part 1. British, French and Italian Influences. *Social Psychiatry, 13*, 1–9, 1978.

Nelli, H.S. Italians. In S. Thernstrom (Ed.), *Harvard Encyclopedia of American Ethnic Groups*. Cambridge: Harvard University Press, 1980.

Opler, M.K., & Singer, J.L. Ethnic Differences in Behavior and Psychopathology: Italian and Irish. *International Journal of Social Psychiatry, 1*(1), 11–17, 1957.

Papajohn, J., & Spiegel, J. *Transactions in Families*. San Francisco: Jossey-Bass, 1975.

Rabkin, J., & Struening, E. *Ethnicity, Social Class and Mental Illness in New York City: A Social Area Analysis of Five Ethnic Groups* (Working Paper No. 17). New York: Institute on Pluralism and Group Identity, 1976.

Ragucci, A.T. Italian Americans. In A. Hargood (Ed.), *Ethnicity and Medical Care*. Cambridge: Harvard University Press, 1981.

Roberts, B., & Myers, J.K. Religion, National Origin, Immigration & Mental Illness. *American Journal of Psychiatry, 110*, 759–764, 1954.

Sanua, V.D. Immigration, Migration and Mental Illness. In E.B. Brody (Ed.), *Behavior in New Environments*. Beverly Hills: Sage, 1970.

Selvini Palazzoli, M., & Prata G. *Trialogue Conference*. Philadelphia, February 12–14, 1982.

Selvini Palazzoli, M., & Prata G. Snares in Family Therapy. *Journal of Marital and Family Therapy*, in press.

Singer, J., & Opler, M.K. Contrasting Patterns of Fantasy and Motility in Irish and Italian Schizophrenics. *Journal of Abnormal and Social Psychology, 53*, 42–47, 1956.

Stein, R.F. *Disturbed Youth and Ethnic Family Patterns*. Albany, N.Y.: State University of New York Press, 1971.

Sternbach, R., & Tursky, B. Ethnic Differences among Housewives in Psychophysical and Skin Potential Responses to Electric Shock. *Psychophysiology, 1*(3), 241–246, 1965.

Stout, C., Morrow, J., Brandt, E.N., & Wolf, S. Study of an Italian American Community in Pennsylvania: Unusually Low Incidence of Deaths from Myocardial Infarction. *Journal of the American Medical Association, 188*, 845–849, 1964.

Tomasi, S.M., Tomasi, C.S., & Engles, M.H. (Eds.). *The Italian Experience in the United States*. New York: Center for Migration Studies, 1970.

Tsushima, W. Responses of Irish and Italian Patients of Two Social Classes under Preoperative Stress. *Journal of Personality and Social Psychology, 8*(1), 43–48, 1968.

Tursky, B., & Sternbach, R.A. Further Physiological Correlates of Ethnic Differences in Response to Shock. *Psychophysiology, 4*(1), 67–74, 1967.

Twaddle, A.C. Health Decisions and Sick Role Variations: An Exploration. *Journal of Health & Social Behavior, 10*, 105–115, 1969.

U.S. Department of Commerce, Bureau of the Census. *Statistical Abstracts of the United States* (98th annual ed.). Washington, D.C.: U.S. Government Printing Office, 1977.

U.S. Immigration and Naturalization Service. *Annual Report*. Washington, D.C.: U.S. Government Printing Office, 1977.

Vecoli, R.J. The Coming of Age of the Italian Americans: 1945–1974. *Ethnicity, 15*, 119–147, 1978.

Wolf, S., Grace, K.L., Bruhn, J., & Stout, C. Roseto Revisited: Further Data on Incidence of Myocardial Infarction in Roseto and Neighboring Pennsylvania Communities. *Transactions of American Clinical Climatological Association, 85*, 100–108, 1973.

Zborowski, M. *People in Pain*. San Francisco: Jossey-Bass, 1969.

Zola, I.K. Problems of Communication, Diagnosis and Patient Care: The Interplay of Patient, Physician and Clinic Organization. *Journal of Medical Education, 38*, 829–838, 1963.

Zola, I.K. Illness Behavior of the Working Class. In A. Shostak & W. Gomberg (Eds.), *Blue Collar World*. Englewood Cliffs, N.J.: Prentice-Hall, 1964.

Zola, I.K. Culture and Symptoms—An Analysis of Patients' Presenting Complaints. *American Sociological Review, 5*, 615–630, 1966.

Zola, I.K. Pathways to the Doctor—From Person to Patient. *Social Science and Medicine, 7*, 677–684, 1973.

17

Jewish Families[1]

FREDDA M. HERZ

ELLIOTT J. ROSEN

There are approximately 6 million people in the United States today who call themselves Jews (Sanua, 1978; Siegel & Rheins, 1980), but, as with many ethnic groups, grouping and classifying them into a single category is impossible (Massarik & Chimkin, 1974). How can we describe an ethnic group on the move, with thousands of years of history, yet no single language or country of origin? This question itself suggests a further peculiarity of this group: Their ethnic identity and religious life are often so interwoven as to be indistinguishable. To understand the complexity of identifying this group, we will consider the demographic and historical roots of the Jewish American community.

A small proportion of the Jews in the United States are descendants of Sephardic (Spanish) Jews who trace their origins in this country back more than two centuries (Glazer, 1957). A somewhat larger proportion are descendants of Western European (primarily German) Jews who immigrated to the United States in the middle of the 19th century (Glazer, 1957; Tsypkin, 1980). However, the bulk of American Jewry (probably 75% or more) has its roots in Eastern Europe (Russia, Poland, etc.) and consists of second- and third-generation descendants of those who passed through Ellis Island from the turn of the century until World War II (Batwin, 1973). Jews have tended to congregate on the east and west coasts of the United States, with California and New York having by far the largest percentage of the Jewish American population today (Siegel & Rheins, 1980).

The fairly recent immigration of Israeli and Russian Jews has added to an already complex mixture. Each of these subgroups has a unique experience and country of origin. The fact that they may identify themselves as Jews does not mean that there is much uniformity in their cultural patterns. If these complexities were not enough, we are also confronted with the fact

---

1. Authors' note. We would like to draw the reader's attention to an old Yiddish saying: "Wherever there are two Jews, you'll find three opinions." We urge the reader's "third" opinion!

Fredda M. Herz. Department of Nursing, Herbert H. Lehman College, Bronx, New York; Faculty, Family Institute of Westchester, Mt. Vernon, New York.

Elliott J. Rosen. Department of Psychology, Pace University, White Plains, New York; Faculty, Family Institute of Westchester, Mt. Vernon, New York.

that there are three main branches of religious Judaism in the United States: Orthodox, Conservative, and Reform (Hertzberg, 1964). Each has its own set of principles, beliefs, and ritual practice, with Orthodoxy claiming the most fidelity to traditional religious observance and Reform the least.

The focus of this chapter will be upon the most typical Jewish Americans, those whose parents and/or grandparents came to this country from Eastern Europe within the last century (Grayzel, 1960; Glazer, 1957). It is this group that has made the most visible "Jewish mark" upon society through its literature, art, music, and religion. We will first consider the characteristics and patterns of the Jewish family and then focus on family treatment in terms of problem definitions, solutions, and therapeutic interventions.

Family Characteristics

Eastern European Jewish families place primary emphasis on (1) centrality of the family; (2) suffering as a shared value; (3) intellectual achievement and financial success; and (4) verbal expression of feelings.

Centrality of the Family

An outstanding study of the Eastern European culture, *Life Is with People* (Zborowski & Herzog, 1952), speaks of the centrality of the family:

> The complete Jew is an adult with a mate and offspring. No man is complete without a wife; no woman is complete without a husband. For each individual the ideal center of gravity is not in himself, but in the whole of which he is an essential part. (p. 124)

While giving priority to the value of the family is hardly unique to Jewish culture, the centrality of the family cannot be underestimated in looking at its dynamics. "Familism" (Bardis, 1961; Zuk, 1978), a belief in the importance of family as a sacred institution, stems from the idea that it is a violation of God's law not to marry. The first commandment in the Torah (Bible) is "You shall be fruitful and multiply." Marriage and raising children —establishing a family—have been the core of Jewish tradition. Historically, asceticism was viewed negatively; celibacy was absolutely condemned. Jewish religious sources speak at length of the responsibility to procreate. Currently, this value is reflected most directly in Orthodox Jewish families who represent a small percentage of the total Jewish population and who explicitly follow the teachings of the Talmud, the traditional compendium of Jewish law, and who see bachelorhood as totally unacceptable (Midrash on Psalm 59; Tsuriel, 1976–1977).

The importance of the family is commonly expressed in the images of the Jewish man as a good father, husband, and provider and the Jewish woman as a devoted wife and mother of intelligent children. The pressure on the Jewish woman to find a husband and her mother's investment in that task have been popularized in movies, television, literature, and jokes. Pressure is also exerted upon men to marry. After marriage, the connections and obligations to the extended family continue to be of great importance. Therefore, young Jewish couples typically spend a great deal of time defining the boundaries, connections, and obligations between themselves and their families. Some young couples seen by the authors have reflected the intensity of this family orientation in their conviction that they would always be children who, in their parents' view, would forever need to be cared for financially and otherwise. As might be expected, along with the very high value placed on the family is the emphasis upon geographical as well as emotional closeness between generations.

Thus living far away is not an acceptable excuse for failing to fulfill family obligations. One family stopped speaking to several family members who had failed to return from Europe to attend an uncle's funeral. Another U.S. East Coast family had not communicated for some time with family members on the West Coast because the latter had not flown in for a family Bar Mitzvah. To those of a different culture this tendency toward cutoffs in response to a perceived breach of commitment to the family may appear extreme.

Intermarriage has always been perceived as the most flagrant breach of family togetherness, and total emotional cutoffs are not uncommon in such instances (Yaffe, 1968). Although there are few reports of it today except in ultra-Orthodox communities, the ultimate cutoff has been represented by families who "sit *shiva*" for a child who intermarries (Gordon, 1964). Today, despite the growth in intermarriage, even the most liberal and assimilated Jewish families remain highly sensitive to the issue, which may continue to signify betrayal of the family and the community (Yaffe, 1968). For example, one client, a fourth-generation Jewish American, recently described a family party:

> "My mother spent half the evening speaking about Jewish cooking and Jewish holidays, peppering her monologue with frequent 'Yiddishisms.' It took me a long while to realize that this uncharacteristic behavior from my 'assimilated' American mother was for the benefit of my non-Jewish wife, whom Mother claims to accept totally."

Divorce, as well, is often seen as a violation of family togetherness. The authors have observed that Jewish parents frequently personalize a child's divorce. As one client reported his mother's response to his divorce: "How could you do this to me?" While divorce is surely a toxic issue in other ethnic groups, an added dimension in the traditional Jewish family is the expectation that a writ of religious divorce (*get*) be obtained as well. Since, in Jewish law only the husband can grant such a decree to his wife, the *get* assumes great importance and may well represent an issue around which a divorcing couple can triangulate.

In addition, Jewish ritual ceremonies in the home and synagogue are family centered and sex roles defined so that following a divorce "open hostility with escalating vindictiveness is often aimed at the rabbi and is frequently followed by withdrawal from Judaism" (Bundt, 1982, p. 74).

Suffering as a Shared Value

Historically, Jews have been persecuted so often that they tend to be on their guard, anticipating attack while privately reassuring themselves that they are "God's chosen people." The assumption is that suffering is a basic part of life. This suffering may even reinforce the notion that they are superior to others by virtue of their burden of oppression. As a popular Yiddish saying goes, *Shver zu zein a yid* ("It's tough to be a Jew").

An interesting comparison can be made between the experiences of suffering by Irish and Jewish families. In both cultures suffering occupies a central position in the family ethos. In Irish families, however, the assumption is that one suffers because one deserves punishment for one's sins. For the Jewish family, the predominant view is that one suffers because "of what the world does to you." This sense of persecution (or its imminence) is part of a cultural heritage and is usually assumed with pride. Suffering is even a form of sharing with one's fellow Jews. It binds Jews with their heritage—with the suffering of Jews throughout history.

Enjoyment for its own sake or the carefree expression of feelings is often disdained, although "having a good time" is thought to be important for social purposes. Jews may have trouble allowing themselves to have simply a good time without "accomplishing" anything. The understanding therapist can often recognize a potential for happiness that a family itself has not only failed to see but has never learned to expect.

Similarly, hypochondriasis is a common Jewish syndrome (Zborowski, 1969). While Jews may complain about their symptoms and constantly seek drugs and doctors, they often do so with a resigned sigh that signifies that they hardly expected any better treatment from life (Zborowski, 1969).

Recently the centrality of suffering for the Jewish family has been drawn to our attention again as the children of the survivors of the Nazi Holocaust have begun to share their experiences (Epstein, 1979; Rabinowitz, 1976; Mostysser, 1975). Although these experiences are unique, they have immeasurably compounded the sense of suffering for all Jews. In the families of actual survivors, however, the issues of suffering and doubts about the right to joy and happiness are even more pronounced. For example, a daughter of concentration camp survivors has said about her growing up: "No discomfort, disappointment, or difficulty seemed worthy of my parents' attention, considering their own experience in the war." Furthermore, she never even felt the right to her feelings since her parents' own suffering was so great that any expression of her own seemed presumptuous. Or, as another young woman pointed out, the constant parental message, "Be happy," took on a grotesque incongruity when coupled with the parents' own bitterness (Mostysser, 1975).

Intellectual Achievement and Financial Success

Success is so vitally important to the Jewish family ethos that we can hardly overemphasize it. The jokes about "my son, the doctor," while often humorously used to ridicule status-seeking Jewish parents, reflect one of the central values of the family. We cannot hope to understand the Jewish family without understanding the place that success, particularly for men (and recently women) plays in the system. In the *shtetl* (small town) of Eastern Europe learning was honored and earned one prestige, respect, authority, and status (Zborowski & Herzog, 1952; Dimont, 1978). This value is reflected in the Yiddish language, which is filled with honorific terms for referring to a learned man (e.g., *Lehrer*, *Hacham*). The high value Jews placed on learning is related to the fact that it was portable, and Jews were always on the move.

Historically, success was not measured according to the standards set by non-Jewish society (Tuchman, 1978). In fact, those standards were considered alien and were eschewed by the family. The possibility of "making it" in Gentile society was rarely an option for Eastern European Jews since, until the present time, they were an alien group in a foreign culture. The openness of American society and the increasing American prosperity of the past 60 years are contributing factors to this commitment to mainstream definition of success (Neusner, 1972). No other era has seen such a commitment to educational, financial, and social success, and pressure upon children to achieve high status is intense. As one patient, a successful accountant, remarked, "Most of my adult life my mother introduced my brother and me as 'This is my son, Dr. ___, and this is Bobby.'" A child's status, particularly when coupled with a doctorate (more specifically, in medicine), reflects favorably upon the family and parents. For daughters, status is often viewed as more secure if attained by marriage than if independently achieved.

Success was and is measured by intellectual (academic) achievement, professional and social status, and money. Rooted in the ancient tradition of learning and the study of Torah, educational achievement was transmuted in American society to include secular study, even to the exclusion of religious study. In the historical context of helplessness, persecution, and suffering described previously, the high value placed on intellectual and educational achievement is quite understandable.

Today, in most Jewish families and communities, it is obligatory that all children go to college; graduate and professional studies are often expected as well (Rosenberg, 1965). When this is not achieved, parents frequently perceive it as a failure requiring therapy.

> For example, a Jewish family seen in brief treatment defined its problem as the fact that the youngest son, Richard, had dropped out of college and was planning to enter a training course for auto mechanics. They hoped the therapist could talk some sense into Richard. The parents had financed the eldest son's education through law school and were presently supporting their daughter in her junior year of college. They refused to pay for Richard's mechanics course and demanded that he get a job and begin to pay rent if he intended to stay at home. Interestingly, the pressure for Richard to continue in college was as great from his brother and sister as from his parents. One major theme from all family members was the embarrassment they would all suffer when the "news got out."

Financial success is also highly valued in the Jewish family. While Jewish attitudes toward money are often stereotypically portrayed, it would be an error of omission to pretend that money has not been an extremely important status symbol for the Jewish family. Having historically been denied access to many crafts and professions, Jews tended to gravitate toward pursuits in which money was handled directly, and it thus became symbolic of status. The New Testament prohibition against a Christian extracting interest payment from his brother made the Jew a vital cog in the economy of feudal society. Medieval European Christians were barred from money lending, an occupation considered by them to be "dirty" (Tuchman, 1978; Marcus, 1960), and they used Jews as money lenders. However, money lending did not guarantee security since rich and poor Jews alike were the objects of anti-Semitic outbreaks. One of the tools of survival is liquidity: Money, jewelry, and other moveables were accumulated (rather than land, business, etc.) so that they could be taken along in flight.

In American society, because Jews have been able to succeed as never before, a conflict has developed between the value of success and the value of family (Zimring, 1980). Previously, discrimination by the outside society curtailed Jewish achievement; thus Jews could achieve within a circumscribed sphere and still stay closely tied to the family. Now, as success often means sacrificing attachment to the family and community, these values are increasingly coming into conflict. This conflict may create particular stress for Jewish men, who are the ones expected to succeed. A couple recently seen by one of the authors poignantly illustrates this dilemma:

> Marla and Robert were referred by an attorney to whom they had turned to arrange a legal separation. They had decided to separate because, as Marla phrased it, "There's no point being married and having a family when Robert is married to his company." In recent years Robert had begun to climb the corporate ladder. With great pride, he told the therapist that he was the highest ranking Jew in a large corporation which had, until recently, not included Jews in any executive positions. He agreed that he

was spending less time with his family and in community and synagogue activities, which had been an important part of their family life in the past. In the first few sessions Robert had little to say about Marla's complaints of his absence except that his job demanded the kind of time he devoted to it. Only later was he able to relate that he, too, felt the loss because he now spent less time with his wife and children.

What was particularly helpful to Robert was to renew contact with his father, a retired city employee who had always been seen as the "loser" in the family. Robert clearly recalled the message received while growing up that he not be like his father. His memories of his father were confused: He felt fondness for his softness and availability and disdain for his vocational failure. A number of conversations with his father allowed Robert to recognize that emotional vulnerability was not inimical in the world of work.

Another common issue in Jewish families, where standards for success are so high, is that almost no one feels he or she can truly meet them. The pressure that family members feel is often exacerbated by expectations that are implicit and unspoken and therefore can never really be met. The following is an example of such a dynamic in another family:

Stephen, a 30-year-old philosophy professor at a major university, sought treatment because of the escalating strife with his parents over a number of issues, particularly the fact that he was still unmarried and "unsettled." Friction with his father was particularly painful for him since his father constantly reminded him that his older brother, Jerry, who had a small manufacturing company, had provided the family with money and grandchildren. Stephen's characteristic way of dealing with his parents had been to provide them with a running account of his frequent academic accomplishments and publications.

He resented their rejection of him and he was confused that his brother was seen as a success while he was viewed as a disappointment. Despite his respected position in the academic world, he often found himself the butt of jokes within the family, usually instigated by his father and Jerry. One way this was done was to ask Stephen's opinion on some issue and then label his reponse as naive because "he lived in an ivory tower." Jerry harassed his brother with the recitation of obscure, and usually erroneous, facts that Stephen felt forced to "correct." The family then joined in with an all-out attack on Stephen's alleged superiority and condescension. Stephen felt relegated to a one-down position knowing that his brother, the financial support of the family, was his father's favorite. While Stephen felt he could never succeed in the family, Jerry's taunts reflected jealousy of his younger brother's intelligence and achievement.

Given the idealistic demands of the Jewish family system for success and achievement, it is hard not to feel a failure no matter how much one accomplishes. As in the case above, this may lead to competition and sibling rivalry that interfere with family intimacy. A vicious cycle may develop in which family members devalue each other in order to bolster individual self-esteem. Once a family member has been subjected to such a putdown, he or she feels like a failure and retaliates. The negative atmosphere engendered by this constant criticism leaves everyone feeling hurt and on guard against future attack. This attitude is extended to the outside world as well, where *Goyim* (non-Jews) are viewed critically and often condescendingly. While this behavior is dysfunctional in present-day Jewish families, it reflects the historical reality that Jews needed to be on guard against persecution by the societies in which they lived.

Giving and receiving play an extremely important role in the Jewish family. In the *shtetl*, the good things of the world such as material goods, wealth, and learning were seen as finite and attainable. They were acquired not only for themselves but also because they made it possible to help weaker, poorer, and more vulnerable families (Zborowski & Herzog, 1952). Even wealthy families had a strong identification with the poor and disadvantaged, in part because their own status in society was so marginal. Thus, a perception of the poor as morally inferior ("He's getting what he deserves") was never part of the Jewish view. In giving to those in need, the giver profited more than the receiver for in the *shtetl* (as well as in today's Jewish community) the prestige value of good deeds was second only to that of learning. "It was chiefly through the benefaction it makes possible, that money can 'buy' status and esteem" (Zborowski & Herzog, 1952, p. 195). Today this tradition is reflected in the tendency of Jewish families to be generous and philanthropic (Freisch, 1924; Grayzel, 1960; Sklare, 1972; Bloom, 1981). This generosity extends to children, extended family, and charitable community causes. At the same time, there is an assumption that such giving entitles them to certain advantages. For example, Jewish grandparents may often feel that they have the right to visit their children's homes at their pleasure because it was their money that provided the down payment. While the money was originally gratefully received, the obligation engendered by its acceptance often creates hostility toward the older generation.

Verbal Expression of Feelings

Jewish Americans value verbal ability, the ability to articulate their thoughts. Being verbal is a by-product of learning and once again reflects skills and knowledge that are portable. In the *shtetl*, the use of argument as an educational method encouraged the development of both rational thought and verbal skills. The Torah and the Talmud were studied by utilizing scholastic methodologies, which suggest varying levels of meaning for scriptural passages. The student's task was to examine various interpretations and to arrive at an understanding of the intent of the ancient arguments.

In many families, children's opinions are highly valued, and it is not unusual for parents to take great pride in the contributions their children make to the solution of a problem. There is a less clear-cut boundary between parents and children than in many other ethnic groups. Family problems are considered from every angle and usually thought to be the entire family's business. Expressing their thoughts and feelings is not only a method of catharsis but an important aspect of family interaction. The importance of verbal skills and self-expression for Jewish families has been documented in a study of cultural reactions to pain. In Zborowski's (1969) classic work, *People in Pain*, Jewish Americans were found to be the best informants of several ethnic groups. They seemed to enjoy the opportunity to express themselves as patients and to elaborate on their negative feelings. Zborowski observed that Jewish patients are less stoic, which is in line with the authors' observations that few Jewish couples are willing "to grin and bear it."

The focus on self-expression, high achievement, and verbal skills interacts with the willingness to express pain and anger to form a pattern typical of Jewish families. For example, couples tend to use language, such as cursing, as an acceptable vehicle for expressing anger. In addition, therapists often note a "carping" negativity (complaining, picking, or nagging) in the interactions between Jewish couples. Cynicism and criticism are frequently used to get others to respond in a certain way. To an outsider, these outbursts appear to be simply anger or hostility. However, such expressions or criticism may actually be ways of showing caring. The therapist can often reframe these verbal attacks by positive connotation, that is, labeling them as expressions of intense caring, thus shifting the family to a more positive direction.

Family Patterns

Men in Jewish Families

In the *shtetl* families prayed that their offspring would be boys since to be male was to be special. Men and boys were expected, if they were sufficiently gifted, to be free from worldly tasks so that they could "learn" (Zborowski & Herzog, 1952). The study of Torah (actually an umbrella term under which all areas of Jewish study are subsumed) was considered the quintessence of life, the lofty pursuit of men alone. The domain of men was the *Bais Midrash*, the House of Prayer and Study, where intellect and a strong male camaraderie were cultivated (Singer, 1962). Tevye's whimsical lament in *Fiddler on the Roof*, that if he were a rich man, he would sit in the synagogue all day and discuss the holy books, was a longing shared by most men in the Jewish community.

However, few men achieved the status desired by Tevye. In fact, there are hints, particularly in the works of Yiddish writers like Isaac Bashevis Singer, that such men were privately scorned as drains upon the family and community. To express such an attitude publicly, however, was considered a sacrilege. "A man who is too good for the world is no good to his wife" (Ayalti, 1976) is just one of several Yiddish proverbs that reflects the private disdain for such men.

The transmission of these values from Europe to America was a complex process. Success outside the family was achieved at the cost of relative devaluation of the husband/father in ongoing family life. Though the father's role became peripheral within the home, the family and Jewish community continued to pay obeisance to his status, for it was his public achievements upon which the family's own status rested. The following case illustrates the dilemma for Jewish men as well as the degree to which success is an expected part of family life.

> Jack, 52, was an extremely successful businessman and the father of three adolescent girls. While revered in the community and the recipient of many awards, Jack felt isolated from his wife and family. He and his wife, Dorothy, came for marital therapy because of his occasional sexual impotence and her anger at his spending more and more time in Jewish philanthropic work and less time with her. What emerged quite early in treatment was Jack's profound sense of alienation from the life of his family. He never felt "permitted" to take an active part in child rearing and was particularly pained at having been excluded from the recent planning of his daughter's wedding. Dorothy expressed great surprise that Jack would want to be involved at home.

The Jewish man is often faced with the paradox of having achieved position and prestige outside the home while feeling unappreciated or ignored within the family. This frequently raises problems of self-esteem for Jewish husbands who see themselves as impotent in the face of powerful wives and demanding children.

Thus, while men are considered important in the Jewish family, it is their public status and the financial support they provide that are most highly valued. Emotional succor and ongoing personal interaction are less expected culturally. Paradoxically, however, the lack of these qualities in a husband/father is often one of the complaints of families coming for treatment.

Women in Jewish Families

> She was a perfect Jewish woman, clear, patient, hardworking, and silent, submissive to God and to her husband, devoted to her children . . . her own well being was unimportant. (Zborowski & Herzog, 1952, p. 138)

The Eastern European Jewish community was a male-oriented culture where women were regarded as subordinate and where men greeted each day by offering thanks to God "that Thou hast not made me a woman" (Hertz, 1960, p. 21). Woman's role was to serve as a helpmate—or complement—to her husband. According to the Torah, God, before creating woman, decided that he would "make a helpmate" for man. A popular medieval Bible commentator adds that if the husband deserves it, his wife will be a help, and if he does not, then she will be his adversary. So while wives may have been regarded as subservient to their husbands, they also occupied a place of importance in the life of the family and were accorded honor by their husbands and children. As a Talmudic homily states: "He who has no wife lives without good . . . or joy. . . . He is not really a complete man" (Genesis Rabbah, XVIII:2).

Since many ritual acts took place at specific times of the day and were tied to the synagogue, women were limited in their ability to participate fully in their religion, and their domain became the home (Baum, Hyman, & Michel, 1975). A woman's role as caretaker and homemaker was, in many cases, augmented by the necessity that she be the breadwinner as well (Priesand, 1976). This often made her more worldly than her husband, and this worldliness was viewed with suspicion.

The sexes were segregated due in large measure to the fear of female sexuality and women's ability (like the Biblical Eve) to lure men into lascivious thoughts or untoward behavior and away from the study of Torah. *Tznius* (modesty) as an ideal for women became at least the external and public way of life, defined by demure dress, shaved and bewigged head, averted eyes, and unobtrusive manner (Ganzfried, 1961). It is important to emphasize the extreme limitations put upon women's public deportment and appearance in traditional Jewish life since it was these public restrictions that greatly contributed to their strong, controlling role in the family.

Women were also viewed as innately more expressive (the Talmud says "light headed")—with tears and laughter and emotions. None of these attributes carried a particularly positive connotation, and wives were often referred to contemptuously and viewed as inferior to their husbands. On the other hand, they were extremely powerful in the primary role that they played in the home. In actual daily living they took the lead and made basic decisions about the destiny of their families. This is, of course, a paradox: women are powerful, while at the same time compelled to deny that they are.

While within Jewish American families women have maintained a central and powerful role, it is not unusual for their external social status to be defined by the men they marry. Since marriage, home, and family are vitally important and since there is a high value placed on academic achievement and financial success, it is no wonder that among the greatest conflicts of present-day Jewish women are the competing demands of family and career (Goldenberg, 1973). For today's Jewish woman, like women in most other ethnic groups, the roles of caretaker and potential career woman are precariously balanced, as the following case example illustrates.

Ruth, a young Jewish woman, entered family treatment for severe depression of eight years' duration. She had been seen in individual treatment for those eight years with no relief of symptoms. When she came with her husband, Bob, she appeared to be a demure, quiet, and adoring wife who admired her husband's great financial success. By the second session Ruth began to tell the therapist that she was a talented dancer who has been on the verge of critical acclaim for several years. When asked why she had been unable to make the move toward professional success, she said, "I guess I wonder how I could dance and keep up what I'm supposed to do— take care of the kids and volunteer for worthy causes. I also think my Bob would be very upset if I were successful."

At the core of Ruth's dilemma is the vital importance of marriage and the family and the roles of husband and wife in Jewish life.

Marriage

Marriage is both the climax and the threshold. From birth on, every step is directed with an eye to the *Khupa* (marriage canopy), and if that goal is missed, life itself seems to be lost. Once attained, however, marriage is merely the background for the great goal, the great achievement, the great gratification: children. (Zborowski & Herzog, 1952, p. 290)

In Eastern Europe, marriages were arranged by a marriage broker, the *shadken*, or by the parents of the couple. It was the bride's responsibility to command (be worthy of) a dowry, a symbol of her family's status. A "good" marriage meant a balance of learning, *yikhus* (pedigree or lineage), and money. The bride's qualifications were also judged by the degree to which her parents had these three essential characteristics (Baum *et al.*, 1976). Today, marriages are no longer arranged, but Jews still tend to have a high rate of marriage (as well as a low rate of divorce) (Sanua, 1978). However, a slightly higher rate of divorce is found among the more acculturated, suburbanites, the better educated, and Reform Jews (Sanua, 1978).

Parental anxiety about their children's marriage is proverbial. Giving their children in marriage is still seen as an obligation which, once discharged, leaves parents free to enjoy the rewards and the *naches* (joys) of parenthood. For women in the *shtetl*, it was the first rite of passage, marking them as full adults and incorporating them into the community through their husbands. Childhood was primarily a preparation for this event, and women were taught practical household tasks. Although marriage is not always a religious ritual for women today, the preparation for marriage is often fraught with as much intensity as it was in the *shtetl*. In preparing for the future, Jewish women are given all that is possible to ensure the best possible match. In more affluent Jewish families (and even in many without financial resources) young girls are given the best clothes, jewelry, and schooling. Physical deviations, such as a "Jewish nose" and "bad teeth" are repaired if at all possible, so that the young women will be more likely to attract successful and prosperous young men.

An interesting paradox is that, although women are encouraged by tradition to care for their husbands, they enter into marriage with the expectation that their spouses will take care of them. As secularization has increased, Jewish women have learned to expect to receive more of the material goods they acquired while looking for a suitable husband. They presume that it is they who will be taken care of.

Jewish men similarly come to marriage expecting to be cared for by their wives. In grooming men for success and achievement, few material provisions are neglected by their parents. Their mothers take good care of them, and their fathers give them the best of schools, cars, and other material goods. Thus, both men and women tend to enter marriage expecting the same caring as they received in their own families of origin. Conflict and disappointment are a common result.

Sex can be a particularly toxic issue with Jewish couples. In traditional Orthodox practice, sex is not to be discussed and women are considered ritually untouchable during their menstrual periods. Before sexual relations can be resumed after menstruation, a wife must go to the *mikveh* (ritual bath) where her immersion purifies her and allows her once again to be sexually available. Since women are not allowed to indicate their sexual desires directly, they indicate accessibility indirectly. Although the ultimate goal of sex is procreation, sexual relations between husband and wife are considered highly sanctified and encouraged as a necessary, and even pleasurable, biological function. Sexual incompatibility is mentioned in the Talmud as grounds for divorce, as is the woman's inability to conceive or bear children.

Although today the *mikveh* and other sexual regulations are practiced only by strictly observant Jews, the sensitivity toward the subject remains. For example, although liberal Jewish mothers may explain the facts of life to their daughters, they may be unable to speak calmly of sex, thus transmitting their own anxiety and ambivalence about the subject. Moreover, watching parents "carping" may suggest to the daughters that all parents relate this way and that intimacy and sex are areas for competition that are maneuvers for control rather than affection.

A Jewish marriage is a marriage of two families, and one cannot discuss marriage without discussing the relationships among in-laws. A vestige of the medieval wedding celebration that is still enacted today in some traditional communities, albeit humorously, is the "quarreling dance." The dance ritual is performed by the new mothers-in-law who stamp, grimace, and lunge at one another, acting out a mock quarrel (Zborowski & Herzog, 1952). The feigned antagonism in the dance dramatizes the concern of each regarding the other's influence on the marital couple. The in-law relationship is considered an important relationship, and, as one client, a middle-aged mother of two married sons, said of her son's in-laws, "There are few relationships that I work at. That one I cultivate."

Another in-law relationship should be mentioned here: the daughter-in-law and mother-in-law relationship. The antagonism in this relationship tends to be increased by the intensity of the Jewish mother–son axis. Jewish daughters-in-law often describe a feeling that they cannot measure up to what their mothers-in-law expect of them as wives for their sons. On the other hand, Jewish men often have good relationships with both their in-laws. In Eastern Europe, when a father-in-law chose a husband for a daughter, it was hoped that he would choose someone with all the ideal traits—someone who would bring honor to their family. To the present day, sons-in-law are frequently viewed as adding to the status of the family.

Children and the Parent–Child Relationship

In the traditional Jewish community, having children is seen as a scriptural and social obligation. "You shall be fruitful and multiply" is the first commandment in the Torah. Children are indicators of a blessed marriage and are viewed as an extension of the worth of the parents (Zborowski & Herzog, 1952).

In the nuclear family, the father and the mother play complementary roles. In the *shtetl*, for example, both parents were addressed as *Tateh-mammeh* in recognition of the duality that composes their union. However, the mother was considered the mother of the whole family, including the father. In this role, the "Jewish mother" is celebrated in story and song. She continually outdoes herself in caring for others and forgoing satisfaction of her personal needs for the benefit of her family (Blau, 1967). No sacrifice is too great, especially for the sake of her children, and she suffers profoundly when her efforts are rebuffed. Children of a mother who sacrifices everything for them and denies all personal needs may feel bound by guilt, for there is no way to repay her efforts adequately. It is important to be aware of the extent to which this guilt pervades the consciousness of Jewish children. Although feelings of betrayal are common between parents and children of every culture, guilt is particularly intense among Jews. For example, a young married daughter who decides to postpone childbearing to pursue a career is very likely to feel that her behavior is a betrayal of her mother. Since children are central to the family system, a daughter's postponement of childbearing not only threatens the mother's familistic values but also rejects the strong tradition that stresses the obligatory interrelationship of the generations. The requirement of "giving parents a grandchild" transcends mere individual choice. In very few cultures can a mother say to adult children who postpone having children, "How can you do this to me?" and be so clearly understood. It is not unusual for a young couple to report that the decision to have a child was based, at least in part, on the desire to make one of the mothers happy.

The unflattering stereotype of the intrusive Jewish mother may often reflect reality, but the meaning of that behavior, particularly its adaptive and maladaptive aspects, is important to examine. The following example of a family seen by one of the authors illustrates the overcentrality of a mother and how the therapist attempts to modify the dysfunctional arrangement.

> The N family came to therapy on the insistence of Sara N, the wife and mother. The problem, as presented by Sara who did most of the talking, was twofold. One relatively minor problem was the continuous verbal clashes between Jennifer, a 16-year-old honor student, and her mother. But the major problem was that Sara's husband, Alan, did not help or support her in any way, particularly in the area of child rearing when she tangled with Jennifer. It became clear, after listening to the couple for only a few minutes, that the family centered around Sara, who could (and did) recite with unerring accuracy the daily schedules of her husband and children in minute detail.
>
> Alan said that he had long ago given up trying to be a part of child rearing because Sara had taken it over completely. A particularly dramatic event occurred in the second session when, upon entering the office, Sara presented a small tin foil packet containing hashish to the therapist. The therapist's surprise was matched by Alan's, who had not known of the packet that Sara had found hidden away in Jennifer's room. After much discussion, the therapist suggested that Sara invite Alan to take charge of the situation. Sara vowed not to interfere in any way, and careful coaching was given to Alan (out of Sara's hearing) about how he might deal with this problem. In the next session Alan reported that Sara had pursued both Jennifer and Alan until she learned exactly how the incident was being handled. She then strongly indicated that she did not approve of how he had managed the situation.

One sign of progress in this family was when Sara took a therapeutic suggestion and began to work parttime outside the home. Since Sara and her family knew that it is the Jewish mother's role to devote her entire emotional energy to nurturing the intelligence and achievement of her children, this decision was momentous.

Mothers view themselves and are viewed by others as the center of family life. When suburban Chicago mothers were asked to name the relative who would take custody of their children in event of their own or their husbands' deaths, nearly 75% of the Jewish mothers chose a relative on their own side of the family. However, only 31% of Protestants and 48% of Catholics chose a maternal relative (Sanua, 1978).

Traditionally, the Jewish mother has been viewed as the primary educator of her children. It has been her job to encourage whatever talents they have, and many generations of highly successful Jewish doctors, lawyers, musicians, accountants, businessmen, *et cetera*, testify to the efficacy of her methods. Since she is merely the instrument of their success, her enjoyment must be vicarious. She values intelligence and achievement, but her mission is to work only for the development of others within the family. She is not expected to use her intelligence and drive for personal accomplishments outside of the home, and thus she finds herself deeply invested in the accomplishments of her children.

The Jewish mother's ambivalence regarding her role often results in tension and conflict between herself and her daughter(s). She may communicate her own ambivalence to her daughter(s) by unclear or unstated expectations regarding a woman's role in life. In contrast, the conflict between a Jewish mother and her son(s) results not from her ambivalence regarding her own or his role, but rather from her disappointment in his failure to meet her expectations.

The ambiguity of the mother–daughter conflict often leaves both frustrated about their ability to resolve the issues, thus creating an intense relationship that may last into the daughter's adult life (Bell & Buerkle, 1962). A Jewish woman may say of her relationship with her mother, "I don't know what she expects of me. I've never been able to figure out how to please her." On the other hand, as a male client of one of the authors recently remarked, "I know what I have to do to please my mother, I'm just tired of doing it."

The pivotal place of the mother and wife in the Jewish family is also reflected in research with families of schizophrenics. In Protestant families, it was found that pathology was more often labeled in fathers, with some 50% identified as emotionally disturbed or socially maladjusted. The trend was reversed in the Jewish families studied, where 50% of the mothers were so diagnosed (Sanua, 1963).

Other cultures appear to be less ambivalent about maternal roles. In Italian families, for example, the mothers are ignored in certain ways, but their worth as cooks and housekeepers is highly regarded. In addition, Italian American mothers may tend to be more traditional in their child-rearing methods (Cohen, 1977). In Jewish families, since the mother instills the educational and achievement values of the culture, she internalizes these values and thus thinks less of her homemaking. This creates a dilemma for the modern Jewish woman. Historical circumstances have given women greater opportunities for personal development and Jewish women have become very successful (Luria, 1974). However, the problem is that the ambivalence of her role often remains unresolved. The competing values of success and caretaking create a conundrum. The Jewish women may express this as, "I'm getting better and better at juggling it, but no better at balancing it."

Despite the expectations of maternal commitment to children, love was often not expressed directly or through physical demonstrativeness by either parent in traditional Jewish homes. Rather, love was demonstrated by constant overfeeding and by unremitting solicitude and worry about every aspect of the child's welfare. This was expressed in neverending verbalizations such as "Have you had enough to eat?" "Are you warm enough?" Inherent in this picture of parental, and particularly maternal love, was boundless suffering and sacrifice for the children. Zborowski and Herzog (1952) claim that in the *shtetl* children were seldom told they were loved nor were they kissed after age 4 or 5.

Child rearing has been accomplished through the use of reasoning, explanation, and rationality. Jewish parents have tended to be permissive, overprotective, and concerned about their children's happiness (Sanua, 1978). However, they have also fostered greater independence in their children when compared to both Irish and Italian families (McClelland, DeCharms, & Rindlisbacher, 1955). Children are viewed as people with drives to act, which require both controls and outlets. The parental task is to guide the flow or to create new channels for the expression of behavior. Punishment is considered only as a method of diverting behavior into new channels.

Between parents and children exist a host of expectations, many of which find their roots in religious tradition. To a large extent, the children's obligations to parents proceed from their role as extensions of the parents. Through the child's success parents are validated; through their defects and wrongdoings parents are disgraced and shamed. Children's duties to parents are also rooted in religious principles, not the least of which is the commandment to honor one's father and mother. This concept of *mitzvah*, or obligation, is central in Jewish tradition and results in a plethora of "shoulds" and "musts" that are an aspect of the family ethos. Ironically, what was originally an aspect of religious obligation may provide a way in which parent and child are permitted intimacy with and responsibility for each other.

All the sacrifice, suffering, and solicitude of the parents help to generate filial indebtedness. A large part of this indebtedness is returned by the child both emotionally and behaviorally through good manners and respect. For example, a son was traditionally referred to by his parents as "our *Kaddish*." The phrase had a variety of implications, but its simple meaning was that the child knew, early on, that he would have the responsibility of reciting *Kaddish* (the memorial prayer) for his mother and father upon their deaths. In common usage, however, it implied comfort and dependence: a parent who reminded a child that he was "my *Kaddish*" reinforced not only that son's responsibility for saying a particular prayer, but also his responsibility for his parent's emotional succor and physical care.

An extension of this idea of "our *Kaddish*" is the concept of *naches* (literally, satisfaction or pleasure in Yiddish). Jewish children learn, early on, that they are expected to provide their parents with *naches*. This can be delivered in the form of achievement, financial success, marriage, and grandchildren, and that it must be delivered is understood by most Jewish sons and daughters. Failure to provide their parents with some *naches* is considered unacceptable and is cause for much guilt. Of course, there can never be enough *naches*, and their failure to provide "enough" inevitably results in guilt. As one of the authors has quipped, "If my autobiography is ever written it will be entitled *What Price Naches?*"

Inducing guilt early in life is thought not only to assure *naches* but to guarantee that children will care for their parents. A young woman client recently commented that she did not think Jewish guilt was so terrible: "It's the best way to remind us that we are responsible for others. How else would I remember to visit my aunt in the hospital or send my cousin a Bar Mitzvah gift. That is why we need guilt. It's a very positive thing and it keeps the family together."

Life Cycle Rituals

The birth of a child, as in any community, is heralded by celebration and ritual. Until recently, such celebration among Jews was restricted to the birth of male children, the ritual *bris* (circumcision) being a universally observed rite. Special ceremonies for the naming of female infants have become more common as well (Strassfeld & Strassfeld, 1976). In recent years some Jewish American families no longer use the traditional ceremony and simply have a party to celebrate the child's birth, leaving the circumcision to medical personnel.

Children are traditionally named for a recently deceased relative; this custom emphasizes again the importance of family relationships and family continuity (Kolatch, 1973). Of course, the choosing of the name can also be a complex matter since feelings in the family about the deceased person may get transferred to the new child. Obviously, the choice of names is seldom simple, and usually both sides of the family expect that a particular name will be chosen. Middle names can be a solution; the child can bear a name from each of the families. This, however, does not always solve the problem.

> Sam and Carol A, new parents, were embroiled in a major battle with Sam's parents because they chose to name their new son for Carol's deceased grandfather, to whom Carol was extremely close. Carol's sister had also named a child for this grandfather a few years previously, and Sam's parents argued that choosing him was not "fair" since there already was a child named for this grandfather. Sam's mother wanted the child named for her brother, who had died long before Sam's birth, and argued that Sam's refusal was an insult to her brother's memory. In an attempt to compromise, Carol suggested that the child be given a middle name for Sam's uncle. Sam's mother was not satisfied and insisted that this was merely second best.

We can see in the above example that Carol's attempt at compromise was unacceptable. She mistakenly assumed that the naming of the child symbolized the blending of two families. Her mother-in-law was more intent upon the traditional use of name giving as allying that child with one of the two families.

In all families, the birth of a child triggers a change in the family balance. For the Jewish family, however, cultural expectations and religious values are brought to bear that often exaggerate tenuous family relationships. While naming a child for a dead relative is not a religious obligation, going against that tradition takes either courage or a dogged determination to enter into a bitter confrontation. Communal and cultural norms die hard. Thus it becomes extremely difficult to strike a balance between a commitment to Jewish tradition and the desire to make independent decisions. (Obviously there are varying degrees of commitment to that tradition and varying degrees of conflict.)

A poignant example of these complicated conflicts was seen in a young man who was faced with the problem of naming his first child. His father had recently committed suicide, and the son had only begun the process of working through his feelings about his father and the suicide. His mother demanded that the child be named for his father which, naturally, created intense conflict within him. Expectations that are a part of Jewish tradition intersect here with intense family issues, leaving it difficult to distinguish between the two. Only after many painful conversations with his mother and a carefully coached trip to visit his father's family was he able to resolve his dilemma.

Another important passage occurs when the child reaches 13 years of age. This ritual passage is the Bar Mitzvah (Bat Mitzvah for girls), which is the celebration of the child's having achieved communal adult status. The core of the ceremony is the child's being called to recite blessings over the reading of the Torah at a regular synagogue service, thus establishing himself or herself as an adult worshipper.

It is important to note that the Bar Mitzvah and Bat Mitzvah are the only life cycle events that do not mark the leaving or entry of a family member. Nevertheless, it is a powerful moment in the life of the family, assuming for many almost gigantic proportions. Families use that occasion as a focus for many issues: loved ones who are ill pray to stay alive at least until that day; families on the verge of breaking up decide to wait until after that day; long-neglected and distant relatives are once again invited back into the family arena. The uninformed therapist may be bewildered by the investment of emotions, thought, and money that are made for this day.

The Bar Mitzvah and Bat Mitzvah were not always such significant events as they have become in today's Jewish community. In fact, a generation ago there was no ceremony for girls and, more often than not, a boy's coming of age was marked modestly by the sharing of some wine by the family and a few friends in the synagogue. The growth of the event to its present-day status is a sociological phenomenon beyond our scope here. It becomes a marker event for today's Jewish family because it is often the earliest moment in the family's life when it can publicly demonstrate the status it has achieved. The day is looked forward to for many years and while the actual event may consist of no more than a few moments of recitation on the child's part, by that point the occasion has already achieved a life of its own. Even among marginally religious Jews, that day takes on great significance and many issues, from the child's performance to the size of a family member's gift, may be talked about endlessly. This is a rite of passage for parents as well as for the child.

While traditional Judaism once had strong views regarding an afterlife, it is safe to say that today the contemporary Jewish community views death as an ending of this life rather than as a beginning of another. There are several aspects of the death ritual in the Jewish culture that are unusual in the mainstream of American life and as such should be noted by the therapist working with Jewish families. In the interest of space, we will note a few of the more typical aspects of the ritual and refer the reader to the excellent text *The Jewish Way in Death and Mourning* (Lamm, 1969) for a more complete presentation.

It is common practice for Jews to bury the dead at the earliest possible time, which is historically within 24 hours, and the mourning ritual does not formally begin until after the burial. The traditional mourning period, called "sitting *shiva*" (or seven), extends for seven days. Although some families cut short the mourning period, it is still referred to by this terminology. There are a number of ritual proscriptions, observed in varying degrees, described in detail in Lamm's book. For example, 11 months following death, the family reconvenes at the cemetery for the "unveiling" or dedication of the tombstone, which marks also the end of the mourning period. *Kaddish* is said daily for the year after burial and on the anniversary of the death.

Major events in any family life cycle produce stress for the family. As such they also represent times during which the family is most amenable to change. They are turning points in family process and ideal moments for therapeutic intervention. Friedman (1980) suggests that at these times it is important for the therapist to maximize the potential of the rituals to promote family strengths and relationships.

The Jewish American Family in Treatment: Problems and Their Resolution

Common Problems

Jewish families are likely to have mild or moderate neurotic symptoms of mental illness, compared to the more severe symptoms found in other populations (Rose & Stuk, 1955; Srole, Langner, Michael, Opler, & Rennie, 1962; Roberts & Meyers, 1954). This finding is further documented in a study of ethnic differences in attitudes toward psychoses. Wylan and Mintz (1976) found that Jewish families were less tolerant of thought disorders but more tolerant of emotionality than Irish families.

Traditionally, Jews, especially Orthodox Jews, have had a low incidence of alcoholism (Snyder, 1958). Several studies have suggested that the moderate use of alcohol and the mild symptomatology (Field, 1962; Farber, Mindel, & Lazerwitz, 1976) in Jewish Americans is related to the pressure for obedience and responsibility. It has also been suggested that the low rate of alcoholism is related to the frequent use of alcohol in ritual ceremonies. Wylan and Mintz (1976) suggest in addition that a group that overemphasizes correct intellectual functioning and feels threatened by its absence can ill afford to get drunk.

Jews are more favorably inclined toward psychotherapy as an effective mode of treatment and are more likely to seek psychiatric outpatient service than are Catholics or Protestant groups (Srole *et al.*, 1962).

Almost 50% of the Jewish respondents in the Srole *et al.* (1962) study suggested psychotherapy as the best resource for a problem in the family. This is in comparison to approximately 24% of the Catholic respondents and 31% of the Protestant respondents. It would seem as though the value placed on verbalizing feelings and sharing suffering are aspects of what motivates Jewish families to see talking and insight as relevant solutions. In fact, it has been demonstrated that among psychiatrists, there is a marked tendency for Jews to hold a psychoanalytic orientation (Hollingshead & Redlich, 1958).

Two other family characteristics also contribute to the Jewish motivation for treatment—their reliance on experts and the value of familism. As mentioned previously, Jewish Americans tend to look to authority figures or experts as relevant problem solvers. Therefore, when they have emotional problems, they seek an expert on "emotional" health—a therapist—rather than an expert on "spiritual" health—a Rabbi. At the same time, the expertise of the "specialist" is always open to question and questioned it is, if the opinion does not match the self-diagnosis of the help seeker (Zborowski, 1969). We have also observed that Jewish families tend to move from one therapist to another in a search for the right answers and to remain in therapy for long periods of time.

Mainly because of the high value placed on the family, Jewish Americans also tend to be sensitive to the continuous changes of family life. Therefore, in our experience, they often seek treatment for problems that appear less severe than those of other groups and often seek that treatment earlier than others do.

Given the value placed on children in Jewish culture, it is not unusual for families to seek treatment for some aspect of their children's behavior. Parents' primary concern often centers around (1) academic performance and (2) leaving home. The following case demonstrates this concern with school performance and also points to certain treatment issues with Jewish families.

Mrs. T called to seek assistance for difficulties she was having with her son, Ed. At the therapist's request, the parents and Ed came for an evaluation session. When the parents were asked if they were in agreement about their son's school problem, Mr. T stated that his wife was more concerned than he. Mrs. T agreed and went on to describe her concern. "I'm so worried that he won't do well. I help him with work every night for a half-hour. I don't do it for him, I just correct his work. But I have to keep reminding him all the time." When Mr. T was asked about his involvement with Ed's work, his wife stated, "He works late every night. I help Ed before he comes home."

This example illustrates several common problems. First, the mother, in keeping with her family focus, called for treatment and appeared to be the one most concerned. Second, the father appeared more distant from the family, the problem, and Ed than his wife was. Third, the mother–son axis is particularly intense and problematic.

This family presents a characteristic triangular configuration frequently seen in child-focused families. What is particularly influenced by the ethnic origin of the family is the stance of each member in the process and the specific problems (in this case, academic performance) for which help is sought.

As has been previously discussed, Jewish families place a high value on academic and intellectual achievement and success, especially for their first-born male children. With so much concern about education, it is not surprising that school achievement is frequently labeled a problem in Jewish families. As stated earlier, with such high expectations for success, it is hard not to feel a failure. That is, no matter how successful Jewish children are, they never quite feel successful enough when compared to the parental and cultural expectations they have internalized.

The second problem area, that of separation or leaving home, derives its intensity from the values placed on children as extensions of their parents and on the importance of family togetherness. These values are so strong that Jewish children rarely leave home without some degree of turmoil in their wake. So difficult is the separation process that it is not uncommon for leaving to be solved by the children remaining emotionally dependent and physically close to the parental home. Enmeshment is a frequent character-istic of Jewish American families. However, the family will not usually be aware that they are upset about the child's leaving. Since Jews tend to be liberal and open to ideas, the last thing they would want is to be seen as unsophisticated, uneducated, or boring. Rather, the problem is presented in a variety of ways, such as not liking the way the child looks, dresses, or behaves or not liking the friends he or she keeps. In one family, the mother felt distressed even when her teenage daughter made plans with her girlfriends for a Saturday afternoon. The mother became depressed and felt that the family was "falling apart." She did not, however, oppose her daughter's independence explicitly but rather saw her plans as not taking the family into consideration. As she said to her daughter in a therapy session: "What if daddy and I had planned something for the family that day?"

If Jewish families seek therapy for marital problems rather than child-related ones, they frequently define the problem as poor communication:

"We don't/can't communicate." After some discussion, it may turn out that the wife views her husband as distant and unaffectionate, while he views her as sexually frigid or at least withholding.

On the surface we see the classic confrontation between the distancer and the pursuer. The distancer, the husband in the example of the T family above, deals with his emotional upsets by moving away from people and toward objects, such as work. The pursuer, the wife in the example above, moves toward people when emotionally tense or upset. Thus the pursuer seeks emotional connectedness such as that achieved in "communicating" while the distancer, usually the husband, moves away from such pursuit and may move toward his wife sexually. These characteristic emotional stances tend to become more complex in Jewish families where the culture prescribes roles and behavior. For example, if mother views her domain as the family and father views his as the outside world, the emotional positions of distancer and pursuer are reinforced. Thus Jewish women tend to overwhelm their husbands verbally, while Jewish men are characteristically less verbal at home.

Sex is one aspect of the wifely role that has had many proscriptions attached to it. Over the centuries, it has continued to be a major source of power that Jewish women have exercised with their husbands. It is reinforced by the fact that Jewish women often think of themselves more as mothers than as wives.

The following anecdote told by a female client illustrates this.

> "On our recent trip Harold, the children, and I shared a hotel room. One evening after the children had fallen asleep Harold wanted to have sex. I kept pushing him away because the children were alseep in the room. Finally in desperation my husband said, 'Let's go into the bathroom.' I turned to him, 'Harold! JAPs [Jewish American Princesses] don't do it in the bathroom!'"

The client then went on to question the therapist as to why her husband could not understand her refusal to have sex in the same room with the children or in the bathroom.

An additional conflict for Jewish women is the dual emphasis on her place in the home and on academic achievement and financial success. Jewish women increasingly are experiencing conflicts regarding their roles. These conflicts usually intensify (1) when a couple decides whether or not to have a child, (2) when the children go to school, or (3) when the children go to college. The manifestation of this conflict may range from the inability to make a decision about career to considering divorce the only way to open the door to a career.

Several other problems that may bring a Jewish family into treatment are difficulties related to extended families and in-law relationships or decisions regarding the care of elderly family members. These issues often reflect the emphasis upon familism, and the problems are best understood when viewed from that uniquely Jewish perspective.

For Jewish American families, psychotherapy, particularly psychoanalytic psychotherapy, meshes with their ethnic beliefs, values, and practices. In fact, Jews often see therapy as a part of life and will be disturbed if the children in the family do not accept its value. While the decision to seek treatment might not be an issue, as it would be in certain other ethnic groups, the therapist's qualifications and the conduct of the therapy are very important to Jewish families.

In light of the previous description of Jewish family characteristics and patterns, the therapist would best be a psychiatrist, a man, and a Jew. While these three key attributes are highly regarded by Jewish families, they will respect and respond to any therapist who is bright, open, and sensitive to family values. However, Jewish families tend to confront the therapist directly, early in treatment, regarding his or her credentials. The further the therapist is from the "ideal," the greater the tendency for questioning and confrontation. While it is easy to become defensive, this must be understood as the way the family relates to authority and professionals (Zborowski, 1969). Where other cultures might regard such questions about credentials and authority as rude or intrusive, the Jewish family views them as perfectly reasonable, legitimate, and necessary reassurance that one is getting the best available help.

Jewish families tend to respond more readily to talking or insight-oriented therapies than to more active change-oriented treatments. In keeping with their cultural tradition, self-expression is important. Complex explanations of problems are preferred and are more readily accepted than simple solutions. They tend to look for various levels of meaning, interpretation, or explanation for a behavior.

Given these values, it is not surprising that Jewish families may seek analytic, individual therapies. However, because of their tendency to be liberal, flexible about accepting new ideas, and knowledgeable about treatment, they may seek family treatment. If they do, they may be more interested in the psychodynamic model of treatment such as that of Boszormenyi-Nagy and Sparks (1973) and Ackerman (1966). Bowen systems therapy (1978) may have considerable appeal because of its complexity, focus on loyalty, and transgenerational emphasis. However, its focus on personal responsibility, change, and individual boundaries may conflict with the strong value of family togetherness and a tendency to scapegoat.

Brief goal-oriented therapy with a specific plan and with right and wrong ways of operating spelled out are less likely to seem satisfying to Jewish families. For example:

A single-parent mother of four children called for assistance with her second child, her only daughter. In addition to numerous difficulties with the school system, such as truancy, the daughter was "hanging around" with "a tough bunch of kids" four years her senior. During the initial treatment sessions, the daughter was out all night and the mother was very upset. After some exploration of the incident, the therapist learned that the daughter had received no punishment for her behavior and that she therefore promptly went out again, cursing at her mother. The therapist suggested that the daughter might profit from learning that negative consequences follow such behavior. After much discussion of the possible consequences and mother's agreement to work on a plan, mother said in leaving, "Yes, this is all fine, but what do I do with my hostility?"

Aside from the typical single-parent issues, this example illustrates the tendency to devalue brief, logical explanations and solutions to problems in favor of more complex, feeling-oriented ones. There is also a devaluation of active change. Talking and expressing their feelings (as hostility above) appears to be more appealing than actively changing their behavior.

Complex solutions may be acceptable if they are made at the level of the family's definition of the problem. While Jewish families often enter treatment describing the problem in relationship terms and sounding more sophisticated than other ethnic families regarding the causation of problems, this may not actually be so. Psychological mindedness and apparent insight into their problems does not necessarily mean they can or are willing to change them. For example, parents may define their inability to set limits on their children elaborately and knowledgeably, but below the surface they may view the basic problem as their children's failure to meet their expectations. This is also in keeping with the tendency to see others as causing the problem and the wish to appear sophisticated.

Therapeutic Dilemmas and Interventions

Recently, one of the authors was showing a tape of a Jewish family in treatment to a group of family therapy trainees. While the author was prepared to identify the therapeutic dilemmas and problems in the case, these trainees viewed the family as "ideal." When asked to state the family characteristics and patterns that led to their conclusions, the trainees stated that the family members were bright, verbal, and had a sense of humor. Furthermore, they thought the family's sense of togetherness was impressive. These same characteristics that make Jewish families strong also may pose difficulties for therapists who attempt to change a system.

Part of the therapeutic process with Jewish (and other) families is to decrease the enmeshed family togetherness that blurs personal boundaries. However, as we have previously discussed, togetherness is valued in Jewish families. A number of techniques can be used to deal with enmeshment. First, the therapist may make structural moves within the session that clarify generational and subsystem boundaries, such as changing seats so that all the children are together and separate from the parents. Second, the therapist can coach one part of the system to reverse a process. For example, a young couple seen by one of the authors felt like children when the wife's parents arrived for a weekly visit and proceeded to take over and do most of the household chores. Instead of attempting to get the wife to set clear boundaries with her parents (who would have been very hurt), the therapist suggested that she think of all the chores that still needed to be done, tell the parents to go ahead and do them when they asked, and then sit back and relax!

A third strategy is utilized when family resistance to change is high; these are paradoxical strategies such as relabeling, reframing, and prescribing the symptomatic behavior. In this type of intervention, an intrusive mother is labeled as very caring and a distant father as trusting and supportive. Parents may also then be encouraged to continue this positive behavior because of the system's need for it.

Since distance may be regarded as acceptable paternal behavior, therapists may have difficulty in engaging and keeping Jewish fathers in treatment. Their distance reflects not a lack of interest but their assumptions about family life. Since home and family are viewed as the mother's domain, therapy may also be viewed as her domain. It is not just his extrafamilial role that promotes his physical and emotional distance, but a long-standing lack of a place for him on the home front. No matter how distant and uninvolved the father may appear, his role is often pivotal in treatment. In child-focused families, his lack of involvement balances the mother's overinvolvement, and only by encouraging his action within the family can the mother gently and safely decrease her overfunctioning. The need for a husband's involvement in marital therapy is obvious since his distance acts as a counterforce to his wife's pursuit.

While dealing with distant husbands may be one difficulty, some therapists have even more difficulty with Jewish women/mothers. They may appear to be intrusive, nagging, and demanding, while they want the best for their family. The therapist should remember that the wife's "overs" are usually balanced by her husband's "unders." Often when therapists meet a Jewish mother, she is viewing herself as "failing" to fulfill her role in the family.

Although it may be difficult for a mother to back off, it becomes more possible when the therapist does not take the same stance as the other family members in regarding her negatively. As mentioned previously, a little positive reframing and empathy may go a long way with her.

A particularly good way of helping to create change in Jewish families is by creating a therapeutic alliance with the children. This is in keeping with the emphasis on children expressing themselves and democracy in the Jewish family. Talking with the children about their school performance and extra curricular activities often is a way to become part of the system.

Misreading the family's use of verbal aggression often creates difficulties for the unaware therapist. As previously discussed, Jewish families utilize verbal anger, criticism, and argument as ways of dealing with problems.

These tools also serve as a major distraction and resistance to therapeutic change. Since Jewish families tend to be verbally sophisticated, the cultural novice often gets caught up in their explanations and does not focus on change. If the therapist does give a therapeutic task or suggest a therapeutic change, it must be couched in terms of the family's own complex explanation of the problem. Otherwise, it may be regarded as simplistic and therefore ignored.

In most instances "carping" is a way for family members to keep each other "in line," let off steam and anger, and even express caring, as described previously. While at times a discussion may get heated, it often appears worse to an outsider than to those inside. If the therapist gets caught up in the negative aspects of this process, he or she may miss the underlying positive feelings and lose opportunities to help the family find other ways of expressing their feelings.

While certain facets of Jewish family functioning pose therapeutic difficulties, others make therapy interesting and rewarding. The Jewish family members' ability to laugh at themselves and at life is a tremendous resource. It has often been said the first step in change is the ability to laugh at oneself. Their brightness and articulateness make them good students of family process. A Talmudic sage once remarked: "From all of my students I have learned." These families, if allowed the opportunity, will readily verbalize aspects of family process, helping the therapist to comprehend more clearly the complex way in which they live with each other. Jewish families are not simple to understand, but their very complexity and richness makes work with them rewarding and growth enhancing.

REFERENCES

Ackerman, N. *Treating the Troubled Family*. New York: Basic Books, 1966.

Ayalti, P.J. (Ed.). *Yiddish Proverbs*. New York: Schocken Books, 1976.

Bardis, P.D. Familism among Jews in Suburbia. *Social Science, 36*, 190–196, 1961.

Batwin, F. *The Jews of America: History and Sources*. New York: Behrman House, 1973.

Baum, C., Hyman, M.S., & Michel, S. *The Jewish Woman in America*. New York: New American Library, 1975.

Bell, R.R., & Buerkle, J.V. The Daughter's Role during the Launching State. *Marriage and Family Living, 25*, 384–388, 1962.

Blau, Z.S. In Defense of the Jewish Mother. *Midstream, 46*, 1967.

Bloom, M. The Missing $500,000,000. *Moment, 7*, 30–35, 1981.

Boszormenyi-Nagy, I., & Sparks, G.M. *Invisible Loyalties*. New York: Harper & Row, 1973.

Bowen, M. *Family Therapy in Clinical Practice*. New York: Jason Aronson, 1978.

Bundt, B.K. The Divorced-Parent Family and the Synagogue Community. *Conservative Judaism, 35*, 74–77, 1982.

Cohen, J.L. *A Comparison of Norms and Behaviors of Childrearing in Jewish and Italian American Mothers*. Unpublished doctoral dissertation, Syracuse University, 1977.

Dimont, M.I. *The Jews in America. The Roots, History and Destiny of American Jews*. New York: Simon & Schuster, 1978.

Epstein, H. *Children of the Holocaust*. New York: G.P. Putnam, 1979.

Farber, B., Mindel, C.H., & Lazerwitz, B. The Jewish American Family. In C.H. Mindel & R.W. Habenstein (Eds.), *Ethnic Families in America: Patterns and Variations*. New York: Elsevier, 1976.

Field, P.B. A New Cross Cultural Study of Drunkenness. In D.J. Pittman & C. Synder (Eds.), *Society, Culture and Drinking Patterns*. New York: Wiley, 1962.

Freisch, E. *An Historical Survey of Jewish Philanthropy*. New York: Macmillan, 1924.

Friedman, E.H. Systems and Ceremonies: A Family View and Rites of Passage. In E. Carter & M. McGoldrick (Eds.), *The Family Life Cycle*. New York: Gardner Press, 1980.

Ganzfried, S. *Code of Jewish Law* (Vol. 4). New York: Hebrew Publishing, 1961.

Glazer, N. *American Judaism*. Chicago: University of Chicago Press, 1957.

Goldenberg, J.O. The Jewish Feminist: Conflict in Identities. *Response*, 7, 11–18, 1973.

Gordon, A.I. *Intermarriage*. Boston: Beacon Press, 1964.

Grayzel, S. *A History of the Contemporary Jew*. New York: Harper & Row, 1960.

Hertz, J.H. (Ed.). *The Authorized Daily Prayer Book*. New York: Bloch, 1960.

Hertzberg, A. The American Jew and His Religions. In O.I. Janowsky (Ed.), *The American Jew: A Reappraisal*. Philadelphia: Jewish Publication Society, 1964.

Hollingshead, A.B., & Redlich, F.L. *Social Class and Mental Illness*. New York: Wiley, 1958.

Kolatch, A.J. *The Name Dictionary*. New York: Jonathan David, 1973.

Lamm, M. *The Jewish Way in Death and Mourning*. New York: Jonathan David, 1969.

Luria, Z. Recent Women College Graduates: A Study of Rising Expectations. *American Journal of Orthopsychiatry*, 44, 312–326, 1974.

Lurie, O.R. Parents' Attitudes toward the Use of Mental Health Sources. *American Journal of Orthopsychiatry*, 44, 109–120, 1974.

Marcus, J.R. *The Jew in the Medieval World*. Philadelphia: Jewish Publication Society, 1960.

Massarik, T., & Chimkin, A. United States National Jewish Population Study. *American Jewish Yearbook*, 74, 264–306, 1974.

McClelland, D.C., DeCharms, R., & Rindlisbacher, A. Religions and Other Sources of Parental Attitudes towards Independence Training. In D.C. McClelland (Ed.), *Studies in Motivation*. New York: Appleton-Century-Crofts, 1955.

Mindel, C.H., & Habenstein, R.W. (Eds.). *Ethnic Families in America: Patterns and Variations*. New York: Elsevier, 1976.

Mostysser, T. The Weight of the Past—Reminiscences of a Survivor's Child. *Response*, 8, 3–32, 1975.

Neusner, J. *American Judaism*. Englewood Cliffs, N.J.: Prentice-Hall, 1972.

Priesand, S. *Judaism and the New Woman*. New York: Behrman House, 1976.

Rabinowitz, P. *New Lives*. New York: Avon, 1976.

Roberts, B.H., & Meyers, J.K. Religion, Natural Origins, Immigration and Mental Illness. *American Journal of Psychiatry*, 110, 759–764, 1954.

Rose, A.M., & Stuk, R. Summary of Studies on the Incidence of Mental Disorders. In A.M. Rose (Ed.), *Mental Health and Mental Disorders*. New York: Norton, 1955.

Rosenberg, S.E. *The Search for Jewish Identity in America*. New York: Anchor Books, 1965.

Sanua, V.D. The Sociocultural Aspects of Schizophrenia: A Comparison of Protestant and Jewish Schizophrenics. In A. Shiloh & I. Selazan (Eds.), *Ethnic Groups of America: Their Morbidity, Mortality, and Behavior Disorders*. Springfield, Ill.: Charles C Thomas, 1974.

Sanua, V.D. The Contemporary Jewish Family: A Review of the Social Science Literature. In G. Babis (Ed.), *Serving the Jewish Family*. New York: KTAV, 1978.

Seligman, B.B. The American Jew: Some Demographic Features. *American Jewish Yearbook*, 51, 3–52, 1950.

Siegel, R., & Rheins, C. *The Jewish Almanac*. New York: Bantam Books, 1980.

Singer, I.B. *In My Father's Court*. New York: Farrar, 1962.

Sklare, M. *American Jews*. New York: Random House, 1972.

Snyder, C.R. *Alcohol and the Jews.* New York: Free Press, 1958.

Srole, L., Langner, T., Michael, S., Opler, M.K., & Rennie, T.A. *Mental Health in the Metropolis: Midtown Manhattan Study* (Vol. 1). New York: McGraw Hill, 1962.

Strassfeld, S., & Strassfeld, M. *The Second Jewish Catalog.* Philadelphia: Jewish Publication Society, 1976.

Tsuriel, Y. The Kadusha of Monogamy. *Response, 10,* 65–70, 1976–1977.

Tsypkin, E. Where We Are Not. *Moment, 5,* 42–45, 1980.

Tuchman, B. *A Distant Mirror.* New York: Knopf, 1978.

Wylan, L., & Mintz, N.L., Ethnic Differences in Family Attitudes towards Psychotic Manifestations. *International Journal of Social Psychiatry, 22,* 86–95, 1976.

Yaffe, J. *The American Jews: Portrait of a Split Personality.* New York: Random House, 1968.

Zborowski, M., & Herzog, E. *Life Is with People.* New York: Schocken Books, 1952.

Zborowski, M. *People in Pain.* San Francisco: Jossey-Bass, 1969.

Zimring, F. Portnoy's Real Complaint. *Moment, 6,* 58–60, 1980.

Zuk, G.H. A Therapist's Perspective on Jewish Family Values. *Journal of Marriage and Family Counseling, 4,* 103–110, 1978.

18

Polish Families

SANDRA M. MONDYKOWSKI

"How can you pick out the groom at a Polish wedding?"
"He's the one in the clean bowling shirt."

"How many Polacks does it take to make popcorn?"
"Five. One to hold the pot and four to shake the stove."

These familiar bits of tasteless humor speak volumes about contemporary society's perception of the Polish American. And, as is so often the case, the wit of the common person has grasped, in a twisted fashion, an underlying reality.

The prejudiced vision of a socially backward groom in a bowling shirt and the absurd spectacle of men shaking a stove both flirt with the reality of the Polish peasant's attitude toward upward mobility and education. These attitudes were born of centuries of exploitation by the Polish nobility and are accentuated by the Pole's fierce resistance to the customs and mores of other cultures. This resistance, in turn, has its roots in a long history of invasion and partition—an experience of statelessness that led the Polish peasantry to absorb the indentity of the Polish nation into their very character. It is the reality of these attitudes in all of their cultural and historical context that we must grasp if we are to deal effectively with the Polish American in a therapeutic setting.

Actually the earliest Polish immigrants are recorded as living in colonial Jamestown; and the Poles can boast of the revolutionary heroes Casimir Pulaski and Thaddeus Kosciuzko. However, the major influx of Poles into the United States began in 1870 and ended in 1913. Exact figures are hard to come by since from 1899 to 1919, Poland was not considered to exist as a country by the U.S. Immigration Bureau (Poland had not existed as a country on the map of Europe since 1795). Many Poles who did not identify themselves as such to authorities were counted as Prussians, Austrians, or Russians, depending upon that part of occupied Poland from which they were emigrating (Lopata, 1976a).

It is estimated that 2 million Poles arrived in search of "bread and freedom" during this period (Greene, 1961). They came in two major waves: 1871 to 1899 and 1900 to 1913 (Kuniczak, 1978). Most were Polish peasants

Sandra M. Mondykowski. Alcohol/Psychiatry Service, Brigham and Women's Hospital, Boston, Massachusetts.

who were suffering the effects of a widespread economic depression and the political and cultural oppression of three foreign nations (Polzin, 1973; Greene, 1980).

Earlier and later migrations were comprised largely of well-to-do Poles who assimilated more easily into the mainstream of American life (Greene, 1975). While some of what is said here may be relevant to these groups as well, this chapter will focus on the values and family patterns of the Polish peasant class (who arrived from 1870 to 1919) and their third- and fourth-generation descendants, whose problems we may confront in therapy.

Historical Setting

Poland came into existence as a political entity in the middle of the 10th century. It derived its name from the Polanes who were the strongest and best organized of the Slavic tribes dwelling between the Oder and Vistula rivers. They produced the Piast dynasty, which ruled Poland until 1370. This dynasty was notable for three contributions to Poland's identity: The first king gave her Catholicism; the second king gave her an autonomous class of nobles that would constitute 10% of the population; and the last king made her a refuge for Europe's wandering Jewish people.

Mieszko I, the first recorded king of this dynasty, married a Bohemian princess and accepted the Roman Catholic faith for himself and for his people. The data ascribed to this event (966) marks the start of the fusion of nationalism and religion into the Polish identity. It is celebrated as both the founding of the Polish state and as the date of the state's conversion to Roman Catholicism. This event also brought Poland into the orbit of Rome and Western civilization. The state's adoption of the Latin alphabet set Poles apart from other Eastern Slavs who were converted to the Greek rite and who adopted the Cyrillic alphabet and Byzantine heritage (Barnett, 1958).

Boleslav the Brave (ca. 992–1025), the second king, spent most of his reign fighting wars to extend Poland's authority eastward, thus opening up commercial routes to the Black Sea and securing Poland's prosperity through the middle ages. In order to attract the manpower to fight these battles, he conferred noble rank on "whosoever possessed a horse and bore arms" (Fournier, 1964). Thus the *szlachta* (the Polish nobility) was born. All those "without horses" were thus relegated to the status of serfs.

Most Western European countries enjoyed long periods of peace that enabled their kings to gain the political and military strength necessary to limit the power of their nobles. These circumstances also provided an atmosphere for social change whereby peasants rose in status and thus checked the nobility. But Poland, because of its geographical location, enjoyed no such long period of security. So, the nobility grew in number, and jealously guarded the rights they had won.

Each Polish noble considered himself to be second to none. Even those nobles whose lands were later confiscated during the partitions were regarded as being entitled to all the rights and privileges of the wealthiest among them. Once born to the gentry, no Polish nobleman could lose his status. Conversely, no outsider could gain admittance to this group either by chivalrous deed or accumulated wealth.

The last Piast king was Casimir the Great (ca. 1332–1370). It was he who invited the Jewish people who were persecuted in the rest of Europe to Poland. In the next two centuries they were granted rights as a semiautonomous community with responsibility for their own educational and social needs. For a while the rise in commerce and trade provided them a necessary role in Poland's economy as merchants, shopkeepers, bankers, and so on, and they flourished. But they remained apart and unassimilated in the mainstream of Polish life (Lopata, 1976a).

Under the Jagiellon dynasty (1386–1572), Poland achieved her greatest territorial gains. By the 16th century, the Kingdom of Poland encompassed all of Lithuania, Belorussia, and the Ukraine.

Several innovations of the Jagiellon dynasty reflected the importance of the nobles' role in the Polish government. At this time the *sejm* (parliament) took control of legislative functions of the state and won the right to elect members of the dynastic family to the throne. The parliament passed the liberum veto, which stated that any member could veto passage of any law indefinitely (Halecki, 1943). It restricted the privileges of the small urban middle class that had flourished during the 14th and 15th centuries. Fearing the growing wealth of this middle class, the nobility passed laws restricting its trade and maintained economic policies that led to the ruin of once prosperous towns (Barnett, 1958). The peasants meanwhile were forbidden to move off their land. Citizenship was restricted to the nobility who considered themselves the "nation."

In 1572 the last Jagiellon king (Sigismund August) died without an heir. Poland's internal weakness was exploited by the Russians, the Turks, and the Swedes. At the same time, internal political anarchy reigned. The gentry would not cooperate with the monarchy to provide money for an army, and the parliament was paralyzed by the liberum veto. The landed gentry treated their serfs so harshly that Poland became known as "the peasant's hell" (Barnett, 1958).

The Polish peasant was socialized by his large family, the village, the local church, and the civic law. All four elements were interdependent and, acting together, provided social control for the individual.

The peasants suffered from the oppression of the upper classes but they also set up a pecking order in their own class. Villagers were judged by how many acres of land and heads of cattle they owned. The wealthiest was accorded the status of village leader, along with the parish priest and the local political leader. The richer peasants sat in the front rows in church since only they could afford those pew rents. The others took their places in descending order of wealth. The renters and lodgers who owned no land stood in the back, and the beggars and servants had to remain outside. Wealth conferred status and with it the right to dominate their families and their villages (Polzin, 1973).

Housing for the peasants usually consisted of a hut with three rooms and an earthen floor. In the summer, life was lived outside, but in the winter the peasants and their cattle had to share the same space. If the peasant was wealthy enough, he could afford wooden floors, glass windows, and a stable for his cattle and his servants.

Educational opportunities varied, depending upon which section of partitioned Poland the peasant was located in. Russia attempted to set up schools, but they prohibited the teaching of the Polish language. These Russian schools were located in towns that were too hard for most children to reach and were not even large enough to accommodate the children who could get to them. But the parish priest was literate and bilingual, and the peasants could turn to him for education. In the German-occupied section of Poland, school attendance was compulsory so the literacy rate was higher. In the Austrian section, city schools were open to Polish children, but most people were so poor that they had neither the time nor the inclination to attend (Thomas & Znaniecki, 1919–1920; Polzin, 1973).

Status was derived from people's positions in the local community rather than the larger world, and families would compete with each other to attain higher positions (Lopata, 1976a). Each family member was expected to participate in this competition. Prestige, and therefore higher positions, came from domestic and agricultural skills. But it was not the individual's position that was to be enhanced; it was the family's. It was the family's background and status that determined the point from which the member would begin the competition, and personal fulfillment was not considered relevant.

This system transplanted itself in the United States and remains strong (Lopata, 1976b).

Polish immigrants often took jobs in mines and factories at lower wages than the English, Welsh, and German workers. These other groups had arrived in America earlier and bitterly resented the Poles who caused wages to be decreased.

The Poles were suspect not only for the lower wages they were willing to take but also for the way they lived. Landlords often took advantage of them, charging such high rents that many were forced to sleep in one room. But even after they could afford to move, many stayed on in substandard housing to save money for their own land or home, which mattered more than maintaining appearances.

Determined to survive, to earn money . . . (the Polish immigrant) accepted low wages, dangerous and unsanitary working conditions, abuse and exploitation. His hungers were not intellectual, his needs were immediate: survival in the present and into the future in its most primitive form. . . . Clannish, suspicious, contemptuous of fine language, dour and unforgiving when oppressed (or when he imagined he had been cheated), the Polish peasant tried to live life wholly in the present, unable to comprehend a life beyond his experience and hostile to everything he did not understand. . . . But he was also painfully honest, self-reliant, and he knew how to bide his time. (Kuniczak, 1978, p. 110)

A cycle familiar to many immigrants was set up. The Poles lived in poor conditions either because they had no choice or because their priorities temporarily precluded better living conditions. But other Americans pointed to them with derision as if to say, "You see, these people live like animals, they must not know any better—how stupid." Several years ago, a Pole who had immigrated to this country in 1912 poignantly expressed to the author some of the contradictions he faced:

"You can never understand what it was like—I was a good farmer and I spoke five languages—you had to in order to get along in an occupied country. But I couldn't speak English and I couldn't read or write. So I come to America and go to work in a mine and I am called a dumb Polack."

Confronting these prejudices gave the Polish immigrants a common problem. They banded together into their own tightly knit communities (known as Polonia) and tried to be as self-sufficient as possible.

Many peasants wanted to preserve as much of their culture as possible, especially those who believed they were going to return to Poland. They became increasingly cautious and defensive. They formed mutual-aid societies that handled insurance, banking, and help for widows and orphans so that they would not have to turn to the outside community (Greene, 1975). Little contact meant less pain and humiliation. In short, a voluntary ghetto grew up around their residences and their parish church.

The subcommunity existed through, or because of, the shared values, attitudes, and activities of Polish-Americans which constituted a way of life relatively distinct from that of the surrounding society. (Polzin, 1973, p. 130)

Going to school provided the first serious break in the continuity of a Polish child's experience. Up to that time children spoke their parents' language and received their values from their parents and the extended family in Polonia. Even if they went to a Polish Catholic grammar school staffed by a Polish order of nuns, children had to confront the English language and "foreign influences" (the dominant culture). They soon began questioning the traditional values of their parents. If they went to public

school, the culture shock was immediate. A patient in her late 50s told me
about her school experience:

> "I was confused and miserable. I didn't even know there was such a lan-
> guage as English. I never heard anyone speak it at home. The teachers
> thought that I was retarded and put me in the slow class. Some of them re-
> fused to try to pronounce my name. The other kids laughed at my clothes
> and my hair because my mother put ribbons in my braids instead of colored
> elastics. My mother said that was how her mother did her hair for school
> and that was how she was going to do mine. She got very angry at me for
> begging her to do it differently. Today if I go to a party, I know in my head
> that my clothes and hair look in fashion but sometimes I have an anxiety
> attack at the door, as if all my old classmates were there on the other side
> waiting to make fun of me." (personal communication)

The Polish Family and Acculturation

Under the circumstances just described, acculturation was slow, and, to a
degree, the family patterns described here may be as true of third-generation
Polish Americans as they were of their grandparents.

In a Polish family, respect, not love, is the binding tie (Thomas &
Znaniecki, 1919–1920). Polish families are characterized by "mutual respect,
support, cooperation, financial and spiritual help, staying together and
sacrificing. . . . Love is expressed in action" (Mostwin, 1980, p. 110). The
father and husband is acknowledged head of the household. His authority is
to be respected and his wishes obeyed. As one Polish patient told me, "When
a Polish husband says, 'Jump!' you ask 'How high?' on the way up."
However, even in the first generation, the dominance of the Polish man is
more theoretical than real (Bloch, 1976). By tradition, the Polish wife not
only brought the requisite dowry into the newly formed household but also
maintained control of the assets that comprised the dowry. The wife not only
contributed assets at the time of the marriage but she herself became an
important source of labor. She worked alongside her husband and took part
in planting and harvesting. The housekeeping and child care were done by an
older female relative or by a young girl. Sanday (1974) suggests that doing
heavy field work gave these women a higher status than their Western
European counterparts, who contributed most of their labor in the home,
and may account for the fact that present-day Polish American women
expect to contribute to the family's income. Wives are expected to stand up
for themselves, sometimes verbally and sometimes physically.

While mutual respect rather than displays of affection is the most
noticeable external trait in the husband–wife relationship (Barnett, 1958),
the Polish wife is still thought of as a sexual partner for her husband, in

addition to her role as mother. Strong sexual feelings are accepted in the family, and sex is not considered bad in and of itself (Novak, 1975).

It would not be unusual for a man to come home from work and, in front of the children, to squeeze his wife's breast or slap her behind playfully saying, "Oh boy, kid, are you going to get it tonight." Within the family, expressions of sexuality have a joyous and overt quality that the Polish Americans consider lusty and that non-Poles have often considered vulgar. This openness included the right of both sexes to make comments about one another's sexual equipment and/or performance. This is very different from the Polish American's ethnic next-door neighbors—the Slovaks—who, as Stein (1978) tells us, considered it bad form to discuss any physical function "all of which are silently performed and intensely private" (p. 37).

Despite its generally accepting attitudes Polish American culture has rules for sexual conduct. Sex was permissible only within marriage or its equivalent (i.e., common-law marriage). While women, too, enjoy sex, the double standard still applies. If men are unfaithful in marriage and discrete about it, then it is understood although not condoned. If they are indiscrete, it is shameful. Premarital sexual activity is expected in men, but not in nice women. Women are expected to be virgins when they marry, but some sexual activity is tolerated, if it is not general knowledge.

Having many children is a source of prestige because of their contributions to the household economy. Children also affirm the parents' status as faithful Catholics since a small family would lead others to suspect that birth control was being practiced—which is forbidden by the Catholic Church.

Children are raised in a strict tradition of discipline (Mostwin, 1980) and are expected to give their fathers unquestioning obedience. Polish American children are disciplined physically, sometimes harshly. This has been especially true of second-generation children because of the conflict in values between the immigrant and the second generation in the United States (Green, 1946). As those second-generation children have grown and become acculturated, they have moderated the disciplining of their own children, but physical discipline is still the norm. Most physical discipline is meted out as punishment for disobeying rules, which in turn is seen as an indication of a failure to respect the parents. Father has chief responsibility for the discipline, but mother is allowed to intervene if she feels the father's punishment is too severe. Punishment is directed toward the child's behavior rather than his or her presumed motivation. This is very different from the Irish Catholic sense of personal badness. As a Polish patient put it, "I would get a beating if I broke a family rule or showed disrespect, but somehow I knew that I was punished not because I was a bad person, but because I had done a bad thing" (personal communication).

Children are not expected to fight back when their parents are disciplining them. In fact, they would be further punished if they did. But children are expected to stand up for themselves outside of the home. They learn early to fight and to take care of themselves. This is as true for girls as for boys.

In a Polish family everyone is expected to work and to pull his or her own weight. Children are instructed in general terms but are supposed to learn the details of their tasks by trial and error. In this way, they are supposed to learn to rely on their own judgment. Parents do not show much affection for their children once they are past the toddler stage for fear of spoiling them, but they will praise them for their performance of chores. Children are also praised for self-control (i.e., bearing pain without crying) (Barnett, 1958). Ideally, a kind of balance exists. Much is expected and little sympathy is wasted on failure, but a child's triumphs are publicly acknowledged and praised.

Second-generation children have experienced terrible conflicts as they sought to fulfill both their parents' and their own dreams. They were told that they were being stuck up if they sought higher education or mobility out of the neighborhood. To call a person "stuck up" was a serious charge that isolated them from the community (Kuniczak, 1978). The outside American world was also considered hostile because children believed that their surface qualifications were not good enough (i.e., dress and manners). Frequently, children from the second (and third) generations became alienated from both worlds.

Therapy with Polish American Families

The ability to function is crucial to Polish Americans for their identity is tied up more with doing than with being. Both men and women greatly fear anything that might cripple or limit their performance. Poles stoically endure physical illness. They may comment on pain matter-of-factly, but they generally work and function despite any discomfort.

Poles find mental illness especially terrifying because it not only impairs performance but also involves loss of control over behavior. Since emotional problems are intangible, they are also harder to forestall. We cannot hide depression the way we can hide the pain of a broken leg.

Family loyalty and mistrust of outsiders is strong, and Polish American families rarely come to a clinic or private practitioner for treatment. When a Polish American family does seek treatment, there is usually a problem that threatens family integrity. Complaints center around the distressing behavior of one family member, which is rarely viewed as a problem for which other family members share responsibility. The most common problems are repeated defiance of a child, refusal of a family member to turn over income for the family's welfare, alcoholism, and sibling conflict over how to care for an ailing parent (Mostwin, 1980; Lopata, 1976b).

The family would first try to deal with such behavior within the family structure, both nuclear and extended. The person is usually told he or she is not behaving correctly and should change. If this approach does not work, the family enlists the help of the community—the Polish resource network. The parish priest, coworkers, members of a mutual-aid society, or fellow club members may be used to pressure an individual to conform. Only after these efforts fail will the family call an outside social agency or the court to intercede with the delinquent family member (Thomas & Znaniecki, 1919–1920; Lopata, 1976b). Several assumptions underlie the Polish American method of problem solving. The first is that the person is refusing, not unable, to change his or her behavior. A second is that behavior is more important than feelings. Personal feelings are allowed as long as external behavior remains acceptable. Thus Poles may at times have trouble reconciling inner feelings with external performance. A third assumption is that results are what matter, not understanding the behavior itself. Poles turn to a therapist to resolve a problem, not to gain understanding of the forces that led to the problem in the first place.

Since the community can have so much influence on Polish American family life, the therapist must know if the family still has extensive contacts with the Polish community, maintains membership in a Polish club, or works in an area with many others of Polish descent. In most Polish communities what happens is everybody's business, and if the family is still connected with Polonia, the community probably knows about the problem that brought the family in for treatment. While the therapist might think she or he is only treating one family, an entire unseen "Greek chorus" might be present at every session. The family will often repeat to the neighbors what the therapist said, and the neighbors will feel free to comment on how the therapist is doing. Thus neighborhood as well as family and individual values will be introduced into the treatment. The therapist must take the opinions of neighbors into account because they may clarify family conflicts.

Traditionally, because the Polish community knew so much about each family, family solidarity was crucial. If the family wished to advance its status, members had to conform with community standards. By the same token, if a family member did something considered deviant, then the family's united front was particularly important to maintain family morale (Lopata, 1976b).

The therapist treating a Polish American family might encounter some special difficulties at points where traditional Polish and dominant American cultural values differ. One difference concerns definitions of deviant behavior. For example, one Polish mother in describing the problem declared, "Doctor, my husband got our son Stanley a good job at his factory, but this ungrateful boy wants to run away to college. How could he do this during a recession when we need the money so badly?" Education-oriented therapists might have difficulty understanding this woman's values and be inclined to ignore them in favor of the son's values since they are closer to their own.

A therapist might also misunderstand the importance of caring for extended family members in a Polish family and the generational conflicts that can develop when children do not want their parents to move in with them (Cohler & Lieberman, 1979; Mostwin, 1979; Fandetti & Gelfand, 1976). One elderly Polish mother complained: "My hot-shot daughters don't want me to move in with them now that my Thomas is dead. They don't think I'll fit into their fancy suburb. They say I'll be trouble getting along with their children! Don't they have respect for their mother anymore!" The therapist from a background that values personal fulfillment and loyalty to the nuclear family over the family of origin must recognize how these family members are violating traditional Polish values.

This is the point where it can be important to pay attention to the "Greek chorus" of the community. The therapist should inquire what solutions have already been suggested by others. Solutions that will be accepted in the community will, in the long run, be the most helpful.

The therapist might also have difficulty with the issue of intimacy. In spite of the expressiveness of Polish Americans, the therapist must not be misled by the easy demonstration of emotions. Often the intense expression of emotions during a family session is a distancing technique to avoid expressing a forbidden need, the need to be taken care of. The lack of acceptance of emotional dependency ranks along with disapproval of higher education and prohibitions against upward social mobility as cultural issues that most adversely effect the accommodation that Polish Americans can make with the dominant culture, not to mention with their own psychological development.

When a Polish American husband and wife talk about supporting each other, they usually mean doing for each other, not emotional support. This has obvious implications for cross-cultural marriages. For example:

> A man of Jewish descent married a woman of Polish background. He had just started a new job and wished to share his anxiety about it with his wife. She was uncomfortable listening to him and he finally accused her of not supporting him. She angrily replied: "How can you say that? Don't I make a nice home for you? Don't I cook just what you like for dinner? Don't I always make sure you have fresh clothes and clean suits?"

But the wife's discomfort did not stem only from these different definitions of support. She was also upset that her husband was expressing anxiety about his performance and angry and fearful about his need to depend upon her in other than tangible ways. In the Polish American community, performance is important as a measure of self-respect. Expressing anxiety about that performance, however, is not allowed. The fear is that the very expression of anxiety will lessen their ability to perform. Expressing anxiety also implies a need for emotional reassurance and support that violates the value of stoicism.

This expectation of stoicism is by no means limited to the husband in the family. A wife who does not work outside the home would be just as upset at the thought of confessing anxiety about her ability to make the Christmas Eve dinner as her husband would be at expressing anxiety over his job. If she sought her husband's reassurance or needed it to get her through the day, she might feel like a failure as a homemaker. And Polish children are similarly expected to inhibit their expressions of need. If children come home crying and say they are afraid of the neighborhood bully, they will not receive much sympathy from their parents. Even a small child cannot voice fears about such things as snakes under the bed or monsters in the closet without risking parental ridicule for "being a baby." "Toughening up the kids" and showing a stoical face to their spouses were probably necessary adaptive behaviors in peasant villages that were continuously subject to invasion and famine. But by the third or fourth generation in the United States, such behaviors may often be maladaptive, though well intentioned and understandable.

Poles also fear dependency because they are expected to take care of themselves. Being taken care of implies weakness and inability to pull their own weight. Feelings of need are not seen as normal and are often connected in the family's thinking with shame and humiliation. The family therapist must, therefore, tread lightly in the area of emotional dependency. To ask a husband or wife to say to the other, "I need you," is to ask the Polish American to confront and reassess a basic part of his or her identity. Yet the issue is important to deal with in family therapy. But since neither the husband, nor the wife, nor the children have permission to express anxiety and dependency needs, there is no ready way to get at them. The level of tension simply rises until the feelings are eventually dispelled in ways, such as violence and alcohol abuse, that may be destructive to the family. There is, in fact, much heavy drinking in the Polish American community, and one of its functions is to give permission to be "weak," to cry, or to "lose control." If they are drunk, they can disclaim responsibility for their actions.

Unfortunately, there is very little written on alcoholism specifically among Polish Americans. It is recognized as a problem in Poland where a national committee against alcoholism had been set up to organize treatment facilities (Tongue, 1962). An international survey on alcoholism and violent crimes showed that over 55% of homicide offenders in Poland were chronic drinkers (Pernanen, 1976). But in a literature survey of drinking behavior in the United States only one relevant citation is to be found, and it is not even specifically about Poles. Namely, 85% of first-generation Eastern European men are drinkers and of these, 16% can be considered heavy drinkers (Cahalan & Cisin, 1976). Heavy drinking is accepted in the Polish American community. It is not considered a problem unless it interferes with work or health. This is an issue that warrants further discussion, but it will have to wait until more studies are done.

Interethnic marriages create special stresses. Differences in the expression of anger and sexuality are common. How the children are disciplined is another problem area. Polish Americans often feel that they have left the old expectations behind, only to find them popping up again once they are married and have children of their own.

In the following examples[1] we will illustrate some of these patterns and the problems they may cause in interethnic marriages.

The Broulards

A Polish American woman, Catherine, was married to a man of French Canadian descent, Henry. They had five children. The eldest daughter, Gloria, became pregnant out of wedlock. Catherine was angry at Gloria because "she was not sensible enough to get some kind of protection," but she came to acept the situation and began to plan a big family wedding. Henry was distraught and drinking heavily.

Gloria then informed her parents that she was not getting married, but she wanted to keep the baby. Catherine still wanted her to get married, and Henry worried that she would be a "bad influence" on her younger sisters, Anna, 14, and Celia, 11. He wanted to send her to a home for unwed mothers and have her give up the baby for adoption. Their two sons, Frank, 18, and William, 16, had been getting into fights in the neighborhood. Catherine and Henry couldn't agree on a course of action, and they were referred to their local mental health center by their parish priest.

Henry felt his daughter was a bad person for having had sex before marriage, and he was deeply concerned with what the neighbors would think if his pregnant daughter stayed in the house. He believed that he should have the final say on all family decisions and that a wife should not question him, let alone disagree with him.

While Catherine was angry at her daughter, she could understand if not condone her sexual behavior. Catherine had provided the sex education the children had received. She accepted her daughter's sexuality and believed there should be a place for Gloria in the family, whether she married the baby's father or not. (In Polish culture, unlike Italian, for example, the loss of a daughter's virginity does not besmirch the honor of the entire family. Nor does it permanently degrade the daughter. "Hate the sin but love the sinner" is a saying that is acted out more in the Polish American community than in other Catholic ethnic groups.)

Catherine was concerned about what her relatives would think if she sent her daughter away to live with "strangers" to have her baby. She also believed that as long as the extended family was behind her, it little mattered what the neighbors thought. Finally, although used to the idea of obeying her husband, Catherine believed that she should stand up to him and even circumvent his authority if it was for the greater good of the family.

---

1. All names in these composite cases have been changed.

The Wadjas

A Polish American, Thomas, was married to a small-town middle-class WASP woman, Linda. They had two small children, Tommy, 3, and Cindy, 8 months. The family was trying to buy a house and Thomas thought Linda should go back to work part time to help with the down payment. Linda refused, saying that the children were too young. Thomas found himself angry and frustrated and resorted to yelling at his wife. Linda then felt that he didn't love her anymore.

Concurrently Tommy had suffered a temporary regression in his toilet training. Linda came home from shopping one day and was appalled to find Thomas spanking the child for soiling his pants. After another fight, during which Thomas slapped his wife, he attempted to have sexual intercourse with her. She accused him of being a "Stanley Kowalski" and demanded that he seek counseling for his "animal behavior" or she would leave him.

Thomas felt that Linda should go to work because the house was for both of them and the wife should take equal responsibility in helping the family to achieve its goal. Linda believed that it was her husband's duty to support her, no matter what their economic circumstances. She was doing her share already by caring for their rented house and for the children. She also felt that by asking her to go to work, her husband was demonstrating his failure to achieve sufficient career advancement and financial recognition, which in turn reflected on her place in the community.

Thomas was picking up Linda's attitude, and since he believed that his ability to work was synonymous with his strength and his manhood, he was enraged and threatened. He felt she was questioning his potency.

Linda reacted to Thomas's anger by withdrawing into silence. She believed not only that expressed anger is bad form, but also that such rage must mean that her husband didn't love her anymore. The quieter Linda got, the angrier Thomas got, for he believed that silence meant lack of love. Finally, enraged, he slapped his wife, who was not respecting his hard work, and he also slapped the child who was not obeying him. He attempted to take his wife to bed to prove to her that he was still to be respected as a man.

Linda was frightened and put off by this combination of anger and sexuality and related it to one of the stereotypes she remembered about Polish Americans—the crude and violent Stanley Kowalski in Tennessee Williams's play *A Streetcar Named Desire*. She was fearful that her husband would now turn into a wife beater and a child abuser. This couple was not aware of most of the assumptions they were making about each other.

The Millers

Paul, a man of German and Austrian background was married to Stella, a Polish American woman. Their first child was 6 months old. Stella had gone back to work two months earlier, even though she had two months left to her maternity leave.

Paul had just been made a partner in his law firm; this meant a significant jump up the socioeconomic ladder as well as increased social obligations. He was furious at his wife for not yet losing the 30 pounds she had gained during her pregnancy. He also wished she would dress more fashionably, in keeping with his new position. She accused him of not appreciating her and refused to attend the required social functions. He in turn accused her of trying to sabotage his career. He brought her into treatment with the belief that the therapist would straighten out her emotional attitudes and make her listen to reason.

Paul put great stock in physical appearance, self-discipline, and the belief that a wife's actions were extensions and reflections of her husband. He felt that if his wife did not look, dress, sound, or act in certain conventionally acceptable ways, it meant she not only did not love him but might actually be mocking him.

Stella felt she was offering her husband great respect by keeping a nice home, continuing to work, and having a child. She felt he did not appreciate her efforts and instead wanted her to concentrate on "trivia."

Paul valued education and social mobility and wished to be considered a well-read, well-spoken man. He looked forward to climbing still another rung on the social ladder.

Stella feared that she would be looked down upon in the circles in which her husband wished to travel. Secretly she wished he would stay on a level in his career where he could make good money but where she would not have to continue to deal with mixed messages concerning "joining the gentry" and being "stuck up."

Paul believed that the outer man was a reflection of the inner man. Being slender, well-dressed, and in good health signified a well-ordered mind, a strong character, and a firm purpose in life.

Stella saw her weight as a positive reflection on her marriage and her position as a wife and mother. Putting on weight meant she was now a "real woman," substantial and strong enough to carry out all of her duties. It also meant contentment with her marriage and satisfaction with her spouse. Losing a great deal of weight could mean that she was frivolous or perhaps looking for an affair. It could also mean she would become too weak and fragile to maintain her responsibilities. Polish Americans share this attitude toward weight with several other peasant ethnic groups, most notably the Italians.

Conduct of Therapy

With Polish American families, above all, the approach of the therapist must be active, practical, and down to earth.

The Novaks

Ted and Lottie were both of Polish American descent. They had two children, Teddy, 19, and Helen, 23. Helen was a nurse at a local hospital and lived away from home. Still single, she planned to go for a degree in psychiatric nursing. Teddy had been in trouble for a number of years. He suffered from school phobia, but when the parish priest suggested counseling, Ted and Lottie refused. They said Teddy was just stubborn, not "crazy." Teddy had also been experimenting with drugs and had been picked up by the police for fighting.

After experimenting with PCP, he had a psychotic reaction and was taken to the emergency ward of the hospital where Helen worked. From there he was sent to the state mental institution for detoxification and psychiatric observation. Ted and Lottie were extremely upset and blamed Helen for "shipping [her] brother off to the funny farm." When Helen stressed the drug reaction rather than the psychosis, they finally accepted her explanation of Teddy's need for treatment.

Through Helen's intercession, Ted and Lottie agreed, grudgingly, to come to one family session (although they did in fact continue for 10 sessions) at the outpatient clinic connected to the state hospital. They would have preferred to deal with the matter themselves or to have the priest "talk some sense into the kid," but they accepted Helen as a liaison because she was a family member who was "in the business"—that is, worked in human services. But her credibility stemmed primarily from her membership in the family, not from her professional status.

Ted and Lottie were afraid that the therapist would present himself or herself as an intellectual and would look down on them. (A therapist who elects a silent style would, therefore, make this family uneasy and only reinforce their fears. They also might interpret silence as lack of interest. The family was present oriented and like most Polish American families, they were looking for instructions and practical solutions. Teddy was the designated patient, and they expected the clinic to "get him off that stuff and back to work.")

Initially the therapist moved to get Teddy out of the scapegoated position by attacking the common enemy, drugs, rather than Teddy's use of drugs. The therapist could sympathize with both sides at once: "Mr. and Mrs. Novak, it is pretty hard to raise children today. You must have worked hard to teach your kids the values that you wanted to hand down. With all these drugs around and all the problems of society, you must feel that the cards are stacked against you." And to Teddy: "You are in a bind. You are trying to grow up listening to your parents, on the one hand, and your peers, on the other. Society tells you that you are an adolescent and, therefore, you are supposed to go through stages and get into trouble. Then when you do what's expected of you, you get called crazy and get put in a hospital."

The therapist's strategy was to separate the "combatants" and to demonstrate that he respected their opinions and their efforts. He could then ask each member to describe how they dealt not with Teddy but with the problem of drugs and social pressures in the society. This approach allowed the therapist to observe how the members interacted as they talked—to note whether they looked or turned toward each other as they spoke, referred to each other in the third person or addressed one another directly. The therapist also learned how they approached problem solving and the extent of their involvement with their extended family and the neighborhood "Greek chorus."

This method of indirect information gathering is much less threatening than that of asking direct family history questions that they might answer with "none of your damn business, Doc." The therapist then described the program Teddy was in at the clinic. This reassured the family that the clinic was not a mysterious authority force seeking to supplant the family. It was emphasized that all therapeutic efforts were supports for the family's own problem-solving efforts. Since in this case the problem had been defined as drugs, the therapist described PCP and its effects and thus helped make the problem more tangible.

Teddy was taking drugs to deal with fears that he was not strong enough to take care of himself. His drug use also masked the issues that he was forbidden to bring up, that is, that he questioned his parents' work ethic and their desire that he live in the old neighborhood. Ted and Lottie needed to see that although Teddy's ideals and goals were different from theirs, he was not disloyal or disrespectful. They also needed to discuss their fears that if Helen got a professional degree she would despise her parents. Helen, in turn, needed to talk out her feelings of isolation and fear of losing her place in the family.

The family learned to talk rather than shout about their feelings and their value conflicts. Helen went on to work toward her degree; Teddy stopped taking drugs and began doing volunteer carpentry work on a neighborhood project. In time he took a carpentry job in another part of the city and moved away from home. Ted and Lottie accepted their children's choices and presented a united front to their community. Once Teddy and Helen felt their parents' approval, they visited home more frequently. They felt safer praising their parents and acknowledging how hard they had worked to get where they were. Ted and Lottie felt properly respected and were more relaxed about their children's life choices, they no longer feared that their children were going to be lost to them.

At some point in the first session the therapist should find one or two points of reference at which to identify with the family experience. The therapist need not relate personal material but could comment on something as simple as having seen the movie one of them mentioned. Polish American patients will take it as a sign that the therapist is secure enough to be a bit human with them. These patients respond best to a style of informal friendliness, sympathetic listening, and nonpatronizing understanding. They are also likely to be more receptive to continued therapy if the therapist can define the family sessions as task-oriented explorations of the problem. He or she can try to sell the family on the idea of coming back by explaining that the program works most efficiently if the clinic does not try to go it alone, if they often consult with one another so the therapist does not say one thing and the parents another. Therapists can invite family members to work with them as guides.

If the family agrees to continue, sessions can proceed on much the same lines as described in the first session. The therapist needs to be active and sympathetic. If the members ask whether the therapist saw a sports event or a movie for example, he or she should respond truthfully and directly. When trust is established, the therapist can ask them what was their perception of the event or movie and in time perhaps relate it to something going on in the family. If the family resists psychological interpretation, then the therapist will do well to offer a self-deprecating humorous response, perhaps joking about his or her own expertise. Power struggles should be avoided.

Over time, more emotion will be expressed. Family members are not necessarily airing their real feelings. Dealing with real feelngs is probably precisely what they want to avoid. They might be using the expression of strong emotion to intimidate the therapist so that he or she will not probe those feelings too deeply, as well as using them as a distancing technique to avoid dealing with dependency needs.

Typically, family members are afraid that if they do express feelings openly, the therapist will label them "crazy." They fear losing control and associate it with mental illness. If the therapist persists in trying to promote expression of feelings without being sensitive to these issues, a Polish American family is likely to drop out.

Since ability to express emotion in and of itself is not usually the problem for these families, what they do need is the therapist's help in structuring angry confrontations. They need to learn to negotiate with each other—to express strong emotions in some effective way, rather than, for example, getting drunk in order to "lose control." They need to be reassured that they are not crazy and that many families have problems similar to their own. An anecdote from the therapist's own family's experiences can at times be very helpful. For example, a therapist dealing with a family where there was intense conflict with teenage children, remarked during a session that he had two teenage sons and "it certainly can be difficult to deal with some of the issues they bring home." The Polish American family felt relieved that the therapist took a personal stance rather than being a "judgmental intellectual."

The therapist may get frustrated when family members listen attentively to all that has been suggested and then come up with completely opposite plans (remember the liberum veto). The members are probably ambivalent about authority, and they may dig in their heels and argue over every insight.

The therapist should try to make Polish Americans respected and trusted partners in their own treatment. Throughout therapy it is best to stay with strengths and to discuss problems in terms of real things that they can do to help themselves. Only then can they gradually learn to deal with dependency issues.

Polish American families do not believe in going down with a sinking ship. If a deviant family member really threatens the family—for example, becomes involved in criminal activity and refuses all efforts to get help—the family will go to court. The court puts the member on probation. If the court action does not work (perhaps the member violates probation), then the family will take the painful step of disowning and ignoring him or her. Rather than have the whole family disgraced and withdrawn from their community, the family members will expel the offender (Lopata, 1976b). This is a kind of family triage that enables the rest of the family to retain unity and to go on with their lives. The family that expels a member under these circumstances will receive support from the community. Friends will confide their similar experiences and provide peer support to ease the family's guilt and sorrow.

Summary

Most Polish American families will not begin or remain in family therapy unless they believe the therapist is going to be of some practical help toward tangible goals. They require practical, action-oriented therapy and will freely express frustration and dissatisfaction with more passive insight-oriented therapy. If therapists demonstrate that they know and respect Polish values, they will be rewarded with interested and cooperative patients who are willing to help themselves.

REFERENCES

Barnett, C.R. *Poland.* New Haven, Conn.: Human Relations Area File Press, 1958.

Bloch, H. Changing Domestic Roles among Polish Immigrant Women. *Anthropological Quarterly, 40*(1), 3–10, 1976.

Cahalan, D., & Cisin, I.H. Drinking Behavior and Drinking Problems in the United States. In B. Kissin & H. Begleiter (Eds.), *The Biology of Alcoholism* (Vol. 4): *Social Aspects of Alcoholism.* New York: Plenum, 1976.

Cohler, B.J., & Lieberman, M.A. Personality Changes across the Second Half of Life: Findings from a Study of Irish, Italian and Polish-American Women. In D.E. Gelfand & A.J. Kutzik (Eds.), *Ethnicity and Aging.* New York: Springer, 1979.

Fandetti, D., & Gelfand, D. Care of the Aged: Attitudes of White Ethnic Families. *The Gerontologist, 16*(6), 544–549, 1976.

Fournier, E. *Poland.* London: Vista Books, 1964.

Green, A.W. The Middle-Class Male Child and Neurosis. *American Sociological Review, 11*(1), 31–41, 1946.

Greene, V. Pre World War I Emigration to America: Motives and Statistics. *Polish Review, VI*(3), 45–68, 1961.

Greene, V. *For God and Country: The Rise of Polish and Lithuanian Ethnic Consciousness in America 1860–1910.* Madison, Wisc.: The State Historical Society of Wisconsin, 1975.

Greene, V. Poles. In S. Thernstrom, A. Orlov, & O. Handlin (Eds.), *Harvard Encyclopedia of American Ethnic Groups.* Cambridge: Harvard University Press, 1980.

Halecki, O. *A History of Poland.* New York: Roy Publishers, 1943.

Kuniczak, W.S. *My Name Is Million.* New York: Doubleday, 1978.

Lopata, H.Z. *Polish Americans: Status Competition in an Ethnic Community* (Ethnic Groups in American Life Series). Englewood Cliffs, N.J.: Prentice-Hall, 1976. (a)

Lopata, H.Z. The Polish-American Family. In C.H. Mindel & R.W. Habenstein (Eds.), *Ethnic Families in America: Patterns and Variations.* New York: Elsevier, 1976. (b)

Mostwin, D. Emotional Needs of Elderly Americans of Central and Eastern European Background. In D.E. Gelfand & A.J. Kutzik (Eds.), *Ethnicity and Aging*. New York: Springer, 1979.

Mostwin, D. *Social Dimension of Family Treatment*. Washington, D.C.: National Association of Social Workers, 1980.

Novak, M. *The Rise of the Unmeltable Ethnics*. New York: Macmillan, 1975.

Pernanen, K. Alcohol and Crimes of Violence. In B. Kissin & H. Begleiter (Eds.), *The Biology of Alcoholism* (Vol. 4): *Social Aspects of Alcoholism*. New York: Plenum, 1976.

Polzin, T. *The Polish-Americans: Whence and Whither*. Pulaski, Wisc.: Franciscan Publishers, 1973.

Sanday, P.R. Female Status in the Public Domain. In M.Z. Rosaldo & L. Lamphere (Eds.), *Women, Culture and Society*. Stanford, Calif.: Stanford University Press, 1974.

Stein, H.F. The Slovak-American "Swaddling Ethos": Homeostat for Family Dynamics and Cultural Continuity. *Family Process, 17*(1), 31–45, 1978.

Thomas, W.I., & Znaniecki, F. *The Polish Peasant in Europe and America*. New York: Octagon Books, 1974. (Two volumes originally published in five volumes, 1919–1920.)

Tongue, A. What the State Does about Alcohol and Alcoholism: An International Survey. In D.J. Pittman & C.R. Snyder (Eds.), *Society, Culture and Drinking Patterns*. New York: Wiley, 1962.

19

Portuguese Families

EVERETT MOITOZA

This chapter identifies culturally influenced mental health attitudes, beliefs, and practices of Portuguese American[1] immigrants and the clinical and cultural implications for family therapy with them. The basic formulations presented here were developed in the course of a study of Portuguese American immigrants and their families conducted in Cambridge, Massachusetts, from 1978 to 1980.[2] Specific findings of that study have been reported elsewhere (Moitoza & Coelho, 1980).

As defined by Giordano (1973):

> Ethnicity from a clinical point of view is more than a distinctiveness defined by race, religion, national origin, or geography. It involves conscious and unconscious processes that fulfill the deep psychological need for security, identity, and a sense of historical continuity. It is transmitted in an emotional language within the family and is reinforced by similar units in the community. (p. 11)

It is from this perspective that this chapter is written.

A note of caution is in order. The author is deeply concerned that readers not be tempted to overgeneralize or engage in ethnic or psychotherapeutic stereotyping of the Portuguese. This chapter is intended only as a modest guide for family therapists working with Portuguese families, and readers are urged, without either divesting the material of its clinical usefulness or overestimating its reliability, to keep this limitation in mind.

Very little research has been conducted on mental health among or on appropriate therapies for Portuguese Americans (Spiegel, 1976). Like (1979), while studying Azorean Portuguese in both the Azores and the United States, and Moitoza (1980), in a study of second- and third-generation Portuguese in the United States, have both observed three features of the

1. The term Portuguese American includes both Azorean and Continental Portuguese. Although differences exist between these two groups, their clinical issues will be treated as similar.

2. This study was based on a group of 146 Portuguese American immigrants and their families who were seen as patients at the Clinica Dr. A. Egas Moniz (a neighborhood mental health center) of the Cambridge Hospital in Cambridge, Massachusetts. The study was primarily based on retrospective qualitative analysis of clinical case data on these patients.

Everett Moitoza. Martha's Vineyard Mental Health Center, Edgartown, Massachusetts; Harvard Medical School, Boston, Massachusetts.

Portuguese culture that have particularly powerful influence in Portuguese approaches to mental health services: (1) the supremacy of the family unit; (2) the reliance on folk medicine practices; and (3) a fatalistic attitude toward life. Indeed, these three features, both independently and in combination, are central to understanding Portuguese Americans in a family therapy context.

The Portuguese Experience

Continental Portuguese had discovered and settled the Azores by 1450. Isolated from, yet politically controlled by Lisbon, the archipelago was slowly colonized by people from the Algarve section of Southern Portugal, from Northern Portugal, and from Flanders. Since the islands are steep and volcanic in origin, they were difficult to cultivate and offered a lean existence to the settlers. Their habitat posed a constant threat of earthquakes and volcanoes. Alone, and essentially abandoned by Continental Portugal, Azoreans were truly littoral frontierspeople. Their rural, insular life was characterized by a sense of confinement and solitude as well as by poverty and limited opportunity. Concomitantly, they relied on superstition, folklore, and Roman Catholic dogma to order and protect themselves from this harsh environment (Moitoza, 1979). Since their lives were subject to the whims and potential devastations of nature, the Azoreans developed a profound sense of fatalism. They viewed life as dangerous and difficult and saw themselves as exercising little or no control over misfortune (Rogers, 1974). This philosophy is also true of the Continental Portuguese. However, their fatalism seems more directly produced by the rigidly two-class society existing in Portugal. This fatalism, central to the Continental and Island Portuguese, is expressed in the following poem (in translation) by the contemporary Azorean poet Otilia Frayão (1959):

Poema
These grayish and very oppressive days
Of an inexpressive void
Which fall upon the land
And leave us all close-lipped and seemingly restless
With a continuing yearning for the world
Which even our ancestors never beheld renew itself.

This sea without end
Which sails do not prefer
And which is the highway always taken
By those of our evasion.

These overlongish nights
Of such gentle silences
Which seem to set free our very hearts
With the prospect of a returning world.

And this awakening always equal
With one's head reposing upon the rock
And one's eyes retaining the eternal bitterness
Little limited and uninteresting. (p. 19)

In reaction to such an overwhelming and isolated environment, as well as to their fatalistic sense of abandonment by Continental Portugal, many Portuguese looked westward to the United States. Beginning in the 19th century, the New England fishing, whaling, and textile industries attracted Azoreans and Continental Portuguese in greater and greater numbers, totaling approximately 64,000 immigrants by 1900 (Bannick, 1971; U.S. Immigration and Naturalization Service, 1979).

Immigrants, largely from the Azores, Madeira, Cape Verde Islands, and Continental Portugal have landed on U.S. shores and now number approximately 1 million (Rogers, 1974). Of these, approximately 161,000 are immigrants who have arrived since 1958 (Rogers, 1980). These recent immigrants are qualitatively different and occasionally in conflict with their third-, fourth-, and fifth-generation fellow Portuguese Americans. Unlike this group, the recent immigrating Portuguese have higher aspirations, are generally less humble, and seek a higher visibility in the American sociopolitical structure. Rogers (1980) believes that these differences are results of events in Portugal, social developments in the United States, and technological advances worldwide.

Portuguese immigration has been heaviest in Massachusetts, California, New Jersey, Rhode Island, and Toronto, although they have also settled in Connecticut, New York, and Hawaii. Since 1972, the Portuguese have been the largest immigrant group in Massachusetts, arriving at the rate of approximately 4000 per year (Massachusetts Department of Education, 1973).

The Azoreans form the largest subgroup of Portuguese immigrants (over 50%). Because the Azores—the nine islands approximately 1000 miles southwest of mainland Portugal—constitute that part of Portugal (and of Europe) closest to New England, the archipelago and the U.S. eastern seaboard have developed close associations. Azoreans can come to the United States quickly—in five hours by jet—and can enter relatively easily under the present immigration laws. Indeed, due to heavy immigration to the United States and Canada, the population of the entire archipelago in the 1970 Census was 291,028, down approximately 11% from 1960 (*Portugal*, 1960, 1970).

Men were the primary immigrants, leaving their families until they earned enough money either to send for them or to return to the Azores financially insured against the hard and ill-fated Portuguese life. This first wave of immigration was stopped in the early 1920s when the United States imposed a strict quota system.

There was tremendous migratory fluidity and some ambivalence about permanent residence in the United States among these first-wave immigrants.

By 1920, approximately 25% had returned to the Azores or Continental Portugal (Taft, 1923). Those who remained in the United States were handicapped by lack of education and language differences. Apparently they retained their sense of passive resignation to their hard and difficult lot in life and, for the most part, stayed in low-level jobs. Until very recently, in fact, the Portuguese have almost totally avoided obtaining "power" in American social and political systems. Unlike other White ethnic immigrants, they have largely remained at the lowest socioeconomic levels in the United States and Canada (Adler, 1972; Anderson, 1974).

Immigration from the mid-1920s to 1958 was only a trickle. But in 1958, due in part to a volcanic eruption near the Azorean island of Fayal a year earlier and in part to the 1965 amendments to the basic Immigration and Nationality Act, a second wave of Azorean immigration began. This wave continues today, principally settling in Massachusetts (U.S. Department of Justice, 1973).

Immigrants in this new wave are, by U.S. standards, poorly educated. The overwhelming majority have completed only four to six years of elementary education, although some have secondary, vocational, and occasionally even college degrees. Like those in the first wave, these new immigrants work in blue collar positions, often gaining employment contacts through older, established Portuguese Americans (Anderson, 1974). At work, they are frequently highly regarded and are described by their supervisors and co-workers as hardworking, earnest, dependable, and self-sufficient.

Historically, Portuguese have demonstrated a seemingly uncanny ability to remain invisible as a U.S. ethnic minority. The apparent ease with which they "melt" into their new surroundings may be a mixed blessing. It may be that the cultural factors that operate so effectively to provide the Portuguese with easy assimilation and a subsequently low profile in their new country may also be the factors that ultimately obscure the Portuguese ethnic identity from that host country. While exerting great effort to live within and to relate to U.S. society, the Portuguese are strongly tied to their traditional beliefs and life-style. The pull both ways is intense and is potentially alienating in both directions. This is not, then, the picture of a particularly assimilated ethnic minority, but rather of a marginal one. Indeed, this marginality is not unexpected, considering the many radical personal, cultural, and familial adjustments the Portuguese immigrants must make when moving from the predominantly rural, agrarian, and fishing economy of Portugal to the urban, industrial economy of the United States.

Family Structure and Values

As in every ethnic group, values, beliefs, and behavior among the Portuguese vary according to socioeconomic status, education, age, and geography. Yet, the illiterate peasant farmer from northern Portugal's Tras-os-Montes region, the hard-working fisherman of the Azorean Island, the cosmopolitan business executive from Lisbon, and the Portuguese immigrant factory worker in the United States, do all appear to share some characteristics, particularly those relating to family. Indeed, the importance accorded the family appears universal among the Portuguese, with differences tending to occur more at the level of structure. Those Portuguese immigrant families followed by the Egas Moniz Clinic have been found to have both significant nuclear and extended components, organized for the most part in a "closed" typology as will be outlined and discussed later in this chapter. The nuclear unit is ostensibly patriarchal, yet, as also described by Smith (1976), much internal and external familial facilitation and negotiation is handled by the female/wife/mother. Authority tends to be organized vertically, flowing from the parental dyad to the oldest son or daughter. All members are expected to make financial contributions so as to make possible the rapid purchase of a house—the repository of family life. This pattern is consistent with Wolforth's (1978) findings:

> No matter where the immigrant settled, he tried as soon as possible to provide a decent home for his family. The sanctity of the family unit and its relationship with other families, often related, was crucial to the immigrant. (p. 80)

Both children and adults are expected to gratify most of their personal, social, and emotional needs within the nuclear or extended family, though family activities may be supplemented with occasional church-based social and religious ones. Parents, in what is seemingly an attempt to insure familial unity, stability, tradition, and ultimate survival, demand loyalty from other family members, with familial needs and goals generally superceding individual ones.

Boundaries between extended and nuclear family membership frequently blur. Variables such as illness of a relative, death of a parent or relative, migration of a family member, need for child care, financial demands, and work schedules, can alter the make-up of the family unit as the nuclear family looks beyond its immediate members to meet its special needs. As a result, both the quantitative size and qualitative functions of the Portuguese family change frequently. Dias (1950) remarks that

> relationships among the members of the [Portuguese] family are almost always very intimate and frequently exclusive. Parents and children, brothers and sisters, aunts and uncles and nieces and nephews, cousins and cousins, are paired for tight and often confusing nets which a stranger penetrates only with difficulty. (p. 19)

In order to insure economic, familial, and social security, Portuguese families sometimes "extend" their membership through such means as cross-cousin marriages, god parentage, and multiple sibling, cross-family marriages. Willems (1963) found similar patterns in upper-class Continental

Portuguese families where consanguine marriages and "cumulative connubial associations" were common. Extending the family in these intrafamilial ways, in fact, further "closes" the system to the outside community.

Family Member Roles

We will now offer a thumbnail sketch of the "typical" character and role of each family member, along with their most frequent psychological complaints.

Men

Portuguese men are expected to maintain great physical and emotional strength in order to combat life's many difficulties. They tend to keep feelings to themselves, lest they suffer a diminution of power or respect. A measure of masculinity is the ability to consume large amounts of alcohol; however, as pointed out by Ferreira (1976), alcohol consumption cannot interfere with daily work or it will be regarded as weakness or illness. Socially, men interact almost exclusively with other men. Dias (1950) notes that even within the home, men and women separate after meals, with men retreating to a separate location to discuss issues of specific interest to them.

The concept of honor is supreme for Portuguese men, especially honor among men. A man might, for example, resist the sexual overtures of a married woman so as not to dishonor her husband or he might avoid placing his girlfriend in a socially or sexually compromising situation out of respect for her father. As a husband, the man is regarded as the primary emotional and physical protector of his family, a position often belied in fact by the wife's many home management activities. As a father, the man is expected to receive respect from his children, respect embodied in their blind and unquestioning obedience to his wishes. Children represent the father's virility, masculinity, and spiritual immortality. The larger number of progeny the better.

Problems most often presented by Portuguese American men seeking psychological help are physical abuse of their children and occasionally of their wives, as well as problems related to alcoholism.

Women

Virtue and purity (as exemplified by the Blessed Virgin Mary) are the most desirable feminine qualities for Portuguese women. The family is careful to protect these qualities, especially in young women. Willems (1963) points out the patripotestal traditions in the Portuguese family, which include hymenolatry and the "virginity complex" associated with well-defined sexual double standards and concern that family honor remain intact. The woman's sexuality is viewed as a powerful and sometimes dangerous thing. It is associated with a multitude of superstitions and, if unrestrained, thought capable of causing physical and mental illness and curses. Fontes (1979) records that in the Tras-os-Montes section of northern Portugal, a menstruating woman is believed capable of transmitting *mau ar*, an evil aura that prevents dough from rising, causes wounds to become infected and exude pus, and turns wine to vinegar.

The wife's role appears, on the surface, to be to love, honor, and obey her husband and to care for her family's many needs. She is particularly responsible for raising the children and apprenticing her daughters. Closer analysis, however, reveals the Portuguese woman's role to be more of an active manager–negotiator and stabilizer, both intrafamiliarly and at the family–community interface. Descamps (1935) writes that in Portuguese society "it is the woman who administers, pays taxes, discharges her obligations to the civil registrar, and solves litigations with neighbors." And during the postimmigration period, she appears to be the one most responsible for the survival of the family (Smith, 1976). Yet, she is an individual who, like women in many other cultures, continuously gives away the by-line to her husband.

Adult Portuguese American women seeking treatment most frequently present anxiety and depressive reactions masked as either vague or specific somatic complaints.

Children

Portuguese children are essentially expected to be seen and not heard. They receive most physical and emotional attention and indulgence from their parents from infancy until about school age. Girls tend to receive overt displays of affection from both parents, whereas boys are often ignored in this area, particularly by the father. Latency age children seem to be much less indulged and are expected to be contributing whatever they can to the household, either financially or in-kind services.

Generally, boys are allowed more time than girls outside of the family. Girls are expected to be with their mothers, acquiring domestic skills.

> The girl learns from direct contact with her mother all the techniques she will need in her future life, ranging from cooking, sewing, and taking part in the preparation of innumerable pork delicacies that always follows the slaughtering of pigs, to the more subtle art of dealing with a husband. (Cutileiro, 1971, p. 74).

Hyperkinetic, impulsive, and aggressive behaviors are major reasons school officials refer boys for psychological intervention. Young girls are not often referred, but those who are tend to present with symptoms such as anxiety attacks and social withdrawal.

Adolescence

Adolescent children are expected to be both financially and emotionally loyal to the family unit. This loyalty often entails quitting school as soon as legally possible and obtaining employment. Wolforth (1978) observes that this pattern of early employment cuts off Portuguese youth from the opportunities education can afford them before they even realize what those opportunities are. While adolescents are expected to work and make financial contributions like adults, they are still subject to the strict demands of both parents, particularly regarding social and courting practices. These demands are often totally at odds with practices in the adolescents' U.S. peer group. For example, a young woman's courtship with a man she is expected to marry is still closely supervised. Adolescents are expected to live at home long enough before marrying to repay some of their own child-rearing expenses and to help the family obtain more financial security. Children who do not marry are expected to remain at home forever. A single young adult (particularly a female) who leaves the parental home seriously risks ostracism by the family and community.

Adolescents often react with frustration and rebellion (both active and passive) to these conflicts between familial and dominant U.S. cultural norms. Men frequently commit antisocial acts (such as auto theft and breaking and entering crimes) that show disrespect for and bring dishonor to the parents. Women often become sexually active and pregnant, necessitating an early marriage, which makes independence from parents and family possible. Psychological problems in adolescence manifest themselves in men through crimes and misdemeanors and in women through various depressive and/or acute psychotic symptoms. Conversely, adolescent men who develop psychotic symptoms are believed to be suffering from lack of an appropriate sexual outlet, or from a curse from a sexually attractive woman, or from some type of toxic drug reaction.

Married Children

Once married, children usually live near their parents. Often they live in the same house or at least in the same neighborhood and maintain frequent, even daily, contact. This is true of both male and female children. Male children are often responsible for the financial support of aging parents, while female children (often the eldest daughter) are responsible for their physical care.

Widowhood

A widowed person enjoys a particularly prestigious status in Portuguese culture. But mores pertaining to widows and widowers differ significantly. The widow is expected to wear black clothing for the remainder of her life and not to remarry. In northern Portugal, for example, a widow who remarries is publicly insulted with a cacophonous mock serenade for nine consecutive nights following her wedding (Willems, 1963). The widow is often recognized as a sexually unavailable community and family member who is accorded great access to and visibility in community activities. The widower, on the other hand, is expected to mourn his wife's passing for one year, wearing black clothing and/or a black arm band and possibly not shaving. Unlike the widow, he retains his sexual availability and, depending upon age, often remarries.

Widowed individuals, especially women, frequently appear for psychological services with various types of unresolved, blocked, or extended grief reactions. Such reactions to the death of a parent or other close relative, are also not uncommon in adult children. Although speculative, these unresolved grief reactions appear connected to the individual's inability and unwillingness to express anger toward death.

Portuguese grief rituals differ from U.S. ones in both practice and duration. Frequent visits to the grave, the wearing of black clothing, having a picture of the deceased in the coffin on display are all practices that may be put aside in an attempt to grieve like Americans. This can result in considerable guilt and depression without resolution of the death.

Godparents

Godparents are extremely close and powerful members of a Portuguese family. There is perhaps no stronger aspect of the Portuguese familial tradition than that of godparentage. For the Portuguese, godparents truly are sponsors in and for life. Perhaps it is because of the Portuguese underlying sense of fatalism that godparentage becomes such an important aspect of the culture. The belief that survival is perhaps insured with a second set of parents is strongly suggested.

Godparents are usually selected within the immediate or extended family or are chosen because of their superior wealth or power in the community. In some cases, children are given to their godparents for rearing. Willems (1963) offers the following description of the intimate and important role godparents play in Portuguese families:

> Theirs is the responsibility to see that the godchild is brought up as a good Catholic, but the mores go beyond such [a] spiritual relationship and impose economic responsibilities in the case of a premature death of either or both biological parents. Marriages between baptismal godparents and godchild are prohibited by church law and custom. In some parts of Portugal people believe that a child born out of an incestuous relationship between godparent and godchild becomes a werewolf. Marriages, or sexual intercourse between godparents and biological parents are likewise regarded as incestuous and an offspring of such a union will be a werewolf unless this state is prevented by the ritual burning of the first shirt worn by such a child. (p. 71)

The Portuguese mark an individual's growth and development with a number of important religious ceremonies. Godparents play an extremely important role in these marker events, accompanying the godchild throughout all of the religious ceremonies in his or her life, beginning with baptism. At age six, when a child receives his or her first communion, the godparents give the child his or her most valuable gift. During the ceremony of confirmation in early adolescence, the child's baptismal godparents may be selected or, if they are not available, their children will be asked to be the confirmation godparents. Ties between the family of the godchild and the family of the godparents are thus strengthened. At marriage, the godchild may select the same-sex godparent to be either matron of honor or best man. And when the godchild has his or her own children, he or she will probably select as godparent a child of the original godparent. When a godparent dies, the male godchildren have the pall-bearing responsibilities at the funeral. They are arranged from the most to the least favored from the head to the foot of the casket. In short, all personal developmental ceremonies include the presence of a person's godparents.

Religion

Ceremonies, both sacred and secular, are designed to deepen an individual's allegiance ot his or her ethnic group. The Portuguese have long marked change points in both the individual's and the family's developmental life cycle with religious and secular ceremonies and celebrations. On a large scale, they maintain a sense of tradition and community with *Festas* (feasts) celebrations which, despite their religious origins, are usually observed outside the Catholic Church. However, the mass offered in the church is always part of the *Festa*. Among the major *Festas* is the Blessing of the Fleet, which is held in seaside Portuguese communities. Traditionally, it is held on St. John's Day, the 24th of June. This *Festa* centers around the community's request to God to provide safety and success for the fishermen who brave the dangers and fickle nature of the sea. Another, the Azorean feast of the Holy Ghost, occurs during Pentecost. The Shrine of the Holy Ghost is placed for one week at a time in seven different households. Prayers are said, the holy rosary is recited, and many special foods are served. Clearly, the celebration demonstrates the powerful interrelationship of home, cuisine, and religion in Portuguese culture. Another large *Festa* is the Feast of the Blessed Sacrament. This religious-based feast included traditional Portuguese foods, dances, and songs and often a large auction of homemade foods and crafts.

These major *Festas* seem important in revitalizing spiritual zeal. They function to maintain communality of the Portuguese, as well as to provide a joyous respite from the drudgery of daily working life.

The Roman Catholic Church provides a spiritual forum for the Portuguese's social and religious lives. This close relationship and religious connection is maintained even if the family does not regularly attend church services. Baptism is considered the most important sacrament for it permits the fated individual to one day enter the kingdom of heaven.

Priests have historically been seen in two different lights by the Portuguese. As learned, educated, and rather worldly paternal figures, they are often seen with a certain amount of suspicion; perhaps even envy. However, as religious leaders of God, they are considered somewhat Holy and are seen as trusted counselors, translators, and mediators for the large society. Priests are often accorded free access into the family unit and often hold substantial influence within it.

Tangled in the Portuguese's religious beliefs and attitudes about day-to-day life, is their reliance on assistance and intercession by numerous saints, Christ, and the Virgin Mary. These "agents" are called upon for luck (destiny) by acting as mediators between the person and God (God is never to be approached directly as He is too powerful and awesome). Much religious metaphor is used in this rather secret and supernatural evocation for assistance. Examples might include asking for assistance with a health problem or seeking better luck for a married son or daughter. This is usually done by women whose role in the family includes the religious and spiritual realm. Vows are also made to saints. These are special promises of deeds to be done by the person as payment for a fulfilled request. The promise might be to make a donation of some money to the church or to perform a particularly charitable act.

Concepts of Psychopathology

Portuguese clients present two prevailing concepts of physical and mental illness, both of which have biomedical and supernatural components. The first is that mental illness is biologically determined and expresses itself primarily in somatic symptoms or bizarre behavior. It is from this biological perspective that the etiology of the major psychotic illnesses and dementia in the elderly, as well as less severe anxious and depressive states (in somatic equivalents) are usually understood. Townsend (1975), Karno and Edgerton (1974), and others have also noted this same concept of mental illness in small towns in rural U.S. populations with non-Portuguese people. Because of this viewpoint, Portuguese often believe that mental illness or its somatic equivalent is incurable, or certainly not curable with mere words. Patients feel that they are not responsible for their problems and that treatment should be actively administered to them. For example, they frequently request medications, particularly liquid preparations. Liquid preparations may be preferred because they resemble a more natural food form and are more like the widely used medicinal herbal teas than are tablets.

Portuguese clients tend to present somatic complaints rather than symptoms of psychological stress. These complaints most commonly involve the gastrointestinal and circulatory systems, the two systems the Portuguese regard as particularly important "barometers" of illness or health. Since they often believe that blood or digestive matrial can "back up" and cause mental problems, they are especially concerned that these two systems function well. In treating Portuguese Americans, therefore, therapists should inquire carefully about circulatory and gastrointestinal functioning and to exercise caution in prescribing medications that can cause either constipation or amenorrhea.

Concern about the gastrointestinal system often centers on constipation, especially among women. Nausea, burping, flatulence, vomiting, and appetite loss may also be reported as symptomatic of some physiological "backing up" problem that often turns out to have anxious or depressive psychological roots. The circulatory system, especially in the head and genitals, is equally of concern since this "backing up" is thought to indicate psychological or physical disequilibrium. The notion that the central nervous and circulatory systems share the same pathways is not uncommon. For example, most Portuguese women are extremely concerned with the regularity and flow of their menses. They often believe that amenorrhea signals the "backup" of menstrual blood to the brain, thereby creating a danger of mental illness.

The second concept of physical or mental illness held by Portuguese patients is that it is caused by supernatural conditions or beings that have to be either negotiated with or appeased. Clymer (1977) in the Azores, Like (1979) in Cambridge, and Moitoza (1980) in New Bedford all found Azorean Portuguese to place strong credence in folk medicine practices, *mau-olhado/quebrando* (curses), *bruxas* (witches), *curandeiros* (curers), and various other superstitions and folk beliefs. These beliefs combine superstitious, religious, and biological elements. Prayers, amulets, teas, herbs, poultices, fumidors (for the burning of incense), and curers are often used concomitantly with more modern medical treatment to ward off or remedy symptoms of physical or psychological discomfort. Whereas Portuguese will usually offer their biological complaints and explanations outright, not surprisingly, they tend to disguise their supernatural beliefs, presenting them indirectly and with some reticence.

In addition to ascribing mental illness to supernatural conditions or to a disruption in normal bodily functioning, Portuguese clients often consider psychological problems, particularly in preadolescent children, to be punishments for parental weaknesses, sins, or failures. Understandably, parents are quite slow to recognize emotional problems in their children and slower yet to seek help for them. The therapist frequently must work with the parents, either simultaneously with or even before initiating treatment with the child, to allay their fears and guilt.

Parents often attribute adolescent psychoses to inadvertent drug ingestion (someone must have given him or her something without his or her knowledge). Additionally, psychiatric problems in adolescent women are commonly believed to be the result of illicit sexual behavior. Interestingly, a significant number of female adolescents presenting with psychotic symptoms do report an initial sexual experience immediately preceding the onset of the illness. In contrast, psychiatric problems, especially psychoses, in late adolescent men are frequently attributed to the inhibition of sexual expression. In both cases, marriage is considered the remedy for the difficulties.

Abnormal behaviors in the elderly are more likely to be attributed to arteriosclerosis than to mental illness. The Portuguese also believe that family inattentiveness to the elderly person—for example, failure to visit or to perform a favor—can result in emotional disturbances.

Family Therapy with Portuguese Americans

Although the Portuguese will rarely seek psychotherapy themselves, when referred by others, family therapy, when based on therapeutic approaches consonant with Portuguese cultural norms, can be simple, effective, and, in the majority of cases, the treatment of choice. In fact, the Portuguese may interpret individual therapy that excludes the nuclear or extended family as an attempt by the therapist to break up family solidarity. As in the Italian culture (Papajohn & Spiegel, 1975), the Portuguese do not single out individuals. In these collateral cultures, any attempt to do so is seen as a threat to the family or to the culture group as a whole. And since success and its opposite, psychological deviance, are similarly viewed as threats to the integrity of the collateral system, the Portuguese family would strongly resist the identification and individual treatment of a patient. Almost surely they would try to join the therapist and, if that failed, withdraw the family member from treatment.

The irony of this press for family over individual psychotherapy is that Portuguese families are extremely "closed" systems. As such, it is difficult for a family therapist to join with the family and engage it in therapy. Kantor and Lehr (1975) describe most clearly the spatial boundary that exists between the closed family system and individuals outside of it.

> In the closed family system, stable structures are relied upon as reference points for order and change. Space in a closed type family is fixed space. The family space is discreet, distinct, and apart from the larger, outside community. Locked doors, careful scrutiny of strangers, parental control over the media, supervised excursions, are all features of a closed type family. The preservation of territoriality, self-protection, privacy, and, in some cases, secretiveness, are often used by the family's authority [usually the father]. In order to preserve the family's closed boundaries, the closed family uses icons and symbols in its space to spread and deepen members' allegiance to the credos that constitute the basis for a closed family. Formal teaching, including the use of moral slogans, homilies, and proverbs, is a popular feature of the closed style, especially as members of the older generation wish to convey and confer their values on the next. (pp. 119–120)

Because of the closed family system, Portuguese families do not actively seek family therapy or, for that matter, any psychological help with either individual or family problems. Rather, the Portuguese attempt to solve their problems via their own extended and nuclear family's resources and support systems. In fact, it has been reported that at least in Massachusetts, the Portuguese use social services less than any other ethnic group (Adler, 1972).

Portuguese families will usually be forced to seek treatment by the police, the local school, the district court, or the family physician. At this point, the therapist must—and this is perhaps the most difficult step in working effectively with Portuguese American families—join the family and establish a working therapeutic relationship from an inside position, for once inside, the therapist will be accorded trust, loyalty, respect, and compliance.

We will now discuss behaviors crucial for therapists if they are to ensure the success of this vital initial stage in family therapy with the Portuguese.

Joining the Portuguese Family in Therapy

Family therapy with Portuguese Americans works best when it takes place in the family's own home. At an office or clinic, the family's suspicion and fear of the therapist, the "outsider" there to inspect them, would be so severe that if they came at all, they would be extremely guarded and either unable or unwilling to engage therapeutically. But the home is where the family, on its own terms, can most safely and comfortably interact with outsiders. Also, by meeting in the home, the balance of safety and power is placed, initially at least, in the hands of the family, especially the father. The therapist, then, is a guest in the patient's home, and as such she or he is accorded the "visiting" privileges that provide the important initial leverage with and access to the family that would be unavailable if the therapist met the family in his or her office.

Lack of observance of scheduled appointment times can be a problem when working with Portuguese Americans, though less so when meeting in the patient's home. Many patients miss appointments, appear at unscheduled times, and give priority to job demands over therapy sessions. This behavior does not necessarily reflect resistance to the therapy. On the contrary, some Portuguese American patients arrive several hours early out of respect for the therapist's time. They want to be sure that he or she will not have to wait for them. Also, it is a display of deference and gratitude on the part of the patient by giving up a considerable part of the patient's time to the therapist. Both of these behavior patterns around appointment times are common among Portuguese Americans (Moitoza & Coelho, 1980) and may well be a manifestation of their ambivalence toward doctors. Again, this issue is eliminated when the therapy takes place in the patient's home.

It is extremely difficult for a woman therapist, especially a young one, to do family therapy with Portuguese Americans by herself. There is strong sexual stereotyping in Portuguese culture, and although the solo female therapist will be accorded a certain measure of politeness and hospitality, she will meet with tremendous resistance from the husband and the wife. This resistance stems from the cultural expectation that only a man can take a superior role. Also, the wife may regard the woman therapist as a potential rival for her husband. What works best is a man and woman therapy team, for there is then no unattached member of either sex to pose a possible sexual threat. In Portuguese culture, unmarried women are considered sexually dangerous and threatening to existing family systems. A woman's sexuality is seen as powerful, even magical, though unconscious, and the man's is thought of as active and conscious. The Portuguese believe that whenever men and women interact, socially or otherwise, they need supervision by some form of chaperone. It is for this reason that the solo therapist, particularly a woman, needs a cross-sex cotherapist.

To work effectively with Portuguese families, the therapist must begin by being a good guest. In the first social/therapeutic encounter at the family's home, the most important factor is the degree of respect shown to the head of the household (father). In fact, this is an act of deference on the part of the therapist, a deferential statement that acknowledges the sovereignty of the family unit.

The therapist will be expected to dress "professionally" (men to wear suits and ties, women dresses and nylon stockings) for two reasons. First, the visit is a formal occasion and although the host may not necessarily dress for it, the guest's appearance should reflect respect for the host and his or her hospitality. Second, "doctors" (as all psychotherapists and, for that matter, all health care providers are seen) are expected to dress according to their station in life. In fact, the doctor's formal dress distinguishes him or her from the majority of blue-collar workers in the society. There is, however, an inherent problem here. In Portugal, education is only for the rich—a class who are alternately envied and mistrusted as representative of power and authority. Since, as Clymer (1977) observes, doctors and other traditional health care providers are considered members of this wealthy class, they are approached with considerable ambivalence. It is precisely this tension that the family therapist is trying to dispel when he or she engages the family in a deferential manner in its own territory. The home visit, then, is a structural move that increases trust of the therapist and allows him or her to enter the affective, spatial, hierarchical, and philsophical dimensions of the family's life.

When entering the home, it is important to remember that all space is private and accessible only with the expressed permission of the head of the family, normally the father but occasionally the mother. Therefore, movement within the home should be limited. There will be "warm-up conversation," which may include discussion of the home itself and its decoration, history, and importance to individual family members. Initially, all remarks should be directed to the father, both as a sign of respect and as a simple courtesy. This courtesy extends even so far as to ask his permission to direct conversation to other members of the family. In this way, it is the father (and later the mother) who introduces the family and family life to the therapist.

The therapist's manner should be formal in a socially polite rather than clinically detached way. Data on the family's immigration experience, as well as its present work and community activity, can be obtained in this relaxed manner. Such discussions are most powerfully supported with family pictures from the "old country" and detailed stories of experiences in the United States. The family may find the use of genograms flattering.

Therapists in cross-sex treatment teams should take care to speak mainly with the marital partner of their own sex since as a general rule in the Portuguese culture, men interact mostly with men and women mostly with women. Direct eye contact between men and women may be considered rude or seductive. The Portuguese sometimes recognize a stare as a sexual overture, which when reciprocated by a woman means she has accepted the man's invitation. (Between members of the same sex, downcast eyes are frequently a sign of deference to the person of superior status.) It would be safe to say that the Portuguese consider most cross-sex interaction on even the most innocent level potentially romantic or sexual.

Physical touching between men is common, especially during conversation. They may interlock arms or put one arm around the other's waist while discussing a particularly important point, or, when sitting down, they may touch each other's hands or knees so as to emphasize their point. A male therapist may reciprocate these gestures but only if they are initiated by the male family head. Women, too, frequently touch and kiss each other, but again, the therapist should avoid touching or, in many cases, even sitting next to a family member of the opposite sex.

Portuguese gesticulate much less while speaking than do the Italians. In fact, the Portuguese often assume a quiescent national pose of interlocking their fingers and holding their hands in the middle of the chest just below the sternum. This position is taken by both men and women when sitting and standing and is associated with a calm state of mind.

Without a doubt, food will be offered at the first session. Indeed, it may be the first thing that occurs upon the therapists' arrival, and it would not be unusual for food and wine to be provided during all family sessions. Often the refreshments will change from store bought to homemade items as the therapeutic relationship develops. This phenomenon seems closely related to the distance and ambivalence Portuguese hold for outsiders, especially those of professional or educated status. In this case, the therapists can gauge their relationship to and acceptance by the family by the appearance of homemade refreshments during the visits.

The practice of giving gifts to the therapists deserves some attention as it can be an area of misunderstanding and mismanagement for the unaware therapy team. In Portugal, cultural and socioeconomic conditions generally dictate a barter-for-service economy. For the Portuguese patient, gift giving is a form of direct payment to the therapist distinct from the third party or sliding scale fee paid to the clinic. The gift is a way of keeping things even— of settling debts among people of honor. The gifts are often of food or drink, starting, as with the refreshments, as items purchased in stores and, as the therapeutic relationship strengthens and trust increases, changing to home-made goods. Should the therapists refuse the gift, the family, especially the father, would be insulted, reading the refusal as a direct statement that the father was not an honorable man. The family would feel tremendous shame or rage and withdraw from therapy.

Therapists will be invited to attend the celebration of marker events (baptisms, graduations, weddings, funerals). These invitations do not seem motivated by an attempt to reduce the power of the therapists by making them friends or equals; rather, they are gestures of respect for the therapists as "insiders," signs that the therapy team has truly entered a family system, which carries rights, privileges, and obligations. To decline these invitations would be to risk insulting and dishonoring the family, particularly the father.

A basic point in family therapy with Portuguese Americans is not to move too fast. Work begins only after adults know and begin to trust one another and, as has been outlined, the process of joining is usually a slow one that cannot be rushed. Similarly, physical action during the family therapy must be approached gradually. Specifically, sculpting and psychodramatic techniques, even when introduced gently, carefully, and clearly, are disliked or resisted by Portuguese families. It is best to avoid offering interpretations of body language, for Portuguese Americans would consider it an invasion of privacy. Furthermore, the Portuguese rarely connect physical expressions or postures with feelings or any conscious motives. Therefore, making such interpretations will seem foolish, if not downright stupid, and consequently may disempower the therapist in the family's eyes.

Family therapists should be very careful about making negative, verbal interpretations of cross-generational alliances within the family. This is particularly important when the therapist is working with a married couple since married children remain dedicated to their families of origin. Thera-peutic attempts to separate of "individuate" husbands or wives from their families is a difficult, if not impossible, task that will be resisted by the couple and sabotaged by the extended family. Instead, engaging the family as possible "assistants" will be most viable structurally in helping the extended family decrease its cross-generational pull on the couple.

Schools of Family Therapy

Without question, the school of structural family therapy, associated with Minuchin, Montalvo, Guerney, Rosman, and Schumer (1967) and Minuchin (1974), and the school of strategic family therapy, associated with the work of Watzlawick, Weakland, and Fisch (1974), are those most effective in working with the Portuguese. Both of these schools are symptom oriented and concerned with how family system boundaries are developed and ordered as well as with what active techniques can be developed to change the symptoms and realign the boundaries (Foley, 1979). And because these two schools are actively directed toward solving the presenting problem and are usually of relatively short duration, they seem most consonant with Portuguese value systems. Yet, a word of caution. It is important to remember that neither of these therapeutic approaches will be of use without an extremely solid joining of the therapists to the family, for within such a closed family system, no therapeutic intervention will be viable until the family has come to trust the therapist and feel confident that he or she poses no threat to the family's traditions or linear power structure. A case example of a strategic family therapy approach utilizing a culturally consonant, paradoxical intervention will now be presented.

> Antonio, a 38-year-old Azorean immigrant, is married to Anna, age 27. They came to the United States eight years ago and have five children, all under the age of 10. Antonio was referred to psychiatric treatment by the local court system following repeated and severe bouts of wife and child beating. On two occasions his wife was taken to the hospital with severe contusions and once with a broken collarbone. Invariably, Antonio would be drunk during these beatings.
>
> Although ordered by the court to attend the local mental health center, Antonio failed to appear for four scheduled appointments. Not surprisingly, however, he was quite amenable to an appointment at his own home with his family present. Indeed, when the family therapist arrived for the first session, the home atmosphere was festive and partylike in honor of the therapist–guest. Cake, coffee, and red wine abounded.
>
> Antonio, a massive man, moved around his home like a proud bull. He noted many times how important it is for a man to keep his wife and children in line. He also reported that he was extremely *ten ciumes* (jealous). When asked further about the beating of his wife, he began to sing this excerpt from a well-known Portuguese song:
>
>> Even the sea is married
>> Even the sea has a wife,
>> He is married to the seashore,
>> He beats it whenever he likes.
>
> The male therapist took on a concerned expression and with some degree of urgency and requested Antonio's permission to meet with him

immediately in another room for some "men talk." Such a quick and direct request would not be used so early in family therapy with the Portuguese; however, the therapist decided to take a calculated risk. Antonio, somewhat nonplussed, yet flattered, agreed and ushered the therapist by the arm into the kitchen. There, the therapist had these words for Antonio.

"Dear Antonio, I know that it is impossible for you to stop beating your wife and children at this time. How sad and embarrassing it must be for you to resort to such a low form of control over them. As you know, a man who is respected in his home never needs more than his words to enforce his wishes. Jealousy is a terrible thing and often strips a man of his dignity and real power. But do not worry my friend Antonio, your secret is safe with me; I shall not inform others [men] of your problem."

Antonio immediately protested that he could stop the beatings at any point. The therapist told him that he did not believe that he could and to do so might increase Antonio's level of jealousy so high that he could not, as a man, control it.

Antonio and his family met with the therapist for four more sessions during which time the therapist also worked with the nuclear and extended family in many combinations. Most of these family sessions centered around the idea of what a "real man" was like in the United States. Antonio, anxious to be an American, listened intently and asked many questions about the role behavior of American men. Most importantly, however, after the first family session, he ceased abuse of his family. Although his "macho" attitude at home continued, he shifted from physical abuse to more verbal domination.

As this case illustrates, paradoxical techniques can be extremely effective with the Portuguese. Selvini-Palazzoli, Boscolo, Cecchin, and Prata (1978) offer an extensive presentation on the use of such techniques when operating within psychotic Italian family cultural systems. Haley (1963, 1976) also discusses such techniques, with special attention to the nonethnic family's presenting problem.

Active Family Therapy Techniques

Family therapy with Portuguese Americans is most effective when active directives rather than cognitions or psychological insights are used as the basic building blocks of change. Perhaps active therapeutic techniques are more successful because they circumvent the typical Portuguese orientation of fatalism and powerlessness. Indeed, talking for the Portuguese is often a process steeped in passive resignation to what is rather than a tool for confronting what might be changed. Their Catholic faith further supports this Portuguese subjugation to the many forces of life, be they natural or supernatural.

While cognitively resigned to a fatalistic design of the world, the Portuguese are surprisingly receptive to changing a behavior if asked to do so by the therapist. Compliance with the therapist's directives seems to decrease, however, as the attempts to provide "psychological explanations" increase, perhaps because such explanations alone challenge the deeply ingrained fatalistic belief systems. The behaviorally directive therapist can sidestep this entire issue by utilizing active family therapy prescriptions that subtly move the fmaily to a position of active collaboration with the therapist. The therapist and family thereby experience mastery over, rather than subjugation to, the presenting problems.

The case of the deMello family exemplifies the use of an active family therapy prescription.

> The mother, Maria, had been referred to the clinic by her general practitioner for panic attacks, somatic preoccupation with her gastrointestinal tract, and an overpowering feeling that she was cursed by someone. These symptoms began several months after her only child had begun elementary school. She had been very close to this child, especially following immigration to the United States just six months earlier. Both Maria and, to a lesser degree, her husband were convinced that she had indeed been given the "evil eye" [cursed] by someone back in the Azores who was envious of her new life in the United States. When Maria arrived for her individual psychotherapy appointment, she was accompanied by her daughter, Flores. When asked about her husband, she stated that he had very little time to be with her (he was holding down two jobs and was looking for a third) and added that they did not have enough "family" in the neighborhood to help her. She outlined how her "nerves" had gone bad when Flores entered school.

The therapeutic intervention was designed to realign and reinforce the marital dyad. This seemed especially important given the particularly distressing postimmigration symptoms and responses Maria was having. Briefly, therapy consisted of contacting Mr. deMello and asking him to "assist" the doctor in treating his wife's "nerves." The therapist also asked, and received, Mr. deMello's permission for the treatment to occur in his home. In the first two sessions, the therapist talked with the deMello's about their life before and after immigration and was served refreshments. The therapist then outlined the following prescription:

Four evenings a week after dinner, Mr. deMello would take Flores to the next door neighbor's apartment to spend the night. When he returned, he and Maria would "measure her nerves" with a small, portable, galvanic skin response (GSR) machine provided by the therapist. Mr. deMello would note her responses and then they would have a glass of wine together while listening to music from their native island of São Miguel. Mr. deMello was instructed to share with Maria his greatest dreams for their future in the

United States as well as to offer statements of devotion and reassurances of their survival. He would then "measure Maria's nerves." Along with this treatment, Maria was also instructed to visit the local Portuguese *curandeira* (curer) where she received an herbal tea mixture for her GI symptoms and "nerves." Following the second evening of "nerve measuring" with her husband, Maria's anxiety, physical symptoms, and feelings of being "hexed" decreased. By the fourth session in family therapy, the symptoms disappeared entirely. Treatment was terminated at that time, and Maria was given a *figa* (amulet) by the therapist to wear around her neck for good luck in the United States. Shortly thereafter, Maria began parttime work at a local factory. Her symptoms have not returned.

Techniques such as the ones used with the deMello family, which blend various aspects of behavior and structural family therapy, seem to be particularly effective with the Portuguese. An extensive presentation of active family therapy prescriptions, which include structurally reorganizing components, have been offered by both Haley (1976) and Minuchin (1974). Although still in the hypothesis stage, it is believed that the Portuguese, like many other rural, agrarian, or maritime cultures, utilize visual learning modes much better than auditory ones. We believe, that for these people, the world is usually negotiated in visual and behavioral terms rather than in cognitive or intellectual abstractions. Along these same lines, therefore, family therapists are advised to use drawings, maps, and family artifacts, such as photos or special possessions, as well as any psychological machines (biofeedback) and teaching aids in their work with the Portuguese. For example, we will engage a Portuguese family more easily and effectively by using a genogram to take a family history. Genograms clearly depict the entire family while they show both therapist and clients the intricacies of the Portuguese extended family. They are particularly useful in working with problems a family may be having with an emerging adolescent man. The genogram points out other men in the family's line who have left their nuclear family to start their own and enables the parents actually to see their own individuating processes and compare them with those of their adolescent children.

One final and important point about the use of active prescriptions is that the therapist should assign the job of "director" of the activity to the mother. In most Portuguese families, the mother is the organizer of family life and the one most often responsible for the running of the household. We can be relatively sure that the prescription will be carried out if the mother is in charge of organizing, directing, and motivating the family members to complete it. The job of the father in active prescriptions should be that of "evaluator," and the therapist should eagerly seek his opinion as to the success or failure of the activity. This role accords the father power, respect, and a superior status that motivates him to participate actively in a prescription. These roles of "director" and "evaluator" also serve to bound off the marital dyad from the rest of the family. When treating an extended Portuguese family, these roles may be given to the grandmother and grandfather or, if the grandparents are unavailable, to the highest ranking (usually the oldest) man and woman present.

In sum, then, when working with Portuguese families, therapists are advised to: (1) employ techniques utilizing pictures rather than words; (2) strive for structured activity over passive understanding; (3) use equipment, family artifacts, and paraphernalia rather than abstract intellectual concepts; (4) assign roles of "director" and "evaluator" in active prescriptions to the mother and father, respectively. Working for change of specific behaviors rather than change of general attitudes will generally prove most successful in the treatment of Portuguese families.

Use of Culturally Consonant Metaphors in Family Therapy

Reframing is an extremely powerful and delicate therapeutic technique (Watzlawick et al., 1974). Often, with a culturally distinct group such as the Portuguese, reframing requires or is enhanced by the use of metaphors, slogans, and proverbs that are close to the day-to-day experience of the patient's home culture. Reframings and clarifying metaphors that draw heavily upon an agrarian existence are generally more meaningful to the Portuguese than those drawn from an industrial or urban experience.

For example, in working with a Portuguese mother and father on the need to allow their adolescent son more freedom and autonomy, the therapist could use the metaphor of a stalk of near-ripe corn. Initially, the plant needs constant nurturing attention from the farmer, but as it matures, the plant begins to stand by itself, tall and straight, and requires of the farmer only the ability to recognize the right time to harvest its mature fruit.

Metaphors and reframings drawn from maritime phenomena—fishing, wahling, ocean storms, aquatic life, and all manners of experience common to a coastal people—can also prove extremely useful in the therapeutic work with the Portuguese. So, too, can reframings based on folk medicine and folklore. In fact, all psychotherapists working with Portuguese should be familiar with their folk medicine beliefs and practices. Since space does not permit a full description of this folk medicine, the reader is referred to the works of Jose Cutileiro (1971), Bruce Clymer (1977), and Everett Moitoza (1980) for more complete descriptions of the folklore and folklore practices of the Azorean and Continental Portuguese.

Godparents and Sponsors in Family Therapy

Because godparents play such a powerful role in the Portuguese culture, they can be extremely useful as therapist assistants. Moitoza, for example, has long enlisted godparents or godparent equivalents as "sponsors"—they typically have high credibility and a strong power base and so can influence a family system or the problemed-system members to change behaviors. Actually called "sponsors" or referred to as *madrinha* (godmother) and *padrinho* (godfather), godparents can be particularly helpful in breaking up over-involved, cross-generational alliances between parents and children, as well as providing support systems for couples experiencing marital difficulties. Sometimes the sponsors are not a family member—in these cases, the individual couple, or even the entire family, chooses a man and woman whom they feel would be ideal godparents and asks them to attend the therapy sessions as "experts on life." The following case illustrates how godparents can significantly enhance a treatment process.

> Manuel, age 21, and his wife of 14 months, Gilhelmina, age 18, were having marital difficulties. Manuel's mother, who worked in the hospital, asked the therapist to call Manuel at home and, as a doctor, to request to see him there. The therapist called and explained his specialty and Manuel agreed, albeit suspiciously, for the therapist to come to the house.
>
> Manuel and Gilhelmina's 14 months of marriage had been stormy. Manuel had refused to accept his role as husband and provider and continued his single life-style, spending most evenings with his friends at the "Luso-American" club, drinking and playing cards. Gilhelmina was now six months pregnant and feeling abandoned by her husband. For some reason, both Manuel and Gilhelmina's families had been unable to persuade Manuel to accept his responsibilities and care for his wife. It was also true that Gilhelmina remained extremely attached to her nuclear and extended families. Even by Portuguese standards, she was overinvolved with her family and neglectful of her husband.
>
> Manuel and Gilhelmina had been born in the same town in Continental Portugal and had immigrated from there to the United States 10 years earlier. Thus, although from very traditional and conservative Portuguese families, they both had experienced adolescence in the United States. Manuel seemed especially torn between the strong family orientation of his native Portugal and the separation/individuation/independence pressures prevalent during his adolescent years in the United States.

Several attempts by the therapist to move the couple closer together as a familial, marital, and parental unit failed. Serendipitously, during the couple's sixth therapy session at the couple's home (a second-floor apartment in Gilhelmina's parents' house), Manuel's godparents dropped in. They lived in a city over 40 miles away and rarely visited except for special holidays and marker events. It was clear to the therapist that Manuel had much respect and affection for his godfather. His godfather, a barber by trade, was surprised and somewhat dismayed to learn about the therapy. The therapist agreed that he, too, had hoped that Manuel and his family could solve their problems alone, but since such was not the case, he wondered if the godparents would be willing to help. They assented, and what followed was a series of five biweekly marital sessions that included both godparents. The sessions alternated weekly between Manuel's and the godparents' homes. In the course of what was a rather simple family therapy, the godparents worked to educate the young couple as to the skills, sacrifices, understandings, and tasks necessary for a successful marriage. They shared with the young couple the arguments they had had and the problems they had faced in their early marital adjustment period, and that explained how they had relied on each other, rather than on family or friends, to make the marriage work. They also showed the couple pictures from their family album to trace visually the development of their own marriage. During the week when Manuel and Gilhelmina were home and arguments would develop, they were able to call the godparents and use them as mediators to help solve these disputes. These godparents were true marital sponsors and were successful in assisting Manuel and Gilhelmina to come closer and to understand better the meaning and responsibilities of marriage. The couple's marital problems decreased, and when their baby arrived, the godparents' oldest son and his wife became godparents to the child.

Summary

Family therapy with Portuguese Americans is an active, visual, gustatory, and social process. The therapist who meets Portuguese families with understanding of and sensitivity to their traditions and values will usually find his or her clients responsive and the therapy effective. The first and most crucial step of the therapist is to approach "joining" of the Portuguese family with care and to tactfully and respectfully enter into participation in the linear power hierarchy and the closed family system. Structural and strategic schools of therapy, which are problem focused and active, will unquestionably be more successful than the more insight-based techniques. Creative use of significant extended family members, especially godparents, will further increase the therapist's repertoire and potential for realizing change in disordered Portuguese families.

ACKNOWLEDGMENT

The author would like to thank Rosie Coelho, MSW, for her invaluable contributions and assistance in the preparation of this chapter.

REFERENCES

Adler, J.P. *The Portuguese* (*Ethnic Minorities in Cambridge*, Vol. 1). Cambridge: Department of Planning and Development, City of Cambridge, 1972 (unabridged).

Anderson, G.M. *Networks of Contact: The Portuguese in Toronto*. Ontario, Canada: Wilfrid Laurier, 1974 (paperback).

Bannick, C.J. *Portuguese Immigration to the United States: Its Distribution and Status*. AB thesis, Stanford University, 1916. (Reprinted, San Francisco: R. & E. Research Associates, 1971.)

Clymer, B. *Traditional Diagnosis and Curing in the Azores*. Unpublished paper, University of North Carolina, Chapel Hill, 1977.

Cutileiro, J. *A Portuguese Rural Society*. Oxford, England: Clarendon Press, 1971.

Descamps, P. *Le Portugal: La Vie Sociale Actuelle*. Paris: Firmin-Didot, 1935.

Dias, J. *Os Elementos Fundamentais da Cultural Portuguesa*. Paper presented at the Colóquio Internacional da Estudos Luso Brasileiros, Washington, D.C., April 25, 1950.

Ferreira, A.G. Alcoholism in Portugal. *International Journal of Mental Health*, 5(1), 63–73, 1976.

Foley, V.D. Family Therapy. In R. Corsini (Ed.), *Current Psychotherapies*. Itasca, Ill.: F.E. Peacock, 1979 (paperback).

Fontes, A.S. *Ethnographia Trasmontana*. Braga, Portugal: Fontes, 1979.

Frayão, O. Poema. *Acoria*, 2, 19, 1959.

Giordano, J. *Ethnicity and Mental Health: Research and Recommendations*. New York: National Project on Ethnic America of the American Jewish Committee, 1973 (paperback).

Haley, J. *Strategies of Psychotherapy*. New York: Grune & Stratton, 1963.

Haley, J. *Problem-Solving Psychotherapy*. San Francisco: Jossey-Bass, 1976.

Kantor, D., & Lehr, W. *Inside the Family*. New York: Harper & Row, 1975 (paperback).

Karno, M., & Edgerton, R.B. Some Folk Beliefs about Mental Illness: A Reconsideration. *International Journal of Social Psychiatry*, 20, 292–296, 1974.

Like, R. *Portuguese Popular Health Culture: A Discussion of Three Case Histories*. Unpublished paper, Harvard Medical School, Boston, 1979.

Massachusetts Department of Education, Board of Education, Division of Immigration and Americanization. *56th Annual Report*. Boston: Author, 1973.

Minuchin, S., Montalvo, B., Guerney, B., Jr., Rosman, B., & Schumer, F. *Families of the Slums*. New York: Basic Books, 1967.

Minuchin, S. *Families and Family Therapy*. Cambridge: Harvard University Press, 1974.

Moitoza, E. *The Azorean Portuguese of Massachusetts: Mental Health Considerations for a Silent Majority*. Paper presented at the Seventh Annual Conference on Ethnic and Minority Studies, La Crosse, Wisc., May 6, 1979.

Moitoza, E. *A Study of Mental Health and Mental Illness Attitudes and Behaviors of the Azorean Portuguese through the Use of Intensive Interview*. Unpublished doctoral dissertation, Boston University, 1980.

Moitoza, E., & Coelho, R. *Ethnic Factors in the Delivery of Psychological Services to Portuguese Americans*. Paper presented at the Annual Meeting of the Northeast Anthropological Association, Amherst, Mass., March 29, 1980.

Papajohn, J., & Spiegel, J. *Transactions in Families*. San Francisco: Jossey-Bass, 1975.

Portugal, Anuário Estatístico I (Continente e Ilhas Adjacentes). Lisbon: Instituto Nacional de Estatística, 1960, 1970.

Rogers, F.M. *Americans of Portuguese Descent: A Lesson in Differentiation*. Beverly Hills: Sage, 1974 (paperback).

Rogers, F.M. Portuguese. In S. Thernstrom (Ed.), *Harvard Encyclopedia of American Ethnic Groups*. Cambridge: Harvard University Press, 1980.

Selvini-Palazzoli, M., Boscolo, L., Cecchin, G., & Prata, G. *Paradox and Counterparadox*. New York: Jason Aronson, 1978.

Smith, M.E. The Portuguese Female Immigrant: "Marginal Man" Par Excellence. In *Proceedings of the Second Annual Symposium on the Portuguese Experience in the United States*. Fall River, Mass.: National Assessment and Dissemination Center, 1976.

Spiegel, J.P. Cultural Aspects of Transference and Counter-Transference Revisited. *Journal of the American Academy of Psychoanalysis*, 4(4), 447–467, 1976.

Taft, D.R. *Two Portuguese Communities in New England*. PhD dissertation, Columbia University, 1923. (Reprinted, New York: Arno Press and *The New York Times*, 1969.)

Townsend, J.M. Cultural Conceptions and Mental Illness. *Journal of Nervous and Mental Disorders, 160,* 409–421, 1975.

U.S. Department of Justice. *Immigration and Naturalization Service Annual Report.* Washington, D.C.: U.S. Government Printing Office, 1973.

U.S. Immigration and Naturalization Service. *Annual Report 1976.* Washington, D.C.: U.S. Government Printing Office, 1979.

Watzlawick, P., Weakland, J., & Fisch, R. *Change: Principles of Problem Formation and Problem Resolution.* New York: Norton, 1974.

Willems, E. On Portuguese Family Structure. In J. Mogey (Ed.), *Family and Marriage.* Leiden, Netherlands: E.J. Brill, 1963.

Wolforth, S. *The Portuguese in America.* San Francisco: Reed & Eterovich, 1978.

20

Norwegian Families

C.F. MIDELFORT

H.C. MIDELFORT

Our intention in this chapter is to give some insights into Norwegian Americans, with particular emphasis on continuities with their Norwegian past. We begin with an account of Norwegian history and values and then describe the deeply embedded contradictions of the culture and the implications for psychotherapy. We have had a unique vantage point to learn about Norwegian families. C.F. Midelfort has practiced psychiatry in the same Midwestern community for over 30 years, giving him the rare opportunity to see several generations of the same Norwegian families. A pioneer family therapist, he began practicing family therapy in 1946. H.C. Midelfort has done anthropological research on present-day Norwegian families in Norway as well as in the United States, which has allowed her to observe in each country the development of different patterns in groups with similar roots in the past.

Our experience has led us to believe that contradictions play a central role in the development of dysfunction and in its cure. The Norwegian character has been profoundly dualistic in its culture, religion, and folklore. Therapy with Norwegian families, therefore, requires mediation between opposites: goodness contends with evil forces, the tendency to rebellion and love of freedom contends with pressure for conformity and obedience to authority. Therapists must work with Norwegian families to transcend the extremes, the polarities of their conflicts, and must support the opposite side in each conflict to rebalance the system.

Much of what follows may apply to Swedish and Danish families as well, but there are important differences among these groups, due, in part, to historical circumstances and to geography—Norway's more extreme isolation and severe climate. The rugged mountains and glaciers, severe spring floods, and long dark winters, when the sun rises at 10 in the morning and sets by 3 in the afternoon, have all contributed to making even survival problematic. The

C.F. Midelfort. Gunderson Clinic, Lacrosse, Wisconsin; Lutheran General Hospital, Park Ridge, Illinois.

H.C. Midelfort. Anthropology Department, Brown University, Providence, Rhode Island.

extreme shortage of arable land (less than 4% is cultivated), frequent famine, and centuries of isolation from the outside world have made the struggle with nature more difficult.

Historical Factors

During Norway's Viking period, independent farms remained within the same families for many generations (Shettelig, 1930). Farmers felt their land was a sacred trust. In fact, in later times they could not leave it without explicit permission from the king (Shettelig, 1930). The farms were closed communities and were the centers of all religious, social, and legal life.

Christianity, which gradually became the official religion in Norway during the 11th century, sought to eliminate old Norse practices such as personal revenge, infanticide, sexual promiscuity, and gruesome punishments for petty crimes. But the pre-Christian gods survived, transformed into various evil spirits. Odin, foremost among the Nordic gods, became equated with the Devil (Bull, 1931).

Prior to the conquest of Norway by the Danes in 1536, the Norwegian farmers were, in effect, the servants of the hereditary kings. However, once Denmark established hegemony over Norway, the farmers rebelled. As an old and settled community, they resented the changes brought about by the new government, "foreign" nobility, businessmen who violated their old laws (the Laws of St. Olaf and of Haakon the Fifth, which had been codified in the Middle Ages).

Under the Danes, farm life was controlled by tight rules set by the (new) king. Taxes and regulations increased. The earlier farming technology continued with no innovations (Steen, 1930). The conflict between town and country increased as the foreigners gradually took over the business sector of town life. A spirit of free enterprise and mercantilism pervaded the towns. Meanwhile, the farmers opposed these "foreign" influences and refused to accept any new ways. For example, they refused to grow potatoes because the potato's skin resembled a leper's skin, and they declared that to sow grass seed demonstrated a lack of faith in God (Steen, 1932). Even the languages were different. The farmers spoke Norwegian, while the townspeople spoke Danish. Although farmers often envied the life of the upper classes in the towns, the split between the cultures increased.

The new religion, Lutheranism, imposed by the Danes also created problems. Catholicism and its priesthood had provided rituals that helped to control the Devil, but Lutheranism emphasized the individual's responsibility in dealing with the supernatural. The world was filled with the temptation of the Devil and fear of God's judgment. A 19-century Dane who wrote about the religious beliefs that reflected this dualism of God and the Devil, as well as the fear of damnation, described it thus:

When a serious mind looked into himself what did he see? Only sin and punishment. Every failure, every disappointment, honestly viewed, was only a finger stretched out to the Devil, who was everywhere present and ready to grasp the whole hand. (Troels-Lund, 1903, Vol. 13, p. 193)

The community provided the only defense against this evil. These beliefs and practices continued unchanged until well into the 18th century. At this point it became possible for Norwegians to move to the towns in search of work. Farmers who moved were both isolated from their families and rejected by the city people. They developed a new religious movement, radical pietism, and formed the beginnings of a Norwegian middle class. They cultivated a sense of personal righteousness and intense religious feelings in contrast to the rationalistic emphasis in 18th-century Lutheranism (Steen, 1932).

The rural farmers, meanwhile, continued to be influenced by a strong sense of custom and history. They occupied the same houses as their fathers, cultivated the same fields, and passed along their stories of the past in the form of folk tales. In short, their traditions were meaningful and they clung to them with a sense of pride (Steen, 1932). As a consequence, by the early 19th century, farmers were seen as enemies of modern education and progress.

Emigration

Norwegian immigration to the United States was primarily a result of episodes of famine, general poverty, and the wish for land and political freedom. The peak periods of immigration were at the beginnings of the decades of the 1840s, 1860s, and 1880s. In the 1880s a total of 186,000 Norwegians came to the United States. By 1915 a total of over 855,000 Norwegians had immigrated to the United States, a number equal to the total population of Norway in 1820. Only Ireland had given up a larger percentage of her population to the United States. The consequence of this outpouring is that there are an estimated 9 million Americans with some Norwegian ancestry in the United States today. By comparison, Norway's present population is approximately 4.5 million persons (Munch, 1980).

Perhaps due to their isolation on farms, Norwegian Americans have been quite successful in maintaining their Norwegianness; often even the third and subsequent generations still speak the native dialect brought over from their home district in Norway. Those who have not preserved the language have at least maintained the values and basic life understandings. It was and is commmon for rural Norwegian Americans to marry other Norwegian Americans. In western Wisconsin they are less likely than any other ethnic group to intermarry. This ethnic loyalty does much to preserve Norwegian traditions and attitudes.

Although it is not usual today for Norwegian Americans to describe themselves as Norwegian, an unpublished study by A. Strickon, Professor of Anthropology at the University of Wisconsin, has shown that friends of the Norwegians are mostly of Norwegian descent. The persistence of the culture is usually greatest within those rural communities peopled by the descendants of Norwegians from a particular valley who had emigrated and settled together.

In the New Country

The love of land and loyalty to family, which had kept Norwegians on the same farm in Norway for hundreds of years, has continued to influence them in the United States. They have also been fervently loyal to the Norway they left. Love for the homeland pervades Norwegian American literature and music (Rolvaag, 1927; Skardal, 1974; Semmingsen, 1980; Wefald, 1971).

Associated with immigration were some changes in family structure and discontinuities with the Norwegian past. In the United States, in contrast to Norway, church and state were separated. The immigrants built their own schools and churches and for the first time controlled them. Although Norwegian farmers were fundamentally conservative, the American experience and new responsibilities led to more liberal attitudes toward such things as education and medicine. More will be said later about changes in the family.

Traditional Family Values

Within the family, the man of the family is in control of major purchases and discipline. The woman is the communication center of the family and establishes the social network among kin, which includes grandparents, aunts, uncles, and cousins. There are implicit duties and mutual obligations in the kinship network, but asking directly for help is uncommon. Assistance must be offered not asked for. When necessary, this is done with a minimum of words and excuses as it is shameful both to need help and to suggest that someone else is incapable of managing on his or her own.

In rearing children, the parents hope to provide the proper atmosphere for the development of considerate, responsible, and obedient adults. Children are supposed to learn what is expected without undue disciplinary action. Each child is understood to have a unique, inborn potential and individuality that must not be hurt, even though she or he must not express that individuality too openly. Direct confrontations of wills are unusual.

Girls begin to assume adult responsibilities earlier than boys. They begin to help their mothers at about the age of eight; boys do not begin helping their fathers until age 11 or 12. A girl's future outcome is her mother's responsibility, a boy's his father's. The eldest son is expected eventually to take over the family farm, although a younger son may inherit it under some circumstances. It is considered a tradgedy if the family farm passes out of the family's hands.

Extended family gatherings are an important part of family life. In rural areas the extended family comes together to celebrate holidays, baptisms, birthdays, confirmations, and funerals. Family unity makes individuation difficult. Attempts to break away from the family are often accompanied by intense feelings of guilt, anxiety, and resentment. In as much as the family conveys a strong sense of continuity with the past (through folk tales, personal myths, and stories regarding various friends and relatives from the past), individuation is also likely to pose a threat to this valued sense of belonging. Finally, the family that successfully engenders a sense of community and acceptance makes it difficult for the individual to choose other than community ideals as a means of self-expression.

In America social, educational, and monetary success were regarded as attainable through hard work and diligence. Farmers and their wives worked hard and rapidly managed to change their socioeconomic position from that of landless farm workers to independent, land-owning farmers. During the 19th century an eighth-grade education was considered more than adequate to give a young person a good start in life. But higher education gradually came to be considered more desirable, particularly with the construction of church-owned colleges.

After the family came to the United States, the father retained his authoritative position but children could leave the farm because new land was more easily available than in Norway. Leaving the farm and the loyalty conflicts associated with it were new sources of friction.

Hard work is highly valued and earns justified rewards. For example, in Norway all young men and women work and earn money. Being on welfare is abhorred. There is no objection to a woman working outside the home, if she accomplishes her home duties as well. She is perceived as industrious and useful.

Leisure time is also devoted to hard physical effort, and idleness is avoided. In Norway athletics are an important aspect of recreation and are tied closely to a mystical appreciation of nature. Having a cabin at the ocean shore on a fjord or in the mountains is a joy that is often regarded as a spiritual necessity, irrespective of socioeconomic position. In the United States, sports, traveling, and camping are valued ways of spending leisure and vacation time.

Sexuality is not regarded as a main issue in life. The body and its functions are seen as natural and good, if kept healthy. Sexual activity is an acceptable but strictly private concern and is not openly discussed. Excessive sexuality, like all other excesses, is frowned upon. Sexuality in itself only becomes problematic if it causes public scandal. In a therapeutic situation it is not advisable to approach the question of sexuality too early, and it should not be brought up at all if children are present.

Among Norwegians and Norwegian Americans emotional expression is strictly controlled. As they see it, resentments must not lead to open confrontations, especially within the immediate family. Overt and direct aggression is rare within the family. In certain situations, however, it is tolerated, as, for example, in the just punishment of disobedience. If wronged, they are permitted to be angry, but not excessively so. Aggression is channeled mainly through indirect means: teasing, ignoring, silence, averting the glance, or staring balefully.

Words at all times are used sparingly and considered powerful. Actions are considered to be more indicative of true thoughts and feelings than are words. When words are used, directness, brevity, clarity, and truth are prized. The nonverbal aspects of communication—a straight glance, a calm tone of voice, and an erect yet respectful posture—are seen as demonstrating the inner motivations of honesty and sincerity. These qualities along with modesty, which is also highly valued, demonstrate respect for others. Any scandal or emotional illness is kept secret since it is thought to reveal an inner taint, a moral weakness in the community. Intimacy between friends is something that develops slowly and is expressed indirectly. This style of intimacy, lacking demonstrativeness, may appear superficial to other Americans.

Norwegians believe that they should not burden their family or even their closest friend with personal problems or feelings of inadequacy. Gossip, although looked down upon, is a common topic of conversation and indirectly comments upon community ideals and individual inadequacies. Friendship is demonstrated through loyalty over time and by spending time together not by sharing intimate problems. Family and friends are united by a silent understanding that life is hard and made more worthwhile by this loyalty and steadfastness.

Norwegians value being *kjekk*, a word meaning courageous, positive, humorous, strong, capable, and industrious. It is demonstrated by a lively sense of humor, a confident tone of voice, and public denial of inadequacy or suffering. They avoid mental and bodily diseases. by remaining active and by living a vigorous life. Among the religious, ill health is seen as resulting from lack of faith. It is either a punishment for sins or a test of their belief. To outsiders Norwegians often appear rather stiff, formal, and reserved. Their stoicism is exemplified by their great tolerance of physical pain. In the experience of P.A. Midelfort, Norwegians in Norway required less local anesthesia for minor surgical procedures than was common in America.

Meals are a very important gathering time for the family. The preparation, selection, and consumption of food are all regulated by family tradition and are invested with symbolic significance. Boiled food, dairy products, and bread are thought of as healthful and are perferred foods. Eating too many sweets is not seen as healthy or "mature." Adults, for example, will usually drink their coffee black.

Alcoholic beverages are allowed in moderation. On certain occasions, such as wedding parties, Norwegians tolerate, in fact expect, a great deal of drinking. It is less common, however, to see women drinking to excess at such occasions. Binge drinking is fairly common among those who have periodic depressions. Those who are strict pietists, on the other hand, see alcohol as sinful and avoid all use of it. Alcohol abstinence societies became popular on both sides of the Atlantic among Norwegians in the 19th century.

Before the 1840s when the Norwegian Parliament forbade the distillation of alcohol on farms, Norwegians considered alcohol a medicine and drank up to four times a day to maintain their health. When Parliament did prohibit its distillation, Norwegians turned to coffee as a replacement. Today when visiting a Norwegian or Norwegian American family, coffee is offered immediately as a symbol indicating the host's desire for the guests to stay.

Since the personal religion of Norwegians has for many centuries been also tied to the landscape and the home, Norwegian Americans feel reverence and a sense that the Church, the home farm, and the land are sacred. As we have already said, this conviction is ancient and can be traced to the days of the Vikings when farmers felt their land was a sacred trust (Shettelig, 1930). In the United States the experience of personal connection with both family and community is centered around the activities of the Lutheran Church. The private myths of Norwegian Americans are also concerned with these two things, God and land. In religion, ritual and action rather than theology are the most important elements of public worship.

Norwegian music and art express mystical feelings about God and nature. Norwegian paintings, of which the people are extraordinarily fond, are unique in their choice of colors. The blues, reds, and earth tones reflect the natural colors of the landscape, water, and sky. Norwegians love to have paintings on the walls of their homes. The paintings are at times misty and dark, but at the same time lively, like music played on the Hardanger fiddle, Norway's national folk instrument. The eight strings of the fiddle produce humming overtones giving a depth and eerie resonance that hint at what is unseen and unheard.

Dualities

Up to this point, the picture that we have painted of the Norwegians has been rather wholesome, as they would like to appear. What is less obvious, but essential to understand in order to be effective as psychotherapists, is the darker side of their profound dualism in which archaic beliefs contend with good intentions.

The Norwegian family system is hierarchical. As we have seen, certain characters personify authority: God, the king, the bishop, the father. Authority is respected, but at the same time there was, and still is, a deep distrust of authority and a desire to rebel against representatives of authority, both within and outside of the family. The origins of this rebellion are deeply rooted in the history of Norway. In that history, we repeatedly find conflicts between loyalty to authority and the assertion of individual freedom.

Dualities are found everywhere. Norwegian life is permeated with the pattern of conflicting extremes: the cold and dark of the winter contrasting with the warmth and continuous light of midsummer; the constant threat of starvation contrasting with the custom of obligatory generosity with food for guests; and isolation contrasting with intense interest in sociability. (After immigration to the United States, Norwegians settled in the northern Midwest where they again found many of these same seasonal extremes.)

A key duality is health and illness. Under the adverse conditions of Norwegian life, physical strength and endurance were and are prized. Norwegians have always attributed great importance to the body—its health and diseases—and have neglected the psychological side of life. They customarily explain their problems in terms of physical causes and are inclined to brood about their inability to change their lives. As a result of this inability resentment smolders within outwardly "cheerful," obedient family members. This resentment is further intensified by the equally traditional Norwegian determination to be true to their ideals at any cost. They strive to be individuals while remaining within the rigid hierarchy of the family.

Similarly, outside the family, Norwegians must loyally conform to community standards, but, at the same time, they will resent any authority and oppose it secretly. In the political and economic arenas of life this leads to Norwegians' firmly opposing the status quo while resisting any change. This is, to be sure, a contradiction, but obvious contradictions are not openly acknowledged or even recognized by Norwegians themselves.

Denial of these and similar profound contradictions and conflicts takes place in every sphere of life. Denial of internal psychological conflict leads to efforts to find external, apparently objective explanations for problems. For example, often emotional ills are thought to be caused by physical weakness or injury. Rural Norwegian Americans believe that health, including mental health, should be maintained through physical fitness, fresh air, sports, and contact with nature. A Norwegian may, therefore, expect that physical appearance and health will be regarded as a direct reflection of inner well-being and personal worth.

Religion

Since the end of the Viking period (ca. 800–1000) Norwegians have had two conflicting religious orientations. The first has been the public, authoritarian national Christian Church. The second has been a secret, archaic folk religion that preserves the old pantheistic Norse religious beliefs as well as some Christian beliefs. In this folk world view profound fatalism is combined with anxious preoccupation with sin and damnation. Fear of God and the Devil and active magical forces of good and evil are all combined into the private faith. Such beliefs are seldom, if ever, expressed verbally: this is the concealed ethos of the family.

Norse myths provide a key to the understanding of the older values. For example, the basic world myth of the Norse was that the world is held together by an enormous evil snake, Midgardsorm. Within its coils Yggdrasil, the Tree of Life, grew and was renewed, while, at the same time, it was dying and withering—a precarious and gruesome balance. The Norse gods were portrayed as capricious and were regarded as being neither infallible nor omnipotent. They could provide humans no ultimate protection. Struggle was endless. For example, in the myth of the end of the world, the catastrophic destruction of the world at Ragnarok, an evil god destroys Balder, the White God, and unleashes a battle in which the gods and the giants, in catastrophic battle, destroy each other and the entire world. Some gods and giants survive to begin the struggle in yet another cycle.

In so uncertain a world, Norsemen believed that the heroism of the individual was the only pathway to immortality. Only heroic commitment to an ideal, a commitment showing an individual's strength of will and stubbornness in the face of great odds, could confer lasting reputation. The pursuit of an ideal did not necessarily bring happiness, but it did earn a certain amount of lasting public validation.

In Norse myths the forces of good and evil, renewal and destruction, and hope and despair contend. Reconciliation takes the form of a balancing or recycling of the struggle. This reconciliation, the therapeutic mediation between opposites, is the particular emphasis of this chapter.

Mediation

Through the centuries Norwegian prophetesses, wise women, priests, pastors, and, today, medical practitioners and psychiatrists have functioned as mediators between opposites. They have always practiced and preached within a community in which a fatalistic world view was normal and a catastrophic end to the universe inevitable: In Viking times it was Ragnarok (Twilight of the Gods), in Christian times it is the day of judgment. These mediators act by recreating myths or explanations of this fate that attempt, ritualistically, to bridge between and transcend extremes and make daily life bearable and meaningful.

During the Catholic period (ca. 1000–1500) the priest protected the parishioners from evil and mediated between Christ and Satan through his use of holy water, extreme unction, and the other sacraments. After the

Reformation, Lutheran ministers used scriptural quotations, hymns, prayers, and ridicule against the Devil (who could not tolerate humor). They used rituals to mediate against overwhelming manifestations of evil, particularly mental illness.

Both priest and minister transformed the uncertainties of everyday life into clear black and white distinctions. This reductionism, or narrowing of attention, was necessary in order for their myths to work the indispensible magic of transforming relationships that had become overly rigid or anarchistic. The sacrament of the Eucharist, for example, is a good model of this process: The bread and wine are transformed by symbolic operations into body and blood that are consumed for spiritual reintegration and healing. The worshipper is transformed by Christ within. Thus, faith in Christ and a relationship with God enables people to transcend their interpersonal grievances and their existential and material limitations. Without a mediator who takes hold of such fundamental spiritual issues, there can be no transformation or healing.

Perhaps this is a universal phenomenon. For a non-Norwegian, the invocation of the mythology of Freud or of Jung may be effective. The opposing forces of superego and id are recognized and mediated by the observing ego, allied with the therapist. But dualism as intense as that of Norwegians is unusual in mainstream American culture and calls for an approach that deals with their specific conflicts.

When Norwegians have become entrenched in their extremes, such as guilt or rebellion, then, the recognition of the opposite and mediation between those opposites is crucial for a return to health. The mediation must be accomplished together by the therapist, the patient, and the family. Joining the culture of the patient and recognizing the underlying myths within the family's private religion is helpful in working with Norwegian families. Their private religion should be tactfully explored to enrich the family's awareness of it. Then the family may accept the contradictions (rebellion vs. authority, sickness vs. longing for health) and achieve some transcendence, peace and wider perspective.

Pathways to Cure

In light of Norwegians' tendency to emphasize their bodies, it is understandable that they turn to surgery and medication as cures for mental illness. Symptoms of emotional illness are interpreted as physical illness with physical causes. Typically, the transformation from illness to health is accomplished through the mediation of surgeons, internists or family practitioners. They become the "priests," possessing supernatural powers and performing the ritual of the surgical or medical procedures. They are accorded great respect.

Family systems theory shows us that the therapist can enter the family at any systems level, be it religious, cultural, social, psychological, or physical, and influence the other levels. However, because it is less effective to enter Norwegian families at the psychological level of conventional psychotherapeutic approaches, entering the family through the physical, religious, or ideological level is more productive. The ethnic level (the level of traditional history and practice) is also generally acceptable and is linked closely to the religious level by Norwegians in the United States.

In the ethnic traditions of every family are found the opposites of respect for authority and rebellion against it in the name of individual rights. Often in families with mental illness this polarization is extreme. Norwegian Americans suffering from depression are usually overly concerned with authority and tradition, while those with character disorders are overly concerned with rebellion.

Psychotherapy may well be described as the discovery of new options not initially remembered by the patient or family. These options, however, are already present as assets within the family and its cultural history.

Often Norwegian families are divided by individuals taking up opposing values. In such cases the therapist should take a position between them. If a family unites on one side of a traditional conflict, the therapist must oppose the family by embodying, in an appealing way, the opposite values. For example, with anarchistic families, therapists should be professional and authoritative. With the overly organized or closed groups, they should be accepting and egalitarian. By taking both sides, supporting both the individual and the family, independence and authority, therapists demonstrate support for the existence of both extremes, embodying the paradox within themselves. Therapists can demonstrate for the family that both extremes can exist in a sane person at the same time.

Case Examples

In each of the cases that follow, the patient, under conditions of great stress, had gone to extremes in one of the fundamental ways that we have described. The therapist, after deciding what was the fundamental conflict, initiated a process of therapeutic mediation.

The setting for therapy was and is important. The therapist behaves in a traditional Norwegian way: serious, respectful, and careful. He or she is firm in handshake and succinct in speech. The sessions are held with as much of the family attending as possible. The entire setting is a ritual in which the therapist conveys a profound understanding of the patient's dilemma. This creates a supportive atmosphere in which the patient's anxiety wanes for a time. Relaxing, the patient joins, indeed identifies, with the therapist and can let go of the extreme and transcend the problem. This experience of transcendence enables the patient to look at the dilemma with a broader perspective. Then new feelings can be experienced and accepted and more reasonable plans can be made. On some occasions it may be possible to talk directly about the problem. More often the therapist must proceed indirectly by choosing subjects for conversation that reflect the values that need support.

A Depressed and Disoriented Widow

An attractive, lively, blond, 26-year-old woman was admitted to the hospital in an acute psychotic depression. Two months prior to admission her husband and only child, a 4-year-old son, were killed in a tragic drowning accident. (They had fallen through rotten boards into an abandoned well on their property and had drowned.) The rural Norwegian community had gathered around her, provided support, but blocked her active grieving by constantly reassuring her that her son and husband were happily rejoined with Jesus in Heaven. She moved back to her parents' home and continued, without interruption, her regular work as a hairdresser and Sunday school teacher. She regarded uninterrupted work as a necessary and essential duty.

She became increasingly agitated and developed bizarre symptoms. Repeatedly and ritualistically, she counted to three and then snapped her fingers. She had visions of an angel coming from Heaven to reunite her with her husband and son. She left cryptic notes with mysterious religious messages around the house for her mother to discover. She alienated her Irish American mother-in-law by insisting on describing the problems in her sexual relationship with her deceased husband.

Like many Norwegian Americans, her account of her problem was strongly flavored with concern about the community's opinions, and she exhibited a particularly Norwegian, legalistic, doom-laden moral preoccupation. She said to the doctor who admitted her, "I pray to God to tell me what to do. I didn't want to go into a depression the way some people do."

During the birth of her son, the patient had been badly torn and the doctor had sewn the vaginal tear too tightly, making sexual intercourse painful. She felt extremely guilty about refusing her husband's sexual advances (in fact she delusionally believed that she was developing cancer as a punishment for this sin). "My vagina was closed. It wouldn't work. It was too painful." Her attempts during her illness to share her feelings of guilt and embarrassment with her family were met with shock and disapproval. Nowhere was she able to talk about her feelings.

Her mother, as she said and as is often true in Norwegian American families, was the family's pillar of emotional strength to whom she could turn in time of need. She also wanted to depend upon the strength and support of the Norwegian community and expressed confusion and anguish over her inability to reconcile their implicit demand that she control herself with her need to express her grief. Therapy focused on mediating the opposites of "good"—being a religious, conforming member of the community, who accepted her fate without protest, and "bad"—her angry, guilt-ridden and depressed reactions to her losses. The therapist moved back and forth, alternately encouraging her expression of grief and guilt and praising her for her acceptance of her situation. He shared with her his own deep religious faith and assured her of God's love, mercy, and ultimate forgiveness. Interventions with her family involved the same kind of mediation, for example, congratulating her mother on her ability to console her daughter and on her equanimity.

During the patient's 21-day hospitalization, the therapist continued to encourage her expressions of grief and guilt. At least one family member was with her at all times and shared in the therapeutic process. Within five days her compulsive symptoms had diminished. Her mother had been the only family member she had allowed to touch her since the death of her husband. Now she sought the comfort of physical touch from the therapist, a kind of ritual of acceptance. She told him, "I decided to slow down. I'm cried out, I guess. I'm not the only one who has problems am I? It's hard for me to cry in front of people, that's all."

After another week the patient's compulsive symptoms were gone, but she continued to experience difficulty in revealing her feelings of grief without the comfort and support of the therapist, her trusted ally, who counterbalanced the emphasis in her family and community on propriety.

A month after her discharge she was seen as an outpatient and felt much better. At each subsequent visit she hugged the therapist and appeared more relaxed and confident.

With the death of her husband and son, the patient had reduced everything to an extreme of spiritualism: The Lord was testing her. She lost contact with the reality of her feelings about the deaths. Intensely involved with her mother, she tried to emulate what she saw as her mother's strength and follow the community's prescription that she be cheerful. In therapy she was given full permission to discover that her desire for love and her expression of unhappiness were acceptable. Her ritual hugging of the therapist (not a part of her usual behavioral repertoire) symbolized their mutual acceptance of a personal religious life where all feelings (sex, grief, anger, and rebellion) were allowed. At the same time, the myth of salvation through faith and confession of sins, the part of her world view that had first appeared in the illness, was also recognized and accepted.

The therapist's mediation consisted of an acceptance of the opposites that are necessary for a healthy daily life. Her religious extremism was opposed and finally neutralized by the reality and involvement of the hospital, family, friends, pastor, local doctor, and therapist. Physical contact brought trust and the discovery of the opposite of religion, the personal side of her life, where her individuality was important and recognized. The therapist, through support of a holding milieu, gave her a place to discover a more balanced, realistic version of her human potential in the context of her familial and religious background.

A Lutheran's Fear of Catholicism

A 30-year-old Norwegian American Lutheran pastor, his wife, and their three children moved from Montana to a small community in Wisconsin, where he served two parishes. His father was a Lutheran pastor as well, and the young pastor, the eldest of three children, had become a minister to please his father. (He had wished to pursue a career as a high school coach and teacher.) The young pastor and his wife felt themselves strangers in the Wisconsin rural community and felt unaccepted by his congregations.

Within a year of their move, the pastor was admitted to the hospital because of acute anxiety after an auto accident occurred outside his home. Describing the accident and its sequelae he said, "I hesitated. I heard it [the accident], but I was afraid. I realized I had to go out there." A Catholic man whose family he knew was lying down in the yard badly hurt. "Since then I've been afraid. I couldn't sleep. My appetite is less. I can't go home because I'm afraid for my wife and three children."

Several years previously the patient's mother had died of a heart attack during an auto accident in which his father had been driving. The patient had blamed his father for her death (in spite of the fact that he was clearly not at fault) and blamed himself as well because the last time he had seen his mother they had quarreled about the father. The patient had accused his father of forcing him into the ministry and of being domineering. His mother had defended her husband. The patient was convinced that, given her chronic heart problems, this quarrel had contributed to her death. He connected this with his present fear that the Catholic family would murder him or his family for his inability to act at the time of the recent accident. The Catholicism was significant because of the long-standing, and often still bitter, antagonism between Lutherans and Roman Catholics.

The patient's wife stayed with him throughout his hospitalization. The therapist talked with them daily and reassured them by accepting, mostly implicitly by empathic listening, the patient's guilty feelings. The patient spoke openly about his hostility toward his father, his feelings of inadequacy in his work, and his fear of Catholics.

The therapist recognized that this was a Norwegian Lutheran who found it very difficult to have feelings of anger and hostility toward Catholics in this instance without subsequently experiencing the dread of death and damnation. As in the first case, the therapist attempted to mediate between these extremes by accepting all of his feelings—fear, hostility, and guilt. The context of the sessions—the safety of a Norwegian Lutheran hospital and a Norwegian Lutheran psychiatrist—helped to give the patient permission to have his feelings.

When confronted with a crisis such as the death of his mother or the threatened death of the Catholic man outside his home, the patient had narrowed his consciousness to focus on fear and guilt. He projected his own feelings of anger and the wish for revenge against his father onto the Catholic family and onto his own congregation. It was as if he embodied a tradition that goes back to the Viking period: Revenge must be exacted for a wrong suffered. He also embodied the next historical development: After the coming of Christianity, strong passion, including revengeful impulses, was condemned and seen as an evil that could cause illness.

For the Norwegian American pastor and his wife, who were afraid of both death and the evil of strong feelings, the therapist and, symbolically Christ, became the mediators. Together, therapist and patient prayed during some sessions. This focus upon transcendence and away from the symptoms of his illness allowed the pastor and his wife enough relief to find their composure and to think and plan in more responsible ways. With support acceptable to a Norwegian Lutheran, the patient was able to begin functioning again as a father, husband, and pastor.

During several of the sessions the patient prayed for the success of the therapy, for his congregations, and for his family. He began to feel sympathy rather than only fear and distrust for the Catholic family. He told the therapist, "I have less fear, less guilt about the accident. The feeling of responsibility for my congregations is coming back."

Within two weeks of hospitalization, the patient was released and could be seen on an outpatient basis. He became progressively less anxious but still experienced fear late at night. He had a feeling of faintness when he had to talk to the president of his congregation. While these symptoms ceased and the patient was able to carry out his duties, he remained a fundamentally pessimistic person and continued to feel ill at ease with the people in his community.

A Depressed Woman

A 64-year-old, second-generation Norwegian Lutheran woman was referred by a surgeon to a therapist. She complained of pain and unhappiness and said that she wanted to have her goiter removed. Her goiter had been unchanged in the past 30 years, and the therapist diagnosed her as seriously depressed.

She lived on her mother's family farm in nothern Iowa with her husband and unmarried son (in his early 40s). Her depression had incapacitated her to the extent that she could no longer function in her home or in her church, where she had been the cook for all community/church activities.

Two years before she had saved her husband's life by pulling him from under the hooves of a cow. It was a serious incident, which left him with a limp. She felt that he was insufficiently grateful for what she had done. This resentment was only one of many that had accumulated over the years. Another blow to her morale had been the recent death of 80 young pigs from hog cholera. They had been, as was traditional, her responsibility.

The last straw, just before her referral, was modernization of her kitchen. Over her objections, her husband and son had replaced the stove, sink, and cupboards and were proceeding to redo the entire room. Despair overcame her, and she ceased to function. She blamed her state on her goiter and accused her husband of neglect for refusing to bring her in for an operation.

Her husband and son had taken her for a series of six electroshock treatments. They had not helped. She was angry at not having been brought to the proper doctor, a surgeon, and believed that an operation at an earlier date would have helped to prevent her depression.

The family sessions included her husband, son, and two unmarried daughters, who had returned from their jobs in Minneapolis and Washington, D.C., to help their mother. Norwegian was spoken. The family told the therapist that she had been depressed on another occasion, 12 years before when house remodeling had also been an issue. The therapist was able to watch the natural progression of the illness over a period of months. (This treatment was conducted before antidepressant medications existed.) He saw the family every two weeks initially and then once a month until the end of the treatment (which happened to occur at Christmas).

From very early on in the treatment it was clear that there were two camps within the family. The father and second child (the daughter who worked in Washington, D.C.) were allied as advocates of change and progress. The son and youngest daughter were allied with the mother as favoring tradition. They felt close to the mother and wept each time she did. She trusted her son and said he could do no wrong. The therapist was careful not to take sides directly with either the patient or her husband. He joined them as a fellow Norwegian, deflected requests for surgery, and was with them in a calm, supportive, ritualized way. He discussed traditions, household activities, and current farm problems with them.

Because of the mother's bitterness toward the father, the therapist gave decision-making power about the patient to the son and helped the family to plan the patient's daily activities. He directed them to accept her as ill and not to expect that she would show initiative in her work as she had done when well. She was kept active as a participant in the household but not as a leader or organizer.

In this case the mediation was between the past and present, with the focus on daily life counterbalancing the patient's obsession with the past. She gradually got better and for the final session of therapy, with the therapist's encouragement, she cooked a cherry cake. The family and the therapist ate the cake together, symbolizing the return to health of the entire family. The patient was able to reassert her leadership in the home and at the church. When seen two years later she was doing fine, and from that time on experienced no recurrence of depression.

The patient's connection with tradition and her family's past was exemplified by the home and kitchen. She was so strongly attached to them that any threat of change precipitated feelings of doom and despair. She saw her husband and oldest daughter as insensitive to her needs and as advocates of change and confusion. She continued to feel that her husband had not shown appropriate gratitude for her having saved his life, and she blamed him for not having cared for her properly during her illness. She believed the source of her illness to be physical. The therapist did not try to persuade them otherwise but instead helped them focus on concrete changes in the family structure, and the requests for surgery ceased.

In this intensely Norwegian milieu, where farm and home were sacred, the therapist's similarity in ethnic and religious background was a tremendous help. He was allowed into the family as an authority figure who knew their traditions and could speak their language. But by focusing attention on the details of daily life, a therapist of any ethnic background could have helped this family overcome the patient's depression.

In all of these cases the therapist was, as a matter of course, placed in a position of authority by the families. Deference and respect are due authority figures in Norwegian culture, but this is combined with a suspicion of authority and outsiders, which must be accepted by the therapist. The therapist addressed the patients as Mr. and Mrs. and maintained a formal and equal relationship. In these situations Norwegians do not equate informality with friendliness or equality. Formality demonstrates mutual respect within a special relationship.

In the above patients, illness was associated with the denial of one of a pair of opposites. In the first situation the patient denied her own emotional needs and was aware only of religious and community demands. The therapist supported both sides of her experience and had the authority to allow her to transcend the conflict and accept both.

In the second case, the therapist allowed the pastor to express his hostility and guilt feelings. The patient had denied his hostile feelings about Catholics and his father to the point where both had become, for him, inhuman monsters. Through a transcendental experience of prayer, the pastor was able to recognize and accept his denied feelings—of Catholics and his father's humanity, as well as his own.

In the third case, the 64-year-old farm wife could not accept modern present-oriented living because it represented a change from the past to which she was devoted. By emphasizing plans for daily living, the therapist allowed the patient to discover that she could live in the present. At the same time, the therapist reinforced the family's Norwegian traditions by discussing their family past and speaking in Norwegian. The culmination of therapy with the sharing of a cake, which the wife had baked at Christmas time, was especially significant for the patient. Christmas is traditionally the time in Norwegian families when women are the center of their families, creating a festive atmosphere in the home. The communal meal with family and therapist symbolized the patient's return to normal functioning in the present as well as an acceptance of her past.

Summary

Cultural and religious subsystems are not the only level of family life that are important in understanding and treating Norwegian American families. We could begin to influence the family system at any level. The surgeon and internist enter at the physical level, the average psychiatrist at the psychological level, and the local physician at the social level.

However, interventions based upon an understanding of history, religion, and myth can all contribute substantially to therapeutic efficacy. In addition, the therapist can help the family to understand itself and thereby contribute to the family's continued welfare. We have emphasized the two types of religion, public and private. They have served the different needs of the Norwegian family for generations. The public religion has to do with the ordering of society and its laws. The private religion deals with the secret, hidden beliefs, the fears and ultimate concerns that are mediated through myths. All the Norwegian healers—the priestesses, priests, pastors, wise old women, and modern therapists—can be understood as mediating between opposites by transcending, without denying, the reality of life's paradoxes.[1]

What has been described here is not a general guideline for family therapy in any culture. But among Norwegian Americans and other similar cultures, where deeply hidden opposites contend and cannot easily be directed, interpreted, and discussed, this approach is likely to be helpful.

REFERENCES

Bull, E. *Det Norske Folks Liv og Historie Gjennem Tidene* (Vol. 2: 1000–1280). Oslo: Aschehoug, 1931.
Levi-Strauss, C. *The Raw and the Cooked* (Vol. 1). New York: Harper & Row, 1969.
Munch, P.A. Norwegians. In S. Thernstrom, A. Orlov, & O. Handlin (Eds.), *Harvard Encyclopedia of American Ethnic Groups.* Cambridge: Harvard University Press, 1980.
Rolvaag, O.E. *Giants in the Earth.* New York: Harper & Row, 1927.
Semmingsen, I. *Norway to America.* Minneapolis: University of Minnesota, 1980.
Shettelig, H. *Det Norske Folks Liv og Historie Gjennem Tidene* (Vol. 1: Oldtiden til 1000). Oslo: Aschehoug, 1930.
Skardal, D.B. *The Divided Heart.* Oslo: Universtetsforlaget, 1974. (American edition, Lincoln: University of Nebraska Press, 1974.)
Steen, S. *Det Norske Folks Liv og Historie Gjennem Tidene* (Vol. 5: 1640–1720). Oslo: Aschehoug, 1930.
Steen, S. *Det Norske Folks Liv og Historie Gjennem Tidene* (Vol. 6: 1720–1770). Oslo: Aschehoug, 1932.
Troels-Lund. *Dagligt Liv i Norden i Det Sekstende Aarhundrede* (Vols. 13–14). Copenhagen: Nordisk Forlag, 1903.
Wefald, J. A Voice of Protest. *Topical Studies No. 1.* Northfield, Minn.: The Norwegian-American Historical Association, 1971.

ADDITIONAL READINGS

Keilhau, W. *Det Norske Folks Liv og Historie Gjennem Tidene* (Vol. 8: 1814–1840). Oslo: Aschehoug, 1929.
Keilhau, W. *Det Norske Folks Liv og Historie Gjennem Tidene* (Vol. 9: 1840–1874). Oslo: Aschehoug, 1931.

1. We have been stimulated by Claude Levi-Strauss's concept of binary oppositions as they illuminate certain aspects of Norwegian American life and history (Levi-Strauss, 1969).

Keilhau, W. *Det Norske Folks Liv og Historie Gjennem Tidene* (Vol. 10: 1875–1920). Oslo: Aschehoug, 1931.

Hasund, S. *Det Norske Folks Liv og Historie Gjennem Tidene* (Vol. 3: 1280–1500). Oslo: Aschehoug, 1934.

Munch, C. *The Strange American Way: Letters from Wiota 1855–59*. London: Feffer & Simons, 1970.

Munch, P.A. Norwegian Settlements. *Norwegian-American Studies and Records 18*. Northfield, Minn.: Norwegian-American Historical Association, 1954.

Munch, P.A. Segregation and Assimilation of Norwegian Settlements in Wisconsin. *Norwegian-American Studies and Records 18*. Northfield, Minn.: Norwegian-American Historical Association, 1954.

Paasche, F. *Hedenskap og Kristendom*. Oslo: Aschehoug, 1948.

Raith, K.B. *The Location of Tobacco Production in Wisconsin*. PhD dissertation, Department of Geography, University of Minnesota, 1973.

Ramsoy, N.R. *Norwegian Society*. New York: Humanities Press, 1960.

Rice, J.G. Pattern of Ethnicity in a Minnesota County 1880–1905: Kandiyohi County, Minnesota. *Geographical Reports No. 4*. Umeaa, Sweden: Department of Geography, Umeaa University, 1973.

Steen, S. *Det Norske Folks Liv og Historie Gjennem Tidene* (Vol. 4: 1500–1640). Oslo: Aschehoug, 1931.

Steen, S. *Det Norske Folks Liv og Historie Gjennem Tidene* (Vol. 7: 1770–1814). Oslo: Aschehoug, 1933.

Terry, P. (trans.). *Poems of the Viking: The Elder Edda*. Indianapolis: Bobbs-Merrill, 1972.

21

British Families

DAVID McGILL

JOHN K. PEARCE

The acronym WASP—White Anglo-Saxon Prostestant—has been used in loose reference to Americans who are White, Protestant, and primarily of early British immigrant origins (Novak, 1973; Simon, 1972). In addition, the terms WASP and Anglo-American have been used to refer to American families who have been in the United States a long time, to those participating in what Margaret Mead has described as the "American Culture" (Mead, 1971), and to refer to White Protestant Americans of vague or mixed national origins, as distinguished from a single ethnic designation, such as Swedish. (People who have old German Protestant origins are consequently often thought of as WASP or Anglo, and, in fact, British and German American cultures have much in common; see Chap. 12.) In this chapter, we will use the more specific term, British American, and will be elaborating their British American ethnicity. British American families are the descendants of English, Scottish, and Scotch Irish immigrants (Anderson, 1970; Erickson, 1972; Leyburn, 1962).

British immigration to the United States can be roughly divided into two major periods: colonial immigration and postrevolutionary immigration. In the early 1600s Puritans settled New England, and Episcopal planters and indentured servants settled Virginia. In 1690, 90% of North American colonists were of English descent, but an analysis of the 1790 Federal Census 100 years later (Erickson, 1980) showed that descendants of the English remained a solid majority (80%) only in New England. In the other areas of the country they accounted for less than half of the total population, outnumbered by the aggregate population of Scots, Scotch Irish, Germans, and Blacks (Seward, 1978; Erickson, 1980).

Postrevolutionary British immigration, which began about 1820, actually surpassed the number of colonial immigrants, and British immigrants continue to constitute one of the major streams of immigration to the United States. The largest number of English came between 1879 and 1893, when 82,000 were arriving annually. English-speaking Canadians have also been a major source of the ongoing British American immigration (Erickson, 1980).

David McGill. Faculty, Smith College Graduate School of Social Work, Northampton, Massachusetts.

John K. Pearce. Faculty, Cambridge Family Institute, Cambridge, Massachusetts.

Values

Knowledge of their values provides the foundation for family therapy with British Americans (Pearce & Friedman, 1979). British Americans are taught that the meaningful issues and struggles of life all lie within the self and that there are few external constraints that cannot be overcome by individual effort (Gorer, 1964).

This empowering of individual effort was reinforced, for British immigrants, by the seemingly limitless possibilities of the North American environment. Over the generations a British American success ethic evolved that partially eroded English class stratification. According to the success ethic, all persons can, and therefore should, be individually successful. Failure is correspondingly almost always ascribed to personal weakness. British Americans' needs to achieve and to be responsible may make it difficult for them to recognize or accept limitations.

> A New England Brahmin couple's marriage was threatened by the wife's irritability and anger as she attempted to cope with her full-time profession, a 6-month-old daughter, and the increasing burden of a serious chronic disease, multiple sclerosis. It was a revelation for her when the therapist suggested that she might be doing too much. The couple was better able to understand the origins of her expectations of herself by exploring her family history. Her ancestors, including the women, had been fiercely independent and had striven to make social contributions through professions or social services. Reviewing this history helped to make sense of her difficulty in accepting any disability or in negotiating further help from her husband. In therapy she revised her expectations to a more realistic level.

British Americans both gain and suffer from their major cultural distinction: hyperindividualism. They tend to be good at self-reliance, self-sufficiency, and self-control and rather less good at maintaining mutually giving relationships, tolerating dependency, and integrating and expressing emotional experience. Keeping a stiff upper lip, muddling through, and taking it like a man, all reflect English values, which British Americans have maintained as the desired responses to pain, suffering, and life's difficulties.

In British American families, one denies, carries on, and, above all, takes responsibility for one's problems by not complaining or involving other people. Likewise, one would not risk interfering in another person's business. A man could be an alcoholic for years, and his closest companion or even business partner might not intervene by suggesting treatment. Individuals "responsibly" keep their problems to themselves and respect the right of others to do the same. For example:

> The father of a British American man developed a melanoma on his back. Eventually it bled so much that he had to change his shirt many times a day,

yet he never sought medical attention. Finally, a tumor developed under his arm that was so painful and disabling that he was "forced to get to a doctor."

Listening to this description, the Jewish therapist suggested that perhaps it was too bad that the father had not gotten some help and relief earlier. The British American patient (who was doing grief work for his father as part of the therapy) replied, "No, my father made his choice and died his own way."

We might hypothesize that it was the nature of this man's illness that prevented him from seeking treatment. He may have assumed that the doctor would not be able to do anything about the cancer and therefore thought it useless to complain (Zola, 1966).

In general, the British American response to pain occupies something of a middle ground between the Irish and the Jewish styles of responding. Zborowski (1969) suggests that whereas Jews strive to identify, discuss, and agonize over pain, the Irish tend to repress and deny it to an extent that they not only do not express pain but often they cannot accurately identify its location. British Americans, in contrast, tend to be aware of their pain and report it fully and accurately to the physician when they think something can be done about it. They want to aid the physician in his work. Elsewhere they do not discuss pain because they value bearing it themselves. Each person is viewed as responsible for his or her own pain (Sanua, 1960).

The isolation and silence of the British American is more than physical; it is emotional self-containment. The image of the silent cowboy or frontiersman who says nothing after returning from months on the trail because "there is nothing to say," while a caricature, nevertheless exemplifies the British American use of speech only to serve a function, not to "waste words." British American words are not for drama as with Italians, nor to elaborate reality like the Irish, nor to share and articulate feelings and thoughts about suffering like Jews. A British American does not share thoughts, feelings, and experiences "just to hear himself talk." Jive and Blarney—some would say nuance and humor—are rather foreign to British Americans.

On Kluckhohn's value-orientation scale of basic cultural choices, British Americans have a strong future orientation for individual achievement, seeing themselves as dominant in their relationship to the natural world (Papajohn & Spiegel, 1975). Thus, past tragedy or difficulty is avoided rather than denied. Their attention belongs elsewhere—on the future, on getting on with it.

What might be regarded as a difficulty with acceptance and lack of a tragic perspective can also be understood as an active British American preference for problem solving. British Americans want to focus on the aspect of the situation that they can do something about. Further, they believe that human nature is fundamentally neutral or mixed (both good and bad) and that it is changeable and perfectable by individual effort.

Above all things, British Americans value work, though sometimes the focus is more on the success that work can bring than on the rewards of work in and of itself. Hard work is equated with virtue. Success is both the path to and evidence of salvation. Thus British American identity, relationships, self-esteem, and sense of adequacy and well-being may all be heavily tied to work, to what they are doing. British Americans have a tendency to transform many aspects of life into work. The man "works" at making a living, and the woman "works" at raising the children and making a successful family. British Americans may talk of "working" on relationships, love, sex, fulfill-ment, and identity. They even take recreation, hobbies, collections, and sports very seriously, with standards of achievement and success in each.

It may be that British American attitudes toward work carry Freud's concept of sublimation to a cultural extreme. Since British Americans often have difficulty directly experiencing and expressing strong emotion, work, whether vocational or avocational, provides an outlet both for their intimacy and their aggression. It is often the main vehicle for both companionship and competition.

Regional Differences

Contemporary British American families vary considerably depending upon many factors: country of origin, migration experience prior to and within the United States, religious differences, urban/rural and regional differ-ences, and socioeconomic status (Adams, 1979; Hardon, 1969; Larsen, 1975; Marsden, 1980).[1] While we cannot address all of these differences here, we have outlined some of the more prominent regional differences and their treatment implications.

The descendants of postrevolutionary British American immigrants are more like other immigrant groups in that they retain some European cultural traits and memories of the immigration. British American descendants of colonial immigrants, on the other hand, are unlikely to have family immigra-tion memories or even to be aware of their origins, except in New England where formal genealogies have often been written. They think of themselves culturally as Americans, although when they look to Europe they clearly consider themselves more akin to the English.

Domestic migration has been crucial in the formation of British Ameri-can family culture and in the evolution of the major regional patterns. British American families today can be divided into two broad groups: (1)

---

1. Paul Adams, from Kentucky, was one of the first professionals to describe WASP culture in mental health treatment.

descendants of those who stayed put in New England and in the South, evolving old regional subcultures and strong family identification with a locality and (2) descendants of the predominantly Mid-Atlantic migrants who moved to the Midwest, and then perhaps on again, until, for some Western families, they became identified with the process of moving.

Southern British Americans

Southern British Americans have long had a very strong regional identification. They are likely to identify themselves culturally as Southern and White rather than as British Americans or Old Americans. Southern White culture has remained more homogeneous and enclosed and less influenced by the influx of European immigrants and internal migration than any other U.S. region in the last 150 years. Religious, military, and local history are alive and important for Southern British American families. History helps them know where they stand and what is important (Cash, 1941; Taylor, 1961; Tindall, 1976).

Attending church has been important for Southerners. The church of status often continues to reflect earliest settlement patterns. In Virginia, for example, Presbyterian Churches of 18th-century Scotch Irish settler origins remain dominant in the Shenandoah Valley while the Episcopal Church tends to be the leader further east.

Southerners take pride in their friendliness and sociability. They consider Northerners (particularly Bostonians) cold and snobbish. They are characteristically interested in local gossip and other people's foibles, but they keep their own problems to themselves, or at least within the family. The family is the core element of identity and is seen as extending meritoriously into the living past. Like other British Americans, Southerners value their individualism and self-control, but they experience and express themselves quite differently. For example, Southerners do not share the practice of intense surveillance of the self for internal righteousness and correct behavior that may still govern New England Congregational Puritans. Puritans behave the same whether alone, in the family, or in public, because they are always in the presence of God. Southern British Americans are usually more concerned about being caught in the public violation of social norms and the consequent loss of family status. They do not go in for the wholesale denial of the pleasures of life.

Appalachian British Americans

Appalachian British Americans are descendants of Scotch Irish and English who settled Southeastern Appalachia from 1717 to 1750. From this period on they have practiced rural subsistence farming on mountainous terrains and have generally remained poor and strongly fundamentalist in their Protestantism. Fiercely independent, they are regarded by outsiders as ornery and resistant to being helped with public services. Like other British Americans, they value individual initiative, but these poor mountain people, who may be recent urban migrants, have not found that initiative and hard work have improved their status (Looff, 1971).

Appalachian families have great mistrust of strangers, a fear of loss of independence and self-sufficiency, and wariness of outsiders' ridicule of their culture and belief systems. A great strength of Appalachian families is their tight, extensive kinship systems that remain continuing sources of loyalty and active, practical support.

Eastern British Americans

Eastern British Americans, like the English, tend to focus on control in their emotional life. They want to keep things to themselves, to remain rational, orderly, and self-contained. In continuity with their Puritan heritage of self-discipline, the individual is raised to feel, think, and behave correctly, that is, according to principle. Middle- and, particularly, upper-class (or Brahmin) Easterners are driven by expectations of high achievement, self-actualization, and obligatory public service. Like Southerners, they retain a pride in family and family-connected local history and are strongly motivated by the desire to live up to past family standards (Bartzell, 1979).

Cooking and eating styles of a group often say much about culture, and Eastern British Americans are no exception. Eastern British American families still tend to have a formal Sunday dinner, with required attendance, to show that family is valued. Roast beef will probably be served. The purpose of the meal is to eat correctly, together, and with a proper family conversation about individual members' efforts and successes during the week. It is not to eat, taste, discuss, or enjoy the food. Eastern British Americans are raised to be indifferent to food and to be in control of impulses and appetites and feelings of all kinds. Women and children may be expected to take very little food on their plates and, in certain circles, to demonstrate control and restraint by leaving food. Meals are daily ritual reminders that appetites are to be ignored or met only for functional purposes, never impulsively or without restraint.

Yankees prefer to understate their large class differences, and different classes may indeed share common values. Poor Northern, New England Yankee farmers are proud, rugged, noncomplaining, self-reliant individuals, just as are their rich Brahmin cousins. However, beneath that rugged individual style, the poor Yankees face the reality of uncertainty, inability to control their lives, and the present-time orientation that are common to poor people everywhere.

Midwestern British Americans

Midwestern British American families began with the same kind of people who migrated all the way to the Far West. Those who stayed in the Midwest developed a close-knit, agrarian, small town, rural culture based on the reliable fertility of the land. Midwest families raise their children to stay with the land and to make their opportunities there, not to move on. Church may still be a cornerstone, not only for religious worship but for most community activities and social life. The Midwestern Protestant Churches (especially Methodist, Church of Christ, and Presbyterian denominations) provide a moral vision of how to live that is echoed and reinforced by the family. If one works hard, is clean and orderly, and organized internally and externally, then life, and its problems, should be well in hand. Midwestern British Americans will make life plans and expect, in a linear fashion, to carry them through. Each step in life has its own fitting time and place. Being productive and doing their duty is tied to a feeling of moral legitimacy, to being responsible in the eyes of God, and to ultimate salvation.

Jean Stamp (1981), a Midwestern family therapist, has suggested that Midwestern British Americans may have qualities of individualism and conformity that are both confusing and problematic for family therapy. Midwesterners experience emotional isolation as something to strive for, interpreting it as independence and a key to success (Lewis, 1920). Seeking help is difficult. While emotional isolation is valued by British Americans of all regions in varying degrees, it is pernicious in the Midwest because it is paired with a general intolerance of deviance. Troubles, especially emotional troubles, are a product of, and certainly may produce, deviance from enactment of the life plan.

Western British Americans

Although the great West could be further divided by sectional subculture, Western families do have some common characteristics.

British American independent individualism evolved to an extreme in the West, where great distance, mobility, and historical aversion to authority has created a form of family that might be viewed by cultural outsiders as embodying pathological denial of family ties. While all British Americans promote individual success, Western British Americans define success with a major emphasis on independence. Independence means moving away from parents and *not* following in the father's footsteps. Multigeneration family businesses are less frequent in the West than in other regions. Western British American families tend to feel they have failed if their children are too much like themselves, if they maintain too much contact, if they live nearby, or if they stay at home. The British American idea that humans could dominate nature came closer to being true on the West Coast than anywhere else in the United States. The Westerners harvested forests of enormous trees, dammed great rivers to make deserts bloom, and mined the ores of the West's great mountains and canyons. In such an environment the role of the family is to raise a child empowered to dominate this world. This is an essentially secular point of view, although God is invoked as the protector and legitimizer of the person who helps himself or herself.

The Western British American's preferred solution to problems is to move on. This is reflected in their handling of adolescence. Typically, they do not go through agonizing separation struggles. A son may be expected to earn his own money, decide on his own career, and drive the family (or his own) car at 14 or 15, even if the law does not yet permit it.

A Jewish family therapist treating Western British Americans may have difficulty learning that for the Western British American, life is not with people. Life may be with ideas, or motorcycles, or stamps, or work, or, in certain families, with the self. They may have particular difficulty sharing experiences with their own families, out of fear of being inadequately self-sufficient. (Indeed, they may find talking to strangers easier.) Parents will feel bad about a child's problems because they are experienced as reflecting a failure to make the child adequately self-sufficient. The parents' first thought will be that they may have indulged the child too much. Adults are likely to compare themselves unfavorably with the mythical exploits of their pioneer ancestors—models of self-sufficiency—unless, of course, they, too, can chop wood until they are 93 years old like the archetypical great-grandfather did.

Family Structure and Life Cycle

Through the stages of the life cycle British American families enact their values within their culturally specific family structures and roles.

Cultures vary in relative emphasis placed on the pursuit of individual versus group or family goals. British Americans heavily favor individual goals. The family is experienced and valued as it sustains the individual, not the other way around. This often results in considerable isolation of family members.

> A successful corporate executive in his 50s, of Scotch Irish ancestry, had been in therapy for two years. His work had been something of an escape. He had little experience with intimacy, and he was quite split off from his own feelings. Part of the therapy consisted of reconnecting him with those feelings. As the therapy progressed he began to express a wish for more of a relationship with his three brothers and sisters, all of whom lived nearby. As the patient put it, "We only get together for Christmas when Mother calls. We enjoy each other, but we all just seem to disappear, except at Christmas."

It was largely the British American family that created the 20th-century American ideal of nuclear family consisting of a breadwinning father and child-rearing mother. The British American ideal had its roots in the nuclear family structure of preindustrial Britain and was modified by the process of adaptation to U.S. conditions. Some contemporary British American families do comfortably fit their nuclear family ideal, perhaps most vividly portrayed by Norman Rockwell's *Saturday Evening Post* paintings of the small town. But since fewer than 10% of U.S. families now fit this "ideal" pattern, the homage paid to this norm of family life may in part be a reaction to the stress of British American cultural loss and vulnerability in the face of new conditions.

British Americans often are guided by their current ideas of what is right or correct. A major concern for many British American families is their uncertainty about how they want their families to be. If a family fails to fit their image of the "right" kind of family, they may experience feelings of failure. Their loss of confidence in their nuclear family ideal, or at least the lack of fit of that ideal with their actual family structures, is part of the context of troubled families seeking treatment.

British American families are especially vulnerable to major external catastrophes such as accidents, serious illness, or economic depression. They have little cultural room for adaptive fatalism, that is, for the acceptance and submission to larger forces and the unknown. They have to control all aspects of life and do not know how to cope with the uncontrollable in themselves, society, or nature.

> The novel *Ordinary People* (Guest, 1977), which documents a family's response to their son's accidental drowning, exemplifies the British American difficulty in dealing with tragedy. Mother, father, and surviving son are all paralyzed by the tragedy. They each overindividualize their response and responsibility, try to be "good" by denying and carrying on, and resent the "mess" of their individual neediness and vulnerability (symbolized by the blood from the surviving son's slashed wrists that spills all over mother's immaculate bathroom).

However, because British American children are not perfect and because they live in an imperfect world, failure and inadequacy of one kind or another is bound to occur. When trying again is not an adequate remedy, the British American family may respond quite harshly with considerable scapegoating and denial, and those who do not measure up may well be cast aside. The inadequate members of families may act out their black sheep status by leaving—running away. They may become marginal, isolated, and eccentric. Even more damaging to WASP family functioning is refusing to leave home, staying and taking the sick, stupid, or crazy role to punish the whole family more aggressively (Adams, 1979).

Marriage and Sex Roles

While subject to the recent changes and stresses experienced throughout our society, traditional British American sex roles were divided much like those of other groups and in the past worked reasonably well in validating both men and women. The hard work of frontier life, for example, joined husband and wife yet provided ample opportunity for individual achievement.

These traditional sex roles are less fulfilling in 20th-century life for both men and women. The British American nuclear family ideal forces British American women into relatively isolated dependency and consequently lower status since it denies them the opportunities for success that their culture so values. Further, asking isolated, dependent women to raise independent children is a cultural contradiction. The "depression" and "inadequacy" of British American women, which has constituted the most common psychiatric patient profile from the 1950s to the present, is in part a product of this devalued, contradictory position. A therapist may help British American women make sense of their anger and modify their cultural tendency to take responsibility and blame for all troubles by ascribing them to their inadequacy as individuals.

This family pattern ultimately proves no more satisfactory for British American men. While the nuclear family supports the man's investment in work, he is reinforced as a workaholic and trained to feel inadequate and irrelevant in child rearing and in maintaining social relationships with his wife, family, and larger social networks.

British Americans tend to experience marriage as a contractual relationship for the negotiation and meeting of individual needs. Sex, money, and even the delivery of happiness are seen as contractual obligations. If a spouse fails to perform adequately sexually, to earn enough money, or to provide enough security, he or she has not kept the bargain. Divorce is then seen as relatively acceptable for British Americans, except perhaps when religion forbids it. British Americans tend to experience divorce as a painful personal failure but not, usually, an indication of badness.

Family communication is often only about business, without direct discussion of emotions (cf. Jewish, Chap. 17, and Italian, Chap. 16, family businesses). Private property and money are often the ties that bind, the source of British American family fights, and the means by which British American families control the behavior of their members, especially that of adult children. The threat of being cut out of the family business or the will gives great power. British Americans also retain the British love of law and litigation as the means of negotiating and regulating relationships. Marital or family disputes may be suppressed or denied through all the early stages and only addressed directly by taking the other family member to court.

Child Rearing

British Americans raise their children to be self-contained, principled, responsible, independent, self-reliant, self-determining, and, perhaps, from the vantage point of other cultures, self-centered individuals (Greven, 1977; Penfield, 1967). The more children begin to demonstrate that they can take care of themselves, the more successful British American parents will feel. British American parents do not depend on communal, oral child-rearing lore as much as do parents from other cultures. British Americans believe in science and in the efficacy of scientific discoveries and methods to solve life's problems. They approach child rearing as a technical business—they want to do it right. Consequently, they try to be modern and respect and avidly follow Dr. Spock or Dr. Brazelton or whoever is deemed the acceptable expert of their era. It may be that British American obstetricians and mothers are responsible for the emphasis on medical technology in childbirth that have made it such an isolated and alienating experience during the last 50 years. British American patients may not be good at expressing feelings of caring and tenderness or at any emotional communication. Criticizing performance may dominate the parent–child relationship.

> An adult male, who came into therapy with problems at work, reported that his relationship with his father had consisted primarily in joining in doing tasks around the house. The father's role was to show his son how to do things right so that the son could take care of himself some day. The patient recalled often feeling ashamed and inadequate because although he had persevered, he could never do things "quite right," and the father would often complete the task himself.

The father's self-absorbed task orientation made the child feel that the work replaced the relationship. In addition it required an attention span and sense of detail beyond a child's reach. British American training for individual adequacy turned out to be training in feelings of inadequacy.

Extended Family

A British American marriage is generally experienced as the marriage of two individuals, not of two families, although, as in all cultures, there is tension between individual choice and family preference.

British Americans' relations with their extended families, communities, and other potential support systems vary considerably by region. Western families tend to have the least contact with extended family. For example, adult siblings frequently have little contact, not even meeting, calling, or writing, except for the yearly Christmas cards. While they often cite physical distance as the reason for this lack of contact, more likely they simply feel they have little in common and therefore have no reason to get in touch. This kind of British American family may consider first cousins distant relatives, if they know them at all.

Western and Midwestern British Americans may feel much closer to members of their local communities with whom they may have frequent, though superficial, contact. Their church activities are a particularly important source of community interaction and may be more valued for this than for religious experience per se.

In the South, Appalachia, and Northeast, extended families are much more likely to live nearby and to play an active role in family life. However, British Americans, in general, do not view their friends, extended families, or church and activity club contacts as a potential support network available to help with problems. Their feeling is that sharing trouble is not really a part of the interpersonal contract and might burden or strain the relationship.

Childhood

British American children often complain that their parents relate to them in a detached manner. They rarely report hovering, worried paternal involvement and, except in some evangelical families, their behavior is not subject to strict authoritarian control. Boys and girls may be treated differently but usually not as distinctly or rigidly as in other ethnic groups. Children are expected to be clean and neat. Developmental stages are typically passed without much notice or ceremony. Going off to school, reaching puberty and menstruating, leaving home, getting married—all of these milestones are greeted with understated attention compared to other cultures, which agonize or celebrate, repress or fight, but do something to acknowledge them. This absence of intensity or even memory of major family developmental stages may be puzzling to the non-British American therapist.

British American parental inexpressiveness or exaggerated self-control may be a problem, especially when joined with uncertainty or inconsistency as in the following case:

> A British American corporate executive sought treatment for depression, apparently precipitated by the sexual activity of his young adolescent daughter. The children did not know what was acceptable sexual behavior. The parents were angry but felt they should not be and did not want to be. As a result they were inconsistent in discipline and unable to respond when things were seriously wrong with the children. The parents had maintained a cool, underinvolved style that deprived the children of the parenting they needed. The course of therapy involved identifying and expressing the family's buried feelings.

British American children typically negotiate school rather well. This is true especially through the latency period, as the tasks of school and of latency are quite syntonic with British American values. The child is encouraged to go off to school by himself or herself, to take initiative, and to achieve. The repeated saying—"If at first you don't succeed, try, try again"— reinforces British American children's perserverance. British American children thus tend to develop a strong sense of their individual capacity and to gain self-esteem from individual achievement.

Going off with peers is also easily accepted by the family. Clubs, sports, hobbies, and church groups help socialize British American children in the twin social modes of competition and conformity. They learn to "play by the rules of the game." The model of peer or chumship relations established in latency remains for many British American men and women a model of peer social relationships in adult life, where they often form elaborate but rather shallow peer relationships based on activity groups.

British American children sometimes have trouble when they are unable to meet their parents' expectations for achievement and performance. British American parents may also need help if for some reason the child is unable to control his or her expression of dependency needs and, therefore, to become relatively self-sufficient emotionally. Extra neediness can come from a child's physical or intellectual limitations or from anxiety about parental conflict. This "bad" neediness can set off feelings of low self-esteem and inadequacy that further heighten dependency. British American families, in short, are fine when things go well. They cope easily with success, not with troubles or failure. This contrasts markedly with many other groups who teach their children to expect problems—whether because of their own "badness" (Irish), anticipation of hostility or racism (Jews and American Blacks), threats from outsiders (Italians), or past experience with a dangerous physical world (Azorean Portuguese).

Adolescence

British American families often have a hard time negotiating the transition from childhood to adulthood. British American culture promotes the early separation of adolescents and the development of individual, self-defined, adult identity and autonomy. British American families do not struggle to keep the children at home or closely involved in family life as do, for example, many Jewish or Italian families for whom adolescence may be a period of open family conflict. The British American difficulty, in today's world, is that adolescents are not always ready to move on when they or their families want them to. It is not so easy today to follow the frontier model, going off on one's own, to one's own work and own new family, whenever one feels it is time.

In 1850, a 20-year-old could be adequately skilled and financially independent with farm, house, and wife established and children on the way. In the 1980s, extended apprenticeship of one form or another in our complex vocational and financial world make buying a house and feeling established in job or career difficult even by age 30.

If a family (father) tries to promote independence by withdrawing physical, financial, or emotional support too soon or too completely, the British American adolescent may feel abandoned. The result may be a kind of false adulthood with premature identity foreclosure. They try on adult careers and relationships as though they were solid choices when, in fact, they are rather desperate efforts to replace the family. British American families carry self-determination to an extreme. They are good at promoting separation but are a little lost when it comes to providing guidance and support.

Elderly, Death, and Dying

British American families tend to undervalue the strengths of the elderly—their wisdom, experience, and companionship. The fear of aging with eventual sickness, incapacity, and dependence may become matters of almost obsessive concern to British Americans of all ages. The youth and future orientation of the British American culture make the elderly particularly vulnerable to loss of self-esteem and depression. At best, an older person in reasonable health is able to sustain feelings of adequacy by continuing self-sufficient, independent living and not becoming a "burden to the family."

When British Americans face extended disability or terminal illness, a stressful situation for any family, their self-contained individualism can be particularly maladaptive. Family members tend, "responsibly," to keep their painful feelings to themselves and to have difficulty negotiating the stages of loss and grief or arranging for extra resources when their own are stretched thin.

Therapy

British Americans are most likely to identify as problems those situations that disrupt autonomous functioning. Feeling inadequate is a core British American symptom. In general they overidentify the seriousness of problems with emotionalism, enmeshment, dependency, depression, and direct expressions of anxiety and overlook emotional isolation and withdrawal. Thus, lack of contact, separation, incapacity to communicate, and schizoid characteristics are less likely to be considered problematic, as are British Americans vulnerabilities to emotional blandness, anomie, and a flat, inadequate sense of self.

British Americans tend also to have difficulties with affiliation and attachment. Distance is the preferred stand for the disturbed British American.

Getting started in treatment is hard for British Americans. They will usually come for help only when the problem is serious and after their efforts to solve it themselves have failed or denial of its importance is impossible. Failing to solve one's own problem evokes the core British American cultural dynamic of guilt for inadequate meeting of one's individual responsibilities. The resulting British American presentation consists of (1) the initial problem, (2) guilt for failing to resolve it oneself, and (3) low expectations of support from others. Asking for help means a loss of self-sufficiency, lower self-esteem, and heightened feelings of inadequacy. Fundamentally, getting professional help is embarrassing. The sense of dependency is uncomfortable, and interviews are likely to be particularly embarrassing because of the public exposure. Therapists should see this initial awkwardness as difficulty in seeking help—not as a reflection of a severe presenting problem. In fact, successful treatment may not reduce British American discomfort with therapy, and positive reinforcement may be experienced as an embarrassment as in the case below:

> A Jewish therapist was bewildered by a British American couple's response to their progress in couples therapy. The therapy had involved increasing each of the partner's awareness of the emotional issues that they had brought to the marriage. At first, the wife did most of the work, but then the husband really caught on. At one point the therapist tried to acknowledge the success of the husband, saying, in effect, "Good for you." Rather than showing pleasure or being able to take credit, the middle-class New England Yankee seemed to wince at the congratulations. The puzzled therapist concluded that the patient's uncomfortable response seemed closest to shame. It appeared to be an embarrassment that he might be praised for doing what was his responsibility. Only a child is praised for meeting responsibilities. The therapist expected the patient to feel good about the psychotherapy, but British Americans do not particularly enjoy therapy, even successful therapy.

The therapist should take these feelings into account, should support rather than confront in the early stages, and should build trust so that this British American sense of vulnerability will not be increased by therapy. British American anxiety about the treatment should also not be the cause of alarm or oversensitivity on the part of the therapist. A calm, easy, straightforward approach is probably all that is needed.

Therapists may have difficulty getting British American families to talk comfortably, but when they do, they are likely to get right to the truth of the matter, at least as they know it. British Americans value insight and reason and are not averse to meaningful discussion. The key here is "meaningful." They tend to be literal, parsimonious, and careful with words, treating them seriously, like contracts ("my word is my bond"). This tendency may be underestimated by Italian, Irish, or Jewish therapists whose traditions all use and evaluate words somewhat differently.

An alliance with the British American family will be facilitated by their need to act "responsibly" and to "face up" to difficulties once they know that they must. British Americans may seek a therapist's assistance in making sense of their pain. They will want to define it as a clear problem that can be worked on. Once this is done, the family can proceed with confidence, believing that hard work in therapy will be sufficient for success, as it is believed to be in other aspects of life.

> A non-British American therapist remarked on a British American family's capacity for sheer hard work once a "contract" for therapy was made. The Smith family, who had been in treatment for a year and a half, illustrate the British American values that the truth is good to hear (no matter how painful), and when you have an issue, you work on it. The focus of the therapy had shifted from (1) sibling conflict, to (2) the marriage, to (3) the mother's lack of individuation. The shifts had taken place without a break, the family remaining serious and task oriented. Composition of the therapy sessions varied considerably. At various stages different members came—the whole family, the couple, the siblings, a parent and child, the mother alone, and so on, depending upon the focus. Each member followed the evolution of the therapeutic contract, saw the problem, and agreed to work on it. In addition to their hard work and perseverance, the therapist noted that the family always felt the therapeutic burden was theirs. They did not struggle with or challenge the therapist or induce him to feel guilty or inadequate. The therapists' role was to help them figure things out; the rest the family perceived as their responsibility.

British Americans come to therapy for help because, despite the discomfort, they are pragmatic and essentially ready to "take the medicine." British Americans will be most comfortable making the therapeutic relationship a contractual one, viewing the therapist as the family's technical consultant. Relationships are expected to be fair, reasonable, technical, and mercantile. British American families will expect to pay a fair fee, clearly negotiated, promptly and without hassle, and they will also expect to get their money's worth in terms of successful treatment.

The therapist should show respect for British American individualism by making contracts with each member of the family, including the children. Often, the therapist will be wise to use an objective method—that is, reason, discussion, education, task assignment, training—as an initial access to the more subjective matters. When approached in a culturally syntonic and nonthreatening manner, British Americans may prove more able to express core emotional issues and to use psychological insights than one might expect at first contact. Effective intervention will usually involve some modification of the emotional isolation that is the British American vulnerability.

Although beginning treatment is uncomfortable for British Americans, they may terminate quite easily. This reverses the natural emotional order of things as expected, for example, by a Jewish family therapist. Since British Americans tend to be understated, they may be making significant progress or be deeply affected without ever telling the therapist. Some British Americans, especially Scots, have an even harder time talking about positive changes in themselves than they do in talking about problems. They may, like some Irish, leave therapy quite satisfied, without a word of acknowledgment or validation, only to tell an astonished therapist some years later how the therapy turned their lives around. British Americans will tend to view the end of therapy as they would the end of other pieces of technical business: when the job is done, the contract ends, one leaves, period. Thus, abrupt departures should not necessarily be attributed to resistance, failure to complete work, or separation anxiety. It is simply in keeping with British American style and approach.

British American Adult and Couples Treatment

British American adults and couples often come to treatment with a controlled style that may make the source and nature of their pain and conflict inaccessible to the therapist. British American aggression is often sublimated into competition at work or recreation rather than acted out in family violence. Alcohol is also heavily used to anesthetize aggressive or other painful feelings. Martinis for lunch and cocktails before dinner on a daily basis are more typical of middle- and upper-class British American drinking patterns than episodic or binge drinking.

British American sexual problems often stem from excessive control, avoidance, and distance in intimate relationships. British Americans suffer more from lack of intensity in their sexual and emotional expression than from repressive inhibition or violent acting out (Albee, 1977).

Worry about adequacy is often a prime component in British American sexual problems. High standards of "production" combined with high expectation of "control" may cause performance anxiety and failure. British American couples often respond to conflict by distancing and avoidance rather than by active confrontation.

A British American couple at the point of separation came to treatment. They were ambitious and perfectionistic, and they tried always to be cheerful and tolerant. It was apparent to the therapist that they had drifted apart and needed help in ending their marriage so that neither would feel irresponsible. They had no norms for conflict expression or resolution and, indeed, had never had any fights, even small fights, along the way. The therapist observed that their cheerfulness, denial, and sense of righteousness had allowed them to carry problems, without directly addressing them, until they were so far apart emotionally that there was nothing left with which to work.

The therapist can teach British Americans an antidote to this cultural pattern that so destructively prevents conflict resolution. They should, on purpose, have small, immediate, frequent, and personal fights instead of letting it all build up.

The most important factor in marital conflict may not be readily apparent. For example, money may well be the dominant factor in family relationships and family conflict without ever being brought up.

As mentioned earlier, both British American men and women are experiencing the stresses of maladaptive cultural roles, evolved earlier in the 20th century, and are searching for more adaptive ones. Very generally, treatment should work to reduce the isolation of British American men, increase the opportunities for independent achievement of British American women, and reintegrate both women and men into the worlds of work, home, and family.

British American couples may not view their families of origin as resources in either childbirth or child rearing. They may not share these experiences with their families. This cultural style leads to isolation—isolation from support, sharing, and the guidance of a cultural tradition. Any change or intervention working toward reducing British American family isolation is likely to be helpful. When a British American couple is able to seek help, contracting techniques, task assignments, and negotiated, even signed, agreements, all make cultural sense. Therapists should not be put off by or over interpret the cool, reasonable, and correct tone of many British American couples in marital conflict. They are trying to maintain self-esteem by doing it right. They may feel humiliated at losing their cool in a fight.

With the elderly, the therapist can help remedy British American family paralysis in the face of what is seen as an individual breakdown. The therapist can actively direct the finding of new resources—sister and brother can be called, a visiting nurse can be arranged. Likewise, education about the stages of grief and loss and their accompanying anger, sadness, dependency, and vulnerability may give British American families permission to acknowledge what they are feeling and to go through the emotional crisis more adaptively.

Family Treatment with British American Children

The response of British American families to a symptomatic child may initially be puzzling to the family therapist. The troubled child is often burdened by his or her isolation within the family. Rather than be over anxious, parents and siblings may feel at a loss as to how they might help the troubled child with what they will see as his or her individual problem.

Adolescent difficulties, in particular, are perceived as the child's own business, not the family's. British American families should be encouraged to stay involved, to provide support, even to retain more responsibility and control. In other words, a little more family struggle may well be good for British American adolescents who would otherwise be left alone to struggle with and for themselves. The antidote is to help place the child emotionally back in the family, to help the child validate and express his or her pain so as to share the load with the rest of the family.

Since middle-class British Americans tend to be self-conscious in their wishes to be effective parents and are good at taking courses and following instructions, preventive interventions, such as Parent Effectiveness Training, are particularly attractive.

Therapeutic Implications of British American Regional Differences

Frank Pittman, a Southern British American family therapist, suggests that a typical Southern family's motivation for seeking help is the experience that something is out of control, that the family needs help doing the right thing (Pittman, 1981). Southern British Americans come for help in order not to change. Pittman also suggests that Southern British American family therapy is a careful, very delicate social transaction. (They may well be concerned about the social standing of the therapist.) The family needs to feel that they are in control, that they can proceed at a moderate pace, and that they are able to solve a problem. Coming to therapy does not mean all family business will be discussed. Indeed, trust is likely to be extended only when the therapist agrees, at least implicitly, that the rules of avoiding certain topics (the family secrets) will continue to be honored. Therapists working with Southern British American families are expected to understand that "their peculiarities are different from their problems" (Pittman, 1981). They do not come to therapy, as do some Northerners, to become better people.

Appalachian families are usually seen by family therapists only after preferred modes of problem solving within the extended family have broken down, perhaps because of isolation within a urban setting in the North. The family therapist may do well to ally with this extended family network, to consider using some form of restorative network family therapy, and to encourage regular visiting back home.

Treatment of Eastern British Americans (especially Brahmins) may usefully include trying to moderate the impact of family history, sometimes by getting the family more directly involved in exploring that history—à la Bowen—in order to sort out the myths from the realities and to try to reclaim realistic expectations. Usually the family needs to have permission to "feed" one another a bit better.

For the Midwest British American, troubles mean failure on two counts —failure to carry on and failure to keep it to oneself. Therapy must proceed in a manner that fits these values. Therapy should be described as reasonably and responsibly "working" on one's problems, dealing with pain, and managing one's life with the goals being restoration of adequate emotional self-sufficiency and a return to the life plan. Of course, to accomplish this, the therapist may well want to help modify extreme emotional isolation and rigid conformity to life plans that are unreasonable.

The Western British Americans, as extreme individualists, are a problem for the family therapist because they believe that life is individually lived, that only individuals have problems, and that certainly only individuals are responsible for them. These beliefs conflict with the central theoretical and therapeutic bias of family therapy, which holds that problems are developed, shared, and best resolved within a family social context. The basis of family therapy and its relevance to the patient must be plausibly explained to the Western British American family. The therapist must be wary of their extreme self-reliance and encourage them to try solutions to their problems, other than moving on to the next town, wife, job, identity, and so on. Training in communication skills and in simple direct group problem solving and conflict resolution may bring quick results.

Theory

Some family therapy theories and techniques fit British American families quite well, others less so. For example, Murray Bowen's systems therapy (Bowen grew up in Tennessee) fits well the values and style of the Southern British American family (Bowen, 1978). Rather than meeting conjointly, Bowen, through individual coaching, promotes the establishment of emotionally mature relationships between individuals within the family. Tracing historical, multigenerational family emotional patterns, as well as those of the present, further helps to differentiate the individual. The individuated person can then confront the emotionally tempestuous family secrets and arbitrary social rules calmly and with a well-defined sense of self. The Bowen model maintains the Southern value that family is the foundation for individual adequacy.

Bowenian family therapy also fits general British American values quite well, especially those of self-determination and emphasis on thinking over feeling. Bowen's advocacy of the establishment of a person-to-person relationship with each member of the family is well designed to counteract the core British American vulnerability—individual isolation and lack of mutuality within the family.

Psychodynamic family therapy is also relatively compatible with British American values. British Americans want to face the truth and gain insight into inner truths. They believe in science and readily accept the mechanistic (hydraulic) psychodynamic model. Evangelical British Americans, like psychodynamically oriented family therapists, are keenly aware of the power and need to defend against unacceptable impulses.

The language, style, and "cure" of structural family therapy fits British

American families rather less well. The structural school's concerns with boundaries, alliances, and barriers are less vital for British Americans than are isolation, lack of mutuality, and communication. While structural theory does recognize isolation as a problem and is goal oriented, it does not articulate solutions in the reasonable, truth-seeking, self-determined manner preferred by the British Americans. As such structural therapy may under-utilize British American family strengths and may not feel like a compatible cure to the degree that Bowenian therapy does.

The problem-focused, goal-oriented therapy of Haley, with his technical explanatory certainty in a brief, impersonal contract, fits with British values. Haley is wary of extended relationships as inherently power abusive rather than curative. He focuses instead on helping the individual establish comfortable separation from others.

The approach of strategic family therapy is one that can contradict British American family values and style and cures (Hoffman, 1981). British Americans expect and trust direct, honest, and aboveboard negotiation. Asking British Americans to maintain secrets and make coached strategic "moves" in alliance with the therapist may seem sneaky and dishonest and may serve to heighten British American emotional isolation by modeling the opposite of direct person-to-person communication of emotional experience for mutual validation that most British Americans need to learn. To ask British Americans to continue what they are already doing conflicts with their desire to work on their problems. However, British Americans share the Strategic school's implicitly egalitarian ideas about balancing and equality. Also, they do appreciate being told that they are doing their best, which they are, and love to hear that they are right.

Of all the family theorists, Virginia Satir's emphasis on "filling the pot," speaks most effectively and directly to core British American self-esteem issues (Satir, 1967, 1972). Satir prescribes hugs (physical and verbal), which help break through British American emotional isolation and self-containment and provide an experience of being filled, in contact and in touch. British Americans do not easily hug or touch to make contact and show affection—today more out of habit than because of repressive Puritan restraint. Thus, Satir's modeling of "stroking" is a form of desensitization, demonstrating that strokes are not painful and may even begin to feel good.

Rogerians may be rare among family therapists, but the focus of Carl Rogers (1951) on empathy addresses quite appropriately the core British American longing for validation. Therapists of non-British American background may underestimate the power of Rogerian empathic listening to bring relief to emotionally isolated British Americans. Satir and Rogers are both from the Midwest, and their work, not surprisingly, is most compatible with Midwestern British American families.

British American positivism, emphasizing the role of will and mastery over nature, is compatible with transactional analysis, behavior modification, and the various self-help, self-instruction, and self-training modes of therapy. Therapies that emphasize the teaching and practice of interpersonal communications skills are, as suggested above, also often of great and immediate benefit to British American families.

British American Families and Non-British American Therapists

Non-British American family therapists may be wary of the ways that British Americans relate to other groups in general and may wonder about potential barriers to relationship with themselves in particular. Therapists may be much more aware of these differences than are the families. As a general rule, British Americans will want to see others as individuals and to think of characteristics and differences as those of individuals and not of groups. This is especially so in personal relationships, as with a therapist. In therapy, British American families may well relate comfortably to therapists of whatever background—by seeing them as individuals. The intolerance and racism of British Americans, when it occurs, may be increased by the envy and heightened defensiveness of the British American, who as an individual standing alone does not feel the support of a clearly identified in-group, as might the Chinese or Jews.

British Americans are not likely to be able to step outside of themselves culturally to provide explanations and will tend to view any problem in understanding between themselves and the therapist as a problem of communication. A practical consequence is that it will be up to the therapist to initiate cultural explaining—describing differences in kinds of experiences and responses and asking the British American family to do the same for themselves.

Other therapist characteristics, such as gender, age, profession, and theoretical orientation, are likewise usually not an issue for families so long as the therapist is seen as an expert who can provide help with their problems.

Summary

British Americans will do well with treatment that recognizes both the costs and benefits of self-contained individualism. The goal of family therapy should be to reduce British American isolation and reclaim important emotional experiences.

REFERENCES

Adams, P.I. The WASP Child. In Noshpitz (Ed.), *Handbook of Child Psychiatry* (Vol. I). New York: Basic Books, 1979.

Albee, G.W. The Protestant Ethic, Sex and Psychotherapy. *American Psychologist, 32*(2), 150–161, 1977.

Anderson, C.H. *White Protestant Americans.* Englewood Cliffs, N.J.: Prentice-Hall, 1970.

Bartzell, E.D. *Puritan Boston and Quaker Philadelphia.* New York: Free Press, 1979.

Bowen, M. *Family Therapy in Clinical Practice*. New York: Jason Aronson, 1978.

Cash, W.J. *The Mind of the South*. New York: Vintage Books, 1941.

Erickson, C. *Invisible Immigrants: The Adaptation of English and Scottish Immigrants in Nineteenth Century America*. London: Leicester University Press, 1972.

Erickson, C. English. In S. Thernstrom (Ed.), *Harvard Encyclopedia of American Ethnic Groups*. Cambridge: Harvard University Press, 1980.

Gorer, G. *The American People: A Study in National Character*. New York: Norton, 1964.

Greven, P. *The Protestant Temperament: Patterns of Child-Rearing, Religious Experience, and the Self in Early America*. New York: Vintage Books, 1977.

Guest, J. *Ordinary People*. New York: Ballantine, 1977.

Hardon, J.A. *The Protestant Churches of America*. New York: Doubleday, 1969.

Hoffman, L. *Foundations of Family Therapy: A Conceptual Framework for Systems Change*. New York: Basic Books, 1981.

Larsen, J.A. *Dysfunction in the Evangelical Family: Treatment Considerations*. Paper presented at a meeting of American Association of Marriage and Family Counselors, Philadelphia, October 1975.

Lewis, S. *Main Street*. New York: Harcourt Brace Jovanovich, 1920.

Leyburn, J.G. *The Scotch-Irish: A Social History*. Chapel Hill: University of North Carolina Press, 1962.

Looff, D.H. *Appalachia's Children: The Challenge of Mental Health*. Lexington: Kentucky University Press, 1971.

Marsden, G.M. *Fundamentalism and American Culture: The Shaping of Twentieth-Century Evangelicalism: 1870-1925*. London: Oxford University Press, 1980.

Mead, M. *And Keep Your Powder Dry: An Anthropologist Looks at America*. New York: William Morrow, 1971.

Novak, M. The World of the WASP. *Christian Century, 90*, 334-335, 1973.

Papajohn, J., & Spiegel, J. *Transactions in Families*. New York: Jossey-Bass, 1975.

Pearce, J.K., & Friedman, L. (Eds.). *Family Therapy: Combining Psychodynamic and Family Systems Approaches*. New York: Grune & Stratton, 1980.

Penfield, W. *The Difficult Art of Giving: The Epic of Alan Gregg*. New York: Little, Brown, 1967.

Pittman, F. Personal communication, January 1981.

Rogers, C. *Client-Centered Therapy*. New York: Houghton Mifflin, 1951.

Sanua, V. Sociocultural Factors in Responses to Stressful Life Situations: The Behavior of Aged Amputees as an Example. *Journal of Health and Human Behavior, 1*, 17-24, 1960.

Satir, V. *Conjoint Family Therapy: A Guide to Theory and Technique*. Palo Alto: Science & Behavior Books, 1967.

Satir, V. *Peoplemaking*. Palo Alto: Science & Behavior Books, 1972.

Seward, R. *The American Family: A Demographic History*. Beverly Hills: Sage, 1978.

Simon, E. *The Anglo-Saxon Manner: The English Contribution to Civilization*. London: Cassell, 1972.

Stamp, J. Personal communication, 1981.

Taylor, W.R. *Cavalier and Yankee*. New York: Harper & Row, 1961.

Tindall, G. *The Ethnic Southerners*. Baton Rouge: Louisiana State University, 1976.

Zborowski, M. *People in Pain*. San Francisco: Jossey-Bass, 1969.

Zola, I. Culture and Symptoms: An Analysis of Patients' Presenting Complaints. *American Sociological Review, 31*, 615-630, 1966.

III
SPECIAL ISSUES

22

Intervention in a
Vietnamese Refugee Family

JAY LAPPIN
SAM SCOTT

> You touch a culture in one place and everything else is affected.
> —Edward Hall, *Beyond Culture*

Family therapy is a multilevel process. Add to this the dimensions of culture, and the process can become so muddled as to lose the forest for the trees. An outpatient therapist is continually faced with families that differ from his or her own cultural background. A lack of understanding about the family's culture can confuse treatment goals and complicate the therapeutic process. This dilemma is compounded by an important therapist tool, namely, language. When the family and the therapist speak different languages, communication difficulties are tenfold and the subtleties of metaphor are often lost to the demand for concrete understanding.

United States society owes its diverse texture to a wide range of cultures and values. Immigrants, past and present, have shared in the struggle of acculturating themselves to a new environment. The process of migration itself is stressful and results in adaptive stages that cross cultural boundaries (Sluzki, 1979). This process is a normal and understandable by-product of being uprooted from the familiar environment that people call "home." Neighbors, streets, sounds, customs, as well as the supportive structure of the extended family and cultural guidelines are erased. Through working with the Indochinese, the authors learned how much every family has its own style of living within its own culture.

In each culture and family, people will use the coping tools most familiar to them in order to carve out their new reality. In some instances, these cultural coping tools may have become artifacts that have lost their effectiveness in the new environment. This upheaval necessarily rattles the family's structural cage and tests the limits of its flexibility. Rules governing interaction and family roles are often challenged and are reformed to adapt to a new context.

Jay Lappin and Sam Scott. Faculty, Philadelphia Child Guidance Clinic, Philadelphia, Pennsylvania.

The Indochinese are now engaged in that struggle. As with many other immigrant groups, the Indochinese have found language to be a major obstacle in the acculturation process. The inability of parents to communicate effectively with landlords, store clerks, school officials, potential employers, and neighbors often leads to a temporary reversal of the family hierarchy. Because children typically learn the new language and customs more quickly, they often become the interpreters for their parents. This throws the patriarchy of the Indochinese family off balance.

This arrangement does not generally cause problems in and of itself. In a short time, the parents gain competency in their new skills, and the children are relieved of their "interpreter" function, free to return to the important business of being children. There are, however, many reasons why this rebalancing of hierarchy may not occur. For example, the unbalancing process of the B family began when Mrs. B left her native Vietnam with her retired G.I. husband in 1975. Mr. and Mrs. B came to the United States with their four children, three boys, ages 11, 10, and 6, and a girl, age 8.

Mrs. B depended heavily on her husband's help to negotiate her new world. Her proximity to her husband and children was further compounded by an Asian cultural value that views wives as being subsumed by their husband's family. Consequently, Mrs. B did not experience a great need for the Vietnamese community.

Shortly after arriving in the United States, Mrs. B's mother passed away in Vietnam. Five months later, her husband died of a heart attack. Because Mrs. B's husband's family was openly hostile to her after his death, Mrs. B stopped all contact with them. Her context became limited to her children. She had no employable skills, and by U.S. standards she was uneducated. She had no car or driver's license and had remained cut off from her own community network. Financial support for the family consisted of a pension and survivor's benefits from the Veterans Administration.

State-mandated social services became aware of the B family when Mrs. B's four children were accused of damaging a neighbor's car. The police were called in to settle the disagreement. Accusations and emotions flared. Mrs. B, who did not fully understand what was happening, began to hurl accusations of her own, in Vietnamese. The situation escalated as Mrs. B became increasingly excited. The police tried to calm her but were unsuccessful. At this point the police felt that Mrs. B needed a psychiatric examination and had her committed to the state mental hospital, where she remained for the next three days. In the interim, her children were placed in foster care.

Through the hospitalization and foster care placement, Mrs. B became connected with the Department of Public Welfare and, because of her children's behavior, with the school social worker. Arrangements were made by the Child Welfare worker to have a volunteer tutor Mrs. B in English. Child Welfare also discovered that Mrs. B was having management difficulties with all the children, not just the eldest child as was originally believed.

In some ways, the state-mandated services replaced the familial and cultural supports the B family was lacking. The interventions of the agencies were helpful and supportive. However, the children still had behavior problems, and the mother was still depressed. Out of concern for these continuing dysfunctional patterns, the family was referred to the Philadelphia Child Guidance Clinic. The therapist, Jay Lappin, and the supervisor, Sam Scott, had available to them the demographic data provided by the Clinic's Intake Department and the information cited above, which was shared by the Child Welfare worker.

Based on the intake information, the authors hypothesized that the dysfunctional cycle this family experienced contained elements that were similar to those in other single-parent families. The mother was overworked and undersupported. She was responsible for parenting 24 hours a day and at the same time was seeking comfort and support from her children. Isolated from outside contacts, her world had narrowed until it included only her children. The cycle of issues most important in this world were death, separation, and grief.

In formulating our treatment strategy, the authors chose goals that were related to single-parent issues. We also wanted to address the cultural aspects of the family's problem and the issues stemming from the family's losses. It was the authors' view that these issues could be contained, if we had clear, concrete, and focused short-term goals: (1) Relieve mother's overwork as a parent and support her parenting by making more effective use of existing resources, that is, the therapist, Child Welfare, volunteers, and school personnel; (2) reduce mother's dependency on the emotional comfort provided by the children; (3) help mother become less dependent on her children as interpreters and use the therapist as a model of direct adult-to-adult communication; (4) normalize mother's feelings of depression by listening.

The Child Welfare worker initially told us that Mrs. B's English was "bad," but she thought Mrs. B could be understood. Since we were not sure what "bad" meant, we decided to have an interpreter available for the first session, but our hope was that he would not be an active participant in treatment. By excluding the interpreter we would support Mrs. B's authority over her children and put her and the therapist in a position of mutual accommodation. Philadelphia Child Guidance Clinic routinely uses live supervision. In this case, the therapist, Jay Lappin, conducted all sessions and was observed from behind a one-way mirror by his supervisor, Sam Scott.

As the therapist, Lappin immediately felt the impact of the decision to exclude the interpreter. As he began to explain the video recording equipment, he soon realized that virtually every word would have to be repeated to ensure understanding. He also saw how readily all the children jumped in to decipher and "interpret" his words. A consequence of this decision was the riptide-like pull the system had on Lappin. The temptation to correct, speak for, and simply speed up the communication process was incredibly strong. It was a slow motion experience that pushed his threshold of patience to new levels. Yet maintaining the slow pace, waiting for understanding, and keeping the children out added an important new dimension to the family. In this struggle for mutual understanding, Mrs. B and her therapist were provided with an activity that became common ground for both of them and left them less self-conscious of their differences. Consequently, they remained firm in the decision to leave the interpreter out.

The following is a verbatim account of a part of the first session, which illustrates the children's activity and mother's inability to stick to one area and follow it through:

LAPPIN: You and I are trying to talk and she [Sally] helps. Is this okay? If they play like this?

MOTHER: No, I don't want them to play.

LAPPIN: (*Sits back.*) Okay, you tell them what you want them to do.

MOTHER: Hey!

JOHN: What?

MOTHER: You sit there.

JOHN: (*Whining.*) No, I wanna play, mom.

MOTHER: No, sit there. You sit there, Ben. (*Ben ignores mother.*) Robert, you sit there, him talk you. Ben after play! (*Ben continues to play.*) Him bad—him never look at me or nothing.

LAPPIN: He doesn't listen to you? This is Ben?

MOTHER: Yeah.

MOTHER: Back of my head hurt, make me sit all time. One do, one be, one beat, one fight, want watch TV, one TV.

LAPPIN: They pull every way, huh?

MOTHER: Yes, one Channel 17, one 29, one 33, I say one TV—what I do? Say I want to watch show, you turn, I say I don't, I never watch TV. My kids—one watch Channel 17, one 48, one Channel 10, one Channel 3, I say one TV, what I do?

In addition to describing her current difficulties with her children, in the following interaction Mrs. B managed to discuss her grief for her husband and mother and her feelings of isolation:

MOTHER: I no like to go out, I no like. I want to stay home and sit and be quiet. My husband, my mother died. My mother dies 4 . . . 5 months, my husband died. I no see my family.

LAPPIN: Must be very hard.

MOTHER: Yes, I cry all day long my husband die.
LAPPIN: Even now you cry?
MOTHER: Yes.
LAPPIN: You still cry?
MOTHER: Yes.
LAPPIN: How often do you cry?
MOTHER: I stay at home by myself all day with my kids. Sometimes, I want to die, I no want to stay. I see my mother die, my father die, my husband die, no my family here. I stay by myself.

It became apparent that the B family provided us with a broad number of issues including culture, communication, grief, depression, disorganization, and separation, all with tempting content in their own right. We felt that if we had tried to deal with more than one issue at a time, we would in effect replicate the B family's disorganized system. For example, to the degree we focused on grief or depression, we would not be able to focus on competence. This is not to say that we saw the two as mutually exclusive, it simply means we would have watered down our own efforts if we tried to address several issues at once.

The B family had evolved its own singular patterns of interacting from adapting to a context that was theirs alone. Appreciating all Mrs. B had experienced, enabled us to maintain a focus on strengths. Having been forced into a new culture, when she suffered the death of a parent she was unable to share this grief with her own people. Her husband died, severing the primary link between her present world and the one she left behind. With no workable skills and little English, Mrs. B had still managed to support herself and her four children. With this kind of success, we could not help but see the B family's "dysfunctional" patterns as adaptive and holding the potential for further change. Part of our task then was to extract elements of strength from the family's culture and to help them graft these strengths onto their new context, one that had changed dramatically since Vietnam. The problem was to find areas in which Mrs. B could demonstrate her competence to her children, thereby reaffirming her position at the top of the hierarchy. While many things Mrs. B had done represented strengths, it was not enough just to discuss them.

Ironically, the key to Mrs. B's competency proved to be the language, which had also been so much of her problem. We decided to put her in the role of teaching both her children and the therapist Vietnamese since her command of her native language was an area in which she was clearly the master.

The children's command of Vietnamese was more limited than the mother's command of English. Now it would be the children and the therapist who would have to struggle to figure out what the mother said. We thought that Mrs. B's use of Vietnamese would sound familiar chords that would eventually tie into her heritage, identity, and pride. Most importantly, the mother would be in charge.

In the beginning session, Mrs. B stated unequivocally that the children did not speak Vietnamese. It was our belief that the children, all born in Vietnam, had brought with them enough of the language and rhythm of Vietnamese to regain what they had already learned. We believed that the more Mrs. B used her native tongue, the more comfortable she would feel, and thus the more competent she would become as a parent. At this session, the supervisor, Sam Scott, was active as a cotherapist.

SCOTT: Do your children speak Vietnamese? Which of them spoke good Vietnamese before, which are . . .

MOTHER: All of them.

SCOTT: I want to see, I want to see if they remember, okay? Ask a question in Vietnamese of each child—ask John a question.

MOTHER: *Ăn cồm* [Eat]—you know?

SCOTT: I don't care whether he says no or not.

JOHN: Yeah.

SCOTT: What—what?

JOHN: What my mom just said.

SCOTT: What's she say?

JOHN: Eat?

SCOTT: Is that what you said?

MOTHER: Yes.

SCOTT: And how do you say that in Vietnamese?

JOHN: *Ăn cồm* [Eat].

SCOTT: In this country we have a game called Simon Says. You know the game?

MOTHER: No.

SCOTT: Okay, in Vietnamese a clown, like a trickster, plays tricks, who can help me with the language? John—do you speak the language well enough to tell her the word for somebody who plays tricks on people?

JOHN: I can't speak Vietnamese.

SCOTT: Well try it.

JOHN: I can't.

SCOTT: Well tell her about people who trick people, you tell her. Go ahead. [The supervisor thought the child would at least use some Vietnamese words.]

JOHN: (*To his mother*) See like a guy dressed up when we went to the Ice Capades and there was this guy who went over a big barrel with big shoes and he had like—he looked like him (*Points to a picture of a clown on one of the toys.*) wear these kinds clothes, and he was all like . . .

It was clear we were again falling into the trap of having the children interpret for the mother. We needed to change direction in a way that would support mother's competency through her culture and language. We arrived at a translation that worked out to be "Boss says stand up, Boss says sit down." Within a few minutes, we saw the transformation of a sad, ineffective, single parent, to a mother who was in full control of her children and having fun with them to boot.

SCOTT: Okay, first practice for a little while, let's practice. *Chủ nói* [Up].
MOTHER: *Dừng dậy* [Stand up].
SCOTT: No, *chủ nói* [boss says], you have to say *chủ nói* [boss says].
MOTHER: *Chủ nói dừng dậy—ngôì xuôńg* [Boss says stand up—sit down].
SCOTT: No, no, no. *Chủ nói—ngôì xuôńg* [Boss says sit down].
MOTHER: *Chủ nói ngôì xuôńg* [Boss says sit down]. *Chủ nói dừng dậy* [Boss says stand up].
SCOTT: *Chủ nói* [Boss says]. Again.
MOTHER: *Chủ nói ngôì xuôńg* [Boss says sit down].
BEN: *Chủ nói* [Boss says].
SCOTT: Again. (*Whispers to mother not to say* "Chủ nói" [*Boss says*].)
MOTHER: *Ngôì xuôńg.* (*Ben, the youngest, gets caught in the game and everyone laughs.*)

Mrs. B got the ideas of how to "trick." At many levels she was beginning to be the "boss" of her family in a way that both she and the family could learn and accept.

The idea of making the mother competent had for the moment become a reality. It was to become a theme that would be played over and over again in therapy with a repetitiveness that would eventually create a new and more functional order for the family. In subsequent sessions, this was reinforced and restated by having mother show the children where they were born and where they traveled in Vietnam. It was done by having them ask for their favorite Vietnamese dishes, in Vietnamese. It was done by having the children at the chalkboard drawing pictures of Buddha and pagodas. At the same time Mrs. B was encouraged to begin to do more things for herself and to do them without the help of the children. Catching the bus, going shopping, studying English, all moved Mrs. B toward effectiveness. Mrs. B also began to show an interest in traditional Vietnamese holidays such as the Tet-lunar New Year. And she involved the children in the celebration. Finally, ending a long self-imposed isolation from her own community, Mrs. B began to take part in local Vietnamese events and community gatherings. In fact, within a few months, this isolated woman took the opportunity to be the guide for non-English-speaking men visiting Philadelphia and had begun her own version of social services.

MOTHER: I say I no got a car, I take the bus.
LAPPIN: So you show them how to take the bus?

MOTHER: I take it, go all way down there. I go all day with new people.

LAPPIN: You take them all day?

MOTHER: In morning I say 10 o'clock meet me down at 69th. (*Laughs.*)

LAPPIN: So you tell them to meet you . . .

MOTHER: Meet me 69th. I take the bus, take people, train and bus 69th. I say wait down at movie. I take a bus. I take—we go all the way down the West Chester. Drive bus one hour. (*Laughs.*)

LAPPIN: How do you feel about that? Does that make you feel good to do that?

MOTHER: Yes, I say—you come here, you can't come here one month, two months, you can't drive car. I say I came here in '75. Five years I can't drive car—you want, I take, you go. I say I no have a car. I help you do papers.

In addition to having increased her competency in and out of the family, Mrs. B began to share what her life was like without her husband. The children, too, began to talk more of the father they had lost and what that meant to them. With order and competency now a larger part of her life, Mrs. B could examine her losses from a position of strength. The strength that she had always possessed flourished when given the proper context.

Mrs. B talked about her losses in a new light. She shared her concern about other family members, still in Vietnam, who in trying to escape, may have died. She talked about how "a lot of people died on the water" and how she worried about her fellow countrymen. More importantly, she began to do something about these concerns. She began to write to the refugee camps to find out about her nephew and her brother. She also began talking to newly arrived refugees, trying to learn about her family.

This was a major shift for Mrs. B. She was now looking to the world outside her children. She was mobilizing her concerns and was beginning to have social contact with other Vietnamese.

Summary

Our intent has been to suggest a method for dealing with cross-cultural issues in family therapy. Families become "stuck" when they cannot adapt effectively to the experiences that impinge on their lives. At one level, helping family members to alter dysfunctional mechanisms is a necessary part of helping them move on. At another level, however, it may be asking the family to give up some of the last remnants of the lives they left behind.

If the therapist makes an ongoing, respectful attempt to bridge the differences between his or her culture and that of the family, he or she creates a framework for understanding that establishes the basic elements of trust, accommodation, and change for the therapeutic contract.

When confidence and competency of the family are restored, then grief, depression, and anger can be dealt with effectively, from a renewed position of strength. To experience some success during extreme depression is far more useful than talking about depression. Our strategy throughout the therapy was based on specific, concrete, short-term steps. By using the idiosyncratic elements of the family and elements of its culture, we concentrated on aspects of the family system that possessed the strengths necessary for moving it toward change.

The strengths of the B family, as of all families, are reflected by the members' ability to survive the changing context of life. War, immigration, loss of family, and loss of cultural context were all factors outside the B family's control, yet they affected their lives tremendously. We needed to reinforce the strength of the family and to support their efforts to cope. We held the conviction that they could succeed. This conviction enabled us to respect the family's adaptive tools so that the functional and unique elements of their culture remained intact and continued to be an important part of their lives.

One of the most striking features of this therapy was the slow, painstaking pace that governed the change process. Sometimes we might spend an entire session just having mother teach the children and therapist a handful of Vietnamese words. Words, sentences, and meanings of words had to be repeated over and over. At times it seemed to take forever. But then all good things take time.

ACKNOWLEDGMENT
Special thanks to Phu Ma for his help correcting and editing the Vietnamese.

REFERENCE
Sluzki, C. Migration and Family Conflict. *Family Process, 18*(4), 379–390, 1979.

23
The Latin Lover Revisited[1]

CARLOS E. SLUZKI

The Latin Lover is a character that has appeared in novels—written by non-Latin authors—and in movies—produced in non-Latin countries. His presence in the products of different cultures is a reality. But is he real or a myth when it comes to identifying him in true life? Maybe both, depending on who the observer is.

As a way of beginning, it should be pointed out that there are no Latin Lovers in Latin countries, at least not in the eyes of Latin people. If a non-Latin travels to a Latin country, however, the person will undoubtedly find arrays of Latin Lovers. We could deduce that travelers bring with them something that transforms a Latin into a Latin Lover. The traveler imports stereotypes from his or her own culture as to how human beings, and subgroups of human beings, are or should be. Actually, the Latin Lover is a stereotype from some non-Latin cultures attributed to people from Latin cultures; it is certainly *not* a stereotype of Latin cultures.

However, we could hardly say that the non-Latin hallucinates. On the contrary, he or she tends to detect quite accurately some behavior patterns that fit into that stereotype. Even more, there is something in the cultural background of the Latins that makes them react according to a fixed pattern when confronted with the behavior of people from a non-Latin culture; there is something in the non-Latin that appears to trigger Latin Lover behavior in Latin people. In fact, as the Latin Lover interactional sequence requires two persons to make sense, we can state that each person's cultural stereotypes contribute to its production.

Two intertwined phenomena contribute to the creation of this sequence: on the one hand, face-to-face distances and the meanings conveyed by their

1. A previous version of this chapter has been published in Spanish in *Acta Psiquiátrica y Psicológica de América Latina, 22*, 107–111, 1976, and in a "priate" printing, in *Psicodeia— Psicología de Hoy* (Spain), *332*, 120–122, 1977.

Its English versions have been rejected by the following journals: *Culture, Medicine and Psychiatry* ("interesting but not suitable"); *Daedalus* (*idem*); *Journal of Communication* (*idem*); *Psychiatry* ("basic idea fairly well known"); *Society* ("we are already publishing another paper on *machismo*"); *ETC, Review of General Semantics* ("interesting and quite probably 'true' but not suitable"); *Voices* ("charming but too technical"); *Urbal Life and Culture* ("beautiful idea, but you do not provide empirical material to lend it plausibility"); *Harper's* (reject slip); *The New Yorker* (*idem*); *Human Behavior* (*idem*); and *Psychology Today* (*idem*).

Carlos E. Sluzki. Mental Research Institute, Palo Alto, California.

variations in different cultures and, on the other hand, some specific sets of culturally bound expectations assumed by and/or attributed to each sex in the specific context of social interaction between sexes.

A clarification is necessary at this point. The hypothetical construct "culture" is particularly elusive and imprecise when applied, as is done in this chapter, to broad ethnic groups. It is often true that a greater difference is found when culture of the various social classes within a given ethnic group are compared than when ethnic groups are compared within each class. The term "Latin culture" is used throughout this chapter as a shorthand that reifies habits, ideas, and attitudes transmitted from generation to generation by the learning process and shared by the majority of the population of countries where a Latin-rooted language is spoken: South and Central America, Mexico, Spain, Italy, France, and Portugal.

The use of genders throughout this chapter should also be commented upon. In order to focus the discussion on the strongest, most prevalent stereotype, a good part of the chapter will be centered on the description of interactional patterns in which the protagonist is a man (and heterosexual) Latin Lover, a woman being his complementary counterpart. It is a sexist choice perhaps, but the above cultural prevalence must be kept in mind.

Face-to-Face Distances

In the context of any social gathering, the mere fact that a person establishes a given distance when starting an exchange provides clues to the interlocutor about how that person is attempting to define the relationship.[2]

Within any culture studied, different face-to-face distances possess different message values, that is, different meanings. However, if we compare the types of meanings attributed to variations in distance in different cultures, the similarities among cultures are striking. For example, in most cultures, a decrease in distance means either a proposition to increase intimacy or a threat, depending on other information conveyed in the communicational "package."[3] A code of meanings is built on the basis of *relative* rather than

2. Gregory Bateson can be credited for having introduced the analytic distinction between "content" and "relationship" levels in human communication (cf. Bateson, 1951, for his original formulation, in terms of "report" and "command," and Watzlawick, Beavin, & Jackson, 1967, for an actualized presentation of the theme).

3. The term "package" was first used by Pittinger, Hockett, and Danehy (1960) to refer to the *gestalten* integrated by signals being sent at the *linguistic, auditive paralinguistic* (tone, volume, rhythm, pauses, etc.), and *nonverbal* (gestures, postures, facial expressions, etc.) levels. The "package" should be expanded, however, to include a fourth series, *the situational context proper* (Veron & Sluzki, 1970a, 1970b): "When a person 'enters' into a social situation (s)he receives arrays of signs from which (s)he classifies the situation (role definitions, hierarchical relationships, shape of the physical environment at the service of the development of certain types of interpersonal relationships, etc.). These elements are always distinguishable from the other three above-mentioned series" (1970a, p. 47).

absolute distances. That is, what is "normal" distance for one given purpose in a given culture may be "normal" distance for another totally different purpose in another culture.[4]

In each culture there is, to start with, a distance we could call "intermediate." This is the one usually expected, and adopted, in a face-to-face formal exchange between two persons in a social gathering, such as a party or occasional encounter in the street. This socially "neutral" distance stands for, or is the equivalent to, a message of the following sort: "My view of our relationship is one of peers, and we should proceed according to the coded sequential pattern expected in our culture for a situation of conversation." If the context is one in which more intimacy is favored—such as a small party—the intermediate distance may mean, in addition to the above: "Intimacy is not encouraged, and any movement in that direction may be met with plain rejection. It is therefore advisable to establish negotiations [i.e., to exchange clues] in other channels before attempting a reduction of distances." If a distance wider than the intermediate is established, the message conveyed may be, according to other clues (such as context, previous conversation, previous distance, relative status): (1) lack of interest in further contact, (2) respect and recognition (the person of lesser rank maintains the distance, thus leaving to the other the right to define whether to remain in the field or abandon it), (3) mistrust, or (4) a combination of the above. If the established distance is shorter than the average intermediate, it is the equivalent, in a social level of informal gatherings, to proposing a relationship with a higher level of intimacy—be it erotic, conspiratorial, or both—or it may mean a threat.

In remarkably different cultures these three distinct, alternative sets of meanings appear to be associated with the corresponding three face-to-face distances in a similar manner. But the absolute *ranges*, that is, the specific number of centimeters, that correspond to the intermediate, distant, and close distances vary noticeably among cultures. A person raised in a country in which the Latin culture prevails, for example, defines as intermediate (neutral, safe, formal) a face-to-face distance that is shorter than the one defined as such by a person raised in a non-Latin culture.[5] Therefore, the

---

4. It should be stressed that we are referring here to face-to-face frontal contacts. The situation varies when two persons stand side-by-side looking straight ahead (such as the case of two strangers in a crowded subway). Under those conditions, distance between faces can be lower than average and the situation would be still qualified as "socially acceptable" by the fact that the actors do not look directly at each other, *plus* the context, *plus* "proper" signs of discomfort such as body stiffness, which informs lack of intentionality on the part of the participants. Excellent descriptions on the codes governing behavior in public places can be found in the work of Erving Goffman (e.g., 1955, 1966).

5. One of the first thorough studies on conversational distances under various conditions of social and psychological closeness is that of Hall (1959). Garfinkel (1964) and Felipe and Sommer (1966), in turn, studied the effect of the violation of individual distance in a series of

distance that the Latin will consider intermediate will be labeled as close—
and loaded with the corresponding meaning—by the non-Latin. And this is
the starting point of a self-perpetuating misunderstanding: *A person raised
in a non-Latin culture will define as seductive behavior the same behavior
that a person raised in a Latin culture defines as socially neutral.*

The probability that spatial configurations may lead to misunderstandings is increased by the fact that the meanings attributed to nonverbal
behaviors are seldom explicitly discussed. The principal source of information
used by the participants in order to confirm or correct meanings is the
context in which the behavior is inserted (e.g., the interactional sequence and
its context or the way in which the signs conveyed though verbal and
nonverbal channels are combined). One of these interpretative contexts that
qualify and provide meanings to the behavior is the information—stereotypical or otherwise—that the receiver has about the culture of the source of
the messages. The fact that we know that the person we are greeting is an
Anglo-Saxon will give a certain meaning to the fact that he does not shake
our hand during the salutation. In the same manner, an Anglo-Saxon will
attribute specific meanings to a spacial behavior of reduced body distance
based on the knowledge that the other one is a Latin; it is classified as a
behavior of a *Latin Lover* (or eventually, his counterpart, the seducing,
tempestuous, hot Latino woman who has broken numerous hearts and
marriages in films and novels).

Punctuations of the Sequence of Events

Let us suppose, following the strongest stereotype, that the non-Latin subject
is a woman. She is approached at a party by a man whose behavior,
according to her understanding, defines his view of the emerging relationship
as one of seduction. She "reads" it in his tone of voice, manners, and,
especially, the face-to-face distance chosen by him and reestablished by him
everytime she withdraws imperceptibly in order to gain her own comfortable
social distance. She does not need to double check the meaning of his
message, for it has been reinforced enough by the (non-Latin) cultural

---

experiments under natural conditions, reporting that the invasion of the individual's "own"
space produces reactions of avoidance, bewilderment, and embarrassment, especially among
males.

This author first heard from Albert Scheflen, at a conference at the MRI, Palo Alto, in
1965, the observation that people raised in Latin countries differ from those raised in non-Latin
countries in terms of the "optimal" distance. His is also the corollary observation that when a
Latin and a non-Latin interact while standing face-to-face (e.g., chatting in a cocktail situation),
they will slowly but steadily perform a sort of dance, the non-Latin withdrawing and the Latin
advancing, each one simply trying to reach their "neutral" distance (a discussion on interpersonal
distance by that author can be found in Scheflen, 1976). It is also relevant to the discussion on
cultural differences in the use of the space during interaction (cf. Watson & Graves, 1966, or
Watson, 1972).

stereotype of the Latin Lover, attributed by her to him, triggered in her mind by his way of handling the face-to-face distance . . . and her knowledge that he comes from a Latin country.

What can she do then? She can either flee or she can respond positively along the same line she attributes to him. If she wishes to flee, she can simply leave the field ("Excuse me, I have to speak a word with someone I see now," or whatever social excuse she may use). She can choose to display signals of discomfort such as increasing *overtly* the face-to-face distance, or displaying body tension, or any other socially acceptable sign she assumes unequivocally reports her wish to withdraw. However, she may wish to respond positively to what she understood was a definition of the relationship proposed by him. In that case, she will start to play her part in the seductive sequence, signaling that she is *in* it, through flirtatious behavior. This can be done in a passive ("Please, seduce me") or active ("I will also seduce you") fashion. Behavior such as lowering the voice—which forces the other to decrease distance—blushing, and lowering the glance belong to the former, while reducing the distance even more, maintaining eye contact longer than customary, slightly touching of the other person's arm or shoulder while speaking belong to the active form of seduction. According to her own understanding, she is only responding to and reinforcing—either positively or negatively—the statement conveyed by his reduced face-to-face distance.

But her behavior, labeled by herself as a mere response to *his* seductive behavior, is for him a first statement in a sequence.[6] According to his own understanding, he did not behave in any way that, from the vantage point of his own culture, could be understood as meaning, unequivocally, seduction. Therefore, according to him, *she* is making a pass *at him*; she is starting to define the relationship as one of seduction.

If he were a non-Latin, he could, in turn, have the same options she had when it was her turn to decode the situation: flight or seduction. But this option, for a person raised in a Latin culture, is totally illusory.

A person raised in any Latin country has incorporated, in one way or another, the local version of the *machismo* cult, which dictates, among other things, that a man must signal that he is always ready for sex. Seductive behavior is expected from him and, even more, is mandatory in most circumstances when engaging in interaction with a woman who is not his wife or his mother, aunt, sister, or equivalent. Therefore, when a woman

6. According to Bateson and Jackson (1964), the "punctuation of the sequence of events" within the continuum of the interpersonal sequence is the arbitrary decision on the part of an actor to define a given message or situation as the "starting" point of the sequence, therefore defining, also arbitrarily, whose intervention is being considered a *stimulus*, whose a *response*, and whose a *reinforcement*. Misunderstandings along this line constitute a most common type of sterile fighting between marital partners: "I withdraw because you nag"; "No, I nag because you withdraw." This subject has been treated in detail in Watzlawick and Beavin (1967) and Watzlawick *et al.* (1967).

starts to send signals that she wishes to engage in a seductive behavior, he is confronted with a situation in which he can only move to a more advanced stage in the seductive process. This behavior in turn, confirms the non-Latin's interpretation of his original behavior. Days, months, years afterward, each will be able to affirm to the other, with equal certainty: "*You* started to seduce me."

Summary and a Moral

To summarize, the steps of our argument have been the following: (1) The neutral face-to-face distance for Latins is similar to the seductive face-to-face distance of non-Latins; (2) non-Latins do not detect the influence of their own stereotype, the Latin Lover, in their perception of the other's behavior; (3) the non-Latin may respond to the supposed Latin Lover by increasing distance and signaling discomfort or by contributing his or her own share of seductive behavior; each behavior will be considered by the non-Latin as a response to the message attributed to the Latin; (4) the Latin, in turn, is forced by the pressure of his own cultural stereotypes to respond to a seductive advance with an increase in his own seductive behavior; he labels his own behavior as a "response" to uncalled for (but always expected) behavior on the part of the non-Latin; (5) the readiness on the part of the Latin to define that exchange as seductive reinforces, in the eyes of the non-Latin, the meaning attributed to that behavior.

Several morals can be inferred from this description: (1) If you are not a native of a Latin country, do not try to act the Latin Lover role; at the most, your interactant will assume that you are nearsighted because, in order for your interactor to perceive you as a Latin Lover, he or she must first believe that you are Latin. (2) If you belong to a Latin culture and you find yourself in a non-Latin environment or in interaction with non-Latins, know that you run the risk of finding yourself bound by your own stereotypes to seduce the member of the opposite sex you are talking with, simply because you forgot that non-Latins adopt a neutral interpersonal distance that you may find uncomfortably wide. (3) If you belong to a non-Latin culture and interact with a Latin person, have mercy on him (or her): The Latin Lover is in YOUR mind. You may be able to materialize it with unusual speed, no doubt about it. However, in that case, who is the Latin Lover?

REFERENCES

Bateson, G. Information and Codification: A Philosophical Approach. In J. Ruesch & G. Bateson, *Communication: The Social Matrix of Psychiatry.* New York: Norton, 1951.
Bateson, G., & Jackson, D.D. Some Varieties of Pathogenic Organization. In D. McRioch, (Ed.), *Disorders of Communication.* Research Publication (Vol. 42), Association of Research in Nervous and Mental Disease, 1964.
Felipe, N.J., & Sommer, R. Invasions of Personal Space. *Social Problems, 14,* 206–214, 1966.

Garfinkel, H. Studies of the Routine Grounds of Everyday Activities. *Social Problems, 11*, 225–250, 1964.

Goffman, E. On Face Work. *Psychiatry, 18*, 213–31, 1955.

Goffman, E. *Behavior in Public Places*. New York: Free Press, 1966.

Hall, E.T. *The Silent Language*. The Hague: Mouton, 1959.

Pittinger, R.E., Hockett, C.F., & Danehy, J.J. *The First Five Minutes: A Sample of Microscopic Interview Analysis*. Ithaca, N.Y.: Paul Martineau, 1960.

Scheflen, A.E. *Human Territories: How We Behave in Space–Time*. Englewood Cliffs, N.J.: Prentice-Hall, 1976.

Veron, E., & Sluzki, C.E. *Comunicación y Neurosis*. Buenos Aires: Editorial del Instituto, 1970. (a)

Veron, E., & Sluzki, C.E. Communication and Neurosis: Semantic Components in Neurotic Verbal Behavior. *Social Science and Medicine, 4*, 75–96, 1970. (b)

Watson, O.M. *Proxemic Behavior: A Cross-Cultural Study*. The Hague: Mouton, 1972.

Watson, O.M., & Graves, T.D. Quantitative Research in Proxemic Behavior. *American Anthropologist, 68*, 971–85, 1966.

Watzlawick, P., & Beavin, J.H. Some Formal Aspects of Communication. *American Behavioral Scientist, 10*(8), 4–8, 1967.

Watzlawick, P., Beavin, J.H., & Jackson, D.D. *Pragmatics of Human Communication*. New York: Norton, 1967.

24

The Myth of the Shiksa[1]

EDWIN H. FRIEDMAN

Here is part of a letter that a Jewish mother sent to her son after learning that he really intended to marry the non-Jewish woman he had been dating:

> Dear Herbie,
>
> Well, if you want to commit suicide, I guess there is nothing I can do. But I can't tell you how much this *shiksa* business is hurting your father and me. I don't know if you realize that this will hurt us financially. We will probably have to leave town and I will certainly have to give up my job teaching Hebrew. . . .
>
> Your father is sick over this—you know he hasn't been well. All I can say is that if he dies, I will hold you responsible.
>
> Mary may say that she loves you, but have you told her that we Jews think of Jesus as an illegitimate son?
>
> Love,
> Mother

For 1000 years, Eastern European Jews and their descendants have used the term *shiksa* to refer to a non-Jewish woman who lures Jewish men away from religion and family. This attractive will-o'-the-wisp, as folk imagination would have it, is seductive, immoral, ignorant, and insensitive to Jewish values. It is not just that she is unsuitable to the warmth of traditional Jewish family life—she will destroy it!

There can be no question that within the Jewish ethnic community intermarriage has long been perceived as a major threat to the survival of the Jewish people and their way of life. Experience with more than 2000 Jewish–Gentile marriages and the reactions of their families has taught me, however, than when it comes to the individual Jewish family, this idea of the shiksa is myth. More important, the false assumptions that support it are hardly confined to Jewish families alone. Such false assumptions are just as

---

1. Several parts of this chapter have appeared elsewhere. The first presentation was at the Georgetown Family Therapy Symposium in 1968 and was entitled: "Ethnic Identity as Extended Family in Jewish–Gentile Marriage." It was later published in *Systems Therapy*, J. Bradt and C. Moynihan (Eds.). The title "Myth of the Shiksa" was first used for a presentation of the culture-family process hypothesis at the Third Annual Family Therapy Conference in Tel Aviv, 1979. An edited version of that paper appeared in *The Family* in October 1980, published jointly by the Georgetown Family Center and the Center for Family Life, New Rochelle, N.Y.

Edwin H. Friedman. Family Center, Georgetown University Medical School, and Family Training, Saint Elizabeth's Hospital, Washington, D.C.

prevalent in cross-cultural marriages of any combination, and they even appear in the families of culturally compatible unions.

Precisely, therefore, because the myth of the shiksa and its constituent myths are so bound up with one another, revealing the falsehood in the particular automatically leads to revealing the truth in the universal. It is the purpose of this chapter to expose the myth of the shiksa in its specific form— the way it surfaces in Jewish families—and, as a by-product, to extract some new ideas about the general relationship of family and culture. Regarding the particular, I will show how matters such as which Jews are most likely to be "seduced," which families and which members of those families are most likely to be reactive, and what strategies maximize keeping those families together all can be understood as matters of family process rather than culture. Then, broadening the perspective, I will show, first, how family process universally wraps itself in the garb of "cultural camouflage" and, second, how focus on background factors by families of any culture, as well as their therapists, supports an unwitting conspiracy of denial.

Clinical Experience

The ideas and examples to be presented here are based on 22 years of continuous experience in the cosmopolitan and international setting of Washington, D.C. During these decades, this area became a "mecca" for people from all over our planet and thus a fertile seeding ground for the cross-pollination of love.

Throughout this period as both a rabbi with a specific responsibility within the Jewish ethnic community and a family therapist with a broadly ecumenical practice, I found myself with an unusual opportunity to view cross-cultural marriage and family reactions within both particular and universal settings. As this situation developed, my position became one of reciprocal feedback. On the one hand, my growing awareness of the universality of family process that had been tutored by my experience with non-Jewish families helped me get past the cultural myths within Jewish families. Then, as I began to understand the emotional processes behind the cultural myth I was observing in Jewish families, I was able to carry that understanding back to all families as universal principles. Eventually I came to see the myth of the shiksa as a prototype, but for two decades it was my laboratory.

I first began to think about the relationship between culture and family process when I tried to understand a paradox about Jewish–Gentile marriage. In my premarital counseling, first, I found that Jews who married non-Jews were not at all uninterested in the survival of their ethnic community, which was contrary to what the community assumed. Second, I noticed that many of the relatives who phrased their opposition to such a marriage in terms of concern for Jewish survival had not themselves led lives evidencing such concern and had become defenders of the faith overnight. Third, and most surprising to me, was the fact that over and over I found the grandparents, though usually more traditional than the parents, generally, were more accepting.

Next I began to see that there were significant correlations between the ideological positions individuals took on such marriages and their positions in their family. This seemed to be true both about which child "married out" and which family member reacted most strongly. Back in the late 1960s, I began to report these findings at symposia of family therapists. Almost unanimously their response confirmed my perceptions. More than that, many began to refer to me mixed couples where neither partner was Jewish, for example, Protestant–Catholic, Black–White, Greek Orthodox–Russian Orthodox, European–Asian, Japanese–Chinese. In all, the number of different combinations probably reached 50.

These referrals gave me the opportunity to realize that certain family emotional phenomena that I had found to be true about Jewish–Gentile mixed marriages—for example, which child in the family tended to intermarry and who threatened to have a heart attack at the wedding—was just as true regarding mixed marriages where neither partner was Jewish.

I then began to see mixed couples in the same counseling groups. Here I found that Blacks and Whites, Turks and Greeks, Russians and Japanese, Puerto Ricans and WASPs, and Germans and Jews could gain as much insight into their own families from observing the emotional processes of these "other" families as from observing families of a similar cultural milieu, sometimes more. At the beginning of these sessions I was so caught up myself in the general mythology surrounding culture and family process that I was astounded by the similarity in the emotional processes between non-Jewish and Jewish family life.

Eventually, the uniqueness of my position in the Jewish and non-Jewish worlds began to pay off. I was able to develop a new hypothesis about the relationship between culture and family process that helped explain and integrate everything I was observing.

My hypothesis, which is the basic premise of this chapter, is as follows: Rather than supplying the determinants of family dynamics, *culture and environment supply the medium through which family process works its art.* Culture and environment may contribute to the morphology of a family's symptomatology, but they do not determine which families or which individuals from which families in a given culture are to become symptomatic. Rather than determining family dynamics, culture and environment *stain* them; that is, they make them visible. It is not that sociologists and anthropologists are wrong in their descriptions of various kinds of family life. What is wrong is to assume that any family, at any given time, is beleaguered by relational conflicts *because* of its culture or environmental setting, even when the family issues are directly related to these factors. In certain situations culture and environment can tip the balance, of course, but, generally, their effect on a given family's emotional processes is not so much to shape them as to supply the fabric for their design.

A simple test of the relative significance of culture and process in understanding the emotional functioning of any family is as follows. Cultural and environmental factors can no more be the sufficient or the necessary conditions for the creation of pathology in a society than paint and canvas can produce artistic accomplishment. Thus even if we could know all the cultural and environmental factors in a given family's background, we could still not posit the future of that family's health. On the other hand, if we could know all the dynamics of that family's emotional heritage and not know anything about their cultural and environmental background, we could posit the future of that family with a high degree of accuracy.[2]

Elsewhere I have shown that it is possible to isolate the family emotional process as an independent force from cultural background by describing 10 rules of family process regarding distance, chronic conditions, symptom formation, cutoffs, secrets, pain thresholds, sibling position, homeostasis, and diagnosis, which have the same validity for all families irrespective of cultural background.[3]

It is the failure to appreciate how emotional processes are camouflaged rather than determined by culture that enables family members to blame the background of others as the source of their discontent and their inability to change. Cultural camouflage encourages family members everywhere to avoid taking personal responsibility for their own points of view. It may be worse. The constant focus on and interminable discussion of background factors either among family members or with family members and their counselors allow important emotional forces to operate in their pernicious way, undetected.

It is only when we can see culture as a stain rather than a cause of family relational problems that we can devise appropriate strategies for affecting the underlying emotional processes that, rather than the cultural factors or

---

2. "Culture and Family Process," delivered originally at the Georgetown Medical School Symposium on Family Psychotherapy, 1971, later published in *Collection of Selected Symposium Papers*, Volume III, R.R. Sager (Ed.), Family Center, Georgetown Medical School, Washington, D.C.

3. This hypothesis should not be seen in any way as an effort to minimize or refute the general importance of ethnic and cultural values and customs in the enriching, developing, and stabilizing of family life everywhere. The emphasis here, rather, is that those same very important factors that ordinarily contribute mightily to the creation of a family, under certain conditions, are used to disguise what is destroying the same family. Ironically, as a rabbi committed to the survival of my people I came to find that I could often further positive feelings about being Jewish through approaches aimed primarily at waning the intensity of a family relationship system, even when, paradoxically, those very approaches seemed to be almost on the opposite side of reinforcing cultural commitment.

differences themselves, have the real power to destroy that family or keep it together.

This chapter is organized into three sections that follow the course of my experience. The first section will describe how ethnic cultural mythology operates in Jewish family life. The second section will show how Jewish families were helped to deal with potentially family-splitting crises when the underlying emotional "demons" in these families lost their cultural masks. The third section will develop the ideas of the first two sections into universal principles about the relationship of culture and family process in all families and then show how those principles feed back to even deeper understanding of the myth of the shiksa in Jewish families.

Ethnic Mythology and Jewish Family Life

The most blatant aspect of the myth of the shiksa today is that she will, or even wants to, attract a Jewish man away from his origins, no less destroy his family. In my experience that is the last thing she wants, generally being attracted herself to that very rootedness that she often lacks. Indeed, if there does exist a "shiksa" today, she is to be found, of all places, among Jewish women. For, in my experience, it is far more likely that when Jews and non-Jews marry it will generally be the non-Jewish partner who is influenced away from his or her origins. When the focus is confined to those marriages in which the Jewish partner is female, then I have to add that I have almost never seen such a union where the non-Jewish male will be the less adaptive partner in family matters.

The myth of the shiksa within the Jewish community today is thus doubly misleading. Not only are the designs of the non-Jewish woman who marries a Jewish man generally toward the preservation of his background rather than its destruction, but that same preservation instinct in Jewish women who marry non-Jewish men generally puts them in the very position that the term shiksa was originally intended to describe, that is, a woman who will seduce her man away from his background.

How then shall we account for the extremely negative reactions, some of them almost psychotic, that can occur in Jewish families when they guess who's coming to brunch?[4]

It is possible to answer this question with some conventional sociological theory. Times have changed; there is a lag in the perception; or any minority

---

4. Throughout this chapter I discuss Jewish–Gentile marriage as though the Jewish partner is always male. This, of course, is not true. The choice was stylistic as well as an effort to catch the traditional flavor of the myth. Previous to the last six or seven years, my own experience showed the Jewish partner to be male most of the time. Since the women's movement began to gather full steam, the curve has flattened out or even begun to bend the other way. I have found little difference, however, in the way family process operates around the issues of mixed marriage when the Jewish partner is female.

group is concerned about its preservation. Given the recent Nazi experience, the threats to Israel, and the long history of deep concern for survival, the Jewish people are naturally going to be even more xenophobic.

In my experience, the problem with such thinking is that I have never been able to find any necessary correlation between the degree of sociological of psychological sophistication in a Jewish family and how they respond to a mixed marriage. Nor have I found that a correlation necessarily exists between past exposure to threats to the Jewish people and how they respond to a mixed marriage. If a family that survived the Holocaust gets upset it is natural to say, "We can understand, given their past." If a deeply assimilated family from an old established, Southern Jewish community is accepting, we may be prone to explain, "What do you expect, given the diluting of Jewish identity in their background?" The problem with these background explanations is that I have often seen survivors from the Holocaust not react negatively, saying, "We have had enough turmoil in our lives," and, on the other hand, I have often seen so-called assimilated fathers take to bed for weeks.

Nor, as my experience increased, did it become possible to predict how any parents might react based on information such as the size of their town; their section of the United States; their degree of Jewish education or synagogue attendance; the amounts they gave to the United Jewish Appeal; or their trips to Israel per year.

Clearly, something deeper than cultural background or lag supported the myth of the shiksa, something else had to be present to modulate the ethnic material. A history of cultural commitment simply was not sufficient to create the reaction, and in some cases it did not even seem necessary.

My first clue to the missing variable came from observing the other side of the issue, namely, who in which Jewish family was most likely to marry an outsider. Here also, I found that the common-sense wisdom did not offer adequate explanation. While broad statistical studies might show inverse proportion between mixed marriage and cultural background factors such as keeping kosher, synagogue attendance, and number of Jewish books in the house, there were too many exceptions when it came down to the specific Jewish families in which mixed marriages were occurring. If deep commitment for Jewish values and customs prevented or inhibited mixed marriage in many situations, why did it not have the same prophylactic effect in many other families? None of the usual assumptions about degree of Jewish education and the inculcation of values necessarily held up. In fact, the correlations linking Jewish values and mixed marriages were skewed further. For it often seemed that the cultural background factors had worked and not worked at the same time. Over and over, I found that the Jewish partners who came from a family with a strong cultural tie felt intensely Jewish despite their decision to marry a non-Jew. *In their own minds one seemed to have nothing to do with the other*.

Finally a factor did begin to show up, a variable that seemed to be more determinative than cultural influence. It did not explain in every single case which Jewish individuals became candidates for cross-cultural marriage, but it seemed particularly important because it also helped to explain why the intensity of family reactions was not necessarily proportional to the degree of cultural commitment. It put both sides of the issue together in a new way, and as things turned out, it eventually led to effective strategies for family harmony.

I began to realize that Jews who married non-Jews overwhelmingly occupied the sibling position of oldest, or only, with only child defined as an actual single child or any child where there was a gap of five or more years between siblings. Such a correlation, I knew, could have meant that they simply exhibited the pioneering or leadership attribute frequently found in individuals from that sibling position. I soon learned, however, that this unusual correspondence between sibling position and the "insider" who married an "outsider" was a hint of something far more significant, something that could be true even when the insider did not occupy that particular sibling position.

As a family therapist who had taken thousands of multigenerational family histories, I knew that the child occupying the sibling position of oldest or only tended to be the focused or triangled child.

As is well known, a major and convenient way that some marital partners reduce the stress and intensity of their own relationship is by tuning down the overall emotional potential in their marriage by siphoning off the excess emotion onto the child. Such a child naturally becomes more important to the balance of the parents' relationship than his or her siblings, and where the resulting balance of the marriage is a calm and seemingly perfect fit, the importance of the child to its balance may not even be realized.

The child most likely to be emotionally triangled in this way does not always occupy the sibling position of oldest or only, of course. The child tends to be either an only, by the nature of things, or a first born simply because he or she was the only one around when the parents' marriage was in its early stages of formation as the parents disengaged from their parents. Any child can occupy this position if the timing is right, for example, when the parents' marriage needs rebalancing such as after a previously triangled child leaves (or dies) or the child is born close in time to the death of a grandparent who has been particularly important to one of the parents. Such a child, regardless of sibling position, might replace that grandparent in a similar emotional triangle that had helped balance the parents' marriage from the beginning.

In any event, if the child occupying such a position in the family does something that is perceived by the parents to be taking him or her out of that set of emotional interdependencies, the parents' anxiety will immediately increase. And it goes without saying that the triangled child will always have more difficulty leaving home!

I began to apply this hypothesis of the *triangled child* to Jewish families involved in mixed marriage, and many things came together. Not only did it help explain the inconsistencies between the degree of exposure to cultural influence and which family member married out or reacted most intensely, but it also helped explain who married further out, that is, interracially as well as interreligiously. For if parents generally have difficulty separating from the emotionally triangled child, the more intense the emotional circuits of that triangle, the more difficulty the child has separating from the parents. More powerful circuits need more powerful circuit breakers.

I thus formed the following hypothesis: In any Jewish (or ethnic) family the child most likely to marry out is the child most important to the balance of the parents' marriage either right then or while growing up. Further, that the parent (or other relative) most likely to react negatively occupied a similar position in his or her own family of origin, either during childhood or right then.

It was, I decided, anxiety over the loss of a previously balanced togetherness that could suddenly turn the genes of cultural commitment on, as in the case of many reacting parents, or slowly off, as in the case of many offspring.

But still a piece was missing. For even if my hypothesis about family position rather than degree of cultural commitment was correct, why this kind of marriage in that kind of family? What was the connection between family process and cultural symptoms?

What I eventually came to learn was that in any family, but particularly in easily identifiable, ethnic families, to the extent the emotional system is intense, members confuse feelings about their ethnicity with feelings about their family. The resulting inability to distinguish one from the other eventually leads to a situation in which reactions in the family relationship system are discussed with the vocabulary of the family's cultural milieu. I soon came to realize that focus on cultural background was a major way members of many Jewish families avoided focusing on their emotional processes.

The inadvertent yet all-encompassing nature of this phenomenon is illustrated by the following list of comments made by Jewish partners in my office. All were spoken in passing as someone was talking about family life back home or expectations about the future.

- I came from a typical Old World Jewish family in which father was the boss.
- I came from a typical Old World Jewish family in which mother was the boss.
- Jews don't talk about death.
- Boating is a Gentile sport.

- Jews don't live near forests.
- I thought Jewish weddings were buffet.
- Jews don't talk about sex.
- I thought Jewish weddings don't have placecards.
- You never can get Jews to be serious when they are eating.
- I thought Jewish weddings were always on Saturday night.
- Jewish families don't joke at dinner.
- I thought Jewish weddings always began when the minute hand was moving up the clock.
- Jewish girls always stay with their mothers.
- Jews aren't interested in watching sports on TV.
- Jewish boys can't get away from their mothers.
- In the Jewish religion we don't tell our ages.
- Why do I worry about him? I'm Jewish.
- My daughter reminds me of a shiksa—she's so cold and distant.
- Jewish women wear knit suits.
- My father was a typical Jewish father; you know, quiet, passive, let mom do all the work in raising us.
- Jewish mothers are dirty fighters.
- I have a typical Jewish girl's build, small on top and big on the bottom.
- Jewish parents don't let their kids sit in the living room.
- Jewish parents don't take vacations without their kids.
- Jewish wives know how to train their husbands.
- Jews like contemporary homes.
- Jewish parents don't charge their daughters rent if they come home again.
- Jewish families don't make big deals over birthdays.
- Jews always buy discount.
- Distance is fundamentally a non-Jewish concept.

As I will show in the third section this phenomenon is hardly confined to Jewish families or even to other ethnic families. The less intense the family, the less likely this is to happen. But a general principle does emerge, namely, that members of families regardless of cultural background, are more likely to fuse cultural values and family processes when an important emotional issue has been touched or when the general level of family anxiety has increased.

In any event, once I began to defocus culture in my work with mixed couples and to pay less attention to the ethnic words, customs, and rubrics usually used by Jewish families to explain intermarriage and personal reactions, a harvest of insights accrued, both about the myth of the shiksa specifically and about the relationship of family and culture generally.

There is one more emotional aspect of ethnicity that needs to be mentioned before showing the therapeutic efficacy of bypassing cultural content.

An ethnic system operates like an extended family composed of nuclear subgroupings. Anxiety in either the nuclear or extended system can escalate anxiety in the other. While this is true for any ethnic group, it has been particularly true about individual Jewish families in relation to what I would call the greater Jewish family (the worldwide Jewish community). Since the Nazi Holocaust and amidst the constant threat to Israel, sporadic anti-Semitic incidents in various countries, the falling Jewish birth rate, and the generally lessened interest in synagogue membership, the greater Jewish family is in a state of chronic anxiety about its survival.

The reciprocal elevation of anxiety between individual nuclear Jewish families and the extended system of the Jewish community works as follows: Members of an individual Jewish family concerned about the survival and togetherness of their own small group become more anxious about their personal family when they read or hear talk from community leaders about the survival and togetherness of the greater Jewish family. Similarly, when the leaders of individual Jewish families anxiously go to the community leaders for help over an issue such as mixed marriage (which in the minds of those family members has to do primarily with worries over their personal families, not worries about the community) the community leaders hear these reports as more proof that their family (the Jewish community) is in danger, and their overall anxiety increases.

This comparison of an ethnic community to an extended family is not inconsistent with the thesis that it is family process that counts, not culture. I am talking about the emotional processes in an ethnic community, not its cultural content. Of all the social groupings that act like a family, none is more like a family than an ethnic group, combining as it does all the same factors that make a family behave with the emotional intensity of a biological organism: genetic pool, long-term association, similar physiognomy, generations of emotional dependency, and so on.

The etymological history of the word shiksa itself is instructive of this relationship between a culture and its constituent families. The Hebrew verb *shakaytz* means to abominate, to utterly detest. In the Bible there are constant admonitions not to eat or take the *shikutz* (masculine noun form), literally, *abominated thing*, into one's house. But why was it necessary to have laws designed to keep people away from that which is abominable? We find no laws today against taking garbage into the house. Obviously whatever the *shikutzim* (plural) were, they were not by nature abominable but were probably attractive and were given this term of opprobrium to dilute people's desire.

There is, by the way, no feminine form of the root *shakaytz* anywhere in the Hebrew Bible; that grammatical construction does not exist. Only in the Middle Ages, in Europe, does the term *shiktsa* (feminine form) begin to surface among the Yiddish-speaking Jews of the ghetto who, obviously hemmed in by their physical and other walls, found the apparent freedom of the non-Jew attractive. The psychology was the same, but the focus had switched from foreign holy objects to foreign (strange?) women.[5]

Family Process and Cultural Costume

In this section I will show how it is possible to understand four basic aspects of the myth of the shiksa in terms of family process rather than culture and how such understanding can help Jewish families thrown into crisis over an impending mixed marriage. They are (1) which family member is most likely to be reactive, (2) what therapeutic strategies are most likely to reduce negative reactions and gain acceptance, (3) which families are most likely to be unaccepting, and (4) what variables have an influence on which given Jewish family is likely to have one of its members marry out.

The Reactive Relative

When some Jewish parents realize that they might have a non-Jewish in-law the reaction can be severe. I have seen Jewish mothers threaten suicide and Jewish fathers go into severe states of depression. I have heard of threats to cut children off emotionally and financially and to get the child kicked out of medical school! I have witnessed harassment in the form of daily letters or phone calls. I have seen parents resort to arguing the Jewish partner out of the potential marriage, and I have seen the effort made with the non-Jewish partner. Whatever form the reaction takes, however, the rationale is usually phrased in terms of, or accompanied by comments on, the survival of the Jewish people. "How can you do this to us?" is usually mixed with "Remember the Holocaust?" The personal qualities of the non-Jew will be attacked along with comments on the superiority of Jewish family life. The impression

5. This theme has been developed further in "The Relationship between Culture and Family Process in the Development of Jewish Identity" delivered at a conference on the psychodynamics of Jewish identity sponsored in March 1981 by the American Jewish Committee and the Central Conference of American Rabbis, the proceedings of which were published in 1982. This paper discusses how it is possible for anxiety in the greater Jewish family (or any ethnic community) to have more of an effect on the identity of its members than the quantity or quality of cultural inputs: libraries, sermons, courses, retreats, celebrations, and so on. It shows how an entire ethnic community can be viewed as one biological organism. Applying some new medical findings on the autoimmune response, trauma, and overcrowding to the "family's" response to the Holocaust it compares that event and its consequences to the kind of debilitating shock wave that can continue down through the generations in any family after a terribly shocking and uprooting event (rape, multiple death, accident, etc.). Here the suggestion is made that if the "family leaders" could shift the concern from how many died to who survived and how, the effect on the emotional processes of the entire ethnic community would then permit the cultural inputs to be far more effective.

that results is that the reacting relative is, if somewhat belatedly, terribly concerned about the survival of Judaism, or at least Jewish family life.

There are reasons for doubting this impression. First, I have only seen failure in efforts to change such reactive family members when the issues were discussed in philosophical or sociological terms of ethnic survival. Over and over, I have seen the Jewish partner go home for a weekend, explain his or her position logically and eloquently, return feeling much better about things, and then receive a letter showing that the parents are back at ground zero. The second problem with automatically assuming that cultural survival or purity is the real issue when it is invoked at such intense moments of family anxiety is the usual response of the grandparents. As I have mentioned, I have almost never seen the grandparents (who are usually more traditional) react more negatively than their less traditional children, the parents. This finding has been so universal that whenever a bride or groom reports that a grandparent is upset, I always ask, "Did you get that directly or hear it from your grandparents' son or daughter?" (i.e., mom or dad). Invariably it was heard from the bride's or groom's parent. Time and time again I have found that the grandparent is more accepting. But how could a leap-a-generation camaraderie overcome so basic an anxiety as in-group survival?

The degree of commitment to Jewish survival is almost irrelevant to the degree of reaction when a family member marries a non-Jew. What is relevant are the following three emotional coordinates of the reacting family member. In other words, irrespective of the language used to phrase the reaction and irrespective of the degree of cultural commitment the reacting relative has shown in the past, the following three emotional factors are always present:

1. There is little distinction of self between the reacting relative and the person getting married. This is so much the case that the reacting relative almost experiences the upcoming marriage as his or her own.

2. There are important issues that have not been worked out in the reacting relative's own marriage. In fact it may be generally true that individuals who are satisfied in their own marriages rarely react intensely to another's.

3. The reacting relative is always caught in some important emotionally responsible position in his or her own family of origin.[6]

The third is really the most important, as I will show shortly, for devising therapeutic strategies, and in some ways it makes the first two redundant. For the former usually follow from the latter.

6. Portions of the following section describing the emotional coordinates of family reactions to a marriage also appear in my chapter "Systems and Ceremonies: A Family View of Rites of Passage" in *The Family Life Cycle*, E. Carter and M. McGoldrick (Eds.), New York: Gardner Press, 1980.

An objection at this point may be, "Surely this would not be true regarding Orthodox Jews." First, that has not always been my experience. Beyond that, however, what is important for understanding and changing the emotional processes in a family is not the cultural position individuals take at such times but *how they function with that position*. Even if it were true that an Orthodox Jew is more likely to object to a mixed marriage (or for that matter an observant Catholic to marriage to a divorcee), the intensity with which that relative reacts is another matter, and that can tell much about the person's family and his or her position in it.

For example, an objection simply stated as such or even a refusal to go to an event because it is against one's principles can be understood as a definition of position. On the other hand, cutting off, disinheriting, constant harassment, saying "This will put a knife in my heart," heavy interference at such moments has little to do with cultural values and traditions, even though the family members who are acting that way may claim their faith supports their behavior and even though at other, less emotional, times the same expressed concern for survival, purity, and so on, reflects positive commitment to and deep involvement in the tradition. The roots of such fanaticism will be found in those family members' unworked out relationships with their own family of origin.

For example, *shiva*, which means *seven*, is the Jewish mourning period for a first-degree relative during which traditional Jews stay at home for a week. Some Jews have "sat *shiva*" for a child who has married out, literally, cutting him or her off from the family. While this would appear to be Jewish because the process is wrapped in a fundamental Jewish custom, nothing could be more misleading. Nowhere has the mainstream of Jewish tradition suggested that this be done, and it is done today (ritually or symbolically) by Jews who are ordinarily so nontraditional that they probably would not go through the ritual of sitting *shiva* when a relative really dies. We have here a good example of the universal emotional phenomenon I shall describe in the next section as the "neurotic usefulness of religious tradition." Family cutoffs are emotional, not cultural, phenomena and always require the consent of the one cutoff. Where that individual will not consent, working on the emotional processes in the cutting-off parent can eventually reconnect the two family members.

Therapeutic Strategies

What has substantiated in my own mind the accuracy of the previously motivated matrix of three emotional factors has been the high degree of success I have had in devising therapeutic strategies for change based on their coordinates. Not only have I found that by ignoring the cultural content of the reacting family member and focusing instead on the family coordinates it is possible to affect the intensity of the reaction, but I found that focus on the family process also can affect the rigidity of the ideological positions! It never works the other way.

Time and again I have seen a family member's most rigid, culturally based positions change when the emotional processes of that family change. But I have never seen the emotional tone, quality, or attitudes of family members change through a direct confrontation on ideological or cultural issues. On the contrary, the latter approach intensified the deeper emotional issues.

The approach I have taken with clients is, first, to help them defocus the cultural issue and, second, to address aggressively the emotional processes that are producing the extreme reaction. Usually it is the bride or groom who is the client. Where that is the case I have through a combination of family history taking and straight teaching about family process first tried to depersonalize the problem. By that I mean I have tried to cut down the bride's or groom's reactivity to parents' emotionality by showing that he or she is the focus of a process that usually goes beyond even the parents.

I try to show how efforts to bring parents around, especially by discussing the content of the charges, only keeps the focus (displacement) on the person. To the extent the bride or groom can understand this I then make direct suggestions for interfering with the multigenerational transmission process that is funneling its way down.

Where the parents are the clients and they have come in to stop the child from "destroying" herself or himself, the goals are the same though the techniques may differ, and the therapy has to be more subtle. I try to switch their goal from stopping the marriage or breaking up the relationship to getting better definition of self between them and their child or showing how when other parents have succeeded in accomplishing this, their children usually respond by drawing closer and either breaking up the relationship themselves (sometimes even after marriage) or forcing the partner to grow. In the process, if the parents' focus can be switched to their marriage, or their own families of origin, the cultural issues tend to disappear. In short, procedures that can refocus the parents on their own marriage or involve parents more in their own extended systems have been successful in eliminating the cultural issues. And this has been true no matter how traditional the parents or the phrasing of their position.

I will give one example with respect to each of the emotional coordinates mentioned in "The Reactive Relative" section.

1. *Lack of differentiation between reacting relative and person getting married.* The general thrust here is to stay out of the "content" of the charges or the pathos of the martyrdom. Paradoxical and playful techniques have proven remarkably effective. For example, "How can you do this to us, after all we have done for you?" can be met with "Mother, why do I have so much power to hurt you?" "Doesn't Jewish survival mean anything to you?" can be met with "The problem is, father, that you didn't keep kosher."

"Where did I fail?" is responded to with "If you had sent me to Hebrew school more often this wouldn't have happened." "We tried, but you wouldn't go," is answered with "But you were the parent, you should have forced me." And it never hurts the process for the child to add, "If your mother were only here now." Such comments, however, only bring breathing space; they do not result in lasting change, though they do reduce the intensity and the reactivity.

But emotional coordinate (1) is always a symptom of (2) and (3). It, therefore, follows that no matter what the focused issue between parent and child and whether or not it is cultural, dealing with coordinate (1) alone never brings lasting change. A fundamental shift only occurs by dealing with those coordinates which underpin it.

2. *Importance of the child to the balance of the reacting relative's marriage.* Parents who are satisfied in their own marriage do not react with prolonged negative intensity to the marriage of one of their children. It follows that one of the most surefire ways of shifting the displacement from the child is to refocus the parent on his or her own marriage. Using as one example, mother–daughter focus, here is content for a speech or letter that I have taught to brides as a way of accomplishing this shift:

> Mother, I know you are opposed to John, and you have a right to your position, but you are still my mother and I believe you owe me one more thing before John and I marry. We have never had a frank talk about sex. What has been the secret to your marital success? How many times a week would you say a man likes it? And when you don't want it, how do you keep a man away?

It is really remarkable how that paragraph will get mothers to cease their efforts to force-feed Jewish history.

Of course, not every daughter can do that little speech. So maybe the success I have seen with this one is that by selection, those daughters who can write it or say it are so well on their own way to disengagement that their own nonreactivity keeps them out of an escalating position, and without feedback to support it, the parents' reactivity wanes.

Whatever the reason, the basic point still holds: Cultural positions are susceptible to change by dealing with the underlying emotional processes.

3. *Extended family of reacting relatives.* If emotional coordinate (1) is symptomatic of processes enumerated in (2) and (3), (2) is also symptomatic of (3). Thus, dealing with (2) effectively will bring more breathing space than dealing with (1) alone, but neither effort will bring the kind of fundamental shift that occurs when dealing with the emotional processes enumerated in (3).

First the extended family of a reacting relative often has not even been told. "This would kill my father." I once saw a situation where a mother, ordinarily obsessed with prestige, censored from a newspaper announcement of her daughter's engagement the fact that her future son-in-law's family went back to the Virginia House of Burgesses, the well-known first legislative body in the United States. For such information would clearly have identified her daughter's future husband as non-Jewish.

I have found that if the bride or groom can outflank the reacting relative in his or her own family of origin, causing members of that family to interact with the parents, then even the most extreme reactions usually go quietly away. One way I have coached the bride or groom to catalyze this process is with a letter such as the one that follows, written preferably to the grandparent but sometimes to another family leader such as an uncle or aunt. That is, it must go to a parent or a peer of the parent.

> Dear Grand . . . , or Aunt, or Uncle,
>
> As you may have heard [they probably haven't] I am going to marry a non-Jew [a Catholic, a Black, a Martian]. I would like to invite you to the wedding even though I know this probably goes so much against your principles that you may feel you can't attend. However, I did want you to know. Also, I wondered if you could give me some advice. Your daughter [or kid sister; not, my mother] is absolutely off the wall about this. She keeps telling me this will be the end of our relationship, calls me every night, says if you found out you would drop dead, etc. I wonder if you could give me any information that would explain why she is behaving this way or any advice on how to deal with her. . . .

Generally the letter writer does not even receive an answer, but the next time the bride or groom has spoken to his or her own parent, there is often a marked change. This approach has worked as well for non-Jewish as for Jewish families. It will work as well in the future when the first Alfa-Centurians arrive and earthling children are warned not to intermarry with creatures who grew up in a different solar system. For it will be the same kind of families that will react and the same kind of families that will produce intergalactic unions.[7]

The universal success of this approach supports, I believe, the basic premise that when it comes to intense moments in a Jewish emotional system, cultural issues are often red herrings, displacement issues, which disintegrate when the emotional processes that spawn them are nullified.

---

7. When this chapter was delivered in Tel Aviv, I suggested that in Israel, where there was not a plentiful supply of shiksas, the children of Jewish families who, had they lived in the United States, would have intermarried with non-Jews, would intermarry with Jews of extremely different backgrounds, for example, German–Yemenite or Russian–Iraqi. I was drawing on my experience that 20 years ago in the United States a high degree of emotional reactivity could get started even in an all-Jewish marriage from different backgrounds, for example, Russian–German. In fact, there was a time when in some cities, Baltimore, for example, Jews of different backgrounds exclusively joined different country clubs. B'nai B'rith, created by German Jews, originally would not allow the admission of Eastern European Jews. In all events, the audience of Israeli therapists immediately informed me that since 1967, when Israel captured the West Bank, the plentiful supply of non-Jews had arrived and that an increasing problem there was Jewish women and Arab men. Their experience with these situations fit with my hypotheses.

Unaccepting Families

A third aspect of the myth of the shiksa that can be explained in terms of emotional process rather than culture is which Jewish families make acceptance of an outsider contingent on conversion. While it is not always true, most reactive family members will accept an "outsider" if he or she converts. In fact, in some families, the immediate focus is conversion, with all efforts going in that direction rather than the direction of preventing the marriage from taking place, though there are situations where a Jewish family or family member will not accept a non-Jew even after properly constituted conversion. Scrupulosity in any tradition is an emotional matter, not a culturally determined phenomenon, usually relating back to one's position in the family or origin, but it is usually so disguised in cultural costume that it is often difficult to discern it from commitment.

In all events, if the myth of the shiksa and its cultural camouflage succeed in their deception, it becomes natural to assume that the families that would be most insistent on conversion would be those families that are most motivated by long-cherished traditional values. In some cases this is true and in some it is not. A more consistent characterization of those families who make conversion into the dominant issue can be found in the following matrix, again phrased in terms of emotional process. The following seven characteristics of the way a family conceives of togetherness, and not any combination of cultural positions, are what I have found to be most true about those Jewish families that focus on conversion as a basis for acceptance.

1. The family is perceived to have a superself to which the self of each individual member is to be adapted emotionally.

2. Undifferentiated closeness is considered an automatic good, and acts of self that convey emotional autonomy are perceived to be "selfish."

3. The whole relationship system is conducive to panic because the circuit-breaker effect of self is missing. In fact, there is so much feedback in the anxiety circuits of such a family that it is almost impossible within such a relationship system to be objective about what is happening.

4. "Members of the tribe" who behave in ways that would take them out of the overall network of emotional interdependencies are perceived to be threatening. For where the whole family system is seen to be so dependent on each member, members of the family will feel they have to change also.

5. The greater family of the Jewish people is perceived in a similar, undifferentiated manner. Such a family tends, therefore, to overemphasize togetherness values in Judaism and to use the customs and traditions spawned by such values to keep its own personal family stuck together. The family members assume it is their Jewishness that is giving their family its kind of togetherness rather than the family that is putting Jewishness to its own neurotic service.

6. Any outsider to such a family is considered automatically threatening since that person has not been programmed to feel as the insiders. Their very inclusion will change the system. The outsider does not have to be a non-Jew, but a non-Jew, because of the melding of feelings about family togetherness, is just that much more threatening.

7. Thinking in such families tends to go to extremes because of the totalistic quality of the emotional climate. A live-and-let-live approach is inconceivable. Solutions tend to be conceived in terms of pressuring the person not to change or to change back, nullifying the effects of the change by changing the outside agent of change (convert the non-Jew), cutting off the family member so the change will not change anyone else (sit *shiva*).

To a large extent, non-Jews change in order to solve the Jewish partner's problems with his or her family.

There is a curious phenomenon about this stuck-togetherness thinking that actually can be used to the advantage of the bride and groom in stripping away the cultural camouflage. The rigidity of position of individuals who think about togetherness in an undifferentiated way makes it appear that they have great conviction about their beliefs. It is, however, not really their values or philosophical position that is paramount but rather their desire for emotional oneness. Thus, often when such relatives realize that there is no hope of swaying the child, it is they who convert, that is, become more accepting, in order to keep the family together, that is, "one."

Family Position and Marital Choice

The fourth aspect of the myth of the shiksa that has more to do with family process than cultural background is the essential question of who is most likely to intermarry. Most explanations have tended to go to one of two extremes: Jews who marry non-Jews are uncommitted, or, when they come from families that are strongly identified in their ethnicity, must be rebelling. Both of these explanations fail to grasp the relationship between family and culture being developed here, especially the role the emotional climate of a family plays in the original inculcation of values. Growing children are affected by their family's background, but I have found that the influence is not direct. The emotional climate of a family acts as a modulating force, screening, filtering, and coloring the background values and customs. Thus, the way any child in any family perceives and is influenced by the culture depends not on his or her position in the culture but on the position within the family.

I knew one mixed couple where the children were raised according to the culture of the same-sex parent. The Jewish father's son was sent to Hebrew school and the Gentile mother's daughter was sent to Sunday

school of her own religious background. Loving his mother, the boy grew up
and married a Gentile woman. Loving her mother, the girl identified with
her, and eventually married a Jewish man.

This emotional screening process exists in any family. It has more effect
in strongly ethnic families. And it is especially present when the emotional
system of the family, ethnic or not, is intense. It is, however, most influential
for the focused child in an intense, ethnic family.

To clarify this relationship between ethnic identity and the family's own
emotional climate, Figures 24.1 and 24.2 show two different examples,
involving two hypothetical Jewish families, the Cohens and the Levys. They
are designed to illustrate how a family's cultural climate and the climate
produced by that family's own emotional history shape the type of family
position that tends to lead to mixed marriages.

The family history of the Cohens and Levys is identical; the degree of
ethnic identification is not. In each family, the son was born within a year
after the death of his paternal grandfather, replacing him in the feelings of
father (B). In each situation the original marriage was balanced by the
mother's intense relationship with her own mother (D-E). Now let us posit
that in each family when the maternal grandmother (E) dies, the wife (D),
Mrs. Cohen or Mrs. Levy, puts the newly available emotional energy that
had been going into her mother (E) into her son (A) when she finds that her
husband (B) was not receptive to it. In each family, then, the son would have
become extremely important to each parent individually, as well as to the
emotional balance of their marriage.

But let us say that one difference between the Cohens and Levys was
that the Cohens were very Jewish whether in a religious, ethnic, historical, or

FIG. 24.1.

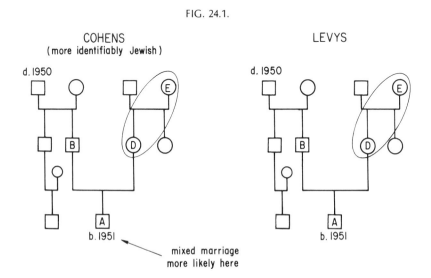

COHENS
(more identifiably Jewish)

LEVYS

mixed marriage
more likely here

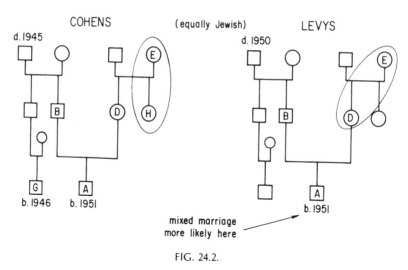

FIG. 24.2.

political way, but the Levys were not. The Levys were Jewish and in no way denied it, but Judaism or Jewishness did not seem to occupy a very significant part of their thoughts or their activities. Then the odds favor the Cohens' son and not the Levys' son contracting a mixed marriage, even though the Cohens are actually "more Jewish."

In Figure 24.2, the variables are reversed. This time let us posit that the Cohens and Levys had identical Jewish histories of deep cultural identification but that the family emotional histories were different.

As the genograms show, this time the Levys have the same family emotional history as in Figure 24.1, with the son consequently triangled deeply into the emotional system of his parents. This is not so with the Cohens, however. For, unlike Mr. Levy, Mr. Cohen was not particularly significant to his own family; his nephew (G), not his son (A), was the grandchild who was born close in time to the death of his father. And as for Mrs. Cohen, it is her sister (H) rather than she (D) who got stuck with the emotional responsibility for their mother. In this situation it would be the Levys with the triangled and emotionally important son and not the Cohens who would be more likely to have their son marry a Gentile, despite the fact that the family Jewish experience in each case was identical and positive.

This coincidence of family and ethnic background does not always create mixed marriage. Nor will it always be found in the background of every mixed marriage. It has shown up, however, more frequently than any set of sociological or cultural attributes and, as already mentioned, has created a theoretical framework for highly successful therapeutic intervention.

In a sense this fourth finding should have come first. It is, after all, more logical to begin with the family factors that influence who contracts mixed marriages and then go on to the emotional matrix that describes reacting relatives. I have purposely gone against that order because it is often only when we understand the reactions that we can understand their causes. So often they are part and parcel of the same process. In many situations the consequences are built in, so to speak. Certainly that is the way my own understanding of the entire phenomenon of Jewish–Gentile marriage unfolded. Only as I began to understand the depth of a parent's reaction to a son's marriage to a shiksa in terms of family history and family process did I then come to understand the depth and lure of her attraction.

The Universality of Cultural Camouflage

But the myth of the shiksa is not just a Jewish myth. First of all, families from almost any culture can be found that perceive outsiders as threats. All the same phenomena of hysteria, depression, and rejection can be found in other cross-cultural situations also. In fact the most severe reaction I ever encountered in a parent was from a Greek Orthodox priest who threatened self-immolation if his daughter married out. And, if we carry things to their logical extreme, it should be pointed out that for a Mormon family in the holy citadel of Salt Lake City, the Jew is the Gentile.

Actually the most famous shiksa in the 20th century did not marry a Jew. She married the King of England. As the Queen Mother told her eldest son bent on that intermarriage, what he was doing was "destructive to his people, shameful to his family, a betrayal of his own upbringing," and, in addition, a relationship that would be "morally destructive to him." All this regal "Mrs. Portnoy" was missing was the culturally appropriate phrase. The true basis for the universality of the myth of the shiksa lies in the universality of the more general erroneous assumptions about family life that support and that really give this Jewish myth in its particular form so much power. Demythologizing the particular leads to exposure of the universals.

Curiously, it is possible to use the in-group concept of the shiksa in reverse. Once it is recognized that the emotional phenomena described in the previous section are not particularly Jewish, then the constituent myths also lose their cover and the oft-hidden universal truths about family emotional process that those supporting myths mask also stand stripped of their disguise.

This section will be divided into two parts. First, I will show the universality of cultural camouflage as an emotional phenomenon. Second, I will show how this hypothesis leads to the unveiling of other displacement myths that feedback and support the myth of the shiksa.

Cultural Camouflage, A Universal Phenomenon

In the first section, "Ethnic Mythology and Jewish Family Life," I presented a list of statements made inadvertently in my office that showed a tendency of Jewish people to color the emotional processes of their family life Jewish. Here is a similar list of statements that I have collected in my office, this time made by individuals of various other cultural backgrounds.

- My husband has a typical Syrian temper.
- That's a typical Prussian way of distancing.
- In Japanese families the mother makes the wedding.
- If you're Catholic, you carry your cross till you die.
- German men are pushy.
- It's my English reserve—one doesn't wear dirty linen in public.
- My parents were Free Methodists—they never bought things on credit.
- The Irish don't bring up divorce at a wake.
- Europeans take things more seriously.
- In Southern families the women are treated like slaves.
- It's my Anglo-Saxon background—peace at any price.
- Korean mothers don't teach their daughters about the kitchen.
- My father was a devout Baptist; that's why we never learned about sex.
- In Indian families bad things come in threes.
- I grew up with the inhibitions of the '50s.
- It was a garden-variety close Huguenot family.
- Pakistani women have no sense of romance.
- I married an Italian; that should tell you something.
- Black women don't hate their mothers.
- In small Pennsylvania towns, you weren't allowed to talk back to your parents.
- I came from a typical European family where father was the boss.
- In those days people didn't get divorced. [Australian]
- In those days people didn't get divorced. [Chinese]
- I grew up in a WASP family; you know—no affection.
- That's his Swiss mentality.
- Once you're baptized, your parents have got you.
- Episcopalians never tell secrets.
- Swedish families can't keep secrets.
- We always tried to date Jewish girls back at school, because everyone knows they're freer.

Clearly the emotional phenomenon by which the family process is disguised in cultural camouflage is universal. Below the surface it operates in two directions, often simultaneously. On the one hand, the family provincializes to its own cultural background something that is really basic to the human condition, to family life in general. On the other hand, the family takes something that is peculiar to its own idiosyncratic process and ascribes it more broadly to its cultural milieu. An example of both is contained in the term "Jewish mother" to describe a woman overly invested in her children, or as one Puerto Rican man described his "typical" Puerto Rican mother, "an energy source in search of an input." Obviously, not all Jewish mothers are "Jewish mothers," but then not all "Jewish mothers" are Jewish.

A more startling example, which also gives insight into the power of family process, is the Unitarian woman who said she was converting to Judaism because "Unitarianism guilts." Of all the "backgrounds," we even hesitate to call it "cultural" because it is so young a tradition and so absent of specific customs, Unitarianism would seem to offer the least amount of cultural camouflage. This woman, however, was a fourth-generation Unitarian whose ancestors were among the New England founders of that church in the United States. For this woman, Unitarianism really was a family affair.

But the very first time I began to question cultural causation was after seeing a mixed couple where neither partner was Jewish. The wife had experienced three "breakdowns" during the 18 years of her marriage to an engineer from Kentucky whose mother was a Christian Scientist practitioner. She was a volatile woman from Mexico with a temperament that might be called "artistic." Her husband had married her because he did not like American women who were always "so serious, so practical, and so concerned with getting things done." She had married him because she "did not like Mexican men who showed such little respect for their wives," unlike American men who "treated them with dignity."

Eighteen years later, he had spent most of his marriage trying to figure out how he had chosen the one Mexican woman who was like all American women, and she was still trying to figure out how she had picked the one American man who was like all Mexican men.

Explaining away a family's emotional process by ascribing them to ethnic cultural causation is not the only way families avoid "owning up" to their own emotional heritage. The culture of the environment, the age, the physical conditions, even the sibling position are other popular forms of disguise. For example:

- My father is cheap because he grew up during the depression. [Despite the fact that his brother, Uncle Harry, can't hold onto a dime.]
- Aunt Rose is a prude because of the times in which she grew up. [Despite the fact that Aunt Mary, her kid sister, is a bunny.]
- I am frigid because I was raised with a very strict Catholic background. [Despite the fact that her sister keeps getting pregnant out of wedlock.]

• Why wouldn't you expect me to be adaptive in my marriage? The whole "culture" taught me to believe that women are the second sex. [Despite the fact that her sister, cousin, friend, or even her mother failed to get the message and are erroneously dominating their husbands.]

Other familiar examples are:

• I think my wife is insecure because her family moved about so much.
• I can't communicate with my son because of the generation gap.
• We should never have exposed him to all that violence on television.
• She is going through the change of life.
• Our child was okay until he started associating with the wrong friends.
• He (I, she) was a middle (oldest, youngest, only) child.

Cultural and environmental explanations for family functioning tend to deny the family's responsibility for that functioning. It is just not evident, for example, that those whose ancestors came to the United States on the *Mayflower* will necessarily be more secure in marriage than those whose folks have just gotten off the boat. Cultural and environmental causation theories almost always fail to account for the fact that there are other families from the same background, or even other individuals from the same family, who are behaving differently.

It is true that sometimes there is the chance synchronization between a given family's style and certain outstanding attributes of that family's culture, so that the family is able to put aspects of the culture to its own neurotic service. When this occurs it is even more difficult to discern cause from effect. Authoritarian fathers who happen to be Mennonite or Catholic, possessive mothers who happen to be Jewish, prudish mothers who happen to be Methodist, adaptive women who happen to be Quaker, all will hear certain aspects of their tradition louder. Actually, what seems to occur is that all families of all cultures have a tendency to select or emphasize from their culture's repertoire of customs and ceremony those modes of behavior that fit their own style. And they hear those values loudest that tend to prevent change!

For example, I was once working with a Catholic family where the wife was the twin sister of a nun. When she went back home and started talking about the importance of self in marriage, her parents, secure in a mutually adaptive relationship in which they had both sacrificed their selves for togetherness, became anxious and told her to stop seeing a "Jewish" therapist since Christians believe in self-sacrifice. Whereupon, the twin sister, whose specialty was theology, quoted a raft of Catholic theologians who had exalted the importance of self-respect and dignity.

If, however, we assume that it is the family emotional system rather than the ethnic or environmental background that does the real "culturing," then it is possible to develop an approach to the relationship of family and culture that keeps the responsibility where it belongs.

Displacement Myths and the Process of Change

I would like to present three examples of how cultural camouflage obscures the lines of responsibility in efforts to change a family. Each involves a widespread myth about family life that is reflected in the myth of the shiksa. But each, also, precisely because it is so widely believed, enhances the displacement and denial power of that particular myth in Jewish families. The areas of concern are compatibility in marriage, focus of discontent, and reasonableness and values as agents of change.

COMPATIBILITY IN MARRIAGE

For the most part, families tend to think about marital compatibility in terms of similarity; incompatibility, in terms of difference. A great deal of emphasis in premarital counseling or matchmaking is placed on finding what individuals have in common. This is especially true when a mixed marriage is being considered, where couples are warned they already have "two strikes against them," but it tends to be true about all premarital ruminations even when the "kids" grew up on the "same side of the tracks." Similarly, when any match needs repairing, the couple will consider themselves as mismatched. That there is some difficulty with this notion is evident from the fact than when individuals with strikingly different sets of interests or backgrounds make it, the explanation usually given is "opposites attract."

The truth, of course, is that differences, whether cultural or of another kind, follow the same rules and play the same roles in all families. At times of stress, they become the focus of attention, and easily identifiable differences become the causes of the stress. But even when a difference becomes an issue, whether it is a difference in cultural background or a differing over anything else, that same difference is not necessarily "differed" over everytime it shows up. What determines whether background or other kinds of differences are repulsive or attractive are factors much more subtle than the so-called basic differences themselves. What seems to be crucial is not the ingredients of the mixture but the overall emotional crucible into which it is poured. Incompatibility in marriage has less to do with the differences themselves than with what is causing them to stand out at that time.

The fact that families tend to ascribe their problems to their differences feeds back to the myth of the shiksa in two ways. First, it increases anxiety in the family and in the couple about their chances for marital success. Second, it does the exact opposite; it deludes the couple into thinking that the mates they have selected are far different (from their opposite-sex parent) than they really are.

A striking example of this phenomenon involved a highly educated, extremely well-traveled and cultured Protestant woman from the Midwest who was marrying a Jewish English professor from New York. Her father, a bigoted bricklayer, was furious about the marriage. During the courtship, her mother, who also opposed, developed cancer and died within a few months. Father (an extremely passive man in his marriage who let mother take all the responsibility and kept her adaptive to him with constant putdowns) then began to blame his daughter for her mother's death. As the woman changed in response to the way she handled both her mother's death and her father's reactions, the fiance made more and more noises about how she had changed, how rigid and cold she had become, and how he could not "get through" to her anymore.

He began to complain that she did not understand his dilemma as a Jew marrying a woman whose father was anti-Semitic. Next he spoke about his fears that with this new pattern of "withdrawal" she might abandon him emotionally in their marriage. He blamed it all on the fact that she was "denying" her mother's death.

Another type of cultural "fakeout" is the situation where, after a period of extreme mutual hostility, Jewish mother and shiksa daughter-in-law gravitate toward one another, drawn by the similarity with which they generally relate, namely, laser-beam focus on another person. In this process, which I have dubbed the *crossover*, the triangle shifts, and instead of Jewish husband and non-Jewish wife being in alliance against Jewish mother, it is now Jewish husband who is the outsider, as the two women exchange recipes from their respective backgrounds. I have seen this occur with Black, Pakistani, Chinese, and Appalachian shiksas.

FOCUS OF DISCONTENT

It is not only distressful issues that family members are prone to consider cause rather than symptom; other members of the family are also often perceived to be a source of anxiety when they are really the focus of the anxiety. Husbands and wives often displace their own existential discontent on their spouse, their discontent with one another on a child, their discontent with a parent on an in-law, and so forth. And it is obviously crucial for effective therapy, as well as long-lasting change, that both the therapist and the family be able eventually to distinguish a cause of discontent from a focus of discontent.

Failure to make this discrimination preserves the focus as a displacement, for, as with the culture–family process syndrome, the content (in this case, the information presented about the focused person) is seen as causative rather than illustrative of the reporter's anxiety, and that is exactly what the myth of the shiksa is all about. Not only is she no longer a non-Jewish woman, today she is not even a woman, that is, a person. The shiksa today is a focus, a focus of discontent, and as I have tried to show, she tends to rise with all her own mythology to the imagination of certain Jewish families not because she is non-Jewish, really, but rather because that given Jewish family at that particular moment does not wish to take responsibility for the way it is put together.

Once again, however, the more general myth not only is reflected in the myth of the shiksa, it supports it. For the widespread fashion whereby families equate the focus on their discontent with the cause of their misery makes it all the more difficult for a given focused couple to understand why they have "triggered" so much emotionality against them or why they have been so unsuccessful in their reasonable efforts to calm the family down. As can be the case with even the most experienced therapist, what the couple has unwittingly done is to accept the focus by their very efforts to change the family's views. Despite their good intentions, because those efforts were directed at the content of the issues, they became part of the family's process of denial.

Of course, the fact that with the shiksa the displaced focus is on culturally different persons adds to the identifying process and creates a doubly reinforced displacement. But all forms of denial are in secret allegiance.

REASONABLENESS AND VALUES AS AGENTS OF CHANGE

In my training and supervising of family therapists, whether they be clergy, social workers, psychologists, nurses, or psychiatrists; whether they live in the East or the West, the United States or Europe; whether they work for organizations or privately; and regardless of their social, religious, or cultural background, I have been struck by one extraordinarily similar aspect of their thinking—their reliance on reasonableness and values as instruments of change. I believe this is part and parcel of the "content thinking" that is the hallmark of cultural emphases.

The kind of experience with mixed marriage that I have been describing in which emotional process almost always overrides cultural values raises suspicions about the efficacy of such reliance on reason.

Blessed with a cortex and the power of speech, it is only logical to assume that members of a family can be changed by resorting to these inherent tools. However, my experience with trying to bring change to families reacting to a mixed marriage suggests generally that families who are in distress tend to "think with their spinal cords" rather than their cortex, and that when thought processes have that quality, expressed values are less evidence of what motivates family members than symptomatic of emotional positions they have already arrived at.

In the above-mentioned paper on the relationship between culture and family process in the formation of Jewish identity, I tried to explain the failure of the emphasis on cultural content to produce a stronger identity. I suggested that such content could be compared to the fuel needed to run a motor, but that we could not make a vehicle go forward by simply enriching the fuel if the "transmission" was in neutral, no less reverse. When the emotional system is ignored and the focus is only on cultural content, communication has the effect of typing a message on an electric typewriter when the current has been turned off. When it comes to changing families since all families are supplied by their culture with an infinite variety of rationalizations for ex post facto justifications of behavior, focus on values and ideological positions is often just another form of displacement. To offer reasonable alternatives to such positions, therefore, is once again only to conspire in the family's denial of its emotional process.

It has been my experience in working with families of all backgrounds that rather than values or reason, it is power that is the most forceful agent of change. This is not the power of conquest and domination but rather the strength to get enough distance from the anxiety malstrom whirling around us to think out our own values, whether or not they coincide with values from our own background, to define them clearly, and then to have the strength to hold that position against the efforts of others to change us back. In other words, the most powerful agent of change comes more out of a focus on our own values than on a focus that tries to define the other's values.

Regarding the myth of the shiksa and Jewish families, the widespread erroneous belief that expressed values are the cause of family members' positions and that, therefore, change in a given family member's functioning can be brought about by appealing to or changing those values, simply escalates anxiety and resistance on both sides. For it encourages a process wherein each side is perpetually trying to define, convince, change, and, therefore, *convert* the other.

Summary

In summary, I have endeavored to demythologize the myth of the shiksa in Jewish families and at the same time to show how that particular myth provides a laboratory for observing the way other widespread myths of family life prevent change in families everywhere. The broader myths all have some relationship to one generally misunderstood notion about the relationship of culture and family process. Once that relationship is understood to be almost the reverse of what is often assumed, new perceptions become available for understanding all families, as well as for creating strategies for therapeutic change.

25

A Social Systems Approach
to Assessment and Treatment for
Chinese American Families

EVELYN LEE

The importance of the family system has been recognized as pivotal in the treatment of Asian Americans (Kim, 1978; President's Commission on Mental Health, 1978; Sue & Sue, 1971; Sue & Wagner, 1973; Shon & Ja, Chap. 10). Although most authors have emphasized family considerations when dealing with Asian American mental health, much of this emphasis has focused on providing background information on the values, attitudes, philosophies, and history of Asian American families and very little has been said about assessment or intervention. This chapter will present practical guidelines for assessing and treating Chinese American families. Obviously, the emphasis on practical considerations has resulted in the omission of much background and theoretical material which the reader is invited to pursue in other publications (Kleinman & Lin, 1981; Sue, 1977; Sue & Morishima, in press; Wong, 1982; Shon & Ja, Chap. 10).

Working with Chinese families requires taking a holistic view of health and an interactive and contextual perspective on behavior. For the Chinese the separation of social, psychological, physical, and cultural phenomena has limited meaning. Although Western clinicians find it helpful to compartmentalize their thinking, for the Chinese the integration of such divisions into a holistic view of health, well-being, and life satisfaction is necessary. For assessment data and treatment interventions to have meaning for Chinese clients, the therapist must focus at the same time on the person, his or her family, and other significant relationships.

This presentation will focus on four aspects of the *client* system and the *treatment* system: (1) assessment and evaluation, (2) therapeutic relationships, (3) treatment considerations, and (4) treatment setting.

Evelyn Lee. Department of Psychiatry, University of California Medical School, San Francisco, California

Assessment and Evaluation

This model focuses on the three major subsystems that define the client system: the *person*, the *family*, and the *community*. Within each of these systems significant variables are organized around three general groupings: (1) physical and manifest features; (2) psychological features; and (3) social, cultural, and ecological determinants. Concrete guidelines are provided for diagnostic inquiry.

The Person System

As in any assessment, it is vital for clinicians to base their evaluation on the three principles mentioned above: the physical (constitutional or somatic organization), the psychological (the ego or self-concept as an organizing force), and the sociocultural (the organizing response to the rules and expectations of society and culture). However, because of the unique aspects of the lives of Chinese families and the impact of their particular environment, the assessment must include information beyond traditional intake data. Culturally specific factors relevant to the client's life experience must be ascertained. Personal data such as language and dialect spoken, physical health status and medical history, Chinese and Western medication used, work roles, help-seeking behavior patterns, and other significant demographic information (years in the United States, country of origin, immigration status, etc.) are helpful in developing a profile of the client. Psychological data, including the client's process of adaptation and acculturation, perception of problems and their solutions, past problem-solving ability, degree of life cycle interruption, and so forth, can provide important clues to the clinician. Social and cultural data such as the client's immigration and relocation history, work hours and environment, and extent of contact with human service networks can help the therapist to understand the degree of support or stress from the external environment.

The Family System

The family is the central unit of social organization for the Chinese. Because of cultural orientation, English-language limitations, separation from friends and extended kin, and other isolating environmental factors, the family often provides the sole means of interaction, socialization, validation, and stabilization. For the treatment of Chinese Americans to be effective, it is critical and take into careful account the impact of family life. To understand the present Chinese American family in treatment, the following factors need to be understood.

PSYCHOLOGICAL ORIENTATION

In Chinese culture, the family, rather than the individual, is the major unit of society. The sense of the family's importance and contribution to the individual's core identity has been molded by cultural norms and values over many centuries. The individual can only be understood in terms of family goals and family developmental history; adaptation and acculturation; the family sense of shame and obligation; the Chinese perception of courtship and marriage relationships; support from siblings, grandparents, and other extended family members; and the Chinese coping styles and perceptions of problems and their solutions. Understanding the psychological significance and centrality of the Chinese family is crucial in formulating any treatment plan.

CURRENT STATUS AND BEHAVIOR

While psychological features frame the limits whereby treatment interventions can occur, attention should be given to the observed behavioral features of Chinese families in treatment. Understanding the specific *interactional* and *behavioral* practices of family members enables the clinician to assess the limits of treatment practices that can be applied. Such specificity should include the nature, extent, and quality of family communication; family composition; languages spoken by family members; the kinship network; financial situation and family income; health status of members, help-seeking behavior; and other demographic data such as the number of male and female children and the living arrangements.

SOCIAL, CULTURAL, AND ENVIRONMENTAL FACTORS

The Chinese American family is shaped not only by past traditions and current life experiences but also by the ongoing political and economic events in the Far East and the United States. Many environmental stresses, such as poor housing, underemployment, discriminatory immigration laws, and individual and institutional racism, exercise a disorganizing influence on the Chinese American family system. The clinician should have a good understanding of the significant social and cultural factors, such as the neighborhood condition; intergenerational differences; family roles and their allocation; and the extent of the family's support system, including sponsors, employers, friends, and family, locally or elsewhere.

The Community System

For many Chinese Americans the Chinese community is the major arena for interaction and exchange. The sense of "we-ness" in Chinatown provides needed security and support to many immigrants and refugees in a very different and difficult environment. The Chinese who move away from

Chinatown still come back to renew themselves and to express their sense of ethnic identity. Therefore, the therapist needs to be particularly sensitive to the impact of the community on the client and the family. In particular, mental illness is still quite stigmatizing to the family. The community's reaction to mental illness may have greater impact than any therapist's interventive activities on whether a client initiates or continues treatment. Key features of the community system that the clinician needs to understand are as follows.

EXISTING COMMUNITY STRUCTURES

Clinicians who are working with Chinese Americans need to have a good understanding of its geographical boundaries, social institutions, demography, formal and informal structures, history, human service agencies, and community leaders. Such information will elucidate the limits and potential impact of interventions within any particular Chinese community.

PSYCHOLOGICAL SIGNIFICANCE OF THE COMMUNITY

Enclaves of Chinese living in Chinatowns across the United States represent not only a physical sense of community but also a psychological one. To many Chinese Americans, especially recent immigrants, the community provides the psychological significance of an extended family. Similar to the support formerly available in their "village," the community provides the family with a network of informal support and a mechanism for socialization into appropriate behaviors needed for survival and adaptation. Chinese depend upon other Chinese to learn about their "new world." The community may have the same psychological, cultural, and relationship bonds as the nuclear family does for many Western families.

SOCIAL, CULTURAL AND ENVIRONMENTAL DETERMINANTS

Because Chinese communities tend to be cohesive, with very good informal communication networks, the therapist must assess the influence of any particular Chinese community as a constraint on treatment of any particular family.

In the following sections the procedures for obtaining additional culturally relevant information about the client system will be provided. Table 25.1 summarizes the kind of information needed in each of the key areas.

The Overall Impact of the Migration and Relocation History

For many immigrants, physical arrival in the United States does not mean their "emotional" arrival. A residence in the United States may not be considered a "home." It is very important for the clinician to map out the client's relocation experience. As a result of the major political changes in

China in the past several decades, many Chinese became refugees even before they arrived in the United States. It is helpful to understand how much energy clients have spent in coping with their losses and separations and how much energy they have left to cope with new demands. The clinician working with immigrant families (see also McGoldrick, Chap. 1) should obtain information regarding the following: How many times did the client move in the past? From where to where? With whom? What were the reasons? Which family members are still behind? What was the order of migration? Were these voluntary or involuntary migrations? To what political and economic systems was the family exposed? When did family members come to the United States? Who is the sponsor? What kind of relationship does the family have with the sponsor? Have family members experienced upward or downward mobility since immigration? How did they cope with all the new changes?

The Individual and Family Life Cycle in the Context of Migration

In addition to the overall impact of relocation, migration disrupts at least two sets of life processes: the course of individual development and the life cycle of the family. For example, how does a child growing up in a refugee camp with no provision for substitute mothering establish a basic sense of trust? How does an adolescent from mainland China integrate old values with the new ones learned from the media, school, and peer groups? How does a Chinese housewife deal with new values in regard to sexual orientation, independence, achievement, and work? How does a newly arrived elderly Chinese man who expects to be supported by his children and grandchildren deal with his loneliness in a housing project for the elderly or in a nursing home? According to the *Task Panel Reports* submitted to the President's Commission on Mental Health (1978), the young, widowed and divorced women, and the aged are high-risk groups among the Asian population. They are disproportionately vulnerable to psychosocial stresses and attendant stress-induced problems and exhibit a higher than average rate of psychopathology in coping with traumatic life events.

If we consider arrival in the United States as the rebirth of the family system, there are at least three types of Chinese families in the United States:

1. Recently arrived immigrant families, for whom the impact of separation and the wish for reunion is still very great. Family energy must be spent largely on the development of basic survival skills for work, housing, and relating in the new land.

2. Immigrant-American families. Such families usually consist of foreign-born parents and their American-born children. The family system usually experiences a greater degree of cultural conflict between parents and children. Younger family members are usually more in-

TABLE 25.1. Summary of Additional Information Inquiry for the Assessment of Chinese American Families

Physical and manifest features	Psychological features, dynamics, and structures	Social, cultural, and ecological features
	Client system	
Language(s) and dialect(s) spoken and degree of fluency	Rate and process of adaptation and acculturation	Migration and relocation process and history
Physical health status and medical history	Perceived problems and solutions	Work hours and work environment
Medications used (including herbs and Chinese medicines)	Attitudes toward Western medicine and help	Extent of contact with social and human services network
Work and job roles	Degree and kind of interruptions to the individual's life cycle	
Help-seeking behaviors and patterns	Perception of past successes and failures in problem solving and coping	
Other significant demographic data (immigration status, age, sex, birth order, male and female siblings, educational background in the United States and elsewhere, marital status, income, years in the United States, country of origin)		
	Family system	
Extent and quality of family interactive and communication behaviors	Role and process of adaptation and acculturation of family members	Degree and kinds of intergenerational differences
Family composition	Members' perceptions of problems and solutions	Family member roles and allocation process
Language(s) and dialect(s) spoken by members and degrees of fluency	Perception of courtship process and marriage relationship	Migration and relocation process and history
Kinship network		Neighborhood conditions

Financial situation and family income	Extent and kind of interruptions to the family life cycle and development	Participation in and meaningfulness of family rituals and celebrations
Health status of members	Role of and perception of support from members (e.g., siblings, grandparents)	Extent of support system (to include sponsors, employers, individuals in China and elsewhere)
Help-seeking behaviors and patterns of family members	Sense of obligation and shame	
Living and household arrangements	Image of family portrayed to others	
Number of children (male and female)	Coping styles of members	
	Individual and family goals of each member	

Community system

Geographic boundaries and location	Extent of informal support network	Impact of immigration and refugee policies
Social and human services agencies	Attitudes toward health and mental illness of community members	Reaching-out efforts of family associations and other political and social organizations
Community developmental history	Perceptions of problems and solutions by community members	Extent of Chinese media and other communication networks
Services available outside of community	Identification of a "Chinatown" by community members	Degree of cross-ethnic relationships (e.g., racism)
Community composition and changing populations (e.g., census data)	Community image portrayed to others	Practice and celebration of Chinese cultural holidays and festivals
Formal referral and helping network	Extent of adaptation and acculturation within community	Reaching-out efforts of human and other service agencies

dividualistic and independent. The individual goals of the children at times conflict with the family goals set by the parents. Lack of a common language may make communication among family members very difficult.

3. Immigrant-descendant families. Such families usually consist of American-born parents and their children. Family members usually speak English at home and are quite Westernized in value orientation.

These families have different help-seeking patterns: Recently arrived immigrant families generally come to agencies in Chinatown with many environmental problems that require concrete assistance and crisis intervention. Immigrant-American families usually require help in resolving generational conflicts, communication problems, and role confusion. Immigrant-descendant families usually live outside Chinatown and seek help from traditional human service agencies or private clinicians with some degree of comfort and little stigma.

In view of the long history of losses and separation in many Chinese families, it is common for the pain and unresolved conflict of one generation to be suppressed or denied and then passed on and expressed in the next generation. It is very important for clinicians to view the pain an individual brings to an agency as pain experienced by the total family, including parents and grandparents. In addition, since the majority of the first-generation immigrants are adults who live and work in an ethnic neighborhood such as Chinatown, conflicts of acculturation may be postponed. Cultural conflict is generally manifested in the next generation, particularly by the American-born adolescent, who is likely to reject the "ethnic" values of parents and to strive to become "Americanized." Assessment of the disruptions to individual and family life cycles provides a framework for understanding and anticipating additional life crises or normal developmental trends.

Differences in Rates of Adaptation and Acculturation

Chinese families differ greatly in their adaptive abilities and motivation to deal with the cultural conflicts inherent in the process of immigration. Individual family members within one household likewise differ greatly in their rates of adaptation and acculturation. Due to discriminatory laws such as the Exclusion Act of 1882, which prohibited the immigration of family members of Chinese who came to the United States for work, Chinatown was "frozen" for many decades into a male society with very few family households. As a consequence of the new, more liberal immigration policy established in 1965, however, the family size in Chinatown expanded. It is estimated that in 1980 60% of all Chinese Americans were first-generation immigrants, many of them women and children who had been separated from the other generations of their families. The extended family is still the basic family structure in Chinatown. Therefore, family assessment must include understanding of generational differences in language, religion, support networks, recreational activities, housing arrangements and neighborhood, significant life events, and patterns of care seeking. (For an exercise to help families deal with such intergenerational differences, see Lee & Ja, 1982.)

There is a great diversity among the Chinese in the United States. Immigrants and refugees have come from many different areas of Asia such as Hong Kong, Taiwan, China, Vietnam, and other Southeast Asian countries. The descendants of immigrants, first, second, or third American-born generations will have varied cultural patterns, and children of "mixed" marriages, where one of the parents is Chinese, will present different patterns still. Given the diversity of languages, norms, mores, and immigration status, therapists are advised to assess a client's acculturation and adaptation in the United States very carefully. In general, four indications can be used:

1. Years in the United States. A non-Chinese-speaking, third-generation person may be very "Westernized" and have a totally different value orientation from a non-English-speaking, newly arrived immigrant or refugee. However, years in the United States cannot be used as the absolute yardstick to measure the degree of acculturation. For example, many older Chinese who came to the United States more than 40 years ago still try to preserve their heritage by "freezing traditions," and, as such, they may be more "Chinese" than newly arrived immigrants from Hong Kong or other parts of China.

2. Country of origin. Political, economic, and educational backgrounds of different Asian countries will also influence the rate of acculturation. A Chinese graduate student from Singapore may absorb American culture much more easily than a young adult from mainland China, because people in Singapore have rapidly adopted many Western practices, whereas mainland Chinese are only beginning to do so.

3. Professional affiliation. An English-speaking Chinese doctor from Hong Kong who works in an American hospital is exposed to many more American practices than a Chinese cook who works in the kitchen of a Chinese restaurant with other non-English-speaking Chinese. Professional affiliation provides avenues through which the acculturation process can be accelerated because of greater access to other Americans and to such resources as money, status, and esteem.

4. Age at time of immigration. A 10-year-old child who immediately enters into the public school system is more easily assimilated than an 80-year-old man who lives in Chinatown.

The rate of adaptation and acculturation are key indicators of a family's ability to change and thus are crucial in diagnostic assessment.

Work Stress

For the Chinese the work environment and work roles contribute greatly to a person's self-definition and self-esteem. Work can be a facilitator or a barrier to life adjustment. Hope of improving the family's financial status is one of the major reasons Chinese immigrate to the United States. However, language barriers and other factors have "trapped" many Chinese in restaurant and garment factory work with no other alternatives. "Status inconsistency," created by underemployment, is one of the major stressors for Chinese in this country. In addition, demands from work have brought about drastic changes in the Chinese family system. Because of long working hours, many Chinese men find it difficult to maintain their traditional family role as husband and father. Women, especially those who did not work before they came to the United States, find it very stressful to be working mothers with little support from their husbands. Becoming the breadwinner is devastating for one who has not faced that responsibility before.

Strengths and Vulnerabilities in the Family System

In every phase of the life cycle, the Chinese family unit is of central importance in providing the necessary resources for growth and the definition of social expectations and responsibilities. Careful assessment needs to be made with respect to the family's strengths in past adaptation, coping, and problem solving, as well as the family's vulnerabilities and areas of deficiency. Several key practices within a Chinese American family may increase vulnerability and disorganization, which can further exacerbate family problems: (1) insufficient energy within the family, as a result of past losses, to meet the demands for adaptation and coping, (2) goals of any member that are in conflict with family goals, (3) disrupted or unclear family communication or role expectations, and (4) environmental stresses when the family is not adequately organized to replace old community and family support systems or to obtain additional energy from the outside. In assessing the family's strengths and vulnerabilities, the clinician needs to consider the sociocultural dimensions that affect family communication patterns and roles.

FAMILY COMMUNICATION PATTERNS

Some of the principal sociocultural factors that influence family communication patterns are the following.

1. Generational differences in language within a family. As a result of different times of immigration by family members to the United States (some members as much as 30 years apart) and different rates of acculturation of these family members, it is not uncommon to find older members speaking only in a dialect of Chinese and younger American-born members speaking only English. As such, family members often lack a common language by which they can communicate or share emotional exchanges. In addition, Chinese Americans speak many different dialects and cannot always understand each other even in Chinese. It is very important for the clinician to find out what language(s) clients use at home, at work, and in other social contexts.

2. *Vocabulary available to family members.* The clinician needs to assess the extent to which family members can communicate complex issues and emotional content in Chinese or English with the lexicon available to them. Chinese terms and grammatical structures that allow for simple social exchanges and for ordering food at a restaurant are not the same as those necessary for discussion of family issues.

3. *Indirect and action modes of communication.* The clinician needs to assess the degree to which family members communicate using suggestions, examples, nonverbal actions, body language, and other indirect modalities.

4. *Differences in temporal and interactive style.* For example, some family members, in pausing after a relatively long statement, may really have more to say, but may pause to get a sense of their impact. A therapist who follows up too quickly may really be interrupting what needs to be communicated.

5. *Primary modes of expression of affect.* Feelings may be shared in different modes—for example, by the induction of affect, by using a familiar philosophical example of Chinese cultural saying.

6. *Taboo topics.* Therapists must assess carefully what topics cannot be discussed openly. For example, families might view comments about illness, accidents, hospitals or death as instigating a chain of "bad luck." Sex should also be approached with extreme discretion. Mention of certain words about sex, illness, or death, especially at significant times like holidays or during a woman's pregnancy, would be serious breaches of acceptable behavior. It is definitely unadvisable to inquire about sexual matters in the first interview, and the therapist would be well advised not to bring up such matters until a very good alliance has been established with the family. Otherwise the therapist can unwittingly trigger in the family the sense of "bad luck" or at least damage the therapeutic relationship.

FAMILY ROLES

In traditional Chinese families interpersonal interactions are determined more by prescribed roles, obligations, and duties than by a person-oriented communication process. Typically, interpersonal interaction takes into account a vertical and hierarchical role structure, which is determined by age, sex, generation, and birth order of family members. Family roles are allocated on the basis of family functions. For example, a Chinese woman is usually placed in a subordinate position in the power structure until she produces sons or becomes a mother-in-law herself. Although she has little overt power, her duties include rearing children and taking care of their emotional development. This, of course, gives her enormous influence over the psychological development of her children. For her the most important bond is likely to be that with her children, especially her sons and above all the oldest son, rather than with her husband. The Chinese husband is usually given the responsibility and power to be the financial provider and the disciplinarian of the children and to handle whatever happens outside the family. His strongest bond is often with his own mother rather than with his wife, the more so for men who have experienced long separations from their fathers.

Because of the unequal power distribution in Chinese families, there is often a large gap or distance between certain family members. The distance may be greatest between the father and the youngest child. Often the gap is so large that no effective communication is possible between certain family members. In these cases an intermediary may be needed to bridge the gap. This special role is typically assigned to the "parental" child, the "well-respected" uncle, a trusted friend from the same village, or perhaps the family therapist.

The positions of oldest son and youngest daughter have been associated with the highest rates of psychopathology in Chinese culture, suggesting that the social roles that go with these positions may at times be highly stressful (Kleinman & Lin, 1981). In the traditional Chinese family the oldest son usually has to assume many special roles. He must provide the major emotional support to his mother and grandmother, he may be used as a pawn in the power struggle between an overinvolved mother and a detached father or as an intermediary to link uncommunicative members, and he has to take care of the educational and character development of his younger siblings and bring honor to the family by being a good student and financial supporter.

The youngest daughter in the Chinese American family usually either came to the United States at a young age or is American born. She usually represents the last task of the parents, and their final hope of a child who will not abandon them by leaving. She may resent bring left with responsibility for her parents as her older siblings leave home and, in addition, the unfair treatment she gets as a daughter in relation to her brothers. Since she is likely to be the most acculturated, she may be the most vulnerable to cultural value conflicts. Her major emotional support is usually from her oldest brother, her grandparents, and her peers. Interruptions in these relationships are likely to be most stressful for her.

As the Chinese American family continues to change its traditional family structure, role allocation and the multiple roles served by family members have also been changing. It is essential for the therapist to pay close attention to these roles as well as to other factors that can influence them. Such factors include the ability to speak English (which may put the person in the role of spokesperson), financial or social status in the outside world (which may lead to particular stress when it conflicts with one's status in the family), and changes as a result of migration, which often puts stern demands on family members to assume roles that conflict with the traditional family structure.

COMMUNITY INFLUENCES ON THE CLIENT AND
ON FAMILY BEHAVIOR

There is increasing recognition among helping professionals that the problems encountered by ethnic minorities cannot be resolved without reference to the community (Sue, 1973). The adjustment of individuals depends upon (1) the nature and extent of community demands and (2) the availability and adequacy of resources (Klein, 1968). Chinatowns throughout the United States are characterized by high levels of stress and low levels of community resources. Many Chinese who live in Chinatown, especially the newly arrived immigrants, are subjected to numerous environmental problems such as inadequate housing, underemployment, and institutional racism. Chinese immigrants have not only come from different social, political, territorial, and linguistic backgrounds, but have been continually subjected to changing social and economic life-styles, both in their other overseas communities and in the United States. As mentioned, the therapist needs to assess carefully the degree of support or vulnerability felt by the Chinese family within its community. Therapeutic problems may arise because of the sense of losing face due to the community stigma of emotional problems, cross-ethnic relationship conflicts involving racism, conflicts within the Chinese community, lack of service alternatives, and the poor reputation of the treatment system in handling Chinese family issues and confidentialities.

Manifestation of Emotional Problems in the Context of the Cultural Environment

Somatic concerns and complaints, sleep or appetite disturbance, depression, job-related difficulties, interpersonal problems, anger and hostility, adaptational concerns, and psychosis are only some of the common problems expressed by Chinese clients in mental health clinics. There are few studies that compare clinical manifestations of mental illness among Chinese Americans with those of other ethnic groups in the United States (Morishima, Sue, Teng, Zane, & Cram, 1979). However, among the unassimilated Chinese population, there are significant differences in the ways mental illness is expressed. It is not within the scope of this chapter to discuss the cultural aspects of different clinical manifestations of emotional problems. However, two areas that deserve attention are the high rates of psychosomatic complaints and suicide among Chinese American patients. Somatization as a cultural mode of expressing emotional distress has been receiving increasing attention by researchers and clinicians (Kleinman & Lin, 1981). For example, one study indicated that Chinese depressives tend to somatize (Marsella, Kinzie, & Gordon, 1973). The very terms Chinese apply to dysphoric states— *may* (depressed, sad), *fan-tsao* (troubled, worried, anxious), *kan huo* (irritable, angry), *shen-k'nei* (kidney weakness or deficiency)—refer to a somatic network. These terms convey psychological meaning through somatic symbols (heart, liver, kidney, nerves, etc.) (Kleinman & Lin, 1981). Since the client may use these symbols to communicate concerns, it is very important to routinely request information on the client's physical condition. The therapist will need special skill in assessing psychosomatic symptoms. Close consultation with physicians and working together as a team whenever possible are highly recommended, since clients are most likely to see the medical system as relevant.

Another problem that deserves attention is suicide. The suicide rate among the Chinese is 27.9 per 10,000 per annum, three times the national average (Bourne, 1973). Bourne, who studied suicides for the period 1952–1968, also found that the suicide rate among Chinese men is four to five times that among women, although in recent years these ratios have gradually begun to change because of the increase of women immigrants and the changing roles of Chinese women. Barbiturate ingestion is noted to be the most common method of suicide for Chinese men. Lonely elderly men who came to America as sojourners and, who were despondent over physical illness constituted a very high-risk group for suicide (Bourne, 1973). For Chinese women hanging is the most common method of suicide. Suicide attempts are usually precipitated by interpersonal conflicts such as chronic family strife, desertion by her husband, or parental scolding (Yap, 1958). Yap borrowed Lindemann's concept of hypereridism to explain the high frequency of interpersonal stresses as a precipitating factor for female suicide. In traditional Chinese culture women are denied opportunities for self-expression and assertion. Interpersonal conflicts may produce a hyperidic state that exerts an impersonal pressure slowly leading to despair, which cannot be alleviated by threats or appeals. Under such circumstances, an acute quarrel or even a minor reprimand can set off an impulsive, poorly planned suicide attempt.

For the Chinese family it is often the suicide attempt of one member that brings the family into treatment. It is critical to understand such manifestations in the context of the family environment.

Therapeutic Relationships: Special Cultural Considerations

The Chinese, like other Asian groups, place great value on relationships (Hsu & Tseng, 1974–1975). Even in contrived and special relationships such as therapeutic relationships, interpersonal issues will play an important role. Differences in language, ethnicity, socioeconomic status, life experiences, and the perception of the therapeutic process, which have been demonstrated to be important factors in psychotherapy outcome (Garfield & Bergin, 1971), are particularly sensitive issues with Chinese families. Western-trained therapists have very different values from Chinese clients in the following areas, which may particularly affect the therapeutic relationship.

Value Orientation

The American-trained therapist is mostly a product of a nuclear family with strong emphasis on individualism, independence, and self-reliance (see Table 25.2). Most new Chinese immigrants come from a nondemocratic society where there is a vertical structure with a rigid set of role expectations. Suppression of critical comments and emotion is encouraged in such family and political environments. In the United States, therapists have been raised in a democratic society where relationships are more equal and horizontal in structure. Expression of negativity, criticism, and emotions is usually openly encouraged. Clinicians need to be aware of cultural value clashes in this area when engaging Chinese families in treatment.

Conceptualization of Mental Illness

Western-trained therapists have paid great attention to the intrapsychic influences that shape life experiences and behavior. In coming to understand the causes of mental illness, the Chinese rarely invoke psychological explanations. The following are some common Chinese beliefs about the causes of mental illness.

TABLE 25.2. Cultural Differences (Basic Concepts)

	East	West
Civilization	Agricultural	Industrial
Religion	Confucianist, Buddhist, Taoist	Christian
Philosophy	Logic of the heart	Logic of the mind
	Suppression of individuality	Individualism, egoism
	Mutual dependence, collective responsibility between kinship members	Independence, self-reliance
	Conformity, harmony	Competition
	Living more with the past (ancestor worship)	Living for the future
	Financial dependence	Financial independence
	Fatalism	Master of one's own fate
	To conserve	To change
	Suppression of emotion	Expression of emotion
	Rigidity of role and status	Flexibility of role and status

Question: What are the treatment implications?

1. Organic disorders. Mental illness is conceptualized as a manifestation of physical disease, especially brain disorders, menstrual disorders, diseases of the liver, sexual frustration or sexual excess, and so forth.

2. Supernatural intervention. Mental illness is seen as some form of spiritual unrest meted out to the individual through the agency of a "ghost" or vengeful spirit.

3. Genetic vulnerability or hereditary weakness

4. Physical and emotional strain and exhaustion caused by external situational factors

5. Metaphysical factors—for example, an imbalance between *yin* and *yang* elements

6. Fatalism

7. Character weakness

"Healing" versus "Talk Therapy"

For Western-trained therapists, great emphasis is placed on the following concepts for the therapeutic "healing" process.

1. Individual growth, change, and development, and individual goal setting for change

2. Long-range goals and future-oriented accomplishments made by slow therapeutic "working through" of issues

3. Individual efforts, self-motivation, and drive, which bring about change (lack of individual motivation is equivalent to "being resistant" in treatment)

4. Psychological deficits and personality shortcomings correctible through a psychological process (as opposed to actual life experience) by means of "corrective emotional experiences")

5. Verbal, intimate, emotional, self-disclosing, and behavioral feedback seen as central in the change process

6. Distinction between the domains of physical health and mental well-being

7. Emphasis on cause-and-effect and if–then relationships as is consistent with Western scientific thought

8. Emphasis on pathology

In contrast, for many Chinese, mental health is achieved through self-discipline, exercise of willpower, and the avoidance of morbid thoughts. Many Chinese are trained to "bear" suffering and emotional stress. There is still much cultural shame attached to being mentally ill. Disclosing illness to anyone outside the family is considered to result in a loss of social status. Therefore, the need for "talk therapy" is not understood and is generally unacceptable.

Process of Healing

A traditional treatment model usually goes through the same sequence of steps with each patient: assessment, formulation of diagnosis, development of treatment goals, development of a relationship, actions and interactions to progress toward these goals, and, finally, termination. In many cases, the evaluation and diagnostic process is quite lengthy. The major activity in the treatment process is verbal communication between the therapist and the patient. Chinese patients will probably have difficulty understanding such therapeutic processes. They seek help from mental health agencies only as the last resort after they have exhausted all other resources and usually come for help in a state of crisis with expectation of an immediate "cure." They are used to the traditional Chinese healing practice, which usually includes diagnosis, a brief physical observation, and prescription writing all in one interview. They do not understand the purpose of lengthy evaluation sessions and the apparent lack of treatment in that initial process. They may also get upset with an initial interview that probes into their family and personal backgrounds. For immigrants who have suffered many losses and separations, this process can be extremely stressful. To reveal family secrets to an outsider also evokes a sense of guilt. Consequently, many Chinese patients drop out of treatment.

Expectations of Treatment

For many therapists the "success" of a case is measured by the "emotional" growth of the individual patient in the ability to communicate and express feelings, including anger and hostility. For Chinese families, the criteria for successful treatment are based largely on physical and behavioral changes and the immediate alleviation of symptoms, such as the ability to work, eat, sleep, maintain good health, and to assume allocated family roles.

Perception of Professional Roles

Because of a lack of experience with mental health professionals in their home countries, many Chinese do not have the sophistication to understand the roles of mental health professionals. A team approach involving many disciplines can be quite confusing to Chinese patients. As mentioned, they do not understand the value of "talking sessions." Since the role of physician is more clearly understood and respected, Chinese patients may expect therapists to conduct themselves in the traditional role of physicians who prescribe medications. Therefore, especially in the initial stage of the therapeutic relationship, it is very important for the therapist to explain his or her role to the patient and at the same time to explore the patient's expectations with regard to the clinician's role.

Language

One of the major barriers in conducting sessions with non-English-speaking Chinese clients is language. If the therapist does not speak the same dialect as the client, the interviews have to be conducted through an interpreter. There are several common problems with this procedure.

1. It is very difficult to establish rapport through a third party.

2. Most of the translators are not trained in or familiar with psychiatric terminology, and it is very difficult to translate English expressions or emotional terms into Chinese.

3. Because Chinese do not want other Chinese to know about their emotional problems, many clients bring their own translators, usually family members, such as the oldest son or daughter. The combined roles of family member and translator can be nonetherapeutic because of the potential conflict of interest.

Education and Social Class

Most Chinese immigrants are not well educated and come from working-class or poor backgrounds. Class-bound value conflicts become one of the barriers in establishing rapport with therapists of middle-class, educated backgrounds. It is important for therapists to see the connection between the relative power of their own group and the feelings, perceptions, and behavior of their patients, who are highly sensitive to status differences.

Special Recommendations in the Establishment of Therapeutic Relationships

1. The therapist should convey expertise and use caution in establishing an initial egalitarian therapeutic relationship. Because Chinese families view family relationships in terms of a vertical hierarchy, extreme caution is advised against adopting a democratic attitude in the therapeutic relationship. The therapist will need to take a much more authoritative attitude than may be customary, since Chinese family members view the therapist as the "problem-solver" and expect him or her to behave in an authoritative or parental manner. They will feel very uncomfortable if put on a peer level with the therapist.

Therapists need to convey an air of confidence. When asked, they should not hesitate to show off their educational background and work experience. Clients need to know that the therapist is more "powerful" than their illness and will "cure" them with competence and know-how. A less than authoritative and assertive attitude conveys to many Chinese clients a sense of self-doubt and, perhaps, of a novice at work.

2. Volunteering information on the personal credentials, qualities, and background of the therapist provides the client with commonalities for establishing rapport. Chinese clients usually do not view their therapist as merely a professional involved in this kind of human service or as just an agency staff member providing valuable services. They expect the therapist to care about them as people. It is not uncommon for clients to ask the therapist many personal questions about his or her family background, marital status, number of children, and so on. The therapist will need to feel comfortable about answering personal questions in order to gain clients' trust and to establish rapport. Clients, in turn, find that they can reasonably depend on the competencies of the clinician because they see areas of mutual compatibility and because they have been able to "evaluate" the clinician's background.

3. Nonjudgmental listening and neutrality in the clinician's responses may be viewed as a lack of interest. Psychotherapy, as practiced in the United States, places considerable emphasis on the therapist's developing a nonjudgmental, noncritical, neutral attitude in order to be effective. Such a passive manner may be interpreted by Chinese clients as noncaring, or lacking confidence. Since verbal expression of feelings is not encouraged in Chinese culture, the client's dissatisfaction may not be made known to the clinician.

4. Flexibility and willingness to assume multiple helping roles enhance the therapeutic relationship. Because of the lack of understanding of the role of mental health professionals, especially among disorganized, multiproblem families, clients expect the therapist not only to be a "talking" doctor, but also to play the role of teacher, advocate, family adviser, consultant to friends and relatives, and so on. Actions such as telephoning the client's physician, making a home visit, or getting the client a job can be very therapeutic. However, the therapist should be aware of which roles are therapeutic to the client. The use of paraprofessionals in a team can be effective in allowing for a diversity of therapeutic roles, although it is important to have one primary therapist.

5. Demonstrations of empathy and caring are often needed. Among Chinese patients with a history of long years of separation from their loved ones, there is a yearning for an actively empathic parental figure. Therapists who exhibit warmth are more able to gain the trust of their clients. This requires not only careful listening to the clients, but also trying to *do* something that will be helpful in relieving symptoms. Due to the strong sense of obligation in Chinese culture, clients may view keeping appointments or taking medication as doing something for the therapist in return for the therapist's concern.

6. Dependency at the onset of the therapeutic relationship is expected and may be prolonged in some cases, because of the English-language

barrier, which requires much reliance on translators and other helpers. The therapist should encourage "healthy dependency" and set up a treatment plan that will foster future independence when the client is ready. Of course, long-term dependency should be discouraged.

7. Special caution is advised for therapists who share similar cultural backgrounds with Chinese clients. Therapists with the same cultural background may have particular difficulties and blind spots. For example, a young Chinese therapist who is still struggling with his or her own cultural identity and dependency toward parents may overidentify with the teenagers in the family. A Chinese woman who is in a hostile dependent relationship with her husband may have difficulties in relating to a male therapist.

8. It is very important for the therapist to identify the decision-makers in the family and gain their support for the treatment plan. Their active participation in the implementation of the plan can be very effective. In the early stages of treatment, individual sessions with the client alone (some Chinese families refer to these as "secret meetings") can foster unnecessary guilt and isolation within the family, and can increase the family's resistance to involvement in treatment.

9. Establishment of relationships with multiple family members is preferred. In view of the strong Chinese family influence on the individual's behavior, family therapy is generally the treatment of choice. This requires the establishment of relationships with the client, the parents, the siblings, the grandparents, and/or significant others. Each set of relationships may require different intervention skills.

10. Flexibility and informality around case entry and exit are necessary. Many Chinese clients come to an agency for help not by formal referral but by word of mouth. They may drop by the office without an appointment because they have heard about the worker from friends with whom they work in the community. They are not used to the formal appointment system. Formal evaluation sessions may scare them away. Termination is another area requiring special attention. The Chinese concept of time and space in relationships is quite different. They invest a great deal of energy in trusting their therapist and in allowing him or her to be part of the family, and they like to maintain contact even after the successful achievement of treatment goals. For many Chinese, a good relationship is a permanent one that should be treasured. It is quite common for Chinese families to send gifts and cards to their therapist during Christmas or Chinese New Year. Many still bring gifts to their therapist years after termination of treatment. When such families need help again, they will normally call upon their therapist, rather than the agency, for help.

11. Appreciating the inherent ambivalence in the relationship with the therapist facilitates the therapeutic relationship. Sharing feelings and family secrets with an outsider can provoke feelings of guilt and uneasiness. On the

other hand, many Chinese clients are yearning for a close relationship with someone who is understanding and supportive. Especially for the Chinese woman whose identity is built around her husband, parents, and in-laws, receiving individual attention with a focus on her own growth and needs can be overwhelming and confusing. She may miss appointments if she feels too close to the therapist, but may show up again without an appointment weeks later when she needs to talk to someone. Such ambivalence should be respected. Helping the client understand the reasons for ambivalence can be therapeutic.

12. Creative use of the client's cultural strengths is encouraged. Strengths such as support from extended family members and siblings, the strong sense of obligation, the strong focus on educational achievement, the work ethic, the high tolerance for loneliness and separation, and the loyalties of friends or between employer and employee should be respected and used creatively in the therapeutic process.

Therapeutic Considerations

Although stress has been placed on the importance of family dynamics in the assessment and treatment of Chinese clients, psychotherapy does not always mean meeting with the whole family together. It is recommended that therapeutic encounters focus on family dynamics, and, in many cases, the family (in part or as a whole) needs to be involved. However, such involvement may include minimal but significant roles for family members at one or more sessions, having several family sessions as an adjunct to the total treatment process, or conducting ongoing family therapy sessions on a regular basis. Therapists should pay special attention to the following areas.

1. Language spoken by the family members. As mentioned above, it is quite common for the parents to speak only Chinese and the children to speak English. Conducting family sessions in different dialects or languages can be confusing, if not impossible.

2. Readiness of family members to communicate as a group. Due to the hierarchical structure of the Chinese family, family members are not used to sitting down together and sharing feelings. Parents' open expression of fear or sadness in front of the children might be interpreted as "losing face" or losing control of their authoritative roles. Children might also resent seeing their parents in a vulnerable position. Verbal abuse by children in front of an outsider can also provoke extreme embarrassment and anger. Therefore the decision of who to see in therapy should be based on careful clinical assessment. A gradual process to link up different family subsystems may be necessary. The therapist can start by working with the identified client and other family

members who are willing to be involved and, after gaining their trust, can then move on to other resistant members. Alliance with the decision-makers in the family is crucial.

3. Time and place for family sessions. Because of the long hours of restaurant work of many Chinese males, finding time for family sessions can be very difficult. The husband's day off seems to be the most appropriate time for family sessions. Many Chinese families prefer to have the family sessions in their home in order to feel safe and in control.

Specific Interviewing Skills in Working with Chinese Families

The following are some suggestions for conducting interviews with Chinese clients.

1. Try to overcome language barriers. Good translation is not equal to good treatment. Ideally, referral to a competent bilingual, bicultural therapist might be the treatment of choice. If using an interpreter is the only alternative, try to use one regular interpreter for all sessions, preferably not a family member. Be sure the interpreter is experienced in psychiatric interviews. It is helpful to have a preplanning interview with the interpreter to establish a trusting relationship, to allow the interpreter to raise questions about the case, and to discuss the best translation format. The therapist should clarify the expectations of the interpreter. Use simple sentences; it is difficult to translate sentences with several conditional clauses. Encourgage both the interpreter and the client to ask questions if the phrasing of a comment is unclear. Allow enough time to conduct the interview since an interview with an interpreter can take two to three times as long as usual. Instruct the interpreter to reassure the client of confidentiality.

2. Help family members set up measurable short-term goals. Treatment contracts should be in realistic, behavioral terms.

3. Focus on external stresses in the beginning stage of intervention and use crisis intervention techniques creatively. Demonstration of care with action instead of "just listening" is essential.

4. Directive, active, and structured participation in discussion during the initial stage of the relationship appears to be most effective.

5. Avoid extensive diagnostic evaluation. The ability to label a problem with confidence is important, as is the ability to provide authoritative guidance.

6. Clarify the treatment process and expectations with the client. The therapist's ability to raise the client's hope for change is also important.

7. Avoid constant direct eye contact, which may give the impression of a challenge or confrontation.

8. Be flexible with regard to office hours, length of interviews, and home visits (which are often very important in establishing rapport).

9. Use medical doctors and medications creatively.

10. Respect family secrets and confidentiality.

Special Issues in Psychopharmacology

Clinical reports from Asian countries and sporadic reports in the United States suggest that dosages based on Caucasian patient populations may not be readily applicable to Asian populations. Experience in mental health centers serving Asian populations in the United States has shown that Asian American patients generally need fewer medications for the same condition, whether depression, psychosis, or mania. Chinese clients are usually unfamiliar with Western medicines and their side effects. Detailed explanations and clarification of appropriate dosages are necessary. The mixing of Chinese and Western medicines is a concern to many therapists. It is advisable to get a detailed medication history from the client and to advise against the use of internal herbal medicines in conjunction with psychotropic or other drugs.

Service Setting

The service setting of mental health services is a major factor to consider in treating Chinese American families. Based on the cultural considerations, the following premises are assumed.

1. Bilingual providers with a good understanding of the distinctive ethnic value system and common life stresses of the client group's environment will make the best therapists.

2. It is important to have culturally relevant services available in the immediate community in areas with a high concentration of Chinese residents.

3. Local control and support by community-based policy and advisory boards with Chinese representatives are most likely to be of use.

4. It is helpful for mental health services to be located close to other service agencies.

5. Services need to be tailored to the needs of the clients (e.g., flexible hours and fees), since most Chinese immigrants work long hours and do not have third-party coverage for services.

Naturally the service organizations that have been found to be consistent with the needs of Chinese Americans are those providing mental health services in conjunction with primary health care, multiservice centers, and community mental health centers, particularly if they have a satellite to serve Chinese Americans.

Conclusion

In recent years there has been a growing need for effective treatment techniques for use with Asian Americans, who bring a particular set of cultural, linguistic, and economic circumstances to the therapeutic encounters. In this chapter variables related to effective treatment of Chinese American clients and their families were identified. Systematic assessment practices and therapeutic recommendations based on the social systems approach were provided in terms of the interplay of two major social systems: the client system and the treatment system. The emphasis has been on offering practical recommendations and guidelines to therapists in the field, with the goal of providing clinicians who may feel at some loss in their therapeutic encounters with Chinese families and with other Asian families, some concrete suggestions for therapeutic action.

REFERENCES

Bourne, P.G. Suicide among Chinese in San Francisco. *American Journal of Public Health,* *63*(8), 744–750, 1973.

Garfield, S.L., & Bergin, A. E. *Handbook of Psychotherapy and Behavior Change.* New York: Wiley, 1971.

Hsu, J., & Tseng, W. Family Relations in Classic Chinese Opera. *International Journal of Social Psychiatry, 20–21,* 159–172, 1974–1975.

Kim, B.L.C. *The Asian Americans: Changing Patterns, Changing Needs.* Urbana, Ill.: Association of Korean Christian Scholars in North America, 1978.

Klein, D.C. *Community Dynamics and Mental Health.* New York: Wiley, 1968.

Kleinman, A., & Lin, T.Y. (Eds.). *Normal and Deviant Behavior in Chinese Culture.* Hingham, Mass.: Reidel, 1981.

Lee, E., & Ja, D.Y. *Migration and the Asian Families: A Multi-Generational Perspective.* Paper presented at the Second Annual Symposium on Cross-Cultural and Trans-Cultural Issues in Family Health Care, University of California, San Francisco, March 1982.

Marsella, A.J., Kinzie, D., & Gordon, P. Ethnic Variations in the Expression of Depression. *Journal of Cross-Cultural Psychology, 4,* 535–568, 1973.

Morishima, J., Sue, S., Teng, L.N., Zane, N., & Cram, J. *Handbook of Asian American and Pacific Islanders Mental Health Research.* Rockville, Md.: National Institute of Mental Health, 1979.

President's Commission on Mental Health. *Report to the President* (Vol. III). Washington, D.C.: U.S. Government Printing Office, 1978.

Sue, S. Community Intervention: Implications for Action. In S. Sue & N. Wagner (Eds.), *Asian Americans: Psychological Perspectives.* Palo Alto, Calif.: Science & Behavior Books, 1973.

Sue, S. Psychological Theory and Implications for Asian-Americans. *Personnel and Guidance Journal, 55,* 381–389, 1977.

Sue, S., & Morishima, J. *Asian American Mental Health: Knowledge and Directions.* San Francisco: Jossey-Bass, in press.

Sue, S., & Sue, D.W. Chinese-American Personality and Mental Health. *Amerasia Journal, 1,* 36–48, 1971.

Sue, S., & Wagner, N.N. (Eds.). *Asian Americans: Psychological Perspectives.* Palo Alto, Calif.: Science & Behavior Books, 1973.

Task Panel Reports (submitted to the President's Commission on Mental Health). *Mental Health of Asian/Pacific Americans* (Vol. III). Washington, D.C.: U.S. Government Printing Office, 1978.

Wong, H.Z. Mental Health Services to Asian and Pacific Americans. In L. Snowden (Ed.), *Services to the Underserved.* Los Angeles: Sage Annual Reviews of Community Mental Health, 1982.

Yap, P.M. Hypereridism and Attempted Suicide in Chinese. *Journal of Nervous and Mental Disease, 127,* 34–41, 1958.

26

Therapy with Families in Cultural Transition

JUDITH LANDAU

> The great aim of culture [is] the aim of setting ourselves to ascertain what perfection is and to make it prevail.
>
> —Matthew Arnold

Change is a natural phenomenon affecting the physical properties, geography, and inhabitants of our world. Perhaps it is in response to the potential threat implicit in this exciting challenge that so many people through the ages have clung to the safety of the traditions and norms created by their own group rather than risk the insecurity of the unknown. As the face of our world has altered, however, so has there been an inexorable transition of its peoples, some of whom have been transformed by forces far beyond their control.

The period of time through which change occurs is perhaps the most crucial factor affecting adaptation. Where change occurs over many generations, the adjustment may be scarcely noticeable and may, in fact, be too gradual to be seen in the space of one lifetime, as in the case of rural Africa (Landau & Griffiths, 1981). All the families discussed in the other chapters of this book, by contrast, have faced the stress of rapid industrialization and urbanization with accompanying attitudinal changes, mass media, alteration in dependency patterns, gender role confusion, and increasing occupational demands. They have, in addition, been precipitated into new and different cultures within the space of one or two generations.

Therapists are well aware of the need to understand the life cycle factors involved in treating adolescent problems, the mourning process, the empty nest, and other intrafamilial changes (Carter & McGoldrick, 1980). An understanding of the relevance of the broader transitional issues and the position of the family system in its community is also necessary. The author and colleagues have worked intimately and at length with many diverse

Judith Landau. Formerly of the Department of Psychiatry, University of Natal, Natal, South Africa, and the Faculty of Health Sciences, University of Durban–Westville, Westville, South Africa. Present address: Philadelphia Child Guidance Clinic Training Center, and private practice, Philadelphia, Pennsylvania.

cultural groups coexisting within the same environment. To our surprise, we eventually began to notice that for all groups, the problems and clinical patterns originating in exposure and adjustment to a new culture differed only in cultural form and presentation. It became apparent that it was necessary to consider the specific stress of migration, the reactions and family patterns arising as a result of it, and possible techniques and modes of therapy to aid in its resolution.

Migration may involve many families from a particular country, region, or culture, or it may be an isolated experience for a single family; more frequently it falls between the two extremes (Sluzki, 1979). The resources needed for handling the transition process are obviously vastly different in each case. It is, therefore, useful to ascertain the transitional history of the migrant group before drawing conclusions as to the stresses affecting any individual family. A working knowledge of the group's developmental history and social and cultural norms will diminish the risk of misinterpretation of the family process.

Cultural Transition

"Culture may be defined as the system of social institutions, ideologies, and values that characterize a particular social domain in its adaptation to the environment. It is also implicit in the concept that these traditions and beliefs are systematically transmitted to succeeding generations" (Hamburg, 1975, p. 387). The rapidity of change in our modern world—and more specifically the threat of cultural migration—commonly leads to an increased intensity of cultural emphasis in a threatened group. It has frequently been surmised that the enormous cultural strength and constancy of the Jews and Poles was based on their being forced to return to the security of their traditional culture when dangers threatened their group existence.

The threat to the group varies greatly according to the pattern of cultural transition. Where the migration is within the same country, the change may be limited to loss of family support systems and alteration of the level of urbanization. Where, on the other hand, a new country is chosen, there may be the question of an entirely new value system and language in addition to the above factors. When outside influences are responsible for altering an existing culture within the home country, there is more likely to be a certain amount of group and family support as the changes impinge on the community as a whole (Landau, 1982).

Factors Affecting Cultural Transition

Several such factors are important, as follows.

Reasons for Migration and Realization of Goals

Migration occurs for diverse reasons, and the adjustment of the family depends on the extent to which its original expectations of the migration compare with its reality.

Availability of Support Systems: Community; Family of Origin

The support systems in the community play an important role in determining the facility with which each family resolves transitional issues. If other families in the social group are at a similar stage of transition, the problems are more likely to be satisfactorily resolved. The attitude of the family of origin and its health and resources are also major determinants in the system's adaptation.

The Structure of the Family

The structure of the family is an important factor in its adaptation to its new environment. The natural development of the family as a sociological unit follows a pattern from extended to nuclear family and from nuclear to newly emergent family forms beyond the nuclear family (Landau & Griffiths, 1981). Migration moves the family along this pathway at a more precipitate rate than factors such as urbanization and industrialization. An individual, or a small nuclear unit moving away from a close traditional extended family into a new culture where nuclear independence is expected, is likely to feel severely threatened. There is a sudden lack of extended family support at a time when it is most needed. The new isolated unit is also, for the first time, responsible for making and maintaining its own set of rules, which, in view of the new situation and its strange demands, needs to be different from those previously maintained and administered by the hierarchy of the extended family (Landau, Griffiths, & Mason, 1981).

Degree of Harmony between Cultures

The relative stress of migration is in part determined both by the country and culture of origin and by the country and culture of adoption. A decision to emigrate from the Far East is likely to be taken by an entire nuclear family, frequently accompanied by one or more members of the extended family. A man from the Western world, by contrast, is far more likely to move alone, followed at most by his immediate family if he has acquired one or, if a bachelor, creating a nuclear family in his country of adoption. An immigrant from the Middle East may choose either of these alternatives but, if emigrating alone, often retains far closer links with his family and country of origin than his Western counterpart.

A Hindu family leaving India in search of better opportunities in the United States or Great Britain will experience the forces of transition from the security of a close traditional extended family to the isolation of a nuclear family. It will also be confronted by the totally foreign values of a country with vastly different culture, language, religion, and life-style.

In contrast, the young Anglo-Saxon bachelor emigrating from Great Britain to Australia or South Africa may have minor difficulty in finding a group with whom he can identify. His problems with language relate to accent only; his religion is no hindrance to the adjustment process; and his family of origin is more likely to accept his decision without question or threat of permanent mourning. His facilities for revisiting Great Britain are great, and the stress of cultural migration slight.

When, however, a young Greek or Portuguese decides to leave his homeland in search of financial improvement and educational opportunities for his children, the bereavement is intense. He may well decide to emigrate alone, send for his wife and children when possible, and spend the rest of his life in sad exile supporting both his family in the homeland and his nuclear family in the country of adoption. He may face both his own difficulties in the process of adaptation and the misery of lack of acceptance by the citizens of his new home.

Incorporation of Transition as a Developmental Stage: Health of System versus Dysfunction

Severe crises frequently result from the lack of resolution of transitional issues. The family's healthy adaptation to transitions may be viewed as a successful negotiation of a developmental stage of the family's growth in society, and unresolved transitional conflict may be regarded as leading to dysfunction in the same sense that the unresolved stages of family life cycle may result in dysfunction of the system.

Changes Associated with Cultural Transition

The visible markers of a family's ethnic background are its language, religion, education, and life-style. A family in cultural transition often must confront change in all of these areas, as is apparent throughout the preceding chapters.

Typical Problems Associated with Cultural Transition

Where the stresses are extreme and the support systems and health of the family insufficient, the family may become isolated, enmeshed, or disengaged. When family members adjust at different rates, the system is severely stressed and transitional conflict may occur.

Isolation

Isolation is a paramount risk of the migrant family. Fear of the new situation and a longing for the safe and familiar may cause the family to remain separate from its new environment. The differences of language, education, religion, and life-style accentuate the difficulties of adjustment, and, where a large extended family has been left behind, the stress of isolation may lead to severe problems of acculturation. Isolation may also result from the strangeness of the new family and its exclusion by the well-established cultural groups in the adopted country.

Enmeshment

The threat of the new culture, fear that the family's youth will be lost to it, and the family's unacceptability in its new environment may lead the system to close its boundaries to the outside world. The family that continues to impose strict traditional values on its members and retains its religion and language is forced to strengthen family bonds in an attempt to cope with the unprecedented stress confronting it. If problems arise, the family is not in a position to make use of the helping facilities of its new community, nor is it able to adapt to new demands. Under stress the family closes ranks and becomes progressively more enmeshed.

Disengagement

In certain instances, individuals in the family become isolated as they no longer accept the family's values and life-style. This leaves them very vulnerable in their new environment. In other cases, the whole family is immobilized, which precipitates the loosening of boundaries to the point of disengagement and ultimate vulnerability of all its members.

Transitional Conflict: Differential Rates of Adjustment of Family Members

The most significant transitional stress occurs when a family member or several members move more rapidly than the others along the transitional pathway. They adapt to the new environment while others remain resistant to the process of change and struggle to retain the traditional culture at all costs. The resultant conflict of direction precipitates severe problems within the family system. *Recognition of transitional conflict is the key to helping families in cultural transition.* For example, severe sibling rivalry may on careful assessment be found to be based on adaptation conflicts. When one spouse is an immigrant or has immigrant parents, the presentation of marital difficulties may signal adaptational stress. The attitudes of an immigrant grandparent may be in serious conflict with those of an adolescent grand-child who presents with behavior disturbance or drug addiction. The re-sultant conflict may precipitate severe problems within the family. Such transitional conflict is rarely presented directly, and very thorough investiga-tive methods must be employed.

> As an example, Andreas Papadopoulos,[1,2] aged 12, experienced severe schooling difficulties, and the family was referred for therapy. At the initial home visit it was apparent that his parents and maternal grandparents were rigidly traditional, as were his three older sisters. His brother, 18-year-old Philotheos, however, spoke excellent English and had made a reasonable adjustment to the new way of life, except that he and his parents argued continually. Mr. and Mrs. Papadopoulos, threatened by the potential loss of their older son, had responded by attempting to close the family's bounda-ries by refusing to allow friends to visit the house as they were bitterly opposed to outside influences. They rigidly enforced Greek tradition and religion.
>
> Young Andreas was caught in an impossible bind. In order to please his parents he had to achieve well at school, but to do this he had to adapt to the new culture and make friends with his peers, thereby risking aliena-tion from his parents. He had to choose between conflict with his grand-parents, parents, and sisters, or with his much admired older brother and peers. Each member of the family was caught in the transitional conflict of the system.

Therapeutic Techniques with Families in Cultural Transition

The range of cultures confronting the family therapist is vast, and the challenge of acquiring a working knowledge of each group's developmental history and norms is overwhelming. An attempt by any therapist to under-stand the values, traditions, and language of all immigrant groups, though ideal, is far from practical. Consequently, the therapist may be aided by conceptual schemata and operational principles that allow him or her to be as effective as possible across diverse circumstances, given limited knowledge. In the remainder of this chapter a model for interventions of this kind will be presented.

The members of the Milan group (Selvini-Palazzoli, Boscolo, Cecchin, and Prata) have devised a form of therapy that they believe cuts across cultural differences through recognition of elements universal to family systems (Cecchin, 1980). Andolfi (1979), too, has a technique of using a common language as a therapeutic tool. In our management of families in cultural transition, the emphasis is on the assessment of the relevant migration

1. All the names of actual families described in this chapter have been changed to maintain confidentiality.

2. The author was the therapist in all the cases presented in this chapter.

and acculturation stress and the presence of typical transition problems as described above. If we approach and analyze the family system in its larger social context, we obtain a leverage that can then be used to effect change. The therapeutic methods used were developed more or less independently. However, the techniques, principles, and thinking often include what we later learned were structural, strategic, provocative, and experiential features (Landau, in press).

Analysis of the System

In a society composed of many different immigrant groups, it is valuable to establish at the outset whether transitional issues are relevant to current difficulties. It is obviously essential to *establish whether transition is in progress and whether transitional factors are relevant to the problems presented to the therapist.* Not all immigrant families are in need of therapy, and the therapist must take care not to overinterpret the cultural phenomena present. Many families negotiate the acculturation process with minimal difficulty if the factors affecting adaptation are favorable. On the other hand, *many families experience differential rates of transition among their subsystems, inevitably leading to transitional conflict. In the latter, therapy is usually indicated.*

The transitional techniques outlined below—transitional mapping, link therapy, and dual sculpting—may be used either as the total focus of therapy or as part of an overall therapeutic plan. Further elucidation of these techniques will be found in Landau (in press). They are used for both diagnostic and therapeutic purposes. In treating families and systems the distinction between diagnosis and treatment is blurred. Any intervention has diagnostic value as the therapist observes the response to it. Any diagnostic action, by its nature, conveys a message from therapist to family and is therefore an intervention (Haley, 1970).

Transitional Mapping

Mapping has become a relatively standard practice in both individual and family therapy and is extremely useful in the assessment of cultural transition. Sluzki (1979), working with migrant families, states categorically that "in the course of the first interview, the therapist should establish which phase of the process of migration the family is currently in and how they have dealt with the vicissitudes of previous phases" (p. 389). *A comprehensive map should extend beyond that of the individual's and family's life cycle to include the transitional position of the multigenerational family in society.* This differential map should include the position of each individual and the family as a whole in life cycle stages, cultural origin, family form, and current status relative to other family members and the community. An example of a family transitional map is given in Figure 26.1, and a fuller explanation of the technique appears in Landau (in press). The role of factors aiding or hindering adaptation should be considered, as should the rates of adaptation of family members and the system as a whole. *Whenever differential rates of adaptation are found, the influence of transitional conflict may be presumed and appropriate therapy instituted.*

> Mrs. C, aged 29, was referred by her general practitioner for treatment of a severe depression. The family map elicited from Mr. and Mrs. C and their 10-year-old son, Reno, at the initial family interview revealed that the family move had been instigated by Mr. C, who had persuaded his wife that there was more opportunity for motor mechanics in South Africa than in Italy. He had adapted extremely well to the move and was anxious for his wife to become more independent both of him and of her own family.
>
> Mrs. C's family of origin was a traditional one, of close extended patriarchal structure. Mrs. C's emigration was the first rupture in her family's stable pattern. The general practitioner had noticed that Mrs. C was most depressed when her mother from Italy visited her in South Africa and when Mrs. C visited Italy. Her parents' response to her depression had been an immediate invitation for the young family to return home.
>
> During the initial interview there were signs of marital conflict. Further evidence of dysfunction in the system was the recent change in Reno. His marks at school had deteriorated, and he had lost interest in sporting activities. His position on the map had changed; where previously he had been adjusting well to his new environment he was now spending more and more time with his parents, not speaking English to his father unless ordered to do so, and spending almost none of his leisure time with his peers. Mrs. C's only social contacts were at the Italian Club. The family was becoming progressively more enmeshed.

The mapping showed that Mrs. C was trying, unsuccessfully, to negotiate both separation from her traditional extended family and acculturation, while Mr. C had successfully negotiated the transition already. Reno, too, was caught in the system's transitional conflict, which had caused decompensation at multiple levels.

Link Therapy

A number of the families discussed in the chapters of this book have moved from close traditional extended families into new situations where nuclear independence is either expected or made inevitable by geographic isolation.

When some members acculturate more rapidly than others, transitional conflict develops. There are two therapeutic dilemmas: (1) whether an attempt should be made to reverse the direction of transition or whether the extended family should be pressurized into accepting the inevitability of the transition;

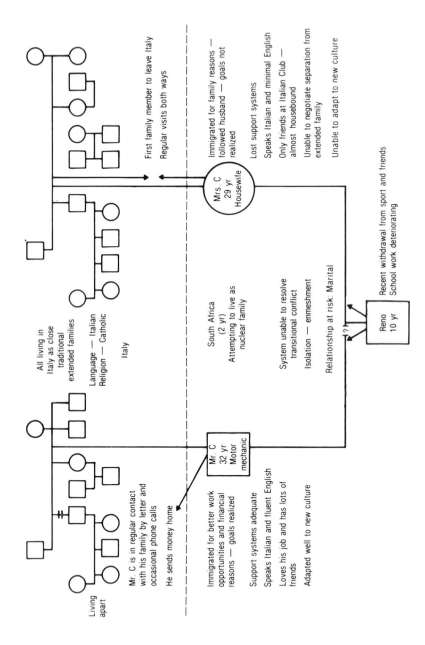

All living in
Italy as close
traditional
extended families

Language — Italian
Religion — Catholic

Italy

First family member to leave Italy

Regular visits both ways

Mrs. C
29 yr
Housewife

Immigrated for family reasons —
followed husband — goals not
realized

Lost support systems

Speaks Italian and minimal English

Only friends at Italian Club —
almost housebound

Unable to negotiate separation from
extended family

Unable to adapt to new culture

Living
apart

Mr. C is in regular contact
with his family by letter and
occasional phone calls

He sends money home

Mr. C
32 yr
Motor
mechanic

Immigrated for better work
opportunities and financial
reasons — goals realized

Support systems adequate

Speaks Italian and fluent English

Loves his job and has lots of
friends

Adapted well to new culture

South Africa
(2 yr)
Attempting to live as
nuclear family

System unable to resolve
transitional conflict

Isolation — enmeshment

Relationship at risk: Marital

Reno
10 yr

Recent withdrawal from sport and friends

School work deteriorating

FIG. 26.1. C family transitional map.

(2) whether the therapist should take control of the family's direction or allow the family to determine its own direction.

Traditional extended families resolve their own emotional difficulties by traditional prescription within the family boundaries and without recourse to outside agencies (Landau & Griffiths, 1981). A decision to work with the more traditional members of the system, therefore, would imply acceptance of their set of values and would lead ultimately to abdication of the therapist. Conversely, a decision to work with the most acculturated member would indicate acceptance of the new set of values. The choice of which family members to involve in therapy can, therefore, artificially determine the transitional direction taken by the family. It is thus necessary to establish methods of selection that will avoid artificial momentum but that will enable the family to resolve the transitional conflict, thereby facilitating further growth and development.

In our initial work we tried network therapy as devised by Ross V. Speck in the mid-1960s (Speck & Attneave, 1974). We found, however, that it frequently failed in the face of resistance from the rigid hierarchical members of the extended family. An additional problem in working with these families was that many of them came from the lower income group and could not afford therapy. There was, therefore, a real need to use brief, strategic intervention wherever possible.

It became apparent to us that a single family member could be used to provide the *link* between the family therapist and the rigid structure of the extended family since extended families generally deny the therapist adequate entry (Landau, 1981). This method allows us to avoid the issue of defining therapy as "family therapy," in that the whole family does not have to be present at one time. For example, many Greek, Indian, African, and Iranian families cannot tolerate discussion between parents in the presence of their children in the typical mode of conventional family therapy. By using link therapy families who would not otherwise become involved in therapy may be treated. It is also an expedient form of therapy, using only one therapist and, for the greater part of the therapy, only one family member.

Link therapy involves the *training and coaching of a family member to function as a therapist to his or her own family system* (Landau, 1981, in press). After initial family assessment, this family member (link therapist) is selected and goes back alone into the family to initiate interventions with the continued guidance and supervision of the family therapist. The link therapist is coached to assist the family in resolving its transitional conflict in a direction of the link therapist's choice.

SELECTION OF THE LINK THERAPIST

The link therapist needs to be both acceptable to and effective with the family, as well as available and amenable to the family therapist. In a patriarchal system the most effective link would obviously be a man of some seniority, such as an uncle or older son.[3]

The therapist should avoid the temptation to select the most acculturated member of the family whose life-style and values most closely approach the therapist's. Selection of either the most traditional or the most acculturated member would give artificial momentum to the direction of resolution of the transitional conflict.

The person seeking therapy is usually either an acculturated member or an entrenched traditional member. In each case the motivation is clear, and agreement to work with either would predetermine the transitional direction taken. Instead, we have found that the most effective link therapist is a family member whose position has not yet been resolved, one who, caught in the system's transitional conflict, is himself in the process of cultural transition. He is generally not the complainant and may even be a peripheral member of the family.

NEGOTIATION AND LOGISTICS OF THE CONTRACT

The initial negotiation occurs during the first consultation or home visit when the link therapist is selected. The therapist explains to the family that there seem to be many difficulties because family members appear to want the family to go in different directions. Some members may want only the traditional language spoken, while others choose only the new one; some may want to live in nuclear units, while others are trying to keep the extended family together. The areas of conflict are simplified in order to illustrate the directional discrepancy to the family.

The link therapist is invited to attend an appointment with the family therapist in order to talk about what is happening in his family and to determine whether the therapist might be able to assist him in helping the family to sort out its difficulties. It is usually a great relief to the link therapist to feel that he is regarded as competent, an aspect that is stressed during the initial invitation.

Arrangements for payment are worked out by having the link therapist ask his family, "How shall we pay for this?" Allowing him to negotiate the issue with his family is further confirmation of his competence. In private practice fees may be covered by medical insurance. Where the family does not fall into this category, the link therapist decides how the clinic fee (usually nominal) will be met.

During the first link session a contract is negotiated for the link therapist to attend four to six sessions with the family therapist over a period of six to eight weeks. Preceding each appointment with the family therapist, the link therapist is encouraged to conduct a weekly session, of at least one or two

---

3. The link therapist is hereafter referred to by male pronouns, as a man is usually selected for this role.

hours, in the extended family's home. Arrangements are also made for a family interview three to six months later.

COACHING OF THE LINK THERAPIST

Coaching commences during the first session with the link therapist. The object of coaching is to supervise the link therapist's work with the family. He needs to be encouraged to decide the direction of resolution of the family's transitional conflict. For him to do this he needs to feel that he is invested with sufficient authority to create change. There is an ambivalent message implicit in this that needs to be reconciled before work can commence.

The coach must work out how to supervise while investing the link therapist with confidence and authority. We have found that the most effective method is to take the one down position, using a lot of gentle humor to make the process enjoyable and to diminish the therapist's authority. Positive encouragement and reframing are used liberally in order to elevate the link therapist. Discussion and supervision are kept as simple and clear as possible.

The following extracts from first and second link sessions are taken from a case discussed in an earlier paper (Landau, 1981).

> The link therapist, Ganesh, aged 22, was the third son of a multiproblem traditional Indian family that had been referred to the university clinic by the local social welfare agency. Ganesh and his wife moved regularly out of the family home and back again, but they had never come for therapy themselves. Ganesh had not been present at the initial family interview and appeared not to be too stuck in the family system.
>
> THERAPIST: What have the problems been in the family?
>
> GANESH: I've had no problems.
>
> THERAPIST: This is the main reason I wanted to meet you. It seems that the rest of the family has had much difficulty and that you hadn't, so I thought maybe you would be prepared to help me help the other members of the family. How would you feel about doing that?
>
> GANESH: Okay.
>
> Ganesh then discussed his feelings about being the brother with the greatest strength and the one best able to control his wife. However, he sounded daunted by the magnitude of the family's problems.
>
> GANESH: Too many problems, too many! It's difficult to stay calm because everyone shouts and swears and there is too much corruption because of my mother letting the girls do just what they want.
>
> THERAPIST: Who is the boss of the house?
>
> GANESH: The head of the house is my father.
>
> THERAPIST: And does he manage?
>
> GANESH: I don't think so.
>
> THERAPIST: Can your father tell your mother what to do?

GANESH: No, she never listens. (*Chuckles.*)

THERAPIST: How would you like to change things in the family?

GANESH: Married ones should live separately.

Ganesh then outlined his ideas of how he would like the family to progress to a point where there was looser bonding of the extended and nuclear units (the constellation most frequently found en route to nuclearization).

THERAPIST: How can we best help the rest of the family?

GANESH: We have regular meetings and discuss like now and I go back to them and help my father stop the women from winning all the time.

At the second link interview two weeks later Ganesh explained:

GANESH: I spoke to my father and saw that it wouldn't work so I called my uncle down and we chatted. I told him of all the carrying on at home and of the corruption. He has a lot of strength and he said that he would help me run the house the right way.

THERAPIST: How are you going to tell the rest of the family?

GANESH: My uncle told them and my father is very glad because my mother will listen to him.

THERAPIST: Do you think that things in the family will work out?

GANESH: Of course. My uncle gave them all lectures about how to behave, especially the girls. My mother is scared of my uncle, and she was silent as soon as he came. She listened to every word.

THERAPIST: So you are happy about things now?

GANESH: Yes, things are coming straight now.

To the therapist's amazement, Ganesh had elected to call in a traditional authority figure to reestablish the hierarchy of the extended family. Ganesh canceled all further link meetings, and at a follow-up home visit three months later the therapist was told that there were no further problems. It was difficult to believe that there was no further dysfunction of the system. What was evident, however, was that the return of the family to its traditional extended form prevented the necessity for outside intervention, as problems were once more resolved according to strict traditional prescription within the boundaries of the family system.

The course of therapy was very different in the case of the Casalviere family.

The Casalviere family had been referred for therapy because 10-year-old Fabrizio was behaving very badly at school. He was "untidy, rude, and constantly getting into fights." His father had given the teachers permission to discipline the boy as was necessary, but they were not able to achieve much change in his behavior.

At the initial family interview it was discovered that Luigi Casalviere, an engineer, aged 36, and his wife, Tiziana, a housewife, aged 34, had immigrated to South Africa with their children (Felice, 14; Fabrizio, 10; and Fabbiola, 8) five years previously. Luigi's parents remained in Italy but

Tiziana's parents, Mr. and Mrs. Girone, had joined the family in South Africa 11 months before the referral. The additional member of the household was Luigi's brother, Aldo, a 30-year-old bachelor who had arrived shortly after his brother.

The interview was very strained, with Mr. Girone keeping tight control of all that was said. He kept reiterating that "everything's fine in this house," and made the therapist feel like an unwelcome intruder. Aldo was very polite and obviously intent on not upsetting Mr. Girone. Luigi, on the other hand, made some hard comments about his son, Fabrizio, and seemed less awed by the situation.

Luigi had apparently made a large circle of friends, which he shared with Aldo and with whom he was spending increasing amounts of time away from home. His job was going well, and he couldn't see that there were any problems apart from his son. Tiziana was relatively silent but looked especially unhappy when Luigi's friends were discussed. She also remarked that the children were forgetting both their Italian and their religion—and their respect for their grandparents. The latter was stated with an accusing look at her husband. It was evident that the traditional members of the family would sabotage therapy, if given the chance, so the link technique was selected.

Aldo was the most suitable link therapist; he was acceptable to the traditional members of the family, was ready to work with the therapist, and was in the process of making decisions about his transitional position. The family agreed, rather reluctantly, to allow him to attend the first link session one week later, "if something can really be done about Fabrizio."

During the first session Aldo expressed his doubts about carrying any weight with Mr. and Mrs. Girone, but he felt competent to talk to the younger members of the family.

ALDO: The kids are good kids, they listen to their uncle most of the time and my brother—well he's okay. But her parents—everything old is good; they don't want to hear.

THERAPIST: I don't know. They seemed pretty fond of you when I saw you all together.

ALDO: Mmm.

The therapist encouraged him to look at how well he got on with the old people, how they shared a sense of humor, and how they all lost patience with Luigi at times. Aldo gradually became aware that he might have some ability to guide their opinions, certainly far more than the therapist—who shared a good laugh with him about that!

Aldo felt that the solution to the family's confusion and conflict was for everybody to learn English better, "but not forget to speak Italian ever," and for Luigi to "make more fuss of Tiziana and take her out more with his friends—she doesn't know them and makes a big noise all the time. If they go out more she won't be hearing her mother all the time and then she won't give Luigi such a hard time." He also felt that the children should spend more time with their schoolmates and be more involved in sports.

Aldo undertook to spend at least two hours a week discussing the plans with the family. With some gentle guidance he agreed that he should work with Tiziana and her parents before "interfering" in this brother's marriage. He decided to encourage Mr. and Mrs. Girone to get out of the house more and planned to take them to the Italian Club.

At the fifth link session, seven weeks after the first consultation, Aldo reported that the situation at home had improved considerably. Tiziana was even speaking English to the children on occasion, and Aldo felt that she was not so much under her father's control. Aldo still felt that Luigi ought to take his wife out more and that they were not getting along well enough. He felt, however, that he would like to continue working without the therapist's supervision, and an arrangement was made for a family meeting three months later. The therapist felt that if resolution of the cultural transition conflict continued and there were still problems in Luigi's marriage, conventional marital therapy could be considered.

The second family consultation was markedly different from the first. Mr. Girone allowed Aldo to say almost as much as he himself, and there appeared to be far less tension (possibly because the therapist was no longer a total stranger). The most significant change was Tiziana's bright appearance and her active participation in the session. Aldo felt that no further help was required at that stage, but he promised to contact the therapist if he felt it was needed in the future.

The school reported a noticeable change for the better in Fabrizio's behavior, and the principal agreed to contact the therapist if there were any further problems. At telephone follow-up six months later the principal stated that all the children were doing fine and that there had been no further difficulties.

The link therapists in transitional families generally elect to move the family along the natural direction of cultural transition, but this is not inevitable. Some choose to return the family to its traditional form as did Ganesh. *Where this occurs, resolution of conflict tends to be temporary and is superseded by further crises of cultural transition until the natural direction is pursued (Landau, 1981).* When the natural direction is followed, as in the case of the Casalviere family, successful resolution of problems is far more likely to result.

Link therapy may be used in any situation of cultural transition where access to the family as a whole is not appropriate. It may be used for a child who presents with problems at school, for adolescent difficulties within a family, or for any instance of cultural transgenerational conflict. In one family where the traditional family members remained in Germany, the son-in-law was sent to do the link work on an intensive basis. He achieved satisfactory resolution of the directional conflict, and the South African part of the family system improved.

We might wonder how this approach differs from that developed by Bowen (1978). The two approaches are similar in that they both employ the coaching of one person and both relate to the total family system. One difference is that the Bowen method emphasizes the dynamics within the multigenerational family system, while the link approach stresses a broader system involving both the multigenerational family and its socioanthropological context. The major distinction, however, is that the Bowen approach aims at differentiating the individual from his family system, whereas the link therapy technique is more problem focused and trains a family member to be the therapist to his own family system.

A further difference is that link therapy is a much more concentrated paradigm, aimed at rapid resolution and change over a brief period of time. A Bowen therapist might meet for sessions monthly or even yearly, whereas the link model usually involves four to six sessions over a period of six to eight weeks, with a follow-up session three to six months later.

Dual Sculpting

The technique of dual sculpting was developed for use in families where members in transitional conflict are amenable to and available for therapy. Where the families of the two sculptors are not amenable to or available for the session, as frequently happens in cases of severe cultural conflict, students, colleagues, or clinic staff may be used to simulate family members.

Dual sculpting has grown out of the original sculpting technique pioneered and developed by such therapists as Virginia Satir, David Kantor, Fred and Bunny Duhl, and Peggy Papp (Duhl, Kantor, & Duhl, 1973). Hoffman (1981) summarizes the use of sculpting as follows:

> To elicit major coalition formations and homeostatic sequences, so that old patterns can be perceived and played out differently. . . . It can also be used by members of a family in therapy as a geospatial metaphor for various aspects of a relationship system; closeness/distance; splits and alignments; the experience of being one up to one down in the reference to another. (p. 250)

Dual sculpting differs from other sculpting in that we use a sculptor from each of the two families (or the two parts of the family) in cultural conflict and assist them in negotiating a joining of the two. Recognition is given to the larger system of the family in its cultural community, and dual sculpting is therefore an invaluable tool for working with families in cultural transition.

In the case of a couple in marital therapy, each member of the couple would sculpt his and her family of origin. In the case of transgenerational conflict, a member from each generation would be invited to sculpt his or her view of the family. Where adolescent–parent conflict occurs, the adolescent would be one of the sculptors and the parent the other. Table 26.1 outlines the various steps.

In dual sculpting one of the two family members selected as sculptors chooses to sculpt first while the other watches. The sculpting may be either in

TABLE 26.1. The Procedure of Dual Sculpting: Sculptors A and B

1. A sculpts	True to life Then according to fantasy	B observes
2. B sculpts	True to life Then according to fantasy	A observes
3. A moves into B's sculpture	True to life Then according to A's fantasy	B observes
B moves into A's sculpture	True to life Then according to B's fantasy	A observes
4. A and B sculpt their own positions relative to each other		
5. A and B	*The dual sculpt* Reassemble original sculptures and negotiate joining of the two	
6. Debriefing		

tableau form (as though posed for a family photograph) or in action, according to the preference of the sculptor. The initial sculpting is nonverbal and as true to life as possible. Once the sculpture is complete the therapist suggests that the sculptor move into fantasy and alter the sculpture according to his or her own personal desires. The therapist as mentor encourages as much change as possible at this stage. When real family members are used, their reactions to both the original sculpture and the changes are gently discussed. The procedure is then reversed with the first sculptor becoming the observer while the previous observer sculpts his or her own family.

When both sculptors have completed realistic and fantasy sculptings, they are asked to reassemble their original sculptures. Each sculptor in turn is then asked to move into the other's sculpture in the position or role of the original sculptor to experience the feeling created by the other. After discussing their reactions, they are encouraged to make alterations with which they feel comfortable. Each then returns to his or her own sculpture to experience the changes brought about, and again their reactions are discussed. Each is usually able to go much further in fantasy in the other's sculpture than in his or her own, and a depth of experience and insight not found in individual sculpting results.

It is frequently useful at this stage to ask the two sculptors to sculpt, without words, their positions relative to each other. Brief discussions may follow this, but the positioning is nonverbal and opportunity for negotiation is not given at this stage.

The final stage of the actual dual sculpting is then started, with the sculptors being asked to negotiate the joining of their two original sculptures. They are given permission to exclude peripheral members of their families if this is appropriate. Often a great deal can be achieved during this final phase.

As the sculptors struggle to impose the transitional directions of their choice and become ultimately aware of the opposing forces, a profound level of insight is often achieved. Family members learn to accommodate and compromise and are also given the opportunity to be creative.

Because the technique of dual sculpting is a very powerful tool, attention must be paid to the debriefing period, which is critical. Participants are encouraged to discuss and share their experiences of the session. We have found it useful to have audiovisual recordings for this purpose. We have also found it necessary that the initial discussion about the sculpting experience occur during the same therapy session as the sculpting, although it naturally continues beyond this into subsequent therapy sessions.

> Eight-year-old Basil W was doing very badly at school, and his father was requested to call at the school. Mr. W, an accountant, aged 33, whose parents were Jewish immigrants from Central Europe, was alarmed to hear that Basil's behavior was intolerable to the teachers and pupils alike, that he was distractible during lessons, violent during breaks, and would have to be removed from the school if matters did not rapidly improve. The school counselor referred Basil and his parents to the family therapist.
>
> At the first family consultation, attended by Mr. and Mrs. W and their two sons, Basil and Julian (aged 3 months), it became evident that the family was on the point of dissolution. There had been underlying, scarcely suppressed, marital strife for many years, which had come to a head with the birth of Julian. Mr. W regarded his wife, a dedicated physiotherapist, aged 30, as far too independent, a hopeless cook (particularly when compared with his mother, whose main purpose in life was baking and cooking for the family), a careless mother, and an undemonstrative wife, who chose to share nothing of her life, verbal or practical, with her husband. Mrs. W, the daughter of Irish immigrants, felt that there were no further sacrifices she could make for her husband and his family. Despite her conversion to Judaism she had never felt accepted by her husband's family. She failed to understand his need for her to give up her job and could not bear his continual demands for public displays of affection and verbalization of every minor situation. It was evident to the therapist that Basil's behavioral disturbance was symptomatic of a stressed parental system and a decision was taken to commence work on the marriage.
>
> Since Basil's problems were the only topic of common interest currently shared by his parents, structural intervention seemed appropriate. However, on the transitional map the cultural conflict was readily apparent, and it was felt that this needed to be resolved before therapy could proceed further. The cultures of Mr. and Mrs. W's parents were very different, as were the needs of the couple, neither of whom seemed aware of the origins of their difficulties. As the therapist felt that the transitional conflict was primary to the problems that the family system was experiencing, a decision was made to use dual sculpting.
>
> Since neither of the families of Mr. or Mrs. W could be appropriately included in the therapy session, a group of family therapy trainees was invited to participate in the sculpting. The therapist chose to exclude the children from the session as the major business was between the parents.

Mr. W was invited to be the first sculptor. He was instructed, with as little use of language as possible, to select people from the group to represent the members of his three-generational family of origin. He was invited to arrange the members of his surrogate family as he saw them in relationship to each other, making use of space and movement wherever possible, but not speaking other than to inform the therapist of the identity of each member. Mr. W arranged his family in a busy domestic scene with his mother actively involved in food preparation in the kitchen, his father reading the newspaper, but observing the family's activities over the top of it from time to time, and he and his siblings comfortably arranged around the dining room table each busily involved in some separate activity but with intermittent marked interest in each other. His youngest sister moved repeatedly to the kitchen to participate in mother's activities.

The therapist then asked Mr. W to move into fantasy and to alter the family in any way he wanted, pretending that any change was feasible. Mr. W's only alteration of the scene was to ensure that his older brother took a greater interest in his writing, discussing it with him at regular intervals. Despite considerable encouragement from the therapist, he was unable to introduce further changes.

Mrs. W, when asked to experience her husband's family as he had arranged it, felt severely constricted and immediately moved both the paternal grandparents, who had been sitting quietly in what appeared to be the living room, away from the sculpture. She informed the therapist that they had both been deceased for a considerable time and decided that it was high time that they were truly buried, as she felt that their influence over the family was iniquitous. The paternal grandparents had died prior to her husband's birth. She further separated the children, moving the married members of the family away. Her last move was to seat her mother-in-law on a chair near her father-in-law.

When Mr. W was asked how he felt about his wife's fantasy he appeared delighted with the burial of his grandparents but found it extremely difficult to take the disruption of the sibling generation. He also enjoyed the proximity of his mother and father and expressed surprise that he had felt unable to institute the necessary change. Mrs. W was able by her fantasy to help Mr. W create changes that he would never have considered.

Mrs. W then proceeded to choose and arrange her own family members. The scene was one of amazing activity. Her father paced restlessly up and down, two of her brothers rushed in and out of the tableau with alarming speed, and her mother repeatedly turned toward her father in supplication and then away in despair. Her younger sister lay on the carpet apparently engrossed in a book, and Mrs. W sat at a table involved with her sewing.

When asked to move into fantasy, Mrs. W brought one brother back into the family and banished the other. She placed her father firmly in a chair with the newspaper and seated her mother nearby. She tried tentatively to make them touch but was unable to sustain the contact and returned her father's hand to his newspaper.

Mr. W, given free reign with his wife's family, reintroduced the missing brother and formed a cozy domestic scene with which Mrs. W felt extremely uncomfortable.

The couple was then asked to show the therapist, nonverbally, where they now were in relationship to each other. Not surprisingly, they placed themselves at opposite ends of the room and, despite Mrs. W's attempts to reach her husband, they remained distant from each other. The therapist realized that her hypothesis that the couple had never really negotiated a marriage was correct. She then requested that the couple, using words where necessary, attempt to negotiate the joining of their two families of origin. They each made vain attempts to introduce their fathers and gave up; they had more success with their mothers, and none at all in a joint arrangement of the family.

The situation was gently interpreted during the session, and the interpretation was continued in the debriefing process. Mr. and Mrs. W spent two more sessions working with the therapist through the video material. After considerable debate they decided they were prepared to put in the work necessary for continuation of the marriage and committed themselves to marital therapy, which was greatly facilitated by the experience of dual sculpting.

During the ensuing six months structural family therapy (Minuchin, 1974; Minuchin & Fishman, 1981) was employed, and the situation improved remarkably. Basil's behavior at school continued to settle and his marks became progressively better. The therapist considered using Mr. W as a link therapist with his family of origin, but this proved unnecessary as the family opened its ranks to accept Mrs. W once the marital situation had improved.

Summary

We have examined some of the specific effects of migration on the family system. It will be evident from the discussion in this chapter that the larger system of the family in its community must be considered and that a knowledge of culture, tradition, and ethnicity is vital in understanding families in cultural transition.

We have used case studies to illustrate the necessity for careful examination of families in order to locate their phase of cultural transition and the presence of conflict. Cultural conflict is usually most intense between parents who retain their traditional values and their children who move more quickly to the values of the new culture. It is all too easy for the therapist to presume that the new or dominant culture of a society must be right for everybody and that the nuclear family structure, or the therapist's own, is the only correct paradigm. Families should be allowed and encouraged to make their own choices, facilitated by the therapist where intervention is appropriate.

The key to treating families in cultural transition is to recognize that their problems arise because different family subsystems adapt at different rates. This notion underlines the framework presented here—a framework that cuts across many dimensions of family functioning, transcends ethnic boundaries, and provides a blueprint for systemic change. The particular therapeutic mode used—for example, link therapy, dual sculpting—is less important than adherence to this transitional paradigm. *Transitional therapy clarifies the differential rates of adaptation and facilitates the family's resolution of transitional conflict.*

ACKNOWLEDGMENTS

The author would like to express her sincere thanks to Mrs. J. Mason, Professor W. Wessels, and Mr. A. Gialerakis for their helpful comments on an earlier version of this chapter; to Dr. M. Duncan Stanton for his invaluable assistance throughout the preparation of the chapter; to Mrs. M. Cowan for her untiring effort; and to Mrs. C. Varley for her 11th-hour typing. A special note of appreciation is extended to Monica McGoldrick for her insightful and painstaking editorial contribution and to Kathy Milea for her helpful editorial recommendations.

REFERENCES

Andolfi, M. *Family Therapy, An Interactional Approach.* New York: Plenum, 1979.

Bowen, M. *Family Therapy in Clinical Practice.* New York: Jason Aronson, 1978.

Carter, E.A., & McGoldrick, M. (Eds.). *The Family Life Cycle.* New York: Gardner Press, 1980.

Cecchin, G. Personal communication, Toronto, Ontario, Canada, November 1980.

Duhl, F.J., Kantor, D., & Duhl, B.S. Learning, Space and Action in Family Therapy: A Primer of Sculpture. In D. Bloch (Ed.), *Techniques of Family Psychotherapy.* New York: Grune & Stratton, 1973.

Haley, J. Approaches to Family Therapy. *International Journal of Psychiatry, 9,* 223–242, 1970.

Hamburg, B.A. Social Change and the Problems of Youth. In S. Arieti (Ed.), *American Handbook of Psychiatry* (2nd ed.). New York: Basic Books, 1975.

Hoffman, L. *Foundations of Family Therapy.* New York: Basic Books, 1981.

Kaslow, F. (Ed.)., International Yearbook of Family Therapy. New York: Bruner/Mazel, 1982.

Landau, J. Link Therapy as a Family Therapy Technique for Transitional Extended Families. *Psychotherapeia, 7*(4), 382–390, 1981.

Landau, J. *The Family in Transition: Theory and Practice.* New York: Guilford Press, in press.

Landau, J., & Griffiths, J.A. The South African Family in Transition—Therapeutic and Training Implications. *Journal of Marital and Family Therapy, 7* (3), 339–344, 1981.

Landau, J., Griffiths, J. & Mason, J. The Extended Family in Transition, Clinical Implications. *Psychotherapeia, 7*(4), 370–381, 1981.

Minuchin, S. *Families and Family Therapy.* Cambridge: Harvard University Press, 1974.

Minuchin, S., & Fishman, H.C. *Family Therapy Techniques.* Cambridge: Harvard University Press, 1981.

Sluzki, C.E. Migration and Family Conflict. *Family Process, 18* (4), 379–390, 1979.

Speck, R.V., & Attneave, C.L. *Family Networks.* New York: Vintage Books, 1974.

About the Editors

Monica McGoldrick

I am a fourth-generation Irish American, although I would never have said so until a few years ago, because the question of ethnicity never occurred to me. I was born in Brooklyn, New York, in 1943, the second of three daughters. My father was a lawyer, politician, and teacher. My mother worked in public relations and, in later life, in the antique business. My grandfathers and great-grandfathers followed traditional Irish job patterns: policeman, government clerk, saloon keeper, political leader, and immigrant laborers. My grandmothers and great-grandmothers were housewives, except for one, who ran a boardinghouse after her husband died.

I grew up having more contact with family friends than with relatives. My family always had friends from many different backgrounds. Visits with relatives were, for the most part, rather perfunctory. I never thought of myself as ethnic. I did have a favorite grandaunt, who had a great affection for all things Irish and often told me stories about "the old days" and who had the very best of Irish good humor.

Until the age of 6 I lived in a mixed ethnic neighborhood in Brooklyn, from the ages 6 to 14 I lived in Bucks County, Pennsylvania, an area with a strong Quaker influence. When I was 14 we moved to Brooklyn Heights.

I was raised not only by my parents, but also by a Southern Black woman, Margaret Bush, who lived with my family from the time I was born until she died. Experiencing her traditions and values was my first exposure to cultural differences and had a profound effect on my development, although I could not articulate it at the time. Her Jamaican husband also lived with us at times.

The only distinctions I was aware of growing up were Black and White, Catholic and non-Catholic, and, after moving back to Brooklyn, Jewish and non-Jewish.

I began studying foreign languages (French and Latin) in high school. In college I studied Russian and German and lived with a family in Vienna during my junior year. I planned to work in international relations. In 1966, after receiving a Masters degree in Russian studies, I decided to switch fields, moving from Dostoevsky to Freud seeking more practical work than I could find in academia. I went into psychiatric social work, a field no one in my family, including myself, had ever heard of.

In 1968 I met my husband, who had emigrated from Greece at age 21. (Prophetically, I had had a Greek godfather, K.P. Tsolainos, who was a close friend of my father.) I began to study Greek and to visit my husband's family in Greece. Meeting my husband and his family was a great cultural lesson, I might better say shock. He did not play by the rules my family always obeyed, like "keeping up appearances," holding hostilities carefully in check, and never "making a scene."

A few years later, having become interested in Bowen systems theory and inspired by working with Phil Guerin, I became interested in my own relatives and my family background. In 1975 my family went to Ireland to celebrate my parents' 35th wedding anniversary. While there I managed to locate members of my mother's family of origin in Cork and my father's family in Donegal. Since that time I have made several return trips to Ireland, where I always have, in some unexplainable way, the overwhelming feeling of having come home and of being in touch with my whole family.

It was only after beginning to look into the issue of ethnicity and family therapy that I came to realize how Irish I still am, in spite of the fact that, apart from my physiognomy, I have hardly any of the obvious trappings. Studying the ethnic patterns of different groups, I became aware that I had been very myopic, thinking everyone else experienced the world as I did—not realizing how many of my attitudes were determined not just by my family, but by a much broader context with a long and rich history in common. Certain of the characteristics I was very happy to recognize: the gift of gab, the humor, the strength of women, the tendency to see the glass as half-full rather than half-empty. Other characteristics I found much harder to deal with: the righteousness, the moralistic rigidity of thought, prudishness, the difficulty dealing directly with strong emotions, except with a moral and just cause (when I love a good fight!).

I struggle with these qualities when I recognize myself in my clients. I still struggle with the embarrassment of my Irish families in therapy, understanding very well how they feel, and yet wishing they could let go. I also struggle with my Italian families, who express their feelings so openly, I am still surprised the sky does not fall. And, I am still mystified by my Jewish patients' enjoyment in sharing their suffering and concern that their child only got a B+. My WASP Brahmin families, with their propriety, love of moderation, and belief in their entitlement, take me back to some historical reactivity that has somehow filtered down.

I have come to a completely different attitude toward my relatives, with whom I sense I share a lot, even with those I meet for the first time, and I feel rooted in our commonality, which once I experienced as awkward distance at best. I have gotten in on something very powerful that I had lost without knowing it.

John K. Pearce

I am from Seattle, a West Coast WASP. Both sides of my family are descended from Scotch Irish and German pre-Revolutionary War immigrants. My mother's family, the Goses, were German Protestants who left Germany to avoid military conscription. They came to Virginia and gradually moved west, with the expanding frontier, to Kentucky. My grandfather Gose traveled all the way west during the 1849 California Gold Rush. He mined dirt, growing vegetables for the hungry miners. With the stake made in California he took his family over the Great Plains and the Rocky Mountains to the Northwest. They traveled in a covered wagon on the Oregon Trail to Walla Walla, Washington, the biggest town in the Northwest Territory. His sons became pioneer lawyers, and our extended family has since continued in the practice of law in Walla Walla and Seattle.

My father's parents arrived later, after the transcontinental railroad had been built. They were from Crawford County, Illinois, where their families had for three generations been farmers and sometimes merchants. My grandparents lived in small logging towns, eventually settling down in Longview, Washington, where my grandmother Pearce ran the Cowlitz County Credit Bureau. She stayed at her business, working, until she was 88 years old. (She died at 91.)

It seemed to me that our family had been in the Northwest from the beginning. And, of course, as a child it seemed to me that the founding of the State of Washington (in the mid-19th century) was, for all practical purposes, the beginning of recorded time.

After graduating from the University of Washington with a degree in forestry, my father took a job in India, setting up logging operations and saw mills. He wrote home proposing marriage to my mother, who, adventurously, took a ship to India to live and have children in a drastically different world.

She enjoyed India tremendously. Having grown up in Walla Walla, a dusty wheat farming town, she had escaped to college in relatively cosmopolitan Seattle, and worked, for those times a pedological pioneer, as a physical education teacher in San Diego. She was not timid and embraced India with a pioneer's zeal. She especially liked the style of the English civil servants and admired the grandeur of the Indian princes. When they needed furniture they could borrow a maharaja's wood carver to build it (with the rosewood that my father had harvested from the rain forest). But in India, primitive living conditions, disease, and poor medical care (which resulted in the loss of their second child) finally led them, wisely, to go back home to Seattle.

India left its mark on my parents' style. When entertaining, my mother always served, with zeal, curry and rice and talked about the way that her production compared with that of her Indian cooks. My father interjected that in India only curry that brought tears to the eyes was considered authentic. During the course of those evenings, my mother gradually spoke with more and more of an English accent. They relished those times.

My older sister had been born in India, but my twin sister and I were born in Seattle after my parents had returned in 1934. Pam, the eldest child, could not remember India (she grew up speaking Hindustani) but we all were familiar with the exotic world of Asia, a world never seen but felt to be not far away—an impression heightened by the stream of Asian students that my father taught as a professor of forestry at the University of Washington.

India was a backdrop to our lives, and, I see now, the life my parents had in India was a powerful symbol of the riches that are to be found by moving on (the common denominator of pioneer experience) and accepting the taking of at least some risks as a usual part of life. Other values of our family were probably typical of Protestant (Congregational) Seattle: My mother emphasized that my sisters and myself should think for ourselves even if she did not much approve of what we thought. She expected rebellion but was also confident that in time we would return to liberal Protestantism and the Republican Party. She hoped and expected that we would have substantial positions within our community.

Unself-consciously, my mother told us what, for her, demonstrated the legitimacy and worth of her father's place in his community: When people, rich or poor, were in trouble, they came to her father, the lawyer, for help. Because this image of legitimacy was deeply held (and conflict free), I took it in and have lived it out myself as a psychiatrist.

In Seattle, everyone was supposed to be more or less the same. We were oblivious to ethnic difference and, to a considerable extent, social class. In fact, the ethnic diversity was tremendous—Scandinavian, WASP, Irish, Jewish, Oriental, and so on. But the shared conviction of Seattle in the 1940s and 1950s was that the melting pot would bring us all together and we would all grow to be much the same. Of course, it may be that, like all children, we thought egocentrically that the endproducts of this melting would be much like ourselves. I certainly supposed that everyone was headed the same way I was, toward a liberal Protestant life-style. Other values were almost invisible to me.

I went through public high school and then studied physics and mathematics at the University of Washington—only four blocks down the street from my house. I left physics (because I did not want to go into the weapons building business) and went off to Yale Medical School to study biophysics or, maybe, psychiatry, and ended up loving psychiatry. Actually, what I liked was not so much academic psychiatry but seeing people in the psychiatric outpatient clinic, where we were allowed to begin working as therapists in the first year.

My psychiatric residencies were at Yale, Austen Riggs Center in Stockbridge, and, finally, Beth Israel in Boston (for child psychiatry)—all psychoanalytically oriented programs. It seemed natural to me to then go on to study what was new and promising in psychiatry—group and family therapy. Furthermore, reaching out for the new was part of both the values of physics and the pioneering tradition of my family. It seemed incredible to me that my young colleagues would study and cling to what was old and established—it still does. The study of families was obviously the appropriate next step in the development of psychoanalytic psychiatry, and I found that I loved seeing families.

As a family therapist, I began being concerned with ethnicity when interviewing Irish American and other ethnic families at the Boston Veterans Administration Hospital. I had been trained at the Family Institute in New York (now the Ackerman Family Institute) to do family therapy with a clientele that was primarily Jewish and secondarily WASP. I recognized that I did not understand those VA families. For example, I was accustomed to parents who were anxious about the safety and achievement of their children. In contrast, Irish parents (at least some) were proud of their sons' heroic risk-taking. For example, one 14-year-old boy was stealing cars and racing them on Boston's most hazardous local expressway where his best friend had been killed in a similar escapade. The parents were proud of him. They were expressing, of course, the Irish fondness for near suicidal courage and, implicitly, the feeling, fatalistically, that death and God's mercy might be preferable to life.

Trying to understand these Irish families started me off on the study of ethnicity in general, which, because it must bring together the experience of many clinicians, is a cooperative enterprise. And, because it is a study of cultures that are always changing, it is endless.

Joseph Giordano

I am the grandson of an Italian immigrant laborer, the son of a steamfitter, the father of two sons, and was married to a dynamic Italian American, Puerto Rican woman for 20 years. In 1979 she died. Two years later I met Mary Ann, a loving, sensitive woman, who just happened to have seven children of her own. So we blended. But my roots start back 47 years ago.

I was born in the Red Hook section of Brooklyn, New York, an Italian neighborhood that was surrounded by a mosaic of different ethnic groups—Swedish, Norwegian, Irish, Puerto Rican, German, and Jewish. My own neighborhood was a network of families that provided many people with a sense of community and security. People helped each other. For example, when a family had a serious problem, the neighborhood went into action—the relatives, priests, local cops, and politicians were all sources of help.

While my family went through the many hardships and crises of most families, the thought of reaching outside was taboo. The use of public institutions was to be avoided and any involvement was to be viewed suspiciously. All was taken care of within the family and neighborhood. I remember my father telling me about the *padrones* and the family connections that existed in our close-knit community.

My father, the oldest of seven children, would not speak Italian at home. It was un-American to do so. My parents, two older brothers, who are also steamfitters, and my sister lived through the Depression and stood on a "bread line," a story I heard many times with little understanding of what it meant.

Mama worked for one week in a factory before she married my father, and this was always related to us as a humorous story. Her role was to cook, clean, and take care of the children; everyone knew that there was no question as to the need to work hard and to earn a living, no matter what the job. However, my family always had the hope of some day "making it rich." My sister who sang and danced was going to be a big star like Judy Garland, or so we all dreamed. I would sit with my parents at American Legion affairs and watch my father silently mouth the words as my sister sang "Somewhere over the Rainbow." The big dream never materialized, however, and life went on.

I remember being a member of a Brooklyn street gang during my teens. While the gang expressed "antisocial behavior" in fighting with other gangs, the cohesion of the group, the loyalty of its members, and the feelings of security and protection became very much part of my own way of relating to people.

Although scholastic achievement was not highly valued by my parents, my father wanted me to be an engineer like his bosses, who drove "Caddies" and paid off people for special privileges. But that was not my interest, and, after a "bumpy road" through high school and college, I decided to enter graduate school. When my father learned that I planned to become a social worker his disappointment was expressed by asking, "Why do you want to give handouts to bums on the corner?"

During the period between my adolescence and completion of graduate school, I became socialized and homogenized into an entirely new set of values. Traces of old neighborhood ties entered into my initial decision to become a street gang worker. But inbetween my first and second years of graduate school the final disengagement occurred. I decided to work in what was called in those days a "special setting (family agency)" rather than in a community center. Later, I went into the psychiatric field, became an administrator, doctoral candidate, social planner, freelance writer, and developed a private practice—in the words of Zorba the Greek, "the full catastrophy."

However, in the process, a heavy price was paid. I disinherited myself from my Italian American working-class background and replaced it with a professional identity. I went from the particularism of group interest to being a "cosmopolitan." I even moved from Brooklyn to Manhattan, à la John Travolta in *Saturday Night Fever*.

I realize today that one identity cannot and should not be rejected for the other. To be an effective professional person, I must be comfortable with both identities. I am finally becoming aware of the continuity—the passing on of emotions, instincts, memories and life-style that are intertwined and span the four generations of my family.

In the final analysis it is not true that "you can't go home again." The fact is we never separate ourselves completely from our early family values. In my own life I have traveled back often, selecting what was good and leaving behind what was not useful for me. I needed to bridge the past with the present in order to better understand how my identity today is interrelated with my working-class and Italian American heritage that has passed on from my grandparents to my parents to me and to my children.

Author Index

579

Subject Index